Readings on
The Exceptional Child

THE CENTURY PSYCHOLOGY SERIES

Kenneth MacCorquodale, Gardner Lindzey, Kenneth E. Clark, *Editors*

Readings on
The Exceptional Child

Research and Theory 　　　　　　*Second Edition*

Edited by

E. PHILIP TRAPP
University of Arkansas

PHILIP HIMELSTEIN
University of Texas at El Paso

New York

APPLETON-CENTURY-CROFTS
Educational Division
MEREDITH　CORPORATION

Copyright © 1972 by
MEREDITH CORPORATION
All rights reserved

This book, or parts thereof, must not be used or reproduced in any manner without written permission. For information address the publisher, Appleton-Century-Crofts, Educational Division, Meredith Corporation, 440 Park Avenue South, New York, N.Y. 10016.

73 74 75 76/10 9 8 7 6 5 4 3 2

Library of Congress Card Number: 74-186622

Copyright © 1962 by Meredith Corporation

PRINTED IN THE UNITED STATES OF AMERICA

390-88484-7

ACKNOWLEDGMENTS

3. Paper delivered November 8, 1967, at Rehabilitation Colloquium, Rehabilitation Counseling Program, State University of New York at Buffalo. To be published in Colloquium Series.
5. Reprinted from *Character and Personality*, 1941, *9*, 251–273, through the courtesy of the publisher, the Duke University Press, and the author.
7. From the *Journal of Abnormal Psychology*, 1968, *73*, 343–352. Reprinted by permission of American Psychological Association.
8. From the *Journal of Abnormal Psychology*, 1968, *73*, 294–304. Reprinted by permission of American Psychological Association.
9. Reprinted by permission from the *American Journal of Mental Deficiency*, Copyright 1969, American Association of Mental Deficiency.
11. Reprinted from *The Gifted Group at Mid-life: Thirty-five Years' Follow-up of the Superior Child*, Vol. V, Genetic Studies of Genius. By Lewis M. Terman and Melita H. Oden. By the permission of the publishers, Stanford University Press. Copyright ©, 1959, by the Board of Trustees of Leland Stanford University.
13. From *Exceptional Children* April, 1963. Reprinted by permission from The Council for Exceptional Children.
14. Reprinted and edited from *Psychological Monographs*, 1951, *65*, No. 15, with the permission of the publisher, American Psychological Association, and the author.
15. From the *British Journal of Medical Psychology*, 1968, *41(3)*, 213–222. Reprinted by permission of The British Psychological Society.
17. Reprinted from the *American Annals of the Deaf*, 1968, *113*, 29–41.
20. From the *Journal of Speech & Hearing Research*, 1970, *13*. Reprinted by permission.
21. From the *Journal of Abnormal & Social Psychology*, 1951, *46*, 51–63. Reprinted by permission of American Psychological Association.
23. Reprinted and edited from the *Journal of Nervous and Mental Disease*, 1942, *96*, 153–172, with the permission of the William & Wilkins Co. and Dr. Werner.
25. From Weiss and Betts in *Pediatric Clinics of North America*, Vol. 14, No. 4, Nov. 1967. Reprinted by permission of W. B. Saunders Company, Philadelphia.
27. From *The American Journal of Public Health*, 1969, *59*, No. 3, 478–484. Reprinted by permission of the author and The American Public Health Association.
28. From the *American Journal of Orthopsychiatry*, 1966, *36*, No. 3, 450–457. Reprinted by permission of Journal and author.
29. From the *American Journal of Psychiatry*, 1958, *114*, 712–718. Copyright 1958 the American Psychiatric Association.
31. From the *Journal of Abnormal Psychology*, 1967, *72*, 529–535. Reprinted by permission of American Psychological Association.
33. From *"Exceptional Children,"* reprinted by permission of The Council for Exceptional Children and the author.
34. From *Review of Educational Research*, 1965, *35*, 377–389. Reprinted by permission of the American Educational Research Association.
36. From *The Bible Translator*, April, 1969. Reprinted by permission of United Bible Societies, London.

Preface to the Second Edition

Research developments over the past ten years point up the need for a revision of our readings book on the exceptional child. The format remains basically unchanged: the reader will encounter the classics in the field along with the trend-forming studies of the present. Some of the original contributions in the first edition have been retained because they have become classic during the past decade.

Research developments, as would be expected, have not progressed evenly in the field of exceptionality. The literature abounds with excellent studies on the mentally retarded and, on the other extreme, is scant with empirical research on the blind. Three areas in particular have seen a burgeoning of research interest: research on learning disabilities, research on socially disadvantaged children, and research on behavior-modification techniques with exceptional children. The revision has attempted to reflect these developments. For example, a new section, *Exceptional Environments,* has been added in recognition of the increased concern with socially disadvantaged children.

In general, the quality as well as quantity of research continues to improve. The field of exceptionality is much too gigantic to do justice to its many facets. Much selectivity had to be exercised. All we could hope to accomplish was to give the reader a reasonable glimpse of the giant and whet his appetite to see and explore more of it on his own. Many excellent scholars and researchers in the field, too many to enumerate, constructively participated in the shaping of this project. The strengths we owe to them; the shortcomings, to us.

E. P. T.
P. H.

Preface to the First Edition

This project, in a large measure, was motivated by our experiences in teaching the introductory course on the Exceptional Child. It has come to be our conviction that the student, whether research- or service-oriented, should acquire first-hand familiarity with significant experimental studies in the field. The student with some concept of the nature and variety of problems that have been experimentally investigated and with some awareness of the variety of research designs that have been effectively employed should be better equipped to pursue more confidently his own research interests, and interpret more intelligently the core of knowledge and developments in the field. Toward these general ends this book of readings is primarily directed.

Two types of articles seem most appropriate for our purposes: specific experimental studies and critical reviews of a group of related experimental studies, pinpointing basic issues or defining major trends. Since the student may be unfamiliar with technical terms and concepts, some attention to definitional, classificatory, and historically slanted articles also seems in order.

Statement of the format is one thing and its implementation is quite another. The difficulty is heightened by the mushrooming of research on many fronts. With the field in such a fluid and expanding state, we recognized the value of going beyond our own subjective evaluations in determining the studies to be retained and the ones to be rejected. The problem was approached three ways.

First, we employed the rather obvious survey method. Requests were sent to over 100 major universities in the United States for copies of required reading lists in courses on the Exceptional Child. Co-operation was enhanced with the statement that a master list would be formed and copies submitted to the respondents. Results of this survey showed surprisingly little overlap between reference lists. We found that many of the bibliographies were grossly outdated or meager in the experimental area, which further intensified our opinion that an experimentally oriented book of readings is needed.

Secondly, we initiated correspondence with many research workers in the field, which led to many fine suggestions and ideas. This was probably our most profitable approach as a sizeable proportion of our final selections grew out of these contacts. Since scores of people were involved, it would not be feasible to cite them individually, but we would like to publicly express our gratitude to them and attribute to them a large measure of what modicum of success the book may gain.

Thirdly, we canvassed the prevailing textbooks on the Exceptional Child and systematically ferreted out the more frequently cited experimental references. These were carefully reviewed and some retained.

An unexpected type of validation of our efforts was the not infrequent casual remark of an author that the reprint demand for the article we selected has exceeded that of his other papers.

A somewhat novel feature of the book is the mixture of previously published studies with original contributions. The need for new material was engendered by the abundance of current research activity, stimulated by unprecedented federal grants. Included in this category are several recent and unpublished doctoral dissertations in condensed forms, several reports from ongoing grants, and several articles canvassing recent research developments.

While the emphasis of the book is on the contemporary scene, we have included a few of the earlier investigations, particularly those that have stimulated considerable research.

A cursory glance at the table of contents will quickly show that certain classes of articles have been excluded; for example, etiological and psychometric studies. These studies, some of them excellent, were considered not germane to our purposes and were omitted in deference to space limitation.

Also, it may be noticed that more articles are devoted to certain areas than others. For example, the largest number of articles is on mental deficiency in recognition of the fact that the majority of experimental studies have been in this area. The relatively few articles on the emotionally disturbed child is a reflection of the small amount of experimental research done on this subject. In fact, the several articles selected in this area were chosen mainly to accent problems of high current interest in need of extensive experimentation.

Some editors of books of readings are disturbed by the variations of styles among the contributors, and are moved to make extensive revisions and depletions. We frankly disagree with this policy. Apart from the inevitable biases this injects into the original studies, it takes away a function that properly belongs to each individual instructor. As we see it, a book of readings is merely the raw material, not the finished product.

Preface to the First Edition

The instructor, guided by his particular frame of reference, determines what use to make of the material. Hence, we have done very little in altering the original form of the articles, although we have added introductory comments and, when appropriate, some post hoc remarks from the authors.

The following agencies have been most helpful and encouraging to us in our project and we thank them for their kind assistance:

Alexander Graham Bell Association for the Deaf
American Association on Mental Deficiency
American Foundation for the Blind
Boston Nursery for Blind Babies
California School for the Blind, Berkeley, California
Central Institute for the Deaf, St. Louis, Missouri
Council for Exceptional Children
Department of Health, Education and Welfare
Industrial Home for the Blind, Brooklyn, New York
Institute for Research for Exceptional Children, Urbana, Illinois
John Tracy Clinic, Los Angeles, California
Lexington School for the Deaf, New York, New York
National Association for the Gifted Children
National Epilepsy League
National Index on Deafness, Speech, and Hearing
National Organization for Mentally Ill Children
National Society for Crippled Children and Adults
New York State School for the Blind, Batavia, New York
Perkins School for the Blind, Watertown, Massachusetts
Quincy Youth Development Project, Quincy, Illinois
St. Joseph's School for the Deaf, New York City
State of California Department of Education
Training School at Vineland, New Jersey
United Cerebral Palsy Association
United Cerebral Palsy of New York City, Incorporated
Wayne County Training School, Detroit, Michigan

E. P. T.
P. H.

Contents

Preface to the Second Edition   v

Preface to the First Edition   vii

I. INTRODUCTION

1. Incidence Figures of Exceptional Children in the United States   *E. Philip Trapp and Philip Himelstein*   3
2. Development of a Revised Scale for the Functional Classification of Exceptional Children   *Ira Iscoe and Sherry Payne*   7
3. Psychological Snares in the Investigative Enterprise   *Beatrice A. Wright*   31

II. EXCEPTIONAL INTELLECTUAL PROCESSES

The Mentally Deficient

4. A Historical Survey of Research and Management of Mental Retardation in the United States   *Eugene E. Doll*   47
5. Experimental Studies of Rigidity: I. The Measurement of Rigidity in Normal and Feebleminded Persons   *Jacob S. Kounin*   99
6. Rigidity in the Retarded: A Reexamination   *Edward Zigler*   123
7. Expectancy of Success and the Probability Learning of Middle-class, Lower-class, and Retarded Children   *Gerald E. Gruen and Edward Zigler*   161
8. Sensory Restriction and Isolation Experiences in Children with Phenylketonuria   *C. Jack Friedman, Maarten S. Sibinga, Ira M. Steisel, and Harry M. Sinnamon*   179
9. Use of Punishment Procedures with the Severely Retarded: A Review   *William I. Gardner*   197

xii   Contents

10. Effects of a Severely Retarded Child on the Family   *Bernard Farber*   225

The Gifted

11. The Gifted Group at Mid-life   *Lewis M. Terman and Melita H. Oden*   249
12. Characteristics of Creatively Gifted Children and Youth   *E. Paul Torrance*   273
13. A Critique of Research on the Gifted   *T. Ernest Newland*   293

III. EXCEPTIONAL SENSORY AND MOTOR PROCESSES

The Aurally and Visually Handicapped

14. Space Perception and Orientation in the Blind   *Philip Worchel*   305
15. Problems of Play and Mastery in the Blind Child   *Doris M. Wills*   335
16. A Review of Recent Personality Research on Deaf Children   *W. John Schuldt and Doris A. Schuldt*   351
17. Early Manual Communication in Relation to the Deaf Child's Intellectual, Social, and Communicative Functioning   *Kathryn P. Meadow*   363
18. Multiply Handicapped Deaf Children: Current Status   *McCay Vernon*   379

The Speech Handicapped

19. A Survey of the Literature on Functional Speech Disorders and Personality: Forty Years of Research   *Leonard D. Goodstein and Ellin L. Block*   399
20. Stuttering and Its Disappearance   *Joseph G. Sheehan and Margaret M. Martyn*   425
21. The Modification of Stuttering through Nonreinforcement   *Joseph G. Sheehan*   437

Brain-Damaged and Physically Handicapped Persons and Learning Disabilities

22. The Problems and Promises of Psychological Research in Rehabilitation   *Franklin C. Shontz*   469
23. Disorders of Conceptual Thinking in the Brain-injured Child   *Alfred A. Strauss and Heinz Werner*   483

xiii   Contents

24. Neurological Abnormality in Infancy, Intelligence, and Social Class   *Raymond H. Holden and Lee Willerman*   501
25. Methods of Rehabilitation in Children with Neuromuscular Disorders   *Herman Weiss and Henry B. Betts*   513
26. Some Aspects of Specific Learning Disabilities in Children   *Sidney Rosenblum*   523

IV. EXCEPTIONAL EMOTIONAL PROCESSES

27. Slicing the Mystique of Prevention with Occam's Razor   *Eli M. Bower*   541
28. Psychiatric Syndromes in Children and Their Relation to Family Background   *Richard L. Jenkins*   551
29. School Phobia: A Study in the Communication of Anxiety   *Leon Eisenberg*   561
30. Operant Conditioning: Breakthrough in the Treatment of Mentally Ill Children   *Bernard Rimland*   573
31. Stimulation-level Preferences of Autistic Children   *J. Richard Metz*   587
32. Behavior Modification with Emotionally Disturbed Children   *Robert M. Leff*   601
33. The Santa Monica Project: Evaluation of an Engineered Classroom Design with Emotionally Disturbed Children   *Frank M. Hewett, Frank D. Taylor, and Alfred A. Artuso*   643

V. EXCEPTIONAL ENVIRONMENTS

34. Characteristics of Socially Disadvantaged Children   *Edmund W. Gordon*   657
35. Linguistic Aspects of Culturally Disadvantaged Children   *Richard B. Dever*   671
36. A Black English Translation of John 3:1–21 with Grammatical Annotations   *Walter A. Wolfram and Ralph W. Fasold*   689

Name Index   699

Subject Index   711

part I

Introduction

1

Incidence Figures of Exceptional Children in the United States

E. Philip Trapp and Philip Himelstein

This summary report is based on a survey conducted by the U.S. Office of Education, Bureau of Education for the Handicapped, for the year 1968.* In interpreting the results, the reader should bear in mind that, while this report is the most accurate document currently available, the statistics do represent only *estimates* and not actual head counting.

Table I presents a categorical breakdown of the number of elementary- and secondary-school-age children who are handicapped. It may be noted from Table I that the number of handicapped children (5,224,705) represents approximately 10 percent of the population of school-age children. The bulk of the handicapped (80 percent) falls into the categories of the speech handicapped, the mentally retarded, and the emotionally disturbed.

Data were also gathered on the manpower situation. Table II reports on the number of teachers and specialists currently employed to serve the needs of handicapped children and the number of additional teachers and specialists needed. The most obvious conclusion to be drawn from Table II is that all categories of exceptionality show serious manpower deficiencies. The most dramatic needs (in terms of percentage increases)

---

* Incidence figures on the mentally gifted were not available in this report.

Introduction

Table I Number of Handicapped Elementary- and Secondary-school-age Children (5–17 Years)

Type of exceptionality	Number of children[a]
Visually handicapped	52,378
Deaf	39,283
Hard of hearing	261,890
Speech handicapped	1,833,230
Crippled and other health-impaired	261,890
Emotionally disturbed	1,047,560
Mentally retarded	1,204,694
Specific learning disabilities	523,780
Total	5,224,705

[a] The estimates are based on a total estimated school-age population (5–17 years) for 1968 of 52,378,000 listed in *Estimates of Current Manpower Needs in Education for the Handicapped, 1968–1969,* Bureau of Education for the Handicapped, U.S. Office of Education, 1968 (mimeographed). Specific estimates by area of handicap are derived by application of incidence rate to this total population.

are in the areas of the emotionally disturbed, specific learning disabilities, and hard of hearing.

Another approach to pointing up the critical manpower (and facilities) shortage for handicapped children is to report on the number of children being serviced in the schools and the number of children who are deprived of such services. Table III furnishes the data for this comparison. Consistent with the figures in Table II, the data in Table III reveal that the relatively most neglected children are those with specific learning disabilities, the emotionally disturbed, and the hard of hearing.

In spite of the manpower needs reflected in this report, there is evidence of increasing public acceptance of responsibility in the area of exceptionality. In 1948, for example, the school systems handled approximately 400,000 handicapped children; the number was doubled in 1958; and the figures have been doubled again over the past ten years. This rate of growth far exceeded the growth rate of regular school enrollments during the corresponding periods.

Table II Number of Teachers and Specialists Currently Employed and Number Needed for Handicapped School-age Children (5–17 Years)[a]

Type of exceptionality	Number currently employed	Number needed[b]
Visually handicapped	2,566	2,877
Deaf	5,205	823
Hard of hearing	1,080	12,100
Speech handicapped	11,067	12,733
Crippled and other health-impaired	12,810	5,674
Emotionally disturbed	9,950	121,794
Mentally retarded	37,241	58,406
Specific learning disabilities	3,940	22,564
Total	83,859	236,968

[a] Data from *Estimates of Current Manpower Needs in Education for the Handicapped, 1968–1969*, Bureau of Education for the Handicapped, U.S. Office of Education, 1968 (mimeographed).
[b] Corrected for 8 percent attrition of those currently employed.

Table III Number of Handicapped School-age Children (5–17 Years) Served in the School Systems[a]

Type of exceptionality	Number in local public schools	Number in residential or state schools	Number not receiving services
Visually handicapped	17,671	7,900	26,807
Deaf	12,000	21,000	5,440
Hard of hearing	20,700	Not applicable	241,190
Speech handicapped	987,000	Not applicable	846,230
Crippled and other health-impaired	144,366	3,489	114,035
Emotionally disturbed	64,700	55,700	927,160
Mentally retarded	500,555	45,000	659,139
Specific learning disabilities	20,388	Not applicable	503,392
Total	1,767,380	133,932	3,323,393

[a] Estimates based on 1966 data; not corrected to current projections. Data from *Estimates of Current Manpower Needs in Education for the Handicapped, 1968–1969*, Bureau of Education for the Handicapped, U.S. Office of Education, 1968 (mimeographed).

2

Development of a Revised Scale for the Functional Classification of Exceptional Children

Ira Iscoe and Sherry Payne

Dr. Iscoe is Professor of Psychology and Education at the University of Texas at Austin and Sherry Payne is an advanced graduate student at the University of Texas. Dr. Iscoe has been concerned with the problems of exceptional children, more specifically with diagnostic and treatment approaches, for over fifteen years. His interests have been reflected in many research articles in professional journals and numerous consultantships in the Austin area. His early recognition that effective treatment procedures require broad community participation placed him among the first group of psychologists to shape and develop the relatively recent field of community psychology. Within the past year he has coauthored a book on the subject.

The present article, a revision of a paper appearing in the first edition of this book, provides additional data and comments on his proposed classification system. As most workers in the field know so well, much confusion in terminology still prevails, with an abundance of conceptual schemes advanced by scholars from many different disciplines. Dr. Iscoe is to be applauded in his effort to work out a classification system designed to cut across disciplinary lines and, hence, improve interdisciplinary communication.

8   Introduction

In the first edition of this book a scheme was presented under the title "The Functional Classification of Exceptional Children." The present article expands this system and presents some data with regard to reliability. Response to the original system was rather widespread, and the author received many requests and suggestions, some of which have been incorporated into the present chapter. Unfortunately a thorough perusal of the literature reveals little or no published results. It is small comfort that in the same search, very little if any mention is made of classification devices other than those traditionally used, such as intelligence, medical reports, and achievement ratings. While these are useful and will and should enjoy continued usage, there is still need for inter- and intradisciplinary communication.

This need is increasing. The last ten years and especially the last seven have witnessed a tremendous expansion in training opportunities, educational facilities, and treatment programs for exceptional children. The impetus for this concentration of resources has its origin in many sources. Perhaps one of the strongest forces has been the work which began soon after World War I and which continued into the 1950s. It was in this era that many theoretical formulations with regard to handicapping conditions were formulated. It was then too that some of the earlier notions with regard to early training and remediation in handicapping conditions had their "field trials" as it were. Another force was the increasing recognition of the incidence and prevalence of exceptionality in children. This was of course buttressed in the early 1960s with the advent of our belated recognition of the effects of cultural deprivation, environmental handicaps, and ethnic disadvantages.

Despite the laudable progress made, and despite the relatively high level of support that is enjoyed today, the whole special educational process, indeed the whole spectrum of exceptionality, is under surveillance. There is need for much more evaluational and longitudinal studies of the various types of exceptionality. It is obvious that an exceptional condition such as mental retardation or cerebral palsy or even a mild learning disability does not stand independent of other factors. For example, in many ways special education teachers determine and influence the success of the child they teach. Also, the encouragement of parents and the needed mutuality of perceptions are factors that have been remarked on often.

Although much improvement has taken place in evaluative instruments designed to measure various types of functioning, such as intelligence, social maturity, language ability, and the like, it is surprising that a rather thorough review of the literature has failed to disclose any attempts to evaluate exceptional children *across or within disciplines*. Thus, while an intellectual assessment made by a psychologist may be communicated to other psychologists and also to other professionals, these same other professionals must often communicate with others via different instruments—if indeed they use any at all. In good clinical practice it is understood, and indeed desirable, that all those associated with the child voice their opinions. According to this technique, each individual reports his observations for the case history, or files a report of work that has been carried out. Such records are of course invaluable and do form the basis for one type of comprehensive planning for the child. However, the literature does not reveal the usage of a methodology whereby professionals, nonprofessionals, parents, and others may compare their observations and predictions about a particular child. It is for this purpose that the expanded methodology reported herein has been devised. Its advantages would seem to lie in its many uses (to be described) and its ability to be used with minimal instruction by a wide variety of individuals. Furthermore, it is hopefully the kind of instrument whereby the perceptions of the school teacher, the occupational therapist, the speech therapist, the parents, and others would have equal weight. Such equal weighting is a product not of the scale itself but of the inherent approach that the perceptions as recorded by any one individual are valid in terms of that particular person's perceptions and thus are important in themselves.

NEED FOR A FUNCTIONAL SYSTEM

The very diversity of specialties concerned with exceptional children is the primary cause of many difficulties in communication between them. The "lingo" or specialized language employed by one group is frequently not understood by another group. This can be most frustrating. It is an axiom of good communication technique that the communicator, or person doing the writing or talking, employ a language and a level that can be understood by the person or persons receiving the message (the communicatee). This does not imply that one discipline "talk down" to another. It does imply that there is a need to establish some common ground to facilitate interdisciplinary communication. It appears that some type of classification, based on principles easily understood by all involved, would be helpful.

RATIONALE OF THE SYSTEM

How may a system be developed to describe exceptional children that is communicable across disciplines, and yet not subject to practice effects? In the present work it is held that exceptional children differ from normal children in a number of domains. If they differ only slightly the chances are that they will not even be called exceptional. Beyond a certain quantitative and qualitative amount of deviation, certain children begin to stand out and they are noticed as "different." Without doubt, much value judgment is involved in classifying exceptional children, and actually there seems no way to avoid such judgments. In fact, it may very well be that value judgments are an extremely important aspect of dealing with exceptional children.

However, it becomes necessary, in the name of parsimony, to select certain aspects of a child's behavior for classification since, understandably, differences in children occur in intellectual capacities, physical capacities, speech clarity, educability, general adjustment to the environment, and countless other domains. In selecting certain domains comparison has been made with the normal child of the same sex and roughly the same chronological age. Implied here is a knowledge of normal child development and of age expectancy. Thus, it is necessary in most cases to use the normal child as a comparison, as indeed is the case in intelligence testing and other measuring devices.

What domains are to be used for classifying exceptional children? For the purposes of this paper three domains are proposed, with three categories in each:

I. Physical Domain
   a. Visibility
   b. Locomotion
   c. Communication
II. Perceived Adjustment Domain
   a. Peer acceptance
   b. Family interaction
   c. Self-esteem
III. Educational Domain
   a. Motivation
   b. Academic level
   c. Educational potential

While the scheme presented may appear broad, one of its strengths is that it furnishes an economic means to obtain significant information about a child's exceptionality. That is, in a minimum amount of time, pertinent information can be supplied about major areas of concern in the several specialties involved. In any case, opportunities for use of the scale need not be limited. Rather, only through continued use and research can the scope of the inherent possibilities be determined.

DESCRIPTION OF THE SCALE

A brief description of domains and categories follows together with a copy of the proposed rating scale.

I. Physical Domain

This domain places primary emphasis on aspects of exceptionality that are more readily observed upon initial contact. The three categories included deal with exceptionality primarily as it relates to physical functioning. In essence, we want to know whether the child looks, communicates, or locomotes differently, as well as how and to what degree.

a. Visibility In its simplest sense, the question is asked: How apparent on immediate or limited contact is this child's exceptionality? Most of the clues here are gained from physical appearance and behavior. It is doubtful whether a gifted child can be recognized as such by physical appearances, certain stereotypes to the contrary. Not every mentally retarded child looks "stupid." Certain conditions are of course highly visible. Blind and some physically handicapped children are easier to recognize than deaf children. The cerebral-palsied child frequently has symptoms that make him highly visible as, for example, an achetoid condition. Emotionally disturbed children do not usually offer a clue based upon physical appearance. Therefore, it is possible only within limits to state how apparent the child's exceptionality is on the basis of first appearance.

The role of various disciplines and specialties deserves comment here. In general, the lower the visibility, the better the initial acceptance of the child, that is, the less likely he is to be classified as different. The reduction of visibility has become the role of several specialties. Teaching orientation to the blind and achieving more effective limb and speech control by physical and speech therapy are examples of reducing visibility. Corrective surgery is another method from another discipline. It follows that beyond a certain point, visibility in most cases cannot be reduced in certain specific disorders. Blindness and limb paralysis stand out as two examples where visibility may remain relatively high despite the best training. A child with a cane, in a wheelchair, or on crutches is noticeable. Judgment as to just how visible the condition is, naturally is a somewhat subjective matter. Nevertheless, the ordering of the judgment to some form of scale allows for comparison between judges. This may be of value in itself, as we shall see later.

b. Locomotion How well does the child get about in his environment without assistance? As a child grows and develops, his repertoire of locomotion skills increases. He goes about the yard, then the neighborhood, then the city. Locomotion after a certain level of maturation obviously involves more than simply being able to walk. A judgment and reasoning process is involved also. A blind child, age 12, may be able to locomote as well or better around a city than a mentally retarded child of the same chronological age but half the mental age, or vice versa. Locomotion should not pose any problem to a gifted child, age 8, free of physical involvement, but will pose one to a child in a wheelchair, despite superior intelligence.

It is not difficult that in this category, as well, many disciplines are involved. There is some relationship admittedly between visibility and locomotion. For our purposes, locomotion is considered a component of action, while visibility has a passive connotation.

c. Communication   The emphasis here is placed on oral communication. Our society is one that dotes on verbal fluency and often makes sport of speech impediments. In brief, then, is the speech clear compared to the speech of normal children of the same sex and age? The question is in the special area of the speech pathologist and speech correctionist, although the psychological and psychiatric aspects of speech are receiving increasing recognition. The mentally retarded, the gifted, the emotionally disturbed may all have problems of speech, as well as those children who have so-called "pure" speech problems.

II. Perceived Adjustment

In this domain the emphasis is placed on the degree of psychosocial adjustment or acceptance that the child has developed about himself as an individual as well as between himself and other individuals in the environment, specifically the peer group and the family.

a. Peer acceptance   In this category several questions are asked. How does the child get along with his peers? How socialized is he? Has he progressed in the socialization process despite, for example, a physical handicap? How well accepted is he by his peers, provided he is at an age and developmental level where peer acceptance is important? In peer acceptance as in the other categories, the "why" is not stressed. The reality of "the way it is" is what is important. Peer acceptance here does not imply passivity or receiving grudging acceptance, having been forced on a group of children. It implies a mentally healthy give and take, of the child working for acceptance and adjusting to his handicap, with both he and the group recognizing limitations. A peer group judges harshly yet realistically. A mentally retarded 9-year-old would certainly have a more difficult time in this area than a well-trained deaf child of normal intelligence. A gifted child with a severe emotional disturbance would conceivably find less acceptance than a blind child of normal intelligence, good training, and social sensitivity.

b. Family interaction   Here we want to know how much consistent difficulty exists between the child and other family members. Once again, we do not want to know why there may be difficulties, nor are we interested in the various problems of an everyday nature that are an integral part of living with other people. We are interested in difficulties that recur fairly consistently and repeatedly between the child and one or several family members to the extent that family integration and welfare appears impaired or seriously threatened. Obviously much of the interpretation of the degree of difficulty experienced and the relationship that it plays within the family structure will be dependent upon the subjective judgment of the rater. What may appear extremely abnormal or exceptional to one individual may appear quite the opposite to another individual with different experiences. Clearly the degree to which the interaction is rated as exceptional depends on the biases and experiences of the rater. Therefore, we again see the importance in some cases of having several individuals who hold differing emphases or outlooks rate a particular category or domain.

c. Self-esteem This category requires additional clarification. Primarily, we want to determine what kind of opinion or regard the child has developed about himself and his capabilities. So we ask the question: How does the child seem to feel about himself as a person? Included in this general question are others, such as: Does he feel comfortable in new settings? Does he become alarmed or frightened easily? Does he constantly seek attention? Does he often depreciate his schoolwork or other products? Is he boastful or shy much of the time or require a lot of attention? The development of a healthy self-esteem depends primarily upon the child's accurate perception of his ability to master certain resistances and obstacles, as well as a realistic appraisal of his areas of weakness. Thus the form that a child's self-evaluation will take is based upon the effectiveness of his own activity in dealing with his environment as well as the opinion that others hold about him.

The child who is exceptional in this area has not developed a successfully integrated personality that can differentiate between his various levels of competencies and weaknesses. On the one extreme of exceptionality in this category is the child who experiences feelings of severe inferiority, which primarily result from an overall inability to establish a sufficient measure of success and worth (esteem) in any area. This is the child who consistently compares himself unfavorably with others based on a range of abilities or accomplishments that is much too wide. It is here that we can see how a crippled or physically handicapped child might have poor self-esteem if he had not sufficiently accepted his limitations. On the other hand, if he has a good realization of his areas of weakness, and these are balanced by feelings of worth in other areas, this would not necessarily be the case. Often the child who feels extremely inferior and unworthy has attempted to compete in too many areas, with little, if any, regard to his own particular strengths; this may take the form of shyness in certain areas or, in more extreme forms, withdrawal. For example, a gifted child might have low self-esteem if he could not successfully complete every task he attempted, without even taking his limitations into regard.

The child at the other end of the continuum has developed extreme confidence in himself and his abilities that is blatantly overabundant, if not conceitful. However, although this child may indeed possess superior capabilities, which lead to additional opportunities to compete and excel, the persistence of such extreme overconfidence is not usually a normal trait. Rather, it is considered an indication of exceptionality.

While it may be difficult for a complete stranger to assess the aspects of a child's self-esteem on immediate contact, it is possible for an individual to make a reasonably accurate rating by utilizing various observational situations. For example, an examination of a child's experiences, attitudes, and coping behaviors at school, at play, and as a member of a family group should provide some significant information.

III. Educational Domain

In some ways this domain has its greatest relevance to teachers of exceptional children. Here we are interested in providing ratings that will aid in developing appropriate and beneficial kinds of educational experiences for exceptional children. It is in this effort that we are focusing on motivational aspects of the child within the classroom, appraising present level of functioning, and making a general determination of the child's educational potential. Since the schooling of a child has often been equated with the demanding occupational experiences of the adult world, the significance placed upon imparting effective and useful academic experiences for the exceptional child is considerable.

a. Motivation In rating this aspect of a child's behavior, we want to know how motivated or responsive the child is to working after some suggestion and/or cooperation has been given from his teacher. That is, how much consistent intervention from the teacher is required as a motivational device? We can perhaps think more clearly of this motivational aspect in terms of degree of teacher–child interaction if we consider the following diagram:

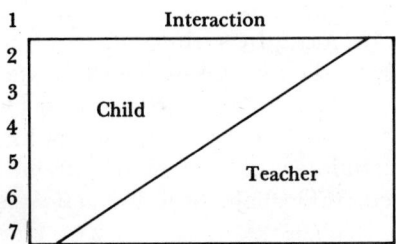

We have started with the assumption that a certain amount of teacher interaction is necessary, and at various times every child requires more or less assistance, there being few times when none is warranted. But we are interested in how much interaction is consistently required from the teacher to provide sufficient incentive that the child will continue primarily on his own, barring difficulties in understanding or explanation. Obviously this teacher–child interaction is not the same as time spent by the teacher with the child in simple clarification of vague or poorly defined aspects of the lessons. It is possible, for example, that a child of superior intelligence in a regular class will require and demand more of a teacher's efforts to motivate him before he will produce the required material than, say, a crippled or physically handicapped child of normal intelligence.

b. *Academic performance level* The question here is whether the child in school is performing at an appropriate academic level for his age. The emphasis is not on the child's innate ability or capacity to perform, since this may be unknown or even in error. In this instance, we can only determine where the child is academically in relation to all other normal school children of the same age. Consistently one of the first questions any teacher of exceptional children asks concerns his present level of performance. Is it below or above that for normal children? It is possible that data received from this inquiry can assist in making determinations late about an appropriate educational program for the child in terms of age as well as ability.

c. *Educational potential* In this category we want to know the rater's estimation of the child's potential in a very general educational sense. How high is his potential for learning and what can he achieve given optimal conditions? Specifically, does his potential to learn and achieve appear to be significantly affected by certain limitations, weaknesses, or educational blocks? Such limitations may be anything that significantly affects or lowers the child's potential to achieve, such as areas of emotional difficulties, level of intelligence, or the ability to achieve abstract thought and associational relationships. These aspects of difficulty may be reflected in subjects such as logic, or higher forms of math, or simply in learning to spell, read, or write. Therefore, we want to assess the child's difficulty, if any, and thus determine how much it may affect his ability to achieve, if given other optimal conditions. It is not intended that a particular child's rating will become fixed, rigid, or perpetuated. The importance of maintaining flexible standards and programs certainly cannot be underrated.

THE RATING FORM

Having described the rationale and purposes of the domains and categories, we may now proceed to illustrate the form of the scale itself.

RATING FORM

Functional Classification System

Date _____

Name _____ Age _____ Sex _____ Problem _____
Rater and specialty _____ Clinic, agency, or school _____
Informant (if any) _____ First time rated? _____ Yes _____ No
Supplemental information _____
_____
_____

Circle the number most appropriate to the child. Ratings are always made comparative to normal children of the same age and sex.

I. PHYSICAL DOMAIN

a. Visibility

0. Little or no opportunity to observe.
1. The physical appearance gives absolutely no indication of the condition. (Note: For gifted children, use this rating unless there is another condition along with being gifted.)
2. There is occasionally a slight indication of the condition, not noticeable to the layman, but apparent after awhile to the trained specialist.
3. There are several indications of the condition, which are immediately apparent to a trained specialist but still not to the layman.
4. There are fairly obvious signs of the disability and it is usually apparent to the layman, although the child may have made some adjustments that still occasionally render the condition unnoticeable to the layman.
5. There are moderately severe indications of the condition. It is readily apparent to the layman at all times.
6. The condition is severe and obvious, but less than in 7, more than in 5.
7. The condition is extremely severe and stands out clearly to everyone.

b. Locomotion

0. Little or no opportunity to observe.
1. No apparent or reported difficulty in this area.
2. A few restrictions but not enough to warrant special help.
3. More restrictions than in 2, and he needs special help occasionally.

4. Moderate restriction. Can keep up with his peers in some ways; in others he needs help or guidance from others.
5. Moderately severe restriction. Needs help or direction more than half of the time.
6. Severe restriction. Needs help and direction almost all the time, although there may be one or a few areas where assistance is not required.
7. Extremely severe restriction of locomotion. Help and direction is needed continuously.

c. Communication

0. Little or no opportunity to observe.
1. No difficulty at all, observed or reported. Speech is entirely normal.
2. Occasional signs of a slight problem. May be apparent to the trained worker but not to the layman.
3. Several indications of difficulty. Readily apparent to the trained worker but not usually to the laymen.
4. Moderate difficulty. Occasionally noticeable to the layman.
5. Moderately severe difficulty. Readily apparent to all.
6. Severe difficulty manifest. More severe than in 5 but less than in 7.
7. Extremely severe difficulty is manifest in this area. Obvious to all who listen or observe.

II. PERCEIVED ADJUSTMENT DOMAIN

a. Peer Acceptance

0. Little or no opportunity to observe.
1. No problem at all exists in this area. Well accepted and sought after by peers. This is mutual.
2. A slight problem, invariably transient in nature, and primarily affects only one or a very few individuals.
3. Occasional difficulties, often transient and not usually evident to any but experienced professionals. Accepted by the majority of his peers.
4. Evidence of much more difficulty. May be noticeable to the layman after awhile, although the problem may still be considered transient in nature. He has some peer approval, but the general relationship to his group is brittle.
5. Evidence that the problems are moderately severe. Accepted by some of his peers but definitely not the majority. The problem is less likely to be transient. However, he occasionally seeks peer approval.
6. The difficulties are severe. He is rejected by almost all his peers. He makes little effort to seek out friends. Social skills are poorly developed.
7. Extremely severe rejection by all his peers. He is not accepted by them and little if any effort is expended in making friends. Socialization is at a minimum and the problem is most likely one of long standing.

18   Introduction

b. Family Interaction

0. Little or no opportunity to observe.
1. No difficulty observed or reported in this area. The child is a well-accepted, integrated member of the family, capable of experiencing mutual respect.
2. An occasional problem may occur between the child and one other family member. Invariably superficial in nature and does not significantly affect overall family relationships.
3. Occasional difficulties occur consistently between the child and one other member of the family. The problem is most likely transient and rarely affects the child's relationships with other family members. The problem is readily apparent to an experienced professional and occasionally to a close friend.
4. Considerable difficulty is displayed consistently between the child and another family member, but this friction may occasionally involve at least one other individual. The problem is evident to most close acquaintances but to few outsiders.
5. Moderately severe problems. The relationships between the child and several (at least half) family members is extremely poor and consistently abrasive. There are a few persons in the family with whom the child can form some type of acceptable relationship, although the alliance is often brittle. Difficulties are immediately apparent to a layman or to outsiders.
6. The difficulties are severe. The child is consistently rejected by almost all family members, or vice versa. On extremely infrequent occasions an association may be initiated or continued but usually proves to be untenable.
7. Extremely severe difficulties observed between the child and the family group. Complete rejection by one or both parties. Interaction (in terms of stable or normal relationships) is at best minimal, and the problem is of long standing.

c. Self-esteem

0. Little or no opportunity to observe.
1. No problem observed in this area. The child's self-esteem appears consistently high but accurate.
2. There is indication of a slight problem. It is invariably transient and is apparent to a trained specialist, usually after examination.
3. More difficulties are evident than in 7, less than in 4, but they are not necessarily of long duration.
4. Considerable difficulties. Problem is eventually, but not immediately, apparent to a layman.
5. The difficulty is moderately severe. Immediately apparent to a layman and less likely to be transient. There are still several areas in which the esteem is accurate or high but the general adjustment is poor and

there are many areas in which his reactions and responses are inappropriate in accord with his actual abilities.
6. The problem is severe. In most areas the child's esteem is poor or inaccurate.
7. The problem is extremely severe and undoubtedly of long standing. Does not consider himself worthwhile in any area, or his perceptions are continually inaccurate, and appropriate responses are at a minimum.

III. EDUCATIONAL DOMAIN

a. Motivation

0. Little or no opportunity to observe.
1. No problem in this area. Schoolwork is primarily self-directed. Requires only a minimum of interaction from the teacher as a motivational aspect.
2. Slight problem in this area. General motivation is good, but he may occasionally become frustrated or bored, requiring intervention from the teacher. Invariably transient, affecting only an occasional subject area.
3. Occasional difficulties. Individual attention from the teacher is needed more than in 2, less than in 4, but still not usually for any prolonged period of time.
4. Signs of considerable difficulty in motivation. Requires assistance from the teacher at least half of the time or he becomes easily frustrated and unable to work.
5. Moderately severe problem. In order to produce any work at all in school, individual assistance from the teacher is required. This occurs about three fourths of the time.
6. The condition is severe and in evidence almost all the time. Only in a few circumstances does motivation to initiate and continue school tasks not appear to be seriously impaired.
7. The condition is extremely severe. The child appears to have a minimal amount of motivation, requiring almost consistent attention from the teacher.

b. Academic Performance Level

0. Little or no opportunity to observe.
1. No problem in this area. Performs well and works up to an appropriate level in all areas of study.
2. A slight difficulty in academic performance. May occur under isolated circumstances only. Almost all work is up to or beyond an appropriate level of performance.
3. Several areas of difficulty where academic performance is below an appropriate level, but this is not usually severe or long lasting. May

occasionally require a tutor for a short time in areas of specific difficulty.
4. Academic performance is restricted in up to one half of his academic subject areas. With a tutor adequate performance can usually be maintained. This assistance is probably not needed for a prolonged period of time.
5. The problem is moderately severe. Performance is below an appropriate level in at least three fourths of his academic subjects. Professional assistance is required in most subjects, although there may be several areas where it is not needed.
6. The problem is severe. Performance in almost all areas is weak and poor. Consistent and prolonged tutoring is most likely necessary in all but one or two areas.
7. Performance in all subject areas is extremely severely restricted and limited. Assistance from a professional is required continuously if any improvement can take place in all areas.

c. Educational Potential

0. Little or no opportunity to observe.
1. Extremely high potential.
2. High potential. May have an occasional weakness which could slightly affect potential.
3. Potential is above average.
4. Average potential.
5. Below-average potential.
6. Limited potential.
7. Extremely limited potential.

DIVISION AND RATINGS OF DOMAINS AND CATEGORIES

The three major domains of behavior have been assigned the following designations:

        Ph — PHYSICAL
        Ad — PERCEIVED ADJUSTMENT
        Ed — EDUCATIONAL

As described earlier, these three domains have in turn been further divided into several categories, each of which have been designated a separate categorical classification:

        Vis — visibility
        Loc — locomotion
        Com — communication

Peer — peer acceptance
Fam — family interaction
Self — self-esteem
Mot — motivation
Aca — academic level
Ptl — educational potential

Each category may be rated directly by the rater using a seven-point scale for each, in which 1 indicates no difficulty or problem in the area being rated and 7 indicates difficulty that is extremely severe or outstanding. It may be advisable, however, in other situations to utilize composite ratings for the three domains, that is, to have one individual rate the Physical Domain, another, such as a teacher, rate the Educational Domain, and so on. This method of adjusting the scores may also be applied to the individual categories. For example, in cases where the child is seen in a clinic situation, several ratings of the same category, such as peer acceptance, or motivation, may be made quite independently and averaged out later (or adjusted by another method) to obtain the child's rated score. Or one individual may rate visibility and another, such as a speech therapist, may rate communication, while a physical therapist may rate locomotion. Thus one or several individuals may utilize the scale at any one time in terms of domains or categories. In cases where it does not seem appropriate to rate the child on the information or observations available, the designation 0 should be used for the domain or category in question. However, this rating should be used sparingly. Estimates may always be changed, and it is always instructive to estimate the child's level of functioning from the point of view of the rater and then compare it with others.

As an adjunct to the maintenance of records or to simplify the keeping of records, it is suggested that each domain and attendant categories be recorded on a profile form as follows:

	Vis	Loc	Com
PH			
	Peer	Fam	Self
AD			
	Mot	Aca	Ptl
ED			

POSSIBLE USES

In using this system of classification, a number of possible uses suggest themselves.

Communication-facilitating Device

One use of the system would be as a shorthand descriptive device that would facilitate communication between disciplines and clinics. For example:

a.

PH	Vis	Loc	Com
	1	4	4

AD	Peer	Fam	Self
	6	3	5

ED	Mot	Aca	Ptl
	5	6	6

Mental Retardation
Sex: male
Age: 8 years

This information conveys the message that this mentally retarded child does not have any physical stigmata or involvements that are readily apparent. The general ratings of the Physical Domain suggest that he has some difficulty which may require the aid of specialists. Specifically, he gets about moderately well (Loc = 4), although there is evidence of some restriction and difficulty in this category, and there are occasional noticeable difficulties in speech (Com = 4). His ratings in the Perceived Adjustment Domain indicate that he has some overall problems in relating to others and forming stable relationships. This is seen primarily in the form of considerable difficulties with and severe rejection from his peer group (Peer = 6). Although he has occasional difficulties with certain members of his family (Fam = 3), it is not serious; but his esteem (Self = 5) of himself as a worthy individual appears to be a definite problem. In terms of educational experiences coupled with the knowledge that he is mentally retarded, there is evidence of rather severe complications. His motivation (Mot = 5) is low, his present level of performance (Aca = 6) appears to be seriously impaired as compared with others of his age, and his potential educationally (Ptl = 6) is limited. Obviously even if the information concerning his intellectual functioning had not been available, we could have concluded from the Aca and Ptl ratings that his performance was considerably retarded, very likely necessitating special class placement.

In the following ratings we see the situation of a 10-year-old girl with cerebral palsy:

b.

	Vis	Loc	Com
PH	6	3	6
AD	Peer	Fam	Self
	4	1	5
ED	Mot	Aca	Ptl
	2	5	4

Cerebral Palsy
Sex: female
Age: 10 years

The general overall indications are that the girl has rather serious physical difficulties, much less serious educational problems, and a good general adjustment. Her appearance (Vis =6) gives evidence of severe physical involvement, but despite this she gets around rather well (Loc = 3). The locomotion rating further suggests that the disability is in the upper portion of the body—she obviously can move about without assistance from another person. Her speech difficulty is quite severe (Com = 6), but her acceptance by her peers is relatively good (Peer = 4). She gets along extremely well with her family (Fam = 1), but her self-esteem (Self = 5) is poor, which could be tied up with her feelings about her physical involvements. Her performance in school (Aca = 5) is fairly low for her age, but even so her motivation (Mot = 2) remains high despite her other difficulties, and her educational potential is average (Ptl = 4). It is possible that her low performance level may be more a result of her physical limitations than any particular lack of ability, as was suggested by the earlier clue, which indicated that her involvement was primarily in the upper part of the body. Placement in a special class could be recommended, in which case a more suitable program may be developed for her which will take into consideration her various abilities and limitations.

Briefly, this example of a 9-year-old boy conveys information that he experiences no difficulty in the general physical domain. However, in terms of adjustment and educational experiences, he has severe problems. Apparently having strong doubts about his worthiness (Self = 6), he also has extreme difficulties with his peers (Peer = 7), and he relates to his

c.

PH	Vis	Loc	Com
	1	1	1
AD	Peer	Fam	Self
	7	6	6
ED	Mot	Aca	Ptl
	5	6	6

Sex: male
Age: 9 years

family only slightly better (Fam = 6). This boy is clearly, then, an emotionally disturbed child who is functioning poorly in school (Aca = 6) and, doubtless because of his emotional difficulties, his educational potential is presently rated quite low (Ptl = 6).

d. A word of caution is in order regarding the use of the scale with the gifted child. Here we face certain limitations. The following rating should convey little more than that this is a gifted child with no problem in the domains we are rating.

PH	Vis	Loc	Com
	1	1	1
AD	Peer	Fam	Self
	1	2	1
ED	Mot	Aca	Ptl
	1	1	1

Sex: male
Age: 7 years
IQ: 140

In terms of logic, this kind of rating indicates that there is not much to significantly distinguish this child from any normal children of his age and sex, and therefore the child is not exceptional by the criteria we are using, which presumes difficulty or handicap in one or more of the areas rated. However, gifted children with other types of exceptionality, such as speech problems or motivational difficulties, may be included within this system. Such a child could have difficulty in communication (for example, Com = 5) or motivation (Mot = 5), without necessarily having other losses, such as in peer acceptance or in academic performance

Planning and Evaluating Programs of Treatment

Perhaps one of the weakest factors in special education and indeed in assessing the effect of therapeutic regimes is the lack of a comprehensive scheme for evaluation. Equally distressing is a failure in some cases to articulate, within realistic limits, a clear treatment program for each child. The employment of the profile scale permits the development of planning interdisciplinary treatment procedures on a basis that will allow, perhaps a year later, individuals to determine for themselves how well the goals have been formulated and met.

As an example, let us return to the previous example of the 10-year-old cerebral-palsied girl.

Present Status

	Vis	Loc	Com
PH	6	3	6

	Peer	Fam	Self
AD	4	1	5

	Mot	Aca	Ptl
ED	2	5	4

Cerebral Palsy
Sex: female
Age: 10 years

It is apparent that while the areas of locomotion, family relationships, and motivation in school work need little improvement, there is a need for further therapy to reduce visability, to help make her speech more comprehensible, to affect a greater degree of acceptance from herself and her peers, and to improve her academic performance in school. The effect of such a program can be grossly judged only after a period of time. The reduction of visibility and the improvement in speech could well result in improved educational and psychological adjustment. Thus the goal for this child for the *immediate* future could be described as aiming for the following:

Therapeutic Goal

PH	Vis	Loc	Com
	5	3	5

AD	Peer	Fam	Self
	3	1	4

ED	Mot	Aca	Pot
	2	4	4

Specifically this involves improvement in the area of visibility (from 6 to 5), in communication (from 6 to 5), in peer acceptance (from 4 to 3), in self-esteem (from 5 to 4), and in schoolwork (from 5 to 4). We must also consider that improvement in one area may also lead to additional improvements in other areas, as in educational potential hopefully from 4 to 3. But failure to achieve in one or all of these goals after a suitable period of time might pose questions as to the efficiency of the remedial procedures or the potential of the child to profit from further treatment. At any rate, the possession of a rating made in the past furnishes a potentially useful base line against which to assess the efficiency of specific procedures as well as overall improvement.

To Judge Congruence or Discrepancy in Estimates of the Child's Ability

It is frequently of value to examine how closely various persons concerned with the exceptional child agree with each other. Does the rating made by the teacher of the exceptional child align itself reasonably well with that of the mother? If not, where do they disagree? Does the estimate of the speech therapist who sees the child for specified periods of time agree with that of the physician who sees the child less frequently? Do two workers in the same specialty disagree? If so, in what area? These are all questions of fundamental importance to experienced workers. The problem is not so much one of determining which rater is "correct" but in recognizing that if raters disagree markedly, their perceptions of the same child are different and the difference could be an interfering factor in the overall planning for the child. However, such differences could also reflect differences in professional orientation. Reasonably good congruence among professional workers would indicate similarity of perception of the present functioning ability of the child.

As an example let us examine briefly the ratings of the following child.

        Cerebral Palsy, Mental Retardation
        Sex: female
        Age: 11 years

Clinic-staff Consensus

	Vis	Loc	Com
PH	4	4	3

	Peer	Fam	Self
AD	4	3	5

	Mot	Aca	Ptl
ED	6	3	4

Mother

	Vis	Loc	Com
PH	6	5	5

	Peer	Fam	Self
AD	5	3	5

	Mot	Aca	Ptl
ED	4	5	6

Clearly, some significant discrepancies exist. It is in such situations that the clinic or school staff can utilize the profile to counsel with the parent if necessary. It may also be used to illustrate discrepancies in perception which could be followed by suggestions from each concerning the subsequent therapeutic treatment deemed most appropriate for the child in the present circumstances.

However, in order to observe differential perceptions more closely, a rater agreement scale is proposed which can also facilitate cooperative

28   Introduction

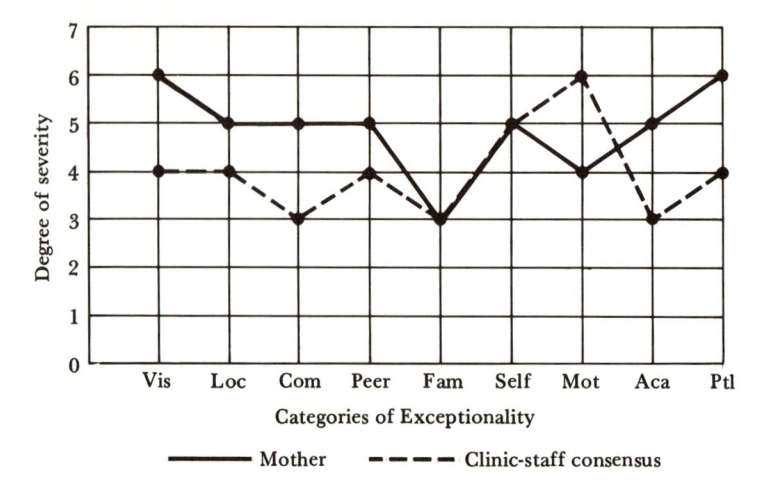

Fig. 1   *Rater agreement scale.*

planning and action for the child. Since the primary interest here is to determine degree of agreement between raters, Figure 1 (based on the example just cited) was devised specifically to clarify such concerns. This technique of plotting scores is especially helpful in instances where a child has failed to make progress despite the reasonable expectancy of his doing so.

For Long-term Follow-up and Longitudinal Studies

As has been previously mentioned, the need for longitudinal follow-up of exceptional children is a crucial one. Since the American population is a highly mobile one, such follow-up studies have become even more expensive than previously. Given the simplicity of the form and knowledge of a particular child's location, the possibility of obtaining a follow-up rating from some source or sources is heightened. It also allows for the validation of predictions, something that is sorely lacking at the present time.

RESEARCH TO DATE

As mentioned earlier, despite great interest, very little quantitative research has been done with the scale. However, one study by the authors has turned up inter-rater reliabilities ranging from .47 to .85. That study was made across disciplines and using professionals as well as nonprofessionals without controls of previous training in use of the scale. These results would suggest that a minimum of training would significantly raise the inter-rater reliability. As it is, the reliabilities are all highly significant.

CONCLUSION

One is always in danger of putting forth or advancing his own methods or pet theories. The classification system presented in this article doubtlessly needs much more refinement, with the ultimate addition of other categories and the deletion of some already in the scale. How can further utilization be encouraged? One tends to become discouraged in that there are sporadic bursts of enthusiasm such as a graduate student using the scale or a derivative in a dissertation and then no more communication. No doubt many systems similar to this one are used at the local level. Some see the light of day briefly; others perform yeoman service within a clinic or a school and that is all. With the millions of dollars expended in the entire field of special education, one sometimes wonders if there would be utility in a state- or federal-supported conference dealing with classification. One begins to feel sometimes that the target population of special education, the children, could get a better deal out of the whole undertaking than they are now receiving. This may be too cynical, but cynicism and skepticism are powerful spurs to progress.

3

Psychological Snares in the Investigative Enterprise

Beatrice A. Wright

Dr. Wright is Professor of Psychology at the University of Kansas. She is one of the most distinguished scholars and research workers in the field of rehabilitation. To give a complete list of her books, monographs, articles, consultantships, and honors would entail pages of fine print. Therefore, just a few of her professional recognitions will be mentioned. Her book Physical Disability: A Psychological Approach *won the Child Study Association of America Book Award for 1960. As a coauthor of the book* Artificial Limbs, *she won the 1959 Research Award of the Division of Rehabilitation Counseling, American Personnel and Guidance Association. She also won the 1959 award by the National Council on Psychological Aspects of Disability for her excellent work as editor of its publication, the* Bulletin. *And, finally, in 1968 she served as the American Psychological Association representative to the International Society for Rehabilitation of the Disabled.*

It is most fitting that we close the introductory section of our book with an article by Dr. Wright which concerns itself with pitfalls in doing psychological research. While Dr. Wright draws heavily on disability research to illustrate her points, her expressed thoughts have very broad applications.

PAPER DELIVERED November 8, 1967, at Rehabilitation Colloquium, Rehabilitation Counseling Program, State University of New York at Buffalo. To be published in Colloquium Series.

In drawing conclusions from observations, there are a number of psychological pitfalls that are so seductive that the investigator, be he the actual researcher or the consumer in search of understanding, must maintain a constant vigilance lest they entrap him. Four such deceptively innocent psychological illusions will be analyzed. They are referred to as (1) the figure–ground problem, or the tendency to perceive differences between groups in terms of the manifest variables; (2) commonsense connections between physique and behavior, or the tendency to select the facts that fit and fit the facts that don't; (3) the problem of stable organization, or the tendency to translate "sometimes" into "always"; and (4) the idolization of quantification, or the tendency to neglect qualitative experience and behavior. Exemplification will be drawn primarily from disability research, but the principles discussed have application to limitless content areas.

THE FIGURE–GROUND PROBLEM

Consider the following statement: The deaf appear to have a higher crime rate than the blind. Take a moment to think of as many reasons as you can to account for this fact. This problem was given to a group of mature scientists, a group of college students, and a group of parents of handicapped children. If your perceptual processes are like theirs, you will offer such reasons as the following:

> You need sight to execute a crime.
>
> Deaf people tend to be suspicious, which more easily gets them into trouble.
>
> Because deaf people can't hear, so it's hard to teach them right from wrong.
>
> The deaf are less accepted by society and therefore are more revengeful.
>
> Blind people seem to be closer to God.
>
> Blindness makes a person noticeable, so he would be less likely to risk a crime.

Notice that these reasons pertain directly to the effects of deafness and of blindness, the two labels by which the groups were explicitly differentiated. And yet there is some evidence that the age distribution among the blind and the deaf is not comparable, that a higher proportion of the blind than the deaf are over 60, an age where crime behavior tends generally to be inconspicuous. Whatever the facts, the possibility that the difference in age distribution of deaf and blind persons could account for the differential crime rate was not entertained by anyone, not even by the most well-seasoned of the experimenters. Evidently one is easily lured into explaining phenomena in terms of what is illumined by a label. The lure of a label is not unlike the misconception of the drunk who, in searching for the keys he dropped by his doorstep, looked under the lamppost a half block away because, he said, that was where the light was.

One can now see why the following study illustrates a type of reasoning common in disability research. The personality of crippled girls 16–25 years of age in a charity summer camp was investigated by means of a personality questionaire (Rosenbaum, 1937). The crippled girls received a mean score within the range of emotional maladjustment as determined by the norms, the standardization population being female college freshmen. The investigator concluded that the less-adjusted scores on the part of the crippled girls was "due in part to their physical handicaps and consequent thwarted activity and development."

And yet, in the wisdom of our detached critical appraisal, we can immediately point out that the results may plausibly be accountable in terms of differences between the crippled and noncrippled groups other than physical disability. It is to be noted, for example, that girls attending a charity camp are quite differently selected than college freshmen. They may be expected to differ in socioeconomic status, intelligence, and personality, factors which can be expected significantly to influence test scores aside from the factor of crippledness. Yet no mention was made of these variables. They were the background factors that did not figure because labeled outlines of them were not drawn.

Any labeled variable seems to have the power to capture under its aegis almost any behavior that may be posited. In fact, one feels let down, fooled, when the manifest variable has no connection with the behavior in question, such trickery being the basis of the humor in the query as to why firemen wear red suspenders. The fact that the color of the suspenders is made explicit *requires* that it enter solution of the problem, but the jokester, by ignoring as incidental what is otherwise manifested as essential, claims another dupe in affirming that firemen wear these suspenders to hold up their trousers.

There is evidence that negative physical characteristics as indicated by such terms as "crippled" and "disabled" are especially powerful in suggesting connections with other facts about the person (Wright, 1960). It is also to be noted that crippling, being a *visible* handicap, emerges as a manifest variable even when not highlighted by an explicit verbal label. A good example is the study in which half a group of high school subjects was shown a photograph of a boy sitting in a wheelchair, and the other half were shown the same picture with the wheelchair blocked out (Ray, 1946). The boy in the wheelchair was judged to be more conscientious, to feel more inferior, to get better grades, to be more unhappy, etc., than when depicted as being noncrippled. The single fact of physical deviation was able to affect the perception of the kind of person being judged. Ichheiser (1949) stresses visibility as a main determinant of what is regarded as reality. Coercion that is evident in violence, for example, is more objectionable than when it is more subtle, although not less devastating.

Precautionary Measures

Precautionary measures can be taken against the tendency to view physical deviation as a key to a person's behavior and personality, that is, against the otherwise irresistible tendency to perceive effects in terms of manifest variables. For example, it has become a working rule in psychological science to give special attention to the possible confounding effects of a least age, sex, intelligence, and socioeconomic status, and to control these factors in the research design when feasible. For certain problems, other factors must come in for careful scrutiny before conclusions can be restricted to the experimental or manifest variables. In somatopsychological research, for example, variable living conditions (such as special schools) of handicapped and nonhandicapped groups often need to be considered in evaluating differences between the groups. This is an important point, for the difficulty of collecting good descriptions of life as it is lived has made it easy to disregard the significance of ecological settings.

Entertaining what my esteemed teacher and philosopher, Herbert Feigl, has called the "something-else-perhaps" query can be amazingly effective in avoiding the all-too-simplified "nothing but" connections between behavior and disability. The query itself opens up a much wider array of factors as possibly having important bearing on physique–behavior connections. Feigl reminds us (1953), however, that in replacing "nothing but" by "something else," the investigator must be pressed to discover "what's what." The problem being researched may lend itself to ruling out the possibly contaminating "elses," or to multivariate analysis. Or it may better be handled by systematic observation and clinical interpretation, which attempt to give full weight to the multiplicity of factors that connect disability and behavior as revealed by real people in real-life situations. In any case, the oversimplification of disability–behavior connections which reflects the tendency to relate effects to manifest variables is at least thwarted.

COMMONSENSE CONNECTIONS BETWEEN PHYSIQUE AND BEHAVIOR

There are very good reasons why prejudices (i.e., prejudgments) have such a strong affinity for being regarded as fact. One of the basic reasons has to do with the powerful role of expectations in coercing perception in general (Wright, 1960). Prejudgments are expectations about how a disability will affect behavior, and as such they influence and in some cases determine to a large degree what we will see and what we will remember.

A nice illustration from another area of inquiry, the analysis of rumor, is provided in the work of Allport and Postman (1947). The following incident took place in a rural Maine community in 1945 shortly before Japan's surrender: A Chinese teacher on a solitary vacation drove his car into the community and asked his way to a hilltop from which he could see the pleasant view pictured in a tourist guide. Someone showed him the way, but within an hour the community was buzzing with the story that a Japanese spy had ascended the hill to take pictures of the region.

The distorting process was initiated by the frame of reference of the Maine residents that any Oriental was a "Japanese Spy." This expectation led to the omission from the rumor of many details: that no one had seen a camera in his possession, etc. It also led to the misinterpretation of certain of the details included; the fact that the visitor had a picture in his hand (the tourist guide) was erroneously translated into the act of "taking pictures," for example.

Because of just this kind of distortion, the perception and recall of facts that "fit" within an organizing principle (e.g., a good deal of knowledge claims in somatopsychology) might more accurately be predicated by "It is rumored that . . ." rather than by "It is a fact that. . . ." Consider such statements as the following:

> There is a distinct psychosis of the deaf . . . marked by suspiciousness, concealed anxiety, dejection, and emotional tension (Hentig, 1948, p. 84).

> Such flights of the imagination (as Robert Louis Stevenson achieved in *Treasure Island)* are characteristic of people who because of handicaps are not able to find adequate self-expression in overt activity (Mitchell and Mason, 1948, p. 80).

Although such statements as the above have a place in a research program where the job is to verify or refute the presumed connections between physique and behavior, they have no place as statements of fact—because there are, in short, no facts to support them. Because they fit in with the lore of common sense, as statements of facts they continue to blind us to the need for investigation.

A striking example of how wrong the "naturally logical" may be is given in the generally accepted notions concerning the proper living arrangements for ex-tubercular patients. It has been pointed out, however,

36   Introduction

that "while it is asserted frequently that exposure to excessive heat or cold, extremes in temperature, dampness, excessive humidity, drafts or fumes, gases, or nonsiliceous dust may reactivate tuberculosis, authorities state that there is no proof for such statements. Equally erroneous is the idea that the extuberculous must live in a special climate" (Rusk and Taylor, 1946, p. 118).

Equally sobering is the thought that we may not only be selecting facts to fit prejudicial expectations but may also be fitting facts that defy them. An especially relevant example is an experiment involving the self-acceptance of a group of stutterers (Berger, 1952). In validating the self-acceptance scale it was expected "on both an *a priori* and an empirical basis" that the group of stutterers should score lower than the group of nonstutterers. When they did not, the investigator, searching for possible uncontrolled factors, matched the stutterers with nonstutterers on the basis of age and sex. The resulting self-acceptance scores came out in the "right" direction—and the investigator stopped controlling! If the results had persisted in being stubborn, socioeconomic status would probably have "come in for its ruling out." The facts we expect can be manufactured by pursuing investigation until we arrange our methods to obtain them.

Precautionary Measures

Such selectivity of perception and procedure need not represent intentional distortion on the part of the investigator. It is precisely because as a human being "he can't help it" that he must exercise extraordinary care in making as much use as possible of precautionary measures against bias.

For example, in an experiment by Kahn (1951) on frustration in normal hearing and impaired hearing children, it became necessary to rate the behavior and verbal responses of the subjects in the experimental setting according to a variety of frustration indices. A not-uncommon expectation or stereotype concerning deafness is that a hearing loss makes for greater irritability and emotional immaturity in frustrating situations. Would not this expectation as an organizing frame of reference bias the ratings in favor of the normally hearing children? Because the experimenter was well aware of this danger, he mitigated it by eliminating the subject identification of the behavior protocols being rated. Other precautions are suggested by the well-known rules for establishing reliability and validity of data.

But because expectations (or mind sets, or theories, or frames of reference) serve as organizing principles for the selectivity of perception, it does not follow that we would be better off without expectations. We merely need to take measures to counteract the distortions introduced by them or, at the very least, to make the biasing assumptions explicit.

Actually, expectations in the form of explanatory hypotheses are necessary in order to broaden understanding of the relationships between physique and its effects. Consider the following statement: "One who is confined to bed with a chronic illness is likely to encounter special difficulty at adolescence when the problem of determining his identity is acute" (Witmer and Kotinsky, 1952, p. 61). Serious consideration of this hypothesis immediately leads to provocative questions. What do we mean by one's identity? How shall we know when a person is experiencing a problem in determining his identity? What kind of special difficulty in adolescence is implied? Does this refer to acceptance of the self, acceptance of the chronic illness, or reaction to and from peers? Other questions arise, too, and in their more explicit formulation research becomes possible and advances. But the tendency of the original statement concerning adolescence and chronic illness to be credited with the reality of fact simply by the coercion of common sense must be guarded against, for the common sense may more fittingly turn out to be common prejudice.

Pronouncements in somatopsychology could well be more frequently limited by such notations as appeared in the following statement: "It seems undeniable *(though scientific demonstration is largely lacking)* that, in one way or another, a deviation sufficient to be labeled a marked physical handicap is likely to be an impediment to personality development as well" (Witmer and Kotinsky, 1952, p. 61, italics mine). When scientific demonstration is forthcoming, even such a seemingly undeniable pronouncement may become most untenable.

THE PROBLEM OF STABILE ORGANIZATION

In an important study of the psychological aspects of facial deformity, the patients were asked to draw a figure of a person (Macgregor et al., 1953). Of the patients with but mild disfigurements, 81 percent produced drawings whose facial features were not disfigured in any way, whereas this was true of only 42 percent of those with severe deformities. In interpreting this difference, the investigators state: "We can perhaps say . . . that the drawings of the mildly deformed suggest the unrealistic nature of the way they perceived the actual deformity . . . The severely deformed on the other hand, reflect either a correct body image of themselves or a preoccupation with deformity . . . which is realistic . . ." (Macgregor et al., 1953, p. 152). Yet, two of five severely deformed patients produced drawings more typical of the mildly disfigured; conversely, one of five of the mildly disfigured produced drawings more typical of the severely deformed group. Although statements can legitimately be made as to how the two groups *as groups* differed, definitive inferences about individuals within the groups cannot be made. The group differences may also be used to indicate how confidently a particular hypothesis has been confirmed or how probable it is that similar differences would be found in comparable groups. (For a discussion of the concept to probability in terms of relative frequency and degree of confirmation see Carnap, 1953.) But if the group differences are used, as they so often are, to define the behavior of a member of the group without probability constraints, the unwarranted leap from "sometimes" to "always" has been committed. Moreover, as Allport (1964) has repeatedly argued, what holds true for aggregates of people cannot be assumed for the individuals in that aggregate. He reminds us with a homely example that "to say that 85 of 100 boys having such and such a background, will become delinquent is not to say that Jimmy, who has this background, has 85 in 100 chances of being delinquent."

The above discussion deals with what might be called *subject* overgeneralization. There is also overgeneralization of a different sort—behavior overgeneralization. On the basis of one behavioral manifestation in one kind of situation, observed group differences not infrequently are vaguely generalized as if they would obtain in any and all situations. And yet it is entirely possible that different situations could yield different results.

This is nicely shown in an experiment on rigidity in the personality of deaf children (Johnson, 1954). The experimenter used not one, but several, tests of rigidity in comparing day-school deaf children with matched hearing children. The results are given in Table 1. Just imagine how different the findings would have looked if only the Block Sorting Test had been used! Then the deaf children would have been shown to be more rigid than the hearing children. Or, if the Hidden Faces Test

Table 1 Comparison of Day-School Deaf Children and Normally Hearing Controls on Several Measures of Rigidity

Test	More rigid group	Significance level
Block sorting	Deaf	.001[a]
Level of aspiration		
total series	No difference	
failure series	No difference	
success series	No difference	
Hidden faces	Hearing	.001[a]
Ambiguous picture	Deaf	.05[b]

[a] Fisher's t-test.
[b] Wilcoxon's T-test.

had been the only measure of rigidity, the conclusion might have been just the opposite. But, because diverse manifestations of "rigidity" were evidenced, the experimenter was led to make a safer and at the same time more far-reaching conclusion: "Deaf children are *not necessarily* more rigid than hearing children . . . Deaf children may sometimes, in some situations, behave less rigidly than hearing children" (Johnson, 1954, p. 71). This conclusion is more far-reaching because it forces further consideration of the conceptual meaning of rigidity. Perhaps rigidity isn't a unitary concept at all. In that event there would be an advantage in employing different verbal designations of the separate personality dynamics involved. Or perhaps rigidity is a tidy concept, its phenotypical variations being an expression of situational factors in interaction with personal variables. In any event, the conclusion is far-reaching because it directs thinking to additional situational and personal variables which can then be pursued in continued investigation. For example, the experimenter in the above study considered the diverse results and the nature of the situations presumed to underlie them and speculated that the deaf will be flexible in many situations that involve acute visual perception (p. 75). The necessity of including an adequate sampling of situations (sometimes designated as "objects") as well as an adequate sampling of subjects has been urged upon psychological science by Brunswik (1947) and referred to as the problem of representative design. Then it is that the overgeneralization of today, instead of becoming the error of tomorrow, has a chance of becoming tomorrow's special case.

One significant factor that feeds into the overgeneralizing tendency has to do directly with principles of perceptual organization; that is, whatever man perceives tends to be or become organized and meaningful. One of the organizing principles is that events will be perceived and remembered in terms of the most stable organization possible.

A laboratory demonstration of this is given in the pioneer experiments of Wulf (1922), who asked his subjects to reproduce visual figures drawn on cardboard from memory after different time intervals:

Stimulus

Reproduction time 1

Reproduction time 2

Reproduction time 3

40 Introduction

He found a marked trend for the reproduced drawings to show a systematic change from the original irregularly formed figures toward figures that showed greater "stability." It seems likely in the context of our discussion that the "always" or overgeneralized statement represents a more stable, less complicated perceptual organization than the "sometimes" or probability statement with its implied "ifs, ands, and buts."

The second factor supporting the overgeneralizing tendency concerns the mission of the researcher as a scientist. As such his goal is to establish laws of behavior that may be generally applied and not merely restricted to the cases on hand. He would like to be able to talk, for example, about how severity of deformity affects perception of deformity in terms that apply to all cases. "Always" seems more scientific than "sometimes." He needs the added reminder, however, that not only in psychology, but also in physics, laws may have the character of statements of probability.

Precautionary Measures

Quipping that "all generalizations are false including this one," Bernard Shaw pointed up the strength of the overgeneralizing tendency. Yet there are at least partial safeguards against this tendency, as already suggested in the preceding discussion. With respect to subject overgeneralization, statements applying to groups should be carefully couched in probability terms, inferences from group data to the individual should be made with great caution, and generalization to wider populations not sampled in the investigation should be made only as hypotheses to be verified. With respect to behavior overgeneralization, research should incorporate diverse situations and diverse measures of the variable being studied. And with respect to semantic issues, it is urged that both the research worker and those interested in the findings keep ready the kind of question that will point up the possibly too-hasty generalization.

The semantic problem is such a telling one that it is well to stress it with an example. Consider the following statement: "A person who is threatened by identification with a particular group will also avoid contact with that group." Whenever a statement appears of this kind, the reader should immediately restrain its uncritical generality by such questions as: Does this mean that *all* persons who are threatened by identification with a given group will *always* try to avoid contact with that group? Or does it mean that there will be a force, however small, in each such person to do so, though in actual behavior he may not display avoidance? Or does it mean that *probably* such a person will try to avoid contact, but that the relationship between threat of identification and avoidance of contact does not hold for all persons? It is in the asking of such questions that at least the first checks to sweeping generalizations are introduced. Perhaps interjecting such syntactical restraints in the reporting of findings as: under certain conditions, may, tends to, probably, not infrequently, sometimes, usually, etc., may help to combat the overgeneralizing tendency. In any case, a precautionary mind set is urged upon the investigator, be he the producer or consumer of research, that looks for exceptions to rules and sees in the exceptions not a hampering of science, but a stepping stone for the discovery of significant understandings.

THE IDOLIZATION OF QUANTIFICATION

The veritable idolization of quantification in the scientific enterprise has led to a disdain for qualitative description of experience and behavior. Not only is measurement generally seen as necessary in any scientific investigation, but not infrequently it also is regarded as a sufficient condition.

This adulated position may be attributed to the convergence of a number of factors in the last half century:

1. The great power of the alliance between physics and mathematics in enabling man to predict and control awesome phenomena.

2. The conviction that anything that is real can be measured.

3. The belief that measurement is fundamental to all scientific advance.

4. The paradigm of the hypothetic-deductive method, which requires measurable predictions.

5. The desire of the social sciences to achieve the scientific status of the physical sciences through emulation of their methods.

6. The development of elaborate statistical procedures enabling the investigator to draw increasingly legitimate conclusions from the data of observation. With this development, a status hierarchy has developed between so-called low-level and high-level statistics, the lowly mean and percentage no longer figuring for much unless they first become embedded within a complex network of statistical manipulation which removes them from their immediate grasp.

7. The appeal of numbers as such in imposing order upon ideas that otherwise appear to remain more diffuse. I recently carried out an experiment in which the ideas in part of a lecture were explicitly enumerated in terms of "one," "two," and "three," whereas other ideas were delivered without such numerical identification. It was strikingly clear that in the former case, the notes taken were both more extensive and more orderly.

I would not quarrel with the guideposts of quantitative methodologies if they were not regarded as the *sine qua non* of science, for certainly they have aided enormously in the discovery of facts and ideas as well as in the validation of them. But by virtually revering quantification, an enormous scope of psychologically meaningful problems become eclipsed from view, either because they are not felt to be researchable in these terms, or because they become distorted by being shaped to fit the requirements of measurement, or because the quantitative treatment of the data so saps the time and energy of the investigator that he has no reserve left for delving into the fullness of qualitative analysis. A number of years ago Dembo and her coworkers cautioned against premature quantification, that is, quantifying behavior before the laborious task of qualitative description of problems and concepts is sufficiently advanced (Dembo et al., 1956). To this we can add that even when conceptualization is sufficiently advanced for meaningful quantification, an important place will remain for qualitative descriptions of experience and behavior.

Because the many problems that are most vitally relevant to living people in living situations are clamoring for a hearing, there is growing acknowledgment that such tender-minded topics as the values people live by, their hopes, moods, feelings, and beliefs must come under scientific scrutiny, but still the model held forth remains that of the "tough-minded approach to the tender-minded topic." Qualitative descriptions of the way people feel, think, and behave are still rarely felt to be legitimate in themselves; at best they are allowed as criteria for categorizing behavior so that such units can be counted and entered as frequencies into the statistical treatment of data.

It is emphasized here that we most certainly also need the tender-minded approach to the tender-minded topic. Although measurement contributes significantly to scientific advance, it is not fundamental to all scientific advance. We know so very, very little about so very, very little that the research enterprise should encourage a diversity of approaches, both tough-minded and tender-minded, on a diversity of topics. One approach is not intrinsically better than the other. Systematic qualitative analysis of interview material and of behavioral descriptions during which the investigator formulates notions as to what is occurring, checks these notions against continuing analysis and observation, and reformulates them accordingly can contribute much to the scientific enterprise. This is not armchair psychology. It is theoretically and empirically guided just as are experimental methods that rest heavily on instruments of measurement. The test of its scientific merit in stimulating further research, in producing concepts of value in understanding behavior, and in opening up new areas for systematic scrutiny is not less valid than in establishing a significance level of .01 or less.

The first three types of psychological problems that were reviewed here all lead to a gross oversimplification between disability as a physical fact on the one hand and behavior as a psychological fact on the other. The figure–ground problem as seen in the tendency to perceive differences between groups in terms of manifest variables, commonsense notions as seen in the tendency to select facts that fit and to fit facts that don't, and the problem of stable organization as seen in the tendency to translate "sometimes" into "always" all make it perceptually easier to grasp certain relationships that may not be there. The last issue, that of idolizing quantification, leads to an exorcism of important problems for investigation. Perhaps the suggested precautionary measures could enhance the self-corrective aspect of science, which "has rightly been stressed as its most important characteristic" (Feigl, 1953, p. 13).

References

Allport, G. W. *Pattern and growth in personality*. New York: Holt, Rinehart and Winston, 1964.

Allport, G. W., & Postman, L. *The psychology of rumor*. New York: Holt, Rinehart and Winston, 1947.

Berger, E. M. The relation between expressed acceptance of self and expressed acceptance of others. *J. abnorm. soc. Psychol.*, 1952, *4*, 778–783.

Brunswik, E. *Systematic and representative design of psychological experiments*. Berkeley: University of California Press, 1947.

Carnap, R. The two concepts of probability. In H. Feigl & M. Brodbeck (Eds.), *Readings in the philosophy of science*. New York: Appleton-Century-Crofts, 1953, pp. 438–456. Reprinted from *Philosophy and Phenomenological Research*, 1945, 5.

Dembo, T., Leviton, G. L., & Wright, B. A. Adjustment to misfortune—a problem of social psychological rehabilitation. *Artificial Limbs*, 1956, *3*, 4–62.

Feigl, H. The scientific outlook: Naturalism and humanism. In H. Feigl & M. Brodbeck (Eds.) *Readings in the philosophy of science*. New York: Appleton-Century-Crofts, 1953, pp. 8–18. This article originally appeared in *Amer. Quart.*, 1949, *1*.

Hentig, H. von. *The criminal and his victim*. New Haven: Yale University Press, 1948.

Ichheiser, G. Misunderstandings in human relations. *Amer. J. Social.*, 1949, *55* (supplement to No. 2), 1–70.

Johnson, D. L. A study of rigidity in the personality of deaf children. Master's thesis, University of Kansas, 1954.

Kahn, H. A comparative investigation of the responses to frustration of normal-hearing and hypacousic children. Ann Arbor: University Microfilms, Publication No. 2766, 1951. Brief summary appears in *Microfilm Abstr.*, 1951, *11*, 959–960.

Krech, D., & Crutchfield, R. S. *Theory and problems of social psychology*. New York: McGraw-Hill, 1948.

Macgregor, F. C., Abel, T. M., Bryt, A., Lauer, E., & Weissmann, S. *Facial deformities and plastic surgery*. Springfield, Ill.: Charles C Thomas, 1953.

Mitchell, E. D., & Mason, B. S. *The theory of play* (rev. ed.). Cranbury, N.J.: A. S. Barnes, 1948.

Ray, M. H. The effect of crippled appearance on personality judgment. Master's thesis, Stanford University, 1946.

Rosenbaum, B. B. Neurotic tendencies in crippled girls. *J. abnorm. soc. Psychol.*, 1937, *31*, 423–429.

Rusk, H. A., & Taylor, E. J. *New hope for the handicapped.* New York: Harper & Row, 1946.

Witmer, H. L., & Kotinsky, R. (Eds.). *Personality in the Making: Mid-century White House Conference on Children and Youth, Washington, D.C.* New York: Harper & Row, 1952.

Wright, B. A. *Physical disability—a psychological approach.* New York: Harper & Row, 1960.

Wulf, F. Über die Veränderung von Vorstellungen. *Psychol. Forsch.*, 1922, *1*, 333–373. (Reported in Krech & Crutchfield, 1948, pp. 126–128.)

part II
Exceptional Intellectual Processes

The Mentally Deficient

4

A Historical Survey of Research and Management[1] of Mental Retardation in the United States

Eugene E. Doll

> *Dr. Eugene E. Doll is Associate Professor of Special Education at the University of Tennessee. This article was written while Dr. Doll was Associate Director of the M. Stuart Walker Clinic School, Philadelphia. Active in the area of mental retardation, his articles have appeared in the* American Journal of Mental Deficiency, Journal of Consulting Psychology, *and* Music Therapy.
>
> *This article, an original contribution in the first edition, has become a classic in the field. It serves as an excellent introduction to the area of mental retardation. Dr. Doll traces the development of philosophies of and facilities for the treatment of the mentally retarded from the pre-Christian era to the beginning of the 1960s. He presents a brief consideration of psychological and anatomical approaches to this problem and concludes with an earnest plea for the further utilization of the abilities and talents of this potentially valuable, though limited, group of individuals.*
>
> *The article should provide the student with a good background to evaluate the developments in what continues to be the most active research area in the field of exceptionality.*

[1] The term "management" is here used generically to include the threefold approach of medical treatment and prophylaxis, educational training, and sociological care and supervision.

48   The Mentally Deficient

"Mental retardation constitutes one of our nation's most extensive health, education, and welfare problems. . . . It is estimated that 300 of the children born every day are destined to be mentally retarded. . . . Of each 100,000 persons in our population, an estimated 200 are blind, 300 are permanently crippled by polio, 350 by cerebral palsy and 700 by rheumatic heart conditions, *but 3,000 individuals are mentally retarded*" (Di Michael, 1956). For over a century the retarded have been the subject of searching and sophisticated scientific study. Perhaps no other special group of children has received more sustained and earnest attention through the years. Yet facilities for their care are still inadequate, publications about them difficult of access, and able personnel for their training hard to find.

Almost from the beginning, the study of mental retardation has been plagued by vagueness and disagreement over definition. Indeed, much of the controversy over the nature and extent of the problem has actually been a confusion in terminology. We shall here use the term "mental retardation," as recently defined by the American Association on Mental Deficiency, to cover "subaverage general intellectual functioning which originates during the developmental period and is associated with impairment in one or more of the following: (1) maturation, (2) learning, and (3) social adjustment." It follows that mental retardation may be either permanent or temporary, and that it may stem from constitutional inferiority, specific maldevelopment, sensory deprivation, social deprivation, accidental trauma, emotional disturbance, or fortuitous circumstance. It is descriptive only of "the current status of the individual with respect to intellectual functioning and adaptive behavior . . . determined in relation to the behavioral standards and norms for the individual's chronological age group." [2]

The term "mental deficiency," on the other hand, will be here used in its original sense, to designate a specific type of mental retardation, (1) developmentally manifest, (2) based upon structural defect, and (3) such as to render the individual socially incompetent. Such *deficient retardation,* being caused by inferiority or maldevelopment of the central nervous system, is irreversible. The failure of some writers to distinguish between mental deficiency so defined and *nondeficient retardation* stemming from sensory impairment, emotional involvement, environmental deprivation, or delayed development, has produced much confusion in diagnosis and prognosis. Both the deficient and the nondeficient retarded, however, are frequently the concern of the same agencies and the objects of similar methods and techniques. They exhibit the common feature of current retardation, and there is frequent embarrassment in accurate differential diagnosis. Consequently, it is both convenient and instructive

---

[2] Quotations from Heber (*1959*).

to treat the two types of retardation in one survey. As the problems of the mentally deficient are socially more urgent than those of the nondeficient retarded, they have received far more attention, study, and care—as will be evident from the following pages. The present survey will confine itself essentially to developments in the United States, with the exception of a few European developments which have been directly influential here.

The oldest written reference to mental retardation in our cultural tradition is said to occur in the Therapeutic Papyrus of Thebes, 1552 B.C. The problem also engaged the attention of several Greek writers. Although Greek contributions were not outstanding, it is worthy of note that both Hippocrates and Plato placed the seat of the soul in the brain, while Galen discussed variations in mental acuity. Aside from these contributions, the Greeks are remembered chiefly for their custom of either abandoning handicapped children to the elements or killing them outright. To such measures the Romans are said to have added the custom of maintaining fools for pleasure. Among the Iranians, on the other hand, Zoroaster reputedly enjoined tender care.[3]

The spread of Christianity, with its compassion for the unfortunate and the downtrodden, also brought hope to the handicapped. The Institutes of Justinian provided caretakers for imbeciles as well as for the deaf and the dumb, while at least one Byzantine nunnery undertook to care for the sick and the idiotic. With the decline of learning, quite variable practices seem to have prevailed in Western Europe—the retarded being variously favored as "innocents," tolerated as fools, or persecuted as witches. Of special interest is the establishment at Gheel, in Brabant, of a religious shrine and asylum, where both the insane and the feeble-minded were cared for in private families—a custom which in recent years became the model for family care in the United States. In twelfth-century England imbeciles were accorded legal status as wards of the king. The Reformation, however, with its emphasis upon personal responsibility, is said to have fostered harsher attitudes. Chains and dungeons were the fate of some, while in colonial New England others were doubtless included among the public charges whose labor was sold to the highest bidder for economic exploitation.[4] Throughout this early period there was no real understanding of the condition nor any co-ordinated plan for dealing with it. The first known glimmer of modern concepts appeared in a legal definition of idiocy in Sir Anthony Fitz-Herbert's *New Natura Brevium (1534)*, which combined the developmental, intellectual, and social aspects of modern terminology:

> And he who shall be said to be a sot [*i.e.* simpleton] and idiot from his birth, is such a person who cannot account or number twenty

[3] Barr *(1913)*; Nowrey *(1944–1945)*; Whitney *(1948–1949)*.
[4] Barr *(1913)*; Nowrey *(1944–1945)*.

pence, nor can tell who was his father or mother, nor how old he is, etc., so as it may appear that he hath no understanding of reason what shall be for his profit nor what for his loss. But if he hath such understanding, that he know and understand his letters, and do read by teaching or information of another man, then it seemeth he is not a sot nor a natural idiot.[5]

In 1690 Locke specifically distinguished idiocy from insanity:

Herein seems to lie the difference between idiots and madmen, That madmen put wrong ideas together and reason from them, but idiots make very few or no propositions and reason scarce at all.[6]

In 1675 Wolfgang Höfer, court physician at Vienna, gave the first-known scientific disquisition on cretinism. Half a century earlier Juan Pablo Bonnet had developed a system for the education of the deaf which led eventually to the development of Seguin's "physiologic" education of the mentally deficient. At the same time, St. Vincent de Paul was establishing his charitable orders in France and gathering together the homeless, the bodily and mentally infirm into the Bicêtre and other hospitals in Paris. Slowly, here and there, interests and formulations basic to the brilliant burst of activity in the early nineteenth century were building up.[7]

THE MOVEMENT FOR TRAINING: 1799–1875

Beginnings of Physiological Education in France

The basis for American work with the mentally retarded was laid in France in the late eighteenth and early nineteenth centuries. Even before Rousseau's call for an education based on nature, and prior to the sensationist psychology of Condillac, Jacob Rodriguez Péreire had established in Paris a school for deaf-mutes, where he evolved a scientific method of instruction which served as the basis for Seguin's subsequent work with idiots. Although Péreire did not work with the mentally deficient himself, his contributions to the philosophy and methodology of their education can hardly be overestimated. Basing his work upon the physiology of the day and upon wide reading among predecessors, he used both scientific observation and the case history in his approach, insisting upon the adap-

[5] Fitz-Herbert, *New Natura Brevium,* quoted in Pintner *(1931).*
[6] John Locke, quoted in Nowrey *(1944–1945).*
[7] Barr *(1913).*

tation of methods to the individuality of the pupil. Péreire viewed all the senses as modifications of the primary sense of touch, and believed them all capable of indefinite intellectualization. He used the intact senses educationally to reinforce or replace the damaged, also strengthening the latter by special exercises. His approach to speech was based not only upon phonetics but also upon a developmental approach to language. He stressed the necessity of methods utilizing the felt needs of his pupils, the importance of an educational program conceived in terms of ultimate social needs, and the fundamental educational principle of proceeding from the known to the unknown.[8]

The first to apply the principles of sensationist psychology to the mentally deficient, albeit unintentionally, was Jean Marc Gaspard Itard, a physician at the National Institution for the Deaf and Dumb in Paris. In 1798 a boy eleven or twelve years of age, found wandering wild and naked in the woods of the Department of Aveyron, was brought to the attention of Professor Bonaterre, of the Central School of the Department. Although Victor, as the "wild boy" came to be called, was not the first such feral human to be discovered in Europe, Bonaterre was the first to supply an adequate description in terms of modern science. He then took the boy to Paris, as an example of the original state of man, and to provide the followers of Condillac with an opportunity to observe the development of primitive faculties—"provided," he added with keen insight, "that the state of imbecility we have noticed in this child does not offer an obstacle to his instruction." [9]

The boy was eventually turned over for instruction to Itard, who undertook the task with enthusiasm, ignoring the warnings of Bonaterre and others as to the possible imbecility of his charge. Itard embarked upon a psychologically oriented course of instruction, by means of which he sought to (1) attach the boy to social life through bodily comfort, (2) awaken his nervous sensibilities by stimulation and by quickening the affections, (3) extend the sphere of his ideas by creating new wants and multiplying his human associations, (4) teach him speech through imitation under the bond of necessity, and (5) exercise the mind upon wants and then apply it to instruction. The combination of scientific sagacity, affectionate humanism, and practical resourcefulness with which Itard labored over his *"sauvage"* for five years makes epic reading. In the end, however, he confessed himself defeated in his attempt to civilize the lad. Victor was, indeed, an imbecile, quite incapable of anything beyond the most elementary stages of learning.

In his disappointment, Itard scarcely realized that the simple elementary instruction he had succeeded in imparting had proved the edu-

---

[8] Fynne (*1924*).
[9] Bonaterre, as quoted in Barr (*1913*).

cability of imbeciles. This won him the applause of the Academy and provided the bases for a new field of educational endeavor. He had demonstrated the feasibility of harnessing natural wants and drives for educational ends. He had proven the possibility of creating new wants and making them operative for future development. He had shown the possibility of refining sensory discrimination from wide to narrow differences. Of still wider significance, he had developed his program in terms of the child's organic needs—mental, moral, social, and esthetic. He had pointed the way to functional education for practical use.[10]

Having concluded his experiment with the "wild boy," Itard returned to the more fertile soil of deaf-mutism. The ground had been broken, however, and a couple of decades later Belhomme undertook the instruction of idiots at the Salpetrière, in Paris. In his *Essai sur l'idiotie (1824)* he noted that diagnosis must precede choice of subject matter, and advised inquiry into inclinations and propensities. During the 1830's schools as both the Bicêtre and the Salpetrière proved that idiots and imbeciles could be improved. Meanwhile, Esquirol addressed himself to the psychiatric aspects of the problem, differentiating imbecility from idiocy and both from insanity. Esquirol defined idiocy, in contrast to insanity, as arrested or imperfect development, incurable, and based upon defects in structure visible at autopsy. He added that it was a condition, not an illness. Imbecility he defined as a similar affliction, but less severe. Esquirol described imbeciles as endowed with feeble intellectual and affective capacities; incapable of attention; with feeble and fugitive sensations and poor memories; lacking in abstract notions, self-direction, and providence; emotionally underdeveloped; and easily influenced. Positively, he noted their ability to do rough coarse work, and to learn reading, writing, and a little music—adding that "in the insane hospitals they are the servants of everybody in the institution." Among idiots, on the other hand, instinct dominates all faculties, speech scarcely exists, physical malformations and afflictions are common, the senses are often enfeebled, and emotions nonexistent. Binet credits Esquirol with being the first to recognize that the basic lack of both classes was primarily intellectual rather than sensory.[11]

Physiological Education Crosses the Atlantic

The systematization, expansion, and implementation of the ideas of Péreire, the experiments of Itard, and the researches of Esquirol fell to Edouard Seguin, perhaps the greatest teacher ever to address his attention to the mentally deficient, and a man whose influence upon education gen-

---

[10] Barr *(1913)*; Fynne *(1924)*.
[11] Esquirol *(1838)*; Wylie *(1930)*.

erally has never received due recognition. At the suggestion of Itard, and under the guidance of Esquirol, Seguin in 1837 undertook the instruction of idiots in a private school in Paris. So great was his success that he was in 1842 made director of the school for idiots at the Bicêtre. He soon withdrew, however, to establish his own school, news of which shortly reached the United States through an enthusiastic article by George Summer in *Chambers' Journal*. An ardent follower of St. Simon, Seguin was in 1850 driven by political developments in France to migrate permanently to the United States.[12]

In this country, work with the mentally deficient began as an outgrowth of work with the blind and the deaf. As early as 1839 Samuel G. Howe, Director of the Perkins Institution for the Blind in Boston, experimented successfully with the physiological education of blind idiots. In 1844 the American Asylum at Hartford is said to have achieved similar success through the use of parallel methods with a deaf idiot. In 1848 Hervey B. Wilbur, inspired by Seguin's work in Paris, opened a private school at Barre, Massachusetts, devoted exclusively to the training of idiots. State training schools followed rapidly in Massachusetts, at South Boston (later moved to Waverly), and in New York at Albany (later moved to Syracuse). In 1852 a private institution with state support, later know as the Elwyn Training School, was opened in Germantown, Pennsylvania. By 1876 there were twelve institutions in eight states, all east of the Mississippi. Seguin himself was actively associated with all of the first four schools. He also served in Ohio and Connecticut before opening his own private school in New York City.[13]

All of these schools, frequently established in the face of public opposition, were conceived primarily as training schools for education and release rather than as custodial asylums. The state, in organizing them as "a link in the chain of common schools," [14] did not undertake to assume permanent care. In some instances retention was specifically limited to those of school age. In 1866 Seguin wrote that in his experience

> more than thirty per cent have been taught to conform to moral and social law, and rendered capable of order, of good feeling, and of working like the third of a man; more than forty per cent have become capable of the ordinary transactions of life under friendly control, of understanding moral and social abstractions, or working like two-thirds of a man; and twenty-five to thirty per cent come nearer and nearer to the standard of manhood, till some of them will defy the scrutiny of good judges . . . .

[12] Barr (*1913*); Fynne (*1924*); Wylie (*1925–1926*); Davies (*1930*).
[13] Davies (*1930*); Nowrey (*1944–1945*); Wylie (*1925–1926*).
[14] S. G. Howe, quoted in Fernald (*1893*).

54   The Mentally Deficient

If these expectations seemed unduly optimistic to his successors, they had at least the virtue of setting high goals. It is interesting to compare them with modern concepts and figures on retention and release.

Seguin's physiological system of education was firmly grounded in current physiology, humane philosophy, keen observation, and practical ingenuity. Resting upon the assumption that the brain could be developed only as an integral part of the nervous system, it was based upon stimulation of the muscles and senses, imitation, reflection, and synthesis. The point of departure was the individual child as he was found by observation to be, with special attention to his individuality, specific limitations, and talents. The aim was the comprehensive harmonious training of the whole child, physically, intellectually, and morally. The program reached from the cradle to the grave—beginning with institutional supervision of home care, and conditioning the child for adult life through a careful program of socialization and the choice of a suitable occupation.[15]

Seguin's procedures involved orderly sequences from passive to active, from sensation to perception, from the gross to the refined, from the known to the unknown, from observation to comparison, from attention to imitation, and from patterned activity to spontaneity. A strong believer in functional education, Seguin advocated teaching in context, teaching by relations rather than by rote, and utilizing the materials and situations of daily life in both intellectual and moral instruction. Sensing the rhythm of life itself, he alternated mobility with immobility, activity with repose, and urged variety and contrast in occupation. He suggested that each day's work begin and end with pleasurable activities, and that the intervening tasks be adapted to the mood of the hour. Despite his emphasis upon sensation, he noted the occurrence of "intellectual deafness." Recognizing the love of the retarded for routine, he based discipline on order; at the same time he made love the basis for altruistic socialization and called attention to the values of group play. Small wonder that his principles have, as he hoped, exerted increasing influence upon the education of normal children as well, at the same time that his name has fallen into ever deeper oblivion.

THE INSTITUTIONAL MOVEMENT: 1876–CA. 1890

The Rise of Custodial Care

In 1866 Seguin proposed a concerted attack on the problem through the formation of a national association. It was not until 1876, however, under the stimulus of the Centennial Exposition, that the Association of Medi-

---

[15] Seguin *(1866)*; Fynne *(1924)*.

cal Officers of American Institutions for Idiotic and Feeble-Minded Persons was formed at the Elwyn Training School, at Media, Pennsylvania. Present were delegates from New York, Pennsylvania, Ohio, Illinois, and Connecticut; actively interested superintendents from Kentucky, Massachusetts, and Indiana were included in the membership.

Down to the present this association, now known as the American Association on Mental Deficiency, has served as the focus for professional work in the field. Although full membership was at first limited to superintendents, associate membership was early available to others active in the field. Women were included among the first of these. Seguin was elected the first president. At once evident in the proceedings is a toning down of Seguin's optimism of the previous decade, and the emergence of a new conception of the role of the institution. "From ten to twenty per cent can be rendered self-supporting," announced the *Philadelphia Medical Times*—adding that many others could be "more cheaply and humanely cared for in asylums than scattered in the community." [16]

Indeed, the training schools were finding themselves unable conscientiously to return to the community a major portion of their students. Methods of custodial care were placed on the agenda for the second meeting. At the third, in 1878, H. B. Wilbur announced the opening of a frankly custodial branch of the Syracuse School, at Newark, New York, to cope with the serious social problem of feebleminded women of childbearing age. Ten years later, New Jersey followed with a similar state school for women at Vineland, to receive female graduates of the Training School. The need for custodial care for the feebleminded of both sexes finally found expression in the establishment of the Rome State Custodial Asylum in New York in 1894. For a number of years thereafter, custodial care became the major concern of the state institutions—although, oddly enough, Rome itself was to become outstanding in questioning this pattern early in the following century. The Association was active in agitating for the establishment and differentiation of institutions in all states. By 1892 there were nineteen state institutions and nine private schools in sixteen states, with a total population of 6,225.[17]

Also in 1876 delegates from France, Germany, Great Britain, Holland, Jamaica, Norway, Sweden, Switzerland, and the United States met in London to evaluate the work among "idiots and imbeciles" in their several countries. Here, too, it was agreed, "A small proportion of idiots and imbeciles may be made self-supporting. Many can be trained to be useful and happy." The conference recommended segregation at an early

---

[16] Quoted in Nowrey (*1944–1945*).

[17] Association of Medical Officers of American Institutions for Idiotic and Feeble-Minded Persons, *Proceedings* (*1876–1878*); Nowrey (*1944–1945*); Davies (*1930*); Fernald (*1893*).

age for distinctive treatment based upon useful training, especially industrial and agricultural. It recommended institutionalization for those liable to retrograde, but also noted that the condition of many could be improved by "boarding out" (*White House Conference on Child Health and Protection, 1952–1953*).

Clinical Types and Classification

Basic to any program of treatment and control were problems of causation and classification; but it was precisely here that the complexity of the problem and the limitations of scientific knowledge placed the resourceful "stalwarts of the past" at their greatest disadvantage. Their clinical medical orientation was well suited to the recognition and definition of the classical clinical types, but it impeded the rise of logical classificatory principles. Ireland's classification, as quoted by H. B. Wilbur in 1877, was based partly on etiology, partly on pathology: (1) genetous idiocy, (2) microcephalic idiocy, (3) eclampsic idiocy, (4) epileptic idiocy, (5) hydrocephalic idiocy, (6) paralytic idiocy, (7) cretinism,[18] (8) traumatic idiocy, (9) inflammatory idiocy, and (10) idiocy by deprivation. To this miscellaneous mélange of types, I. N. Kerlin in 1887 added the still less precise "moral imbecile," characterized by an undeveloped will. Despite the dubious psychological definition of this type, it was to prove a useful concept—serving as the basis for the definition of the "defective delinquent" of the early twentieth century.[19]

Earlier classifications of Esquirol and Seguin, while more logical than Ireland's, were inadequately differentiated, difficult of application, or of doubtful medical validity. It was Wilbur who pointed in the proper direction in calling upon all to address themselves to the problem of standardized description and analysis of the educational path for better evaluation, prognosis, and training. Despite the chaotic state of standards, both Kerlin and Knight in the 1890's were urging the value of large institutional populations which permitted classification for effective institutional administration and training.[20]

Broadening the Educational Base

Oddly enough, the outstanding achievements of these physicians were pedagogical. The year following his plea for descriptive analysis, H. B. Wilbur presented a developmental analysis of speech in terms of physio-

---

[18] Mongolism was by some considered a modification of cretinism.
[19] Association of Medical Officers of American Institutions for Idiotic and Feeble-Minded Persons, *Proceedings* (*1877, 1887, 1895*).
[20] *Ibid.*

logical, kinesthetic, associative, imitative, and volitional levels. He is said to have taught aphasics to read before they spoke. He was perhaps most influential through his "object system of teaching," which stressed concrete presentations and training for use. His papers before state and national teachers' conventions are said to have influenced the entire educational system of New York state. At Elwyn, Kerlin introduced the kindergarten in 1879 and explored the values of musical instruction. He anticipated returning the brighter children to their families in from five to ten years. For those needing permanent institutional care, H. B. Wilbur emphasized industrial training, while Doren, in Ohio, stressed agriculture. Walter E. Fernald reported on the training of low-grades in body care, gymnastic drill, self-help, habits and discipline, and in domestic chores—which both gratified their egos and helped to defray their expenses.[21]

The final major contribution of the nineteenth century lay in anthopometry and pathology. In 1881 G. G. Tarbell, statistically comparing institutionals with 25,000 normals, suggested the physical as well as the mental inferiority of the feebleminded. By 1887 Wilmarth, at Elwyn, was laying the basis for modern pathological work. Working with mongoloids,[22] he found characteristic a small pons and medulla, structural abnormalities of cells and blood vessels, and a lack of vascular tone throughout the brain. At about the same time Bournéville, in France, identified microcephaly as arrested cerebral development, blasting the older theories of cranial etiology. By the end of the century he and others had added tuberous sclerosis, scaphocephaly, and oxycephaly to the clinical types. In 1895, following years of experimentation, the successful treatment of cretinism with thyroid extract was announced.[23]

In reviewing the achievements of the nineteenth century, one cannot fail to be impressed with the wisdom, resourcefulness, and energy of these pioneers—who in a very real way prefigured the shape of things to come. With the exception of mental testing, Freudian psychology, and biochemical techniques, there was probably no major current point of view which did not find expression among them. By 1890 the responsibility of the state for the care of the retarded was finding general acceptance; supplementary private agencies were also among the foremost in the field.

[21] Association of Medical Officers of American Institutions for Idiotic and Feeble-Minded Persons, *Proceedings (1878, 1893)*; Wylie *(1925–1926)*; Fernald *(1893)*; *Psychol. Clin.* 1911–1912, 5.

[22] Mongolism as a clinical type of mental deficiency must, of course, be distinguished from Mongolism as a racial type. Interestingly enough, Mongoloid mongoloids do occur.

[23] Association of Medical Officers of American Institutions for Idiotic and Feeble-Minded Persons, *Proceedings (1881, 1887, 1895)*; Pichot *(1948–1949)*.

Although institutional segregation, either temporary or permanent, was deemed the most effective means of operation, the special-class movement —already well under way in Germany—was being urged here as well. Educational theory was firmly based upon developmental concepts and the unity of the personality; it was implemented in terms of practical use and adapted to the peculiarities and level of the individual child. The severely retarded and the "moral imbecile" had been recognized as in need of lifetime control. Others were being set at gainful employment. Anatomical advances included the discovery of bulbar underdevelopment, cerebral agenesis, structural anomalies, and vascular deficiencies. Etiological theory recognized genetic, physiological, and environmental factors. On the other hand, after fifty years of effort, in the United States these striking accomplishments were confined to sixteen of thirty-four states. Even in these, they reached only a small proportion of the retarded. Moreover, there is little evidence to indicate how widely the progressive programs of the half-dozen outstanding schools were imitated.

MENSURATION AND SOCIAL CONTROL: 1890–1919

The Rise of Normative Tests of Intelligence

The second great impetus to the field came again from France, in the work of Alfred Binet. Binet was the first to identify central intelligence— as opposed to peripheral disturbances—as the essential problem with the mentally deficient. He also supplied a scientifically reliable means for evaluating intelligence which opened new vistas in clinical diagnosis, classification, and educational planning. As it was a psychologist who solved what had passed as a medical problem, so in the new era of mensuration and social control, the leadership of the physician was disputed and shared by the psychologist, the educator, and the sociologist. In the words of Goddard, the most effective approaches were now conceived to be psychological and educational rather than anatomical. This was perhaps best symbolized by the establishment in 1906 of the first psychological laboratory for the study of mental deficiency, at the Training School at Vineland. Although this period merged imperceptibly into the one which was to follow, we may for purposes of organization use the publication of Goddard's *Psychology of the Normal and Subnormal (1919)* as a point of demarcation between the two.

The Binet-Simon Scale, radical as it appeared, was actually preceded by nearly a decade of previous psychological work. As early as 1890 James McKeen Cattell had advocated the standardization of methods and the establishment of norms in psychological testing. His sensory and sensory-motor tests, however—reflecting his training under Wundt—were ill-suited to the differentiation of intellectual abilities. In 1893 Jastrow devised tests of memory and Gilbert introduced age norms. In 1897 Ebbinghaus, viewing synthesis as the test of intelligence, introduced his completion test—which was, however, slow to spread in this country.[24]

The pioneer testing of the feebleminded here was carried out at the turn of the century by A. R. T. Wylie at the Faribault State School in Minnesota. In 1899 Wylie found his subjects markedly deficient in sensation, but with a high mean variation which emphasized the importance of individually variable sensory training. In a series of incisive papers he reported rigid memory with defective associations, deficient muscular control, deficient endurance, and feebleness of instinctual elaboration and emotional inhibition. In 1906 Naomi Norsworthy, citing the lack of agreement in the fields of brain histology and physiological chemistry, and criticizing the narrow range of previous psychological testing, contrived a battery of tests for the measurement of mental ability. Expressing her norms in terms of group variability, she found idiots to fall within the curve of normal distribution. Her results showed the feebleminded subnormal in all mental functions—with perception stronger than memory, and memory stronger than intellect. She considered their motor difficulties a reflection of the intellectual.[25]

Norsworthy's able study was rapidly overshadowed by the more comprehensive work of Binet, the first to achieve an objective normatively standardized scale for the measurement of human intelligence. In 1904 Binet, as a member of a French commission on the education of defective children, was faced with the problem of devising an objective basis for selecting retarded children for the special classes of Paris. He rejected the current etiological and symptomatic classifications by clinical type as pedagogically unfruitful in not giving the degree of handicap. For the evaluation of educable potential, he concluded that psychological evaluation of intelligence was needed. For objectivity he considered mensuration essential. He proposed a graduated scale which would allow comparison with normals. The basis for intelligence Binet found in the mental process of *judgment*. He added that attention and memory could serve as useful indicators of intelligence before the development of the higher intellectual processes.

In 1905 Binet published a convenient, precise, and rapidly administered series of heterogeneous tests of intelligence. In 1908, having standardized this on normals in the primary schools, he grouped the tests under normative age levels, introducing the concept of mental age. This revision, he suggested, indicated the maturational level for instruction and offered a standard for the evaluation of medicopedagogical treat-

[24] Pintner (*1931*).
[25] Wylie, *J. Psycho-Asthenics*, 1899–1900, *4;* 1900–1901, *5;* Norsworthy (*1906*).

ment. *Prognosis,* however, was reserved, and for pedagogic *diagnosis* he recommended use of the scholastic record as well as the test score. In view of the deceptive simplicity of the scale, Binet set forth detailed instructions for its administration, stressing the importance of trained examiners, and warning against trusting gross results without recording psychological observations. Keenly critical of his own instrument, Binet labored constantly for its improvement up to the time of his death.[26]

Henry Herbert Goddard, Director of Research at the Training School,[27] discovered the Binet tests while traveling in Europe in 1908. At first antipathetic, he became more enthusiastic with increasing study, finally finding in the scale the possibility of bringing new order to the investigation, classification, and treatment of mental deficiency. Upon his return to Vineland, Goddard published an immediate translation of the 1905 series. In 1910 he brought out an American standardization of the 1908 scale. In 1916 he and Elizabeth S. Kite offered a translation of Binet's five major papers on the analysis and measurement of intelligence. In 1918 one of his assistants, Edgar A. Doll, published a brief form of the scale (for use in situations which did not admit of the longer scale) which correlated highly with the complete series. Meanwhile other workers hastened to address themselves to the tasks of restandardization and refinement—notably Town, Wallin, Kuhlman, Yerkes, Bridges, and Terman, who in 1916 introduced the Intelligence Quotient earlier suggested by William Stern.[28]

The entire Binet movement underwent bitter attack. Skeptics at once pointed out the danger of losing the unique quality of performance in mathematical scores, as well as the inadequacy of a single diagnostic instrument. Especially unpopular was the concept of the IQ—the constancy of which was questioned even within the Binet ranks, by Doll in his doctoral dissertation *(1921).* The Binet was, indeed, susceptible and subject to serious abuse in the hands of the untutored and the inept, but its role in explaining, diagnosing, and rejuvenating the treatment of mental retardation was revolutionary.

It was immediately reflected in the classification of feeblemindedness adopted by the American Association on Mental Deficiency in 1910. Formulated largely by Goddard, this classification was based directly on Binet's mensuration of social adequacy in terms of intellectual level. The older terms, idiot and imbecile, were retained—differentiated now at the upper limit of Mental Age 2 by a variety of performances, rather than by the earlier single criterion of speech. For the highest grade of social inade-

[26] Binet and Simon *(1916).*
[27] The Training School at Vineland, New Jersey, commonly referred to simply as "The Training School."
[28] Pintner *(1931);* Doll, "Brief Binet-Simon," *Psychol. Clin.,* 1911–1912, *5;* 1913–1914, *7;* 1914–1915, *8.*

quacy—reaching from MA 8 to MA 12—Goddard coined a new word, *moron*, from the Greek, meaning deficient in judgment, sense, or intelligence. The older clinical designations were retained as adjectival qualifying prefixes.[29] With its logically consistent differentiation in terms of ability, its scientifically validated uniformity, and its useful implications for differential training, the new classification rapidly replaced the older pathological systems and became standard throughout the country.

The Investigation of Nonintellectual Factors

Among the first to express his dissatisfaction with the Binet constructively was William Healy, of the Chicago Juvenile Court. Faced with linguistic problems in his work, and distrustful of the facile verbalist, Healy in 1911 presented additional aids to diagnosis which discriminated conditions and the need for more items testing the "thing thinker," as opposed to the Psychological Clinic of the University of Pennsylvania, complained that the tests currently in use did not distinguish "mentally defective children" from "children with mental defects." In the same year, W. E. Fernald contended that the problem of borderline diagnosis was still unsolved. Terman himself, occupied with the Stanford Revision of the Binet, noted the need for more items testing the "thing thinker," as opposed to the "idea thinker." In 1915 S. D. Porteus, complaining that the Binet was influenced by previous training, and that it penalized certain temperamental and sensory defects, brought out a new series of "motor-intellectual" mazes calculated to test prudence, foresight, and mental alertness in a relatively concrete setting. In 1916 Edgar A. Doll, in discussing the elements of comprehensive clinical evaluation, listed—in addition to tests by Binet, Otis, Whipple, and Healy—the formboard and the maze, anthropometric measurements, tests of learning, tests of educational achievement, familial and personal history, and clinical impression, with emphasis on the total picture. In 1917 W. E. Fernald, in formulating his ten-point "fields of inquiry," added the assessment of practical knowledge and general information, social history and reactions, economic efficiency, and moral reactions. In the same year Rudolf Pintner and D. G. Paterson, working with the deaf and the linguistically handicapped, brought out their Scale of Performance Tests as a clinical corrective to the linguistically weighted Binet. This was based upon a whole decade of work with formboards, mazes, puzzle boxes, and picture-completion tests, developed by Norsworthy, Goddard, Knox, Healy, Porteus, Pintner, and Paterson.[30]

[29] *E.g.*, Microcephalic idiot. See Goddard on classification, *J. Psycho-Asthenics*, 1910–1911, *15*.

[30] *Psychol. Clin.*, 1910–1911, *4;* 1913–1914, *7;* 1916–1917, *13*. Terman in *J. Psycho-Asthenics*, 1913–1914, *18*, 31. Davies (*1930*). Pintner and Paterson (*1917*). Porteus in *J. Psycho-Asthenics*, 1915, *19* (4), 200–213.

As is evident from these protests, warnings, and supplementary devices, Binet's central theory of retardation as intellectual deficiency in judgment was immediately qualified by correlaries of individual variation based upon sensory defects, special abilities and disabilities, temperamental pattern, and environmental deprivation. With the first numbers of *The Psychological Clinic*, in 1907, Lightner Witmer had called attention to the variability of retardation. In these and subsequent numbers, he discussed the etiological importance of emotional deprivation, lack of experiential stimulation, functional nervous disease, inadequate or improper nutrition, sensory defects, physical illness, and improper discipline. By 1911 he asserted, "Retardation is not a disease, it is not a brain defect, nor is it necessarily the result of a brain defect. It is not even a condition with a definite number of assignable characteristics. It is a mental status, a stage of mental development." [31] The pages of his journal were rich with theoretical and practical materials on such problems as aphasia, laterality, and word-blindness.

Healy, Emerick, and V. V. Anderson, working with defective delinquents, also devoted attention to personality differences and special abilities. In 1915 Schlapp, discussing "simulated feeblemindedness," called attention to neurotic and physiological components. In 1917 Augusta Bronner added epilepsy, overindulgence, physical trauma, brain-disease, alexia, and low motivation to the conditions already mentioned, and elaborated the educational implications of individual variation. Meanwhile Kuhlmann and Bliss investigated the problems of borderline diagnosis. Phillips had already noted variations in test patterns between racial-cultural groups.[32]

In contrast to the brilliant and burgeoning advances in psychology, pathology constituted a declining interest during these years. This was partly owing to the complex and contradictory nature of findings, partly to their limited practical application. Mierzejewski's findings with respect to the deficiency of association fibers in idiocy were sound. Also fundamental were the discoveries of Hammarberg and Tredgold with respect to the numerical deficiency and irregular arrangement of nerve cells. Such contributions, however, led nowhere in terms of training and control. The anthropological studies of Hrdlicka and the biochemical studies of Peters, while suggestive, did not pass beyond the preliminary stages.[33]

[31] *Psychol. Clin.*, 1910–1911, *4*.
[32] *Psychol. Clin.*, 1907–1908, *1;* 1910–1911, *4;* 1911–1912, *5;* 1914–1915, *8*. *J Psycho-Asthenics*, 1911–1912, *16;* 1914–1915, *19;* 1916–1917, *21;* 1917–1918, *22;* 1918–1919, *23*. Bronner (*1917*).
[33] Mierzejewski in *J. Psycho-Asthenics*, 1900–1901, *5*. Potter in AAMD, Proceedings, 1925, *30*, 258–265. Hrdlicka in *J. Psycho-Asthenics*, 1898–1899, *3*, 47–75, 99–136, 153–190. Peters in *Train. Sch. Bull.*, 1912–1913, *9*, 70–73.

Institutional Differentiation and Extension

The institutions, meanwhile, were faced with challenging problems of increasing population and inadequate financial resources. Disappointed in their overly optimistic expectations of cure and discharge, they found themselves the victims of their own agitation for laws of permanent custody. With the development of more sensitive diagnostic instruments and with the increasing awareness of the problem, pressures increased still more. Now was added the staggering responsibility for the social menace of the thousands of marginally intelligent but socially irresponsible morons brought to light by Goddard's investigations. To meet this multiple challenge, the monolithic institutions differentiated their programs and extended their activities.

Earlier hopes for large institutions so classified as to provide the advantages of intimate care and a diversified program were realized toward the close of the century by the development of the "cottage" plan at the Training School. In 1907 this was used as the basis for the new institution of Letchworth Village in New York.

Antedating even the cottage plan was the colony—born partly of the desire for greater occupational and social opportunity for high-grades, partly of the thrifty hope of rendering them self-supporting. A colony has been defined as "a number of mentally deficient persons living together under supervision and control outside of, but in affiliation with, an institution and supported more or less by group earnings" (*White House Conference on Child Health and Protection, 1933*). Wylie has credited Illinois with the establishment of the first farm colony, for older boys, in 1881. The Syracuse State School of New York opened a similar undertaking at Fairmount in 1882. Indiana and Massachusetts followed in the 1890's. The colony achieved its most effective organization, however, at the hands of Charles Bernstein, of the Rome State School, who, in 1919 estimated that his moron population had increased from about 15 to about 80 per cent. By 1916 Bernstein had purchased or rented five farms in the vicinity of Rome, New York, where boys and men were living freer, happier, and more productive lives than in the institution. In 1914 he had obtained a house in a residential section of Rome as a home for fourteen girls who earned their living as domestic servants in the community. In 1917 the wartime shortage of labor enabled him to establish a similar industrial colony for girls in cooperation with a knitting mill in Oriskany Falls. Not only were the inmates of these colonies enabled to live much more nearly normal lives but they had also been turned from economic liabilities into assets, freeing expensive institutional beds for more needy cases.[34]

[34] Wylie (*1925-1926*); Davies (*1930*); Bernstein (*1919*).

At the Training School, under E. R. Johnstone, the institutional program underwent extension as well as differentiation. We have already mentioned the establishment of the Vineland Laboratory, which undertook the study of the characteristics, classification, and etiology of mental deficiency with reference to methods of treatment, training, social control, and prevention. This ambitious undertaking would hardly have been possible without the formation, in 1902, of the "Feeble-Minded Club," a group of philanthropic and public-spirited citizens and specialists who both interested themselves in the problem and provided financial assistance. In the same year Johnstone instituted a Summer School for professional workers. The far-reaching influence of this program, which subsequently enjoyed university affiliations, can be comprehended only by comparing the names of subsequent leaders in the field with the rosters of summer students. In 1909 there was formed at Vineland a state-wide committee which within three years had obtained a legislative program providing for medical inspection and special classes in the public schools, custodial retention of the socially incompetent, parole, a marriage prohibition law, and the appointment of a state commission. In 1913 the Training School organized a permanent Department of Extension to publicize findings in the field. In 1914 it gave birth to the Committee on Provisions for the Feeble-Minded, which agitated throughout the country before legislative bodies, professional groups, and the general public. Eventually the program of the Committee included 1,100 lectures in thirty-three states and Canada, and was responsible for new or increased provisions in nineteen states. Johnstone's early dream of a Central Bureau for the collection and circulation of data was only recently independently realized, with the establishment of the AAMD Project by the American Association on Mental Deficiency in 1956.[35]

The Movement for Segregation and Sterilization

In 1896 Martin Barr, in an investigation of 1,034 idiots, found 38 per cent with family histories yielding insanity or imbecility, 57 per cent with histories yielding "other neuroses." These findings were confirmed by the British Royal Commission in 1908, when Tredgold went so far as to suggest that 90 per cent of feeblemindedness was familial in origin. In 1910 Goddard, in a paper before the American Breeders Association (*Goddard, 1910*) distinguished between hereditary and nonhereditary types and presented family charts showing recurring feeblemindedness extending back three, four, and five generations. In 1912, in a popular work on the "Kallikak family" (*Goddard, 1912*), he presented striking parallel hereditary lines extending five generations in a single New Jersey family—an illegiti-

[35] Johnstone (*1949*); Johnson (*1923*).

mate line shot through with feeblemindedness, and a legitimate line of normal and superior descendants. In 1914, in an elaborate scientific study (*Goddard, 1914*) based on 327 genealogies, he outlined his thesis of the inheritance of feeblemindedness as a Mendelian unit character in about 70 per cent of the cases. Although Goddard's work shows some need for correction in terms of modern procedures and discoveries, it set a new standard of scientific discipline for the day and dispelled much of the older folklore concerning etiology.[36]

The British Royal Commission also pointed up strikingly the significance of mental deficiency as a cause of crime and delinquency. It reported 20 to 40 per cent of the inmates of prisons and reformatories, and about 30 per cent of unwed mothers as intellectually incapable of economic self-sufficiency or prudent management of their affairs. Anne Moore, in a study of the situation in New York, stressed the endemic nature of the problem and the need for concerted action to provide life-long supervision and care, with particular attention to the reproductive years. In 1917 V. V. Anderson's summary of various studies reported estimates of the proportion of feeblemindedness in prisons, reformatories, poorhouses, and houses of refuge ranging from 16 to 50 per cent. The study of the "criminal imbecile," or "defective delinquent," was pursued intensively by Healy, Emerick, Goddard, and W. E. Fernald, who pointed out the difficulty of caring for this type in either reformatories for the normal or the regular institutions for the feebleminded. In 1911 Massachusetts passed a law providing for the separate segregation of defective delinquents, which was not, however, implemented until 1922.[37]

Faced with such an alarming indictment of the social consequences of feeblemindedness, as well as with disturbing evidence of fertility rates and sexual irresponsibility, authorities logically turned to sterilization as the complement to segregation for effective control of the problem. Early in the 1890's Kerlin had recommended its serious consideration. Before the advent of legal provision, Pilcher, in Kansas, had performed eighty-five operations, on the grounds of expediency. The passage of the first sterilization law, in Indiana in 1907, was followed by 800 operations in that state within a year. A permanently continued and widely utilized program, however, was first achieved in 1917 in California, where sterilization became a customary provision for parole and was made available to extra-institutional idiots upon request. Faced with popular opposition, professional doubts, and legal uncertainties, sterilization was slow to achieve acceptance outside of California, until the upholding of the Vir-

---

[36] Barr, in *J. Psycho-Asthenics*, 1895–1896, *1;* Davies (*1930*); Goddard (*1910, 1912,* and *1914*).
[37] Davies (*1930*).

ginia sterilization law by the United States Supreme Court in 1927 opened the way for its continued slow but steady growth.[38]

The Rise of the Special Class

While the early training schools of this country were developing along the lines of segregation, diversification, and social control, Germany, the cradle of public education, was already dividing its retarded children between institutions and the public schools. Although special classes for the mentally retarded began at Halle-an-der-Saale in 1859, they had their first extensive development in Saxony in the 1860's. By 1905 Saxony alone boasted more than 10,000 children in 492 special classes in 180 cities. Based upon Froebelian precepts of the educational value of play, as well as upon Seguin's physiological methods, these schools and classes advocated a flexible program which included spontaneous activity, stimulation of latent abilities, "realistic studies," a delayed and modified academic program, the project method, projective techniques, and socially useful education (*Maennel, 1909*).

Continued reports of the practical success of these schools led to the establishment of special classes in half a dozen of the larger American cities at the turn of the century. The beginnings of the movement are somewhat unclear, for in some of the early classes the retarded were mixed with other problem children. Specific classes for the backward are reported in Cleveland in 1875 and again in 1893. Between that date and 1905 classes specifically for the retarded appear to have been initiated also in Chicago, New York, Providence, Springfield, Philadelphia, Boston, and Portland.[39]

The model class conducted at the University of Pennsylvania by Lightner Witmer and Elizabeth Farrell, who had studied in Germany and Belgium, combined and extended earlier American and European methods. On the basis of case histories, Witmer and Farrell grouped their children according to abilities. Proceeding from the concrete to the abstract, they utilized and directed the constructive, proprietary, and play "instincts" in freely conceived projects and activities. Providing a variety of activity within the classroom, they also took measures to control the outside environment (*Witmer, 1911*).

Goddard, at Vineland, also fostered the utilization of psychological

---

[38] Nowrey (*1944–1945*); Davies (*1930*); Cave on early sterilizations in Kansas, *J. Psycho-Asthenics*, 1910–1911, *15;* Hawke on *ibid., Amer. J. ment Def.*, 1950–1951, *55*, 220–226.

[39] Steinbach on special classes in Cleveland, AAMD, *Proceedings,* 1918; Mitchell (*1916*); Davies (*1930*); *Psychol. Clin.*

research in the classroom and urged his teachers to pedagogical experimentation. To the older emphases on individuality, meaningful repetition, and nonacademic instruction, he added the physiological and psychological importance of enthusiasm, happiness, and concrete motivation. Suggesting that the estimate of retarded children as 2 per cent of the school population was probably too low, he urged the importance of special provision in small educational systems as well as in large. He set the maximum feasible class size at fifteen. The Vineland Summer School, always enriched by a galaxy of guest specialists, addressed itself to the urgent problem of teacher-training.[40]

Among its outstanding graduates was Meta Anderson Post. In 1917 Dr. Anderson, Director of "Binet Classes" in the public schools of Newark, New Jersey, codified the principles of curriculum and method (*Anderson, 1917*). Acknowledging her debt to both Goddard and Tredgold, she recommended an ungraded sequence of kindergarten, departmental, and vocational work. She centered the elementary curriculum about self-care, exercises in practical living, sensory training, speech training, manual dexterity, physical training, and practical academic essentials. Vocational training she based on a combination of individual assessment with practical possibilities for employment—stressing training for employee attitudes as well as for occupational proficiency. She related her students to the community through entertainment and home visitation. In method, Dr. Anderson warned against the limitations of any single technique and stressed the necessity for continual improvisation. She did, however, call special attention to the procedures and techniques of Maria Montessori—who, after applying the principles of Seguin to retardates in Italy with striking effect, had evolved an elaborate system of principles and practical materials which exercised considerable influence upon the education of both retardates and normals.

Following the lead of New Jersey in 1911, fifteen states had made the establishment of special classes or schools permissive or mandatory by 1927. By 1923 special classes in 171 cities claimed an enrollment of nearly 34,000. Meanwhile, in Cleveland, Rochester, and elsewhere, elementary vocational schools and trade extension classes were organized for specific needs. These positive advances, however, were matched by negligence in other parts of the country; and even where the spirit was willing, the know-how and the means were often lacking. The high cost of an adequate program ($83 per year in Cincinnati for retardates, as compared to $35 for normals) and the inherent difficulties of the work undoubtedly had much to do with this lag.[41]

---

[40] Goddard (*1914, 1915–1916,* and *1919*).
[41] Davies (*1930*); Wylie (*1925–1926*); Mitchell (*1916*).

INDIVIDUAL VARIABILITY AND THE CO-ORDINATION OF SERVICES: 1920–1941

Parole, Community Services, State-wide Programs

The 'twenties and 'thirties saw the increasing study of the individual variability of the mentally retarded and state-wide co-ordination of varied services for their care, training, and supervision. Although by 1927 there were seventy-three institutions in forty-three states, it was obvious that their capacity of about 58,000 was far from sufficient for the demands of the problem. They were learning that some of their greatest contributions were to come by moving out into the communities and integrating their special knowledge with other services.

Bernstein had already proved the colony capable of rehabilitating numbers of deficient retardates and returning their services to society. By 1921 the Rome State School counted twenty-five colonies scattered about the state. In view of the values of the colony in stimulating self-sufficiency, self-respect, and independence, Bernstein was soon recommending it as a halfway station for parole. In 1912 the legislature granted him discretionary power to grant paroles and leaves of absence. By 1921 he had trained and paroled 130 males and 102 females, either to their families or to homes which could use their services. One-third of his total institutional population was now self-sustaining—in colonies, on parole, or on leave. The fact that twenty-two of the females had reproduced, Bernstein considered a small price to pay for the human and financial values of the successful cases.[42]

Massachusetts also pioneered in the study and practice of controlled release. In 1919 W. E. Fernald had published a study of discharges from Waverly over a period of twenty-five years—runaways, patients discharged over institutional protest, and approved discharges. Of the females he found only 27 per cent sexually immoral; 30 per cent were earning their own way economically. Of 470 males, 191 were employed, either gainfully or at home; arrests, commitments, and readmissions numbered 166. Considering the unselected nature of the group and the lack of systematic supervision, Fernald considered the amount of crime, sexual offense, and illegitimacy surprisingly small. He concluded that an appreciable percentage could be trained for successful extra-institutional adjustment. Already in 1918, before the publication of the study, both Fernald at Waverly and G. L. Wallace at Wrentham instituted parole, although legal sanction for Massachusetts came only in 1922.[43]

[42] Davies (*1930*); Bernstein (*1919* and *1921*).
[43] Davies (*1930*).

In the latter year V. V. Anderson brought out a study of the community adjustment of graduates of the special classes of Cincinnati. Of 301 cases diagnosed as mentally defective by the public schools or the Vocation Bureau, he found about half gainfully employed, about 20 per cent with court records—suggesting the need for a more purposeful program of selection, training, and supervision (*Anderson, 1922*).

Fernald also extended institutional services into the community by means of the out-patient clinic. As early as 1891 he had operated such a clinic at Waverly. In 1915 he provided for traveling clinics to adjacent towns for purposes of diagnosis and to suggest methods of training and treatment. Between 1891 and 1920 the Waverly clinics had served 6,000 patients. In 1922, under Fernald's leadership, Massachusetts inaugurated a state-wide system of mental clinics for examining mentally retarded children, suggesting procedures, and making the resources of the institutions generally available. G. S. Stevenson has claimed that these innovations set the pace for early child-guidance clinics throughout the nation.[44]

More and more studies and investigations were pointing to two conclusions. Substantial numbers of both institutional parolees and extra-institutional retardates were capable of successful adjustment in the community. In most tallies the "good" appeared to outnumber the "bad." At the same time, many of these adjustments were obviously marginal, in that as much depended upon the environment as upon the retardate himself. It was obvious, with lengthening waiting lists and increasing attention to the needs of nondeficient retardates, that new methods of meeting the problem in the community were urgently needed. By 1930 the White House Conference on Child Health and Protection was to report 15 per cent of the population below MA 12 (*White House Conference on Child Health and Protection, 1933*). The new program was phrased in terms of guardianship rather than institutionalization (*Kuhlmann, 1940–1941*).

In 1920 Florentine Hackbusch pointed out the urgency of comprehensive state programs supervising all aspects of the problem—recommending differential placement, exercising continuing legal supervision of cases, operative through state and local clinics, and utilizing and integrating the work of all available agencies (*Hackbusch, 1920*). In 1922 Pauline Hoakley defined the model institution as "a clearing house, a training school, and a welfare center for our high-grade defective population," as well as a "permanent home" for the "lower-grade and emotionally unstable high-grade." Her survey showed seventeen institutions utilizing parole (*Hoakley, 1922*). Groves Smith, deploring political interference and financial retrenchment, called for comprehensive registration and care for the retarded from the cradle to the grave (*Smith, 1925*). As "waiting-list care" took its place on the agenda, Edward Humphreys cited

---

[44] Davies (*1930*); Fernald (*1920* and *1922*); Stevenson (*1947*); Wylie (*1930*).

the need for immediate care for the low-grades (*Humphreys and McBee, 1939*). At the other end of the scale, placement specialists began the charting of occupations in terms of minimum intellectual levels, giving rise to a list of 118 occupations suitable to Mental Ages 5 to 12 (*Burr, 1925; Beckham, 1930*). In New York City the Vocational Adjustment Bureau was early established as a private agency to find gainful employment for deficient, maladjusted, or delinquent girls (*Davies, 1930*).

The 'thirties saw the introduction into this country of family care of the mentally deficient. Agitated by H. M. Pollock and E. A. Doll, this was first instituted by C. L. Vaux, of the Newark State School, in New York. In the quiet rural village of Walworth, Vaux placed thirty-two cases in various families, with good effect upon both patients and families. As contrasted to parole for wages, this was strictly a program of care, chiefly for the placement of inmates who were felt incapable of benefiting further from institutionalization, but for whom no suitable home placement was available. Despite decided benefits to the children and financial saving to the state, this warmly human experiment was slow to gain recognition— although a similar program was instituted a few years later at the Belchertown State School in Massachusetts.[45]

Many of these new developments and interests were incorporated into comprehensive state programs in which the central state agency, the mental clinic, and the social worker were prominent. In both New York (*1919*) and Pennsylvania (*1923*) state field agents were appointed to assist and oversee local agencies in the examination and supervision of cases. In New York the State Department of Mental Hygiene instituted statewide records. In New Jersey the State Department of Institutions and Agencies made both information and consulting services available throughout the state. In Massachusetts, under a law of 1921, commitments were made directly to the Department of Mental Diseases, which was then responsible for suitable assignment and proper supervision. In Minnesota, in the face of inadequate institutional space, the supervision of retardates became the concern of county welfare boards which directed planning in local terms under state supervision.[46]

The best of these programs, however, drew continuing criticism from within the ranks. In 1932 Florentine Hackbusch complained that the zeal for community placement was outrunning sober judgment and available facilities (*Hackbusch, 1932–1933*). In 1935 Clara Harrison Town, in a scrupulous scientific investigation of familial feeblemindedness, attacked the adequacy of community control in New York, the home state of parole. In 141 families she found 31 of 73 matings illegitimate, 398 of 1,384

---

[45] Vaux (*1935*); Pollock et al. on family care, *Amer. J. ment. Def.,* 1940–1941, *45;* 1945–1946, *50.*
[46] Davies (*1930*); Thomson (*1939*).

members professionally diagnosed as feebleminded (chiefly morons), and only 96 definitely normal. Whether from hereditary or environmental causes, these homes were proven foci of disease, alcoholism, destitution, criminality, and vice. Noting that the graduates of special classes moved on to nothing but the streets and idleness, she urged that permanent, ever-present supervision and help were needed. Temporary supervision and parole, as used with normals, were worse than useless, she warned (*Town, 1939*). It would be unfair, however, to charge such conditions solely to professional overzealousness and incompetence; more culpable were political interference, public apathy, the inadequacy of state and local appropriations, and specific provisions disqualifying the mentally deficient with respect to specific federal welfare funds.

Psychological Emphases on Personal, Social, and Developmental Factors

Both the psychological emphasis on individual variation and the sociological emphasis on care of the retarded as a community problem led to increasing interest in personality structure, social competence, borderline diagnosis, and the defective delinquent.

As opposed to the earlier view of the overwhelming menace of feeblemindedness to society, Healy and Bronner in 1926 found only 13.5 per cent of juvenile offenders clearly mentally deficient, 9.1 per cent borderline subnormals (*Healy* and *Bronner, 1926*). Other similar studies yielded estimates ranging from 10 to 24 per cent. While this implied that serious delinquency was five to ten times more common among the deficient than among the general population, it was also pointed out that the less intelligent criminal is more liable to arrest. Both William Healy and Pearce Bailey maintained that among the retarded, as among the normal, environment was probably as potent a causative force for delinquency as was mentality. Lawson Lowrey called attention to the psychological "conflict over difference," found among gifted children as well as among the retarded. The differentiation of the defective delinquent as a relatively small distinctive class within the mentally deficient group led to the establishment of segregated institutions for them in New York, Massachusetts, and other states, with appropriately modified programs and more stringent provisions for discharge (*Davies, 1930*).

Interest in differential and borderline diagnosis went hand in hand with increasing attention to the scientific evaluation of nonintellectual aspects of behavior. W. E. Fernald, in 1922, was among the first to contend that the integration of mental functioning in terms of character was decisive in distinguishing between social adquacy and inadequacy at the borderline level. In the same decade H. W. Potter's pioneer studies of instinct, emotion, and intelligence led to an ordered guide for securing information for personality studies. At Vineland, Yepsen developed a behavior adjustment score card, while Aldrich found differences in emotional function, distractibility, motivation, and personality organization even among idiots. Witmer's early interest in the relationship between juvenile psychosis and retardation was revived by both Piotrowski and Drysdale, the latter laying special stress on environmental etiology. In 1937 Patterson and Magaw found the Rorschach a useful tool in the diagnosis of personality problems, although not discriminative at the borderline level. Grace Arthur's restandardization and revision of earlier performance scales set new standards in revealing characteristics of behavior and in vocational prognostication.[47]

The call went out for a new developmental schedule which should offer holistic evaluation of the total personality (*Stevenson, 1926–1927*). In 1925 Gesell had devised a developmental schedule for appraising the maturation of the preschool child in terms of normal expectation and individual variation. Working with both the retarded and the normal, he combined both mensuration and descriptive evaluation in normative summaries—synthesized in a single estimate, qualified by descriptive comment, and providing a standard for periodic reappraisal. As early as 1921 the problem of social evaluation had been tacked at Vineland by S. D. Porteus, whose social rating scale provided for the scoring of eleven asocial traits arranged in experimentally weighted order.[48]

In the early 1930's E. A. Doll succeeded in combining the maturational and social aspects of the problem in his Vineland Social Maturity Scale—the first standardized instrument for the objective evaluation of the total personality in maturational terms from infancy to adulthood. The scale presented in 1935 (*Doll, 1936*) consisted of a series of 117 items arranged in order of increasing average difficulty, organized in categories of self-help, self-direction, locomotion, occupation, communication, and socialization. The constellation permitted evaluation of objective nontest performance in terms of integrated personal and social functioning. Based upon an analysis of social competence comparable to Binet's pioneer work with intelligence, this instrument lends itself to a wide variety of clinical uses—as a schedule for reviewing developmental histories, a normative scale for the repeated measurement of individual growth or change, a quantitative and qualitative statement of individual differences for differential diagnosis and placement, a method for estimating basic potential with allowance for specific defects, and a basis for the planning and evaluation of treatment or training. Doll's study *Measurement of So-*

---

[47] Fernald on character, AAMD, *Proceedings,* 1921–1922, *26;* Potter on personality, *ibid.,* 1922–1923, *27;* Sarason and Gladwin (*1958*); Piotrowski (*1932–1933*); Drysdale (*1920*); Arthur (*1930*).

[48] Gesell (*1925*); Porteus in *Train. Sch. Bull.,* 1921–1922, *18.*

cial Competence, tardily published in 1953, presented a statistically elaborate normative standardization, a validation for the mentally deficient, and an impressive series of exploratory studies of growth rates, inheritance, developmental periods, socioeconomic variables, ethnocultural differences, conduct disorders, physical and mental handicaps, clinical types, educational applications, and differential diagnosis. Although the Vineland Scale has taken its place as an almost universal element in clinical evaluation, its deceptive simplicity calls for a highly sophisticated examining technique and lays it open to serious abuse in untutored or unskilled hands.

The Vineland Laboratory was also active in the early application of electrophysiology to mental retardation. In 1935 George Kreezer found a higher level of chronaxy among low-grades (*Kreezer, 1935*). In 1936 he reported his early electroencephalographic studies of the brain waves of the mentally deficient (*Kreezer, 1936–1937*). Cautiously suggesting the possibility of variation with mental age and with clinical type, Kreezer viewed his findings as suggestive rather than conclusive—prophetically anticipating the best present-day usage of this technique.

Educational Classification and Methods

Educational methods continued to be conceived in terms of psychological theories and findings. So incisive and inclusive had been the views of Witmer, Farrell, Anderson, and other pioneers that the 'twenties and 'thirties saw largely a systematization and elaboration of concepts and procedures implicit in earlier work. The fundamental goals of scientific diagnosis, differential instruction, vocational utility, good citizenship, and personal happiness have remained constant down to the present day.

Basic has been the increasing recognition of individual variation. In 1923 Leta Hollingworth developed the educational implications of psychological studies of such special abilities and disabilities as laterality, mirror-writing mechanical ability, and specialized defects in tool subjects (*Hollingworth, 1923*). In 1924 Wallin's inclusive *Education of Handicapped Children,* distinguishing sharply between the needs of the mentally deficient and the backward, called for segregated schools for the mentally deficient, ungraded classes and prevocational schools for borderlines, and grading within groups. It also noted the "track plan" of differential instruction and the unassigned teacher as possible variant approaches.

The needs of the special class teacher herself were well served by Helen D. Whipple (*1927*) and Annie D. Inskeep (*1926*), who in the 1920's presented a wealth of practical procedures and materials for classroom use. Alice Descoeudres (*1928*) stressed experimental learning and the desirability of controlling the extraclassroom environment. To assist in this last, the visiting teacher movement was developed (*Davis, 1930*).

Christine Ingram (*1953*) devoted special attention to the development and elucidation of the project method of units related to the child's needs, condition, and experiences. For the small-school system, where the retarded child was still retained in the regular classroom, Gesell (*1925*) published a useful guide, suggesting the utilization of help from other children.

Numerous special studies also yielded renewed and shifting emphases as well as specific techniques. The scientifically controlled preacademic training program of the Wayne County Training School, under the direction of Thorleif Hegge and Ruth Melcher Patterson, proved the motivational and intellectual value of a prolonged period of constructive, group, and readiness activities. Hegge also called attention to the role of individual maturation and emotional difficulties in reading and presented elaborate phonetic drills. In Virginia, Mabelle Stuart Walker devised a speech method for the cerebral palsied based upon muscle-training and phonetics. Orton, finding confusion in handedness frequently associated with speech and reading disorders, as well as with emotional disturbance, urged the importance of training in lateral dominance. Elise Martens, reviewing the status of occupational education, found the closing of industrial opportunities by the depression unreflected in training programs. Urging increased training for service occupations, she called for more scientific studies of individual ability, realistic placement service, and follow-up on the job.[49]

Scientific Differentiation of Secondary Types

In medicine, as in education, refined scientific methods were brought to bear upon older concepts. The period was notable for increasing awareness of the implications of secondary types and more searching investigation of their characteristics.

Foremost among these developments was the study of birth injury as associated with either deficient or nondeficient retardation. The studies of W. S. Cornell in etiology, of Groves Smith on evaluation and minimal damage, of Paul Schroeder on behavioral manifestations, and of Crothers on neurological aspects were all basic to the work of Doll, Phelps, and Melcher in outlining the implications of birth injury for mental deficiency. This classic presentation of 1932 established the birth-injured as a major etiological group, with incidence ranging from 5 to 10 per cent and individual involvement ranging from minimal to mortal. It investigated appropriate methods of mental mensuration, evaluated the prospec-

---

[49] Melcher on preacademic program, AAMD, *Proceedings*, 1939–1940, *44;* Hegge (*1932, 1933–1934,* and *1934–1935*); Walker (*1939–1940*); Orton (*1929*); Martens (*1936–1937*).

tive benefits of physiotherapy, and called attention to theoretical implications. In 1933 E. W. Martz, in reviewing an already extensive literature on birth injury, called special attention to brain damage without neuromuscular impariment. In 1937 Crothers (*1937–1938*) elaborated the postnatal aspects of brain damage, while Phelps (*1937–1938*) pointed up the implications of multiple handicap.

Other clinical types to receive special attention included mongolism —represented by an extensive literature—endocrine disorders, and idiocy owing to maternal pelvic irradiation—first reported by Murphy and Doll in 1929.

The study and theory of heredity also underwent extensive revision. As early as 1912 Davenport and Danielson had suggested that inherited deficiency involved a combination of traits rather than a Mendelian unit character. In 1925 Jennings not only pointed out the complexity of the combinations of genes but also called attention to their chemical interactions. In 1935 Davenport differentiated defects as those arising in the germ cell, those involved in fertilization or implantation, those arising in the embryonic period, those arising in the fetal period, those stemming from birth injuries, and those originating in infancy and childhood. Adding that the gathering of statistics was an inadequate approach to the complexities of genetics, he urged experimentation on lower mamals. In 1936 Jervis suggested the biochemical hereditary basis of a number of conditions characterized by both the genetic behavior of Mendelian recessivity and the lack of specific enzymatic action. Prophetically he included phenylpyruvic oligophrenia and amaurotic family idiocy in this group.

Pathological anatomy, on the other hand, remained neglected and controversial. Potter's comprehensive summary of 1925 could as well have been written a decade earlier. In this he described the secondary cases as stemming from a variety of pathological defects ranging from general or focal agenesis to extensive replacement or degenerative changes—massive or diffuse sclerosis; degenerative changes in blood vessels, ganglionic cells, or medullary substance; atrophy due to old cerebral hemorrhage; porencephaly; hydrocephaly; pachymeningitis; or brain tumor. Among hereditary cases, on the other hand, various observers had variously reported "irregularity in position of nerve cells in . . . the gray matter, reduction of the number of cells in the gray matter, and reduction of association fibers in the white matter."

At the opposite pole from such biochemical and anatomical approaches, H. M. Skeels and others at the University of Iowa revived the interest in retardation owing to environmental deprivation earlier noted by Witmer. Most of the contributions of Skeels and his associates dealt with follow-up studies of adoption in which a correlation was shown between the IQ of adopted children and their foster parents, following placement. Their most clearcut study, however, dealt with the placement of thirteen mentally deficient children from an understaffed orphanage on wards in a home for older mentally deficient girls, usually one to a ward (*Skeels* and *Dye, 1938–1939*). In this new environment the orphans became centers of attention subject to increased verbal communication and affection from the older girls. Skeels and Dye found an average increase of 27.5 points in IQ over a two-year yeriod. During the same period the IQ's of twelve average-to-dull normal children left in the orphanage dropped an average of 26.2 points. Skeels and Dye concluded that normals may show retardation under a continued nonstimulating environment, and that an intimate relationship between the child and an interested adult is important for development. Although the dramatically extreme results of these studies raised a storm of critical controversy among older workers in the field, the Iowa studies had the virtue of forcing a reassessment of the importance of environmental stimulation in mental development.

TOTAL MOBILIZATION: 1941–1960

Despite the obvious advances and broadening programs of the 'twenties, 'thirties, and early 'forties, there were increasing complaints and misgivings that the personal and social problems of mental retardation were not being adequately met. In addition to the passing of the outburst of others at the beginning of the century, the depression of the 1930's and the distraction of World War II had left their marks. During the 1930's admissions to institutions actually declined in proportion to the general population, despite increasing waiting lists. The same was true of both the number and enrollment of special classes from 1936 to 1940 (*Malzberg, 1940; Martens* and *Foster, 1942*). Despite this retrenchment, the early 'forties quietly laid the groundwork upon which future developments were to rest. The resumption of normal activity following the war brought to the field a new generation of professionals, largely unacquainted with the accomplishments of their predecessors and frequently uninterested to learn from their experience. In the late 'forties there broke in upon this shifting scene, with ever-increasing volume, the demands of the parents of retarded children, impatient of the inadequacy of immediate help, and frequently unacquainted with available resources. Eventually the naive enthusiasm of young "discoverers" of the field— backed by federal, state, and private funds beyond the wildest dreams of the stewards of the lean years—merged with the richer experience of older leaders to create a renewed attack upon the problem. Not, however, before much time and money had been wasted on ill-conceived programs and numerous old truths had been energetically rediscovered.

Conspicuous among current developments have been (1) an impressive revival of anatomical and biochemical research; (2) significant advances in the study of sensory deprivation and integrative anomalies; (3) the application of the principles of Freudian psychology; (4) special interests in the severely retarded, the cerebral palsied, and the vocationally trainable, and (5)—perhaps most important—increasing co-operation between the various disciplines, parents, administrators, and the general public in a total attack on the problem. So numerous and varied have been the advances and discoveries that it will be impossible here to more than briefly allude to general trends.

Anatomical and Biochemical Approach

The last two decades have seen especially marked strides in the fields of neurology, neuroanatomy, and biochemistry. Conspicuous developments have been the meticulous re-examination of clinical types in modern medical terms and the experimental use of the lower mammals for purposes of research. The great wealth of careful descriptive and interpretative studies has already been productive of general trends significant for both etiology and training. These may be most clearly summarized under the three headings of neuroanatomy and neurophysiology, etiology and management, and distinctive clinical types.[50]

The classic pathological descriptions of the period have been those of Clemens E. Benda *(1946–1947)* at Waverly, based upon two hundred cases of deviations at various developmental stages. Concentrating upon pathology, and viewing biochemical research as the next step, Benda sought first to describe the deviations and to determine onset in terms of ontogenetic development. He distinguished developmental anomalies as (1) prenatal, natal, or postnatal in time, and (2) traumatic, infectious, or degenerative in type, seeking definite implications for etiology and management. Benda successfully correlated pathology with clinical types, and even—in some instances—with metabolic and behavioral manifestations; yet he found diverse etiologies frequently productive of similar manifestations. On the basis of his researches he suggested a new etiological category—chronic rheumatic encephalitis. He also announced the discovery of distinctive anatomical abnormalities which he hoped might eventually clarify the distinction between familial retardation and dull normality.

Despite these advances, practically all authorities agree on a disappointingly limited correlation between the locale and distribution of

[50] Except where otherwise indicated, the comments of the following section are based upon Whitney *(1951, 1952, 1953, 1954, 1955a, 1955b, 1956, 1957)*; Wearne *(1948–1949)*; Masland *(1958)*; The Training School Conference on Diagnosis in Mental Retardation *(1958)*; Brecher and Brecher *(1959)*.

lesions and manifestations in terms of mental defect. Similarly disappointing, although somewhat more controversial, has been the use of the electroencephalogram in diagnosis. This has proved useful chiefly in combination with other clinical data—as in pointing out organic bases for behavioral disorders, or in the diagnosis of convulsive disorders.

Studies in etiology, management, and prevention have laid bare the amazing complexity of human reproduction and development. Current research recognizes three major types of pathology of the central nervous system: (1) genetic maldevelopment, (2) prenatal developmental arrest, and (3) pre-, para-, and postnatal destructive processes. These chronologically differentiated basic etiological types have been credited with quite distinctive pathological results in terms of underdevelopment, symmetrical maldevelopment, or assymetrical lesion or degenerative conditions. As various specific etiologies may produce similar results, however, pathological findings must be correlated with complete history and comprehensive examination. Findings in humans have been supplemented by suggestive investigations of cortical lesions in monkeys.

Effective genetic analysis in mental retardation has in many instances been held up by the lack of accurate definition of specific abnormalities or traits. Recent advances in biochemistry, however, have made possible the study of genetic variation. Not only are abnormalities of body chemistry among certain types of retardates probably significantly related to the mental defects, but the genes themselves are thought to act through enzymes. Several types of mental defect, notably Mongolism, have been associated with the occurrence of an extra chromosome.

Reproductive efficiency has been shown to vary somewhat obscurely with parental age, socioeconomic class, familial tendency, and other factors. The importance of the physiochemical environment of the fetus has been shown to vary appreciably with fetal age. Experimentation with animals has suggested various teratogenic agents. Following conception, the fetus is subject to the deleterious influences of such maternal infections as rubella or syphilis—although either mother or fetus may suffer from infection without apparent manifestation in the other. During the late prenatal period, erythroblastosis foetalis may give rise to kernicterus. During the prenatal period, prematurity, birth trauma, and anoxia are all proven causes of destructive lesions. Postnatal hazards include cerebral vascular disease and such inflammatory or degenerative processes as acute or subacute encephalitis, postinfectious encephalomytitides, primary demyelinating diseases, and the leukodystrophies.

These new approaches and discoveries have resulted in a downward revision of the role of heredity from about 80 to about 30 per cent. In contrast to former alarmist positions, Penrose has gone so far as to posit a population in equilibrium through assortive mating and differential fertility, in which the large birth rate among the intellectually inferior group replaces low fertility in the upper levels from a reservoir of diverse genes.[51]

Anatomical, biochemical, and orthopedic researches have also shed considerable light on several clinical types with reference to definition, management, and prevention. The research of Benda and others on Mongolism has clarified the clinical picture in terms of anatomical and biochemical characteristics, has suggested a still unclear relation to temporary or permanent reproductive exhaustion, has made possible its detection *in utero,* and has proven a rather limited response to endocrine therapy. Special strides have been made with the cerebral palsies, which constitute another major secondary group. The American Academy for Cerebral Palsy has elaborated an extensive classification scheme in terms of diagnosis and prognosis (*Minear, 1956*). Phelps, Perlstein, Fay, Crothers, Benda, and others have established the relationship of cerebral palsy to mental retardation and the incidence of retardation in the cerebral palsies; they have evaluated etiological factors and developed a wide range of therapeutic methods. Operative procedures for the arrest of further damage in some instances have been devised. Even more striking has been the work with phenylketonuric oligophrenia in Norway, England, and the United States. This hereditary condition can now be detected early in life and its mental manifestations seemingly prevented by dietary control. Dietary procedures, operative procedures, and injections have also been devised for the control of galactosemia, hydrocephalus, and encephalitis due to measles. Mental deficiency from kernicterus owing to incompatibility of maternal and fetal blood-types has been proven preventable by neonatal exchange transfusion. Both amaurotic family idiocy and gargoylism have been developmentally described and demonstrated to be probably endogenous [52] in origin.

Somewhat related to the biochemical approach has been considerable experimentation with drug therapy. Based upon a somewhat doubtful rationale, and initially administered without foreknowledge of ultimate side-effects, these attempts have been generally disappointing. Frequently, upon continued administration, a drug either loses its effect or produces opposite results. The hopeful predictions that glutamic acid would raise the intellectual level were quickly discredited. Claims have since been made for the value of various drugs in improving intellectual function through controlling hyperactive behavior. Others have been used in the control of spasticity and athetosis. Most useful have been phenobarbitol and dilantin in the control of convulsive seizures—although even here

---

[51] Penrose on population, *Amer. J. ment. Def.,* 1948–1949, 53.

[52] In 1942 A. A. Strauss introduced the terms *endogenous* and *exogenous* as more precise terms for the older dichotomies of *hereditary* and *environmental, familial* and *nonfamilial, primary* and *secondary.*

the importance of emotional factors is gaining increasing recognition. Some authorities have opposed all drug therapy on the grounds of its alleged deadening of the intellect.

Sensory Deprivation, Integrative Anomalies, and Social Deprivation

These neurological and biochemical investigations into etiology, prevention, and amelioration have been paralleled by increasing psychological interest in pseudofeeblemindedness, especially in the study of sensory deprivation, integrative anomalies, and social deprivation.

Outstanding has been the work of Strauss, Werner, Kephart, Lehtinen, and others, at the Wayne County Training School and the Cove Schools, in studying the characteristics of brain-injured children and in devising methods to deal with their handicaps. Strauss found these children—who may or may not suffer from neuromotor involvement as well—likely to show any or all of the following symptoms: weakened emotional inhibition; fragmented perception; distractability; figure-ground disturbance; perseveration in perception; bizarre concept formation; stereotypic tendencies in classification; associations based on minor details; pedantic, meticulous, formalistic patterns of behavior; and strong dependence on adults for assistance and attention. He and his associates have been especially successful in utilizing these psychological findings to devise an effective educational program based upon the reduction of external stimuli, education in progressive voluntary control, small classes, emphasis upon concrete manipulative materials, reinforcement through color stimulation, and gradual return to the normal classroom situation (*Strauss* and *Lehtinen, 1947*).

Lauretta Bender has also contributed considerably to the critical analysis of the extent and nature of brain damage in individual cases, calling attention to anxiety states, negativism, and specific disabilities. Pedagogically she has recommended emphasis on the patterning of all impulses through games and the arts, as well as specific training for specific disabilities (*Bender, 1942* and *1951*).

Many of these techniques developed in work with the brain-injured are reflected in the successful educational programs recently developed for aphasic children. H. R. Myklebust uses a developmental language approach based upon the ordering of life experience and the primacy of symbolic "inner language." At the Central Institute for the Deaf, McGinnis, Kleffner, and Monsees have worked out an elaborate associational system proceeding from articulation and cursive script to meaningful expression. Both systems stress concrete objects and a multisensory approach.

These years have also seen a spectacular rise in the interest in the etiological significance of environmental deprivation. These studies are especially difficult to evaluate, not only because of the difficulty of controlling experimentally the multiplicity of variables, but also because the expectations and social philosophy of the investigators are so likely to skew the interpretation of results. An increasing number of studies have claimed to find an appreciable increase of IQ in favorable institutional or foster-home settings, following initial intellectual and affective deprivation. Many of these, however, have been questioned on methodological grounds, while others are contradicted by opposing studies of apparently equally sound methodology. In England, Harold Bourne, finding a remarkable preponderance of destructive social influences among nonorganic "defectives" with IQs below 50, revived Clark's earlier theories of pathological ego-formation and aborted organization of the personality. Probably the soundest interpretation is that of Boyd McCandless, who has posited intellectual level as a function of the amount of material available for learning and the types of learning which take place. Other writers have stressed the importance of proper stimulation at the proper time.[53]

Studies of cultural and ethnic variation have been at least equally controversial in interpretation, although somewhat more consistent in experimental findings. Ginzberg and Bray found rejection rates for mental deficiency in World War II to vary with regional-cultural differences, racial-cultural group membership, and the rate of expenditure for educational facilities. Gibson and Butler, studying institutional retarded children in Canada, found a high proportion of foreign parentage and socioeconomic deprivation among retardates of undetermined etiology with IQs above 50. A. M. Shotwell, working with institutionalized Mexicans in California, obtained scores in or near the normal range on the Arthur Performance Scale. Lee and others found the IQs of southern Negroes to rise with continued residence in northern cities, as compared with a relatively constant group of northern Negro controls. Pasamanick, in Baltimore, found both gross defects and minor brain damage greater among Negroes than among whites. Garrett, reviewing a number of studies, called attention to the consistently lower IQ of Negroes. Rosen, studying motivation, found social class a stronger determinant than ethnicity. Klineberg, however, early questioned the validity of comparing the test scores of culturally varying groups.[54]

Whatever the interpretation of these results, it is obvious that many subcultural and economically marginal groups contribute to the problem of retardation all out of proportion to their numbers. There has been little progress in attributing this definitely to heredity, environment, or differential migration. After fifty years, we are still facing the tumult over whether this problem can best be met by attempting to control the reproductive proclivities of these groups—with their frequently high percent-

[53] McCandless (*1951–1952*); Sarason and Gladwin (*1958*); Whitney (*1957*).
[54] Studies reviewed by Sarason and Gladwin (*1958*).

age of illegitimacy—or by attempting to raise their socioeconomic and reproductive status by paternalistic programs.

Study of the Total Personality

In all of this study of specific defects and their origins, however, there has been increasing emphasis upon the study of the integration of the total personality. This has been reflected in the development of new diagnostic devices and procedures, as well as in new uses of older instruments. The Vineland Social Maturity Scale has proven more useful than mental-age scales for borderline diagnosis, and has found a wide range of special applications. Jack Birch has revived the interest in the use of abbreviated forms as exploratory devices and has pointed out the potentialities of the Goodenough Draw-a-Man Test as a measure of the total personality. Jastak has abandoned the concept of central intelligence in favor of the measurement of personality variables. Thus his method ingeniously projects in terms of a personality profile, with graphic implications for diagnosis, remedial procedure, and prognosis. Myklebust has called for cooperative diagnosis by specialists of various disciplines in cases with multiple handicaps.[55]

Another approach has been in the direction of the analysis of test patterns and psychometric patterns. Werner and Strauss early suggested a distinctive exogenous test pattern characterized by incoherent, unsystematic, poorly integrated behavior, with visual–motor and figure-ground disturbance. They found the typical *endogenous* retardate characteristically more global in approach. Sloan and Cutts found defective delinquents to conform to the Wechsler pattern for adolescent psychopaths. Bijou found cases with relatively high performance quotients generally characterized by behavioral efficiency and inherent stability, as compared with cases with relatively high IQs. He joined Wallin, however, in warning against the dogmatic application of the pattern approach.[56]

Especially marked have been advances in the use of projective techniques. Kelley and Berrera early found the Rorschach ink-blot test useful in differentiating between genuine capacity and actual efficiency. Hackbusch and Klopfer found it indicative of intellectual potential, in conjunction with other tests. The work of Abel and Kinder has suggested its possible use in differentiating groups of similar intellectual level but different behavioral patterns. Piotrowski has summarized its usefulness in

---

[55] Bice (*1948–1949*). Birch on the Goodenough and abbreviated scales, *Amer. J. ment. Def.*, 1949–1950, *54;* 1954–1955, *59*. Jastak on the endogenous slow learner, *Amer. J. ment. Def.*, 1950–1951, *55*. Myklebust (*1954*).

[56] Bice (*1948–1949*). Bijou on psychometric patterns, *Amer. J. ment. Def.*, 1941–1942, *46*, 354–371; 1942–1943, *47*, 171–177.

describing current personality traits, including motivation and social relationships. Goldfarb has warned against its use in isolation, without other clinical instruments. The use of the Thematic Apperception Test with retardates was pioneered by S. B. and E. K. Sarason. Not only have they found it useful in the approach to personality problems and placement, but their results have done much to weaken the older view of deficient retardates as too rigid for effective psychotherapy.[57]

Psychiatric diagnosis has meanwhile investigated the border zone of psychogenic retardation. Bradley, in 1941, found the concept of childhood schizophrenia poorly developed, despite an interest dating back to 1919. Describing the conditions as characterized by a diffuse retraction of interest from the environment, a diminution of appropriate affective contact with reality, and a withdrawal into an inner life of fantasy, Bradley observed that aberrant behavior was usually already present in infancy in the lack of response to stimulation.

Picking up the developmental aspect, as opposed to the retrogressive aspects of schizophrenia, Kanner in 1943 proposed a distinctive category of early infantile autism, related to but differentiated from the schizophrenias. His syndrome included (a) a profound withdrawal from contact with people, (b) a generally skillful relation to objects, (c) an obsessive desire for sameness, (d) the retention of an intellect, (e) pensive physiognomy, (f) characteristic anomalies precluding effective interpersonal communication, and (g) distortion or irregularity in the conception of wholes and parts. He also mentioned a frequent combination of lack of parental warmth with seemingly inborn autistic disturbances of affective contact in the child. Interest and affection are therapeutically indicated. Richards has called attention to the dangers of misdiagnosing these schizoid and autistic tendencies as true mental deficiency.[58]

Quite aside from such extreme deviations, other writers have called attention to such dynamic factors as the needs of the retarded in terms of security and personal expression, aggression based on insecurity, and destructive fantasies as an impediment to learning.[59]

The Integration of the Retarded into the Community

Current thinking and action is progressing along the lines of integrating the retarded effectively into the community rather than segregating them

[57] Kelley and Berrera (*1940–1941*); Hackbusch and Klopfer (1946–1947); Sarason (*1953*); Piotrowski, reported in Whitney (*1951*).
[58] Bradley (*1941*); Kanner (*1943* and *1951*); Richards, reported in Whitney (*1952*).
[59] Walker (*1950–1951*); see also Whitney (*1954* and *1955b*).

for life. C. J. De Prospo (*Whitney, 1956*) has formulated educational goals as the achievement of self-realization and the development of proper human relations, economic efficiency, and civic responsibility. Noting that 54 per cent of jobs require no schooling beyond the elementary level, he has analyzed employers' complaints against the retarded with an eye to educational implications. In all programs of integration, however, it is important to bear in mind E. A. Doll's warning (*1946–1947*) of the previous decade concerning the constitutional nature of deficient retardation, the limitations of amelioration through therapy, and the fallacy of considering change in IQ as indicative of clinical recovery. Both aspiration and realism are necessary in implementing the comprehensive program formulated by S. G. Di Michael (*1956*) in the mid-'fifties: (1) community diagnostic-treatment clinics, with professional counseling for the family; (2) home-visiting counselors to help parents in training the infant or child; (3) nursery classes; (4) special education, with improved vocational training for the "educable retarded"; (5) special education with improved social training for the "trainable retarded"; (6) training centers and sheltered workshops; (7) community centers to fill in gaps left by other services; (8) integration of the retarded in society, including selective placement in regular employment; (9) dynamic community-minded residence centers (the revitalized institution); and (10) an adequate program of research and training.

Although a large proportion of the retarded have always been cared for in the home, assistance in home training received little systematic attention before the early 1940's, when Massachusetts inaugurated one of the early programs and Katharine Ecob published a pioneer handbook. Of outstanding interest has been the program in New Jersey, under the direction of Vincentz Cianci (*1955–1956*), implemented by educators rather than social workers. This provides, for the severely retarded, a comprehensive program in self-help, emotional control, language, and preinstitutional training; for the "trainable," it offers handicraft, modified primary work, and household skills. Social needs are also given consideration. Family care in foster homes has increased rapidly. In 1956 a survey (*Thomas, 1955–1956*) of practices in eighty-four institutions reported that twenty-seven schools in thirteen states and two Canadian provinces offered family-care programs of some sort.

The role of the institution has been thoroughly overhauled. In 1943 Storrs found the large state schools in crisis—facing lower budgets with which to meet both critical overcrowding and an increasing percentage of infirm and defective delinquent inmates. This very overcrowding has forced intensive efforts at placement. Illinois initiated a system of planned institutional depopulation. In Michigan the wartime vocational achievements of parolees from the Wayne County Training School initiated a new era of thinking in vocational training. At Pacific Hospital in California, Tarjan and Benson succeeded in nearly doubling the number of "indefinite leaves" through a program of psychotherapy, psychiatric casework, recreational and occupational therapy. In Colorado social-orientation courses have yielded substantial gains in self-control, contentment, responsibility, confidence, and emotional stability. Both Waverly, in Massachusetts, and the Lapeer State School, in Michigan, have inaugurated day classes as another aspect of the movement of the institution into the community. The Brandon Training School, in Vermont, has initiated a joint program with the Office of Vocational Rehabilitation which includes the use of rehabilitation homes. At the other end of the scale, the tendency to lower the age of admissions began in New Jersey, following World War II.[60]

Programs of sterilization have seen considerable quiet growth both in this country and abroad. Butler's survey of 1951 revealed compulsory or voluntary laws in twenty-eight states and eleven foreign countries. Of a total of 26,858 operations performed in the United States since 1907, California had contributed the largest number. The most active programs, however, were those operative in Utah, North Carolina, Delaware, and Virginia. Nine laws permitted extramural sterilization. The programs have met with general satisfaction. The procedure has not proven conducive to increased promiscuity, as fear of childbearing is apparently not an appreciable deterrent with the mentally deficient anyway.[61]

Educational programs have experienced expansion, differentiation, and proliferation. Outstanding developments have been the definition of new methods based upon psychological findings, the patterning of new programs in terms of social and personal needs and potentialities, and the rapid expansion of programs for the trainable and severely retarded.

Current estimates, ranging from 3 to 5 per cent of the school population, place the number of children in need of special class or institutionalization at upwards of 2,000,000. Elise Martens (1950), reviewing curriculum in 1950, found goals essentially the same as fifteen years earlier, but now applied more earnestly to the seriously retarded, implemented by improved techniques, and more commonly the concern of the smaller school districts. She noted especially the adaptation of the secondary curriculum to IQs below 75, largely through the use of core curricula based on units of experience and related to specific social and civic situations. She found many adolescents with serious intellectual deficiency now considered capable of a reasonable degree of social competence if provided with proper guidance and educational opportunities.

In the development of new educational techniques, the Wayne County Training School has continued outstanding. There, intensive

[60] Davies and Ecob (1959); Whitney (1955b).
[61] Butler on sterilization, *Amer. J. ment. Def.*, 1944–1945, 49; 1951–1952, 56.

86   The Mentally Deficient

work with psychometric patterns and functional analysis emphasized the qualitative heterogeneity of the group. Careful study of specific learning disabilities and mental structures were used as the basis for a diversified program of techniques applied to a comprehensive preacademic, academic, and vocational program. A whole series of papers elucidated findings and applications with respect to specific techniques for exogenous cases, projective techniques, play therapy, psychological counseling, social and industrial training.[62]

In Detroit, and later in New York City, a new approach to education appeared in the "occupational education" of R. H. Hungerford and his colleagues. Convinced that changing technology and ineffective methods demanded a thorough reorganization, Hungerford made occupational education basic to the curriculum at all levels. The system provides for the co-operative evaluation of pupils in terms of an employability scale, for pretrade, sheltered-helper, or custodial training. It orders minimum occupational MA levels in terms of social and vocational skill sequences which recognize personal and social factors as vital to successful placement. It provides for the "core" teaching of social skills, realistic counseling, and the enlistment of community understanding and co-operation. In 1943 the Barden-LaFollette Act made federal funds available for specific services relative to placement and follow-up. In 1952 Rockower called for more sheltered workshops, psychiatric help, personal adjustment training, and organized recreation for successful social integration.[63]

The past decade has also seen increasing attention to educational services for the trainable and the severely retarded. In 1952 A. S. Hill estimated that about 15 per cent of the "severely retarded" were receiving instruction in public or private schools or institutions—including the facilities of about 730 school districts. Responsibility for their care was still being debated between public schools and welfare agencies. Hill felt that possibilities for occupational contribution and acceptable dependent status in the community were being grossly neglected. In 1957 I. I. Goldberg estimated that about 19,000 or 20 per cent, of the "trainable" were attending public or private schools. Although basic curricular content for this group has not changed appreciably, it has been more optimistically approached, more effectively systematized pedagogically, and more practically oriented vocationally.[64]

Other educational developments have included (1) continuing attention to the enrichment and differentiation of the preschool program; (2)

[62] Hegge on Wayne County Training School program, *Amer. J. ment. Def.*, 1951–1952, *56,* 665–670.

[63] Hungerford (*1941–1942*); Hungerford, De Prospo, and Rosenzweig on the nonacademic pupil 1948–1949, *53;* Engel (*1952*); Rockower (*1952*).

[64] Hill (*1952*); Goldberg (*1957–1958*); Rosenzweig (*1954–1955*).

organization of curriculum around the items of the Vineland Social Maturity Scale; (3) the use of structured settings for the brain-injured child; (4) the use of controlled environment for the autistic child; (5) Kirk and Johnson's progressive levels from preschool stimulation to postschool supervision; (6) the Woods Schools conferences on planning at various life ages; and (7) the renewed emphasis by G. N. Getman and N. C. Kephart on the fundamental importance of motor and sensory training in mental development.[65]

In addition to ouright instruction, psychotherapeutic techniques are finding increasing use with the retarded. Cotzin, Sarason, I. N. Wolfson, and others have demonstrated favorable results from both individual and group psychotherapy and have urged a regular place for them in institutions—in both in-service and out-patient settings. Reported benefits include both the detection of pseudofeeblemindedness and significant changes in institutional assignments and behavior patterns. Special techniques have included psychodrama, play therapy, and art therapy. Whitney, however, has warned against overemphasis on psychological analysis at the expense of other approaches.[66]

Co-ordinated Implementation

The need for over-all planning and co-ordination has grown with the expansion of services and the differentiation of approaches. W. J. Ellis early called attention to the responsibility of the state in co-ordinating the activities of many private, state, and federal agencies. More recently Gunnar Dybwad has suggested the importance of community planning bodies in determining responsibilities and fostering co-operation among agencies to insure a comprehensive and balanced program.

Co-ordination of activities at the national level was undertaken in 1946 by the American Association on Mental Deficiency, in its three-year "Project on Technical Planning in Mental Retardation," operating under a grant from the National Institute of Mental Health. This project, including specialists from both within and without the ranks of the Association, set as its tasks the compilation of information, the evaluation of data, the dissemination of new and current information, the delineation of new and profitable areas for study, the development of new methods, and the stimulation of interest and activity. It sought to assess and explore current situations, to define urgent research tasks, to formulate bet-

---

[65] Kirk on preschool curriculum, *Amer. J. ment. Def.*, (1949–1950), *54*, 305–310; (*1951–1952*), 56, 692–700; Wallin (1955); Kirk and Johnson (*1951*); Woods Schools (*1953–1960*); Getman (*1958*); Kephart (*1960*).

[66] Cotzin on psychological services, *Amer. J. ment. Def.*, 1951–1952, 56, 60–73; Sarason (*1953*); Stacey and Martino (*1957*).

ter methods of care, and to propose ways of integrating the problems of the retarded into the ongoing organizations and structures of society. By 1959, at which time the Project was extended for another two years, it had provided for the periodic publication of abstracts covering the entire field, inaugurated a news sheet of current developments, published a ten-year index to the *American Journal of Mental Deficiency,* brought out a new manual on classification, and undertaken a guide for program planning at state and community levels. It had also begun studies of co-operation between universities and institutional centers of the training of specialists, and of programs of vocational rehabilitation.[67]

In 1950 the Association extended its interests to the international level by joining the World Federation of Mental Health.

Within the past decade great impetus to the work has come from the formation and program of the National Association for Retarded Children, an organization of the parents of the retarded and other interested laymen, with local chapters in forty-nine states. By the late 'forties the inability of many services to meet the growing demands placed upon them moved parents to concerted action. Even the declining enrollments in special classes were generally restricted to the high-grade "educable retarded." Child-guidance clinics, often initially instituted for the benefit of the retarded, were increasingly turning their attention to the emotionally disturbed and other more "hopeful" cases. The reduction of infant mortality had led to a burgeoning population of severely retarded which was straining already inadequate institutional provisions to the limit.

Parents' organizations had their origin in Cleveland's Council for the Retarded Child in Cuyahoga County, organized in 1933 to assist children excluded from the public schools. By 1940 there were about 10 such groups—including parents' groups of institutionalized children—scattered about the country. The beginning of 1950 found 88 groups in thirty-eight organizations in nineteen states; its close saw the formation of a national organization. By 1959 the National Association for Retarded Children boasted 50,000 members in 750 local units, representing all states except Alaska. In line with the growing interest in vocational rehabilitation, the Association numbered among its first projects the fostering of sheltered workshops.[68]

In 1956 S. G. Di Michael, Executive Director of the NARC, addressed to the House of Representatives an appeal (*Di Michael, 1956*) for an effective federal program. To assist in the development of his ten-point plan, Di Michael urged federal subsidy of research commensurate with the incidence of mental retardation, grants for a specific program

---

[67] Nisonger (*1955–1956*). See also subsequent annual reports in *Amer. J. ment. Def.*

[68] National Association for Retarded Children (*1954*); Boggs (*1960*).

for the recruitment and training of specialized personnel, and the expansion of federal services to provide effective leadership in education and community services. He also requested an enlarged and revamped program of public assistance, reinterpretation of the hospital survey and construction act to include institutions for the retarded, the establishment of a federal Secretariat in Mental Retardation, and the earmarking of federal funds for specific grants-in-aid to further sheltered workshops and other services for vocational rehabilitation.

In 1960, in anticipation of the White House Conference on Children and Youth, the NARC prepared an evaluation report of progress during the first decade of its existence. Although the NARC can by no means claim sole credit for the impressive advances of these years, its dynamic leadership, aggressive campaigning, and effective financial solicitations have constituted important driving forces. The field of family services has seen tremendous strides in the dissemination of information to family physicians, the establishment of seventy comprehensive clinics devoted solely to the diagnosis *and placement* of the retarded child, the establishment of seventy-five programs of parent-motivated discussion groups, a substantial growth in literature addressed to parents, a study of family living with the retarded, and the enlistment of adolescent interest and participation in programs for the retarded.

The number of states providing special classes for the retarded has increased from twenty-four to forty-eight. Twenty states have enacted permissive or mandatory legislation extending the privileges of such classes to the "trainable" (roughly characterized by IQ 25 to 50), while seventeen have held such extension to be authorized by more general laws. Federal statutes now provide for teacher training and research in both techniques and curriculum. Nursery schools and day care centers are developing rapidly. Summer day camps and other recreational facilities have been not only expanded but also more specifically adapted to the needs of the retarded.

Social caseworkers are undergoing reorientation in terms of a more diversified and sophisticated approach to the retarded referred to their agencies. Social security laws have extended survivors' benefits beyond the age of eighteen for permanently disabled persons. Institutions have lowered ages for admissions and have resumed extensive building programs. Local councils of social agencies are beginning to review available services in terms of the retarded. Sheltered workshops and training centers number about one hundred, somewhat more than half of them operated by member units of the NARC. The whole question of the legal status of retarded persons is undergoing reconsideration.

Thus have the mentally retarded progressed from total rejection by society, through imprisonment and grudging acceptance, through a century of devoted care by a handful of professionals and philanthropists, to emerge as a major concern of the welfare state. The present day is seeing increasing acceptance of the "rights" of the retarded laid down by the NARC—the right of each to full realization of his potentialities, the right to affection and understanding from those charged with his care and guidance, the right to stimulation and guidance from a program of free public education. In the increasing realization of these rights, it is to be hoped that society may not lose sight of the still greater dignity of a reciprocal privilege—the obligation of the retarded, in return, to contribute to that society to the fullest extent of his limited abilities.[69]

References

The author wishes to express his appreciation to Walter Jacob, Director of the Training School at Vineland, and to Johs. Clausen, Chief of Psychological Research, for hospitality and access to the Library of the Department of Research.

Abbreviations used in footnotes and bibliography:

AAMD   American Association on Mental Deficiency

Amer. J. ment. Def.   *American Journal of Mental Deficiency*

American Journal of Mental Deficiency. Begun as *Proceedings and Addresses of the Association of Medical Officers of American Institutions for Idiotic and Feeble-Minded Persons* (1876–1895). Continued, in new series, as *Journal of Psycho-Asthenics* (1896–1917/18). Continued as *Proceedings of the American Association on Mental Deficiency* (1918–1939) (begun as *Proceedings and Addresses of the American Association for the Study of the Feeble-Minded*). Continued as *American Journal of Mental Deficiency* (1940–   ).

American Association for the Study of the Feeble-Minded, *Proceedings and Addresses . . . Comprising the Journal of Psycho-Asthenics.* See *American Journal of Mental Deficiency.*

American Association on Mental Deficiency. *Proceedings.* See *American Journal of Mental Deficiency.*

Anderson, Meta L. *Education of defectives in the public schools.* Yonkers-on-Hudson: World Book Company, 1917.

Anderson, V. V. A study of the careers of 321 feeble-minded persons who have been in the special classes and are now out in the community. AAMD, *Proceedings,* 1922, *27,* 138–149.

Arthur, (Mary) Grace. *A point scale of performance tests.* New York: Commonwealth Fund, 1930.

Association of Medical Officers of American Institutions for Idiotic and Feeble-Minded Persons. *Proceedings and Addresses.* See under *American Journal of Mental Deficiency.*

Barr, Martin W. *Mental defectives: Their history, treatment, and training.* Philadelphia: Blakiston, 1913.

Berrera, S. Eugene. See Kelley, Douglas McG. The Rorschach method. . . , 1940–1941.

[69] Thomas (*1957*).

Beckham, Albert Sidney. Minimum intelligence levels for several occupations. *Personnel J.*, 1930, *9*, 309–313.
Benda, Clemens E. Ten years research in mental deficiency. *Amer. J. ment. Def.*, 1946–1947, *51*, 170–185.
Bender, Lauretta. Post-encephalitic behavior disorders in childhood. In Josephine B. Neal et al. *Encephalitis: a clinical study.* New York: Grune and Stratton, 1942.
Bender, Lauretta. The psychological treatment of the brain damaged child. *Quart. J. child Behav.*, 1951, *3*, 123–131.
Bernstein, Charles. Rehabilitation of the mentally defective. AAMD, *Proceedings*, 1919, *24*, 125–155.
Bernstein, Charles. Colony care for isolation of defective and dependent cases. AAMD, *Proceedings*, 1921, *26*, 43–59.
Bice, Harry V. A decade of psychology: a review based on reports in the *American Journal of Mental Deficiency*. *Amer. J. ment. Def.*, 1948–1949, *53*, 57–64.
Binet, Alfred, & Simon, Th. *The development of intelligence in children.* Trans. by Elizabeth S. Kite. Publications of the Training School at Vineland . . . No. 11, May, 1916.
Boggs, Elizabeth (Mrs. Fitshugh W. Boggs). Remarks at the Conference of Rehabilitation of the Mentally Retarded at Southern Methodist University, Dallas, Texas, February 10th to 12th, 1960. Ms.
Bradley, Charles. *Schizophrenia in childhood.* New York: Macmillan, 1941.
Brecher, Ruth, & Brecher, Edward. Saving children from mental retardation. *The Saturday Evening Post,* Nov. 21, 1959.
Bronner, Augusta F. *The psychology of special abilities and disabilities.* Boston: Little, Brown, 1917. Reprinted, 1929.
Bronner, Augusta F. See also Healy, William, *Delinquents and criminals.*
Bronner, Augusta F. See also Healy, William, *Delinquents and criminals.*
Burr, Emily T. Minimum intellectual levels of accomplishment in industry. *Personnel J.*, 1925, *3*, 207–212.
Cianci, Vincentz. Home training. *Amer. J. ment. Def.*, 1955–1956, *60*, 622–626.
Crothers, Bronson. Birth injuries and the illnesses of infancy in the etiology of mental deficiency. *Amer. J. ment. Def.*, 1937–1938, *48*, 26–31.
Davenport, Charles B. Causes of retarded and incomplete development. AAMD, *Proceedings*, 1935–1936, *41*, 208–214.
Davies, Stanley Powell. *Social control of the mentally deficient.* New York: Crowell, 1930.
Davies, Stanley Powell, & Ecob, Katherine G. *The mentally retarded in society.* New York: Columbia, 1959.
Davis, David B. Encephalography—the method and its use in mental deficiency. *Amer. J. ment. Def.*, 1938–1939, *44*, 72–78.
Descoeudres, Alice. *The education of mentally defective children.* New York: D. C. Heath and Co., 1928.
Di Michael, Salvatore. Proposals on a federal program of action in 1956–1957 for America's mentally retarded children and adults. Respectfully submitted . . . to the . . . Chairman, House of Representatives Sub-Committee on

Appropriations for the Departments of Health, Education and Welfare, and Industry. Mimeographed ms. 1956.
Di Michael, Salvatore. *Speaking for mentally retarded children in America.* New York: National Association for Retarded Children (ca. 1956).
Doll, Edgar A. Preliminary note on the diagnosis of potential feeble-mindedness. *Train. Sch. Bull.,* 1916–1917, *13,* 54–61.
Doll, Edgar A. A brief Binet-Simon scale. *The psychol. Clin.,* 1917–1918, *11,* 197–211, 254–261.
Doll, Edgar A. Growth of intelligence. *Psychol. Monogr.,* Vol. 29, Princeton: Psychological Review, 1921.
Doll, Edgar A. *The Vineland social maturity scale. Revised condensed manual of directions.* Publication of the Training School at Vineland, Department of Research. Series 1936, No. 3, April 1936.
Doll, Edgar A. *The measurement of social competence: A manual for the Vineland social maturity scale.* Philadelphia: Educational Test Bureau, 1953.
Doll, Edgar A. Is mental deficiency curable? *Amer. J. ment. Def.,* 1946–1947, *51,* 420–428.
Doll, Edgar A., Phelps, Winthrop M., & Melcher, Ruth T. *Mental deficiency due to birth injuries.* New York: Macmillan, 1932.
Drysdale, H. H. Juvenile psychosis. AAMD, *Proceedings,* 1920, *25,* 34–44.
Dybwad, Gummar. Community organization for the mentally retarded. *Community Organization,* 1959, pp. 108–121.
Ecob, Katharine G. See Davies, Stanley Powell. *The mentally retarded in society,* 1959.
Engel, Anna M. Employment of the mentally retarded. *Amer. J. ment. Def.,* 1952, *57,* 243–267.
Esquirol, E. *Des maladies mentales.* Paris: Baillière, 1838. 2 vols.
Fernald, Walter E. The history of the treatment of the feeble-minded. *Proceedings of the National Conference on Charities and Correction.* 20th Annual Session, 1893, pp. 203–221.
Fernald, Walter E. An out-patient clinic in connection with a state institution for the feeble-minded. AAMD, *Proceedings,* 1920, *25,* 81–89.
Fernald, Walter E. The inauguration of a state-wide public school clinic in Massachusetts, AAMD, *Proceedings,* 1922, *27,* 200–215.
Foster, Emery M. See Martens, Elise H. *Statistics of special schools and classes . . . ,* 1942.
Fynne, Robert John. *Montessori and her inspirers.* London: Longmans, Green, 1924.
Gesell, Arnold. *The mental growth of the pre-school child . . . including a system of developmental diagnosis.* New York: Macmillan, 1925.
Gesell, Arnold. *The retarded child: how to help him.* Bloomington, Ill.: Public School, 1925.
Getman, G. N. *How to develop your child's intelligence.* Luverne, Minn.: privately printed, 1958.
Gladwin, Thomas. See Sarason, Seymour B. Psychological and cultural problems . . . , 1958.
Goddard, Henry Herbert. Heredity of feeble-mindedness. *American Breeders Magazine,* 1910, *1,* 165–178.

Goddard, Henry Herbert. *The Kallikak family.* New York: Macmillan, 1912.

Goddard, Henry Herbert. *Feeble-mindedness: its causes and consequences.* New York: Macmillan, 1914.

Goddard, Henry Herbert. *School training of defective children.* Yonkers-on-Hudson: 1914.

Goddard, Henry Herbert. The size of the special class. *Train. Sch. Bull.,* 1915–1916, *12,* 106–107.

Goddard, Henry Herbert. *Psychology of the normal and subnormal.* New York: Dodd, Mead, 1919.

Goldberg, I. Ignacy. Some aspects of the current status of education and training in the United States for trainable mentally retarded children. *Except. Child.,* 1957–1958, *24,* 146–154.

Hackbusch, Florentine. Organization of clinics and extra-institutional supervision. AAMD, *Proceedings,* 1920, *25,* 192–200.

Hackbusch, Florentine. Special classes as a dysgenic factor. AAMD, *Proceedings,* 1932–1933, *37,* 67–70.

Hackbusch, Florentine, & Klopfer, Bruno. The contribution of projective techniques to the understanding and treatment of children psychometrically diagnosed as feeble-minded, with sample cases. *Amer. J. ment. Def.,* 1946–1947, *51,* 15–34.

Healy, Augusta Brooner. See Bronner, Augusta.

Healy, William & Bronner, Augusta F. *Delinquents and criminals: their making and unmaking.* New York: Macmillan, 1926.

Heber, Rick. (Ed.). *A manual on terminology and classification in mental retardation.* Monograph Supplement to the *Amer. J. ment. Def.* (Sept., 1959).

Hegge, Thorleif. Reading cases in an institution for mentally retarded problem children. AAMD, *Proceedings,* 1932, *37,* 149–212.

Hegge, Thorleif. Special reading disability with particular reference to the mentally deficient. AAMD, *Proceedings,* 1933–1934, *39,* 297–344.

Hegge, Thorleif. A method for teaching mentally deficient reading. AAMD, *Proceedings,* 1934–1935, *40,* 476–484.

Hill, Arthur S. *The forward look: the severely retarded child goes to school.* Federal Security Agency, Office of Education, Bulletin 1952, No. 11.

Hoakley, Z. Pauline. Extra-institutional care for the feeble-minded. AAMD, *Proceedings,* 1922, *27,* 117–137.

Hollingworth, Leta S. *Special talents and defects.* New York: Macmillan, 1923.

Humphreys, Edward J. Investigative psychiatry in the field of mental deficiency. AAMD, *Proceedings,* 1935, *40,* 195–206.

Humphreys, Edward J., & McBee, Marian. Present needs in the care of mental defectives in New York City, *Amer. J. ment. Def.,* 1939, *44,* 264–273.

Hungerford, Richard H. The Detroit plan for the occupational education of the mentally retarded. *Amer. J. ment. Def.,* 1941–1942, *46,* 102–108.

Ingram, Christine P. *Education of the slow learning child* (2nd ed.). New York: Ronald, 1953.

Inskeep, Annie Dolman. *Teaching dull and retarded children.* New York: Macmillan, 1926.

Jervis, George A. Inherited biochemical alterations in certain types of mental deficiency, AAMD, *Proceedings,* 1936–1937, *42,* 101–115.

Johnson, Alexander. *Adventures in social welfare.* Fort Wayne: Author, 1923.

Johnstone, Edward R. The extension of the care of the feeble-minded. *J. Psycho-Asthenics,* 1949, *19,* 3–15.

Journal of Psycho-Asthenics. See *American Journal of Mental Deficiency.*

Kanner, Leo. Autistic disturbances of affective contact. *Nerv. Child,* 1943, *2* (3), 217–250.

Kanner, Leo. A discussion of early infantile autism. *Dig. Neurol. Psychiat.,* 1951, *19,* 158.

Kelley, Douglas McG., & Berrera, S. Eugene. The Rorschach method in the study of mental deficiency. A resume. *Amer. J. ment. Def.,* 1940–1941, *45,* 401–407.

Kephart, Newell C. *The slow learner in the classroom.* Columbus: Charles E. Merrill, 1960.

Kirk, Samuel A., & Johnson, G. Orville. *Educating the retarded child.* Boston: Houghton Mifflin, 1951.

Kite, Elizabeth S. See Binet, Alfred, *The development of intelligence . . . ,* 1916.

Kleffner, Frank R. *Teaching speech and language to aphasic children.* Washington: Volta Bureau, 1958.

Klopfer, Bruno. See Hackbusch, Florentine. The contribution of projective techniques . . . , 1946–1947.

Kreezer, George. Motor studies of the mentally deficient: quantitative methods at various levels of integration. *Amer. J. ment. Def.,* 1934–1935, *40,* 357.

Kreezer, George. Electrical phenomena of the brain among the feeble-minded. *Amer. J. ment. Def.,* 1936–1937, *42,* 130–141.

Kuhlmann, F. One hundred years of special care and training. *Amer. J. ment. Def.,* 1940–1941, *45,* 8–24.

McBee, Marian. See Humphreys, Edward J. Present needs . . . , 1939.

McCandless, Boyd. Environment and intelligence. *Amer. J. ment. Def.,* 1951–1952, *56,* 674–691.

McGinnis, Mildred A., Kleffner, Frank R., & Goldstein, Robert. *Teaching aphasic children.* Washington: Volta Bureau (ca. 1956).

Maennel, B. *Auxiliary education: the training of backward children.* Trans. by Emma Sylvester. New York: Doubleday, Page, 1909.

Malzberg, Benjamin. Trends in the growth of population in the schools for mental defectives. AAMD, *Proceedings,* 1940, *45,* 119–126.

Martens, Elise H. Occupational preparation for mentally handicapped children. AAMD, *Proceedings,* 1936–1937, *42,* 157–165.

Martens, Elise H. *Curriculum adjustments for the mentally retarded.* Federal Security Agency, Office of Education. Bulletin 1950, No. 2.

Martens, Elise H., & Foster, Emery M. *Statistics of special schools and classes for exceptional children: 1939–1940.* Biennial survey of education in the United States, Vol. II, Chapter V. Federal Security Agency, U.S. Office of Education, 1942.

Martz, Eugene W. Recent trends in the problem of cerebral birth lesions. *Amer. J. ment. Def.,* 1932–1933, *38,* 311–327.

Masland, Richard L. The prevention of mental retardation: a survey of research. *Amer. J. ment. Def.,* 1958, *62* (6), 991–1112.

Melcher, Ruth T. A program of prolonged pre-academic training for the young mentally handicapped child. AAMD, *Proceedings,* 1939, *44,* 202–215.

Melcher, Ruth T. See also Doll, Edgar A., *Mental deficiency due to birth injuries,* 1932.

Minear, W. L. A classification of cerebral palsy. *Pediatrics,* 1956, *18* (5), 841–852.

Mitchell, David. *Schools and classes for exceptional children.* Cleveland: Educational Survey (Vol. X). Cleveland Survey Committee of the Cleveland Foundation, 1916.

Myklebust, Helmer R. *Auditory disorders in children.* New York: Grune and Stratton, 1954.

Myklebust, Helmer R. *Teaching aphasic children.* Washington, D.C.: Volta Bureau.

National Association for Retarded Children. A history of the National Association for Retarded Children, Inc. Offprint from *Blueprint for a Crusade,* 1954.

National Association for Retarded Children. *Decade of decision: An evaluation report prepared . . . for the 1960 White House Conference on Children and Youth.* New York: National Association for Retarded Children, 1959.

Nisonger, Herschel. Special AAMD project, technical planning in mental retardation. *Amer. J. ment. Def.,* 1955–1956, *60,* 690–695. See also subsequent annual reports in *Amer. J. ment. Def.*

Norsworthy, Naomi. The psychology of mentally deficient children. *Arch. Psychol.,* No. 1. New York: Science Press, 1906.

Nowrey, Joseph E. A brief synopsis of mental deficiency. *Amer. J. ment. Def.,* 1944–1945, *49,* 319–357.

Orton, Samuel T. The relation of the special educational disabilities to feeblemindedness. AAMD, *Proceedings,* 1929, *34,* 23–32.

Paterson, Donald G. See Pinter Rudolf, *Intelligence testing,* 1931.

Phelps, Winthrop M. Motor handicaps and retardation. AAMD, *Proceedings,* 1937–1938, *43,* 26–31.

Phelps, Winthrop M. See also Doll, Edgar A., *Mental deficiency due to birth injuries,* 1932.

Pichot, Pierre. French pioneers in the field of mental deficiency. *Amer. J. ment. Def.,* 1948–1949, *53,* 128–137.

Pintner, Rudolf, & Paterson, Donald G. *A scale of performance tests.* New York: D. Appleton & Company, 1917.

Pintner, Rudolf, *Intelligence testing: methods and results.* (New ed.) New York: Holt, Rinehart and Winston, 1931.

Piotrowski, Zygmunt A. The test behavior of schizophrenic children. *Amer. J. ment. Def.,* 1932–1933, *38,* 332–347.

Post, Meta Anderson. See Anderson, Meta.

Potter, Howard W. A review of the literature on the brain pathology of mental deficiency. AAMD, *Proceedings,* 1925, *30,* 258–265.

The Psychological Clinic: A Journal for the Study and Treatment of Mental Retardation and Deviation. Philadelphia: 1907–1935.

Raymond, C. S. Intellectual development in morons beyond the chronological age of sixteen years. AAMD, *Proceedings,* 1926–1927, *32,* 243–248.

Rockower, Leonard. A study of mentally retarded applicants for vocational rehabilitation in New York City. *Amer. J. ment. Def.,* 1952, *57,* (2), 268–269.

Rosenzweig, Louis E. Report of a school program for mentally retarded children. *Amer. J. ment. Def.,* 1954–1955, *69,* 181–205.

Sarason, Seymour B. *Psychological problems in mental deficiency.* (2nd ed.) New York: Harper & Bros., 1953.

Sarason, Seymour B., & Gladwin, Thomas. Psychological and cultural problems in mental subnormality: a review of research. *Amer. J. ment. Def.,* 1958, *62* (6), 1113–1307.

Seguin, Edward. *Idiocy: and its treatment by the physiological method.* New York: Wood, 1866.

Simon, Th. See Binet, Alfred, *The development of intelligence . . . ,* 1916.

Skeels, Harold M., & Dye, Harold B. A study of the effects of differential stimulation on mentally retarded children. AAMD, *Proceedings,* 1938–1939, *44,* 114–136.

Smith, Groves B. Modern trends in the study of mental deficiency. AAMD, *Proceedings,* 1925, *30,* 227–244.

Stacey, Chalmers L., & De Martino, Manfred F. *Counseling and psychotherapy with the mentally retarded.* Glencoe: Free Press, 1957.

Stevenson, George S. The need for a biological approach to an understanding of the feeble-minded. AAMD, *Proceedings,* 1926–1927, *32,* 26–30.

Stevenson, George S. Where and whither in mental deficiency? *Amer. J. ment. Def.,* 1947, *52* (1), 43–47.

Strauss, Alfred A., & Lehtinen, Laura E. *Psychopathology and education of the brain-injured child.* New York: Grune and Stratton, 1947.

Thomas, David H. H. Cultural attitudes to mental subnormality. *Amer. J. ment. Def.,* 1957, *61* (3), 467–473.

Thomas, Ethelbert, Jr. Family care. *Amer. J. ment. Def.,* 1955–1956, *60,* 615–619.

Thomson, Mildred. Social aspects of Minnesota's program for the feebleminded. *Amer. J. ment. Def.,* 1939, *44,* 238–243.

Town, Clara Harrison. *Familial feeble-mindedness, a study of one hundred and forty-one families.* Buffalo: Foster and Stewart, 1939.

The Training School at Vineland. Conference on Diagnosis in Mental Retardation. Report on Conference on Diagnosis in Mental Retardation. *Train. ch. Bull.,* 1958, *55* (2), 17–44.

The Training School Bulletin. Vineland, New Jersey, 1904.

Vaux, Charles L. Family care of mental defectives. AAMD, *Proceedings,* 1935, *40,* 168–189.

Walker, Gale H. Social and emotional needs of mentally retarded children. *Amer. J. ment. Def.,* 1950–1951, *55,* 132–138.

Walker, Mabelle Stuart. Speech therapy with the cerebral palsied: spastics and athetoids. AAMD, *Proceedings,* 1939–1940, *44,* 145–155.

Wallin, J. E. Wallace. *The education of handicapped children.* Boston: Houghton Mifflin, 1924.

Wallin, J. E. Wallace. *Education of mentally handicapped children.* New York: Harper & Bros., 1955.

Wearne, Raymond G. A. A résumé of medical and psychiatric developments in mental deficiency during the past ten years. *Amer. J. ment. Def.*, 1949, *53*, 47–56.

Weisenberg, Theodore, & McBride, Katharine M. *Aphasia: a clinical and psychological study.* New York: Commonwealth Fund, 1935.

Whipple, Helen Davis. *Making citizens of the mentally limited.* Bloomington, Ill.: Public School, 1927.

White House Conference on Child Health and Protection. IV. The Handicapped. The Committee on Physically and Mentally Limited. Subcommittee on Problems of Mental Deficiency. Problems of mental deficiency. In *The Handicapped Child.* New York: The Century Co., 1935. Pp. 329–390.

Whitney, E. Arthur. The historical approach to the subject of mental retardation. *Amer. J. ment. Def.*, 1948–1949, *53*, 410–424.

Whitney, E. Arthur. Mental retardation—1950. *Amer. J. ment. Def.*, 1951, *56* (2), 253–263.

Whitney, E. Arthur. Some stalwarts of the past. *Amer. J. ment. Def.*, 1952–1953, *57*, 345–360.

Whitney, E. Arthur. Mental deficiency—1951. *Amer. J. ment. Def.*, 1952, *56* (4), 737–746.

Whitney, E. Arthur. Mental deficiency—1952. *Amer. J. ment. Def.*, 1953, *58* (1), 1–12.

Whitney, E. Arthur. Mental deficiency—1953. *Amer. J. ment. Def.*, 1954, *58* (4), 583–593.

Whitney, E. Arthur. Mental deficiency—1954. *Amer. J. ment. Def.*, 1955, *59* (4), 549–556. (a)

Whitney, E. Arthur. Current trends in institutions for the mentally retarded. *Amer. J. ment. Def.*, 1955, *60* (1), 10–20. (b)

Whitney, E. Arthur. Mental deficiency—1955. *Amer. J. ment. Def.*, 1956, *60* (4), 676–683.

Whitney, E. Arthur. Mental deficiency—1956. *Amer. J. ment. Def.*, 1957, *61* (4), 656–661.

Witmer, Lightner. *The special class for backward children: an educational experiment for the instruction of teachers and other students of child welfare by the psychological laboratory and clinic of the University of Pennsylvania.* Philadelphia: Psychological Clinic, 1911.

The Woods Schools. Child Research Clinic, Spring Conferences.
    1953. The pre-adolescent exceptional child.
    1954. The adolescent exceptional child.
    1955. The exceptional child faces adulthood.
    1960. (To deal with old age.)

Wylie, A. R. T. The development of institutional care for the feeble-minded. *Bull. Mass. Dept. Ment. Dis.*, 1930, *14*, 40–60.

Wylie, A. R. T. Fifty years in retrospect. *J. Psycho-Asthenics*, 1925–1926, *21*, 219–233.

5

Experimental Studies of Rigidity:
I. The Measurement of Rigidity in Normal and Feebleminded Persons

Jacob S. Kounin

Dr. Kounin is Professor of Educational and Clinical Psychology at Wayne State University. A productive research worker for many years, his current research interests focus on teaching emotionally disturbed children in regular classrooms.

This particular study on rigidity, suggesting that rigidity is directly related to the degree of mental retardation, has stimulated a vast amount of research regarding the role of this variable in the behavior of the mentally defective child. Therefore, it seems most appropriate that the student get acquainted with the pioneering work. Dr. Zigler's article summarizes the subsequent research.

In the editors' correspondence with the author, he wished to advise and remind the reader that the definition of rigidity as used in the study refers to a postulated property of inner regions of the person, which is different from the commonsense meaning of rigidity, which usually refers to a quality of overt behavior such as inflexibility or stereotype.

Any system of psychology which attempts to deal with problems of personality has to postulate some kind of structure for a person in order to

REPRINTED FROM *Character and Personality*, 1941, *9*, 251–273, through the courtesy of the publisher, the Duke University Press, and the author.

100   The Mentally Deficient

be able to account for certain behavioral events of a nonreflexive character. Whether stated explicitly, or whether implicitly assumed, wherever constructs of a psychoanalytical, neurological, typological, or any other variety have been utilized, all psychological theories have dealt with problems of personality "structure." The following investigation is an attempt to give precise formulation to, and to achieve co-ordinating and operational definitions for, one of a number of basic concepts utilized in problems of personality structure, namely, the concept of rigidity.

The concept of rigidity has its place in a series of interrelated statements and constructs which are postulated in topological and vector psychology. Briefly, the "person" is said to be structured and differentiated into parts. The unit of structure is co-ordinated to a geometrical region, or "cell," which occupies a certain position among other regions. The psychological environment in which a person behaves is also structured into regions. Behavior is said to be a resultant of certain forces functioning in and relating to the personal and environmental structures. The structural and positional properties constitute topological psychology. The functional relationships and forces which determine the behavior that occurs within the given structure make up vector psychology.

The construct of rigidity deals with the closeness of the functional relation between cells of the person; in other words, it refers to that property of the functional boundary between the cells of the person which represents the relative independence (degree of segregation) of different regions of a person. Occurrences in one region may have quite different effects upon other regions. A change in a region A of a person may produce more change in a region B than the same amount of change in a region X produces a change in a region Y; i.e., tension may spread more easily from region A to region B than from region X to region Y. There may be such differences in rigidity of the boundary between different regions of the same individual and differences in rigidity between comparable regions of different individuals.

The concept of rigidity, particularly as applied to a theory of feeblemindedness, has been tentatively formulated by Lewin (*1935a*). This theory is based upon unpublished studies dealing with the comparative behavior of moron and normal children in experiments concerned with the process of satiation, the resumption of interrupted tasks, and the substitute value of substitute actions. The findings revealed decided differences between the feebleminded and normal children. After becoming satiated with an assigned drawing activity, the feebleminded children refused to continue with free drawing, while the normal children did not refuse. The feebleminded children were said to have been either satiated or "not satiated," whereas the normal children were "partly satiated." In experiments on resumption of interrupted activities, the feebleminded children manifested a greater fixation upon goals than did normal children. This was evidenced by their more frequent resumption of interrupted activities. In studies of substitution it was found to be more difficult to create satisfying substitute goals for the original goals in the case of the feebleminded than in the case of the normal children. The differences between the two groups of individuals were summarized as indicating that the moron children behaved more "rigidly," i.e., in a pedantic, "all-or-none," "either-or" manner. The construct of rigidity was utilized to derive these differences.

It would seem that rigidity of overt behavior cannot be directly coordinated with rigidity of the boundaries of the regions making up a person's structure, i.e., with his dynamic rigidity. Factors other than dynamic rigidity may operate to produce phenomenological rigidity. There are three such uncontrolled factors which may have influenced the results obtained in the experiments cited by Lewin. (1) *The degree of differentiation of the person*. Lewin states, in fact, that "one might consider reconstructing the theory so as to place at the center lack of differentiation rather than material properties, or one might dispense altogether with the assumption of a difference in material" (*Lewin, 1935*, p. 228). The mental ages and related degrees of differentiation of the moron and normal children used in the experiments cited by Lewin were not equated. (2) *Degree of differentiation of the relevant areas*. One can speak of the degree of differentiation of the person "as a whole" and of the degree of differentiation of particular areas. Two persons may have the same total degree of differentiation, yet one of them may behave in a more stereotyped manner in a particular situation because the relevant and applicable regions are less differentiated in his case. In the experiments on satiation, after being satiated with drawing "moon faces" the normal children were disposed toward drawing other things in a free drawing situation, while the moron children refused to do free drawings. It is possible that the area of drawing was more differentiated in the normal children and that they could "think of" more to draw. The moron children, on the other hand, may not have had "anything else in mind" and, as a result, were not inclined to continue drawing. (3) *The security of the two groups*. It is not within the scope of this paper to define security within a strict conceptual framework. One might include under this concept such factors in the psychological environment as the fear of failure and the relative barrier quality of unknown regions. If an individual feels insecure, he may exhibit phenomenologically rigid behavior, not because of dynamic rigidity but because he is afraid of attempting the new and so clings to what he does know.

THE PROBLEM

The problem of this series of experiments is to evaluate the concept of rigidity, to develop methods of measuring its properties, and to ascertain its validity in theories of age and of feeblemindedness. More specifically, with factors such as degree of differentiation and security controlled, can one speak of rigidity of boundaries of regions? If so, can the concept be related to theories of feeblemindedness and of age?

A related problem is to ascertain the predictive value of the construct of rigidity and related topological and dynamic concepts. To be specific: Does the theory permit one to state the consequences to be obtained in defined conditions?

The problem of measurement, testability, and predictive-power is one of attempting to ascertain concrete events which may be regarded as symptoms or signs of the postulated causal conditions and relationships. This implies not merely direct operational definitions of a construct but also the use of the "hypothetico-deductive" method of prediction and verification. A theory is proposed, implications of an "if this is so . . . then" proposition are deduced by relating one construct to another, and these deductions are put to experimental test, i.e., "proof." Such a procedure provides the framework for measurement and for explanation. A combination of the definitions of constructs, and the derivation of behavioral events which can be used as signs of the construct and therefore as means of measurement, and the testing to ascertain whether predictions maintain, is the plan of procedure utilized in the following research.

Definitions, Theory (Postulates), and Derivations (Theorems) [1]

Definition Rigidity is that property of a functional boundary which prevents communication between neighboring regions. The degree of communication of a region A with a region B refers to the degree of influence of A on B, or vice versa. Regions A and B are communication to the degree to which a change of the state of A changes the state of B. The degree of rigidity can be regarded as determining: (a) the difference in tension (or other states) which can be maintained by the boundary between neighboring regions and (b) the degree of functional segregation of neighboring regions.

The rigidity of the boundaries of different regions of the same person varies. Nevertheless, it is possible to speak of the rigidity of a Person-1, R(P-1), as compared to the rigidity of a Person-2, R(P-2), when: (1) we compare equivalent regions (a) of the individuals, i.e., regions which correspond to activities of the same psychological meaning, and (2) we further assume that the rigidity of the boundary of region A is representative of the rigidity of the boundaries of other regions (B, C, D . . . X) of the person.

---

[1] Definitions of related concepts can be found in Lewin (*1935, 1936*) and in Barker, Dembo, & Lewin (*1941*).

The general theory The general theory postulates that rigidity is a positive monotonic function of chronological age. A corollary of this theory is that rigidity is a positive monotonic function of the degree of feeblemindedness. The latter theory follows if one assumes that mental age corresponds to the degree of differentiation of a person, since the degree of feeblemindedness is defined as the ratio between mental age and chronological age (IQ).

Derivations The complete logical steps involved in the following derivations are not presented here for the sake of brevity. It is hoped that the brief descriptions of the experiments will indicate how these derivations were obtained. To restate the derivations in their entirety would require more complete definition of all terms used. The derivations are as follows: the older and/or more feebleminded an individual:

1. The less effect a change of state in one region will have upon the state of neighboring regions.

2. The less likely he is to be in an overlapping situation.

3. The more difficulty he will have in the performance of a task which requires him to be influenced by more than one region.

4. The more likely is he to structure a new field which is perceptually ambiguous into a relatively large number of separate, independent regions (achieve a less integrated structure).

5. The less easily can he perform a task which requires that he restructure a given field.

THE EXPERIMENTS

Subjects Three groups of subjects of equal Binet mental ages were utilized. Table I presents a summarized description of the subjects.

The feebleminded subjects were all inmates of the Iowa State Hospital for Feebleminded Children at Glenwood, Iowa. All the subjects were diagnosed as functional cases by resident physicians. The normal subjects were all enrolled in one of the elementary public schools of Iowa City.

SUBJECTS	$\dfrac{\text{Time for D}}{\text{Time for A}}$	$\dfrac{\text{Time for D}}{\text{Time for B}}$	$\dfrac{\text{Time for D}}{\text{Time for C}}$	Mean Number of Errors
Old feebleminded	302	224	187	3.7
Young feebleminded	225	174	145	1.7
Difference	77	48	44	2.0
Critical ratio	4.14	2.90	4.44	2.0

104 The Mentally Deficient

Table I

MEASURE	Old Feeble-Minded Subjects (OF)	Young Feeble-Minded Subjects (YF)	Normal Subjects (N)
Number	21	21	21
Mean mental age	80 mo.	82 mo.	82 mo.
Range	69 to 94	72 to 96	72 to 92
Mean chronological age	41.7 yrs.	14.5 yrs.	6.8 yrs.
Range	29 yrs. 3 mo. to 53 yrs. 9 mo.	10 yrs. 10 mo. to 17 yrs.	6 yrs. 0 mo. to 7 yrs. 9 mo.
Mean IQ*	42	48	99.76
Range	38 to 52	38 to 63	88 to 109

* For those subjects whose chronological ages were above sixteen years, a chronological age of sixteen years was used in computing their IQs.

Experiment I: Satiation and Cosatiation

Derivation-1 This experiment was designed to test Derivation-1. The general plan was to create experimentally a differentiation of an equal number of regions of security for all subjects, to produce a change in one of the regions, and to ascertain the effect this change had upon the state of the neighboring regions, i.e., to determine the degree of communication between these regions.

As an example indicating how the derivations in this study were arrived at, Derivation-1 is stated below:

1a. The older the individual, the less effect a change of state in one region will have upon the state of neighboring regions.

1b. The more feebleminded the individual of a given mental age, the less effect a change of state in one region will have upon the state of neighboring regions.

If we let DC equal the degree of communication between the two neighboring regions, CA equal chronological age, and FM equal the degree of feeblemindedness, then:

(1a) $DC = F(1/CA)$ (1b) $DC = F(1/FM)$

1. Let us suppose, as represented in Figure 1, that an old feebleminded individual and a young normal individual are both equally differentiated in equivalent areas, and that a change of state is effected in one of the regions (OF = old feebleminded; YN = young normal).

2. According to postulates 1a and 1b, an old feebleminded individual is to be characterized by a greater degree of rigidity than a young normal individual.

105 Jacob S. Kounin

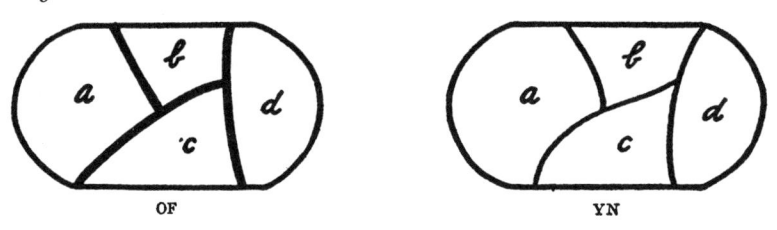

Fig. 1 *Schematic representation for derivation 1.*

3. It follows from 2 and the definition of rigidity that regions a and b (and other regions) of an old feebleminded individual will be in less communication with each other than will be regions a and b of a young normal individual.

4. Therefore, it follows from 3 that the older and/or more feebleminded the individual, the less effect an occurrence in one region will have upon the state of neighboring regions.

Each subject was presented with four drawing activities, placed on separate tables in a room. These drawing activities are illustrated in Figure 2. The subject was shown how to draw cats, bugs, turtles, and rabbits until he felt confident and secure in these activities. He was then allowed to draw cats until he became satiated and wanted to draw no more. After having become satiated with the drawing of cats, he was asked if he wanted to draw more bugs. After becoming satiated with drawing bugs, he was asked if he desired to draw more turtles. Finally, he was asked whether or not he felt like drawing more rabbits after having become satiated with drawing turtles. The situation was made as free as possible, and a minimum of pressure to continue drawings was placed upon the subject. (The degree of freedom actually created in the situations was indicated partly by the spontaneity in the general behavior and verbal expressions of the subjects, and partly by the fact that over 50 per cent of the subjects with which the experiment was started felt sufficiently free to

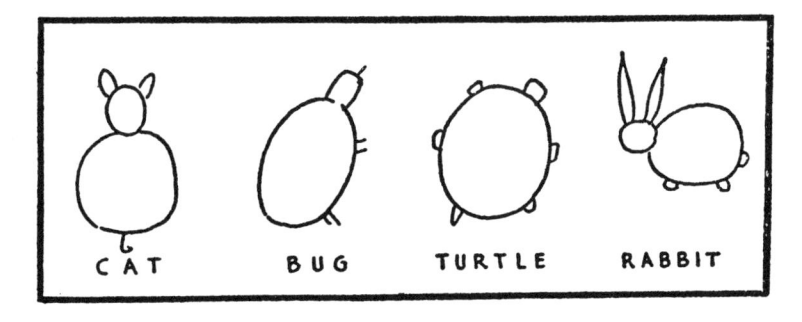

Fig. 2 *Objects drawn in experiment 1.*

106   The Mentally Deficient

refuse after the experimenter demonstrated the activities to them, or else drew objects entirely unrelated to the experimental situation.)

Since the old feebleminded subjects can be characterized by a greater degree of rigidity (by postulation), satiation of the region of "drawing cats" should not markedly cosatiate the neighboring regions. The young normal subject is characterized by less rigidity; therefore the neighboring regions should be partly cosatiated in the process of satiating the "drawing cats" region.

An index of cosatiation was computed for each subject by using his satiation time on the first drawing activity as the basis of comparison. This cosatiation index was expressed by a percentage. The formula used was:

$$\frac{\text{Satiation time on cats minus satiation time on bugs (or turtles, rabbits)}}{\text{Satiation time on cats}}$$

An index of 0 per cent or below (negative percentage) means that satiation of the cat-drawing activity had no effect upon the bug-drawing activity. That is, the subject spent as much time drawing bugs as he did drawing cats. Conversely, a cosatiation index of 100 means that satiation of the cat-drawing activity resulted in complete cosatiation of the bug-drawing activity.

The mean cosatiation indexes of the three groups of subjects are given in Table II [2] and are graphically represented in Figure 3.

It can be seen that the least amount of cosatiation was evidenced in the old feebleminded group, and the greatest amount of cosatiation obtained in the normal group. The differences between the three groups of subjects in the degree of cosatiation were revealed by quantitative time measures, by the qualitative nature of their overt behavior, and by the nature of their drawings. The behavior of the old feebleminded subjects while drawing bugs, turtles, and rabbits was no different from their behavior while drawing cats. In contrast, cosatiation effects in addition to the quantitative time measures were markedly revealed in the case of the young normal subjects. They exhibited more tendencies to leave the field while drawing bugs, turtles, and rabbits than they manifested while drawing cats. They paused more frequently and for longer time intervals, engaged in nondrawing activities more often, and generally exhibited relatively more satiation symptoms (such as variations and mistakes) in the later drawing tasks than in the first drawing task.

[2] The number of subjects is not constant for all of the cosatiation indexes. This is due to the fact that some subjects spent so much time on the first few drawing activities that it became necessary to interrupt the experiment in order for the subject to have his noon or evening meal.

Jacob S. Kounin

Table II   Mean Cosatiation Indexes of the Three Groups of Subjects for the Different Drawing Tasks

SUBJECTS	SATIATION-TIME							
	$\dfrac{Cats - Bugs}{Cats}$		$\dfrac{Cats - Turtles}{Cats}$		$\dfrac{Cats - Rabbits}{Cats}$		$\dfrac{Cats - (Bugs + Turtles + Rabbits + Turtles)}{Cats}$	
	Number	Per cent	Number	Per cent	Number	Per cent	Number	Per cent
Old feebleminded	14	−28	12	−8	12	8	12	−10
Young feebleminded	17	39	17	52	16	66	16	54
Young normal	17	90	17	90	17	96	17	92
Old feebleminded minus young feebleminded	—	67	—	60	—	56	—	64
T (Fisher's)	—	3.9	—	3.3	—	2.3	—	3.3
Old feebleminded minus young normal	—	118	—	98	—	88	—	102
T (Fisher's)	—	7.6	—	6.2	—	4.0	—	6.0
Young feebleminded minus young normal	—	51	—	38	—	30	—	38
T (Fisher's)	—	6.2	—	4.5	—	3.2	—	5.1

There were also marked differences among the three groups of subjects with respect to the process of satiation, as such. The general progress of satiation in the old feebleminded subjects revealed a more sudden and "all-or-none" character. They appeared to be either satiated or not satiated. The process of becoming satiated occurred in a much more gradual manner in the young normal group. These differences can be summarized as follows:

1. It required the most time to satiate the activity in the case of the old feebleminded subjects, and the least time to satiate the same activity in the case of the young normal subjects. The differences in absolute sati-

108   The Mentally Deficient

[Bar chart showing Per cent co-satiation on y-axis, ranging from -30 to 100]

Index: 1·2/1   1·3/1   1·4/1   1·x/1

No. of
subjects: 14 17 17   12 17 17   12 16 17   12 16 17

☐ Old feeble-minded   1 = satiation time, cats
▨ Young feeble-minded   2 = satiation time, bugs
■ Normal   3 = satiation time, turtles
                             4 = satiation time, rabbits
                             $x = \frac{2+3+4}{3}$

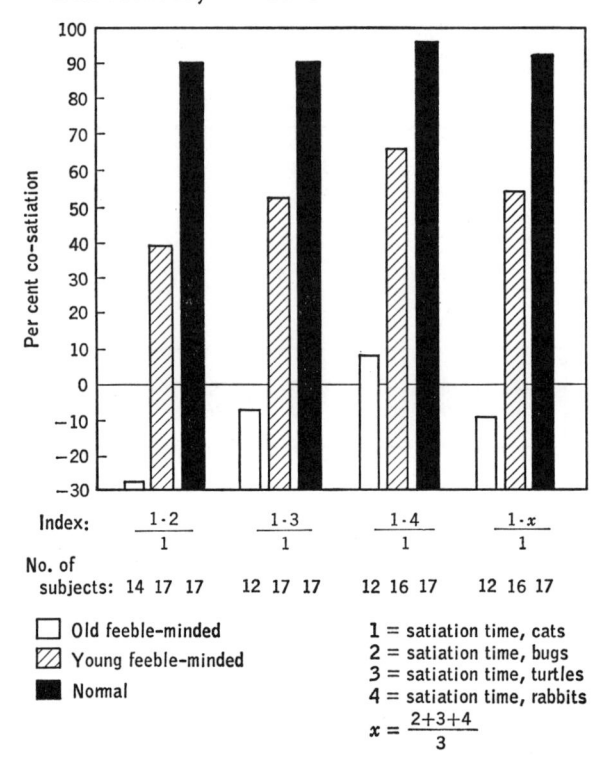

Fig. 3   *Mean cosatiation indexes.*

ation-time between any two of the three groups of subjects were all large and statistically significant.

2. The young normal subjects spent the greatest amount of time in nondrawing activities relative to the time they spent drawing, and the old feebleminded subjects spent the least amount of time in nondrawing activities relative to the time spent in drawing.

3. The greatest number of old feebleminded subjects stopped drawing only after finishing the last page upon which they were working. The greatest number of young normal subjects stopped drawing before finishing the last page upon which they were working.

4. The drawings of the old feebleminded subjects were more regular with respect to size and other variations in the nature of the objects drawn; the drawings of the young normal subjects tended to be the least regular.

5. The drawings of the old feebleminded subjects were most regular with respect to positional order on the pages (rows and columns); those of the young normal subjects displayed the greatest amount of positional variation.

It should be pointed out that the smaller amount of cosatiation found among the old feebleminded subjects obtained *in spite of* their larger absolute satiation-times. Actually, the more time an individual spends in doing one activity, the less time he is likely to spend in subsequent related activities. The latter statement is supported by studies on satiation and cosatiation as well as by studies concerned with fatigue (Crawley, *1926,* and Karsten, *1928*).

Experiment II: Transfer of Habit

Logically, it is possible to derive certain effects of rigidity upon the psychological environment by assuming that the rigidity of inner-personal regions parallels the degree of functional segregation of neighboring regions in the psychological environment. This may apply to the independence of a region from its background. The more rigid the structure of the person, the more does the degree of influence (potency) of an immediate region approach unity, and the less does the background situation affect his behavior. By definition, it is necessary for two situations to have an effective degree of influence (potency) upon the person, in order for the person to be in an overlapping situation. It follows that the more rigid the inner personal regions of an individual, the less likely is he to be in an overlapping situation.

This experiment was designed to test Derivation-2. The general plan was to create a specific situation for each subject (Situation-1), to place the subject in another situation (Situation-2), and to note what effect Situation-1 had upon the subject while he was in Situation-2—i.e., to determine the degree to which the subject was in an overlapping situation.

The apparatus used was similar to that designed by Schwarz (Schwarz, *1927* and *1933*) in his studies on unlearning. This consisted of a box into which marbles were introduced, one at a time. The subject could release the marble either by depressing or by raising a lever at the side. The mechanism was so designed that either depressing or raising the lever would release the marble.

Each subject was given three series of thirty trials each in which he released the marbles, one at a time, by depressing the lever. One-third of the marbles were red, one-third were black, and one-third were blue. After each marble was released by the apparatus to fall into a container, it was placed by the subject in a compartment corresponding to the color of the marble. This was done as rapidly as possible. Part of the situation was then changed by instructing the subject to raise instead of to depress the lever. There were two series (referred to as Situations D and E in Table III) of thirty trials each in which the subject was required to raise the lever. The effect of the previous situation was determined operationally by the number of times the subjects entered (i.e., behaved appropri-

110   The Mentally Deficient

ately to) that situation after having been placed in the second situation. Thus, the more errors made by the subject (depressing the lever), the more he was in an overlapping situation (being influenced by Situation-1 while in Situation-2).

On the basis of the theory, one would predict that the normal subjects would make the most errors—be most likely to be influenced by Situation-1 while in Situation-2—and that the old feebleminded subjects would make the least number of errors or would be least likely to be in an overlapping situation.

A summary of the results are given in Table III and Figure 4. These results support the theory by showing that the normal subjects made the

Table III   Error Records* of the Three Groups of Subjects in the Transfer of Habit Experiment (20 Subjects in Each Group)

MEASURE	Old Feeble-Minded	Young Feeble-Minded	Young Normal	DIFFERENCE BETWEEN Young Feeble-Minded and Old Feeble-Minded	Young Normal and Old Feeble-Minded	Young Normal and Young Feeble-Minded
Total errors on Situation D	13	27	89	14	76	62
Total errors on Situation E	11	30	51	19	40	21
Total errors	24	57	140	33	116	83
Mean number of errors	1.20±.47	2.85±.97	7.0±.99	1.65	5.8	4.15
Critical ratio of differences in means				1.53	5.32	3.01
Per cent of subjects making zero errors	55	15	0	40	55	15
Critical ratio of differences in percentages				2.92	4.95	1.88

* Perseveration-errors (repetition of down strokes in consecutive sequence) were counted only as *one* error. The concern was with the number of times the subject entered the situation of pushing the handle down, and not with how long he stayed in that region after having entered it. Such repetition of single errors did not occur frequently, and would not change the results to any appreciable extent. (The investigations of Schwarz definitely show the difference between errors of relapse and perseveration-errors.)

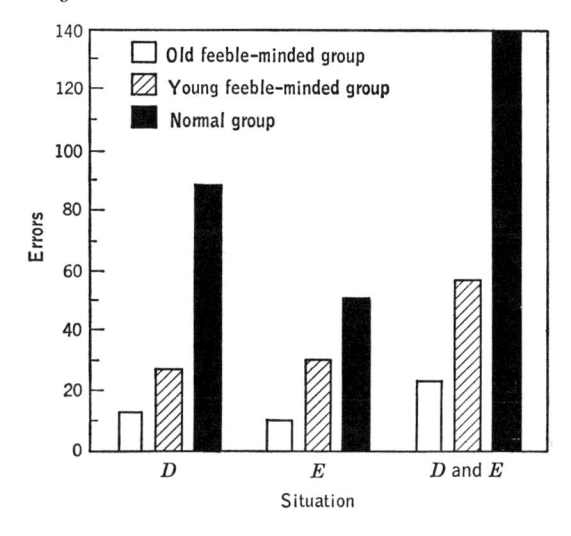

Fig. 4 Errors made in transfer of habit experiment.

greatest number of errors, and the old feebleminded subjects made the fewest number of errors. Thus, the old feebleminded subject is least likely to be in an overlapping situation. He is either in the one situation, "pushing the handle down," or in the other situation, "pulling the handle up," but is rarely influenced by both situations simultaneously.

Experiment III: Card Sorting in Simple and Overlapping Situations

This experiment was designed to test Derivation-3. The general plan was to determine the ratio of the difficulty (as measured by time and errors) each subject had in the performance of a particular activity in a simple situation to the difficulty he had in the performance of the same activity in a more complex and more overlapping situation. Card sorting was the activity utilized. Each subject sorted cards in three simple situations and in one overlapping situation. The relative difficulty of the overlapping situation was determined for each subject, by comparing the time that he required to complete the activity in an overlapping situation with the time that he required to complete the activity in the three simple situations.

The equipment consisted of fifty-two solidly colored cards, equally divided into four colors—red, yellow, black, and green. Four bottomless boxes each colored to correspond to one of the card colors were fitted into a large carton.

Following are the three simple situations, in order of their performance:
  a. The subject was required to deal the cards onto the table, one at a time, as rapidly as possible.
  b. The subject was required to place the cards, one at a time, into one of the boxes, as rapidly as possible.
  c. The subject was required to place the cards, one at a time, into a regular sequence of boxes, from the left side to the right side and back to the left to repeat the process, as rapidly as possible.

The overlapping situation is as follows:
  d. The subject was required to place each card into the box of the corresponding color as rapidly as possible. The cards were thoroughly shuffled, no two colors following one another consecutively. The subject had to keep in mind both accuracy and speed, and both the color of the card and the color of the box. Since the boxes were bottomless, the subject was unable to correct an error, thus enabling the time-score to be more accurate by not involving the time used in correcting errors. The cards fell into compartments and it was possible to record the locus, sequence, and total number of errors.

The extent to which Situation-D (the overlapping, complex situation) was more difficult than the others, was measured by determining the percentage more time required for each subject to complete the activity in Situation-D than to complete the activity in the three preceding simple situations. Below is a tabulation of the results, including the mean number of errors made by each group of subjects. The results are presented graphically in Figure 5. There were twenty subjects in each group.[3]

The above ratios were not functions of the absolute time required for the completion of the tasks. The same results obtained with pairs of young and of old feebleminded subjects who were equated in terms of the absolute times required in the sample situations. The fact that the old feebleminded subjects found the performance of a task in an overlapping situation relatively more difficult than did the young feebleminded subjects tends to add additional support to the proposed theory of rigidity. The difference is not explainable by postulating a greater

---

[3] This experiment was conducted with the old feebleminded and young feebleminded subjects. The number of times that the young normal subjects could be taken from their classrooms was limited. It was felt that this experiment could be eliminated with less loss than one of the others, since the young normal subjects' lack of the necessary motor coordination for the performance of this activity would complicate the comparative measures.

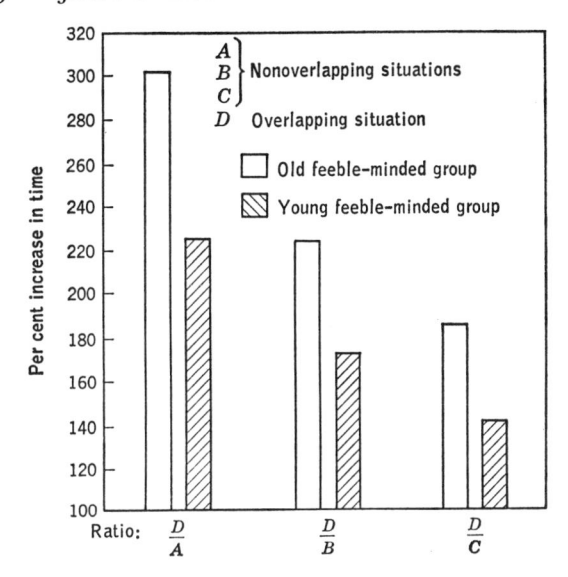

Fig. 5 Relative difficulty of an overlapping situation.

"cautiousness" in the case of the older subjects, since they actually made more errors than did the younger subjects.

Experiment IV: Integration by Classification

The following experiment was designed to test Derivation-4. The general method employed in this and in the following experiment, Experiment V, has been used rather widely by other investigators for various problems (*Bolles, 1937; Hanfmann* and *Kasanin, 1937; Vigotsky, 1934*). The procedure is to present a group of objects to a subject, some of which belong together in one "class," and to instruct the subject to arrange them in groups or categories. Such a method has been utilized in studies related to the thinking processes of individuals, especially with reference to "concrete" and "abstractmindedness."

In this study, certain modifications were made in the general method in order to make it more applicable to the problem and suitable for the mental ages used. One general type of classification-test was utilized, but with four modifications. The modifications were proposed partly in order to attain the initial conditions required in the derivations, and partly in order to avoid the all-or-none character of "abstract- *vs.* concrete-" mindedness tests and theories as applied to feeblemindedness.

Set-up A The initial condition specified by Derivation-4 supposes that the subjects are equally differentiated in equivalent areas. Set-up A was performed as a control experiment to insure the equivalent degree of differentiation of the different subjects.

Twenty-five cards were presented to each subject who was required to classify them into five groupings. There were five cards of each of the following five colors: black, yellow, green, pink, and red. The instructions for all of the classification tests were:

> Here are some things all mixed up. Some of these are the same and belong together. Here are five boxes. Suppose you find some that are the same and belong together and put them in one of the boxes. Then find some others that are the same and put them in another box, then find some others that are the same and put them in another box, and keep on going until you have all those that are the same together.

All subjects succeeded in classifying the cards into five color categories without any apparent difficulty. This indicated that the subjects understood the directions and possessed the necessary color concepts.

Set-up B The purpose of this set-up was to ascertain the comparative behaviors of the subjects when required to structure a more ambiguous field than that of the first set-up. Twenty-five cards were used, five each of the following forms: triangles, squares, circles, crosses, and five-pointed stars. Those cards were painted with water colors in five shades of blue. The colors were perceptually of three rather distinct categories: five purplish-blue, five navy blue, and fifteen light blue. Of the light blue cards there were five of each of three shades, which varied little from one another. The cards can be described as possessing various forms easily discriminated from one another, as having some colors which were readily distinguished from one another, and as having still other colors which could be distinguished one from the other only with considerable difficulty. At times the individual perceived form to be more outstanding and at other times, color. No time limit was stated in either set-up, nor did the experimenter suggest in any way that speed was a factor in sorting.

Table IV summarizes the results obtained from the three groups of subjects.

The behavior of the majority (62 per cent) of the old feebleminded subjects can be summarized as follows:

1. The cards were classified in more than five groupings.
2. The groupings were not consistent with one another. Some were made on the basis of form; others, on the basis of color.
3. Minor differences between the cards were not overlooked.
4. The subjects compared but two or three of the cards at a time.
5. The general behavior of the subjects was of a typical trial-and-error variety.

Jacob S. Kounin

Table IV Number of Subjects Changing Classifications

TRIAL OF CHANGE	Old Feeble-Minded (N = 20)		Young Feeble-Minded (N = 20)		Young Normal (N = 21)	
	Number	Cumulative Per cent	Number	Cumulative Per cent	Number	Cumulative Per cent
2	1	5	1	5	0	
3	0	5	0	5	0	
4	3	20	4	25	11	52
5	0	20	1	30	5	76
6	1	25	3	45	4	95
7	0	25	1	50	1	100
8	0	25	1	55		
9	0	25	1	60		
10	1	30	0	60		
Per cent changing		30		60		100
Per cent not changing		70		40		0

6. The subjects manifested extreme "immediate-mindedness." Their classifications were dependent upon the specific card or pair of cards they happened to be considering. What they did in the "past" or planned to do in the "future" apparently had little or no influence upon their present behavior.

The majority (60 per cent) of the young feebleminded subjects classified the cards into five form categories, without any evidence of confusion or consideration of color.

The behavior of the normal subjects differed from the behavior of both the young feebleminded and the old feebleminded subjects. The majority (44 per cent) of the normal subjects originally classified the objects on the basis of fewer than five color categories. Some of them put all of the "dark" blue cards in one category and all "light" blue cards into another. Others in this group classified the cards into three color categories: purplish blues (5), dark blues (5), and light blues (15). After the experimenter corrected them by saying: "There are supposed to be five in a box," the subjects classified the cards into five color categories. They evidenced no difficulty in making the correction.

Two other behavior categories were obtained with the normal subjects which were not observed in any of the other subjects. Twenty-eight per cent of the normal subjects started to classify the objects on the basis

116   The Mentally Deficient

Table V   Behavior of the Three Groups of Subjects in Set-up B

BEHAVIOR CATEGORIES	Old Feeble-Minded (N=21) Per cent	Young Feeble-Minded (N=20) Per cent	Young Normal (N=21) Per cent
Classify objects on the basis of form without verbal or behavioral consideration of color	19	60	19
Spontaneous classification on the basis of form, after having started on the basis of color	0	0	28
Inconsistent classifications (failure) followed by correct classification on the basis of form after experimenter's corrections	5	15	0
Classification on the basis of color*	5	0	0
Spontaneous classification on the basis of color, after verbal or behavioral consideration of form	0	0	9
Classified cards in fewer than five color categories, and changed to five categories after experimenter's correction	0	0	44
Inconsistent classifications, followed by classification on the basis of color after experimenter's correction	9	20	0
Failure to classify the objects consistently on the basis of form or color even after corrections of experimenter	62	5	0

* A color classification was correct if there were fewer than five errors, since some of the differences between colors were very difficult to discriminate.

of color, but before completing the sorting, spontaneously changed to a form classification. Nine per cent of the normal subjects started to classify the objects on the basis of form but spontaneously changed, before completing the trial, to sort the cards into five color categories. In all, 37 per cent of the normal subjects spontaneously changed their method of classifying the cards.

It has been shown that the concept of rigidity of boundaries in the structure of a person makes it possible to derive the relative independence of a region in the psychological environment from the regions neighboring and surrounding it. This proposition can then be applied to problems of the segregation of an immediate region from its background, to problems of overlapping situations (which, by definition, require at least two situations to have an effective degree of potency ("weight") in influencing behavior), to problems of the degree of unity and integration of paths, to problems of the effect of "past" and "future" upon a "pres-

Jacob S. Kounin

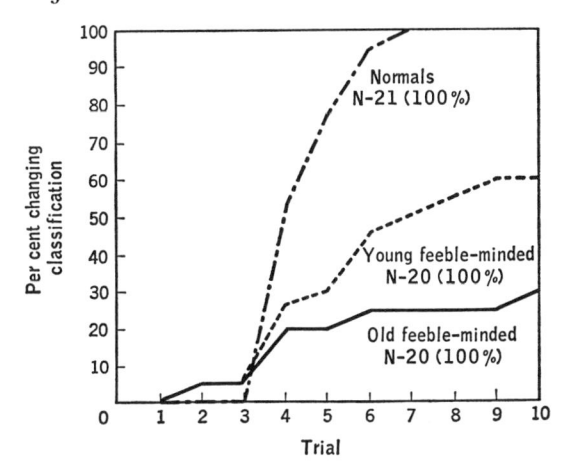

Fig. 6 Cumulative per cent of subjects changing classification.

ent" field, and to any problem which involves the interdependence of regions.

The old feebleminded subject is to be characterized by the greatest degree of rigidity, by postulation. Thus, the older and/or more feebleminded an individual, the more is any subregion of activity involved in a task independent from the other subregions of activity. This prevents the activity as a whole from becoming unified. All the behaviors exhibited by an old feebleminded subject can be shown to result from the more general premise of the relative lack of interdependence of regions in his psychological environment. The different units of activity in his path toward the solution of the task are functionally more segregated; as a result, the particular region in which he happens to be, dominates his behavior at the time. If the form quality of a pair of cards is perceptually most outstanding, he places the cards in a form-pile; if the color quality is most dominant in the next pair of cards, he places them in a separate color-pile; and he continues to make a considerable number of separate, independent classifications. The other types of behavior exhibited in the process of trying to solve the problem, such as the "immediate-mindedness," the lack of relationship between a "present" classification (i.e., form) and an immediately "past" classification (i.e., color), likewise follow from the general statement of the functional separation of one region from the others. The end-results of the performance are also derivable from the general proposition presented in the preceding paragraph. Thus, the old feebleminded subject ends with more than five groupings (more independent regions), and with groupings inconsistent with one another (functionally separated).

118   The Mentally Deficient

In the case of the young feebleminded subject, both the form and color paths are unified and segmented into five regions. He takes the path which, as a whole, is more potent. As a rule, form is perceptually more outstanding than color due to the nature of the cards, and he takes the form path of classification. While in the region of form, however, the influence of color is negligible. As a result, the young feebleminded subject neither changes his basis of classification spontaneously, nor does he give any indication of considering color.

The normal subject appears to be influenced by what he did in the past, and is in more of an overlapping situation than the feebleminded subject. Hence, since he classified the cards in Set-up A on the basis of color, he classifies the cards in Set-up B on the basis of color, in spite of the fact that it is harder to do than it is to group the cards on the basis of form. In addition, there are fewer than five segmented regions in the color path of his initial classification; i.e., he groups the cards in two or three classifications. He easily segments the cards into five categories after the experimenter's correction. The fact that the normal subjects are in an overlapping situation to a greater extent and more readily restructure a field than the feebleminded subjects (note Derivations 2 and 5) is indicated by their spontaneous changing of classifications from color to form, or vice versa.

Experiment V: Restructuring by Classification

This experiment was designed to test Derivation-5. The method is essentially that used in Experiment IV. The subject was experienced in both form and color classifications (in the previous set-ups). He was then presented with a group of cards, which consisted of the same forms and colors that he had experienced, to see whether he could make a change from one type of classification to the other while using the same group of cards. In addition, a method was planned to determine the amount of force necessary to apply to the different subjects in order to produce a change of their classifications, in order to get away from the "all-or-none" nature of "ability-to-change" concepts.

Set-up C   The twenty-five cards were made of the same forms utilized in set-up B of Experiment IV. All cards were made of yellow cardboard. The procedure was the same as that employed in the other classification tests. This was used to give all subjects the experience of a form classification, as well as to insure that all could make form-abstractions.

All subjects were able to classify the cards into five form categories without any noticeable difficulty.

Set-up D   Twenty-five cards were used whose colors were the same as those used in set-up A of Experiment IV and whose forms were the same as those used in set-ups B and C. They were presented to the subject as previously (Trial 1). After he had classified the objects correctly, either on the basis of color or form (*all* subjects successfully performed the task by one method or the other), the experimenter reshuffled the cards and returned them to the subject with the instructions to "do them again" (Trial 2). If the subject did not change his method of classifying the cards after the second trial, the cards were reshuffled and he was asked to sort the cards "again" (Trial 3). Should the subject have continued on the same basis of grouping on Trial 3, the experimenter reshuffled the cards and gave them to the subject with the instructions to "put them together some other way" (Trial 4). If the subject still did not change his method of grouping the cards, the procedure was repeated, with the instructions stated as follows: "No, find some *different* way. See if you can find some *other* way that they belong together" (Trial 5).

This was continued for a maximum of ten total trials. In case the subject at any time refused to continue, he was urged to continue trying by such comments as: "Sure you can do it. If I thought that you couldn't do it, I wouldn't have asked you to come up. Go ahead, I know that you can find some other way to do it." Such statements always resulted in inducing a renewed effort from the subject.

All subjects were able to classify the cards into five groupings either on the basis of five forms or on the basis of five colors. Approximately the same number of subjects chose to classify the cards into color groupings as classified the cards into form groupings.

The relative number of subjects of each group who changed their classifications (restructed the paths) are presented in the Table V and in Figure 6.

It can be seen that the old feebleminded subjects were least able to change from one to the other method of classification, and that the normal subjects were most able to change from one classification to the other. In spite of the fact that the greatest number of normal subjects changed their classifications, it required the least force to produce (in terms of the number of trials necessary and the strength of the experimenter's request).

SUMMARY AND CONCLUSIONS

The purpose of this study was twofold: (1) to arrive at a dynamic theory of age and of feeblemindedness; (2) to determine the predictive value of some topological and vector constructs, especially those related to the concept of rigidity.

Two general theories were proposed: (1) that rigidity is a positive monotonic function of chronological age; (2) that rigidity is a positive monotonic function of the degree of feeblemindedness. The latter is in reality a corollary of the first theory.

On the basis of the concept of rigidity in its postulated relationship to chronological age and to the degree of feeblemindedness, five derivations were arrived at by means of a hypothetico-deductive method. These were:

Other things being equal, the older and/or more feebleminded an individual:

1. The less effect a change of state in one region will have upon the state of neighboring regions.

2. The less likely he is to be in an overlapping situation.

3. The more difficulty he will have in the performance of a task which requires him to be influenced by more than one region.

4. The more likely is he to structure a new field which is perceptually ambiguous into a relatively large number of separate independent regions (achieve a less integrated structure).

5. The less easily he can perform a task which requires that he restructure a given field.

Experimental situations were devised to test each of the derivations. Three groups of subjects of equal Binet mental ages were utilized: (1) an old feebleminded group; (2) a young feebleminded group; and (3) a young normal group.

The results obtained showed definite differences between each of the three groups of subjects with respect to the propositions tested, thus indicating the validity of the theories.

The general conclusion is to the effect that any performance which requires a certain degree of communication between neighboring regions (the degree of communication being inversely proportional to the degree of rigidity) is to such an extent made difficult for the older and/or more feebleminded individual. As far as these experiments permit one to generalize, the phenomenological nature of the performance is unimportant. The task may be predominantly of a cognitive nature (as in the classification experiments), of a motor nature (as in the card-sorting experiment), or of a "volitional" nature (as in the experiments on satiation and cosatiation). If a task is facilitated by the lack of communication between neighboring regions, such a task will be more efficiently and accurately performed by an older and/or more feebleminded individual (as indicated by the "transfer of habit" experiment).

References

Barker, R., Dembo, T., & Lewin, K. Frustration and regression. A study of young children. Univ. of Iowa, Stud. in Child Welfare, 1941.

Bolles, Mary M. The basis of pertinence. *Arch. Psychol.*, 1937, No. 212. Pp. 51.

Crawley, S. L. An experimental investigation of recovery from work. *Arch. Psychol.*, 1926, No. 85. Pp. 66.

Hanfmann, Eugenia, & Kasanin, Jacob. A method for the study of concept formation. *J. Psychol.*, 1937, *3*, 521–540.
Karsten, Anitra. Untersuchungen zur Handlungs- und Affectpsychologie. V. Psychische Sättigung. (Investigations of the psychology of action and affection. V. Psychic satiation.) *Psychol. Forsch.*, 1928, *10*, 142–254.
Lewin, Kurt. *A dynamic theory of personality: selected papers.* Trans. Donald K. Adams and Karl E. Zener. New York: McGraw-Hill, 1935. Pp. ix, 286. (a).
Lewin, Kurt. *Principles of topological psychology.* Trans. Fritz and Grace Heider. New York: McGraw-Hill, 1936. Pp. vii, 231. (b).
Lewin, Kurt. The conceptual representation and the measurement of psychological forces. *Contrib. Psychol. Theory*, 1938, *1*, No. 4. Pp. 247. (c).
Schwarz, Georg. Untersuchungen zur Handlungs- und Affectpsychologie. IV. Über Rückfälligkeit bei Umgewöhnung, Teil I. Rückfalltendenz und Verwechslungsgefahr. (Investigations in the psychology of action and affection. IV. On relapses with the changing of habits.) *Psychol. Forsch.*, 1927, *9*, 86–158.
Schwarz, Georg. Untersuchungen zur Handlungs- und Affectpsychologie. XVI. Über Rückfälligkeit bei Umgewöhnung, Teil II. Über Handlungsganzheiten und ihre Bedeutung für die Rückfälligkeit. (Investigations in the psychology of action and affection. XVI. On relapses in the changing of habits. Part II. On act totalities and their importance for relapses.) *Psychol. Forsch.*, 1933, *18*, 143–190.
Vigotsky, L. S. Thought in schizophrenia. *Arch. Neurol. Psychiat.*, 1934, *31*, 1063–1077.

6

Rigidity in the Retarded:
A Reexamination

Edward Zigler

Dr. Zigler is Professor and Director of the Child Development Program at Yale University and is currently the Director of the Office of Child Development in the Department of Health, Education, and Welfare. He is one of the most prolific research workers in the field of mental retardation. His many published papers and those by his students and colleagues in isolating and identifying the factors that lead to rigid behaviors in the mentally retarded places him as the premiere scholar in this area of research.

This paper, supported, in part, by United States Public Health Service Research Grant HD-03008 and the Gunnar Dybwad Award of the National Association for Retarded Children, is a revision of his paper appearing in the first edition of this book. It brings the reader up to date with respect to the Lewin–Kounin rigidity formulation.

The implications of this paper go far beyond the empirical studies reported. They affect attitudes toward the mentally retarded and strike at the core of the traditional methods of caring and treating the mentally retarded. The student interested in doing research or planning educational programs for the mentally retarded will find this article invaluable.

The reader is also referred to the preceding article by Kounin and the following one by Gruen and Zigler.

Few views in the mental retardation area have had the staying power of the Lewin–Kounin formulation that retarded individuals are inherently rigid. Not only has this formulation precipitated numerous empirical investigations, but, as Sarason and Gladwin (1958) have noted, it has had considerable influence on the care, training, and treatment of the retarded. Although widely accepted as a major theoretical breakthrough for the understanding of the behavior of the retarded, it should be noted that, since its inception, this formulation has had a particularly stormy career, being continuously surrounded by controversy. Much of the early controversy appears to have stemmed from the failure of concerned investigators to deal adequately with both the definitional and methodological demands of the formulation. A particular source of confusion has been the failure of certain critics and defenders of this view to grasp fully the theoretical foundation of the rigidity hypothesis as advanced by its early proponents, Kurt Lewin and Jacob Kounin.

In an effort to extricate the hypothesis that retarded individuals are rigid from the controversy and confusion that has surrounded it, the present paper will present an historical overview of this issue. Within the scope of this historical perspective, some empirical efforts related to the Lewin–Kounin formulation will be reviewed. Finally, a brief overview of the motivational work of the author and his colleagues will be presented. The latter body of work represents a counterview to the Lewin–Kounin position and indicates that much of the rigid behavior of the retarded can be attributed to a variety of motivational factors rather than to an inherent cognitive rigidity.

THE LEWIN–KOUNIN FORMULATION

In Lewin's general theory, the individual is treated as a dynamic system with differences among individuals derivable from differences in (1) structure of the total system, (2) material and state of the system, or (3) its meaningful content. The first two factors play the most important role in Lewin's theory of mental retardation. In respect to structure, Lewin viewed the retarded child as being cognitively less differentiated (i.e., having fewer regions in the cognitive structure) than a normal child of the same CA. Thus, in respect to the number of regions in the cognitive structure, the retarded child resembles a normal younger child. However, in relation to the material and state of the system, Lewin stated that even though retarded children corresponded to normal younger children in degree of differentiation, they were not to be regarded as entirely similar. He explicitly stated that he conceived "the major dynamic difference between a feebleminded and a normal child of the same degree of differentiation to consist in a greater stiffness, a smaller capacity for dynamic rearrangement in the psychical systems of the former" (Lewin, 1936).

Lewin presented a considerable amount of observational and anecdotal material as well as the findings of one experiment to support his theoretical position concerning the rigidity of the retarded. Lewin's experimental procedure consisted of having groups of normal and retarded children of differing CAs draw moon faces until they were satiated on this activity. The persistence (i.e., longer satiation time) displayed by the 10-year-old retarded children as compared to the 10-year-old normals was used by Lewin as evidence of the greater rigidity of the retarded.

A serious difficulty in Lewin's study was that comparisons were made between groups having different MAs, thus varying in their degree of differentiation. This placed Lewin in the position of being faced with a behavioral manifestation of rigidity without being able to ascribe it solely to the principle that the 10-year-old retarded are less differentiated than the 10-year-old normals, or to the principle that, differentiation notwithstanding, the retarded as compared to normals are characterized by a lessened fluidity between regions of the dynamic system. Thus, in accounting for his results, Lewin vacillated between an explanation in terms of degree of differentiation and one in terms of fluidity of the system.

Although Lewin undoubtedly felt that lack of differentiation could lead to rigid behaviors (e.g., pedantry, fixation, stereotypy, inelasticity, concreteness, etc.), he was quite clear that this lack of differentiation was not what he meant by rigidity. To Lewin, lack of differentiation referred to the number and hierarchy of regions within the total system, while rigidity was defined in terms of the fluidity existing between regions. It follows from Lewin's theory that if an individual's system is characterized by lack of differentiation or by rigidity or both, that individual is more likely to emit behaviors commonly referred to as rigid. Lewin's failure to draw a clear distinction between the meaning of rigidity, as he employed it, and rigid behaviors, as such, appears to be a major factor leading to the subsequent controversy in this area. This difference between rigidity, as defined by Lewin, and the concept of rigidity, as employed to characterize a particular class of phenotypic behaviors, must be kept firmly in mind.

Lewin also suggested a motivational explanation, centered around the high incidence of failure experiences, for the rigid behaviors observed in the retarded. However, he quickly dismissed it as inadequate. In addition, Lewin issued a warning that psychologically comparable situations must be employed if differences in rigidity are to be assessed correctly. Lewin here was suggesting that a particular situation may constitute a conflict situation for a retarded individual while presenting no conflict for a normal individual.

An examination of Lewin's work thus discloses at least four factors which must be taken into consideration when assessing differences in the occurrence of rigid behaviors in normal and retarded individuals. These four factors may be summarized as follows:

1. *Degree of differentiation.* Of two individuals of the same CA, one normal and one retarded, it is assumed that the retarded individual is less differentiated (i.e., has fewer regions) than the normal individual. Owing to this lesser degree of differentiation, the retarded individual will manifest more rigid behaviors over a wide range of tasks than will the normal individual of the same CA.

2. *Rigidity.* Of two individuals having the same degree of differentiation, one a younger normal and one an older retarded, the boundaries between the regions in the retarded individual will be less permeable, thus making the total system less fluid and more rigid. Owing to this rigidity within the system, the retarded individual will manifest more rigid behaviors over a wide range of tasks than will the chronologically younger normal possessing an equal degree of differentiation.

3. *History of the individual.* Any individual who is frequently faced with problems beyond his capacity and who experiences an inordinate number of failures may adopt a life style characterized by rigid behaviors. Such behaviors would not be considered the result of the innate rigidity of the individual but rather the product of a unique history of environmental events.

4. *The psychological situation.* In assessing differences in the amount of rigid behaviors between any two individuals, care must be taken that the overall assessment situation be psychologically equivalent for both individuals. Otherwise, differences in the amount of rigid behaviors may be due to the individuals operating in phenomenally different situations rather than to actual differences in the amount of rigidity possessed by the two individuals.

In any individual these factors would interact, the interaction of factors 3 and 4 being especially obvious. While the last two factors played a relatively minor role in the early efforts to analyze the high incidence of rigid behaviors in the retarded, factors of this type are prominent features of the more recent studies conducted by the author and his colleagues.

The clearest experimental support for the position that retarded individuals are more rigid than normal individuals having the same degree of differentiation is contained in the work of Kounin (1939, 1941a, 1941b, 1948). Kounin, building upon Lewin's work, advanced the view that rigidity is a positive, monotonic function of CA. Again, it is imperative to note that by "rigidity" Kounin, like Lewin, was referring to "that property of a functional boundary which prevents communication between neighboring regions" and not to phenotypic rigid behaviors as such. Thus, with increasing CA, the individual becomes more differentiated (i.e., has more cognitive regions), which results in a lower incidence of rigid behaviors, while the boundaries between regions become less and less permeable. Furthermore, while this lack of permeability in the boundaries between regions often results in behaviors which would be characterized as rigid, in some instances it leads to behaviors which could be characterized as indicative of "flexibility." (For an example of the latter possibility, see the results of Kounin's lever-pressing task presented below.)

Kounin offered the findings of five experiments in support of his formulation. In these experiments he employed three groups: older retarded individuals, younger retarded individuals, and normals. (It should be noted that the two retarded groups resided in an institution, whereas the normal children did not.) In view of the inadequacies of Lewin's satiation study, Kounin instituted certain experimental controls. He defined the degree of differentiation as the MA of an individual and controlled for this factor by equating the three groups on MA. He also attempted to reduce what he later referred to as "motivational factors (such as low success expectation, hesitance to enter unfamiliar regions, etc.) that might produce those very types of behavior that are sometimes lumped together in the pseudo-descriptive category of behavioral rigidity" (Kounin, 1948). Kounin attempted to control for these factors by having his subjects engage in each of the activities prior to the experiment proper, thus attempting to make each subject feel confident and secure during the experimental tasks.

As Kounin predicted, the three groups differed in certain instruction-initiated tasks (e.g., drawing cats until satiated and then drawing bugs until satiated) and lowering a lever to release marbles and then raising the lever to release marbles. As predicted from the Lewin–Kounin hypothesis, the normals showed the greatest amount of transfer effects from task to task, the younger retarded a lesser amount of transfer and the older retarded the least amount of transfer. That is, on the drawing task, the retarded individuals drew longer on the second task following satiation on the first task than did normals, with the least cosatiation effects being observed in the older retarded group. On the lever-pressing task, the greatest number of errors, lowering rather than raising the lever on task 2, was made by the normals, the least number of errors by the older retarded, with the younger retarded falling between these two groups.

One should note that on this task the lesser "rigidity," as defined by Lewin and Kounin, of the normals results in a higher incidence of a behavioral response often characterized as rigid (i.e., perseverative responses). One should further note that this lack of influence of one region on another in the performance of the retarded would only be predicted in those cases where the retarded individual is "psychologically" placed into a new region by employing an instructional procedure. In those instances where the individual must on his own move from one region to another, the Lewin–Kounin formulation would predict that such movement would be more difficult for the retarded than for the normal individual. This prediction was also confirmed by Kounin in his concept-switching experiment, in which the child was given a deck of cards which could be sorted on the basis of either one (form) or another (color) principle. In this experiment the subject, after voluntarily sorting the cards on the basis of either color or form, was asked to put the cards together some other way. Here the normals evidenced the least difficulty in shifting and the older retarded the most difficulty in shifting, with the younger retarded again falling between these two groups. Thus, in the instance where a movement to a new region is self-initiated, it is the retarded who evidence the higher incidence of perseverative responses.

The Lewin–Kounin theory of rigidity is a conceptually demanding one in that it sometimes predicts a higher and sometimes a lower incidence of phenotypically rigid behaviors in retarded as compared to normal individuals. However, the fact that it generates specific predictions as to when one or the other state of affairs will obtain is a tribute to this theory. Kounin thus offered impressive experimental support for the view that, with MA held constant, the older and/or more retarded an individual is, the more will his behaviors be characterized by dynamic rigidity (i.e., greater rigidity in the boundaries between regions).

THE CRITICISMS OF GOLDSTEIN AND WERNER

Both Lewin's and Kounin's positions on rigidity in the retarded were soon criticized by Goldstein (1942–43). Although taking issue with those earlier investigators on several points, Goldstein clearly stated: " . . . I do not deny at all that rigidity is an important symptom of feeblemindedness." He disagreed with Kounin that rigidity was a positive monotonic function of chronological age and with both Kounin and Lewin on their conception of rigidity. He offered in its place a two-factor theory of rigidity which differentiated between primary and secondary rigidity.

A comparison of the views of Goldstein with those of Lewin and Kounin presents certain difficulties. Lewin implicitly and Kounin explicitly applied their theory only to the familial retarded. Goldstein treats mental retardation as a homogeneous entity having a common organic etiology, drawing no distinction between the organic and the familial retarded. Another problem lies in Goldstein's use of the term "rigidity." He sometimes employs it as a physiological construct having organic referents, while at other times he uses it to describe the behaviors themselves. As noted earlier, failure to make this differentiation explicit has caused considerable difficulty. Goldstein's failure to comprehend fully Kounin's definition of rigidity led him to what appears to be a misdirected criticism of Kounin's satiation experiment in which the subjects drew pictures of animals.

Goldstein argued that the four tasks in this experiment were in reality just one task, drawing four objects one after the other which required but a single *Einstellung*. He notes the ease with which the retarded shifted from drawing one animal to another and uses this fact as indicating that all the drawings comprised one task, for Goldstein felt that "if it were a new task, rigidity would appear." Thus, Goldstein treats Kounin's concept of rigidity as involving no more than ease of shifting. However, Kounin (1948) has clearly pointed out that in this experiment he was not measuring the ease of shifting but was instead measuring the degree to which the satiation of one need cosatiated a neighboring need. Kounin further pointed out that no predictions concerning the ability to shift in this particular experiment could be derived from his concept of rigidity. Once again, Goldstein's error appears to lie in his insistence on interpreting Kounin's concept of rigidity as referring to a type of behavior, rather than a hypothesized quality of the boundaries between cognitive regions.

One aspect of Goldstein's criticism of the satiation experiment does merit further consideration. Goldstein states, in effect, that Kounin's four drawing tasks did not require the person to move from one region to another. It would appear that anyone who uses a theory that employs such concepts as "degree of differentiation," "region," "overlapping situation," "restructuring a given field," *"Einstellung,"* "mental set," etc., to predict behaviors must make an effort to define these concepts independently of the operations which constitute the predicted behaviors.

With the exception of Kounin's defining the degree of differentiation as the MA of the individual, this has never been clearly done. It is true that to the extent that one employs his theory, implements such concepts in any single experimental procedure, and obtains positive results, not only is the general theory supported but the implication is that the implicit requirements of the concepts have been fulfilled. It is, however, only to the extent that these requirements be made explicit and the concept divorced from any single experimental procedure, as such, that one can unequivocally state that the demands of the concept have been met. Goldstein's criticism of Kounin's satiation experiment stands as evidence on this point. It is difficult for Kounin to show that drawing bugs after drawing cats requires the individual to "move to a new region." Goldstein's criticism further illustrates that not dealing with this problem invites different interpretation of positive results.

The issue becomes even more critical in respect to negative findings. A requirement of any theory is that it produce testable hypotheses which are open equally to both proof and disproof. It would appear that, in their present state, the theories so far discussed do not meet this requirement. Since the concepts referred to above are not independently defined, any negative results obtained employing them can be explained away by stating that the demands implied in these concepts were not met. For example, had Kounin found no differences between the three groups in the satiation experiment, these results could have been discarded on the grounds that this particular experimental procedure did not really involve movement to a new region. In this respect, the theory is receptive only to positive results and not to findings which may constitute a disproof. This shortcoming is a serious one and must be kept in mind when evaluating the various theories under discussion.

Returning to Goldstein's distinction between primary and secondary rigidity, Goldstein felt primary rigidity involved "an abnormality of the *Einstellung* mechanism, most frequently observed in lesions of the subcortical ganglia." Goldstein advanced the position that primary rigidity is independent of an impairment of higher mental processes, manifesting itself in a lack of ability to change from one "set" to another. This deficiency becomes apparent only when the individual attempts to shift from one task to a second unrelated task. The difficulty is not related to the various tasks themselves, for Goldstein felt that an individual suffering from primary rigidity is quite capable of solving individual tasks even if such tasks demand a high level of abstraction.

Goldstein viewed secondary rigidity as being "due to a primary defect of the higher mental processes occurring in cortical damage and cortical malformations, such as feeblemindedness." Underlying secondary rigidity is an impairment of abstract thinking. The ability to think abstractly can be positively related to the concept of degree of differentiation. In a manner reminiscent of Kounin's equating degree of differentiation with MA, Goldstein equates ability to think abstractly with "mental capacity." Indeed, at one point, Goldstein makes the translation and places lack of differentiation at the center of the problem of rigidity in the retarded. Goldstein, thus, agreed with Lewin and Kounin that lack of differentiation results in a high incidence of rigid behaviors but disagreed with them concerning their assumption of a primary abnormality in the boundaries between regions. Goldstein suggested that all differences in the incidence of rigid behaviors in the retarded stem from their relative lack of differentiation and from this factor alone. To Goldstein, secondary rigidity is a result of an individual's dealing with a problem beyond his mental capacity. Rigid behaviors, such as perseveration, are adaptive mechanisms which allow the individual to escape frustration. The retarded emit more of such behaviors because they encounter problems beyond their capacity more frequently than do normal individuals.

Goldstein, feeling that Kounin had not considered this problem, tried to explain away Kounin's findings. He attributed Kounin's positive results to Kounin's experimental tasks varying in the intellectual demands they made on the three groups of subjects. This criticism of

Kounin's work by Goldstein would only be appropriate if Kounin had either given tasks differing in complexity to three groups of individuals having the same mental capacity or had given the same task to three groups differing in mental capacity. Actually, Kounin did neither. In each experiment, all subjects performed the same task. As to mental capacity, not only did Kounin equate his three groups on MA, but he made a further effort to see that his three groups were equated in ability to perform the specific experimental task employed. Therefore, as interesting as Goldstein's concept of secondary rigidity is, it can in no way explain the differences found by Kounin.

There appears to be another difficulty in Goldstein's distinction between primary and secondary rigidity. One wonders exactly how his secondary rigidity is any more "secondary" than his primary rigidity. Primary rigidity implies subcortical damage, which results in an inability to change "sets," from which ensue certain definite behaviors (i.e., inability to shift to a new task). Secondary rigidity implies cortical damage which results in an inability to think abstractly, from which ensue certain behaviors (i.e., perseveration or distractibility). How, then, is one "primary" and one "secondary" unless these terms have as a referent only the level of the central nervous system involved? It is only to the extent that secondary rigidity is divorced from organic involvement that the distinction "secondary" becomes meaningful. If this were done, then Goldstein's secondary rigidity would become simply a general behavior mechanism, unrelated to retardation, that appears when any individual is confronted with a problem beyond his capacity. It is of interest to note that such a general behavior mechanism has indeed been utilized to account for the appearance of certain rigid behaviors when individuals are faced with difficult or insoluble tasks (Maier, 1949; Stevenson & Zigler, 1957).

Werner (1940, 1948) has also advanced the view that the retarded are rigid. He has, however, taken exception to Kounin's concept of rigidity and especially to Kounin's hypothesis that rigidity is a positive monotonic function of CA. Werner ascribed differences in behavior between normals and the retarded to lack of differentiation in the retarded and to such descriptive generalizations as "feebleminded children are less easily satiated than normal children," "everybody familiar with feebleminded children has noticed the stereotypy even of their free activity," and, "as a rule feebleminded children are not opposed to monotonous work; they rather like it." Werner felt that Kounin's hypothesis on the relationship of rigidity and age was erroneous since as a person grows older, he becomes more differentiated, with his behavior becoming less stereotyped, less perseverative, less concrete, more plastic, etc. As Kounin (1948) has noted in a reply to Werner, this controversy appears to be the result of Werner's failure to distinguish between "behavioral rigidity" (rigid behaviors) and "dynamic rigidity" as Kounin defined it.

Werner's attempt to relate the differences obtained by Kounin between his normal and retarded subjects to differences in degree of differentiation also appears inadequate. As noted earlier, Kounin obtained these differences after equating the groups on degree of differentiation. Werner nowhere stated that Kounin's equating procedure failed to achieve its purpose. It thus appears that Werner's criticisms of Kounin's work suffer from some of the same shortcomings as did those of Goldstein. One can only conclude that Goldstein's and Werner's critiques of Kounin's work have cast very little doubt on Kounin's position that retarded subjects emit more rigid behaviors than do normal subjects of the same MA, and that the older and/or more retarded an individual is, the more will his behavior be characterized by rigidity as defined by Kounin. (For a further discussion of the Kounin–Goldstein–Werner controversy, the reader is referred to Leach [1967].)

However, this review of the Goldstein–Werner criticisms does allow for the clarification of certain issues. It is clear that all investigators agree that the greater the degree of differentiation (i.e., mental capacity or MA of the individual), the lower will be the incidence of rigid behaviors manifested across tasks. There is thus no argument that the mentally retarded child will emit more rigid behaviors than a normal child of the same CA. It is, therefore, surprising that some investigators (Spitz & Blackman, 1959) continue to report differences in the incidence of rigid behaviors in retarded and normal subjects equated on CA and offer such findings as supporting Lewin's view, while negating views that are in opposition to that of Lewin. Although such studies are interesting in their own right, they cast little light on the controversial issue contained in the Lewin–Kounin formulation. This issue, stated in its simplest form, is that with the degree of differentiation (i.e., MA, held constant), a difference in the incidence of rigid behaviors will be found between normal and familial retarded individuals.

It is also clear that Lewin and Kounin felt that their formulation applied only to the endogenous retarded. It therefore becomes difficult to evaluate the pertinence of certain studies (O'Connor & Hermelin, 1959) which investigate the relative flexibility of retarded individuals without considering the etiological variable. It would appear that much preliminary work must be done before the Lewin–Kounin formulation can be extended to the exogenous retarded.

This overview of the efforts of the early investigators also reveals an awareness that numerous motivational factors (e.g., fear of failure, conflicts raised by the experimental situation, etc.) can give rise to behaviors often labeled rigid. Thus, one can find in the work of Lewin, Kounin, Goldstein, and Werner the seeds of the hypothesis that, with MA held constant, it is motivational factors rather than inherent rigidity that result in the greater incidence of rigid behaviors in the retarded.

This hypothesis will play a major role in the body of work discussed in the final section of this paper.

EMPIRICAL TESTS OF THE LEWIN–KOUNIN FORMULATION

In Kounin's work, the MA was employed as a general measure of the individual's cognitive differentiation. However, even though equated on this measure, Kounin's three groups differed on several tasks. Thus within the Lewin–Kounin position, the MA is viewed as an adequate referent of one important developmental dimension (i.e., differentiation) but is not seen as a very good predictor of tasks sensitive to cognitive rigidity defined in terms of the permeability in boundaries between cognitive regions. The very procedure by which an MA score is obtained makes the Lewin–Kounin view of the MA a perfectly reasonable one. An individual's overall MA is obtained by employing a heterogeneous collection of test items and summing across those items which the individual passes. Thus, two individuals may obtain identical MAs, although one has succeeded at certain items, while the other person has succeeded at different items. The Lewin–Kounin formulation would, therefore, lead us to expect that retarded and normal individuals having the same MA will pass different items on the intelligence test with the retarded doing especially poorly on those test items sensitive to cognitive rigidity.

An empirical test of this expectation was conducted by Thompson and Magaret (1947). These investigators examined the Stanford-Binet test performance of normal and retarded individuals equated on MA. Consistent with the Lewin–Kounin expectation, they found that the normals did significantly better on a number of the subtests than did the retarded, while the retarded did significantly better on a number of the other subtests than did the normals. [The reader is referred to a recent paper by Achenbach (1969), who found that retarded and normal individuals of the same MA did not differ on nearly as many Stanford-Binet subtests as reported by Thompson and Magaret.] However, most relevant to the Lewin–Kounin expectation is not that retarded and normals of the same MA differ, but that the retarded would be inferior on those subtests sensitive to cognitive rigidity. Thompson and Magaret tested this specific prediction by having two judges well versed in the Lewin–Kounin formulation (Jacob Kounin and Roger Barker) rate the items for their sensitivity to cognitive rigidity. No support for the prediction was obtained inasmuch as the rigidity ratings of those items on which the normals excelled were strikingly similar to the ratings for those items on which the retarded excelled.

Viewed historically, the negative findings of Thompson and Magaret do not appear to have unduly impeded the popularity of the Lewin–

Kounin rigidity formulation. It was shortly after the report of the Thompson and Magaret findings that Kounin and Werner engaged in the controversy reported in the previous section. There can be little question that Kounin got the better of this particular exchange of theoretical papers. One is tempted to conclude that by simply pointing out the error in Werner's view of the Lewin–Kounin formulation, Kounin further convinced workers of the validity of this particular formulation. In any case, almost a decade passed before the rigidity hypothesis was subjected to another rigorous empirical test.

This test was conducted by Plenderleith (1956), and her findings represent a serious contradiction to the Lewin–Kounin formulation. In her experiment, subjects were required to learn to choose one of two stimuli. After this discrimination was learned, the stimuli were reversed and the subjects were required to shift their response to the previously incorrect stimulus. Contrary to the predictions derived from the Lewin–Kounin formulation, the retarded children did not differ from the normal children in learning the discrimination nor in reversal trials that were given after 24 hours. Plenderleith's study has been criticized at some length by the present author (Zigler, 1958). It is sufficient to note here that these criticisms have been directed at the inappropriateness of certain of Plenderleith's derivations from the Lewin–Kounin theory, the overly easy nature of the experimental task, and the failure to equate carefully certain of the groups on pertinent variables.

Stevenson and Zigler (1957) conducted a study that was similar to Plenderleith's in that it was also designed to test the validity of the Lewin–Kounin theory of rigidity and in that it also investigated the ability of normal and retarded subjects to acquire one response and then to switch to a new response in a discriminative learning situation. Moving from Kounin's postulate that the boundaries within the life space are more rigid in the retarded than in normals, they hypothesized ". . . that the solution of a reversal problem would require movement to a new region of the life space and that such movement would be more difficult for the feebleminded subject because of the more rigid boundaries separating the regions of the life space." As to the actual rigid behavior resulting from such rigidity in a reversal problem, Stevenson and Zigler chose as their measure the relative incidence of perseverative responses in which the subject continues during the solution of the second problem to make the response which was previously correct but is no longer appropriate. It would appear that such a perseverative response following the switch is the most direct evidence that the subject has remained in a prior region and has not moved to a new region.

Three groups of subjects were used: an older retarded group, a younger retarded group, and a group of normal children, with the groups being equated on MA. The results indicated a striking equivalence in performance among the groups. They did not differ significantly on the number of trials required to learn the initial discrimination problem, the number of correct choices on the reversal problem, the number of subjects in each group who learned the reversal problem, or on the direct measure of rigidity employed—the frequency with which subjects of each group made the response on the reversal problem which had been correct for them on the initial discrimination problem.

Although the switching problem employed by Stevenson and Zigler was more difficult than Plenderleith's reversal problems, the possibility still remained that the switching problem they employed was too easy to allow differences between the groups to become manifest. In order to investigate this possibility, Stevenson and Zigler conducted a second experiment, designed to investigate the performance of normal and retarded individuals on a more difficult reversal problem than that employed in their first experiment. On the basis of the findings of the first experiment, Stevenson and Zigler rejected the Lewin–Kounin hypothesis, assuming instead the hypothesis that rigidity is a general behavior mechanism, from which it may be deduced that the frequency with which rigid behaviors are shown is a function of the complexity of the problem. Stevenson and Zigler then predicted that the frequency of rigid responses (perseverations) would be greater for both the normal and retarded groups in the second experiment than in the first experiment, but that there would be no differences between the groups in the number of such responses. All predictions made for the second experiment were confirmed.

The reversal learning tasks employed by Plenderleith (1956) and Stevenson and Zigler (1957) have become relevant for theories concerning mental retardation other than that proposed by Lewin and Kounin. O'Connor and Hermelin (1959), employing Luria's (1961) formulation that the retarded suffer from a dissociation between the motor and verbal systems, generated and confirmed the prediction that normals would have greater difficulty on a discrimination reversal learning task than would retarded children. This prediction is antithetical to that derivable from the Lewin–Kounin formulation. Balla and Zigler (1964), in an effort to resolve contradictory findings of earlier studies, failed to replicate O'Connor and Hermelin, finding instead a general similarity between the performance of normals and retarded children of the same MA. The findings of Balla and Zigler were, thus, generally consistent with those reported by Plenderleith and Stevenson and Zigler. A number of other studies involving comparisons of normal and retarded subjects on reversal learning tasks have now been conducted and these studies have been reviewed by Wolff (1967). The findings of these studies led Wolff to conclude that, with MA held constant, there is no consistent evidence indicating that performance on reversal learning tasks is related to IQ. This failure to find consistent differences between normals and retarded of the same MA thus calls into question not only the Lewin–Kounin rigidity formulation, but Luria's verbal mediation deficiency hypothesis as well.

In spite of the failure to find consistent support for the Lewin–Kounin formulation, a number of studies employing a variety of tasks have discovered the type of difference in perseverative behavior between normals and the retarded that is in keeping with the general views of Lewin and Kounin. Thus, Kaufman and Peterson (1958) found that retarded, as compared to normal, children made a significantly greater number of stimulus-perseveration errors on a learning set task, leading these investigators to conclude that stimulus perseveration was a characteristic of the learning approach of retarded, but not of normal, children. Greater perseveration by retarded than by normal children was found by Siegel and Foshee (1960) on a task quite different from that employed by Kaufman and Peterson. Siegel and Foshee presented normal and retarded children with a task in which pushing any one of a number of buttons could turn on a light. The normals showed much greater variability in their selection of buttons than did the retarded children. Perseveration by the retarded of a somewhat different sort was also found by Terdal (1967). This investigator compared the performance of normal and retarded children when confronted with the task of attending to designs projected alternately on the left and the right of the subject. The results indicated that, compared with normals, retarded subjects showed marked position (spatial) preferences. Greater perseveration in retarded than in normal children was also found by Penney, Croskery, and Allen (1962) on a habit-reversal task, leading these investigators to conclude that the retarded were more rigid than normals. Greater perseveration of habit in retarded than in normal children in drawing tasks was found by Carkhuff (1962, 1966).

An interesting study specifically designed to test the Lewin–Kounin formulation was that conducted by Kern (1967). In this study, normal and retarded children were required to perform three sorting tasks: sorting first by shape, then by color, and, finally, by color and shape. The children did not have to generate the sorting concept but merely had to comply with the instructions to sort in a particular way. Thus, Kern's series of sorting tasks was a parallel to Kounin's lever-pressing task. The Lewin–Kounin formulation would generate the prediction that the normal, as compared to the retarded, children would make more errors on Sorting Tasks 2 and 3 due to the greater negative transfer. The degree of negative transfer was found to be related to the MAs of both the normal and retarded children, but not to the IQs of the two groups. The performance of the normal and retarded children was found to be quite comparable and, thus, Kern's study provides no support for the Lewin–Kounin formulation. Another explicit test of the rigidity hypothesis was conducted by Corter and McKinney (1968), who compared the performance of normal and retarded children on five tests of cognitive flexibility. The findings of this study do lend some support to the Lewin–Kounin rigidity hypothesis. Normal children were found to be superior to retarded children on an object-sorting test reminiscent of the concept-shifting task employed by Kounin. However, the support for the Lewin–Kounin formulation provided by the Corter–McKinney study must be considered equivocal in that no significant differences between normal and retarded subjects were found on any one of the other four cognitive flexibility tasks. (However, the total scores obtained by summing across the five tasks was significantly greater for the normal than for the retarded children.)

Sorting tasks on which normals have been found to be superior by both Kounin and Corter and McKinney have also been employed in studies conducted by Backer (1966) and Budoff and Pagell (1968). Backer employed five card-sorting tasks and analyzed the performance of normal and retarded subjects on these tasks several ways; his overall findings were rather complex. Although there were certain findings consistent with the Lewin–Kounin rigidity formulation, the bulk of Backer's findings were not consistent with the rigidity hypothesis and led Backer to conclude that the inherent rigidity position was not capable of encompassing the complex findings revealed in his study. Budoff and Pagell employed an adaptation of Kounin's card-sorting task and compared the performance of three groups of children equated on MA, normal children and retarded children who were and were not able to profit from coaching on a block-design task. The retarded gainers required fewer trials to switch concepts than did the retarded nongainers. However, most relevant for our discussion here was the finding that neither retarded group differed significantly from the normal group on the concept-switching task.

In an effort to directly investigate the replicability of Kounin's original findings, Zigler and Butterfield (1966) compared the performance of younger and older retarded individuals in two institutions and a group of noninstitutionalized normals (all groups equated on MA) on three of Kounin's tasks, the cosatiation drawing task, the lever-pressing transfer-of-habit task, and the card-sorting task involving the switching of concepts. The general findings of this study were not consistent with those reported by Kounin. On the drawing task, the one significant finding obtained was in a direction opposite to that reported by Kounin. On the lever-pressing task, no significant differences were found between the groups. There was a trend of borderline significance indicating that the older retarded made more errors than the younger retarded. This trend is in opposition to the rigidity formulation and to the findings of Kounin. On the concept-switching task, the young retarded did not differ significantly from the normals. The one result of Zigler and Butterfield consistent with the rigidity formulation was the finding that the older retarded had more trouble switching concepts than did the other groups. In view of the tendency of the older retarded to manifest the least rigidity on the transfer-of-habit task, it is difficult to interpret their performance on the concept-switching task as clearly indicating greater rigidity. Making any straightforward interpretation of the concept-switching findings even more difficult was Zigler and Butterfield's discovery that the retarded residing in the institution with a poor social climate did better on the concept-switching task than did the retarded residing in the institution having a better social climate.

What can we, therefore, conclude from the empirical findings relevant to the Lewin–Kounin formulation reviewed in this section? Over the years there has certainly been a smattering of findings consistent with the rigidity hypothesis. However, the Lewin-Kounin formulation has certainly not received the sort of strong and consistent empirical support that would generate great confidence in the validity of this particular theoretical formulation. The question may, therefore, be raised as to whether the phenotypic rigidity grossly observable in the retarded and manifested in certain of the studies noted above may not reflect a variety of factors other than the inherent dynamic rigidity postulated by Lewin and Kounin. Just such an alternative interpretation of the greater phenotypic rigidity of the retarded as compared to normals of the same MA is represented in the motivational approach espoused by the author and his colleagues.

THE MOTIVATIONAL APPROACH *

Social Deprivation and Motivation for Social Reinforcement

As noted above, Stevenson and Zigler (1957) obtained findings inconsistent with those of Kounin. In an effort to reconcile these disparate findings, Stevenson and Zigler directed their thinking at the differences in tasks employed across the two sets of experiments and, probably more importantly, the characteristics of the subjects, over and above their formal cognitive characteristics, which could have influenced their performance. In respect to the retarded groups, their most obvious characteristic was that they were residing in institutions. Thus, Stevenson and Zigler evolved the view that the performance of such subjects on tasks like those em-

* Space limitations do not permit a comprehensive review of studies that have been conducted indicating that rigid behaviors emitted by the retarded can often be attributed to motivational differences between the retarded and normals of the same MA rather than to differences in cognitive rigidity. For such a review, the reader is referred to Zigler (in press).

ployed by Kounin could, at least in part, be ascribed to the social deprivation experienced by institutionalized subjects. Stevenson and Zigler noted that, in their experiments, the subjects were required to learn two successive discriminations in which there was minimal interaction with the experimenter, while in Kounin's task the response had been made primarily on the basis of instructions. Thus, differences in rigid behaviors between normal and retarded individuals of the same MA in the instruction-initiated tasks may be related to differences in the subjects' motivation to comply with instruction rather than to differences in cognitive rigidity. This hypothesis was based on the assumption that institutionalized retarded children tend to have been relatively deprived of adult contact and approval and, hence, have a higher motivation to procure such contact and approval than do normal children. At the time, this assumption appeared congruent with the view advanced by other investigators that both institutionalized retarded and institutionalized normal individuals exhibit an increased desire to interact with adult figures (Clark, 1933; Sarason, 1953; Skeels, Updegraff, Wellman, & Williams, 1938).

The first test of this motivational hypothesis was contained in a study of Hodgden, Stevenson, and Zigler (Zigler, Hodgden, & Stevenson, 1958). In an effort to employ tasks comparable to Kounin's instruction-initiated satiation task, they constructed three simple motor tasks, each having two parts and each allowing the experimenter to secure a satiation, cosatiation, and error score. The study deviated from Kounin's procedure in that two conditions of reinforcement were used. In one, the experimenter maintained a nonsupportive role and did not reinforce the subject's performance; in the second, the experimenter made positive comments and in general reinforced the subject's performance.

Two specific hypotheses were advanced: (1) support has a reinforcing effect which results in an increment in performance over that found in nonsupport conditions; and (2) interaction with an adult and adult approval provide a greater reinforcement for the responses of institutionalized retarded subjects than they do for those of normal subjects. Two retarded groups (a support and a nonsupport) equated on CA and two normal groups (a support and a nonsupport) equated on CA were employed. All four groups were equated on MA. Six predictions were derived from the two hypotheses. Five of the six predictions were fully or partially confirmed.

It was found that

1. Retarded subjects spent a significantly greater amount of time playing the games under the support than under the nonsupport condition, while normal subjects did not.

2. Retarded subjects spent more time on the games than the normal subjects in both reinforcement conditions.

3. There was a significantly greater difference in length of performance between support and nonsupport conditions for the retarded than for the normal subjects.

4. There was little difference in the cosatiation scores for normal subjects between support and nonsupport conditions. However, for retarded subjects, support not only resulted in lower cosatiation scores, but in scores that were negative in value (the subject plays longer on part 2 of the game than on part 1).

5. Cosatiation effects were generally less for retarded than for normal subjects under both conditions of support and nonsupport.

6. The proportion of errors was not significantly different for normal than for retarded subjects. In addition, a significantly greater number of retarded subjects stopped the games at points where the experimenter asked them if they wanted to play other games. This was interpreted as further indication of their greater compliance with instructions. (The error in this interpretation will be pointed out later in the section dealing with the phenomenon of outerdirectedness.)

The marked sensitivity of the retarded as compared to the normals to variations in the degree of social reinforcement, as well as the marked shift by the retarded from one social reinforcement condition to another in behavioral indices thought by Kounin to reflect cognitive rigidity, lent a certain amount of support to the social-deprivation hypothesis. However, the findings of the study by Hodgden, Stevenson, and Zigler were not of the sort that would lead one to abandon totally the Lewin–Kounin inherent rigidity formulation. In fact, certain of the Zigler, Hodgden, and Stevenson findings were reminiscent of those found by Kounin. Consistent with Kounin's results, they found that, regardless of social reinforcement condition, their retarded subjects performed an inordinately long time on relatively boring and monotonous tasks. As Kounin surprisingly found with his older group of retarded, they found that their retarded subjects in the support condition played the second part of a two-part cosatiation task longer than they did the first part, even though both parts of the task were extremely similar. This phenomenon will be discussed at some length in the next section. In light of this, the Zigler, Hodgden, and Stevenson findings hardly constitute any death blow to the Lewin–Kounin rigidity formulation. At most, these findings indicate that the production of phenotypically rigid behaviors is also influenced by motivational effects, a view not very much at variance with Lewin and Kounin's own stance concerning motivational factors. At this point, what appeared to be in order was a more convincing test of the view that the Lewin–Kounin rigidity formulation lent little to the understanding of the grossly observable high incidence of rigid behaviors emitted by the retarded.

In what was hoped to be a more definitive test of the view that the rigid behaviors emitted by the retarded were a result of the social deprivation they had experienced rather than a product of any inherent cognitive rigidity, Zigler (1958, 1961) did a study in which it was hypothesized that, within an institutionalized retarded population, a relationship should exist between the degree of deprivation experienced and the amount of rigidity manifested. The specific hypothesis tested was the following: The greater the amount of preinstitutional social deprivation experienced by the retarded child, the greater will be his motivation to interact with an adult, making such interaction and any adult approval or support that accompanies it more reinforcing for his responses than for the responses of a retarded child who has experienced a lesser amount of social deprivation.

On the basis of preinstitutional social deprivation ratings, 60 retarded children were divided into two groups. The groups did not differ significantly on either MA, CA, or length of institutionalization. The study employed a socially reinforced, instruction-initiated, two-part satiation game similar to those used in earlier studies. Three of the four predictions derived from the hypothesis were confirmed. The more socially deprived subjects (1) spent a greater amount of time on the game, (2) more frequently made the maximum number of responses allowed by the game, and (3) evidenced a greater increase in time spent on part 2 over that spent on part 1 of the game. The fourth prediction, that the more socially deprived subjects would make fewer errors, only reached a borderline level of significance.

Results consistent with these were recently obtained by Zigler, Balla, and Butterfield (1968). These findings would appear to call into question the Lewin–Kounin rigidity formulation, since it is difficult to derive from this formulation an explanation of differences in rigid behaviors between groups of retarded children equated on both CA and MA. The findings offer further support for the view that the rigid behavior observed in retarded individuals is a product of higher motivation to maintain interaction with an adult and to secure approval from him through compliance and persistence. These results also offer evidence that the institutionalized retarded subjects' higher motivation to interact with an adult is related to the greater preinstitutional social deprivation such subjects have experienced. Furthermore, individual differences among the retarded in persistent and/or compliant behavior can be related to differences in the amount of social deprivation experienced. Since the persistence and compliance exhibited by retarded subjects have been found to be related to social deprivation, the hypothesis was generated at that time that these characteristics would also be shown by subjects of normal intelligence who have experienced similar social deprivation. (As can be seen below, this hypothesis was confirmed in subsequent studies.)

Another test of the view that the incidence of rigid behaviors is a function of the greater social deprivation experienced by the institutionalized retarded child rather than a function of his inherent rigidity was carried out by Green and Zigler (1962). The investigators used three groups of subjects: institutionalized retarded, noninstitutionalized retarded, and normals. It was assumed that the noninstitutionalized retarded child has suffered less social deprivation than the institutionalized retarded child. All three groups were equated on MA, and the two retarded groups were also equated on CA. As in the earlier studies, only familial retarded children were employed. Again, a two-part satiation-type task was used.

The Lewin–Kounin rigidity formulation would generate the prediction that the performance of the two retarded groups would be similar and that their performance would differ from that of the normal group. The social-deprivation hypothesis would generate the prediction that the performance of the normals and the noninstitutionalized retarded would be similar and that their performance would differ from that of the institutionalized retarded. The latter hypothesis was supported with no significant differences in performance found between the noninstitutionalized retarded and normals. Both of these groups differed significantly from the institutionalized retarded. Again, it was the institutionalized retarded who showed the relatively long satiation times, a perseverative behavior that has been employed as evidence for the inherent rigidity of the retarded.

Zigler (1963) conducted a further test of the view that perseveration on open-ended satiation-type tasks is a result of an enhanced effectiveness of social reinforcers stemming from the greater social deprivation experienced rather than a product of an inherent cognitive rigidity. This study differed from that conducted by Green and Zigler primarily in that it included a group of institutionalized normal children. In this study, institutionalized children of both normal and retarded intellect were found to play a socially reinforced satiation-type task longer than did groups of noninstitutionalized normals and retarded of the same MA. This greater effectiveness of social reinforcement for both institutionalized normal and retarded children as compared with noninstitutionalized normal and retarded children has also been found by Stevenson and Fahel (1961).

Crucial to the motivational interpretation of many of the studies discussed above is the view that the institutionalized retarded have been deprived of adult social reinforcement and are, therefore, highly motivated to obtain this particular class of reinforcers. Evidence offering further support for this view is contained in a recent study by Harter and Zigler (1968), which found that an adult experimenter was a more effective social reinforcer than a peer experimenter for the institutionalized retarded, but not for the noninstitutionalized retarded. Thus, it would appear that the institutionalized retarded child's motivation to obtain social reinforcement is relatively specific to attention and praise dispensed by an adult rather than a more generalized desire for reinforcement dispensed by any social agent (e.g., a peer). This differential effectiveness of peer and adult social reinforcement further argues against the view that the retarded are inherently rigid and will, therefore, perseverate on a dull, monotonous task. Rather, how perseverative the retarded child is would appear to depend on the valence of the social reinforcers dispensed during the task.

The studies outlined above indicate that certain behaviors of the institutionalized retarded that have been attributed to their inherent rigidity can more parsimoniously be viewed as a product of the greater social deprivation experienced by the institutionalized retarded child. Although the hypothesis that social deprivation leads to increased compliance and persistence is an important one, it is clear that this factor alone cannot account for all the findings contained in the literature concerned with rigidity in the retarded.

Social Deprivation and the Negative-reaction Tendency

A phenomenon which appears to be at considerable variance with the retarded individual's increased desire for social reinforcement (a phenomenon the author has labeled the positive-reaction tendency) has been noted: the retarded child's reluctance and wariness to interact with adults (Hirsh, 1959; Sarason & Gladwin, 1958; Wellman, 1938; Woodward, 1960). This orientation toward adults (which the author has labeled the negative-reaction tendency) appears capable of explaining certain differences between the retarded and normals reported by Kounin, differences that have, heretofore, been attributed to the greater cognitive rigidity of retarded individuals. As noted earlier, Kounin employed a cosatiation-type task as one measure of rigidity. In this type of task, the subject is instructed to perform a response and is allowed to continue until he wishes to stop. He is then instructed to perform a highly similar response until again satiated. The cosatiation score is the measure of the degree to which performance on the first task influences performance on the second task. The theoretical position of Lewin and Kounin, as well as Stevenson and Zigler, would predict that the absolute playing time of subjects on task 2, after satiation on task 1, would be greater than that of normal subjects. However, neither of these positions can explain the recurring finding (Kounin, 1941a; Zigler, 1958; Zigler et al., 1958) that, as a group, retarded subjects, under certain conditions, perform longer on task 2 than they do on task 1. Groups of normal children, on the other hand, have invariably been found to perform longer on task 1 than on task 2.

In an effort to explain the longer playing times of the retarded on task 2 relative to task 1, the author (1958) advanced the following hypothesis:

> Institutionalized feebleminded subjects begin task one with a positive-reaction tendency higher than that of normal subjects. This higher positive-reaction tendency is due to the higher motivation of feebleminded subjects to interact with an approving adult. At the same time, feebleminded subjects begin task one with a negative-reaction tendency higher than that of normal subjects. This higher negative-reaction tendency is due to a wariness of adults which stems from the more frequent negative encounters that feebleminded subjects experience at the hands of adults. If task one is given under a support condition, the subject's negative-reaction tendency is reduced more during task one than is his positive-reaction tendency.

The institutionalized child learns during task 1 that the experimenter is not like other strange adults he has encountered who have initiated painful experiences (physical examinations, shots, etc.) with supportive comments. This reappraisal of the experimental situation results in a reduction of the negative-reaction tendency. When the deprived child is then switched to task 2, he meets it with a positive-reaction tendency which has been reduced less than has been his negative tendency. The result, then, is that his performance on task 2 is lengthier than it was on task 1. The finding that normal children exhibit a decrease in length of performance during task 2 as compared to task 1 follows if one assumes that they have a relatively low negative-reaction tendency when they begin task 1. When normal subjects are switched to task 2, it is the positive-reaction tendency which has been reduced more, through fatigue and satiation effects, than any negative-reaction tendency they might have had. The result, then, would be a briefer performance on task 2 than on task 1.

Thus, the author suggested that the cosatiation score mirrors a particular set of motivational determinants, rather than inherent rigidity. This view was first tested in a study by Shallenberger and Zigler (1961). The cosatiation score was obtained on a two-part experimental task similar to those used in the earlier studies. The study differed from the earlier cosatiation studies in that three experimental games preceded the two-part criterion task. These experimental games were given under two conditions of reinforcement. In a positive reinforcement condition, all the subject's responses met with success, and he was further rewarded with verbal and nonverbal support from the experimenter. It was assumed that this reinforcement condition reduced the negative-reaction tendency which the subject brought to the experimental setting. In a negative reinforcement condition, all the subject's responses met with failure, and the experimenter further negatively reinforced the subject by noting this lack of success. It was assumed that his reinforcement condition increased the negative-reaction tendency. (Ignoring the positive-reaction tendency was dictated by the assumption that this tendency was less open to experimental manipulation than was the negative tendency.) Two groups of retarded and two groups of normal subjects, all matched on MA, were employed. One normal and one retarded group were given the positive experimental condition, while the other two groups received the negative condition. All subjects performed on the criterion task under identical conditions (i.e., during both part 1 and part 2, all subjects received liberal amounts of verbal and nonverbal social reinforcement).

The most striking finding of this study was the confirmation of the prediction that both negatively reinforced groups would evidence a greater increase in time spent on part 2 over that spent on part 1 of the criterion task than would the normal and retarded groups who played the experimental games under the positive reinforcement condition. This difference was such that the two groups receiving the negative condition played part 2 longer than part 1, while the two groups receiving the positive condition played part 1 longer than part 2. These findings indicate that cosatiation effects are not the product of inherent rigidity, but rather of the relative strength of certain motivational variables (i.e., positive- and negative-reaction tendencies). These tendencies, and their relative strengths, seem to be the product of particular environmental experiences and apparently are open to manipulation and modification. Thus, the Shallenberger and Zigler study presents further evidence that differences in the performance on certain tasks of retarded and normal individuals of the same MA can be attributed most parsimoniously to different environmental histories and motivations.

The findings of this study did require a broadening of the approach to motivational factors in the behavior of the retarded. Whereas the earlier studies emphasized the increased motivation to interact with and receive the support of an adult, the Shallenberger and Zigler study demonstrated the role of another motivational variable, the negative-reaction tendency. It would seem that the experiencing of that population of events which has been described as socially depriving gives rise to an increased desire to interact as well as a wariness to do so.

The view that the genesis of the negative-reaction tendency was to be found in early socially depriving experiences rather than in mental retardation per se was central to a study conducted by Harter and Zigler (1968). In this study, the two-part cosatiation task was employed to compare the negative-reaction tendencies of institutionalized retarded children with those of noninstitutionalized retarded children living at home with their parents, in homes that could be considered at least fairly adequate. In order to investigate just how general the child's wariness (i.e., the negative-reaction tendency) was, the subjects were further subdivided so that half of each group was socially reinforced by an adult and the other half by a child of normal intelligence. The institutionalized retarded were found to manifest a higher negative-reaction tendency than did the noninstitutionalized retarded. This greater wariness on the part of institutionalized as compared to noninstitutionalized retarded was found in both the adult and peer reinforcement conditions. Thus, it appears that the institutionalized retarded suffer from a generalized wariness of strangers, regardless of whether the strangers are adults or children. The co-satiation scores used to measure the negative-reaction tendency of the noninstitutionalized retarded were very similar to those found with normal children of the same MA.

The Reinforcer Hierarchy

Another concept which has been advanced to explain differences in performance between normals and retarded of the same MA is that of the reinforcer hierarchy. This reinforcer hierarchy pertains to the ordering of reinforcers in the individual's motivation system from most to least effective. While the motivational factors noted previously can explain many of the normal–retarded differences found by Kounin, they cannot handle parsimoniously Kounin's finding that the retarded evidence greater difficulty than do normals on a concept-switching task. What should be noted about Kounin's card-sorting task was the relative weakness of the reinforcer employed by Kounin to motivate his retarded subjects. The only reinforcer obtained by Kounin's subjects for correctly switching concepts was whatever reinforcement inheres in being correct. Being correct is probably more reinforcing for the performance of normal than for retarded children, who may value the interaction with, and attention of, the experimentter much more than the satifaction derived from performing the task correctly.

The hypothesis suggested here is that if equally effective reinforcers were dispensed to normals and retarded of the same MA for switching concepts, no difference in the ability to switch would be found. Such a hypothesis demands the assumption that the positions of various reinforcers in the reinforcer hierarchies of normal and retarded children differ. Basic to this assumption is the view that for every child there exists a reinforcer hierarchy, and the particular position of various reinforcers is determined by (1) the child's developmental level, (2) the frequency with which these reinforcers have been paired with other reinforcers, (3) the degree to which the child has been deprived of these reinforcers, and (4) a variety of other experiential factors.

Considerable evidence has now been presented either indicating or suggesting that the reinforcer hierarchies of middle-class children differ from those of lower-class children (Cameron & Storm, 1965; Davis, 1944;

Douvan, 1956; Ericson, 1947; Terrell, Durkin, & Wiesley, 1959, Zigler & Kanzer, 1962). Emanating from this body of work is the view that middle-class children are more motivated to be correct for the sheer sake of correctness than are lower-class children. These studies attest to the feasibility of attributing the differences in performance between normal and retarded children on a concept-switching task to such differing reinforcer hierarchies rather than to the greater cognitive rigidity of the retarded. Terrell et al. (1959) and Cameron and Storm (1965) found that middle-class children did better on a discrimination learning task when an intangible rather than a tangible reinforcer was employed, while lower-class children evidenced superior performance when the reinforcer was a tangible one. This social class finding is pertinent to the relatively poor performance of the institutionalized familial retarded on concept-switching tasks since such individuals are drawn predominantly from the lowest segment of the lower socioeconomic class (Zigler, 1961). The importance of the specific reinforcer dispensed, in studies of the retarded, is further suggested by the Stevenson and Zigler (1957) findings that when tangible reinforcers were given, the institutionalized familial retarded were no more rigid than normal subjects of the same MA on a discrimination reversal learning task. Furthermore, on a concept-switching task identical to Kounin's (1941a), both retarded and upperclass children switched more readily in a tangible than in an intangible reinforcement condition. Contrary to Kounin's findings, no significant main effect associated with the normal–retarded dimension was found (Zigler & Unell, 1962).

This suggests that the differences obtained by Kounin (1941a) on his concept-switching task resulted from the comparison of retarded with middle-class children who valued the intangible reward of being correct much more than did the retarded. These studies further suggest that not only retarded, but lower-class children, in general, would be inferior to middle-class children when such a reinforcer is employed. However, middle-class children should not be superior to either retarded or lower-class children of the same MA when these latter children are rewarded with more optimal reinforcers (i.e., reinforcers high in their hierarchies).

This view was tested by Zigler and deLabry (1962) in an experiment utilizing Kounin's concept-switching task under two reinforcement conditions with groups of institutionalized familial retarded, lower-class, and middle-class children. In one condition, Kounin's original reinforcer, the reinforcement that inheres in a correct response, was employed. In a second condition, the reinforcer was a tangible reward, a small toy. Half the subjects in each group received the tangible reinforcer and half received the intangible reinforcer for switching from one concept (either form or color) to the other. The reinforcement hypothesis, and the predictions derived from it, were supported by the findings. The retarded and normal lower-class children did better (fewer trials to switch in the tangible than in the intangible condition), while the normal middle-class children did slightly better in the intangible than in the tangible condition. Reminiscent of Kounin's results was the finding of significant differences among the three groups who received intangible reinforcers. However, no differences were found among the three groups who received tangible reinforcers. Furthermore, no differences were found among the three groups that exhibited maximal performance (retarded–tangible, lower-class–tangible, and middle-class–intangible).

The finding that with proper motivation retarded children perform as effectively as normal children of the same MA on a concept-switching task is congruent with the findings of Osborn (1960), who also reported that retarded and normal children of the same MA did equally well on a concept-formation task. Again the implication is that differences in the performance of normal and retarded children, matched on MA, are a result of motivational differences which arise from diverse environmental histories and conditions.

Expectancy of Success

Another motivational factor advanced to explain the phenotypic rigidity of the retarded is their high expectancy of failure. This failure expectancy has been viewed as an outgrowth of a lifetime characterized by frequent confrontations with tasks with which the retarded are intellectually ill-equipped to deal.

Assuming that the inordinately high incidence of failure experienced by retarded children produces a failure set, Stevenson and Zigler (1958) tested the hypothesis that the retarded would be willing to settle for a lower degree of success than would normal children of the same MA. To test this hypothesis, they employed a three-choice discrimination task in which only one stimulus was partially reinforced, the other two stimuli yielding zero reinforcement. Although it is now clear that performance on such a task is influenced by a number of other factors (Gruen & Weir, 1964; Lewis, 1965, 1966; Stevenson & Weir, 1959, 1963; Weir, 1962, 1964), the Stevenson and Zigler (1958) rationale was that maximizing behavior (persistent choice of the partially reinforced stimulus—a behavior describable as "rigid") should be more characteristic of the retarded than the normal child since retarded children have come to expect and settle for lower degrees of success than have normal children.

Further support for the expectancy-of-success hypothesis was found in a second experiment (Stevenson & Zigler, 1958), in which normal children were given either a success or failure condition prior to performing on the partially reinforced three-choice learning task. It was hypothesized that a preliminary failure experience would lower the expectancy of success and, thus, lead to a higher incidence of maximizing behavior. As predicted, a higher incidence of maximizing behavior was found for children who had experienced prior failure than for children who had experienced success. Again it can be seen that if normal children receive the experimental analogue of the real-life experiences of retarded children (in this instance, a low degree of reinforcement across a number of tasks preceding the criterion task), they behave in much the same manner as do the retarded.

It should be noted, however, that in the first Stevenson and Zigler experiment, the obtained difference in maximizing behavior between the retarded and normals is consistent with the Lewin–Kounin rigidity formulation. Within this framework, maximization (consistently responding to one stimulus) could be conceptualized as perseverative, stereotyped behavior, thus, generating the prediction that the inherently more rigid retarded child would maximize more than the less rigid normal child of the same MA. A further test of the validity of the motivational explanation for the differences found in the performance of retarded and normals of the same MA on a partially reinforced three-choice problem was conducted by Gruen and Zigler (1968). A procedure for differentially testing the Stevenson–Zigler motivational and Lewin–Kounin inherit rigidity positions suggested itself. If it is the lowered expectancy of success stemming from a high incidence of failure experiences that causes the retarded to manifest maximizing behavior, then this same type of behavior should be found in children of normal intellect who have also experienced relatively high amounts of failure. Lower-class children would appear to have had such a background (see Gans, 1962). The motivational position would, therefore, predict similarity in performance by retarded and lower-class children on a partially reinforced three-choice problem. The position that rigidity is inversely related to IQ would lead one to expect a dissimilarity in the performance of these two groups and a similarity in the performance of lower-class and middle-class children matched on IQ.

In the Gruen and Zigler study, groups of middle-class normal, lower-class normal, and noninstitutionalized familial retarded children of comparable MAs (approximately seven) performed on the partially reinforced three-choice learning task employed by Stevenson and Zigler (1958). Consistent with the motivational position, both the normal lower-class and retarded children made more maximizing (persistent choice of the correct knob) responses than did the normal middle-class children. Contrary to the expectation generated by the Lewin–Kounin formulation, the lower-class normal children showed more maximizing behavior than did the retarded children, although this difference did not reach a conventional level of statistical significance.

Reminiscent of the findings of the Gruen and Zigler study are those of Odom (1967). Employing the expectancy of success hypothesis, this investigator also found that lower-class children were more willing to employ a maximization strategy on the three-choice task than were the middle-class children. However, what must be emphasized is that it is not social class or intellectual level, in and of themselves, which determine the child's expectancy of success and, thus, his performance on this particular learning task. Rather, it is the particular incidence of success or failure experienced by the individual crild that determines his expectancy of success. Certainly, a very protected retarded child who may not experience as much failure as one who is less protected, will, thus, have a higher expectancy of success. Analogously, not every child in the lower socioeconomic class has the same history of success and failure. Thus, the performance of the child is more predictable when it is approached from a psychological point of view rather than from a demographic, economic, or social class membership frame of reference.

Outerdirectedness

Another line of investigation has indicated that, in addition to a lowered expectancy of success, the high incidence of failure experienced by the retarded generates a style of problem-solving characterized by outerdirectedness. That is, the retarded child comes to distrust his own solutions to problems and, therefore, seeks guides to action in the immediate environment. In certain instances this results in behavior that could be characterized as rigid or inflexible.

In an early study Zigler et al. (1958) found that the institutionalized retarded tended to terminate their performance on experimental games following a suggestion from an adult experimenter that they might do so. Normal children tended to ignore such suggestions, stopping instead of their own volition. Originally this finding was discussed in terms of social deprivation and heightened motivation for social reinforcement and was interpreted as reflecting a greater compliance on the part of the institutionalized retarded. The position here was that social deprivation resulted in an enhanced motivation for social reinforcers and, hence, greater compliance in an effort to obtain such reinforcement.

However, Green and Zigler (1962) found that, while normal children again exhibited little tendency to do so, a higher percentage of the noninstitutionalized than the institutionalized retarded terminated their performance upon a cue from the experimenter. This finding is incongruent with the social deprivation interpretation, which would generate the prediction that the noninstitutionalized retarded would be similar to normal children in their sensitivity to adult cues. This dissimilarity in the performance of the noninstitutionalized retarded and normals led Green and Zigler to suggest that such sensitivity to external cues is most appropriately viewed as a general component of problem-solving, having its antecedents in the child's history of success or failure.

Of the three types of children which Green and Zigler (1962) employed, the normal child would be expected to have had the highest incidence of success emanating from self-initiated solutions to problems. As a result, such a child would be the most willing to employ his own thought processes and the solutions they provide in problem-solving situations. Antithetically, the self-initiated solutions of the retarded would be expected to result in a high incidence of failure, thus making the retarded wary of the solutions provided by their own thought processes. This type of child should then evidence a greater sensitivity to external or environmental cues, particularly those provided by social agents, in the belief that these cues would be more reliable indicators than those provided by his own cognitive efforts. The retarded, in general, then, would be more sensitive to external cues than would normal children. The institutionalized retarded live in an environment adjusted to their intellectual shortcomings and should, therefore, experience less failure than the noninstitutionalized retarded. This latter type of child must continue to face the complexities and demands of an environment with which he is ill-equipped to deal and should, as was found, manifest the greatest sensitivity to external cues.

This general position was first tested by Turnure and Zigler (1964). In a first experiment, they examined the imitation behavior of normal and retarded children of the same MA on two tasks. One task involved the imitation of an adult and the other the imitation of a peer. Prior to the imitation tasks, the children played three games under either a success or a failure condition. The specific hypotheses tested were that retarded children would be generally more imitative than normals and that all children would be more imitative following failure experiences than following success experiences. These hypotheses were confirmed on both imitation tasks. To the extent that the behavior of normal children is considered the preferred mode, this study indicates that the outerdirectedness of the retarded child results in behavior characterized by an oversensitivity to external models with a resulting lack of spontaneity and creativity. However, it must be emphasized that heightened outerdirectedness is not invariably detrimental to performance on problem-solving tasks.

Turnure and Zigler (1964) conducted a second experiment in order to test further the hypothesis that retarded children are more outerdirected then normal children of the same MA. In this study an effort was also made to demonstrate that outerdirectedness may be either detrimental or beneficial, depending upon the nature of the situation. Normal children and noninstitutionalized retarded children of the same MA were instructed to assemble an item, reminiscent of the object-assembly items on the WISC, as quickly as they could. While the subject assembled the item, the adult experimenter put together a second object-assembly item.

The hypothesis was that the outerdirectedness of the retarded child would lead him to attend to what the experimenter was doing rather than concentrating on his own task, thus interfering with his performance. When the child had completed his puzzle, the experimenter took apart the puzzle that he himself had been working on. He then gave this second puzzle to the child and told him to put it together as quickly as he could. Here the cues that the retarded child had picked up as a result of his outerdirectedness should facilitate performance on the second puzzle. The predictions were again confirmed. The normal children were superior to the retarded on the first task, whereas the retarded were superior to the normal children on the second task. No statistically significant differences were found in the control condition in which the experimenter did not put together the second object-assembly task while the subject was working on the first. Further confirmation of the outerdirected hypothesis was obtained by a direct measure of the frequency with which the children actually glanced at the experimenter. As expected, the retarded subjects were found to glance at the experimenter significantly more often than the normal children.

The findings of this study not only confirmed the hypothesis that retarded children are more outerdirected in their problem-solving, but also suggested the process by which the outerdirected style of the retarded is reinforced and perpetuated. There are undoubtedly many real-life situations in which the child is rewarded for careful attentiveness to adults. However, it is also clear that there will be many situations in which such attending will be detrimental to the child's problem-solving. Across tasks, optimal problem-solving requires a child to utilize both external cues and his own cognitive resources. The retarded child's overreliance on external cues is understandable in view of his life history. The intermittent success accruing to the retarded child as a result of such a style, in combination with his generally lowered expectation of success across problem-solving situations, suggests the great utility which such outerdirectedness would have for the retarded.

A further test of the hypothesis that retarded are more outerdirected than normals was conducted by Sanders, Zigler, and Butterfield (1968). The central question addressed in this study was whether or not the outerdirectedness of the retarded, found on simple imitation and object-assembly tasks, also manifests itself in a standard discrimination-learning situation. The discovery that the retarded child's outerdirectedness influences even his performance on a discrimination-learning task would indicate that this style of problem-solving is a relatively pervasive one which should be taken into consideration in evaluating the general behavior of the retarded child. Groups of normal and retarded children of the same MA were compared on a size discrimination task which involved the presentation of an additional cue which the subject could use in making his choice of stimuli. Three conditions were employed: (1) one in which the subject's response to the cue would lead to success (positive condition), (2) one in which it would lead to failure (negative condition), and (3) one in which no cue was presented (control condition). The expectation was that the cue would be more enhancing in the positive and more debilitating in the negative to the performance of the retarded than for the normal children. Although some rather complex findings were obtained in the positive condition which lent some weight to the outerdirectedness hypothesis, this hypothesis received its strongest support under the negative conditions. The retarded made significantly more errors than normals in the negative conditions. Furthermore, the retarded made significantly more cued than noncued errors, while there was no difference between cued and noncued errors for normals. Thus, the retarded relied heavily upon the negative cue even though it led to errors, while the normals did not. This study, thus, provides further evidence of an outerdirected style of problem-solving in retarded individuals. Especially relevant to the rigidity issue is the fact that, on the discrimination-learning task, the retarded subjects preseverated in their selection of the cued but erroneous stimulus.

Further work on the outerdirectedness hypothesis was conducted in a series of three experiments by Achenbach and Zigler (1968). Although their procedure varied somewhat across the three experiments, essentially Achenbach and Zigler utilized a three-choice size-discrimination task in which a light came on in association with the correct stimulus. On the first few trials of this learning task, the light came on almost immediately. As the trials progressed, however, the interval between the onsets of the trial and of the light became longer and longer. Throughout the trials, the subject was occasionally prodded to make his choice of stimulus as quickly as possible. This procedure was intended to create a somewhat ambiguous situation in which the child could either continue waiting for the light to direct his choice or begin responding to the abstract relation (relative size) among the problem elements. Correct responses before the light onset were utilized as the measure of the successful employment of the problem-learning strategy. Control groups were also employed in which groups of subjects learned the discrimination without any light cue present.

In their first experiment, Achenbach and Zigler examined the performance of institutionalized retarded, noninstitutionalized retarded, and normals matched for MA. (As noted above, the noninstitutionalized retarded should be even more reliant on external cues than should the institutionalized retarded because the environment of the latter, which is geared more to their abilities, reduces the failure experiences leading to reliance on external cues.) In the control condition, the learning performances of the three groups were quite comparable. As predicted, however, in the cue condition, the retarded relied on the cue significantly longer than the normals. Furthermore, the noninstitutionalized retarded relied on the cue significantly longer than the institutionalized retarded.

In a second experiment, groups of normals and noninstitutionalized retarded were presented the learning tasks immediately after experiencing either success or failure. In this second experiment, Achenbach and Zigler replicated the findings of their first experiment. However, contrary to their expectations, their failure and success manipulations did not significantly influence the reliance on cues either by normal or by the retarded. Nevertheless, during this study, Achenbach and Zigler obtained some rather serendipitous support for their view that it is the relative incidence of success and failure experienced by the child that determines his outerdirectedness as defined by reliance on cues. Achenbach and Zigler discovered a class of 16 retarded children whose teacher employed teaching methods directed to the long-term manipulation of precisely those variables which have been thought to determine outerdirectedness. Observation of his classroom made it clear that he showered new pupils with success experiences and attempted to increase their self-esteem. Thereafter, he specifically reinforced what he called "figuring things out for yourself," rewarding independent thought more highly than correct responses. Achenbach and Zigler examined the performance of these 16 retarded subjects on their learning task and discovered not only that they relied on cues significantly less than their other retarded subjects, but that they relied on them less, albeit not significantly so, than did the subject of normal intellect. Again, we see that it is not the retardation per se that produces the behavior but rather the particular experiences to which retarded children are subjected. In a third experiment, Achenbach and Zigler (1968) found a significant correlation between imitation of an adult and the number of trials taken to give up reliance on the cue in the learning task by the retarded but not by normals. This suggested that the reliance on external cues constituted a more general, less task-specific strategy for the retarded than for the normal child. However, the findings of a recent study by Achenbach (1969) indicated that for normal children the cue-learning strategy is not necessarily task-specific, since such cue dependency was found to be related to the normal child's impulsivity as well as to the higher intellectual processes involved in analogical reasoning. It, thus, appears that for normals and retarded, reliance on cues in a discrimination learning problem is but one manifestation of a general style of problem-solving.

CONCLUSIONS

What then is the current status of the Lewin–Kounin rigidity formulation? One is tempted to argue that, in view of the many negative and inconsistent outcomes of direct experimental tests of this formulation, as well as the alternative motivational interpretation of the positive findings outlined in the preceding section, that the rigidity hypothesis has become a closed issue. However, the continuing discovery, from time to time, of supporting evidence, as noted in a previous section of this paper, suggests that such a viewpoint would be premature. Nevertheless, the evidence presented in the preceding section strongly indicates that the rigid behaviors observed in the retarded are most appropriately viewed as phenotypic phenomena stemming from a multitude of developmental and motivational factors rather than being a direct outgrowth of the inherent rigidity of the retarded as postulated by Lewin and Kounin. These factors may be summarized as follows:

1. Institutionalized retarded children tend to have been relatively deprived of adult contact and approval, and hence have a higher motivation to secure such contact and approval than do normal children.

2. While retarded children have a higher positive-reaction tendency than normal children, owing to a higher motivation to interact with an approving adult, they also have a higher negative-reaction tendency. This higher negative-reaction tendency is the result of a wariness which stems from retarded children's more frequent negative encounters with adults.

3. The positions of various reinforcers in a reinforcer hierarchy differ as a function of environmental events. Owing to the environmental differences experienced by institutionalized retarded children, the positions of reinforcers in their reinforcer hierarchy will differ from the positions of the same reinforcers in the reinforcer hierarchy of normal children.

4. Institutionalized retarded children have learned to expect and settle for lower degrees of success than have normal children.

5. An inner versus outerdirected cognitive dimension may be employed to describe differences in the characteristic mode of attacking environmentally presented problems. The innerdirected person is one who employs his own thought processes and the solutions they provide in dealing with problems. The outerdirected person is one who focuses on external cues provided either by the stimuli of the problem or other persons, in the belief that such attention will provide him with a guide to action. The style which characterizes the individual's approach may be viewed as a result of his past history. Individuals whose internal solutions meet with a high proportion of failures will become distrustful of their own efforts and adopt an outerdirected style in their problem-solving. Since the retarded experience a disproportionate amount of failure, they are characterized by this outerdirectedness. Many behaviors that are thought to inhere in mental retardation (e.g., rigidity) may be a product of this cognitive style.

The studies generating these conclusions indicate that the retarded person must be viewed as an individual and is not to be understood in terms of some stereotyped view of retardation. Furthermore, these studies disclose that the retarded are shaped by and respond to their environment in much the same way as does the normal individual who possesses the same amount of intellect (of the same MA). The author has opposed emphasizing the inherent differences between the retarded and normals. His position has been that all that is required to understand the performance of the familial retarded individual is his MA and the particular environmental conditions which underlie his motivation.

The motivational studies dealing with the rigid behaviors of the retarded appear to be of practical as well as theoretical import. As Sarason and Gladwin (1958) have noted, the characterization of the retarded as rigid has had far reaching consequences in the treatment and training of the retarded. These latter investigators attribute to this view the reluctance to do psychotherapy with subnormals. Sarason and Gladwin have also noted the tendency of institutions to capitalize on the hypothesized rigidity of the retarded by applying certain placement and training practices. The motivational studies noted in this paper indicate not only that such practices should be discontinued but also suggest specific patterns of social interactions as well as certain types of learning situations which would eventuate in the retarded child maximizing his potential on a number of types of tasks. Finally, these studies offer further evidence of the danger in describing a group as though its members uniformly possess a particular characteristic (e.g., rigidity) without considering such factors as historical differences among the individuals, variability in motivation, the nature of the reinforcement provided, or the tasks employed.

References

Achenbach, T. Cue-learning, associative responding, and school performance in children. *Developmental Psychology,* 1969, *1,* 717–725.

Achenbach, T., & Zigler, E. Cue-learning and problem-learning strategies in normal and retarded children. *Child Development,* 1968, *39,* 827–848.

Backer, M. H. An experimental investigation of the motivational hypothesis of rigidity in retardates: A comparison of retarded and normal performance on a series of card sorting tasks. *Dissertation Abstracts,* 1966, *26,* 4068–4069.

Balla, D., & Zigler, E. Discrimination and switching learning in normal, familial retarded, and organic retarded children. *Journal of Abnormal and Social Psychology,* 1964, *69,* 664–669.

Budoff, M., & Pagell, W. Learning potential and rigidity in the adolescent mentally retarded. *Journal of Abnormal Psychology,* 1968, *73,* 479–486.

Cameron, A., & Storm, T. Achievement motivation in Canadian Indian middle- and working-class children. *Psychological Reports,* 1965, *16,* 459–463.

Carkhuff, R. R. Perseveration of habit in drawing tasks as a characteristic distinguishing mental defectives from normals. *Journal of Clinical Psychology,* 1962, *18,* 413–415.

Carkhuff, R. R. Variations in performance of non-institutionalized retardates. *Journal of Clinical Psychology,* 1966, *22,* 168–170.

Clark, L. P. *The nature and treatment of amentia.* Baltimore: Wood, 1933.
Corter, H. M., & McKinney, J. D. Flexibility training with educable retarded and bright normal children. *American Journal of Mental Deficiency,* 1968, *72,* 603–609.
Davis, A. Socialization and adolescent personality. *Adolescence, Forty-third Yearbook, Part I.* Chicago: National Society for Study of Education, 1944.
Douvan, E. Social status and success striving. *Journal of Abnormal and Social Psychology,* 1956, *52,* 219–223.
Ericson, M. Social status and child rearing practices. In T. M. Newcomb & E. L. Hartley (Eds.), *Readings in social psychology.* New York: Holt, Rinehart and Winston, 1947.
Gans, H. J. *The urban villagers.* New York: Free Press, 1962, pp. 129–136.
Goldstein, K. Concerning rigidity. *Character and Personality,* 1942–1943, *11,* 209–226.
Green, C., & Zigler, E. Social deprivation and the performance of retarded and normal children on a satiation type task. *Child Development,* 1962, *33,* 499–508.
Gruen, G. E., & Weir, M. W. Effect of instructions, penalty, and age on probability learning. *Child Development,* 1964, *35,* 265–273.
Gruen, G. E., & Zigler, E. Expectancy of success and the probability learning of middle-class, lower-class, and retarded children. *Journal of Abnormal Psychology,* 1968, *73,* 343–352.
Harter, S., & Zigler, E. Effectiveness of adult and peer reinforcement on the performance of institutionalized and noninstitutionalized retardates. *Journal of Abnormal Psychology,* 1968, *73,* 144–149.
Hirsh, E. A. The adaptive significance of commonly described behavior of the mentally retarded. *American Journal of Mental Deficiency,* 1959, *63,* 639–646.
Kaufman, M. E., & Peterson, W. M. Acquisition of a learning set by normal and mentally retarded children. *Journal of Comparative and Physiological Psychology,* 1958, *51,* 619–621.
Kern, W. H. Negative transfer on sorting tasks, MA, and IQ in normal and retarded children. *American Journal of Mental Deficiency,* 1967, *72,* 416–421.
Kounin, J. S. Experimental studies of rigidity as a function of age and feeble-mindedness. Unpublished doctoral dissertation, State University of Iowa, 1939.
Kounin, J. S. Experimental studies of rigidity: I. The measurement of rigidity in normal and feeble-minded persons. *Character and Personality,* 1941, *9,* 251–272. (a)
Kounin, J. S. Experimental studies of rigidity: II. The explanatory power of the concept of rigidity as applied to feeble-mindedness. *Character and Personality,* 1941, *9,* 273–282. (b)
Kounin, J. S. The meaning of rigidity: A reply to Heinz Werner. *Psychological Review,* 1948, *55,* 157–166.
Leach, P. J. A critical study of the literature concerning rigidity. *British Journal of Social and Clinical Psychology,* 1967, *6,* 11–22.
Lewin, K. *A dynamic theory of personality.* New York: McGraw-Hill, 1936.

Lewis, M. Social isolation: A parametric study of its effect on social reinforcement. *Journal of Experimental Child Psychology*, 1965, *2*, 205–218.

Lewis, M. Probability learning in young children: The binary choice paradigm. *Journal of Genetic Psychology*, 1966, *108*, 43–48.

Luria, A. R. *The role of speech in the regulation of normal and abnormal behavior.* New York: Pergamon Press, 1961.

Maier, N. R. F. *Frustration: The study of behavior without a goal.* New York: McGraw-Hill, 1949.

O'Connor, N., & Hermelin, B. Discrimination and reversal learning in imbeciles. *Journal of Abnormal and Social Psychology*, 1959, *59*, 409–413.

Odom, R. D. Problem-solving strategies as a function of age and socio-economic level. *Child Development*, 1967, *38*, 753–764.

Osborn, W. J. Associative clustering in organic and familial retardates. *American Journal of Mental Deficiency*, 1960, *65*, 351–357.

Penney, R. K., Croskery, J., & Allen, G. Effects of training schedules on rigidity as manifested by normal and mentally retarded children. *Psychological Reports*, 1962, *10*, 243–249.

Plenderleith, M. Discrimination learning and discrimination reversal learning in normal and feebleminded children. *Journal of Genetic Psychology*, 1956, *88*, 107–112.

Sanders, B., Zigler, E., & Butterfield, E. C. Outer-directedness in the discrimination learning of normal and mentally retarded children. *Journal of Abnormal Psychology*, 1968, *73*, 368–375.

Sarason, S. B. *Psychological problems in mental deficiency.* New York: Harper & Row, 1953.

Sarason, S. B., & Gladwin, T. Psychological and cultural problems in mental subnormality: A review of research. *Genetic Psychology Monographs*, 1958, *57*, 3–290.

Shallenberger, P., & Zigler, E. Rigidity, negative reaction tendencies, and cosatiation effects in normal and feebleminded children. *Journal of Abnormal and Social Psychology*, 1961, *63*, 20–26.

Siegel, P. S., & Foshee, J. G. Molar variability in the mentally defective. *Journal of Abnormal and Social Psychology*, 1960, *61*, 141–143.

Skeels, H. M., Updegraff, R., Wellman, B. L., & Williams, H. M. A study of environmental stimulation. *University of Iowa Study of Child Welfare*, 1938, *15*, No. 4.

Spitz, H., & Blackman, L. A comparison of mental retardates and normals on visual figural after-effects and reversible figures. *Journal of Abnormal and Social Psychology*, 1959, *58*, 105–110.

Stevenson, H. W., & Fahel, L. S. The effect of social reinforcement on the performance of institutionalized and noninstitutionalized normal and feebleminded children. *Journal of Personality*, 1961, *29*, 136–147.

Stevenson, H. W., & Weir, M. W. Variables affecting children's performance in a probability learning task. *Journal of Experimental Psychology*, 1959, *57*, 403–412.

Stevenson, H. W., & Weir, M. W. The role of age and verbalization in probability learning. *American Journal of Psychology*, 1963, *76*, 299–305.

Stevenson, H. W., & Zigler, E. Discrimination learning and rigidity in normal and feebleminded individuals. *Journal of Personality,* 1957, *25,* 699–711.
Stevenson, H. W., & Zigler, E. Probability learning in children. *Journal of Experimental Psychology,* 1958, *56,* 185–192.
Terdal, L. G. Complexity and position of stimuli as determinants of looking behavior in retardates and normals. *American Journal of Mental Deficiency,* 1967, *72,* 384–387.
Terrell, G., Jr., Durkin, K., & Wiesley, M. Social class and the nature of the incentive in discrimination learning. *Journal of Abnormal and Social Psychology,* 1959, *59,* 270–272.
Thompson, C., & Magaret, A. Differential test responses of normals and mental defectives. *Journal of Abnormal and Social Psychology,* 1947, *42,* 285–293.
Turnure, J. E., & Zigler, E. Outer-directedness in the problem-solving of normal and retarded children. *Journal of Abnormal and Social Psychology,* 1964, *69,* 427–436.
Weir, M. W. Effects of age and instruction on children's probability learning. *Child Development,* 1962, *33,* 729–735.
Weir, M. W. Developmental changes in problem-solving strategies. *Psychological Review,* 1964, *71,* 473–490.
Wellman, B. L. Guiding mental development. *Childhood Education,* 1938, *15,* 108–112.
Werner, H. Comparative psychology of mental development. New York: Harper & Row, 1940.
Werner, H. The concept of rigidity: A critical evaluation. *Psychological Review,* 1948, *53,* 43–53.
Wolff, J. L. Concept shift and discrimination-reversal learning in humans. *Psychological Bulletin,* 1967, *68,* 369–408.
Woodward, M. Early experiences and later social responses of severely subnormal children. *British Journal of Medical Psychology,* 1960, *33,* 123–132.
Zigler, E. The effect of preinstitutional social deprivation on the performance of feebleminded children. Uupublished doctoral dissertation, University of Texas, 1958.
Zigler, E. Social deprivation and rigidity in the performance of feebleminded children. *Journal of Abnormal and Social Psychology,* 1961, *62,* 413–421.
Zigler, E. Rigidity and social reinforcement effects in the performance of institutionalized and noninstitutionalized normal and retarded children. *Journal of Personality,* 1963, *31,* 258–269.
Zigler, E. The retarded child as a whole person. In H. E. Adams and W. K. Boardman, III (Eds.), *Advances in experimental clinical psychology,* Vol. I. New York: Pergamon Press, in press.
Zigler, E., Balla, D., & Butterfield, E. C. A longitudinal investigation of the relationship between preinstitutional social deprivation and social motivation in institutionalized retardates. *Journal of Personality and Social Psychology,* 1968, *10,* 437–445.
Zigler, E., & Butterfield, E. C. Rigidity in the retarded: A further test of the Lewin-Kounin formulation. *Journal of Abnormal Psychology,* 1966, *71,* 224–231.

Zigler, E., & deLabry, J. Concept-switching in middle-class, lower-class, and retarded children. *Journal of Abnormal and Social Psychology,* 1962, *65,* 267–273.

Zigler, E., Hodgden, L., & Stevenson, H. W. The effect of support and nonsupport on the performance of normal and feebleminded children. *Journal of Personality,* 1958, *26,* 106–122.

Zigler, E., & Kanzer, P. The effectiveness of two classes of verbal reinforcers on the performance of middle- and lower-class children. *Journal of Personality,* 1962, *30,* 157–163.

Zigler, E., & Unell, E. Concept-switching in normal and feebleminded children as a function of reinforcement. *American Journal of Mental Deficiency,* 1962, *66,* 651–657.

7

Expectancy of Success and the Probability Learning of Middle-class, Lower-class, and Retarded Children

Gerald E. Gruen and Edward Zigler

Dr. Gruen is Associate Professor of Psychology at Purdue University. The reader is referred to the article Rigidity in the Retarded: A Reexamination *for a brief description of Dr. Zigler's duties and research activities.*

Doing research mainly with children, Dr. Gruen has been particularly interested in variables affecting probability learning. His active research program has led to publications in six major journals within the past five years.

This well-designed, carefully conceived study is a good example of the type of research conducted by the Zigler group. It supports the motivational approach espoused by Zigler. The reader is referred to the Kounin article and the Zigler article.

A major controversy in the mental retardation area is that between general developmental and defect theorists (see Zigler, 1966a, for a complete discussion of this issue). The general development theorists (Zigler, 1966b) have argued that the familial retardate's cognitive development differs from that of the normal only in respect to its rate and the upper

FROM THE *Journal of Abnormal Psychology,* 1968, 73, 343–352. Reprinted by permission of American Psychological Association.

limit achieved. Such a view generates the prediction that when level of development is controlled, as is grossly done when groups of retardates and normals are matched on MA, there should be no difference in formal cognitive processes related to IQ. The defect theorists (Ellis, 1963; Goldstein, 1943; Kounin, 1941a, 1941b; Lewin, 1936; Luria, 1956; O'Connor & Hermelin, 1959; Spitz, 1963; Zeaman, 1959) have argued that the retardate suffers from a specific physiological or cognitive defect over and above the slower general rate of cognitive development. This view generates the prediction that even when level of cognitive development is controlled, as in the matched MA paradigm, differences in conceptual functioning related to IQ should be found. At face value, the repeated findings of differences in performance between groups of normals and retardates matched on MA have lent credence to the defect position and have cast doubt on the general developmental formulation. The general developmental theorist's response to these frequently reported differences has been to point out that performance on any experimental task is not the inexorable product of the S's cognitive structure alone, but is also influenced by a variety of emotional and motivational factors as well. According to this argument, differences in performance are more reasonably attributed to motivational differences which do not inhere in mental retardation but are rather the result of the particular histories of the typical retarded S.

While a number of such motivational differences have now been investigated (Zigler, 1966b), this paper shall be confined to a consideration of the expectancy-of-success variable studied by Stevenson and Zigler (1958) and by Cromwell (1963) and his students. Stevenson and Zigler (1958) hypothesized that the inordinately high incidence of failure experienced by retarded children leads to a lowered expectancy of reinforcement which in turn could account for certain differences in performance between normals and retardates matched on MA. To test this hypothesis, these investigators employed a three-choice discrimination task in which only one stimulus was partially reinforced, the other two stimuli yielding zero reinforcement. Although it is now clear that performance on such a task is influenced by a number of other factors (Gruen & Weir, 1964; Lewis, 1965, 1966; Stevenson & Weir, 1959, 1963; Weir, 1962, 1964), the Stevenson and Zigler (1958) rationale was that maximizing behavior (persistent choice of the partially reinforced stimulus) should be more characteristic of the retarded than the normal child since such children have come to expect and settle for lower degrees of success than have normal children. This rationale is consistent with Goodnow's (1955) analysis of the determinants of choice behavior. Goodnow suggested that greater maximizing behavior will be found when an S will accept less than 100% success as an acceptable outcome, while less maximizing behavior will be found when an S is expecting 100% success, or a level of success greater than that allowed in the situation. As Stevenson and Zigler (1958) predicted, retarded children were found to maximize their choice of the partially reinforced stimulus to a greater degree than normal children. Further support for the expectancy-of-success hypothesis was found in a second experiment (Stevenson & Zigler, 1958) in which normal children were given either a success or failure condition prior to performing on the partially reinforced three-choice learning task. It was hypothesized that a preliminary failure experience would lower the expectancy of success and thus lead to a higher incidence of maximizing behavior. As predicted, a higher incidence of maximizing behavior was found for children who had experienced success.

It should be noted, however, that the difference in maximizing behavior between retardates and normals found by Stevenson and Zigler in their first experiment is consistent with a number of defect positions. These findings are certainly consonant with the Lewin–Kounin rigidity formulation (Kounin, 1941a, 1941b; Lewin, 1936). Within this framework, maximization (consistently responding to one stimulus) could be conceptualized as perseverative, stereotyped behavior and the prediction generated that the inherently more rigid retarded child would maximize more than the less rigid normal child of the same MA. Some support for this interpretation of the Stevenson and Zigler (1958) findings is contained in the work of Siegel and Foshee (1960) who found that retarded children were less variable in their response patterns than were normal children of the same MA.

The major purpose of the present study was to provide a further test of the validity of Stevenson and Zigler's (1958) motivational explanation for the differences found in the performance of retardates and normals of the same MA on a partially reinforced three-choice problem. A procedure for differentially testing the Stevenson-Zigler motivational and Lewin–Kounin inherent rigidity positions suggests itself. If it is the lowered expectancy of success stemming from a high incidence of failure experiences that causes retardates to manifest maximizing behavior, then this same type of behavior should be found in children of normal intellect who have also experienced relatively high amounts of failure. Lower-class children would appear to have had such a background (cf. Gans, 1962). The motivational position would therefore predict similarity in performance on a partially reinforced three-choice problem by retardates and lower-class children. The position that rigidity is inversely related to IQ would lead us to expect a dissimilarity in the performance of these two groups and a similarity in the performance of lower-class and middle-class children matched on IQ.

In the present study, groups of middle-class normal, lower-class normal, and noninstitutionalized familial retarded children of comparable MAs were run on the partially reinforced three-choice learning task

164   The Mentally Deficient

employed by Stevenson and Zigler (1958). In order to throw further light on the possible motivational dynamics influencing performance on this task, two experimental manipulations were also utilized. As in Stevenson and Zigler's (1958) second experiment (which employed only children of normal intellect) the degree of success experienced by children immediately prior to performance on the learning task was manipulated. One third of the children in each group were administered a number of pretraining tasks in which they experienced a high degree of success; one-third were given pretraining tasks in which they experienced a very low level of success; one-third did not receive any pretraining. The expectation here was that the low, as compared to high, success condition would lower the child's general expectancy of success and thus result in more maximizing behavior on the learning task.

Penalty and no-penalty conditions were also included. Gruen and Weir (1964), employing the same three-choice probability learning task as Stevenson and Zigler (1958), found that penalizing children by having them give up a previously won reward for an incorrect response (defined as a trial on which S received no reward) resulted in greater maximizing behavior than did reward alone. In the present investigation, then, a $3 \times 3 \times 2$ factorial design was employed involving three types of children (retarded, normal lower-class, and normal middle-class), three pretraining conditions (success, failure, and control), and two penalty conditions (penalty versus no penalty).

METHOD

Subjects

A total of 180 Ss, 90 boys and 90 girls, was employed. Sixty noninstitutionalized retarded children were drawn from special classes in the public schools of Worcester, Massachusetts. These Ss were all diagnosed as familial retardates and none exhibited gross sensory or motor disturbances. The 60 normal children constituting the lower-class group all resided in a government housing project for low-income families. No family earning more than $4,000 per year was allowed to live in the project, and the average yearly income was less than $3,000. This definition of lower socioeconomic class is consistent with that now being employed by governmental agencies. The 60 normal children constituting the middle-class group were drawn from various schools in predominantly middle-class areas of Worcester. The fathers of these children were all employed in occupations conventionally designated as middle-class (Warner, 1960). The mean CA, MA, and IQ of each group of children are presented in Table 1. As can be seen in Table 1, the mean IQ of the lower-class group was approximately 10 points lower than that of the middle-class group. Such

Table 1 *Mean CA, MA, and IQ for Each Type of Subject*

Group	N	CA (in years) M	CA (in years) SD	MA (in years) M	MA (in years) SD	IQ M	IQ SD
Retarded							
Success—penalty	10	11.40	1.20	6.79	.22	67	5.69
Success—no penalty	10	11.38	1.01	6.86	.48	68	9.44
Failure—penalty	10	11.10	.68	6.78	.38	69	5.53
Failure—no penalty	10	11.85	1.27	6.98	.67	66	6.62
Control—penalty	10	11.29	1.13	7.12	.32	70	7.17
Control—no penalty	10	11.68	1.42	6.90	.57	66	8.07
Total	60	11.45	1.12	6.90	.48	68	7.06
Normal—lower class							
Success—penalty	10	6.95	.51	6.82	.48	97	7.02
Success—no penalty	10	6.93	.56	7.07	.54	101	5.45
Failure—penalty	10	7.25	.67	6.80	.54	97	7.69
Failure—no penalty	10	6.96	.40	6.73	.48	96	4.45
Control—penalty	10	6.78	.44	6.64	.36	96	5.78
Control—no penalty	10	7.14	.30	6.94	.66	98	5.88
Total	60	7.0	.48	6.83	.51	98	6.04
Normal—middle class							
Success—penalty	10	6.43	.43	7.08	.44	112	11.92
Success—no penalty	10	6.78	.47	6.95	.43	104	10.70
Failure—penalty	10	6.86	.41	7.26	.54	107	11.02
Failure—no penalty	10	6.42	.33	6.97	.44	109	8.26
Control—penalty	10	6.38	.44	6.88	.48	109	4.09
Control—no penalty	10	6.72	.50	7.05	.59	109	14.29
Total	60	6.60	.43	7.03	.49	108	10.05

a difference is typically found in social-class comparisons. Given the distributions of IQs found within the middle- and lower-class populations, it was impossible to equate the two groups on IQ while at the same time equating them on MA. (As will be seen below, this difference in the mean IQs was taken into consideration in the analysis of the findings.) The Ss of each type were assigned randomly to the six experimental groups except for the provision that all groups be matched on MA and contain five boys and five girls. The IQ score for each S was obtained on an individually administered Peabody Picture Vocabulary Test, form B (Dunn, 1959).

Apparatus

Four tasks were used, three experimental games and the criterion learning task. Two of the three experimental games used, the Pick-a-card Game and the Which School Game, were patterned after games previously employed by Stevenson and Zigler (1958) and Butterfield and Zigler (1965). All three experimental games were quite simple with performance depending primarily on compliance with E's instructions.

Materials for the Pick-a-card Game consisted of 10 cards, 5 of which had a red spot and 5 of which had a black spot on one side. The cards were constructed of 2 × 3 inch cardboard on which were mounted small rectangles of black or red paper. Materials for the Which School Game consisted of ten 3 ×5 in glossy pictures of children which were placed into one of two boxes constructed to resemble buildings. One building was painted green and the other was painted pink. The boxes were placed about 6 in. apart and 12 in. in front of the S with their open sides facing S. The apparatus for the Drop-a-marble Game, the third experimental game, was a slanted 18 × 22 in. board on which parallel rows of nails formed maze-like pathways. These pathways led from a point at the top of the board to two separate boxes, a green one and a black one, at the bottom of the board. This apparatus had an equal number of paths leading into the green and the black boxes through which marbles could be delivered. However, the openings of the lower pathways leading to the black box were slightly narrower than the openings of the pathways leadings to the green box. Thus, only smaller-sized marbles could go into the black box, whereas marbles of two sizes could go into the green box. Ten marbles of ½ in. in diameter and 10 of ⅜ in. in diameter were used.

The appartus for the probability learning task has been described in detail elsewhere (Stevenson & Zigler, 1958). Essentially, it consisted of a yellow panel with a horizontal row of three circular, black knobs on its face. A red signal light was centered at the top of the panel, and a hole through which marbles could be delivered was centered at the bottom of the panel. The marbles fell into a plastic container. For Ss in the penalty condition, who were required to give up a marble each time they made an incorrect response, a marble board with 50 holes in it was used into which S could place the marbles he had to give up.

Procedure

Each S was tested individually. The Ss in the success and failure conditions were initially presented the three experimental games in the order of Pick-a-card Game, Which School, and Drop-a-marble and then received the learning task. The Ss in the control group were presented with only the criterion learning task. The E met S in his classroom and then conducted S to the experimental room which was arranged as constantly as possible from school to school. Upon entering the experimental room with S, E pointed to a variety of inexpensive toys spread on a table and said: "Do you see all these toys here? If you could choose any of them to keep, which would you take?" After S made his choice, E said:

> Fine. Now we're going to play some games. By playing the games well, you can win marbles. If you win enough marbles, you can trade them in for this [indicating the toy of the S's choice] when we are all through playing these games.

For *S*s in the success and failure conditions, *E* introduced the first experimental game, Pick-a-card:

> Here's the first game. It's called Pick-a-card. Here are the cards. Some have red spots on one side and some have black spots on one side. [The *E* shows *S* a red and a black card from the deck.] Your job is to pick up cards whose spots are the same colors as the colors I have written down here on this piece of paper. Sometimes a red one is right and sometimes a black one is right. I'll spread the cards all over the table, like this [the *E* spreads the 10 cards before *S*, plain side up]. When it's time for you to begin, you'll guess by turning the cards over one at a time and handing them to me. Every time you hand me a right colored card, I'll give you a marble. If you have enough marbles after we have played four games, you can have this [indicating the object of the child's preference]. You can keep the marbles in this marble board, and we'll count them after we have played several games to see if you have won enough marbles. All right, now you may begin picking up the cards, turning them over, and handing them to me one at a time. When you give me a right card, I'll give you a marble to put in your board.

In the course of turning over the cards *S*s in the success condition received nine marbles and *S*s in the failure condition received only one marble. The point(s) at which the marbles were given differed for each *S* according to a predetermined random schedule.

Following the game, *E* said: "Well, that's all of that game." The *E* then introduced the second experimental game, Which School:

> Now here's the next game. It's called Which School. Here are the two schools. One is pink and one is green. Here are some pictures of children. Each of these children goes to one of these schools. Your job is to guess which school each child goes to. You guess by taking the pictures one at a time and putting them in the school you think that child goes to. When you put the picture in the right school, I'll give you a marble. Here are the pictures. You put them in the schools one at a time.

The *S*s in the success condition were given a marble on 9 of their 10 responses, regardless of which school they placed the pictures in. The *S*s in the failure condition were given a marble on only 1 of their 10 responses. Following this game, *E* said: "Well, that's all of that game." The *E* then introduced the third game, Drop-a-marble:

> Now, here's the next game. It's called Drop-a-marble. When marbles are dropped in here [the *E* holds a marble at the top of the maze],

168   The Mentally Deficient

> they roll down this board into one of these two boxes. Your job is to get as many of the marbles as you can to roll into the green [black] box. You may drop only one marble at a time, but you may make it roll down either side of the board that you want. Here is the first marble. Remember, you want it to fall into the green [black] box. At the end of the game you can put the marbles that you get to roll into the green [black] box into your marble board.

The E gave S 10 marbles, 1 at a time. The Ss in both the success and failure conditions were given smaller marbles until one of them fell into the black box. From then on they were given larger marbles, which could only fall into the green box, until they had nine marbles in the green box. Thus, for all Ss, 90% of the marbles fell into the green box; E had designated this box as the correct box for Ss in the success condition and the incorrect box for Ss in the failure condition.

In each of the three experimental games, Ss in the success condition were given a marble on 90% of the trials. In addition, E made three positive statements to S at predetermined points during each of the experimental games. These statements always occurred on a response for which S was given a marble. The positive statements were: "That's good." "You really know how to play this game." "That's fine." In the failure condition, Ss were given a marble on only 10% of the trials in each experimental game. In addition, E made three negative statements at predetermined points during each of the experimental games. These statements always occurred following a response for which S was not given a marble. The negative statements were: "That's not good." "You don't play this game very well." "That's bad."

For Ss in the success and failure condition, following the last experimental game the E introduced the criterion task (the only task given to the control group):

> Now let's play this game. Do you see this light up here? [The E points to red signal light.] Well, every time it goes on you may push one of these three knobs. If you push the correct knob, a marble will fall out of this hole right here, like this [the E drops a marble through the hole in the plastic container]. So, every time this light goes on, your job is to push whichever knob you think will get you a marble. Try to win as many marbles as you can.

From this point on, the instructions for Ss in the penalty and no-penalty conditions differed.

> [No-Penalty Group] When we're finished with this game, I'll count the number of marbles you have won to see if you have won enough to get a prize. Any questions?

[Penalty Group] When you do win a marble, leave it in this box. But when you push a knob and you don't get a marble, I want you to take one marble from this box and give it to me. Now there may be times when you don't have any marbles in this box to give me. When that happens I'll just put a check here on this piece of paper so that I can keep track of how many you owe. At the end of the game, I'll count up the number of marbles you have won and the number you owe and if you have done well enough you'll win a prize. Any questions?

On this task, one knob was reinforced 66% of the times it was chosen and the other two knobs were never reinforced. Reinforcement was thus available on 66% of the responses to the correct knob, rather than on 66% of the total trials. The 66% reinforcement schedule was randomized in four blocks of 30 trials, and these were then broken down into 12 ten-trial blocks with the following restrictions: No S was allowed to have more than one nonreinforcement on the reinforcing knob prior to his first reinforcement on that knob. Also, no S was allowed to receive more than three consecutive nonreinforcements of his choices on the correct knob. Thus, 12 ten-trial blocks were constructed and Ss in each group were randomly started with 1 of these 12 blocks. Each S continued for 100 trials on this task. For each S one of the three knobs (either left, middle, or right) was designated as the correct knob. Three Ss in each group were reinforced for choosing the left knob, four for choosing the middle knob, and three for choosing the right knob.

At the end of the experiment, each S was instructed to count the number of marbles he had won and was told that he had won three more marbles than he needed to win his prize. All Ss were then given their prize, were praised extensively for their performance, and were returned to their classroom.

RESULTS AND DISCUSSION

Correct Response Analysis

Preliminary analyses revealed that neither sex of the child nor knob position influenced performance, and, for the sake of simplicity, these variables were ignored in the analyses of the correct responses (CRs) reported below. The term "correct responses" refers to the trials on which S chose the reinforcing stimulus rather than one of the other two, regardless of whether or not it paid off. In keeping with the typical evaluations of this type of data, two major analyses were conducted, one including all experimental trials and the other including only the last block of 20 experimental trials (Trials 81 through 100).

The Type of S × Preliminary Condition × Penalty × Trials analysis of variance performed on the total number of CRs revealed significant main effects for type of S ($F_{2/162} = 9.44$, $p < .005$) and penalty condition ($F_{1/162} = 7.17$, $p < .01$). (See Figure 1.) There was no significant effect due to the success-failure manipulations ($F < 1$). The mean number of CRs made by retarded, lower-class, and middle-class Ss were 68.4, 71.2, and 55.5, respectively. The means of the retarded Ss and normal lower-class Ss were both significantly greater than the mean of the normal middle-class Ss ($t = 7.45$, $p < .001$; and $t = 9.13$, $p < .001$, respectively). There was a tendency for the mean number of CRs to be greater for lower-class than for retarded Ss ($t = 1.67$, $p < .10$). The significant penalty effect reflects the higher number of CRs in the penalty ($\overline{X} = 69.2$) than in the no-penalty condition ($\overline{X} = 60.8$). The only other significant effects revealed in this analysis were the trials effect ($F_{4/648} = 130.5$ $p < .001$), which reflects the increase in CRs over trials; and a significant Penalty × Trials interaction ($F_{4/648} = 4.50$, $p < .01$). As can be seen in Figure 1 this interaction was due to the steeper slopes of the learning curves in the penalty as compared to the no-penalty conditions.

The Type of S × Preliminary Condition × Penalty analysis of variance performed on the total number of CRs made during the last 20 experimental trials also revealed significant main effects for type of S

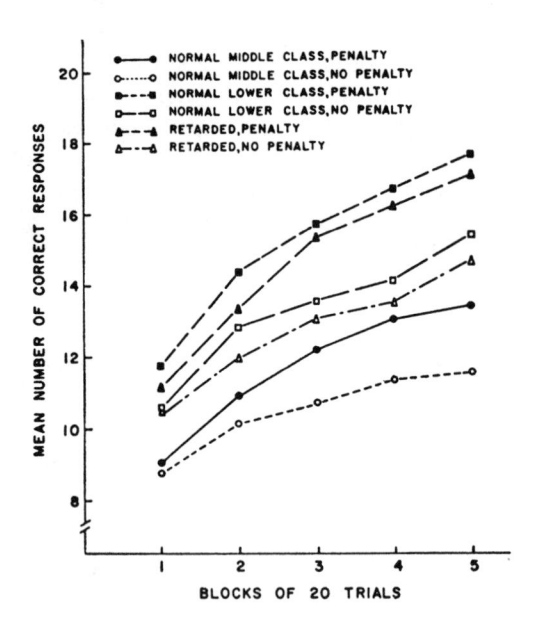

Fig. 1 Mean number of correct responses for each type of subject in the penalty and no-penalty conditions.

($F_{2/162} = 11.87$, $p < .001$) and penalty condition ($F_{1/162} = 8.96$, $p < .005$). Further analyses revealed that the means of the retarded ($\overline{X} = 15.9$) and the normal lower-class ($\overline{X} = 16.5$) were both significantly greater than the mean of the normal middle-class ($\overline{X} = 12.5$) Ss ($t = 3.84$, $p < .01$; and $t = 4.52$, $p < .01$, respectively). The means of the retarded and lower-class Ss did not differ significantly ($t < 1.0$).

The failure to find any significant effects associated with preliminary conditions ($F < 1$, in both analyses) is surprising in light of the Stevenson and Zigler (1958) finding of more maximization following preliminary failure than preliminary success experiences. It should be noted that the Stevenson–Zigler finding was obtained with children who were probably of the middle socioeconomic class. In order to assess the replicability of the Stevenson and Zigler (1958) finding, an individual analysis on the preliminary condition effects for each of the three types of S was performed. The data for these analyses are presented in Figure 2. As can be seen in Figure 2, no preliminary condition effects were found in the retarded and lower-class groups, findings consistent with the overall analysis. However, for middle-class children the preliminary success condition results in less maximization than the other two conditions. Employing the final 20 trials measure, the difference in CRs between the failure ($\overline{X} = 13.8$) and success ($\overline{X} = 11.0$) conditions was found to be significant ($t = 1.74$, $p < .05$; one-tailed test), a finding consistent with that reported earlier by Stevenson and Zigler (1958).

In order to partial out any effects of differences among the groups on IQ, CA, and MA, three analyses of covariance were conducted on the data of the last 20 trials, employing each of the three subject variables as covariates. These analyses resulted in essentially the same findings reported in the original analysis.

Patterns of Response Analyses

It was felt that a more fine-grained analysis than that provided by overall performance curves would throw further light on the mechanisms underlying the differences in performance found between the groups. Earlier studies (Gruen & Weir, 1964; Stevenson & Weir, 1959; Weir, 1962) have demonstrated that when confronted with this task a common strategy of MA-seven children is a left, middle, right (LMR), or a right, middle, left (RML) response pattern, which accounts for about 50% of the total number of responses made. This pattern of responding can be viewed in two distinctly different ways: (a) the probability learning task is an insoluble one if the child assumes that there must be some way of obtaining a reward each time the knob is pressed. Given such a belief, the pattern response may represent a rather high-order strategy among a hierarchy of strategies whose order and total number are primarily a function of the child's MA level. Within this conceptual framework, perseveratively responding to a single knob would be thought of as a more primitive strategy, low in the strategy hierarchy of the MA-seven child though high in the hierarchy of the MA-three child: (b) the pattern response may be simply a stereotyped response which reflects the cognitive rigidity of a child.

If *a* is true, the pattern response is essentially a product of the cognitive level (e.g., MA) of the child and one would expect no differences between the three groups in the occurrence of such responding. If *b* is correct, then the Lewin–Kounin formulation generates the prediction that the amount of pattern responding should be inversely related to the IQ within an MA level. This implies that the retardates should have more pattern responses than the other two groups, with the middle-class group having the least number of such responses, since they have the highest IQ.

These possibilities were investigated in the present study by calculating the number of LMR and RML pattern responses made by each S. In addition, the total number of variable responses made by each S was counted. A variable response refers to a trial on which S chooses a stimulus different from the one he chose on the immediately preceding trial.

A Type of S × Preliminary Condition × Penalty × Trials covariance analysis was then performed on the pattern responses, with the variable responses as the covariate. This type of analysis was used in order to

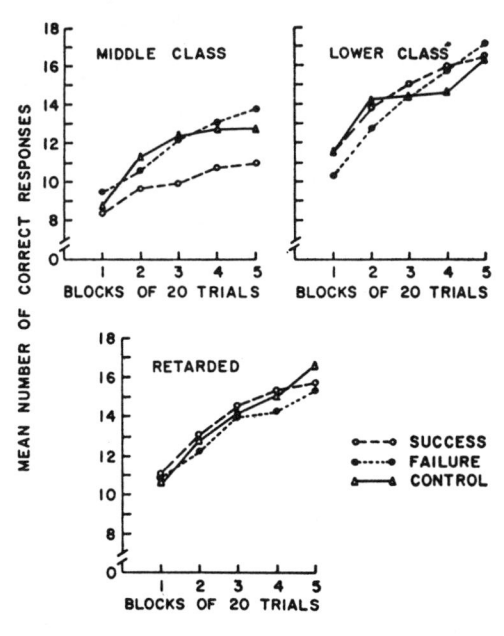

Fig. 2 Mean number of correct responses of each type of subject in each preliminary condition.

be sure that any group differences obtained in response patterning would not be attributed simply to the fact that certain groups made more variable responses (and thus, by chance, more patterns) than other groups.

This analysis revealed a significant penalty effect ($F_{1/161} = 11.05$, $p < .001$) and a difference of borderline significance between the three types of S ($F_{2/161} = 2.30$, $p < .10$). (See Figure 3.) The mean number of pattern responses, controlled for variable responses, made by Ss in the penalty and no-penalty groups was 13.7 and 27.9, respectively. The mean number of pattern responses made by retarded, lower- and middle-class Ss was 20.6, 17.6, and 25.3, respectively.

The tendency of the groups to differ and the ordering of the three groups on the patterning measure calls into question both the notion that the pattern response reflects a strategy dictated by the MA alone and the notion that it is a manifestation of rigidity which is greater at lower levels of IQ. That the pattern response is greatest in the middle-class group and that the partially reciprocal maximization response is least in this group is not without its importance. Some insight as to the exact relationship between the pattern-response strategy and maximization is provided by another significant effect found in the pattern analysis, a significant Type of S × Preliminary Condition interaction ($F_{4/161} = 3.18$, $p < .05$). This interaction reflects the fact that, whereas in the retarded and lower-class groups there was no significant variation in pattern re-

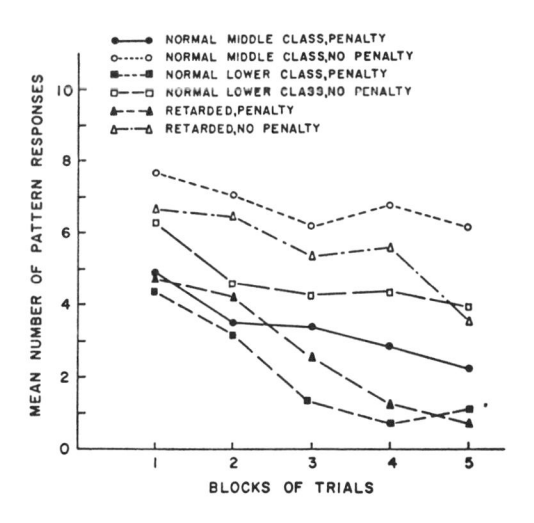

Fig. 3 The adjusted mean number of left-middle-right and right-middle-left pattern responses of each type of subject in the penalty and no-penalty conditions.

sponses associated with preliminary condition, the condition did affect the number of pattern responses in the middle-class group ($F_{2/54} = 3.65$, $p < .05$). In this group the mean number of pattern responses made by Ss in the failure, control, and success conditions was 17.3, 24.3, 33.3, respectively.

The pattern analysis also revealed a significant trials effect ($F_{4/647} = 10.2$, $p < .001$), which reflects the decrease in pattern responses over trials, and a significant Trials × Type of S interaction ($F_{8/647} = 6.29$, $p < .001$). As can be seen in Figure 3 this interaction was due to the greater decrease over trials in pattern responses in the normal lower-class and retarded groups than in the middle-class group. The more rapid decrease in pattern responses in the penalty than in the no-penalty conditions resulted in a significant Penalty × Trials interaction ($F_{4/647} = 10.65$, $p < .001$). The Type of S × Preliminary Condition × Penalty × Trials interaction was also significant ($F_{16/647} = 3.79$, $p < .001$).

CONCLUSIONS

The findings obtained on the correct-response measure in conjunction with those obtained on the pattern-response measure permit certain conclusions concerning the process which mediate the performance of the three types of children. During the early trials, all children rely rather heavily on the pattern response, a strategy dictated by their cognitive level as defined by MA. Subsequently, the operation of a number of factors appears to determine the child's willingness to give up this cognitively congruent strategy for a maximization strategy which, though not meeting the goal of 100% success, does provide the best possible payoff. One such factor is the penalty involved in continuing to utilize the pattern strategy. Across all groups the penalty condition (punishment) causes the child to give up the pattern response in favor of the maximization strategy. This shift to a different strategy in the strategy hierarchy would appear to be predictable from the Law of Effect. However, independent of penalty effects, the three groups continue to differ in their tendency to make patterns which in turn produces differences among the three groups in the number of maximization responses.

These remaining differences between the groups are not at all consistent with the position of a greater rigidity with lower IQ. The findings do appear consistent with the expectancy-of-success hypothesis advanced initially. In the middle-class child this expectancy is relatively high, and therefore he is unwilling to settle for that degree of success provided by the maximization response. Given such a situation he can do little more than continue with the patterning response which at this MA level would appear to represent a relatively complex strategy. On the other hand, the retarded and lower-class children have a lower expectancy of success and are therefore more willing to give up the patterning response in favor of the maximization response. The tendency for lower-class children to make fewer patterning and more maximizing responses is understandable if one remembers that the retardates in this study were obtained from special classes, whereas the lower-class children were obtained from classes in which they probably had to compete continually with brighter children. While this factor may be offset by nonschool experiences, it is very possible that the lower-class child in the middle-class-oriented schoolroom has more failure experiences than retardates in special classes conducted especially for them.

The importance of these success and failure experiences is suggested by the impact of the success-failure manipulations on the middle-class children in this study. As in the Stevenson and Zigler (1918) study greater maximization was found following failure than following success. At the same time success resulted in an increase and failure in a decrease in pattern responding in middle-class children. It would appear that the preliminary success experience enhances the child's confidence in the pattern strategy dictated by his cognitive level and thus increases his reluctance to give up this strategy when confronted with a problem that he thinks can be solved. This reasoning would appear to represent an extension of Stevenson and Zigler's expectancy-of-success hypothesis. The smaller number of correct responses on a probability learning task by a middle-class child would appear to be determined not only by the amount of success he is willing to settle for, but also by the amount of confidence the child has in his own cognitive strategy. That the retarded child has little confidence in his own cognitive resources has now been demonstrated (Turnure & Zigler, 1964). It would not be surprising to discover that the lower-class child who typically experiences a high incidence of intellectual failure also distrusts his own cognitive strategies and is therefore more willing to give them up than is the middle-class child.

This argument would have been strengthened had the success-failure effects found with the middle-class group also been found in the retarded and lower-class groups. However, as has been noted and demonstrated (McCoy & Zigler, 1968; Zigler, 1964), it is naïve to believe that simple short-term experimental manipulations of the sort used in this study would inexorably affect all children to the same degree. How these short-term operations influence behavior will ultimately depend on how they are mediated by the S. The findings of the present study suggest that, unlike the middle-class child, the retardate and the lower-class child have such entrenched attitudes and expectancies that short-term experimental manipulations of success and failure have little effect on their performance. The fact that lower-class children of normal intellect are more similar in their performance to retardates than to middle-class children of the same MA is consistent with other findings (Zigler & deLabry, 1962) and allows the conclusion that differences between retardates and middle-class children on a probability type task are due to motivational factors of the type which have been discussed rather than to any inherent cognitive rigidity of retarded individuals.

References

Butterfield, E. C., & Zigler, E. The effects of success and failure on the discrimination learning of normal and retarded children. *Journal of Abnormal Psychology,* 1965, *70,* 25–31.

Cromwell, R. L. A social learning approach to mental retardation. In N. R. Ellis (Ed.), *Handbook of mental deficiency.* New York: McGraw-Hill, 1963.

Dunn, L. M. *Peabody Picture Vocabulary Test.* Minneapolis, Minn.: American Guidance Service, 1959.

Ellis, N. R. The stimulus trace and behavior inadequacy. In N. R. Ellis (Ed.), *Handbook of mental deficiency.* New York: McGraw-Hill, 1963.

Gans, H. J. *The urban villagers.* New York: Free Press, 1962. Pp. 129–136.

Goldstein, K. Concerning rigidity. *Character and Personality,* 1943, *11,* 209–226.

Goodnow, J. J. Determinants of choice distribution in two-choice situations. *American Journal of Psychology,* 1955, *68,* 106–116.

Gruen, G. E., & Weir, M. W. Effect of instructions, penalty, and age on probability learning. *Child Development,* 1964, *35,* 265–273.

Kounin, J. Experimental studies of rigidity: I. The measurement of rigidity in normal and feebleminded persons. *Character and Personality,* 1941, *9,* 251–273. (a)

Kounin, J. Experimental studies of rigidity: II. The explanatory power of the concept of rigidity as applied to feeblemindedness. *Character and Personality,* 1941, *9,* 273–282. (b)

Lewin, K. *A dynamic theory of personality.* New York: McGraw-Hill, 1936.

Lewis, M. Social isolation: A parametric study of its effect on social reinforcement. *Journal of Experimental Child Psychology,* 1965, *2,* 205–218.

Lewis, M. Probability learning in young children: The binary choice paradigm. *Journal of Genetic Psychology,* 1966, *108,* 43–48.

Luria, A. R. *Problems of higher nervous activity in the normal and nonnormal child.* Moscow: Akademiia Pedagogicheskekh Rank RSFSR, 1956.

McCoy, N., & Zigler, E. F. Children's responsiveness to social reinforcement as a function of short term preliminary social interactions. Unpublished manuscript, Yale University, 1968.

O'Connor, N., & Hermelin, B. Discrimination and reversal learning in imbeciles. *Journal of Abnormal and Social Psychology,* 1959, *59,* 409–413.

Siegel, P. S., & Foshee, J. G. Molar variability in the mentally defective. *Journal of Abnormal and Social Psychology,* 1960, *61,* 141–143.

Spitz, H. H. Field theory in mental deficiency. In N. R. Ellis (Ed.), *Handbook of mental deficiency.* New York: McGraw-Hill, 1963.

Stevenson, H. W., & Weir, M. W. Variables affecting children's performance in a probability learning task. *Journal of Experimental Psychology,* 1959, *57,* 403–412.

Stevenson, H. W., & Weir, M. W. The role of age and verbalization in probability learning. *American Journal of Psychology,* 1963, *76,* 299–305.

Stevenson, H. W., & Zigler, E. F. Probability learning in children. *Journal of Experimental Psychology,* 1958, *56,* 185–192.

Turnure, J., & Zigler, E. Outer-directedness in the problem solving of normal and retarded children. *Journal of Abnormal and Social Psychology.* 1964, *69,* 427–436.

Warner, W. L. *Social class in America.* New York: Harper, 1960.

Weir, M. W. Effects of age and instruction on children's probability learning. *Child Development,* 1962, *33,* 729–735.

Weir, M. W. Developmental changes in problem-solving strategies. *Psychological Review,* 1964, *71,* 473–490.

Zeaman, D. Discrimination learning in retardates. *Training School Bulletin,* 1959, *56,* 62–67.

Zigler, E. The effect of social reinforcement on normal and socially deprived children. *Journal of Genetic Psychology,* 1964, *104,* 235–242.

Zigler, E. Mental retardation. Current issues and approaches. In M. L. Hoffman & L. W. Hoffman (Eds.), *Review of child development research.* Vol. 2. New York: Russell Sage Foundation, 1966. (a)

Zigler, E. Research on personality structure in the retardate. In N. R. Ellis (Ed.), *International review of research in mental retardation.* Vol. 1. New York: Academic Press, 1966. (b)

Zigler, E., & de Labry, J. Concept-switching in middle-class, lower-class, and retarded children. *Journal of Abnormal and Social Psychology,* 1962, *65,* 267–273.

8

Sensory Restriction and Isolation Experiences in Children with Phenylketonuria

C. Jack Friedman, Maarten S. Sibinga, Ira M. Steisel, and Harry M. Sinnamon

Dr. Friedman is Senior Research Psychologist at the Philadelphia Psychiatric Center and is active in psychological research in chronic disease at St. Christopher's Hospital for Children. Dr. Sibinga is Associate Professor of Pediatrics at Temple University School of Medicine and Chief of the Department of Gastroenterology at St. Christopher's Hospital for Children. Dr. Steisel is Chief Psychologist at St. Christopher's Hospital for Children. Mr. Sinnamon is an advanced graduate student in psychology at the University of Rochester.

These scholars, engaged in an active research program on phenylketonuria (PKU), have published many excellent studies advancing our understanding of this disorder. They have demonstrated that factors other than organic can play an important part in the deficit behavior observed in PKU. In the well-designed study reprinted below, the authors have shown the importance of psychosocial factors on the development patterns of children diagnosed PKU.

FROM THE *Journal of Abnormal Psychology,* 1968, *73,* 294–304. Reprinted by permission of American Psychological Association.

To assist the reader in his orientation to this research area and to bring the reader up to date on their current thinking on the topic, the authors have kindly consented to introduce their article with a brief prologue.

PROLOGUE

In 1934 Følling identified a genetic link between mental retardation and the inability of some children to metabolize phenylalanine. More than three decades later, the optimism generated by Følling's discovery has been partially realized by the favorable response of many children with PKU to a diet which nearly excludes phenylalanine. However, many basic questions remain and numerous issues over which controversy continues constitute an intriguing area for research. Findings of recent studies support the relevance and etiological importance of individual behavioral, psychological, and ecological factors in the intellectual performance of children with PKU.

The diagnosis of PKU has undergone further refinements in the last several years and many patients with hyperphenylalaninemia have probably been included in previous groups of patients reported upon. Nevertheless, there are occasional untreated patients with PKU who have normal or near-normal intelligence. The clinical picture of the treated patient thus encompasses a wide range of intelligences, growth patterns, and behavioral disturbances influenced by the biochemical abnormality and the dietary and ancillary treatment. Birch and Tizzard have stated that differences in intelligence levels between children on the diet and those not treated by the diet are attributable to selection. The method of case finding varies extensively. Some children are diagnosed in early infancy by blood screening tests done because of legality or the identification of PKU in an older sibling, while others come to medical attention because of mental retardation or slow development, eczema, seizures, or behavioral problems several years in duration. The fact that treatment by means of a diet low in phenylalanine has been considered mandatory has obscured the effect of this diet and has made prospective studies unfeasible. Nevertheless much remains to be learned about the natural and the iatrogenically altered history of this disease.

We have identified a similar course of illness in two groups of patients. Thirty-seven patients who were diagnosed and put on a low-phenylalanine diet before the age of 7 months had a mean earliest IQ of 82.5 (S.D. 20.6) as compared to a mean initial IQ of 55.8 (S.D. 19.4) of a group identified at a later age because of developmental problems ($t = 5.82$, $p < .005$). The last repeat evaluation of intelligence on these same subjects yielded IQs of 84.7 (S.D. 18.9) and 57.6 (S.D. 19.4), respectively. The average increase in intelligence over 3 years in the two groups was 2.63 and 1.96, neither of which was significant by *t* test. Fifteen children who were never on any diet had an average IQ of 64.2 with an IQ range of 20 to 117. This illustrates some of the methodological problems in research in PKU when dietary treatment is confounded by the mode of identification of the patient.

We also systematically investigated the relationship of severity of the intellectual deficit in PKU to socioeconomic, psychosocial, and environmental factors, relative to dietary treatment, by analysis of variance. While it was found that mothers with more schooling had children whose IQ scores were higher, no relationship between IQ and occupation or education of the father was obtained.

Additional research sought to determine whether parents of children with PKU who fail to adequately understand the disease or who distort factual medical information tend to have children with greater intellectual and behavioral deficits. From responses to a questionnaire of mothers and fathers representing 42 families, only three mothers and two fathers provided completely accurate descriptions of the mature, cause, consequences, and treatment of PKU. By more liberal scoring, fifteen parents provided adequate responses after many sessions with pediatricians and study of written handouts given to them. Apart from the tendency to omit factual information, approximately half of the mother and father groups were judged to display distortion in their concept of the etiology, nature, consequences, or symptoms of PKU. Contrary to generally accepted belief, in this study better educated fathers and mothers were no more accurate or less distorting in their description of PKU than less educated parents. Fathers and mothers were not significantly different in the degree to which they omitted or distorted medical information. A crucial question concerns the relationship of parent lack of understanding and distortion to the intellectual and behavioral (i.e., Interaction Situation, total score) functioning of their children. Of all possible comparisons, the only significant find ($p < .06$) was the tendency for fathers who distort more to have children who obtained lower scores.

Phenylketonuria (PKU) is a recessive disorder of phenylalanine metabolism, caused by the absence of the enzyme phenylalanine hydroxylase in the liver, which normally metabolizes phenylalanine. Mental deficiency is found in the great majority of affected individuals, although dietary restriction of phenylalanine instituted in early infancy may prevent the development of mental retardation.

The presence of symptoms of emotional disturbances and behavioral deviations in phenylketonuria has been the subject of considerable interest and controversy (Bjornson, 1964; Jervis, 1954; Kaplan, 1962; Karrer & Cahilly, 1965; Lyman, 1963; Steisel, Friedman, & Wood, 1967; Yaker & Goldberg, 1963). Reported behavioral aberrations range from mild or moderate neurotic to psychotic symptoms. After reviewing 300 case records of patients with PKU, Jervis (1954) concluded that 277 presented evidence of emotional disturbance. He described the behavior as typically either "hyperactive-destructive" or "passive-apathetic" in nature. Subsequent reports of behavioral deviations (Bjornson, 1964; Koch, Fishler, Schild, & Ragsdale, 1964) have alluded to the similarity between the more severe personality disturbances in children with PKU and childhood schizophrenia. In light of the wide range of deviant behavior reported for this population, Steisel et al. (1967) compared the interpersonal behavior patterns of a heterogeneous group of children with PKU to the behavior patterns of groups of children who were: (*a*) normal, (*b*) retarded and/or brain damaged without PKU, and (*c*) psychotic. In a standardized interaction situation which provided a more objective frame of reference than global clinical impressions, the group of children with PKU was found to display greater impairment of interpersonal behavior than the normal children and the group of children who were retarded and/or brain damaged without PKU. The findings also indicated that there were, among the children with PKU, some who functioned interpersonally like the normals, others who functioned like the retarded and/or brain damaged, and yet others who were indistinguishable from the psychotic children. The disparities in behavior among children with specific metabolic disturbance suggested that the occurrence of behavioral aberrations was not the inevitable consequence of this inborn error of metabolism.

There are two somewhat divergent viewpoints regarding the origin of emotional difficulties in children with PKU. Woolley (1962, 1965) states that the chemical imbalance and the changes resulting from a diet low in phenylalanine are of primary etiological importance. Other investtigators (Bjornson, 1964; Steisel et al., 1967) maintain that the child's past and current life experiences interact with the chemical disturbance as additional important factors. Bjornson (1964) cited the case history of an 11-yr.-old girl with PKU who manifested a schizophrenia-like thinking disturbance. He suggested that the emotional difficulty was largely the result of turbulent and chaotic early experiences, characterized by separation from the biological parents, frequent changes in residence, and numerous changes in parent surrogates. He also called attention to such environmental factors as placement of the child with PKU in a large, undersupervised, and isolating institution which he believes may account for the reported "catatonic posturing" and the "mute-like facies."

Evidence of the importance of psychosocial influences was provided by Wood, Friedman, and Steisel (1967) who emphasized difficulties in enforcement of the stringent diet, the influence of the parents' distorted understanding of PKU, and the impact upon the parents of the implicit or explicit idea of genetic impairment. Direct observations of parents and their children in a simulated eating situation suggested that the parents' feelings of desperation and helplessness created a pervasive need to monitor, control, and restrict not only the child's eating behavior but his exploratory and play behavior as well. Similar findings regarding parental reactions have been reported by Keleske, Solomon, and Opitz (1967). These investigators found that parents of children with PKU reacted to the diagnosis with generalized anxiety, followed by feelings of guilt and ambivalence, and finally by confusion. Rather striking in these two studies was the finding that the parents of children with PKU often distorted information supplied by medical personnel. Inasmuch as beliefs and attitudes of parents rather directly affect parental reactions to child behavior and their child-rearing practices, these studies point up potentially significant etiological factors in the emotional disturbances of PKU.

The present investigation focuses upon a source of psychological influence in PKU heretofore not emphasized, namely the impact on the child of experiences during hospitalization, illness, and routine diagnostic testing. Conceptualization of the hypothesis comes from several converging lines of research. These include the potential traumatic effect of hospitalization on children and infants (Robertson, 1962), the evidence of unusual emotional reactions to some medical treatment procedures in adults (Fiske, 1960), and the striking similarity of a variety of routine pediatric procedures to experimental conditions designed for the study of the effect of sensory deprivation and sensory restriction (Schultz, 1965; Solomon, Kubzansky, Leiderman, Mendelson, Trumbull, & Wexler, 1961). Specifically, various illnesses and disabilities in children require confinement of the child to an oxygen tent, immobilization of the child to maintain quiescence or to permit intravenous feedings, isolation of the child in a dimly lit, monotonous room with little or no opportunity for contact with others, or the use of casts, splints, or braces in hospital or home as an adjunct to postsurgical recovery or for correction of orthopedic difficulties. Such practices all have in common the reduction or alteration in sensory stimulation.

Although there has been relatively little systematic research concerning the influence of such experiences on the develpoing child, Friedman, Handford, and Settlage (1964) have reported on children subjected to varying degrees and durations of physical restraint during the first 3 yr. of life. One finding was the tendency for such children to become hyperactive or unusually passive, or react selectively in these ways to different stimuli. In addition, it was found that these children late in life displayed difficulty in many complex psychological functions including family and peer relations, object relations, verbal communication, and perceptual ability. Idiosyncratic and often peculiar behavior was noted, which sometimes occurred spontaneously, but at other times seemed elicited by circumstances recalling an earlier restricting experience. In this instance it was not possible to show a direct causal relationship between the early restraint experiences and subsequent developmental disturbances, because the observations were made on children originally seen for emotional difficulties. The plausibility of such a formulation was strengthened, however, by findings from extensive animal and human studies (Fiske, 1960; Schultz, 1965; Solomon et al., 1961). Some of the children in the study sample diagnosed as having organic brain damage showed more severely disturbed behavior than could be attributed to either the organic problems or the early stress experiences alone, which could suggest potentiation of these factors.

The resemblance of the problems and behavioral traits encountered in some of the more disturbed children with PKU to those described by Friedman et al. (1964) suggested that early restraint experiences might be implicated in the parallel disturbances noted in the two population samples. On this basis, it was reasoned that children with PKU subjected to early restraint experiences would display greater impairment in overall adaptive behavior than a group of children with PKU who did not have such early stressful experiences. The purpose of the present investigation, then, was to test the hypothesis that children with PKU subjected to sensory restriction, immobilization, or isolation in the first 3 yr. of life would show greater impairment of interpersonal and social behavior, receptive and expressive language ability, and intelligence than a control group of children with PKU.

METHOD

Subjects and Procedure

Thirty Caucasian children with the diagnosis of PKU were selected from a pool of 38 such patients seen regularly in an evaluation and treatment program at St. Christopher's Hospital for Children, Philadelphja, Pennsylvania. Eight children who were otherwise eligible as Ss for the study were not included because the families had either moved or could not be contacted.

The parents, most often the mothers of the Ss, were interviewed to determine the occurrence of sensory restriction or isolation experiences of the child during the first 3 yr. of life. Initially, the parents were asked whether their child had ever been hospitalized. Affirmative answers were followed by inquiry regarding the use of physical restraints, special apparatus, or isolation procedures. Information was also obtained to ascertain the nature of past illnesses, orthopedic corrections, intravenous feedings, restraint to prevent scratching of skin irritations, and quarantine. Special attention was devoted to the methods used by parents to control indiscriminate eating, hyperactive or destructive behavior, and annoying habits such as fingernail biting, head banging, or running away. Toward the end of the interview, the parents were asked whether they could recall any instances in the life of the child of physical restraint, isolation, or temporary deprivation of any sense modality.

Assignment of Subjects

On the basis of the interview data, Ss were placed into either a Stress group which included those children who were reported to have had at least one experience of sensory restriction, physical immobilization, or isolation prior to age 3, or a Control group comprised of those children for whom no such experiences were reported.

The Stress group consisted of 16 Ss, 12 boys and 4 girls. Ages ranged from 4.14 to 12.67 yr. with a mean age of 9.47. Of the Ss in the Stress group, 6 were currently on a low phenylalanine diet, 6 had formerly been on the diet, and 4 had never been on the diet. Of the 12 Ss who were formerly or currently on the diet, 10 had started it between the ages of 3 and 5. The remaining 2 Ss were put on the diet prior to reaching 1 yr. of age. Dietary effectiveness was judged by the pediatrician to be optimum, fair, or poor on review of data regarding phenylalanine levels, reports from the parents, and medical examination of the child. Of the 6 currently dieting Ss, dietary effectiveness was judged to be optimum for 4 and poor for 2 of the children.

The Control group consisted of 14 Ss, 8 boys and 6 girls. These Ss ranged in age from 7.08 to 13 yr. with a mean age of 9.54 yr. Of these 14 Ss, 9 were currently on the low phenylalanine diet, 1 had formerly been on the diet, and 4 had never been on the diet. Of the 12 Ss in the Control group, currently and formerly on the diet, 9 were started on the diet between 3 and 5 yr. of age. The 3 remaining Ss had started the diet prior to reaching 1 yr. of age. Of the 9 children in this group currently on the low phenylalanine diet, dietary effectiveness was judged to be optimum for 4, fair for 3, and poor for the remaining 2 children. Although the assignment of children to the Stress and Control conditions was made without regard to sex distribution, age, diet status, age at which the diet was instituted, or dietary effectiveness, the two groups were relatively well matched on these variables.

Three of the children assigned to the Control group had been hospitalized one time before the age of 3. These children were assigned to the Control group since the parents reported brief durations of hospitalization, freedom of motility in a ward situation with other children, and minimal parent-child separation.

Of the 16 Ss assigned to the Stress group, 14 had had at least one hospitalization before age 3. The most frequent reported mode of stress was physical restriction. In this regard, 8 of the children in the Stress group had been wholly or partly tied down continuously for a period of 3 days or longer. One 12-yr.-old girl, hospitalized for a period of 14 days had, on alternate days, been placed in a special, immobilizing apparatus (viz., a Bradford frame) for the purpose of collecting urine samples. In this case, the child had been subjected to more than 150 hr. of physical restraint during a 2-wk. period of time. Of the 10 children who were physically tied down, 6 were restrained for treatment of upper respiratory infections associated with dehydration for which intravenous fluids had been given. The remaining 4 children were hospitalized for diagnosis or for institution of a suitable diet, which necessitated repeated urine analyses. Three children were reported to have had fractures or orthopedic difficulties: 2 had been in a leg cast for 3 and 4 wk., respectively, while the third was in a hip cast for 6 mo. The remaining 3 children had been subjected to an isolation experience. One of these, a 12-yr.-old girl, just under the age of 3 at the time, had been hospitalized for a duration of 30 days, most of which was spent in the absence of parents or other familiar persons. She remained in a private room and, according to the mother, received attention only for meals and going to the toilet. Regarding the 2 remaining cases, male siblings of 15 and 27 mo. old, the mother reported that she locked both boys in their bedroom from 6:30 P.M. until 7:30 A.M. daily for a period of 2 yr. The room was described as empty except for beds and dressers, on account of the destructiveness of the children. The mother stated that she intended to prevent indiscriminate eating in violation of the diet.

In summary, of the 16 children in the Stress group, 10 had experienced physical restraint for tests or treatment, 3 had experienced immobilization by means of casts, and 3 had been subjected to prolonged isolation or confinement. Of the 14 children in the Control group, only 3 had been hospitalized and none had been subjected to the stress as defined.

Testing

Psychological data on the PKU children in the present sample were collected routinely as part of ongoing research in PKU. Upon arrival at the hospital, usually in the morning, each child was seen for about 30 min. in an experimental interaction situation. Following this, the child was taken to a different room for further psychological testing.

The interaction situation took place in an office room equipped with a one-way mirror, free of enticing, distracting objects. The furniture consisted of two chairs and a desk. A shelf, 8 in. deep and 6 ft. long, was attached to the wall 7 ft. from the floor opposite the one-way screen. On it, in full view of the child, were the various toys available for use (e.g., a dart game, cars, toy soldiers, puppets, balls, guns, etc.). The placement of the toys on the shelf made them relatively inaccessible to the child unless he was helped. The inaccessibility of the toys was intended to stimulate the child to seek interaction with the experimenter (*E*) in order to obtain them. The experimental procedure was divided into three parts as follows: (1) interaction was *solicited* by *E*; (2) interaction attempts made by the child were *rejected* by the examiner; and (3) interaction was neither *solicited* by the adult nor *rejected*, but was *awaited* and, when it occurred, was responded to.

There were four tasks in the first phase, during which interaction was *solicited*. The first of these, a variation of the task found in the Stanford-Binet, required the child to alternate stringing beads with the *E*. In the second task the child alternated turns with *E* in throwing quoits at a stake. For the third task the child and *E* raced cars on the floor. Finally they alternately shot darts at a target. The second phase of the interaction situation, during which the child's efforts to engage *E* in play or talk were *rejected*, was introduced by *E* asking the child which one of all the toys he would like to have to play with. If the child made no choice, *E* provided him with a hammer and peg board. The child was then told that the examiner would be busy for a while. The *E* then occupied himself by making notes or reading. Subsequent overtures from the child were ignored or rejected by *E*. After this period was completed, the *awaited* phase was started. The *E* indicated his availability and asked the child what he would like to do. The child's lead was then followed by *E*. Two or more observers, behind the one-way screen, independently rated the child's interactive efforts during all phases of the procedure.

The rating scale used by the judges had seven subparts: (*a*) paying attention to *E* or instructions (not scored during the *rejected* period); (*b*) paying attention to the tasks or objects; (*c*) following instructions, cooperating, and complying (omitted during the *rejected* and *awaited* periods); (*d*) initiating or instigating interaction with *E* (not rated during the *solicited* period); (*e*) willingness and degree of investment in interaction; (*f*) communicative sounds; and (*g*) response to *E*'s interactive efforts (not rated during the *rejected* period). Each of these variables was scored on a 5-point scale: a scale rating of 5 represented a maximum of the attribute being assessed. A scale rating of 1 represented the minimum of the attribute being measured. Ratings of 2 or 4 were assigned when the child's behavior tended in the particular direction of the behavior being rated but was not characteristically or consistently at one extreme or the other. A score of 3 was given when the child fluctuated from one end of the continuum to the other without consistently being at either.

Judges for the interaction procedure were hospital personnel trained in the fields of psychology, social work, and public health nursing. Trial runs with other patients were used to clarify the procedure and the rating of the scales and to establish reliability. At the end of each trial session, the judges discussed their ratings. After several trial runs there was no marked discrepancy between judges. In the event that more than two judges observed and rated the interaction, two sets of ratings were selected at random.

Language comprehension was measured by the Peabody Picture Vocabulary Test (PPVT) which was administered and scored according to directions in the manual. Five of the patients with PKU were untestable by this procedure. The youngest of these was 8 yr., 7 mo. old at the time of testing; and the oldest was 12 yr., 8 mo. of age. For these Ss, an arbitrary procedure was used to derive a PPVT IQ. Two of the children who were totally unresponsive to the examiner and who according to the parents did not use speech at all were given a PPVT IQ of 25. One child who rejected the testing but used sounds to approximate "mother," "father," and "sister," but otherwise did not talk, was assigned a PPVT IQ of 30. The two remaining children, who could repeat monosyllabic words but did not spontaneously use language beyond this, received PPVT IQs of 40.

Attempts were made to administer the Wechsler Intelligence Scale for Children (WISC) to all Ss over 5 yr. of age. (The Verbal Scale IQ of the WISC was prorated from scaled scores on the Information, Comprehension, Similarities, and Digit Span subtests. The Performance Scale IQ was prorated from scaled scores on Picture Completion, Block Design, and Coding subtests. The Full Scale IQ was derived according to the standard procedure of combining the Verbal and Performance Scale scores.) For the two children (one in each group) less than 5 yr. of age, the Stanford-Binet (L-M) was substituted for the WISC. For five untestable Ss, all in the Stress group, the Vineland Social Maturity Scale was used as the measure of mental development, the parents serving as informants.

Diagnostic impressions on the 30 Ss in the study were derived from observations of the child during psychological testing by the first author. Such factors as the child's reality contact, emotional spontaneity and control, his relationship to the examiner and awareness of external events, the presence of bizarre ideation or behavior, autistic gesturing, or emotional outbursts of rage or fear were all taken into consideration to arrive at a diagnostic impression. The Ss were classified as to the severity of emotional disturbance. Those described as *clearly psychotic* presented the more severe symptoms, while those classified as *questionably psychotic* or *severely disturbed* displayed evidence of considerable disorganization and maladjustment but were neither so uncontrolled nor unrelated as to be regarded as psychotic. Those rated *clearly not psychotic* showed indications of relatively little or no psychological distress. The classification, although relatively imprecise, nevertheless provided three categories of psychopathology which permitted differentiation of Ss in terms of adequacy of behavioral adjustment.

Twenty-two of the Ss, 11 in each group, were seen for a routine psychiatric interview. The psychiatrists were asked to state, on the basis of the the material obtained in the interview, whether the child was clearly psychotic, questionably psychotic or severely disturbed, or clearly not psychotic.

The data from the interaction situation, and from the PPVT and the WISC, along with the diagnostic impressions of the child were all obtained and scored prior to the interviews with the parents and hence before the children were assigned to the Stress and Control groups.

RESULTS

The data from the interaction procedure were scored according to methods described previously (Steisel et al., 1967). This entailed computing a mean scale score separately for the *total, solicited, rejected,* and *awaited* parts of the interaction situation.

Reliability, in terms of interjudge agreement, was measured by Spearman rank-order correlations (rhos). At least two judges had contributed ratings on 28 of the children in the sample. For two children, one in each group, scale ratings were available from only one judge and these were excluded from the analyses on interjudge agreement. Rhos were computed on the paired judges' ratings for the *total* and three-part scores of the interaction situation for the 28 Ss. The obtained values were .94 for the total score, .79 for the solicited, .93 for the rejected, and .71 for the awaited scores. Converting the rhos into t values after a procedure described by Siegel (1956), all were significant at or beyond .001.

Three of the scales in the interaction ratings were selected for separate analysis because of their specific relevance to the nature of the behavioral descriptions reported both for children with PKU and those without PKU who were physically restrained during the first 3 yr. of life (Friedman et al., 1964). These were (1) *attention to the experimenter* which may be regarded as a measure of the child's ability to relate, (2) *attention to toys and objects* which provided the best available index of object relations, and (3) *communicative sounds* which characterizes the child's ability to mediate between his needs to play with the toys and the reality circumstances of the interaction situation. The scores for each of these variables were obtained by summing the number of times they were rated during the entire interaction period. In this regard, the communicative sounds and attention to toys and objects were rated four times during the solicited period (e.g., during bead stringing, throwing quoits, racing cars, and shooting darts) and once each during the rejected and awaited periods. The scores for attention to the experimenter were derived in the same way except that this variable was not rated during the rejection period. Rhos were again used to determine interjudge agreement on these measures of inteactional behavior on the 28 Ss for whom two judges had contributed ratings. These analyses yielded a rho of .80 for attention to the experimenter, .81 for attention to toys and objects, and .89 for communicative sounds. Converting the rhos to t values (Siegel, 1956), all were significant at or beyond .001.

For the subsequent analyses of the data, the paired judges' ratings were summed and averaged and the ratings on two children for whom only one judge's ratings were available were included. Comparisons of the Stress and Control groups on the interaction scores, PPVT, and WISC IQ scores were made by t tests. The results of these analyses are summarized in Table 1.

The Stress group, as hypothesized, demonstrated greater impairment in interpersonal behavior than the Control group with respect to total, solicited, and awaited mean scale scores. These findings indicate that children in the Stress group in comparison to those in the Control group displayed less adequate interpersonal responsiveness overall, and particularly under conditions which required the active participation of the child and E. The two groups, however, were not significantly different in interactive behavior during the rejected period when the E purposely avoided or ignored the child's interactive efforts.

Comparisons between the Stress and Control groups by t tests revealed the Control group to be significantly higher on measures of attention to the experimenter, attention to toys and objects, and communicative sounds. Hence, it was concluded that children subjected to early stress by sensory restriction or isolation displayed greater impairment of interpersonal relations, object relations, and communicational skills.

Table 1 Means and t Ratios for Differences between Stress and Control Groups on Measures of Social Interaction, Language Comprehension, and Intelligence

Measure	Stress group	Control group	t ratio
nteraction total[a]	2.88	3.80	2.14**
Interaction solicited[a]	3.14	4.40	3.15***
Interaction rejected	2.64	3.02	.78
Interaction awaited[a]	2.95	4.21	2.52**
Attention to E[a]	16.03	23.00	3.50***
Attention to objects[a]	20.19	27.68	3.30***
Communicative sounds[a]	17.03	22.54	1.84*
Language Comprehension (PPVT IQ)	53.69	78.93	3.46***
Intelligence (WISC IQ)	51.88	71.86	3.57***

Note.—Stress group ($n=16$); Control group ($n=14$).
[a] Test of significance between means of samples with heterogeneous variances (Edwards, 1960, pp. 106–107).
* $p < .05$.
** $p < .025$.
*** $p < .005$.

Comparisons of the Stress and Control groups on PPVT IQ scores yielded a mean difference of approximately 25 points. Analysis of the PPVT scores revealed that the Stress group was significantly more impaired in language comprehension than the Control group. Comparing the intelligence test scores of the Stress and Control groups by t test, a significant difference (or approximately 20 IQ points) was found between the means ($p < .01$). As with the PPVT, the Control group performed significantly higher than the Stress group on these measures of intellectual functioning.

Diagnostic Impressions

Of the 14 Ss in the Control group, all were judged to be clearly not psychotic during the psychological testing. Of the 16 Ss in the Stress condition, 5 were judged to be psychotic, 5 were judged to be questionably psychotic or severely disturbed, and 6 were judged to be clearly not psychotic. Combining the categories for clearly psychotic and questionably psychotic or severely disturbed, analysis by chi-square yielded a value of 10.5, $df = 1$, indicating that the two groups were significantly ($p < .01$) different on diagnostic impression from psychological testing.

The diagnoses of all the 11 Ss in the Control group given a psychiatric interview were all clearly not psychotic. Thus there was exact agreement between the two diagnostic impression procedures for these 11 children in the Control group. Of the 11 children in the Stress group seen in the psychiatric interview, 5 were diagnosed as clearly psychotic, 3 others were classified as questionably psychotic or severely disturbed, and 3 were judged to be clearly not psychotic. Collapsing the categories of clearly psychotic and questionably psychotic or severely disturbed, the chi-square was 11.8 with $df = 1$ which was a significant ($p < .001$) difference between the Stress and Control groups for the psychiatric diagnostic impression. In summary then, both the psychological and psychiatric diagnostic impressions indicated that children in the Stress group manifested significantly more severe and frequent symptoms of emotional disturbance than children in the Control group.

Several additional analyses of the data were performed to determine the relationship of (a) the age of the child at the time of the initial stressful experience, (b) the duration of the sensory restriction to the response of the child to the interpersonal behavior, and (c) the intelligence and the language ability of the Ss in the Stress and Control groups.

The age variable was the reported age of the child at the time of the stressful experience. This ranged from 3 to 36 mo. for the children in the Stress group, with a mean of 19.06 mo. Analyses were by means of Spearman rank-order correlations (Siegel, 1956). The rho between age and total interaction scores was .84, which indicated that the older the child was at the time of the initial stress experience, the greater the degree of impairment to social or interpersonal behavior. The rho between age and IQ scores or social quotients derived from the Vineland Social Maturity Scale was found to be .67, suggesting that the older the child at the time of the stress experience, the greater the impairment to intellectual functioning. Finally, the rho between age and PPVT IQ scores was .74 which suggested that the older the child at the time of the initial immobilization, sensory restriction, or isolation experience, the greater the impairment to language comprehension ability. Conversion of these rhos to t values (Siegal, 1956) indicated that all were significant at or beyond .01.

Duration of stress was defined as the length of time reported by parents that the child was immobilized, isolated, or subjected to a sensory restriction experience. For those children who were not continuously immobilized or isolated, but who were intermittently subjected to such experiences within a given segment of time, an estimate was made of the approximate duration of stress. Duration of stress for the children in the Stress group ranged from 3 to 365 days. In computing a mean duration for the stressful experiences, the two male siblings who were isolated daily in their rooms from evening until morning and one other male S who was immobilized for 30 days during hospitalization and then immobilized daily by means of a sheet wrapped around the body to foster feeding of the dietary preparation for approximately 2 yr. were excluded. For the remaining 13 children in the Stress group, the mean duration of stress was 14.6 days. The rho for duration of stress for all 16 children in the Stress group in relation to total interaction scores was .17, to the intelligence estimates was .28, and to the PPVT IQ scores was .16. All failed to reach significance at .05.

CONCLUSIONS AND DISCUSSION

The findings of this study show that children with PKU who were immobilized, subjected to sensory restriction and/or isolation during the first 3 yr. of life in comparison to children with PKU for whom no such experiences were reported were: (*a*) more impaired in social and interpersonal behavior under conditions of active play, and specifically less related to the examiner, less interested in toys and objects, and less communicative by words or sounds; (*b*) more impaired in language comprehension ability; (*c*) more impaired in intellectual functioning; and (*d*) more often characterized by manifestations of moderate to severe personality disturbances.

This study documents and emphasizes the importance of certain psychosocial influences in the mental retardation and behavioral disturbance of children with PKU as was previously suggested by the clinical report of Bjornson (1964) and the findings from studies by Wood et al. (1967) and

Keleske et al. (1967). Most important, the early experiences of sensory deprivation and immobilization identified and studied have implications for prognosis, prevention, and treatment of children with PKU.

The present study does not resolve the dilemma of whether the greater intellectual and behavioral deficits noted in children with PKU subjected to early stressful experiences were not in fact the outgrowth of preexisting differences of a biochemical or constitutional nature. It would seem reasonable to assume that children who developed serious upper-respiratory infections or required casting to correct congenital orthopedic difficulties or needed repeated urine samples which necessitated restraint procedures were somehow initially different from those for whom such therapeutic or diagnostic measures were not necessary. From the details of the individual cases presented, however, it becomes clear that the need for physical restraint or isolation was not necessarily created by the severity of the mental retardation or the presence of symptoms of psychological distress. Furthermore, the review of available case materials did not reveal any initial differences between children who experienced sensory restriction or immobilization and those who did not. It is only logical to conjecture that children with PKU might manifest symptoms of the nature described by Mendelson, Solomon, and Lindemann (1958) who reported psychotic-like symptoms, disorientation, confusion, delusions, and hallucinations in adults with poliomyelitis who were physically immobilized and subjected to the sensory deprivation of artificial tank-type respirators. While such symptomatic changes which have been reported in adults are typically of a transitory nature, there is reason to believe that comparable kinds of stresses in children, and in particular those with PKU, lead to permanent changes. In discussing the influences of early environmental experiences, and in particular those which alter normal patterns of sensory stimulation, Fiske and Maddi (1961) mention the primacy of early events, the plasticity of the developing organism, and the relative lack of differentiation as factors in favor of producing more severe, pervasive, and permanent adverse changes in the young child.

In the early studies on experimental sensory restriction emanating from the McGill group (Bexton, Heron, & Scott, 1954; Doane, Mahatoo, Heron, & Scott, 1959; Heron, Bexton, & Hebb, 1953; Heron, Doane, & Scott, 1956), Ss who were restricted to limited areas, or put in gloves, or immobilized by cardboard cylinders on the arms or legs, displayed hallucinations, perceptual disturbances, and decrements in intellectual performance. Fiske and Maddi (1961) have emphasized two features bearing on the severity of aftereffects: the degree of physical immobilization and the number of sense modalities affected. Zubek (1963a, 1963b, 1964a, 1964b, 1964c, 1968) has elucidated the nature of immobilization by itself and in conjunction with other means of sensory restriction in adult volunteers. One of the more striking findings is the tendency for some of the volunteer Ss to find the stress situation intolerable and to quit the experiment. Zubek (1968) recently reported that the "quitters" in his study excreted initially less urinary catecholamines than Ss who were able to tolerate the procedure for longer durations. This is of interest since a deficiency in epinephrine and norepinephrine is known to exist in PKU (Nadler & Hsia, 1961). The suggestion that profound changes caused by immobilization and sensory restriction in children with PKU may be related to disturbed synthesis of epinephrine and norepinephrine in this disease opens up additional lines of research. It needs to be emphasized, however, that there are no systematic investigations available concerning the effects of immobilization on children suitable for comparison with the results of this study.

Of major importance is the present finding that brief periods of sensory restriction in children with PKU may produce pervasive and permanent changes. It is perplexing to realize that 3 days of physical immobilization or sensory restriction may be capable of producing or exacerbating the entire spectrum of personality, social, and intellectual changes suggested by the present results. As Ss of this study were all under 3 yr. of age, it is conceivable, however, that the child's inability to judge and discriminate time, and likewise his limited capacity to understand and appreciate the need for treatment or diagnosis, is somehow implicated in the severity of changes which follow early immobilization or sensory restriction. A study of the effects of Ss' uncertainty regarding the planned duration of restriction has been reported by Cohen, Silverman, and Shmavonian (1962). Their study revealed that reactions to the shortest periods of confinement, when Ss were told nothing with respect to the planned duration, were as severe as reactions to the longest durations of confinement for Ss who were told when the restriction would be terminated. It could be argued that the child's limited conception of time and the nature of the planned procedures to some extent parallels the condition imposed by Cohen et al. (1962), and accounts in part for the severity of reactions to brief periods of immobilization or sensory restriction.

The behavioral characteristics of the majority of the children subjected to these stressful experiences, and specifically the hyperactivity and passivity patterns, resembled manifestations of psychological disturbance for children with a history of physical immobilization reported on by Friedman et al. (1964). The hyperactive children with PKU in the present study frequently displayed exaggerated startlelike responses to relatively low level stimulation (i.e., physical contact, the sound of a passing truck, etc.). In contrast, children who manifested the passivity pattern, and these were in the minority, showed little if any observable responses to relatively high intensities of external stimulation (i.e., being spanked by the parents, physical injuries, loud noises, etc.). Since these similarities between Ss in the present study and those in the Friedman et al. (1964)

sample in overt responses to environmental stimulation have in common a history of early physical immobilization or sensory restriction, there is reason to suspect that early alterations in sensory environments are somehow implicated in the subsequent behavioral reactions in the two study groups. Evidence of such a link comes from Melzack and Burns (1963), who reported exaggerated reaction patterns to normal and intense environmental stimulation in dogs subjected to prolonged sensory deprivation early in life. Such preliminary observations of deviant activity patterns in children with PKU suggest future studies on arousal, sensitivity thresholds in various sense modalities, and habituation in response to high and low level stimulation.

It can be stated that PKU, with its biochemical substrate, is a most complex disorder. The evidence at this juncture suggests that the variations in outcome are in part related to the influence of early stress of physical immobilization, sensory restriction, and isolation experiences.

References

Bexton, W. H., Heron, W., & Scott, T. H. Effects of decreased variation in the sensory environment. *Canadian Journal of Psychology,* 1954, *8,* 70–76.

Bjornson, J. Behavior in phenylketonuria. *Archives of General Psychiatry,* 1964, *10,* 89–94.

Cohen, S. J., Silverman, A. J., & Shmavonian, M. B. Psychophysiological studies in altered sensory environments. *Journal of Psychosomatic Research,* 1962, *6,* 259–281.

Doane, B. K., Mahatoo, W., Heron, W., & Scott. T. H. Changes in perceptual function after isolation. *Canadian Journal of Psychology,* 1959, *13,* 210–219.

Edwards, A. L. *Experimental design in psychological research.* New York: Rinehart, 1960.

Fiske, D. W. Variability among peer ratings in different situations. *Educational & Psychological Measurement,* 1960, *20,* 283–292.

Fiske, D. W., & Maddi, S. R. *Functions of varied experience.* Homewood, Ill.: Dorsey Press, 1961.

Friedman, C. J., Handford, A. H., & Settlage, C. Child psychologic development: The adverse effects of physical restraint. Paper presented at the meeting of the Regional American Psychiatric Association, Philadelphia, April 1964.

Heron, W., Bexton, W. H., & Hebb, D. O. Cognitive effects of a decreased variation in the sensory environment. *American Psychologist,* 1953, *8,* 366. (Abstract)

Heron, W., Doane, B. K., & Scott, T. H. Visual disturbances after prolonged perceptual isolation. *Canadian Journal of Psychology,* 1956, *10,* 13–18.

Jervis, G. A. Phenylpyruvic aligophrenia (Phenylketonuria). *Proceedings of the Association for Research on Nervous and Mental Disease,* 1954, *33,* 259–282.

Kaplan, A. R. Phenylketonuria. *Eugenics Quarterly,* 1962, *9,* 151–160.

Karper, R., & Cahilly, G. Experimental attempts to produce phenylketonuria in animals: A critical review. *Psychological Bulletin,* 1965, *61,* 52–64.

Keleske, L., Solomon, G., & Opitz, E. Parental reactions to phenylketonuria in the family. *Journal of Pediatrics,* 1967, *70,* 793.

Koch, R., Fishler, K., Schild, S., & Ragsdale, N. Clinical aspects of phenylketonuria. *Mental Retardation,* 1964, *2,* 47–54.

Lyman, F. L. (Ed.) *Phenylketonuria.* Springfield, Ill.: Charles C Thomas, 1963.

Melzack, R., & Burns, S. K. Neuropsychological effect of early sensory restriction. *Boletin de Estudios Medicos & Biologicos,* 1963, *21,* 407–425.

Mendelson, J., Solomon, P., & Lindemann, E. Hallucinations of poliomyelitis patients during treatment in a respirator. *Journal of Nervous and Mental Disease,* 1958, *126,* 421–428.

Nadler, H. G., & Hsia, D. Y-Y. Epinephrine metabolism in phenylketonuria. *Proceedings of the Society for Experimental Biology and Medicine,* 1961, *107,* 721–723.

Robertson, J. *Young children in hospitals.* New York: Basic Books, 1962.

Schultz, D. P. *Sensory restriction.* New York: Academic Press, 1965.

Siegel, S. *Nonparametric statistics for the behavioral sciences.* New York: McGraw-Hill, 1956.

Solomon, P., Kubzansky, P. E., Leiderman, P. H., Mendelson, J. H., Trumbull, R., & Wexler, D. (Eds.) *Sensory deprivation.* Cambridge, Mass.: Harvard University Press, 1961.

Steisel, I. M., Friedman, C. J., & Wood, A. C., Jr. Interaction patterns in children with phenylketonuria. *Journal of Consulting Psychology,* 1967, *31,* 162–168.

Wood, A. C., Friedman, C. J., & Steisel, I. M. Psychosocial factors in phenylketonuria. *American Journal of Orthopsychiatry,* 1967, *37,* 671–679.

Woolley, D. W. *The biochemical basis of psychosis.* New York: Wiley, 1962.

Woolley, D. W. New insights into mental illness: Philosophical implications. *Atlantic,* 1965, *216,* 46–50.

Yaker, H. M., & Goldberg, B. R. Some preliminary comparisons of phenylketonuria with childhood schizophrenia. *Pennsylvania Psychiatric Quarterly,* 1963, *4,* 10–17.

Zubek, J. P. Counteracting effects of physical exercises performed during prolonged perceptual deprivation. *Science,* 1963, *142,* 504–506. (a)

Zubek, J. P. Pain sensitivity as a measure of perceptual deprivation tolerance. *Perceptual and Motor Skills,* 1963, *17,* 641–642. (b)

Zubek, J. P. Behavioral and EEG changes after 14 days of perceptual deprivation. *Psychological Science,* 1964, *1,* 57–58. (a)

Zubek, J. P. Behavioral changes after prolonged perceptual deprivation (no intrusions). *Perceptual and Motor Skills,* 1964, *18,* 413–430. (b)

Zubek, J. P. Effects of prolonged sensory and perceptual deprivation. *British Medical Bulletin,* 1964, *20,* 38–40. (c)

Zubek, J. P. Urinary excretion of adrenaline and noradrenaline during prolonged immobilization. *Journal of Abnormal Psychology,* 1968, *73,* 223–225.

9

Use of Punishment Procedures with the Severely Retarded: A Review

William I. Gardner

Dr. Gardner is Professor and Chairman of the Department of Studies in Behavioral Disabilities at the University of Wisconsin. He is also Director of Laboratory of Applied Behavior Analysis and Modification at the University of Wisconsin.

Dr. Gardner's research interest lies primarily with the mentally retarded and the emotionally disturbed child. His research studies on these children have appeared in seven major professional journals.

There have been many published studies over the past ten years concerned with the effects of punishment on the behavior of severely retarded children. Dr. Gardner presents an excellent summary and evaluation of such studies, and concludes that the use of aversive stimuli does have a place in the treatment and rehabilitative repertoire of the severely retarded.

Recent interest in providing a rehabilitation environment for the severely and profoundly retarded has produced a number of studies describing

REPRINTED BY permission from the *American Journal of Mental Deficiency*, Copyright 1969, American Association of Mental Deficiency. The preparation of this manuscript was facilitated by Grant No. RT 11 from the Social and Rehabilitation Service, Department of Health, Education, and Welfare, Washington, D.C.

treatment procedures for work with the developmenal and behavioral problems present in this group (e.g., Bensberg, Colwell, & Cassel, 1965; Giles & Wolf, 1966; Hamilton, Stevens & Allen, 1967; Henriksen & Doughty, 1967). The treatment strategies reported in many of these studies have been based on principles derived from learning theories. As is apparent in the recent review by Watson (1967), the most influential of these models has been that of operant learning.

A significant aspect of a treatment program designed for the severely retarded is that of eliminating or reducing in frequency or severity specific inappropriate behavior patterns. According to reinforcement theory, any operant behavior, desirable or undesirable, can be decreased and eventually eliminated merely by discontinuing those stimulus conditions which reinforce it. An example of the application of this extinction procedure is provided by the work of Wolf, Birnbrauer, Williams, and Lawler (1965) with an institutionalized retarded child. In this study operant vomiting and temper tantrums which occurred at a relatively high rate were both eliminated by removing a positively reinforcing consequence. Further support for an extinction procedure is represented by Spradlin and Girardeau (1966), who, in discussing such problems as tantrums, aggressiveness, self-destructive acts and the like which frequently characterize the institutionalized moderately/severely retarded, suggested, "Probably the most effective procedure for reducing the frequency of these behaviors is to withhold reinforcement when they occur, i.e., extinguish them" [p. 290]. The authors did note, nevertheless, that to be most effective this procedure should be used in combination with one of teaching other acceptable responses which compete with the inappropriate behavior.

Serious limitations in the application of an extinction procedure, however, are encountered frequently when working with the retarded. As has been suggested by Hamilton and Stephens (1967), analyzing and controlling the reinforcing contingencies, especially of complex behavior and behavior of the long standing, may be a most difficult undertaking. First, it is difficult to identify the reinforcing events and to control them once identified. Even with the severely retarded it must be concluded that for a large class of behaviors the complete elimination of reinforcement is impossible. Thus, as Azrin and Holz (1966) suggested "Some other reductive method, such as punishment, must be used" [p. 433]. Secondly, as noted by Lovaas, Freitag, Gold, and Kassorla (1965), in the early phase of extinction there may be an actual increase in the rate of behavior prior to a decremental effect. This characteristic renders this procedure highly undesirable in those instances in which the behavior is either highly disruptive or of potential danger to the client or others. In such cases there is need for a treatment procedure which would result in immediate reduction in the frequency or intensity of the problem behavior. Furthermore, as most behaviors have developed under and are maintained by a partial reinforcement schedule, a strategy of behavior elimination based solely on extinction operations promises to be a slow undertaking. This was noted by Birnbrauer, Bijou, Wolf, and Kidder (1965) in attempting to eliminate behavior problems of groups of retarded boys in a classroom setting by an extinction procedure, i.e., by ignoring instances of inappropriate behavior. After some experience, a time-out procedure was added "since extinction is often difficult to implement effectively in a classroom . . ." [p. 360].

Bucher and Lovass (1968) used an extinction procedure with a seven year old severely retarded boy who, due to high-rate self-injurious behaviors, was kept in complete restraints on a 24-hour a day basis. After eight days of being released from restraints for one and one-half hours daily, the behavior was gradually reduced to near extinction level by removing a presumed source of reinforcement. However, during this extinction process the child hit himself in excess of 10,000 times. In another case of severe self-destructive behavior in a 16 year old retarded girl with psychotic features, these writers reported that "because of the extreme severity of her self-injurious behavior . . . it is impossible to place such a child on extinction. Marilyn could have inflicted serious self-injury or even killed herself during an extinction run" [p. 91].

Watson's observation (1967) is also quite pertinent:

> When a child is engaged in acts that are physically damaging, such as breaking windows with his head, arms, or hands, beating his head against the wall, stabbing himself or others with a safety pin, or throwing another child down with great force, the cottage staff cannot wait for the effects of extinction to gradually end or eliminate the behavior. Someone might be injured severely before the effects of extinction could eliminate the behavior in question [p. 13].

In light of these considerations it must be concluded that, even though from a theoretical viewpoint removal of reinforcement may be a most reliable and effective manner of eliminating behavior, considerable difficulty is frequently encountered in its application in a field situation, especially with cases of extreme behavior deviation. In these instances such a procedure at times is a highly inefficient and thus impractical procedure. Obviously more humane behavior deceleration procedures should be available in an effective treatment program.

Certain characteristics of the severely mentally retarded further emphasize the need for utilizing every useful treatment approach that is available. Limited language and general cognitive skills, a rather primitive social motivation system, and a restricted range of stimulus events which are controlling or reinforcing, all render behavior shaping treatment attempts with this group quite difficult. In addition, for a large number of severely and profoundly retarded, a disproportionate amount of their total behavior is of a sort that creates a considerable management problem. It is not unusual to find in this group such behaviors as dangerous self-mutilation, rectal digging, feces smearing and eating, violent and unpredictable temper outbursts, physical attacks on peers and attendants, chronic and high rate repetitive movements, disruptive screaming and crying, and destruction of windows, clothing, furnishings and the like. These characteristics greatly increase the importance of an unbiased, objective evaluation of the efficacy of all possible behavior change techniques.

Some treatment procedures which have gained recent consideration in work with the severely retarded are those having punishment or aversive components. Many of the reports describing experience with punishment have been products of relatively new clinical research programs aimed at creating a more effective total rehabilitation environment for the retarded. Few have been products of systematic experience in clinical treatment programs. This is not surprising as most clinical treatment personnel categorically reject the use of punishment procedures as legitimate behavior change approaches. Punishment procedures are typically viewed as inhumane, deplorable, unethical, and non-professional. This attitude is perhaps understandable in relation to the mentally retarded in residential settings, as various punishment techniques all too frequently have been used as punitive measures instead of as treatment techniques used in a deliberate systematic fashion. In addition it is assumed by many that the decelerating effects of punishment are temporary and that punishment produces undesirable side effects, including disruptive emotional states and disruption of social relationships. It even appears that these attitudes and extrapolations from animal research have greatly restricted research on use of punishment with the retarded. For example, a recent review chapter (Spradlin & Girardeau, 1966) on the moderately and severely retarded reported no studies in this area. The major portion of the studies reviewed in the present paper has been published within the last two years. In general it appears that punishment is frequently rejected as a treatment procedure, not on the basis of an objective evaluation of scientific data, but rather on the basis of ethical, philosophic, and sociopolitical considerations or as a result of what Solomon (1964) referred to as unscientific legends concerning the effects of punishment.

In view of this restrictive attitude and in consideration of the recent experience which numerous people are reporting, it should be valuable to examine the question, "What does punishment do to the behavior of the severely and profoundly retarded?" To accomplish this, studies which evaluate the use of punishment with children and adults exhibiting severely retarded behavior are reviewed, including a few studies with children who have been labeled autistic or schizophrenic. More specifically, information relevant to the following and related questions will be sought: How effective are punishment procedures in treatment of inappropriate behaviors of the severely retarded? If effective, are such behavior changes temporary? What "side effects" are produced by punishment? With what types of behavior is punishment most effective? Such an evaluation of available data will provide an empirical basis for decisions by treatment personnel concerning the use or rejection of punishment procedures. In addition, a critical evaluation of the studies will provide direction to future investigations, both in terms of identifying design/methodology deficiencies which must be considered if more reliable data are to be obtained and in terms of identifying a range of parameters in need of study.

Punishment procedures which have been used with the severely retarded can be grouped into two classes on the basis of the operations followed. The first class includes those procedures which result in the *presentation* of certain stimulus conditions following a response to be eliminated. These would include: (a) primary aversive stimuli, e.g., electric shock (Tate & Baroff, 1966), food seasoned with hot pepper (Blackwood, 1962), (b) physical restraint, e.g., strapping to chair or bed (Hamilton, Stevens & Allen, 1967), placing in restraining jackets (Giles & Wolf, 1966), and (c) conditioned aversive stimuli, e.g., "No" paired previously with primary aversive stimuli (Watson, 1966), "No" paired previously with removal of food and physical restraining (Henriksen & Doughty, 1967). The second class includes those procedures which result in the *removal* of certain stimulus conditions following the to-be-eliminated behavior. Various procedures of time out from positive reinforcement, e.g., placement in an isolation room following inappropriate behavior (Wiesen & Watson, 1967) illustrate this class of procedures. On occasion the time-out is used in combination with a response cost (Weiner, 1962) procedure, e.g., subject is isolated and in addition loses certain tangible positive reinforcers which are available to him (Hamilton & Allen, 1967).

REVIEW

The reader should note that in most of the studies to be described, regardless of the specific punishment procedures used, subjects not only had alternative response possibilities available in the punishment situation but in addition were provided positive reinforcement for more suitable alternative behaviors. Azrin and Holz (1966) emphasize that such an alternative response situation results in maximum suppression by a given intensity of punishment. Although desirable as a treatment strategy, such a procedure does, however, confound the contributions of punishment and positive reinforcement in subsequent behavior change except in those studies which utilize a precise functional analysis design. Further, the reader should note that the applied research reports reviewed vary greatly in terms of the nature of the data presented. As much of the work represents recent pioneer efforts at studying the effects of punishment on human problem behavior in a clinical setting, it is mostly of a preliminary and/or case study nature. Only a few of the studies used analytic designs (e.g., a reversal or ABAB technique) which would render possible the demonstration of reliable control over the observed behavior changes. In most of the work reviewed, a therapy procedure (i.e., baseline-treatment) was followed which precluded the demonstration of a reliable (replicated) functional relationship between punishment and subsequent behavior changes. Finally, except in a few instances, no objective data were obtained concerning "side effects." The limitations which these design characteristics place on both the reliability and generality of the reported results will be discussed following a review of the studies.

Primary Aversive Stimulus Presentation

Although electric shock has been the primary aversive stimulus most frequently used in animal research in which punishment effects have been investigated, only recently has shock been used as a punishing stimulus in work with problem behaviors at the human level (Azrin & Holz, 1966; Solomon, 1964). Lovaas and his colleagues reported its use in a successful program designed to decelerate behaviors through its presentation (self-destructive and tantrum behavior) and to accelerate other behaviors through its removal (hugging experimenter) in work with autistic children (Lovaas, Freitag, Kinder, Rubenstein, Schaeffer, & Simon, 1964; Lovaas, Schaeffer, & Simmons, 1965).

In a recent report, Bucher and Lovaas (1968) described the application of electric shock in suppressing the high-rate self-destructive responses of three retarded subjects with psychotic-like behavior. All had long histories of self-injurious behavior, all were hospitalized, and all were kept in constant restraints. In all cases the self-destructive behaviors were suppressed immediately and virtually eliminated after a series of response contingent electric shocks (1,400 volts at 50,000 ohms resistance usually delivered by a hand-held inductorium) distributed over a small number of sessions.

Risley (1968) used shock to control dangerous climbing behavior in a hyperactive six year old brain damaged girl described as asocial, with no speech or imitative behaviors. Repetitive head twisting was eliminated by a procedure of shouting at and shaking the child. Previous withdrawal of attention, isolation for ten-minute time-out periods contingent upon the climbing behavior and reinforcement of incompatible behaviors all proved noninfluential. As the behavior was dangerous to the child and destructive to the home, and as the child's aggressive behavior toward her younger brother was causing considerable parental concern, it was felt that an effective control procedure having immediate effects was needed.

Shock in the range of 300–400 volts was applied by a hand-held inductorium to the child's leg, contingent upon climbing behavior. Climbing behavior, which was occurring at the rate of one climb every 10 minutes, was eliminated in a laboratory room after six contingent applications of the shock over eight sessions. No climbing occurred in the therapist's presence during the subsequent 12 sessions but did reappear in the following session. No shock was administered during the subsequent 11 sessions, with climbing occurring an average of 4.9 times per hour. As the author emphasized, "Clearly, the effects of the shock punishment were reversible (not permanent)" [p. 29]. A single response contingent shock again eliminated the response, with no further climbing occurring during the next 59 sessions.

The procedure was applied in the home where the inappropriate climbing was at an average rate of 29 times daily. The rate was reduced to two per day within four days of response contingent shock, with a zero rate obtained within a few additional days. Aggressive behavior against the younger brother resulted in shock. Within three weeks this behavior rate was reduced to zero and was not reported to occur during the subsequent 70 days of follow-up.

The repetitive head rolling behaviors were virtually eliminated within 10 sessions of response contingent shouting ("stop that!") and vigorous shaking.

Tate and Baroff (1966) described the successful use of response contingent electric shock in work with a nine year-old blind boy residing in a state institution for the mentally retarded. The boy engaged in various self-injurious behavior (SIB) including head-banging, face slapping, punching his face and head with his fist, hitting his shoulder with his chin, and kicking himself. He was reported to enjoy bodily contact with others. Subject spent most of his time restrained in bed. Electric shock was used in this case on the assumption that such aversive consequences would result in rapid deceleration of the SIB. This was deemed essential as the risk was present that further SIB would completely destroy the retina of his right eye in which some light-dark vision was present.

Shock was delivered to the lower leg contingent upon SIB. Previous baseline rate of SIB was approximately two per minute. Following response contingent shock a rapid deceleration effect was noted, with only 20 SIBs of light intensity observed during a five and one half hour period (average of .06 responses per minute) on the first day following shock. On the second day there were only 15 SIBs during the entire day (rate of .03 per minute). During subsequent days subject spent nine hours daily out of bed. Subject was observed for 167 days after the beginning of shock, with no SIBs observed during the last 20 days of treatment.

Hamilton and Standahl (1967) reported success with the shock-punishment procedure in obtaining rapid deceleration of a variety of behavior deviations in the severely and profoundly retarded, including such problem areas as window-breaking, rectal digging, rumination, and physically abusing other residents. In each instance a brief electric shock was administered following the occurrence of the target behaviors. These writers noted however, that in some cases responses which occurred at a high rate were not rapidly suppressed. Furthermore the decelerated behavior did not readily generalize to no shock conditions in all cases. A procedure for dealing with these problems was evaluated in work with a 24 year old female institutionalized for over 14 years who exhibited limited self-care skills and no intelligible vocalizations. Her most characteristic behavior consisted of low pitched high intensity screams which occurred during most of her waking hours. Two other types of vocalizations described as "mooing" and "chattering" were also present.

During base rate sessions consisting of eight daily one-half hour periods, a shock apparatus was strapped about subject's waist to acclimate her to this equipment. During treatment (days 9–26) shock was administered following each growl which occurred during the last 15 minutes of each daily 30-minute session. The shock intensity was increased after day 18 following an apparent adaptation effect. During base rate sessions growling was emitted at an average half hour rate of 330. No effect on growling was evident during the first two days of the treatment sessions. During the next three treatment sessions there was a sharp reduction in growling during the shock periods and to a lesser extent during the no shock periods. During the next five days of treatment there was a change from a generalized marked suppression of growling to a return to pretreatment level during both shock and no shock periods. After the shock intensity was increased, an immediate suppression effect was evident. Growling was effectively eliminated during the shock condition. Examination of the frequencies of chattering and mooing, however, indicated that the training was singularly specific to the growling as no effect was noted on these other classes of vocalization. In the second phase of the treatment program, shock was administered whenever growling occurred during two one-half hour periods five days a week. At this time subject was allowed to wander freely on the ward or in the outdoor play yard. By the 18th treatment day, growling was practically eliminated during these two one-half hour sessions. The average growling frequencies dropped from 25.5 in the morning and 19.2 in the afternoon during the first 17 treatment sessions to an average rate of 2.2 and .8 respectively during sessions 18–32.

During phase three the program was expanded to a 24 hour basis. Shock was delivered on a loosely defined intermittent punishment schedule by a shock stick carried by ward personnel. Growling responses gradually diminished over the next three months of the treatment program. Subject was followed for one year with the observation that the behavior rarely occurred at all. Thus it appears that a disturbing behavior which initially had occurred many thousands of times daily had been, for all practical purposes, eliminated following the contingent use of mild shock.

White and Taylor (1967) administered electric shock as a consequence or ruminating gestures of two profoundly retarded adults. Although not presenting adequate quantitative data, the writers reported an impression that the response contingent shock did significantly interrupt the ruminating behavior in these two subjects. In a related study, Luckey, Watson, and Musick (1968) reported the use of mild electric shock to reduce the frequency of vomiting and chronic ruminating by a severely retarded six-year-old boy. Rumination had been present for over a year in the hyperactive, destructive boy. Vomiting episodes started about 12 months prior to initiation of the response contingent shock. Medical and psychiatric treatment had failed to control these behaviors. With the use of a portable radio controlled shock apparatus, the therapist delivered shock immediately following vomiting or rumination behaviors. These behaviors dropped from a daily average of 13 occurrences during the first 4 days of treatment to a near zero level during the following 94 days of treatment and follow-up.

Blackwood (1962) reported the use of aversive stimuli in an attempt to control vomiting behavior in a 16 year old profoundly retarded male. Cayenne pepper used as the aversive stimulus was sprinkled on the vomitus as soon as possible after the regurgitating response. At the beginning of treatment an average of nine vomiting responses per day was recorded. Deceleration of the vomiting response gradually occurred over a 45 day period and was maintained at zero level for approximately 20 additional days. However, following this time and corresponding with several environmental changes, the writer reports gradual acceleration of the response to approximately the original level.

Banks and Locke (1966) studied the effects of mild punishment on self-destructive behaviors of three profoundly retarded subjects ranging in age from four to seven. All were blind and each exhibited a high rate of eye gouging. Punishment, consisting of slight hair pulling delivered during a ten minute period over three consecutive days, produced immediate and pronounced suppression effects for two of the three subjects. However, following termination of the punishment regimen, the response rate quickly recovered. The reader can only speculate about the long-term suppression effects had the therapists continued punishment for a longer period of time.

In addition to these studies using obvious primary aversive stimuli as the major treatment strategy, a few studies are available which report the use of a combination of primary and secondary aversive stimulus consequences or stimulus conditions which differed noticeably in physical intensity. Wiesen and Watson (1967) in an attempt to eliminate soiling in a six-year-old institutionalized severely retarded boy required him to remain in the soiled clothes for five minutes prior to bathing. In addition bathing was completed in water which was maintained at below room temperature. The writers reported that soiling which had occurred as often as nine times per day before treatment was extinguished with very rare reoccurrences. Evaluation of the specific effects of these punishment procedures was not possible as these contingencies were one aspect of a program which also used a time-out procedure in an effort to extinguish other undesirable behaviors. This study will be discussed in more detail in the following section concerned with procedures using removal of stimuli conditions. Marshall (1966) reported success in toilet training an eight-year-old autistic child through use of mild punishment consisting of slaps on the buttocks for soiling behavior and food reinforcement for correct responses.

Physical Restraint

Henriksen and Doughty (1967), Giles and Wolf (1966), and Hamilton, Stephens, and Allen (1967) all report the use of physical restraint as a deceleration procedure. Henriksen and Doughty in a program to eliminate undesirable mealtime behaviors of rapid eating, eating with hands, stealing food, hitting others at table, and throwing trays on floor interrupted the misbehavior and held the subject's arm down in his lap. Secondary aversive cues of verbal disapproval were developed by pairing these cues with movement restraint.

Giles and Wolf placed subjects in restraining jackets, attached them to the end of a rope, and/or retained them in a crawl pen as a negative consequence of soiling behavior. These events were not used to physically restrict behavior but rather as aversive consequences to suppress its occurrence. The authors conclude "This study suggests that aversive stimuli, such as restraining jackets, can be used briefly, yet effectively, to modify inappropriate behavior when distributed for short intervals contingent upon that behavior" [p. 780].

Hamilton, Stephens, and Allen (1967) used a combination of time-out from positive reinforcement and physical restraint in a program to eliminate a variety of aggressive and destructive behaviors in five severely and profoundly retarded adolescents and adults. Following occurrence of the target behavior the subject was placed in a time-out area from 30 to 120 minutes, during which time she was either restrained to a padded chair bolted to the floor or, with one subject, restrained to her bed. High-frequency head and back banging was quickly eliminated in the first subject. The second subject's behavior of frequent undressing throughout the day (e.g., 12 times on the day preceding initiation of program) was reduced to an occasional occurrence after one week.

Subject three illustrates the value of application of response contingent punishment over the use of the same negative conditions in an unsystematic manner. Due to a number of bothersome behaviors, including the habit of breaking windows with her head, subject three was restrained to her bed for extended periods of time prior to initiation of treatment. She averaged one broken window daily during the short periods when she was released for eating, bathing, toileting, and exercising. Following initiation of the program whenever a window was broken, the subject was immediately restrained to her bed for two-hour periods, with no attention provided beyond that essential for medical treatment of cuts for the broken glass. Within a week this behavior had dropped to a minimal frequency. During the next seven weeks only eleven windows were broken, after which the behavior did not reoccur during an eleven-month follow-up period.

Following the elimination of prolonged restraint and window breaking, two other classes of behavior, body-slamming and clothes tearing, were selected for deceleration programming. The occurrence of either behavior resulted in immediate bed restraint. After a few weeks the behavior virtually dropped out and remained so over an extended follow up period.

Abusive behavior occurring at an average rate of five incidents a week was reduced within a month to an average of one incident a week in subject four following systematic response contingent restraint in the time-out chair. Subject five exhibited a wide range of disruptive behavior, mostly involving fighting, making intolerable demands on staff, and defying authority. Much of this behavior was eliminated and that which remained was reduced in severity following response contingent time-out in the restraint chair.

Conditioned Aversive Stimulus Presentation

As suggested earlier Henriksen and Doughty (1967) paired facial and verbal disapproval with the onset of movement restraint and later used the aversive stimuli alone to suppress inappropriate eating behavior. Although unable, due to the confounding effects of other variables, to account for the ensuing behavior changes solely in terms of the presentation of conditioned aversive stimuli, the writers did speculate that the obtained results could be attributed to these aversive cues. Whitney and Barnard (1966) used a similar procedure with positive results in elimination of inappropriate eating behavior in a profoundly retarded 15-year-old girl.

Giles and Wolf (1966), after exploring the effects of a variety of stimuli in an effort to eliminate inappropriate toilet behavior in an eight year old severely retarded boy, found that placing a blindfold on him created an aversive condition. The use of this consequence in combination with physical restraint was followed by the elimination of inappropriate behaviors.

Watson and Sanders (1966) and Watson (1966) used a chain of aversive stimuli as a means of eliminating undesirable behavior of severely retarded boys after experiencing little success in eliminating these following attempts with extinction and a drl schedule (see Watson, 1967). A response in the absence of the discriminative stimulus produced a time-out signal that the S^D would not reappear for 15 seconds. Continued responses produced a firm and moderately loud vocal "No," with an electric shock following subsequent responses. In this higher-order conditioning paradigm, the vocal "No" and the time-out stimulus gained aversive properties. The writers reported this to be a very effective procedure and found it necessary to use the shock very infrequently after an initial introduction to this technique.

In the Tate and Baroff (1966) article discussed earlier, the writers reported that the buzzing sound produced by the shock stick which occurred upon delivering electric shock became an effective conditioned aversive stimulus following a few pairings. Refusal to eat and drink, inappropriate hand posturing, saliva-saving and excessive clinging to people were all brought under control by use of the buzz without actually delivering the electric shock. Similar conditioning effects were reported by Risley (1968).

Removal of Stimulus Conditions

In addition to the typical extinction procedure of removal of the reinforcing consequences associated with the given behavior, a time-out from positive reinforcement has been used successfully as a deceleration procedure with the developmentally retarded. Although experimental demonstration of the possible aversive properties of time-out was reported over a decade ago (Herrnstein, 1955) and has gained the attention of a number of laboratory research projects (e.g., Ferster & Appel, 1961; Ferster & Skinner, 1957; Holz, Azrin, & Ayllon, 1963; Zimmerman & Baydan, 1963), Azrin and Holz (1966) in a recent review suggested "the means whereby a time-out stimulus acts as a punishing stimulus is not completely clear at the present time" [p. 390]. Nevertheless, as implied earlier, a time-out procedure has enjoyed considerable popularity among those working with the developmentally retarded.

Although Verhave (1966) defines a time-out procedure rather simply as a period of time during which positive reinforcement is not available, Leitenberg (1965) indicates that there is no single set of operations which adequately defines time-out from positive reinforcement. It becomes apparent in reviewing various time-out procedures used in studies with the retarded that considerable variation exists among the specific operations followed.

Time-out procedures used with the retarded usually include any of three elements, each of which could contribute to the deceleration effects frequently obtained. The typical operation involves the removal of some aspect of the present stimulus environment which is identified either as a reinforcing stimulus or as a discriminative stimulus for the occurrence of reinforcing events. In some studies with the retarded, (a) a positive reinforcer has been removed for a designated period of time following negative behavior, e.g., consumption of food has been interrupted for 30 seconds for inappropriate response, or food is lost as a response cost, or (b) subject either has been removed from the general stimulus environment in which he typically receives reinforcers or from a present source of reinforcing stimuli, e.g., subject is removed from peers who provide social reinforcement and placed in an isolation area following disruptive behavior, thus reducing the possibility of further social reinforcement. In addition, in instances of withdrawal of social reinforcement or when the child is placed in isolation, conditions are created which may contain conditioned aversive properties, e.g., removing a child to an isolation room when the child is fearful of being left alone. Further, merely turning your back on someone or not responding for a designated period of time may be a discriminative stimulus for "rejection," or other unpleasant affective responses as suggested in a review by Hill (1968). Thus a time-out may be effective either due (a) to the *removal* of the possibility of positive reinforcement for the negative behavior or of the child receiving *any* positive reinforcers for any behavior for a period of time or (b) to the suppressing effects of the *presentation* of conditioned aversive stimuli. It has also been suggested that factors relating to the reinforcing properties of the end of time-out may be operating. The separate contributions of these have not been evaluated in studies involving retarded subjects.

As will be reported subsequently, studies have demonstrated that both isolation from social reinforcement and interruption of consummatory behavior involving primary positive reinforcement have influenced the rate of the behavior which preceded these events. It should be noted, on the other hand, that isolation or the removal of social reinforcers for a period of time does not prove to be aversive universally. Isolation may be neutral or even positively reinforcing for some. Striefel (1967), after studying the effects of isolation as a behavior management procedure with a group of retarded children residing in an institution, concluded that:

> the data support the contention that isolation is not very effective as a means of behavioral management when used indiscriminately. Rather the effects of isolation vary from child to child and in many cases with an individual child, from one time to the next. In many cases isolation actually reinforces the very behavior one is trying to eliminate, since some children find stimuli associated with isolation reinforcing [p. 8].

Wiesen and Watson (1967) reported the use of removal from social reinforcement in eliminating the excessive attention seeking behavior of a six year old severely retarded boy. When the boy engaged in inappropriate attention seeking behavior, a pre-time-out stimulus consisting of a verbal command "No" was followed by the child's removal from the room for five minutes. There was a rapid and steady decline of this behavior over a 21-day conditioning phase. Blackwood (1962), Giles and Wolf (1966), and Whitney and Barnard (1966) all used brief interruption of meals as an aversive event to eliminate behaviors of profoundly retarded subjects which interfered with development of simple self care skills. Peterson and Peterson (1967), in a program designed to eliminate the self-injurious behaviors of an eight year old severely retarded, successfully used time-out from primary (removal of food) and secondary (brief termination of social interaction) reinforcement. An additional punishment procedure of requiring the child to walk across the room and sit in a chair was included. These procedures functioned as mild forms of punishment and facilitated the reduction of the inappropriate behaviors.

Edwards and Lilly (1960) and Hamilton and Allen (1967) used time-out plus response-cost to control inappropriate mealtime behavior of severely and profoundly retarded females. Both report virtual elimination of a wide range of bothersome behaviors including line-breaking, food-throwing, food stealing, food-smearing, and tray-throwing. The basic treatment procedure was one of removing the subject from the dining area without the rest of her meal. Hamilton and Allen obtained a rapid and permanent reduction in inappropriate dining room behavior from the daily average of 60 during baseline. A 12-month follow-up revealed a daily average of less than one inappropriate response.

As reported earlier Hamilton, Stephens, and Allen (1967) were quite successful in the use of time-out plus physical restraint in eliminating a variety of inappropriate behaviors in severely retarded subjects. Hamilton and Stephens (1967), in work with a moderately retarded 19 year old girl, and using the same procedure of time-out plus physical restraint, were successful in rapid elimination of inappropriate behaviors including floor-rolling and screaming. Success with a social isolation consequence was evident in this case even though the subject was described as being consistently socially isolated, withdrawn, and interacted with no one on the ward. Follow-up for six months and longer revealed only infrequent recurrences of these behaviors.

Tate and Baroff (1966) used a brief time-out from physical contact in an effort to eliminate undesirable self-injurious behavior in a nine year old blind boy. Previous observations of this subject strongly indicated that physical contact with people was reinforcing to him and that being alone, especially when he was standing or walking, was aversive. A three second time-out from physical contact period immediately followed each occurrence of a self-injurious response. In addition during the time-out period the therapist ceased conversation with the subject. A median average rate of 6.6 responses per minute was obtained for five control days prior to the initiation of time-out procedure. This average declined sharply with the initiation of the time-out procedure to an average of .1 responses per minute. The results of this study indicated that the relatively simple procedure of immediate brief withdrawal of physical contact produced a dramatic reduction in the frequency of chronic self-injurious behavior. The usual extinction procedure of ignoring the behavior was not effective in reducing its frequency of occurrence.

As suggested earlier, in all studies using a time-out procedure alternative behaviors were not only present but routinely were reinforced positively in a systematic manner. These studies support the statement of Azrin and Holz (1966) which reflected the animal and laboratory human research that "time-out can be a very effective punishing stimulus if the organism has available an alternative response that is unpunished and that will produce the reinforcement" [p. 392].

DISCUSSION

As documented in recent reviews (Azrin & Holz, 1966; Church, 1963; Marshall, 1965; Solomon, 1964) the effects of punishment depend upon the parameters of the aversive stimuli in combination with characteristics of the subject being punished. In the studies reviewed in this paper, types of punishment and subject characteristics as well as behavioral effects varied greatly. These effects will be summarized in this section and similarities to results of general laboratory research noted.

The reader should note that most of the treatment studies reviewed were conducted in the natural setting in which the subjects resided. The primary focus of most studies was that of applied or treatment research and not of basic research, although some would qualify as acceptable behavior modification research endeavors. Furthermore, as suggested earlier, few of the treatment studies utilized a punishment procedure in isolation. Most frequently, alternative responses concomitantly resulted in reinforcement. Finally, subjects continued to live in a rather complex social environment which was not under control of the treatment personnel. In this environment it was not unusual, once the punished behavior reduced in intensity and frequency, for the social environment to attend to and reinforce appropriate behaviors of subjects who were previously ignored or actively avoided due to the obnoxious and inappropriate responses which they exhibited (e.g., Hamilton & Stevens, 1967; Tate & Baroff, 1966; Whitney & Barnard, 1966). Even though punishment was the only independent variable which was manipulated in a systematic manner, other reinforcement variables were possible contributing factors to resulting behavior changes. Therefore, behavior changes should be viewed in such cases as a combination of punishment effects and positively reinforced competing responses.

In evaluating the question of the reliability of the data reported in the studies, certain deficiencies in experimental design are evident. None followed a treatment versus control group procedure. Only a few (e.g., Lovaas et al., 1965; Risley, 1968; Tate & Baroff, 1966) met the rigorous requirements of a "single organism, within-subject design" (Dinsmoor, 1966; Honig, 1966; Sidman, 1960, 1962), i.e., provided demonstration of a causal relationship between punishment and behavior change through a replication design. Most are case studies which described the treatment procedures used in work with single subjects or with small groups of subjects. In most instances the results must be viewed as therapy data, i.e., data showing only a non-replicated correlation between behavior change and punishment. These deficiencies however, are generally characteristic of most behavior modification/behavior therapy studies as documented in recent *Psychological Bulletin* reviews by Gelfand and Hartmann (1968) and Leff (1968). In fact, as Baer, Wolf, and Risley (1968) have suggested, the very nature of applied behavior analysis frequently renders a reversal or replicated procedure impossible. These authors commented, "Application typically means producing valuable behavior; valuable behavior usually means extra-experimental reinforcement in a social setting; thus, valuable behavior, once set up, may no longer be dependent upon the experimental technique which created it" [p. 94].

For those studies which produced therapy data, additional criteria must be used in evaluating the adequacy of the results obtained. In most of the studies reviewed (a) the target behaviors were specified and well delineated, enabling reliable observations of the occurrence-nonoccurrence of the behavior being treated; (b) reliable (over time) base-rate information was provided: (c) description of the specifics of the treatment procedures was provided: (d) quantitative measures of treatment effects were obtained, and (e) follow-up data extending beyond the treatment period were provided. Leff (1968), recognizing the general deficits in experimental design in behavior modification studies dealing with a wide range of techniques and behavior problems, additionally suggested that the studies should be evaluated with respect to the extent to which dramatic changes in behavior followed treatment and which were maintained over a period of time following termination of treatment. He implied that procedures which evoked behavior changes meeting these criteria and which contribute substantially to the general prosocial development of the individual should be viewed as having clinical treatment significance. Many of the studies concerning the mentally retarded did report dramatic, long term changes which evidently contributed significantly to the general adaptation of the individual to his social and physical environment. In conclusion, although the results should be interpreted with caution as most studies reported could be criticized from a rigorous experimental design viewpoint, the consistency of positive results along with a consideration of the nature of the behavior change do provide a basis for the following generalizations.

Is Punishment Effective with the Severely Retarded?

As noted earlier punishment as a behavior modification procedure has been rejected by most treatment personnel as an appropriate or effective strategy. The question of the effectiveness of punishment as a treatment procedure in use with the severely and profoundly retarded, nonetheless, is an empirical one and cannot be answered on an a priori theoretical or philosophic basis.

The studies reviewed provide support for the general conclusion that punishment procedures do contribute to behavior change in the severely and profoundly retarded. Studies which utilized response contingent electric shock, physical restraint, conditioned aversive stimuli, and timeout from primary and/or secondary reinforcement all reported success in the deceleration of a wide range of inappropriate behaviors in both children and adults.

In the majority of the studies reviewed, especially those involving intense stimulation, punishment procedures were used only with chronic high frequency behavior which occurred in individuals who potentially were only minimally responsive to the more typical procedures of behavior change. In many cases punishment was used as a "last resort" strategy, only after other procedures of behavior change produced minimal results. For example, Watson (1966) reported little success in eliminating undesirable responses in severely retarded boys when using extinction or a drl reinforcement procedure. The writer reported that the behaviors were quickly eliminated following the use of a chain of aversive consequences, consisting of time-out, a vocal "No," and electric shock. Likewise, Bucher and Lovaas (1968), Giles and Wolf (1966), and Risley (1968) reported that aversive consequences were used only after positive reinforcement had been found to be ineffective in modifying the behavior.

In summary, studies have reported the deceleration of behavior of severely and profoundly retarded individuals following response contingent punishment. Further, punishing one response does appear to greatly aid the acquisition of other available one (e.g., Blackwood, 1962; Henriksen & Doughty, 1967; Risley, 1968; Whitney & Barnard, 1966).

Are the Effects of Punishment Temporary? Is There a Relationship between the Intensity of Punishment and the Degree of Response Deceleration?

In contrast to Skinner's position (1938, 1948, 1953, 1961) that punishment does not weaken operant behavior but merely produces temporary suppression, recent studies provide support for the position that punishing stimuli may produce long term deceleration effects (e.g., Appel, 1963; Azrin & Holz, 1961; Karsh, 1963; Walters & Rogers, 1963). This is especially true, as Solomon (1964) has noted, when "the response-suppression period is tactically used as an aid to the reinforcement of news responses that are topographically *incompatible* with the punished ones" [p. 241]. Azrin and Holz (1966) in evaluating the "temporary effect" question conclude from their comprehensive review of basic laboratory studies that "punishment really does 'weaken' a response in the same sense that other procedures for reducing behavior 'weaken' behavior. Indeed, punishment appears to be potentially more effective than other procedures for weakening a response" [p. 436].

With few exceptions, the studies involving retarded subjects described in the present review reported deceleration results which extended considerably beyond the treatment period. As noted earlier, in most instances positive reinforcement was used for the instatement and acceleration of alternative, although not in every case incompatible responses, e.g., attention and praise was provided following desirable behavior, food which was withdrawn after inappropriate behavior was returned following prosocial responses. Although few of the studies provided data relative to the theoretical issue of whether the deceleration of performance of the punished response was due to a weakening of the habit or whether the reinforced competing responses merely displaced the punished behavior, such an issue is of minor importance in a program designed to evaluate treatment procedure as long as the punished behavior does not reappear. In summary, there is some support for the position that the deceleration effects of punishment are not temporary when used in a broader program of behavior instatement and acceleration of prosocial responses.

Bucher and Lovaas (1968), in commenting on the durability of behavior suppression following electric shock, suggested that the "post-treatment" environment would be rather critical as subjects in their studies demonstrated rather extensive discriminations among adults, physical settings, and the like. That is, if behavior is suppressed in one environment, it is not necessarily suppressed in another. This was supported by Hamilton and Standahl (1967) and Risley (1968). If the environment that previously reinforced the shock-suppressed behavior remains unchanged, it is highly likely that the behavior would reappear. These studies demonstrated however, that response contingent punishment provided in new situations did result in systematic elimination of the behavior.

Although no study was concerned with a parametric analysis of punishment (i.e., none evaluated the possible effects, for example, of varying the length of time-out or the length or frequency of electric shock), the studies using electric shock do provide some suggestions concerning the relationship between the intensity of the punishing stimulus and the behavioral effect. White and Taylor (1967) reported that their subjects adapted fairly quickly to a mild shock of approximately 400 volts at 1 milliamp. The writers felt that shock at this intensity might have functioned even as positive reinforcement. The voltage was increased to approximately 500–700 volts before it appeared to exert a punishment effect. Hamilton and Standahl (1967), after obtaining behavior suppression effects initially, found an adaptation effect to electric shock delivered through two electrodes attached to a belt worn around the subject's waist. The punished behavior returned to pretreatment level and was decelerated only after the shock intensity was increased. Banks and Locke (1966) obtained only temporary suppression of self-destructive behavior with the use of mild physical punishment. However, as noted earlier, the punishment regimen was so limited in time that no meaningful generalization is possible from that report. Although no definitive position evolves from the data, there does appear to be some suggestion that for the severely/profoundly retarded a relationship does exist between intensity of punishment and behavior suppression effect. Obviously studies which vary intensity of punishment in a systematic manner are needed.

Does Punishment Produce Disruptive and Chronic Undesirable Emotional States or General Chronic Behavioral Disruption?

Punishment frequently is not used in a behavioral modification program due to the belief that aversive stimuli produce undesirable emotional states. Behavioral rigidity, general disruption of cognitive processes, production of neurotic syndrome, suppression effects not specific to the responses punished, and chronic emotional maladjustment are but a few of the negative side effects attributed to punishment (Azrin & Holz, 1966; Church, 1963; Solomon, 1964).

The question was not evaluated satisfactorily by the studies reviewed. However, many expressed a concern for this question and presented relevant anecdotal reports. Contrary to expectations, widespread behavioral improvement rather than disruption was generally reported. Risley (1968), after careful evaluation of behaviors which occurred in the punishment (shock) sessions, concluded, "No suppression of other behaviors was noted, either through generalization of the punishment effect or through conditioned 'emotional' suppression, correlated with the punishment of the target behaviors. . . . The brevity of the general suppression directly produced by the shock, if any, is indicated by the subject obtaining and consuming food within 70 sec. after the first shock" [p. 33].

Tate and Baroff (1966) reported that on control days when no response-contingent punishment was in effect, the subject "typically whined, cried, hesitated often in his walk, and seemed unresponsive to the environment in general" [p. 283]. On experimental days, during which withdrawal of physical contact followed a self-injurious response, subject "appeared to attend more to the environment stimuli, including the experimenters; there was no crying or whining, and he often smiled" [p. 283]. This provides a dramatic example of the possible beneficial effects which response contingent punishment can exert on individuals who exhibit chronic high frequency maladaptive responses. After initiating use of electric shock, these writers reported the observation that shock produced no observable deleterious effects in emotional state or in social interaction. On the contrary, punishment frequently resulted in a more alert, cooperative, smiling, and relaxed child. Bucher and Lovaas (1968), Lovaas et al. (1965), and Luckey, Watson, and Musick (1968) reported highly similar reactions of decrease in whining, fussing, and crying and an increase in alertness, affection, and general social responsiveness in their work with severely retarded and autistic children. These changes in behavior were reported to result in a positive change in the behavior of attendants and nurses toward the subjects. As valuable behavior appeared, the social environment was more likely to attend to and reinforce a wide range of other appropriate behaviors.

In summary, although caution must be exercised in generalizing from these reports, the impression is gained that emotional or behavior disruption is not a necessary result of punishment when used with the severely and profoundly retarded. Conversely, it should not be assumed that the side-effects of punishment should always be neutral or desirable. As suggested by Bucher and Lovaas (1968) the reinforcement history of subjects should influence the specific side-effects which result. Obviously, this complex question requires further investigation.

Is Social Disruption a Consequence of the Use of Punishment with the Severely Retarded? Do Symptom Substitution and/or Other Negative Side Effects Occur?

The purpose of punishment is to eliminate specific inappropriate behaviors and to leave intact other behavior patterns. One of the dangers of using a punishment procedure is that the treatment personnel will acquire some properties of an aversive stimulus and evoke escape and avoidance behavior. Thus, potentially social disruption may occur in subjects who least need such behavior strengthened. The present writer agrees with Colwell's (1966) argument that punishment as frequently used in institutions for the mentally retarded is likely to produce negative reactions to authority figures. In such settings, punishment often is inappropriate both in frequency and intensity and in its proximity to the punished behavior.

Punishment applied appropriately, however, holds promise of being effective without precipitating harmful side effects of social disruption. This is supported by data and anecdotal reports from studies of Risley (1968), Hamilton et al. (1967), and Whitney and Barnard (1966). Risley (1968) evaluated the effects of electric shock on frequency of eye contact with the adult delivering the punishment. Hutt and Ounsted (1966) have predicted that increasing the level of arousal and anxiety of a child would result in a decrease in eye contacts. Contrary to this theoretical position, frequency of eye contact actually increased. This was the only observed change in the subject's behavior toward the therapist. No punishment related aggressive behavior was noted toward any person or object in the laboratory or in the home, even following punishment of the subject's aggressive behavior toward his brother. One side effect which could be labeled as "symptom substitution" was observed. When climbing on a bookcase was punished, the subject began to engage in a topographically similar behavior of chair climbing. This behavior was quickly eliminated when also punished and no other undesirable behaviors appeared. Risley concluded that, "The most significant side effect was the fact that eliminating climbing and autistic rocking with punishment facilitated the acquisition of new desirable behaviors" [p. 33]. Both frequency of eye contact and rate of imitation behavior were increased. Risley suggested the possibility that stereotyped behaviors of deviant children are "functionally incompatible" with the development of new socially desirable behaviors. In this case reported, socially appropriate behaviors were established as stereotyped behaviors were eliminated through punishment.

Hamilton, Stevens, and Allen (1967) reported no cases of negative symptom substitution or any other undesirable side effect. These writers concluded "On the contrary, residents whose unacceptable behaviors were suppressed as a result of the punishment procedure were judged by the ward personnel to be more socially outgoing, happier, and better adjusted in the ward setting" [p. 856]. Whitney and Barnard (1966), after controlling inappropriate eating behavior by means of physical restraint, verbal punishment and time-out, noted that subject no longer removed her clothing, did not play with her feces, nor take food from other residents.

White and Taylor (1967) presented some interesting ideas concerning the positive side effects of electric shock punishment in their comments that the procedure:

> . . . appears to afford a means of developing an interpersonal relationship as it presents a stimulus to the subject which is powerful enough to serve as an identifiable reinforcer. Both subjects, apparently as a consequence of the treatment, appeared to be more aware of and interact more with the examiners than other personnel and other staff members [p. 32].

And later, "the noxious conditioning procedure seems to work well in eliminating responses in patients where it is important to communicate on a physiological level . . ." [p. 33].

In summary, although the data are limited, the studies reviewed would support the cautious position that it is possible to use punishment with the severely and profoundly retarded without producing social disruption or other negative side effects.

Is Punishment Effective in Eliminating Self-destructive Behavior?

It is not unusual for the retarded in a residential setting to be placed in restraints throughout the day due to high rate self-destructive behavior (e.g., Bucher & Lovaas, 1968; Hamilton, Stevens, & Allen, 1967; Tate & Baroff, 1966). When physically possible subjects engage in head banging, window breaking, slapping, scratching, biting, eye gouging, and the like. Basic laboratory research (e.g., Holz & Azrin, 1961; Muenzinger, 1934) provides a possible explanation for the development of this rather paradoxical masochistic behavior. The aversive stimulation of self-injurious responses becomes discriminative for subsequent presentation of positive reinforcement and, theoretically, acquires secondary reinforcement properties. It is difficult in analyzing such behavior in the retarded, however, to identify any subsequent reinforcement conditions and to control the contingencies so as to reduce the discriminative and reinforcing properties of such self-destructive behaviors.

Response contingent application of aversive stimuli differing from those which are directly related to the self-destructive behaviors has been used successfully to disrupt and eliminate such habits. Bucher and Lovaas (1968) and Tate and Baroff (1966), using electric shock, and Hamilton, Stephens, and Allen (1967), using a physical restraint-time-out procedure, reported dramatic treatment results. Apparently the punishing stimuli can be effective in these cases due to their pure aversive properties, i.e., these stimuli have not acquired positive reinforcing function.

Is Punishment Effective with the Unsocialized Profoundly Retarded?

For many severely/profoundly retarded with minimal social language or social conscience, such behaviors as chronic masturbation, rectal digging, feces smearing and eating, chronic self-stimulation, and reingestion of vomitus are correct—incorrect or acceptable—unacceptable only in terms of the immediate stimulus consequences. No social amenities, supergo, internal controls, or the like can be counted on to provide controlling cues of conditioned aversive consequences for such unacceptable behavior. In addition, in many instances it is difficult to identify reinforcers which are powerful enough to compete successfully with those that apparently maintain these behaviors.

In such instances response contingent aversive stimuli in combination with systematic positive reinforcement would appear to facilitate the development of alternative behaviors which would replace these highly socially unacceptable responses. Punishment would be used to "define" the incorrect response and to render more likely the occurrence of correct ones (e.g., Blackwood, 1962; Edwards & Lilly, 1966; Hamilton & Standahl, 1967).

With What Types of Behavior Is Punishment Most Effective?

As noted in the review of studies, punishment operations have been effectively used with a wide class of behaviors, ranging from specific habit disorders to chronic high rate stereotyped responses. While no research program has reported systematic investigation of this question, Hamilton et al. (1967) have provided some observations concerning the types of behavior which responded most favorably to punishment procedure. These observations provide a suggestive basis for further research. In work with a number of retarded subjects presenting a variety of problem behaviors, these writers reported punishment to be very effective in rapid and total elimination of single specific behavior which occurred with little variation in frequency or type and which seldom involved direct interaction with others (e.g., clothes tearing, head-banging). Single specific behaviors which occurred with variable frequency and/or intensity and which typically involved interaction with others (e.g., physical abuse of others) required longer treatment periods and seldom were completely eliminated. General misbehavior consisting of a wide variety of inappropriate behaviors was reported to show least dramatic improvement, although marked improvement was obtained even in complicated cases of this kind. These observations were generally supported by the punishment studies reviewed.

CONCLUSIONS

As Solomon suggested in 1964, studies of the effects of punishment have been hampered unnecessarily by certain unscientific legends concerning this stimulus condition. Although most of the studies reviewed could be criticized from a rigorous functional analysis position, the deficiencies in methodological sophistication are somewhat offset by the consistency and nature of results provided which call into question some of the more stultifying of the legends. As a general conclusion, the studies reviewed lend some support to the feasibility of application of a variety of punishment procedures in work with the severely and profoundly functioning person and, as Risley (1968) has suggested, "do serve to limit the generality of extrapolations from past research which contraindicates the use of punishment" [p. 34]. The results call for an empirical approach to the question of the efficacy of punishment and rejection of a categorical position that would not facilitate continued investigation of the behavior effects of these procedures.

It is quite apparent that considerable research must be completed prior to the general acceptance of punishment as a treatment approach. Examples of specific research questions which evolve out of the studies reviewed include: (a) Are the behavior suppression effects of punishment specific to the behavior punished as well as to the situational cues present during punishment? Bucher and Lovaas (1968), Hamilton and Standahl (1967), and Risley (1968) all commented on the highly specific suppressive effects of punishment. Risley reported that suppressive effects did not even generalize to behavior that was topographically quite similar to the punished behavior. How reliable are these observations? (b) What are the specific side effects of punishment? Writers who commented on this question expressed surprise that there were significant positive side effects. How general are these effects? (c) Is the "functional incompatibility" hypothesis of Risley (1968) tenable? If so, with what classes of stereotyped behaviors? Could such a concept lend some assistance in decision making concerning the appropriateness of punishment in specific cases?

These are merely representative of the extensive work with a wide range of problems, types and intensities of punishment stimuli, and subject characteristics which must be completed prior to presenting a definitive statement of the effects of punishment. Until further data are available, use of punishment techniques in clinical practice should be preceded by a careful consideration of alternative procedures. In those instances in which punishment is the treatment of choice, highly controlled procedures of delivery of punishment and measurement of effects as dictated by a functional analysis of behavior approach should add considerably to its clinical value.

References

Appel, J. B. Punishment and shock intensity. *Science,* 1963, *141,* 528–529.

Azrin, N. H., & Holz, W. C. Punishment during fixed–interval reinforcement. *Journal of Experimental Analysis of Behavior,* 1961, *4,* 343–347.

Azrin, N. H., & Holz, W. C. Punishment. In W. K. Honig (ed.), *Operant behavior: Areas of research and application.* New York: Appleton-Century-Crofts, 1966. Pp. 380–447.

Banks, M., & Locke, B. J. Self-injurious stereotypes and mild punishment with retarded subjects. Working Paper #123. Parsons Research Project, University of Kansas, 1966.

Bensberg, G. J., Colwell, C. N., & Cassel, R. H. Teaching the profoundly retarded self-help activities by behavior shaping techniques. *American Journal of Mental Deficiency,* 1965, *69,* 674–679.

Birnbrauer, J. S., Bijou, S. W., Wolf, M. M., & Kidder, J. D. Programmed instruction in the classroom. In L. P. Ullman & L. Krasner (eds.), *Case studies in behavior modification.* New York: Holt, Rinehart & Winston, 1965. Pp. 358–363.

Blackwood, R. O. Operant conditioning as a method of training the mentally retarded. Unpublished doctoral dissertation, Ohio State University, 1962.

Bucher, B., & Lovaas, O. I. Use of aversive stimulation in behavior modification. In M. R. Jones (ed.), *Miami symposium on the prediction of behavior, 1967: Aversive stimulation.* Coral Gables, Florida: University of Miami Press, 1968. Pp. 77–145.

Church, R. M. The varied effects of punishment on behavior. *Psychological Review,* 1963, *70,* 369–402.

Colwell, C. N. The role of operant techniques in cottage and ward life programs. Paper presented at the meeting of the American Association on Mental Deficiency, Chicago, 1966.

Dinsmoor, J. A. Comments on Wetzel's treatment of a case of compulsive stealing. *Journal of Consulting Psychology,* 1966, *30,* 378–380.

Edwards, M., & Lilly, R. T. Operant conditioning: an application to behavioral problems in groups. *Mental Retardation,* 1966, *4,* 18–20.

Ferster, C. B., & Appel, J. B. Punishment of $S^{\triangle}$ responding in match to sample by time out from positive reinforcement. *Journal of Experimental Analysis of Behavior,* 1961, *4,* 45–56.

Ferster, C. B., and Skinner, B. F. *Schedules of reinforcement.* New York: Appleton-Century-Crofts, 1957.

Gelfand, D. M., & Hartmann, D. P. Behavior therapy with children: A review and evaluation of research methodology. *Psychological Bulletin,* 1968, *69,* 204–215.

Giles, D. K., & Wolf, M. M. Toilet training institutionalized, severe retardates: an application of operant behavior modification procedures. *American Journal of Mental Deficiency,* 1966, *70,* 765–780.

Hamilton, J., & Allen, P. Ward programming for severely retarded institutionalized residents. *Mental Retardation,* 1967, *5,* 22–24.

Hamilton, J., & Standahl, J. Suppression of stereotyped screaming behavior in a profoundly retarded institutionalized female. Unpublished paper, Gracewood State School, Georgia, 1967.

Hamilton, J., Stephens, L., & Allen, P. Controlling aggressive and destructive behavior in severely retarded institutionalized residents. *American Journal of Mental Deficiency,* 1967, *71,* 852–856.

Hamilton, J., & Stephens, L. Reinstating speech in an emotionally disturbed mentally retarded young woman. Unpublished paper, Gracewood State School, Georgia, 1967.

Henriksen, K., & Doughty, R. Decelerating undesirable mealtime behavior in a group of profoundly retarded boys. *American Journal of Mental Deficiency,* 1967, *72,* 40–44.

Herrnstein, R. J. Behavioral consequences of the removal of a discriminative stimulus associated with variable-interval reinforcement. Unpublished doctoral dissertation, Harvard University, 1955.

Hill, W. F. Sources of evaluative reinforcement. *Psychological Bulletin,* 1968, *69,* 132–146.

Holz, W. C., Azrin, N. H., & Ayllon, T. Elimination of behavior of mental patients by response-produced extinction. *Journal of Experimental Analysis of Behavior,* 1963, *6,* 407–412.

Honig, W. K. (ed.). *Operant behavior: Areas of research and application.* New York: Appleton-Century-Crofts, 1966.

Hutt, C., & Ounsted, C. The biological significance of gaze aversion with particular reference to the syndrome of infantile autism. *Behavioral Science,* 1966, *11,* 346–356.

Karsh, E. B. Changes in intensity of punishment: Effect on runway behavior of rats. *Science,* 1963, *140,* 1084–1085.

Leff, R. Behavior modification and the psychoses of childhood: A review. *Psychological Bulletin,* 1968, *69,* 396–409.

Leitenberg, H. Is time out from positive reinforcement an aversive event? A review. *Psychological Bulletin,* 1965, *64,* 428–441.

Lovaas, O. I., Freitag, G., Gold, V. J., & Kassorla, I. C. Experimental studies in childhood schizophrenia: Analysis of self-destructive behavior. *Journal of Experimental Child Psychology,* 1965, *2,* 67–84.

Lovaas, O. I., Freitag, G., Kinder, M. I., Rubenstein, D. B., Schaeffer, B., & Simmons, J. Q. Experimental studies in childhood schizophrenia. Developing behavior using electric shock. Paper presented at the meeting of the American Psychological Association, Los Angeles, 1964.

Lovaas, O. I., Schaeffer, B., & Simmons, J. Q. Building social behavior in autistic children by use of electric shock. *Journal of Experimental Research in Personality,* 1965, *1,* 99–109.

Luckey, R. E., Watson, C. M., & Musick, J. K. Aversive conditioning as a means of inhibiting vomiting and rumination. *American Journal of Mental Deficiency*, 1968, *73*, 139–142.

Marshall, G. R. Toilet training of an autistic eight-year-old through conditioning therapy: a case report. *Behavior Research and Therapy*, 1966, *4*, 242–245.

Marshall, H. H. The effects of punishment on children: A review of the literature and a suggested hypothesis. *Journal of Genetic Psychology*, 1965, *106*, 23–33.

Muenzinger, K. F. Motivation in learning: I. Electric shock for correct responses in the visual discrimination habit. *Journal of Comparative Psychology*, 1934, *17*, 439–448.

Peterson, R. F., & Peterson, L. R. Mark and his blanket: a study of self-destructive behavior in a retarded boy. Paper presented at meeting of Society for Research in Child Development, New York, 1967.

Risley, T. The effects and side effects of punishing the autistic behaviors of a deviant child. *Journal of Applied Behavior Analysis*, 1968, *1*, 21–34.

Sidman, M. *Tactics of scientific research*. New York: Basic Books, 1960.

Sidman, M. Operant techniques. In A. L. Bachrach (ed.), *Experimental foundations of clinical psychology*. New York: Basic Books, 1962.

Skinner, B. F. *The behavior of organisms*. New York: Appleton-Century, 1938.

Skinner, B. F. *Walden two*. New York: Macmillan, 1948.

Skinner, B. F. *Science and human behavior*. New York: Macmillan, 1953.

Skinner, B. F. *Cumulative record*. New York: Macmillan, 1961.

Solomon, R. L. Punishment. *American Psychologist*, 1964, *19*, 239–253.

Spradlin, J. E., & Girardeau, F. L. The behavior of moderately and severely retarded persons. In N. Ellis (ed.), *International review of research in mental retardation*. Vol. 1. New York: Academic Press, 1966. Pp. 257–298.

Striefel, S. Isolation as a behavioral management procedure with retarded children. Working Paper #156. Parsons Research Project, University of Kansas, 1967.

Tate, B. G., & Baroff, G. S. Aversive control of self-injurious behavior in a psychotic boy. *Behavior Research and Therapy*, 1966, *4*, 281–287.

Verhave, T. *The experimental analysis of behavior*. New York: Appleton-Century-Crofts, 1966.

Walters, G. C., & Rogers, J. V. Aversive stimulation of the rat: long term effects of subsequent behavior. *Science*, 1963, *142*, 70–71.

Watson, L. S. Application of behavior shaping devices to training severely and profoundly mentally retarded children in an institutional setting. Paper presented at the meeting of the Midwestern Psychological Association, Chicago, 1966.

Watson, L. S. Application of operant conditioning techniques to institutionalized severely and profoundly retarded children. *Mental Retardation Abstracts*, 1967, *4*, 1–18.

Watson, L. S., & Sanders, C. C. Stimulus control with severely and profoundly retarded children under varying stimulus conditions in a free-operant situation. Paper presented at the meeting of the American Association on Mental Deficiency, Chicago, 1966.

Weiner, H. Some effects of response cost upon human operant behavior. *Journal of Experimental Analysis of Behavior,* 1962, *5,* 201–208.

White, J. C., Jr., & Taylor, D. Noxious conditioning as a treatment for rumination. *Mental Retardation,* 1967, *6,* 30–33.

Whitney, L. R., & Barnard, K. E. Implications of operant learning theory for nursing care of the retarded child. *Mental Retardation,* 1966, *4,* 26–29.

Wiesen, A. E., & Watson, E. Elimination of attention seeking behavior in a retarded child. *American Journal of Mental Deficiency,* 1967, *72,* 50–52.

Wolf, M. M., Birnbrauer, J. S., Williams, T., & Lawler, J. A note on apparent extinction of the vomiting behavior of a retarded child. In L. P. Ullman & L. Krasner (eds.), *Case studies in behavior modification.* New York: Holt, Rinehart & Winston, 1965. Pp. 364–366.

Zimmerman, J., & Baydan, N. T. Punishment of S^{Δ} responding of humans in conditional matching-to-sample by time-out. *Journal of Experimental Analysis of Behavior,* 1963, *6,* 589–597.

10

Effects of a Severely Mentally Retarded Child on the Family

Bernard Farber

Dr. Farber is Professor in the Department of Sociology at the University of Illinois. He has published several monographs on the impact of a mentally deficient child on the family structure and factors in the family setting that should be considered in determining whether or not to institutionalize the child. More recently he has written a book, Mental Retardation: Its Social Context and Social Consequences, *which appeared in 1968.*

The investigations summarized in this paper were supported by grants from the Psychiatric Training and Research Fund of the Illinois Department of Public Welfare and the National Institute of Mental Health, U.S. Public Health Service, while Dr. Farber was associated with the Institute for Research on Exceptional Children at the University of Illinois.

In this provocative and frequently quoted article, the author has summarized his research in this important area and suggests further problems to investigate. The student should be aware of the crisis inflicted upon families of mentally deficient children, and how research tools in the field of psychology and sociology can be applied to the study and understanding of these families.

In recent personal communication with Dr. Farber, he commented on an unpublished Ph.D. dissertation at the University of

Illinois which has relevance to his article. These comments appear at the very end of his article under the section "Epilogue (1972)."

Parents, teachers, social workers, and other educational and medical personnel have long recognized the marked impact of a severely mentally retarded child on family relations. In the course of their work, they have had to offer suggestions to parents regarding the handling of the child based on personal opinion. Even with persons of long experience, the opinions may have been derived from atypical cases which stood out in the professional person's mind.

Decisions regarding the handling of a retarded child in relation to the rest of his family can have a profound influence on the lives of all of the family members. To provide a factual or objective basis for judgment, it is necessary to investigate effects of the child on the family in a systematic way. Research, however, can reveal only general tendencies. For each particular family the situation differs somewhat. In making decisions, the parents and professionals must determine the way in which that family is atypical and make appropriate allowance.

Below, two types of family crisis precipitated by the severely mentally retarded child are described as a basis for understanding how parents react to the child. The studies, which are then summarized, deal with three problems relating to the family crisis. These problems are: (a) effects of a retarded child on families trying to handle the child in the home, (b) family factors in the decision to institutionalize the child, and (c) adjustment of the family to the institutionalization of the child.

DESCRIPTION OF THE SAMPLES AND PROCEDURES OF THE STUDIES

The findings presented here were based upon interviews with two samples of families living in the Chicágo area. The first sample (Sample A) consisted of 240 families; the interviewing for the first sample took place in 1955–56. The second sample (Sample B) consisted of 268 families with a retarded child living at home; the interviewing for the second sample took place in 1958–59. Samples A and B included 40 of the same families.

The parents included in Sample A had been contacted through the mailing lists of the parent associations for promoting the welfare of the retarded. Of the 240 families included in Sample A, interviews with both husband and wife were conducted in 233 families; the husbands in the remaining seven families did not participate *(Farber 1960a)*. In order to define the limitations of the applicability of the findings, analysis was restricted to families with the following characteristics:

1. Both parents were Caucasian.
2. Only one child in the family was regarded as severely mentally

retarded by the parents. (With minor exceptions, the child had an IQ of 50 or under.)

3. The retarded child was aged 16 or under.

4. The parents were married and living together in the Chicago area at the time of the study.

5. The retarded child was born in the present marriage.

The characteristics of the 233 families in Sample A in which both parents were interviewed are presented in Table I.

The parents included in Sample B had been contacted through (a) the mailing lists of parent associations and (b) the waiting lists of the state institutions for the mentally retarded. The sample restrictions were the same as those placed upon Sample A except that nonwhites were included and the maximum age of the retarded child was changed to 15. Furthermore, Sample B included only families with a retarded child at home. The characteristics of the 268 families in Sample B appear in Table II *(Farber, Jenne, and Toigo, 1960)*.

The data in the studies were gathered in interviews with the parents of the retarded child conducted in the home. Two trained interviewers (usually social workers) visited the home by appointment. While one interviewer talked with the husband, the other interviewed the wife. This eliminated the possibility of collusion. The interviews consisted of two parts: An oral, face-to-face interview, and a questionnaire completed by the parents in the presence of the interviewer. The oral section of the interview permitted the parents to elaborate responses pertaining to the child's retardation and his impact on the family. The questionnaires consisted mainly of scales and indices pertaining to family relations and personal reactions to the child. Questions in the interview as well as the techniques of analysis are described elsewhere *(Farber, 1959)*.

TYPES OF FAMILY CRISIS

The existence of a family crisis depends upon the extent to which the family members regard an event as disrupting or frustrating present or future family life. If the event is defined by the family members as *no different in any* way from the situation they had expected to encounter and if these individuals believe that the family routines they have developed will meet the situation, there is no crisis. A retarded child (as defined medically and psychologically) is regarded as injecting the *potentiality* of crisis into family relations. Once the parent considers his child as severely mentally retarded, he must then revaluate the efficacy of the norms and roles in the family for meeting the situation of having a mentally retarded child. Only when the parents perceive this child as mentally retarded and define their present norms and roles as inadequate does the crisis develop.

Table I *Characteristics of Members of 233 Families Included in Sample A*

ATTRIBUTE OF INDIVIDUAL OR FAMILY	Categories	Summary Description
1. Number of families studied	—	233
2. Sex of the retarded child	Boy	142
	Girl	91
3. Residence of the retarded child	At home	168
	Public institution	49
	Private institution	16
4. Mean number of years parents of retarded child had been married	—	14.6 years
5. Mean age of parents of retarded child	Mothers	38.7 years
	Fathers	41.1 years
6. Percentage of parents in their first marriage	—	90%
7. Percentage of parents who had completed high school (12 years of education)	Mothers	63%
	Fathers	69%
8. Religious preference or affiliation of the husbands	Protestant	106
	Catholic	80
	Jewish	30
	None or unknown	17
9. Median income of families in 1955	—	$5,900
10. Percentage of 233 husbands at each socioeconomic occupational level	Professional and technical workers	24%
	Managers and proprietors	24%
	Clerical and sales workers	11%
	Craftsmen and foremen	24%
	Semiskilled and unskilled workers	16%
	Others (unknown; farm occupation)	1%
11. Mean number of children per family	—	2.7 children
12. Mean age of retarded child	—	8.6 years

Table II Characteristics of Members of 268 Families with a Retarded Child Living at Home Included in Sample B

ATTRIBUTE OF INDIVIDUAL OR FAMILY	Categories	Summary Description
1. Number of families studied	—	268
2. Percentage of retarded children of each sex	Boy	61%
	Girl	39%
3. Percentage of families with both parents Caucasian	—	91%
4. Mean number of years parents of retarded child had been married	—	13.8 years
5. Mean age of parents of retarded child	Mothers	37.6 years
	Fathers	40.5 years
6. Percentage of parents in their first marriage	Mothers	89%
	Fathers	88%
7. Percentage of families in which both parents are native-born	—	89%
8. Percentage of parents who had completed high school (12 years of education)	Mothers	62%
	Fathers	62%
9. Percentage of wives with religious preference or affiliation	Protestant	47%
	Catholic	39%
	Jewish	11%
	Other, none, or unknown	3%
10. Median family income in previous year	—	$6,155
11. Percentage of 268 husbands at each socio-economic occupational level	*High:* Professional and technical workers, sales workers, managers and proprietors	42%
	Middle: Clerical workers, craftsmen and foremen	32%
	Low: Semiskilled and unskilled workers	26%
12. Mean number of living children in each family	—	2.8 children
13. Mean age of retarded child	—	7.5 years

In the studies reported here, two kinds of crisis were considered: The tragic crisis and the role-organization crisis. These types represent different ways by which the parents perceive disruption in family life *(Farber, 1960b)*.

Tragic Crisis

In the tragic crisis, the aims, aspirations, and anticipated "happy" family life are frustrated. The retardation is regarded by the parents as an uncontrollable event preventing fulfillment of their hopes and aspirations. Since the retarded child himself is identified as the reason for their frustration, hostility tends to be directed toward him.

While the retarded child is regarded as the precipitator of frustration, various factors prevent the parent from acting aggressively against the child. First, the parent cannot regard the child as having become retarded intentionally. Secondly, the parent may even view the child's retardation as only one link in a chain of events resulting from the parent's own activity or personal attributes. Hence, he cannot easily rationalize his hostility toward the child; he is motivated to continue in his parental role of providing love and care for the child.

In high socioeconomic status families there is a tendency for individuals to give conformity to expectations and obligations priority over expression of impulsive personal gratification. Since parents in high socioeconomic status place much emphasis on attainment of longe-range ends, there are especially vulnerable to the development of the tragic family crisis.

Role-Organization Crisis

In the role-organization crisis, the predicament facing the parents is not one of frustration of aims and aspirations but one of coping with a seemingly interminable care problem during which the normal family lifecycle is arrested. Ordinarily, mothers with normal children can visualize that eventually the children will achieve independence; the mother with severely retarded child faces a prolonged infancy period and the prospect that socially the child will never achieve adulthood.

Essentially, whereas the tragic crisis develops mainly through the emergence of problems regarding ends of family life (i.e., aims, aspirations, values), the role-organization crisis is concerned with the inability to organize a system of workable roles or means. The presence of a system of workable roles implies an ability to control activities of the individual members. Hence, unlike the tragic crisis, role-organization crisis occurs in the realm of what is regarded as controllable by the family members.

The probability of the occurrence of a role-organization crisis would be high among those groups in which emphasis upon parental control is great, but long-range ends of family life are not especially stressed. According to a study by Kohn (*1959*), working-class mothers emphasize obedience and responsiveness to parental authority as values in the socialization of children. Since these values are related mainly to parental control, we would expect to find role-organization crisis most pronounced in families of low socioeconomic status.

Tragic vs. Role Organization Crisis: Empirical Data

The distinction between the tragic crisis and role-organization crisis was assumed to be one of concern over future aspirations and aims as opposed to concern over immediate organization of family roles. This difference in emphasis provided a basis for classifying mothers by their reported reactions to the retarded child.

To provide a classification which would utilize the more extreme cases, mothers were categorized as "nervous," "sick," or control group (i.e., neither). The basis for this classification was as follows:

If the parent faced with a tragic crisis regards her responsibilities to the child as of utmost importance, she must consider herself physically capable of assuming these responsibilities. Since the role of a sick person implies inability to carry out ordinary expectations, the parent feels constrained against assuming this role. Hence, the parent tends to view herself as being in good health.

Thus, the parent in the tragic crisis situation (a) regards herself as being in good health and (b) experiences tension over the conflict between her hostility for the retarded child and her sense of parental responsibility. Recognition by the mother of this personal tension was indicated in her report of treatment for a nervous condition following the diagnosis of retardation.

A mother faced with a role-organization crisis becomes increasingly involved with the retarded child and isolated from the rest of the family. She cannot develop roles (acceptable to her) which can control husband-wife and mother-child interaction. The strain and overwork in trying to develop acceptable roles could easily affect her physical being. The presence of physical symptoms may offer to her a solution to what seems an impossible situation. By definition, a sick person is incapable of acting on conformity with high expectations through no fault of his own. A profound sense of incapability to perform roles adequately together with the physical symptoms would make it possible for the wife to assume the role of a sick person. Therefore, if the mother perceives the child as making very great demands on her, which she cannot satisfy regardless of her effort, to defend herself from a complete breakdown, in the extreme case, she may develop a self-identity as a person in poor health. (Supporting this contention are the findings of Hinkle (*1959*) that unhealthy people tend to be more nonconformist and more highly emotionally involved with other persons than are healthy persons.)

The control group consisted of mothers who reported that they were in good health and that they had *not* been treated for a nervous condition. The presence of a control group does not imply that there was no crisis in these families. Instead, crisis for the control-group mothers is regarded as having been somewhat less severe than that for the others.

Pertinent information for the study was obtained through several scales:

Scale of initial emotional impact of the diagnosis of severe mental retardation The scale consisted of responses to the question: When you found out definitely that your child was mentally retarded, how did you react? The items used in the scale had been developed from open-ended responses of parents in an earlier study *(Farber, 1959)*. The respondent was asked to check "very much," "somewhat," or "not at all" for the following items, which are listed in order of increasing impact according to Guttman scale analysis:

1. I felt is was the biggest tragedy of my life (item of least impact).
2. I was very bitter and miserable.
3. I went to pieces; my world fell apart.
4. I felt the whole world was against us.
5. I avoided telling relatives.
6. I felt somehow that is was my husband's fault (item of highest impact).

The response categories were combined to form dichotomies; the scale met Guttman criteria for unidimensionality.

Scale of demands of the retarded child on the mother This unidimensional scale was regarded as a scale of the current personal impact of the retarded child on the mother. Each respondent was asked the extent to which the following items, derived from open-ended responses in an earlier study *(Farber, 1959)*, were descriptive of the situation:

1. Our retarded child needs patience and understanding.
2. Our retarded child is hard to handle.
3. I feel worn out from taking care of our retarded child.
4. My life revolves around the retarded child.

Response categories were combined to form dichotomies; the scale met Guttman criteria for unidimensionality.

Willingness to institutionalize the retarded child This scale was developed with the following items in response to "Below are statements concerning you and your retarded child. For each statement, please check the answer that best describes you." The response categories were "very much," "somewhat," and "not at all." The statements were:

1. My husband and I have discussed the possibility of placing our retarded child at (names of state schools) or other residential school.

2. I have thought about placing our retarded child at . . . .
3. I am willing to place our retarded child at . . . .
4. I am too attached to our retarded child now to place him at . . . .

The willingness scale consisted of the above four items, which were scored as trichotomies to form a unidimensional Guttman scale.

Index of marital integration The index of marital integration has been applied in several studies *(Farber, 1957, 1959, 1960a)*. The index consists of two parts: (a) a consensus index or extent to which husband and wife agree in their ranking of a list of ten domestic values in order of their perceived importance for family success and (b) an index of tension in the marital role system.

The results of the study *(Farber, 1960b)* are described below:

1. Mothers who had been treated for a nervous condition reported a greater initial impact of the diagnosis of retardation than did control group mothers. The mothers who had been treated for a nervous condition tended to agree only with the statements, (a) "I felt that it was the biggest tragedy of my life"; (b) "I was very bitter and miserable"; and (c) "I went to pieces (and) my world fell apart." The mothers in the control group, however, tended to agree with the first two statements (a and b).

2. Mothers who had been treated for a nervous condition generally had a lower marital integration score than did control group mothers.

3. Mothers who had been treated for a nervous condition tended to preceive the retarded child as making greater demands upon them than did control group mothers. The control mothers, generally responded "very much" to the item, "Our retarded child needs patience and understanding." The mothers treated for a nervous condition, in addition, tended to agree that "Our retarded child is hard to handle."

4. There was little difference in willingness to institutionalize the retarded child between mothers who had received treatment for a nervous condition and mothers in the control group. With respect to scale type, on the average, the mothers responded "not at all" to being willing to institutionalize the child.

In an analysis of data relating to health, the control group mothers were split into two subgroups: Mothers reporting good health without qualification and mothers reporting good health with some qualification.

5. There was little difference in initial impact of the diagnosis of mental retardation upon the mothers in the unqualified good, qualified good, and poor health categories. On the average, the mothers agreed only with the statements that "I felt that it was the biggest tragedy of my life" and "I was very bitter and miserable."

6. Mothers who reported that they were not in good health had a lower marital integration score than did the mothers in the good-health and qualified-good-health categories.

7. Mothers reporting themselves not in good health generally per-

ceived the retarded child as making greater demands on them than did mothers in the good-health and qualified-good-health categories. In terms of scale type, the good-health mothers mean fell *below* the type requiring agreement with the statement, "Our retarded child is hard to handle," while the mean for mothers reporting poor health was between the scale type requiring agreement with the above statement and the more extreme statement, "I felt worn out from taking care of our retarded child."

8. Mothers who reported that they were not in good health tended to have higher scores on willingness to institutionalize the retarded child than did mothers in good-health and qualified-good-health categories.

9. In the sample, mothers who had been treated for a nervous condition generally had a higher initial impact score than did mothers who reported that they were not in good health. These results, however, were not statistically significant.

10. In the sample, degree of marital integration of mothers reporting poor health was lower than that of mothers who had been treated for a nervous condition. The results bordered on statistical significance.

11. In the sample, mothers reporting poor health perceived the demands of the retarded child as greater than did mothers treated for a nervous condition. As anticipated in the hypothesis, however, the results were not statistically significant.

12. Mothers who reported themselves not in good health indicated a greater willingness to institutionalize the retarded child than did mothers treated for a nervous condition.

13. The social status of families in which the mother had been treated for a nervous condition was higher than those in which the mother reported poor health.

The distinction between the "sick" and "nervous" mothers is highlighted by the findings concerning social participation. As compared with mothers treated for nervousness, "sick" mothers attended church less frequently, belonged to fewer organizations, and were less motivated toward upward social mobility *(Pocs, 1960)*.

In general, the results relating to the mother's reports of poor health and treatment for a nervous condition supported the speculation that two kinds of family crisis can occur as a reaction to the retarded child.

Inasmuch as the role-organization crisis is concerned with an inability to organize a system of workable roles, the findings that the mothers reporting themselves not in good health had the lowest marital integration and perceived the retarded child as making the greatest demands were expected. Similarly, the finding that the marital integration of mothers reporting treatment for nervousness was lower than that of control group mothers was consistent with the speculative formulation of the types of crisis.

If the findings had indicated that mothers who received treatment for a nervous condition were more willing than control group mothers to institutionalize the child, the assumption that the "nervous" mothers were highly motivated to continue caring for the child would have been contradicted. However, the results indicated that in neither group did the mother indicate much willingness to institutionalize the retarded child. The control group mothers were probably reluctant for various reasons—perhaps because these mothers found they had developed effective means in family relations for keeping the child at home.

If results had indicated that mothers who regarded themselves as being in poor health also reported a *higher* initial impact than mothers treated for a nervous condition, the assumption of a differential process in family crisis would have been invalidated. Then, we would have had to regard the role organization crisis as an unresolved tragic crisis and "poor health" merely as an extreme nervous condition. Examination of scale types closest to the corresponding mean scores, however, revealed that the mothers treated for a nervous condition tended to indicate that "I went to pieces; my world fell apart" more often than mothers who regarded themselves in poor health.

TYPES OF FAMILY CRISIS AND OTHER VARIABLES

The classification of family crises as tragic and role-organization provided a basis for interpreting findings which had been obtained in the Chicago studies of families with a retarded child. Viewing the results as they relate to type of crisis could then indicate ways in which family crisis is related to other factors in effects of the retarded child on the family. The results are described below in terms of: (a) the family with a retarded child at home, (b) family factors in the decision to institutionalize the retarded child, and (c) family adjustment to the institutionalization of the retarded child. The findings have been reported in monograph form (*Farber, 1959, 1960a; Farber, Jenné, and Toigo, 1960*).

The Family with the Retarded Child at Home

Marital integration In families with a high estimated marital integration prior to the birth of the retarded child, the extent of emotional impact of the diagnosis of retardation reported by the husband was found to be inversely related to the degree of marital integration at the time of the study—the greater the initial impact, the lower the current marital integration. This finding suggests that the crisis for these particular fathers tended to be tragic. A similarity between reaction to the diagnosis and bereavement can be noted. In bereavement, personal impact would be greatest in those families whose members had been close and highly interdependent prior to the death of one member. It would be interesting to determine empirically whether the death of a child affects his parents in a way similar to the diagnosis of retardation.

The relationship between initial emotional impact and current marital integration described above can be contrasted to that in families in which marital integration prior to the birth of the retarded child was estimated to be low. In families with a low early marital integration, there was no relationship between the emotional impact on the husband and the marital integration of the couple at the time of the study. For these families, apparently, low current marital integration results from a variety of factors (in which initial emotional impact upon the husband may add only silghtly to the difficulties). This chronically low integration suggests that families initially low in marital integration might have been prone to role-organization crises whether or not the retarded child had been born.

Sex of the retarded child In the study of the effects of the sex of the retarded child on the relationship between the parents, it was found that among families with a retarded child at home, the parents of a retarded boy had a lower degree of marital integration than did the parents of a retarded girl. To provide further insight into this finding, further analyses were made by social class of the family. The investigation of social-class influence showed that whereas there was little difference in the marital integration of parents of retarded boys and girls in the middle class, in low-social-status families, parents with a retarded boy had a markedly lower marital integration than parents with a retarded girl. This finding suggested that the parents in the low socioeconomic group found greater tension in the marital system when the retarded child was a boy than when the retarded child was a girl.

In order to investigate more systematically effects of the sex of the retarded child on the parent, the emotional impact of the child on each of his parents was studied. The over-all trend was that at the time of the diagnosis of the child as retarded, a boy had a greater emotional impact than a girl upon the father, but generally the sex of the child made little difference in the initial emotional impact upon the mother. With the passage of time, however, the pattern of emotional impact changed. At the time of the investigation, the mothers regarded their boys as making greater demands upon them than did their daughters. The results suggested that the tragic crisis tended to be sex-linked especially for the father but that the role-organization crisis was especially strong for the mother. That boys rather than girls produced greater demands on the mother is understandable in view of the general role expectations for children by sex. The girl's life career is defined primarily in terms of home and family. Evaluation of her role would therefore be based upon her help in the household and her personal appearance. Even the retarded girl is frequently able to fulfill some elements of this role. A boy's role, however, is ordinarily evaluated primarily with respect to extrafamily relations—progress in school leadership, or prowess in athletics. The retarded boy can conform with few of these expectations if any. He thus performs a more deviant role in the home than does a girl and makes greater demands upon his mother.

Supportive versus *nonsupportive community participation* With normal children the parents would require support to stimulate further development of *conventional* family norms. Various studies have found that high community participation is conducive to healthy family life. However, the parents of a retarded child require support for a *different* kind of role. These parents' interests and routines differ from those of parents of normal children of the same chronological age. Discipline, play, development, etc., are not comparable for the retarded and the normal. Ordinarily, kinship, friendship associations, and activity in formal organizations are based on the dominant values and norms of the community, and community participation gives support to these values. Such participation would not, however, give support to parenthood norms revolving around the mentally retarded. On the contrary, these associations may be used for escaping problems, duties, and responsibilities connected with the retarded child. In evaluating his home life, the parent with high participation in these associations may adopt a point of reference prevalent in these associations. These associations would foster values which are inappropriate for the parent whose child is mentally retarded. For the parent of the retarded child, these community relations are thus nonsupportive.

To determine the effects of nonsupportive community relations, the families were divided into two groups on the basis of a battery of questions: Families in which marital integration had been low prior to the birth of the retarded child, and families in which early marital integration had been high. It was found that estimated early marital integration in combination with nonsupportive community participation did affect marital integration at the time of the study. Results relating to nonsupportive community relations were especially clear-cut for families in which early marital integration had been low. In these families, wives who had a high degree of neighborliness tended to have a lower marital integration score than wives who were relatively isolated from their neighbors. In addition, with respect to husbands in low early-integration families, high activity in formal organizations tended to produce a disruptive effect on the marriage. It is probable that the parents whose early marital integration had been low were precisely the ones who required much support for family behavior from their friends, neighbors, and organizational participation. These parents would be more vulnerable to the effect of nonsupportive interaction than would other parents. Participation in formal organization for the husbands, and neighborly and friendly interaction for the wives possibly provided a means of escape from the burdens of the home. In these families the presence of a role-organization crisis may well have been the normal state of affairs.

In contrast to nonsupportive community relations, certain individuals and groups can provide understanding and sympathy necessary for the development of new roles as parents of a retarded child. A major supportive relationship is that between the wife and her mother (maternal grandmother of the retarded child). One of the clearest findings in the study of effects of the retarded child on marital integration was that when the parents were in contact with the wife's mother frequently, their marital integration tended to be high. However, when they were in frequent contact with the husband's mother, marital integration tended to be low. A review of case material provided insight into the findings. Ordinarily, the wife's mother showed much sympathy and understanding for her daughter's situation whereas the husband's mother generally blamed the wife for the retarded child. Sometimes, there was an implication that the mother-in-law regarded the retarded child as punishment for her daughter-in-law's wrong-doing. To gain additional information on the relationship between the wife and her own mother, the effect of seeing the wife's mother on the couple's marital integration was related to the extent to which the parents regarded the retarded child as highly dependent. Presumably, if the contact with the wife's mother were related simply to the degree of dependence on the child, we would expect a good deal of the supportive relationship to come from physical assistance provided by the grandmother. Such was not the case. The findings suggested that the effect of seeing the mother rather than her assistance had a noticeable influence on marital integration.

It had been anticipated that participation in church activities also provided emotional support for the parents. However, there was no marked difference in the marital integration of those parents who attended church services frequently and those who did not. Unfortunately, the number of cases was too small to permit a separate analysis by religion of the parents. Such an analysis might have produced more meaningful results.

Normal siblings of the retarded child Most findings indicated that the effects of the retarded child on his normal sister were generally greater than upon the normal brother. An exception to this general tendency was the relationship between the mother's perception of the extent of her retarded child's dependence and her perception of the personal adjustment of the normal siblings. The measure of her perception of the normal siblings' adjustment was based upon her rating of the siblings on a number of personality traits—nervousness, irritability, stubbornness, moodiness, and depression, etc. Both normal brothers and sisters of those retarded children seen as highly dependent by the mother showed poorer adjustment than those whose mothers saw her retarded child as independent. One possible interpretation is that the mothers who saw her retarded child as highly dependent concentrated much time and attention upon that child. It is likely that these same mothers are those who perceived the retarded child as making great demands upon them. Hence, these would also be the mothers who were faced with a role-organization crisis. The normal siblings in these families, who suffered from lack of attention by the mother, would show many signs of maladjustment.

Effects of interaction between the normal and retarded siblings were studied. Girls who interacted a great deal with their retarded sibling were affected more adversely than girls who were less involved with the retarded child. The degree of interaction between the normal brother and retarded sibling was found to have little effect on normal sibling maladjustment. In her interaction the normal sister generally would be acting as a parent substitute. This places the normal sister in much the same position as the eldest daughter in families with normal children.

In the study of parents' dissatisfaction with their children's performance of various activities, it was found that parents are generally more dissatisfied with their sons; however, dissatisfaction with girls was more affected by relationship between the parents and by the birth order and sex of the retarded sibling. For example, the degree of dissatisfaction with the normal daughter (but not the son) was found to be related to the extent of marital integration of the parents. Moreover, in families in which the oldest child was retarded, fathers of a retarded boy indicated more dissatisfaction with normal daughters than did fathers of a retarded girl. Furthermore, in families with a retarded boy, fathers indicated more dissatisfaction with normal daughters when the retarded child was the eldest than in families when he was not the eldest. The reverse was true in families with retarded girls. There were no comparable significant findings for the normal brothers.

The reasons for these findings on birth order and sex are not clear. They do indicate the great involvement of the sister in all family problems arising from the presence of a retarded child. Presumably the findings are related to the parent surrogate role of the daughter. Possibly, mothers who are faced with a severe role-organization crisis demand much assistance from their daughters and at the same time are highly critical of them. This interpretation suggests that the role-organization crisis especialy has profound mental health consequences for the sister of the retarded child.

Findings on the effects of the size of the sibships on parental dissatisfaction with the behavior of normal children were inconclusive. There was, however, an indication that smaller families affect adversely the parents' perception of their daughter's behavior when a retarded child is present.

In the larger family we might expect care of the retarded child to be divided among several sisters. In the small family however, the work could not be so divided.

Family factors in the decision to institutionalize the retarded child
Although many factors are involved in the decision to institutionalize the retarded child, this study concentrated upon those aspects of family life which influence this decision. Certainly, such nonfamily factors as the adequacy of institutional facilities, the quality of care, and the financial obligation involved enter into the decision to place the child.

In the section on role-organization crisis it was indicated that mothers who reported that they were in poor health were more willing to institutionalize their retarded child than were other mothers. The decision to institutionalize the child would therefore have to be considered in terms of the role-organization crisis. However, many family life factors other than the type of crisis may influence the decision.

Commitments in the community define the tolerance limits in managing a deviant family member (such as the retarded child) at home. Insofar as social class and religious group permit exclusion of a deviant family member through institutionalization, this solution may be accepted by the family. However, the norms relating to tolerance of deviants must be consistent with those for the maintenance of the family's status in the community. Presumably, the higher the socioeconomic status, the greater is the importance assigned by family members, especially the husband, to norms and values of status maintenance. Consistent with this tendency is the finding that generally the higher the social status, the greater was the willingness of the husband as compared with the wife to place the retarded child in an institution. For low-social-status families it was the wife who was somewhat more willing on the average to institutionalize the child; for the high socioeconomic groups the husband was the more willing parent.

With emphasis on expectations required for status maintenance, the higher status families would have a lower tolerance level for deviants, and in addition, status-related considerations (such as planning for normal children's future) would influence the decision to institutionalize the retarded child. In low-status families, on the other hand, where less emphasis is placed on maintenance of status, the relationships between family members can exert a greater influence on the decision to institutionalize the child. It was found that the lower the marital integration, the more willing were husbands in low status families to institutionalize the retarded child. However, the influence of marital integration on husbands' willingness to institutionalize the child was small in high-status families. While, for husbands, marital integration in combination with social status was found to be important in the decisions to institutionalize, for wives the influence of marital integration did not change with social status. Regardless of social status, wives in the middle range of marital integration tended to be more willing than those in the extremes to place the retarded child in an institution. The significance of these findings on the mother is not clear.

The part played by tragic and role-organization crises in institutionalization was revealed in two findings. The first finding was that the lower the social status, the more willing were the mothers of retarded boys rather than mothers of retarded girls to institutionalize their retarded child. This finding is consistent with the low-status mother's perception of the retarded child's extreme demands as described in the section on role-organization crisis. Regardless of status, however, fathers were more willing to institutionalize a retarded boy than a retarded girl. In combination with the finding of a high initial emotional impact of a boy on the father, this result suggests that the tragic crisis has a greater effect on the father's willingness than upon the mother's.

The second finding concerned the parents' dissatisfaction with their normal daughter. Among families with a high or middle degree of marital integration, there was little relationship between parental dissatisfaction with their normal child and willingness to institutionalize their retarded child. Only for parents with low marital integration was a strong association found and then just for dissatisfaction with normal daughters. For these couples there was a high correlation between the father's dissatisfaction with his normal daughter and the willingness of both parents to place the retarded child in an institution. (The rank correlation coefficient between husband's dissatisfaction for and his own willingness score was $-.73$ and between the husband's satisfaction score and his wife's willingness score the rho was $-.65$.) The results were much less striking with regard to the effect of the wife's dissatisfaction score for her normal daughter upon willingness to place the retarded child in an institution. Thus, the combined effect of low marital integration and the father's rejection of the daughter's behavior were especially important in the decision to place the retarded child in an institution. When the wife's inability to maintain an integrated family life generates tension not only in the parent–child relationships but also in the marital system, the husband seems to regard institutionalization as perhaps the only possible solution to the family difficulties.

Findings on the relationship between number of other children and willingness to institutionalize a retarded child provide additional insight into the role of socioeconomic status in the decision to place the child. For high status families, there was a linear, positive relationship between the number of children in the home and husband's willingness to institutionalize a child. In contrast, in low-status families, although there was a linear negative relationship between marital integration and the father's willingness score, the relationship score between willingness to institutionalize and the number of other children was not linear. On the basis of these findings, social status appears to influence institutionalization through the definition of family problems. In the high socioeconomic status families, planning and concern for the future life of the children are consistent with the delayed gratification patterns generally found in families with fathers who are professionals or proprietors. Delayed gratification norms, in turn, are related to the maintenance of status. On the other hand, the closer relationship between low marital integration and willingness to institutionalize in the low-status family suggests institutionalization as a strategy to counteract a more immediate family problem.

The influence of religion upon the decision to institutionalize the retarded child was also investigated. There is some suggestion that Protestant husbands in families with low marital integration were more willing to place their retarded child in an institution than were Protestant husbands in more highly integrated families. On the other hand, Jewish husbands, regardless of marital integration or degree of emotional impact, showed much reluctance to place the retarded child in an institution. Catholic husbands showed only a very slightly greater tendency to place the retarded child when marital integration was low than when marital integration was high. Generally, the willingness scores for Catholic husbands fell between those of Protestant fathers and Jewish fathers.

The Jewish mothers generally showed even greater reluctance to place the retarded child than did their husbands. No similar pattern was found for Protestant and Catholic wives. For mothers in all three religious groups, those with marital integration scores in the middle range indicated a greater willingness to place the child than did mothers in the more extreme high and low marital integration ranges.

In general, the findings on factors involved in the decision to institutionalize the child indicate that not only is the type of family crisis an important determinant, but also the place of the family in the community with respect to both social-economic status and religious group.

Family adjustment to institutionalization of the retarded child Little analysis has been made thus far of data relating to the parents' adjustment to institutionalization of the retarded child. However, several analyses were made comparing families having a child at home with those whose child was in an institution.

In an analysis by religion, the parents were divided into Catholic and non-Catholic groups. Especially among non-Catholic parents, those with a retarded boy at home had a lower marital integration than parents with a boy in an institution. The analysis of all families indicated, however, that marital integration of parents with a retarded girl at home was not markedly different from that of parents with a retarded girl in an institution. Furthermore, parents with a retarded boy in an institution generally had about the same degree of marital integration as parents of a retarded girl in an institution.

These results suggest that the role-organization crisis which was most profound when a retarded boy was at home tended to occur more frequently in non-Catholic families. The findings also suggest that for Catholic parents the church affiliation provides some emotional support. The basis for this emotional support is not immediately apparent although other studies have also shown that Catholic families withstand crisis situations with less disastrous effects than families of other religious backgrounds.

The comparison between parents who have a child in an institution and those with a child at home revealed that age of the retarded child has some effect upon the marital relationship. There was little difference between marital integration of parents with a *young* boy at home and parents with a *young* boy in an institution. Arbitrarily, a young boy was defined here as one aged 9 or younger, 9 being the median for the sample. However the degree of marital integration of parents with an older boy at home (i.e., 10 to 16 years of age) was lower than that of parents with an older boy in an institution. The results suggest that as the retarded boy grows older the role-organization crisis tends to increase in severity.

This finding on age is related to one regarding the interaction of normal siblings with a retarded child. It was found that when the siblings and retarded child were approximately the same age (about one year apart) the interaction of these children at a very early age was on equalitarian basis, but as the children grew older the retarded child more and more took the role of a younger sibling. This finding suggests that socially the retarded child tends to become the youngest child in the family and to assume the special role of that birth order. As the discrepancy between chronological age and social age increases, the organization of an appropriate set of roles would become more difficult.

With respect to effects of institutionalization upon siblings, the results showed that normal girls with a retarded sibling in an institution were characterized by less maladjustment, as perceived by the mother, than were those girls with a retarded sibling at home. Normal brothers of retarded children, however, were affected adversely by institutionalizing the retarded child. That is, the mothers of retarded children in an institution tended to see their normal boys as more maladjusted than did mothers whose retarded child was at home. Taking into consideration the different family roles for normal boys and girls, the interpretation was that boys and girls had different responsibilities toward a retarded child at home. Taking the retarded child out of the home would then have a different effect on their adjustment to his institutionalization. With a retarded child at home, girls could be expected to help care for the retarded child. Normal brothers, however, would be expected to give the mothers as little trouble as possible when the retarded child was at home.

With the retarded child in an institution, the normal girl would be relieved of her surrogate responsibilities, but the normal boy would face many demands which he had escaped earlier.

The retarded child in the institution no longer diverts attention from the normal brother, nor is the mother so inclined to permit deviant activities by the normal brother. The mother now expects the normal brother to conform rigorously to family routines. It is also possible that institutionalizing the retarded child is the result of a final realization that he will never become normal. The mother, therefore, may compensate by being especially severe in her demands upon the normal children. Several parents reported that after institutionalization of the retarded child, their young *sons* (but never daughters) became anxious that they too would be placed in an institution. It is speculated that the normal brother's role in the family is expanded after the retarded child is institutionalized, and greater demands are made upon him. This interpretation should, of course, be re-examined in another study.

EPILOGUE

The studies cited above were concerned with types of family crisis, special difficulties induced by the presence of a retarded child at home, factors in the decision to institutionalize the retarded child, and family adjustment to the child's institutionalization. Many gaps existed both in findings and interpretation. Little systematic study was made of some areas such as family adjustment to the child's institutionalization. In other areas, specific findings such as the relationship between marital integration and the wife's willingness to institutionalize the child could not be readily interpreted. However, tenuousness of findings and interpretation should provide a stimulus for further investigation of families with a mentally retarded child.

References

Farber, B. An index of marital integration. *Sociometry,* 1957, *20,* 117–134.

Farber, B. Effects of a severely mentally retarded child on family integration, *Monogr. Soc. Res. Child Develpm.,* 1959, *24,* No. 2 (Serial 71).

Farber, B. Family organization and crisis: Maintenance of integration in families with a severely mentally retarded child. *Monogr. Soc. Res. Child Develpm.,* 1960a, *25,* No. 1 (Serial 75).

Farber, B. Perceptions of crisis and related variables in the impact of a retarded child on the mother. *Hlth. & Human Behav.,* 1960b, *1,* 108–118.

Farber, B., Jenné, W. C., & Toigo, R. Family crisis and the decision to institutionalize the retarded child. *Council of Except. Child., NEA, Res. Monogr.,* 1960, Series A, No. 1.

Hinkle, L. E. Physical health, mental health, and social environment: Some characteristics of healthy and unhealthy people. In R. H. Ojemann, *Recent contributions of biological and psychosocial investigations to preventive psychiatry.* Iowa City: University of Iowa Dep. of Publ., 1959, pp. 80–103.

Kohn, M. L. Social class and parental values. *Amer. J. Sociol.*, 1959, *64*, 337–351.

Pocs, O. Community participation of mothers with mentally retarded children. Unpublished Master's thesis, University of Illinois, 1960.

EPILOGUE (1972)

One neglected area of investigation is that of effects of a severely mentally retarded child on his family's social mobility. In general, little is known about the life chances of parents and siblings of retarded children.

Using the data described in the paper above, Max Culver investigated social-mobility patterns of parents of severely retarded children. He compared the occupations of the fathers with those of the retarded children's grandparents. His main findings was that the timing of the birth of the retarded child was associated with the movement of the parents upward or downward in the social structure. The earlier in the marriage the child was born, the greater were the chances of his having a depressing effect on his parents' social mobility. A retarded child born early in the marriage tended to impede his father's chances of upward mobility. In those families in which the grandfathers had had white-collar occupations, the parents who kept their severely retarded child at home were more often *downwardly* mobile than were those who institutionalized their retarded child. Culver also found that parents who had attended college were more likely to place their retarded child in an institution than were parents with a high school education or less.

The Culver analysis raises important questions regarding effects of a retarded child on the family as well as reasons for institutionalization. In an interview parents seldom report that the child is an obstacle to upward social mobility. That response would likely be considered immoral or selfish. Although such a response might be repressed by the parents, very likely the frustration of life goals (which probably involves a style of life different from that which parents are forced to lead because of the presence of the retarded child) may provoke much covert hostility toward the child. In the long run, keeping the retarded child at home under these conditions may be harmful for the mental health of everyone concerned.

While the findings of the Culver study are merely suggestive and do not show the large variety of ramifications deriving from the presence of a retarded child on his parents' position in the social structure, it does point to an area of research which may be very fruitful.*

* See Max Culver, "Intergenerational Social Mobility among Families with a Severely Mentally Retarded Child," unpublished Ph.D. dissertation, University of Illinois, 1967. See also Bernard Farber, *Mental Retardation: Its Social Context and Social Consequences.* Boston: Houghton Mifflin, 1968, pp. 163–165, 192–198.

The Gifted

11

The Gifted Group at Mid-life

Lewis M. Terman and Melita H. Oden

At the time of his death in 1956, Dr. Terman was Emeritus Professor of Psychology at Stanford University. He is well known for his longitudinal studies of gifted children and for his efforts in revising the Binet-Simon intelligence tests in the form of widely used Stanford-Binet tests. Mrs. Oden is a research associate in the Department of Psychology at Stanford University and has been associated with Dr. Terman's longitudinal study of the gifted since 1927.

This selection is drawn from the first and final chapter of Volume V of the series, "Genetic Studies of Genius" entitled The Gifted Group at Mid-Life. *It represents thirty-five years of follow-up study of gifted children selected by Dr. Terman in 1921–1922. This monumental study has had tremendous influence in charting the exploration of the characteristics of the gifted. The study of this group, now in their middle years, is being continued by Mrs. Oden and her associates. The most recent published work, "The Fulfillment of Promise: 40-Year Follow-up of the Terman Gifted Group,"* Genetic Psychology Monographs, *1968, 77, 3–93, should be read by the serious student.*

In this monograph a separate section is devoted to the life histories of 100 men rated the most successful and 100 men rated the

REPRINTED FROM *The Gifted Group at Mid-Life: Thirty-five Years' Follow-up of the Superior Child,* Vol. V, Genetic Studies of Genius. By Lewis M. Terman and Melita H. Oden. With the permission of the publishers, Stanford University Press. Copyright ©, 1959, by the Board of Trustees of Leland Stanford University.

> least successful from the standpoint of vocational achievement in the attempt to identify critical nonintellectual factors that influence achievement among men of superior intelligence. The important variables that emerged were: a home background in which the parents place a high value on education, expect a high level of accomplishment, and stress initiative and independence; good all-round social and emotional adjustment; and personality characteristics of perseverance, integration in working toward goals, self-confidence, interest in being a leader, in having friends, in excelling in work, in obtaining recognition for accomplishments, and in achieving vocational advancement.
>
> The overall study continues to strongly repudiate the notion that the gifted tend to "burn out" early and fall far short of their potential. In personal communication with Mrs. Oden, she commented that after 40 years of study the promise of youth has been more than fulfilled for the overwhelming majority of subjects. The large majority of gifted children do indeed live up to their abilities.

Many philosophers and scientists from Plato and Aristotle to the present day have recognized that a nation's resources of superior talent are the most precious it can have. A number of factors, however, have operated to postpone until recent years the inauguration of research in this field. Among these are: (1) the influence of long-current beliefs regarding the essential nature of the genius, long regarded as qualitatively set off from the rest of mankind and not to be explained by the natural laws of human behavior; (2) the widespread superstition that intellectual precocity is pathological; and (3) the growth of pseudodemocratic sentiments that have tended to encourage attitudes unfavorable to a just appreciation of individual differences in human endowment.

The senior author's first exploration into the problems posed by intellectual differences occurred over a half-century ago when, as a graduate student, he made an experimental study of two small contrasting groups of bright and dull children. His interest was heightened a few years later when, in standardizing the 1916 Stanford-Binet Intelligence Scale, he located and studied about a hundred children whose IQs were above 130. He then decided to launch, at the first opportunity, a large-scale investigation of the physical, mental, and personality traits of a large group of exceptionally gifted children and, by follow-up studies, to find out what kind of adults such children tend to become. It was obvious that no intelligent program for training the gifted child could be laid down until the answers to these questions had been found.

In 1921 a generous grant from the Commonwealth Fund of New York City made possible the realization of this ambition. The project as outlined called for the sifting of a school population of a quarter-million in order to locate a thousand or more of highest IQ. The subjects thus selected were to be given a variety of psychological, physical, and scholastic tests and were then to be followed as far as possible into adult life. The investigation was expected to tell us (1) what intellectually superior children are like as children; (2) how well they turn out; and (3) what are some of the factors that influence their later achievement.

THE SELECTION OF SUBJECTS

The problem was to discover in the schools of California a thousand or more subjects with IQs that would place them well within the highest 1 per cent of the school population. For financial reasons it was not possible to give mental tests to the entire school population. Instead, the search was limited chiefly to the larger and medium-sized urban areas. The following procedures were used to identify the children of highest IQ in the areas surveyed.

In grades three to eight each classroom teacher filled out a blank which called for the name of the brightest child in the room, the second brightest, the third brightest, and the youngest. The children thus nominated in a particular school building were then brought together and given a group intelligence test (National Intelligence Test, Scale B). Those who scored promisingly high on the group test were given an individual examination on the Stanford-Binet test. In grades below the third, only the Stanford-Binet test was given to those nominated by the teacher, since no suitable group test was available at that time for younger children. In high schools the selection of subjects was based on the Terman Group Test scores of students nominated by the teachers as being among the brightest in their respective classes.

Checks made on the method of selection indicated that the method used was identifying close to 90 per cent of all who could have qualified. The proportion was high enough to insure that the group selected for study constituted a reasonably unbiased sampling and that whatever traits were typical of these children would be reasonably typical of gifted children in any comparable school population. The original criterion for inclusion for the Binet-tested subjects was an IQ of 140 or above, but for various reasons sixty-five subjects were included in the IQ range of 135 to 139. Most of those below 140 IQ were either siblings of subjects already admitted to the group or were older subjects whose scores were deemed to be spuriously low because of insufficient top in the 1916 Stanford-Binet. The standard set was purely arbitrary and was intended to insure that the subjects included for study should be in the highest 1 per cent of the school population in general intelligence as measured by the test used. Its choice was not based on any assumption that children above this IQ level are potential geniuses. The standards for admission on the Terman Group

252 The Gifted

Test and other group tests also required the subject to score within the top 1 per cent of the general school population on which the norms were established.

The nature and results of the early stages of the investigation have been fully described in an earlier publication and will be summarized in the following pages.

COMPOSITION OF THE GROUP

The gifted subjects whose careers we have followed number, in all, 1,528 (857 males and 671 females). This figure includes a few who were selected before 1921, and 58 who were not selected until the field study of 1927–1928. These 58 were siblings of previously selected subjects who were too young to test at the time of the main search for subjects in 1921–1922.

The Binet-tested group made up more than two-thirds of the total and included 1,070 subjects (577 boys and 493 girls). Selected by the Terman Group Test given in high schools were 428 subjects (265 boys and 163 girls). The remaining 30 subjects were chosen on the basis of scores on the National Intelligence Test or the Army Alpha Test.[1] The average age of the total group at the time of selection was 11 years; the Binet-tested subjects averaged 9.7 years and those qualifying on a group test, 15.2 years.

The mean IQ of subjects who were given the Stanford-Binet was 151.5 for the boys, 150.4 for the girls, and 151.0 for the sexes combined. The IQ range was from 135 to 200 with 77 subjects scoring at IQ 170 or higher. The mean IQ of high-school subjects tested by the Terman Group Test was 142.6 and the range of IQ was from 135 to 169. These figures, however, were estimates based upon norms which were inadequate and were perhaps 8 or 10 IQ points too low. Later follow-up of the high-school subjects indicated that they were as highly selected as the Binet-tested group.

The sex ratio among the Binet-tested subjects was approximately 116 boys to 100 girls. The much higher sex ratio for the high school subjects—roughly 160 boys to 100 girls—is probably due to the less systematic procedures used in locating gifted subjects in the high schools. A sex ratio of 116 males to 100 females may be fully accounted for by the greater variability of males. McNemar and Terman, in a survey of sex differences on variability in such tests as the Stanford-Binet, the National Intelligence

[1] This group includes 24 pre-high-school pupils with National Intelligence Test scores and 6 high-school students with Army Alpha Test scores who were not tested in the formal search for subjects, but were brought to the attention of the study by their schools and included because of their very high test scores.

Tests, the Pressey Group Test, and Thorndike's CAVD test, found that 29 of 33 sex comparisons based on age groupings showed greater variability of boys. In Scotland, 874 of 875 children who were born on four particular days of the calendar year 1926, and were still living in 1936, were given a Stanford-Binet test at the age of ten years. The S.D. of the IQ distribution for this perfect sample was 15.9 for boys and 15.2 for girls—a difference sufficient to give a sex ratio of 134 boys to 100 girls scoring as high as 140 IQ.

KINDS OF INFORMATION OBTAINED

Besides the intelligence test scores on which the selection of subjects was based, information of many different kinds was obtained. The chief sources were as follows.

1. A 12-page Home Information Blank was filled out by the child's parents. This called for information on developmental case history, circumstances of birth, early feeding, ages of walking and talking, illnesses, nervous symptoms, home training, indications of intelligence, age of learning to read, reading habits, educational and occupational achievement of parents, genealogical records, and ratings on twenty-five traits.

2. An 8-page School Information Blank was filled out by the child's teacher. The blank called for information on school health records, quality of school work in each separate subject, evidence of superior ability, amount and kinds of reading, nervous symptoms, social adjustment, and ratings on the same twenty-five traits that were rated by the parents. This information was also obtained for a control group of 527 unselected school children.

3. A one-hour medical examination was given to 783 gifted subjects. The examination covered vision, hearing, nutrition, posture, teeth, heart, lungs, genitals, glandular disorders, blood pressure, and hemoglobin tests, pulse and respiration rates, urine tests, and neurological conditions.

4. Thirty-seven anthropometrical measurements were made of nearly 600 gifted subjects.

5. A 3-hour battery of achievement tests was given to 550 gifted subjects in grades two to eight. The battery covered reading, arithmetical computation, arithmetical reasoning, language usage, spelling, science information, language and literature information, history and civics information, and art information. The same tests were given to a large control group of unselected subjects.

6. A 4-page Interest Blank was filled out by all the gifted subjects who were able to read and write and by a large control group of unselected subjects. The blank called for information on occupational preferences, reading interests, school-subject interests, relative difficulty of school

subjects, number and size of collections, and various activities and accomplishments.

7. A record of all books read over a period of two months was obtained from some 550 gifted subjects and from a control group of 808 unselected children. Each book read was rated by the child for degree of interest.

8. A test of play interest, play practice, and play information was given to all the gifted subjects above grade two, and to a control group of nearly 500 unselected children. This test yielded scores on masculinity, maturity, and sociability of interests, and a play information quotient.

9. A battery of 7 character tests was given to 550 gifted subjects and 533 unselected children of a control group. These included two tests of overstatement; three tests of questionable interests, preferences, and attitudes; a test of trustworthiness under temptation to cheat; and a test of emotional stability.

Family Background

All racial elements in the areas covered were represented in the group, including Orientals, Mexicans, and Negroes. They came from all kinds of homes, from the poorest to the best, but the majority were the offspring of intellectually superior parents. The tendency to superiority in the social and cultural background of the subjects is shown in many ways. Nearly a third of the fathers as of 1922 were in professional occupations, and less than 7 per cent in semiskilled or unskilled work. The mean amount of schooling of both fathers and mothers was approximately 12 grades, or about four grades more than the average person of their generation in the United States. A third of the fathers and 15.5 per cent of the mothers had graduated from college. Twenty-eight fathers and six mothers had taken a Ph.D. degree—numbers which were considerably increased later. By 1940 the number of parents listed in *Who's Who in America* were 44 fathers and 3 mothers.

The number of books in the parents' homes, as estimated by the field assistants, ranged from almost none to 6,000, with one home out of six having 500 or more. The median family income during 1921 for a random sample of 170 families in the group was $3,333; the average for the sample was $4,705. Only 4.4 per cent reported $1,500 or less, while 14.1 per cent reported $8,500 or more, and 4.1 per cent reported $12,500 or more. The field assistants rated a random sample of 574 homes on the Whittier Scale for Grading Home Conditions. Rating superior to very superior were 60.3 per cent, as contrasted with 9.5 per cent rating inferior to very inferior.

Additional evidence of the superiority of family background is the fact that 182 of the families contributed two or more subjects to the group. Among these were 2 families of five children, all of whom qualified for the gifted group, 10 families each of whom contributed four children to the group, and 20 families who contributed three children each to the group. There were also 28 families whose children, often two or more in a family, were first cousins. Since not more than one child in a hundred of the general school population could qualify for the group, the likelihood that two such children would be found in one family would be almost infinitesimal by the laws of pure chance. That so many families contributed two or more children to the group means that something besides chance was operating, such as common ancestry, common environment, or, more probably, both of these influences.

Physique and Health of Gifted Children

Anthropometric measurements were made of a random gifted group of 312 boys and 282 girls, all but a few of whom were between the ages of 7 and 14. The results showed that the gifted children as a group exceeded the best standards at that time for American-born children in growth status as indicated by both height and weight, and that they were also above the established norms for unselected children in California.

Information on physical history was obtained from parents and teachers for nearly all the subjects, and information on health history was also obtained from the teachers for a control group of 527 unselected children enrolled in the classes attended by members of the gifted group. The mean birth weight reported by the mothers of the gifted was about three-quarters of a pound above the norm according to the commonly accepted standards of the time. About 17 per cent of male births and 12 per cent of female births involved instrumental deliveries; these rather high figures probably reflect the quality of obstetrical service obtained by parents of superior intelligence and above-average income. The proportion of breast feeding was considerably in excess of the figures reported for the general population. The reported ages of learning to walk averaged about a month less, and the age of learning to talk about three and one-half months less, than the mean ages reported for unselected children. Among the older children, the onset of puberty, as indicated by change of voice in boys and by first menstruation of girls was, on the average, earlier than for children of the general population. About a third of the gifted subjects had suffered one or more accidents, 8 per cent having had bone fractures. The number of surgical operations averaged one per child, over half of which were for adenoids or tonsils.

The School Information Blank filled out by teachers of the gifted subjects, and also for a control group attending the same classes, furnished interesting comparative data. These reports indicate that "frequent headaches" were only half as common among the gifted as among the controls, "poor nutrition," a third as common, "marked" or "extreme" mouth-breathing two-thirds as common, and defective hearing half as common. The two groups did not differ significantly with respect to frequency of colds, "excessive timidity," or "tendency to worry," but "nervousness" was reported for 20 per cent fewer gifted than controls.

The medical examination was given to 783 of the gifted subjects who lived in or near Los Angeles or the San Francisco Bay area. The examinations were made by two experienced child specialists, both of whom had had two years of postgraduate work in the department of pediatrics at the University of California Medical School. All examinations were made in the physician's office, to which the child was brought by a parent, usually the mother. The incidence of physical defects and abnormal conditions of almost every kind was below that usually reported by school physicians in the best medical surveys of school populations in the United States. This is certainly true for defects of hearings and vision, obstructed breathing, dental caries, malnutrition, postural defects, abnormal conditions of the heart or kidneys, enlargement of the bronchial glands, and tuberculosis. The sleep and dietary regimes of the group as a whole were found to be definitely superior. The incidence of nervous habits, tics, and stuttering was about the same as for the generality of children of corresponding age. The examining physicians, notwithstanding occasional disagreement in their results, were in complete accord in the belief that, on the whole, the gifted children of this group were physically superior to unselected children.

The combined results of the medical examinations and the physical measurements provide a striking contrast to the popular stereotype of the child prodigy so commonly depicted as a pathetic creature, overserious, and undersized, sickly, hollow-chested, stoop-shouldered, clumsy, nervously tense, and bespectacled. There are gifted children who bear some resemblance to this stereotype, but the truth is that almost every element in the picture, except the last, is less characteristic of the gifted child than of the mentally average.

Educational History

The average age on entering school (above kindergarten) was six and a quarter years. Low first grade was skipped by 21 per cent of the children, and the entire first grade by 10 per cent. The average progress quotient for the entire gifted group was 114, which means that the average gifted child was accelerated to the extent of 14 per cent of his age. According to the testimony of their teachers, the average gifted child merited additional promotion beyond where he was by 1.3 half-grades. "Strong" liking for school was reported by parents for 54 per cent of boys and 70 per cent of girls, as compared to only 5 per cent of the sexes combined for whom parents reported either "slight liking" or "positive dislike."

Nearly half of the children learned to read before starting to school; 20 per cent did so before the age of five years and 6 per cent before four years. Other early indications of superior intelligence most often mentioned by parents were quick understanding, insatiable curiosity, extensive information, retentive memory, large vocabulary, and unusual interest in number relations, atlases, and encyclopedias.

The Stanford Achievement Tests were given in the spring of 1922 to a random group of 565 gifted children in grades below the ninth. The tests provided separate scores for reading, computation, arithmetical reasoning, language usage, spelling, and four different fields of information. The average achievement quotient for the school subjects combined was 144, and only one quotient in six was as low as 130. The difference of 30 quotient points between the average achievement quotient of 144 and the average progress quotient of 114 (noted above), means that the average gifted child was retarded in grade placement by 30 per cent of his age below the level of achievement which he had already reached. More than half of those tested had mastered the school curriculum to a point two full grades beyond the one in which they were enrolled, and some of them as much as three or four grades beyond. For the fields of subject matter covered by our tests, the superiority of the gifted subjects over unselected children was greatest in reading, arithmetical reasoning, and information; it was least in computation and spelling.

Another question answered by the achievement tests was whether the gifted child tends to be more one-sided in his abilities than the average child, as so many people believe to be the case. Analysis of the subject-matter achievement quotients of the gifted group as compared to a group of unselected children shows that the amount of unevenness in subject-matter profiles of the gifted does not differ significantly from that shown by unselected children.

Childhood Interests and Preoccupations

The 4-page Interest Blank was filled out by all of the gifted who were old enough to read, and also by a control group of unselected children. In a long list of school subjects the children were asked to rate on a 5-point scale their liking for each of the school subjects they had studied. We will consider here only the ratings given by children of ages 11 to 13, inclusive. Analysis of the ratings showed that gifted children were more interested than were unselected children in school subjects which are most abstract, and somewhat less interested in the "practical" subjects. Literature, debating, dramatics, and history were rated much more interesting by the gifted, while penmanship, manual training, drawing, and painting were rated somewhat higher by the control group. When cross-sex comparisons were made, it was found that in their scholastic interests gifted girls resembled boys far more closely than they resembled control girls.

In the same Interest Blank was a list of 125 occupations and the child was told to place one cross before each occupation he might possibly wish to follow and two crosses before his one first choice. The data were treated for ages 8 to 13 for both gifted and control groups. Analysis of the data revealed that the gifted showed greater preference for professional and semiprofessional occupations, and the control group greater preference for mechanical and clerical occupations and for athletics.

The test of interest in 90 plays, games, and other activities was designed in such a way as to yield a preference score on each of the 90 items for each age and sex group of gifted and control subjects. Comparison of boys and girls in the control group with respect to kinds of plays and games preferred made it possible to derive a masculinity-femininity index for each child. Similarly, by comparison of preferences expressed at different ages in the control group, an index of interest maturity was derived for each child. Finally, an index of sociability was computed which was based on the extent of a child's preference for plays and games that involve social participation and social organization. Comparison of the gifted and control (i.e., unselected) children on these three indices yielded the following conclusions: (1) Gifted boys tended to be somewhat more masculine in their play interests than control boys at all ages from 8 to 12 years, after which there was little difference. Gifted and control girls did not differ significantly at ages 8, 9, and 10, but at ages 11, 12, and 13 the gifted girls tended to be more masculine. (2) Comparisons of maturity indices for gifted and control subjects showed greater maturity of play interests for the gifted of both sexes at all age levels; i.e., they were ahead of their years in play interests. (3) Comparisons on sociability indices showed gifted subjects of both sexes significantly below control subjects at all ages; i.e., age-for-age, the control subjects had somewhat more interest than gifted subjects in plays that involve social participation. Much of this difference can be accounted for by the fact that the gifted child is more self-sufficient and thus more able to amuse himself.

A test of play information (composed of 123 items that could be scored objectively) was devised which yielded a play information quotient based on age norms for unselected children. The average play information quotient of the gifted was 137, and only 3 per cent of the group were below 100. The average gifted child of 9 years had acquired more factual information about plays and games than the average unselected child of 12 years.

Information on the amount and kind of reading done was obtained by having 511 gifted children and 808 children of a control group keep a record of each book read during a period of two months. The records revealed that the average gifted child was reading about 10 books in two months by age 7, and 15 books by age 11, with little increase thereafter. Few of the control group read any books below 8 years, and after 8 years the average number read in two months was less than half that of the gifted. Classification of the books read showed the gifted children reading over a considerably wider range than the control children. The gifted, much more often than the control group, preferred science, history, biography, travel, poetry, drama, and informational fiction.

Character Tests

Do children of superior intelligence tend to be superior also in character traits? An answer to this question was sought by giving a battery of seven character tests to a random group of 532 gifted children aged 7 to 14 years and to a control group of 533 unselected children aged 10 to 14 years. The battery included two tests of the tendency to overstate in reporting experience and knowledge; three tests of the wholesomeness of preferences and attitudes (reading preferences, character preferences, and social attitudes, respectively); a test of cheating under circumstances that offered considerable temptation; and a test of emotional stability. The tests were so devised that they could be scored objectively and could be given to the subjects in groups. The nature of the several tests is described in an earlier report.

The tests of cheating and emotional stability were selected as among the best of a battery of character tests used by Cady; the others were all from a battery devised by Raubenheimer. Both of these batteries had been found to yield satisfactory reliability coefficients and to discriminate rather effectively between boys of known delinquent tendencies and boys of superior social and behavioral adjustment. Total scores of the seven character tests have a reliability of .80 to .85 and a validity (based on discrimination between delinquent and well-adjusted boys of ages 12 to 14) of approximately .60. Whether the validity is equally high for girls is not known.

The results of the character tests were decisive; the gifted group scored "better" than the control group on every subtest at every age from 10 to 14. Below the age of 10 no comparison was possible because the control subjects below this age were not sufficiently literate to take the tests. Table I shows, for the sexes separately, the proportion of gifted subjects who equaled or surpassed the mean of the control group on each subtest and on the total score for ages 10 to 14 combined.

The question may be raised whether a part of the superiority is spurious because of the possibility that bright subjects would be more likely to divine the purpose of the tests and so respond in the socially approved

260   The Gifted

Table I Proportion of Gifted Subjects Who Equaled or Surpassed the Mean of Control Subjects in Each of Seven Character Tests and in Total Score

TESTS	Boys %	Girls %
1. Overstatement A	57	59
2. Overstatement B	63	73
3. Book preferences	74	76
4. Character preferences	77	81
5. Social attitudes	86	83
6. Cheating tests	68	61
7. Emotional stability	67	75
Total score	86	84

way. This factor, if present at all, would be most likely to influence scores on reading preferences, character preferences, social attitudes, and emotional instability. It is believed hardly to have entered at all in the cheating test (disguised as a test of motor accuracy) or in the two overstatement tests, all three of which gave highly reliable differences between the gifted and control groups. In his study of delinquent and well-adjusted boys, Raubenheimer questioned his subjects after they had completed the tests, to find out whether they had guessed their purpose. Less than 5 per cent of his subjects (all 13 years old) guessed correctly.

Trait Ratings

The plan of trait rating used with the gifted subjects was the result of several years' experience in trying out various rating schemes with children of average and superior ability. The traits finally selected for rating numbered 25 and can be classified in the following categories: intellectual (4), volitional (4), moral (4), emotional (3), aesthetic (2), physical (2), social (5), and the single trait, mechanical ability. The individual traits are listed by category in Table II. However, in the blanks in which the ratings were made, the traits were presented in a mixed order.

A cross-on-line technique was used in getting the rating for each trait and the ratings were scored in intervals of 1 to 13. Nearly all of the gifted subjects were rated both by a parent and by a teacher. Teacher ratings were also obtained for 523 children of ages 8 to 14 in a control group composed of unselected children enrolled in the same classes as the gifted.

Table II *Percentages of Gifted Subjects Rated by Teachers Above the Mean of the Control Group*

SUBJECTS		*Percent*
1. *Intellectual traits*		
General intelligence	97	
Desire to know	90	
Originality	85	
Common sense	84	
Average of intellectual traits		89
2. *Volitional traits*		
Will power and perseverance	84	
Desire to excel	84	
Self-confidence	81	
Prudence and forethought	81	
Average of volitional traits		82.5
3. *Emotional traits*		
Sense of humor	74	
Cheerfulness and optimism	64	
Permanence of moods	63	
Average of emotional traits		67
4. *Aesthetic traits*		
Musical appreciation	66	
Appreciation of beauty	64	
Average of aesthetic traits		65
5. *Moral traits*		
Conscientiousness	72	
Truthfulness	71	
Sympathy and tenderness	58	
Generosity and unselfishness	55	
Average of moral traits		64
6. *Physical traits*		
Health	60	
Physical energy	62	
Average of physical traits		61
7. *Social traits*		
Leadership	70	
Sensitivity to approval	57	
Popularity	56	
Freedom from vanity	52	
Fondness for large groups	52	
Average for social traits		57.4
8. *Mechanical ingenuity*	47	

Parents and teachers agreed fairly well regarding the traits on which the gifted children were most or least superior to average children. The rank order of the traits from highest to lowest mean rating by parents correlated .70 with the corresponding rank order based on teachers' ratings. However, the agreement was much less in their ratings on individual children; for most of the traits it was represented by a Pearsonian correlation of only about .30. This figure should not be regarded as a reliability coefficient in the true sense, for the reason that a child's personality behavior in the school is often very different from that which he exhibits in the home.

More important is the comparison of gifted and control subjects on ratings given to both groups by the teachers. Table II gives the comparative data on both for the 25 individual traits and for groups of traits as classified in various categories. The figures in Table II are for the sexes combined and for all ages combined, since the mean ratings varied only slightly either with age or with sex. The slight variation by age and sex was to be expected in view of the fact that raters were instructed to rate each subject in comparison with the "average child of his age and sex."

The superiority of the gifted over the control subjects as shown by teachers' ratings agrees fairly well with the data from other sources. This is especially true in regard to the kinds of traits in which the superiority of the gifted is most or least marked. At the top of the list are the four intellectual traits, with 89 per cent of gifted rated at or above the mean of control subjects. Especially high were the ratings of "general intelligence" and "desire to know." Next highest were the four vocational traits, with percentages in the narrow range of 84 to 81. Third highest are the three emotional traits, with "sense of humor" (74 per cent) the highest of the three. The two aesthetic traits rank fourth with percentages of 64 and 66. Of the four moral traits, "conscientiousness" and "truthfulness" are rated reliably higher than the other two ("sympathy" and "generosity"). The two ratings on physical traits, which rank next, agree fairly well with the physical data obtained from medical examinations, health histories, and andthropometric measurements. Ranking seventh are the five social traits; of these, only "leadership" (with 70 per cent) is rated very much above the mean of control children. The ratings on "leadership" are consistent with the later follow-up studies which have shown the high frequency with which gifted subjects have been elected to class offices and honors despite their usual age disadvantage.

"Mechanical ingenuity" was the one trait in which teachers rated the gifted below unselected children. It is certain that the teachers were in error here, for test scores in mechanical ability have been consistently found to yield positive, not negative, correlations with intelligence scores. This is a trait which the average classroom teacher has little opportunity to observe; moreover, she is prone to overlook the fact that the gifted child in her class is usually a year or two younger than the others.

SUMMARY PORTRAIT OF THE TYPICAL GIFTED CHILD

Although there are many exceptions to the rule, the typical gifted child is the product of superior parentage—superior not only in cultural and educational background, but apparently also in heredity. As a result of the combined influence of heredity and environment, such children are superior physically to the average child of the general population.

Educationally, the typical gifted child is accelerated in grade placement about 14 per cent of his age; but in mastery of the subject matter taught, he is accelerated about 44 per cent of his age. The net result is that during the elementary school period a majority of gifted children are kept at school tasks two or three full grades below the level of achievement they have already reached.

The interests of gifted children are many-sided and spontaneous. The members of our group learned to read easily and read many more and also better books than the average child. At the same itme, they engaged in a wide range of childhood activities and acquired far more knowledge of plays and games than the average child of their years. Their preferences among plays and games closely follow the normal sex trends with regard to masculinity and femininity of interests, although gifted girls tend to be somewhat more masculine in their play life than the average girls. Both sexes show a degree of interest maturity two or three years beyond the age norm.

A battery of seven character tests showed gifted children above average on every one. On the total score of the character tests the typical gifted child at age 9 tests as high as the average child at age 12.

Rating on 25 traits by parents and teachers confirm the evidence from tests and case histories. The proportion of gifted subjects rated superior to unselected children of corresponding age averaged 89 per cent for four intellectual traits, 82 per cent for four volitional traits, 67 per cent for three emotional traits, 65 per cent for two aesthetic traits, 64 per cent for four moral traits, 61 per cent for two physical traits, and 57 per cent for five social traits. Only on mechanical ingenuity were they rated as low as unselected children, and this verdict is contradicted by tests of mechanical aptitude.

Three facts stand out clearly in this composite portrait: (1) The deviation of gifted children from the generality is in the upward direction for nearly all traits; there is no law of compensation whereby the intellectual superiority of the gifted is offset by inferiorities along nonintellectual lines. (2) The amount of upward deviation of the gifted is not the same for all traits. (3) This unevenness of abilities is no greater for gifted than for average children, but it is different in direction; whereas the gifted are at their best in the "thought" subjects, average children are at their best in subjects that make the least demands upon the formation and manipulation of concepts.

Finally, the reader should bear in mind that there is a wide range of variability within our gifted group on every trait we have investigated. Descriptions of the gifted in terms of what is typical are useful as a basis for generalization, but emphasis on central tendencies should not blind us to the fact that gifted children, far from falling into a single pattern, represent an almost infinite variety of patterns.

THE FULFILLMENT OF PROMISE

In the past 35 years we have watched the gifted child advance through adolescence and youth into young manhood and womanhood and on into the fuller maturity of mid-life. The follow-up for three and one-half decades has shown that the superior child, with few exceptions, becomes the able adult, superior in nearly every aspect to the generality. But, as in childhood, this superiority is not equally great in all areas.

The superiority of the group is greatest in intellectual ability, in scholastic accomplishment, and in vocational achievements. Physically the gifted subjects continue to be above average as shown in their lower mortality record and in the health ratings. While personal adjustment and emotional stability are more difficult to evaluate, the indications are that the group does not differ greatly from the generality in the extent of personality and adjustment problems as shown by mental breakdowns, suicide, and marital failures. The incidence of such other problems as excessive use of liquor (alcoholism) and homosexuality is below that found in the total population, and the delinquency rate is but a small fraction of that in the generality. Clearly, desirable traits tend to go together. No negative correlations were found between intelligence and size, strength, physical well-being, or emotional stability. Rather, where correlations occur, they tend to be positive.

The Maintenance of Intellectual Ability

But if gifted children are not prone to die young or, as they advance in years, to become invalids or to suffer to any extent from serious personality or behavior difficulties, there remains the question of the degree to which their intellectual superiority is maintained. The evidence on this score is conclusive. Test scores of 1927–1928, 1939–1940, and 1950–1952 showed the majority of the subjects close to the 99th percentile of the generality in mental ability. This is true even of those who careers have not been particularly notable. It was especially interesting to find that the average Concept Mastery test score in 1950–1952 of the subjects who did not go beyond high school was exactly the same as that of a group of candidates for advanced degrees (Ph.D. or M.D.) at a leading university. Of additional interest are the results of a comparison of Concept Mastery test scores of 1939–1940 and 1950–1952 of the same individuals. The test-retest comparisons showed a reliable gain in the 11-to-12 year interval with increases occurring at all educational and occupational levels, in all grades of ability, and at all ages. The data indicate that not only do the mentally superior hold their own but that they actually increase in intellectual stature as measured by the Concept Mastery test.

Appraisal of Achievement

From a practical and utilitarian point of view the real test of the significance and value of this high degree of mental ability is the use that is made of such gifts. The record points to the conclusion that capacity to achieve far beyond the average can be detected early in life through tests of general intelligence. Such tests do not, however, enable us to predict what direction the achievement will take, and least of all do they tell us what personality factors or what accidents of fortune will affect the fruition of exceptional ability. The appraisal of achievement of our gifted subjects will be concerned with their educational attainments, their vocational records, their contributions to knowledge and culture, and the recognitions that have been won.

The educational record is a distinguished one. More than 85 per cent of the group entered college and almost 70 per cent graduated. The latter figure is about ten times as high as for a random group of comparable age. Graduation honors and elections to Phi Beta Kappa and Sigma Xi were at least three times as numerous as in the typical senior college class, with better than 35 per cent of the graduates winning one or more of these distinctions. Of the college graduates, two-thirds of the men and nearly three-fifths of the women continued for graduate study. The Ph.D. or comparable doctorate was taken by 80 men and 17 women, or about 14 per cent of men and 4 per cent of women graduates. The proportion of the generality of college graduates of corresponding age who have taken a doctorate is less than 3 per cent.

The occupations and occupational status of the men and women of the gifted group have been evaluated separately since the pattern in this regard has been so different. The careers of women are often determined by extraneous circumstances rather than by training, talent, or vocational interest. Whether women choose to work and the occupations they enter are influenced both by their own attitudes and by the attitudes of society toward the role of women. These attitudinal factors also influence the opportunities for employment and for advancement. But in spite of the fact that American women on the average occupy positions of lesser responsibility, opportunity, and remuneration than do men, the gifted women have a number of notable achievements to their credit. That 7 women should be listed in *American Men of Science,* 2 in the *Directory of American Scholars,* and 2 in *Who's Who in America,* all before reaching the age of 43, is certainly many times the expectation from a random group of around 700 women. Publications of the gifted women include 5 novels; 5 volumes of poetry and some 70 poems that have appeared in both literary and popular journals; 32 technical, professional, or scholarly books; around 50 short stories; 4 plays; more than 150 essays, critiques, and articles; and more than 200 scientific papers. At least 5 patents have been taken out by gifted women. These figures do not include the writings of reporters and editors, nor a variety of miscellaneous contributions.

Our gifted women in the main, however, are housewives, and many who also work outside the home do so more to relieve the monotony of household duties or to supplement the family income rather than through a desire for a serious career. There are many intangible kinds of accomplishment and success open to the housewife, and it is debatable whether the fact that a majority of gifted women prefer housewifery to more intellectual pursuits represents a net waste of brainpower. Although it is possible by means of rating scales to measure with fair accuracy the achievement of a scientist or a professional or business man, no one has yet devised a way to measure the contribution of a woman who makes her marriage a success, inspires her husband, and sends forth well-trained children into the world.

As for the men, close to three and a half decades after their selection solely on the ability to score in the top 1 per cent of the school population in an intelligence test, we find 86 per cent in the two highest occupational categories: I, the professions, and II, the semiprofessions and higher business. Eleven per cent are in smaller retail business, clerical, and skilled occupations. Farming and related occupations account for nearly 2 per cent and the remaining 1 per cent are in semiskilled work. The representation in the two highest groups is many times their proportionate share, with a corresponding shortage of gifted representation in the middle occupational levels. No gifted men are classified in the lowest levels of the occupational hierarchy (service workers and slightly skilled or unskilled laborers), whereas 13 per cent of the total urban population are in these categories.

A number of men have made substantial contributions to the physical, biological, and social sciences. These include members of university faculties as well as scientists in various fields who are engaged in research either in industry or in privately endowed or government-sponsored research laboratories.[2] Listings in *American Men of Science* include 70 gifted men, of whom 39 are in the physical sciences, 22 in the biological sciences, and 9 in the social sciences. These listings are several times as numerous as would be found for unselected college graduates. An even greater distinction has been won by the three men who have been elected to the National Academy of Sciences, one of the highest honors accorded American scientists. Not all the notable achievements have been in the sciences; many examples of distinguished accomplishment are found in nearly all fields of endeavor.

Some idea of the distinction and versatility of the group may be found in biographical listings. In addition to the 70 men listed in *American Men of Science*, 10 others appear in the *Directory of American Scholars*, a companion volume of biographies of persons with notable accomplishment in the humanities. In both of these volumes, listings depend on the amount of attention the individual's work has attracted from others in his field. Listings in *Who's Who in America*, on the other hand, are of persons who, by reasons of outstanding achievement, are subjects of extensive and general interest. The 31 men (about 4 per cent) who appear in *Who's Who* provide striking evidence of the range of talent to be found in this group. Of these, 13 are members of college faculties representing the sciences, arts, and humanities; 8 are top-ranking executives in business or industry; and 3 are diplomats. The others in *Who's Who* include a physicist who heads one of the foremost laboratories for research in nuclear energy; an engineer who is a director of research in an aeronautical laboratory; a landscape architect; and a writer and editor. Still others are a farmer who is also a government official serving in the Department of Agriculture; a brigadier general in the United States Army; and a vice-president and director of one of the largest philanthropic foundations.

Several of the college faculty members listed in *Who's Who* hold important administrative positions. These include an internationally known scientist who is provost of a leading university, and a distinguished scholar in the field of literature who is a vice-chancellor at one of the country's largest universities. Another, holding a doctorate in theology, is president of a small denominational college. Others among the college faculty include one of the world's foremost oceanographers and head of a well-known institute of oceanography; a dean of a leading medical school; and a physiologist who is director of an internationally known

[2] A detailed study of the vocational correlates and distinguishing characteristics of scientists and nonscientists among the gifted men was made in 1952 under the sponsorship of the Office of Naval Research and has been published in a separate monograph and also appeared in an abbreviated version as an article in the *Scientific American*.

laboratory and is himself famous both in this country and abroad for his studies in nutrition and related fields.

The background of the eight businessmen listed in *Who's Who* is interesting. Only three prepared for a career in business. These include the president of a food-distributing firm of national scope, the controller of one of the leading steel companies in the country, and a vice-president of one of the largest oil companies in the United States. Of the other five business executives, two were trained in the sciences (both hold Ph.D.'s) and one in engineering; the remaining two were both lawyers who specialized in corporation law and are now high-ranking executives. The three men in the diplomatic service are career diplomats in foreign service.

Additional evidence of the productivity and versatility of the men is found in their publications and patents. Nearly 2,000 scientific and technical papers and articles and some 60 books and monographs in the sciences, literature, arts, and humanities have been published. Patents granted amount to at least 230. Other writings include 33 novels, about 375 short stories, novelettes, and plays; 60 or more essays, critiques, and sketches; and 265 miscellaneous articles on a variety of subjects. The figures on publications do not include the hundreds of publications by journalists that classify as news stories, editorials, or newspaper columns, nor do they include the hundreds, if not thousands, of radio, television, or motion picture scripts. Neither does the list include the contributions of editors or members of editorial boards of scientific, professional, or literary magazines. There have also been a sizable number of scientific documents reporting studies in connection with government research which are restricted publications. We do not have information on the exact number or content of these.

The foregoing are only a few illustrations of conspicuous achievement and could be multiplied many times. They by no means represent all of the areas or types of success for there is scarcely a line of creditable endeavor in which some member of the group has not achieved outstanding success. There are men in nearly every field who have won national prominence, and 8 or 10 who have achieved an international reputation. The latter include several physical scientists, at least one biological scientist, one or two social scientists, two or three members of the United States State Department, and a motion picture director. The majority, though not all so outstanding as those mentioned, have been highly successful vocationally from the standpoint of professional and business accomplishment as measured by responsibility and importance of position, prestige, and income.

There is, however, another side to the picture. There are various criteria of success, but we are concerned here with vocational achievement, and success has been defined as the extent to which the subject has made use of his intellectual ability. This calls for a very high level of accomplishment since the intellectual level is so high and not all have measured up to it vocationally. Although not more than three or possibly four men (again women are not included) could be considered failures in relation to the rest of the group, there are 80 or 90 men whose vocational achievements fall considerably short of the standard set by the group as a whole.

Since the less successful subjects do not differ to any extent in intelligence as measured by tests, it is clear that notable achievement calls for more than a high order of intelligence. After the 1940 follow-up a detailed analysis was made of the life histories of the 150 most successful and 150 least successful men among the gifted subjects in an attempt to identify some of the nonintellectual factors that affect life success. The results of this study indicated that personality factors are extremely important determiners of achievement. The correlation between success and such variables as mental health, emotional stability, and social adjustment is consistently positive rather than negative. In this respect the data run directly counter to the conclusions reached by Lange-Eichbaum in his study of historical geniuses. A number of interesting differences between the two subgroups were brought out but the four traits on which they differed most widely were "persistence in the accomplishment of ends," "integration toward goals," "self-confidence," and "freedom from inferiority feelings." In the total picture the greatest contrast between the two groups was in all-round emotional and social adjustment, and in drive to achieve. This study is fully reported in *The Gifted Child Grows Up.*

Outlook for Future Achievement

The careers of the gifted subjects, now in their mid-forties, are pretty well set in their present courses. In a very few cases, there are no higher rungs on the particular professional or executive ladder they have climbed. But for most of the group, advances to greater levels of achievement and more important roles can be looked for. Lehman has shown that the median age at which positions of leadership are reached has greatly increased in the last 150 years. In field after field the increase has amounted to 8, 10, or even 12 years and numerous positions of high-ranking leadership are most likely to be acquired and retained from fifty to seventy years of age. Lehman has also shown that in nearly all fields of intellectual achievement the most creative period is between thirty and forty-five years. But here Lehman is concerned with *quality* of achievement. Productivity as measured by quantity is often greater after forty than before. And regardless of the merit of one's work, the peak of recognitions, honors, and earned income is usually not reached until the fifties.

On the basis of Lehman's data as well as on the evidence from their own records, the peak of achievement for this group is not yet reached.

More than half were still under age 45 in 1955 and there was little evidence of any slackening of pace. Whether the rise in the next 10 years will be as steep as that between 1945 and 1955 is doubtful, principally for the reason that they are so much nearer the top. The group has made tremendous strides in the past ten or fifteen years. This is true in every field and in every walk of life. There is almost no one who has not improved his status, even though he may still be well below the average of the group in terms of realizing his intellectual potential in his vocational accomplishments.

We said some years ago, that only a professed seer would venture a statistical forecast of the future achievements of the group. However, we did venture some predictions on the basis of the data to 1945, among which were the following:

> The peak of *recognition* for achievement will come much later, probably not before another fifteen or twenty years have elapsed. Listings in *American Men of Science* may well be doubled by 1960, and listings in *Who's Who* may be trebled or quadrupled by 1970. In the decade 1960 to 1970 there should be several times as many holding positions of high responsibility as in 1945, and several times as many of national or international reputation in their special fields of accomplishment.

These were indeed conservative estimates. Instead of the doubling of listings in *American Men of Science* which was thought might take place by 1960, the number has quadrupled, with 77 names (70 men and 7 women) compared to the 19 men and no women in 1945. The list in *Who's Who in America* has grown from 5 names (all men) to 33 (31 men and 2 women), an increase of more than six times rather than the trebling or quadrupling cautiously predicted for the still-distant 1970.

In 1945 probably not more than a half-dozen had a national reputation, and perhaps one was internationally known. By 1955 several dozen at least have become national figures and 8 or 10 are known internationally. Moreover, the group now includes three men who have been elected to the National Academy of Sciences as compared with only one at the earlier date.

It is hard to say in which fields the greatest advances will take place in the next five or ten years. Business will certainly be one, and law another. The scientists are probably nearer their peak than are the rest of the group but even here there are a number of younger scientists with great promise. Regardless of the degree of productivity yet to be attained, the number of those winning special honors and distinctions will increase. This is true because of the time lag between achievement and recognition. Although *American Men of Science* listings are probably now close to their maximum, at least one and possibly two scientists are so outstanding that eventual election to the National Academy of Sciences can be predicted for them. There will undoubtedly be a considerable increase in the number of *Who's Who* biographies but we hesitate to estimate the ultimate number.

There are, however, a few fields, all dependent on special talent, in which there has been a lack of outstanding accomplishment. These are the fine arts, music and, to a lesser extent, literature. The group has produced no great musical composer and no great creative artist. Several possessing superior talent in music or art are heading university departments in these fields and have produced some excellent original work, but none seems likely to achieve a truly great piece of creative work. There are a number of competent and highly successful writers among the subjects but not more than three or four with a high order of literary creativity. Perhaps it is not surprising, in view of the relatively small size of our group, that no great creative genius in the arts has appeared, for such genius is indeed rare. In any case these are the only major fields in which the achievement of our group is limited.

Some Comments on Success

Our discussion so far has been concerned with achievement of eminence, professional status, and recognized position in the world of human affairs. But these are goals for which many intelligent men and women do not consciously strive. Greatness of achievement is relative both to the prevailing patterns of culture and the individual's personal philosophy of life; there neither exists nor can be devised a universal yardstick for its measure. The criterion of success used in this study reflects both the present-day social ideology and an avowed bias in favor of achievement that calls for the use of intelligence. It is concerned with vocational accomplishment rather than with the attainment of personal happiness. And the record shows that the gifted subjects, in overwhelming numbers, have fulfilled the promise of their youth in their later-life achievements.

There are other criteria of success and other goals and satisfactions in life, however, and in the biographical data blank the gifted men and women have expressed their own opinions on what constitutes life success. The final question in the blank was worded as follows: *From your point of view, what constitutes success in life?* There was a wide range of replies, often overlapping, and frequently a respondent gave more than one definition. The definitions most frequently given fall into five categories, each noted by from around 40 to 50 per cent of the group (with the exception of category *c*). None of the other definitions of success was mentioned by more than 15 per cent, and only two by more than 10 per cent of the subjects. The five most frequently mentioned definitions of life success are:

1. Realization of goals, vocational satisfaction, a sense of achievement;

2. A happy marriage and home life, bringing up a family satisfactorily;

3. Adequate income for comfortable living (but this was mentioned by only 20 per cent of women);

4. Contributing to knowledge or welfare of mankind; helping others, leaving the world a better place;

5. Peace of mind, well-adjusted personality, adaptability, emotional maturity.

We would agree with the subjects that vocational achievement is not the only—perhaps not even the most important—aspect of life success. To many, the most important achievement in life is happiness, contentment, emotional maturity, integrity. Even failure to rise above the lowest rungs of the occupational ladder does not necessarily mean that success in the truest sense has been trivial. There may have been heroic sacrifices, uncommon judgment in handling the little things of daily life, countless acts of kindness, loyal friendships won, and conscientious discharge of social and civic responsibilities. If we sometimes get discouraged at the rate society progresses, we might take comfort in the thought that some of the small jobs, as well as the larger ones, are being done by gifted people.

12

Characteristics of Creatively Gifted Children and Youth

E. Paul Torrance

Dr. Torrance is Chairman of the Division of Educational Foundations at the University of Georgia. Outstanding in the field of the gifted, he has written six books, published numerous articles, and authored several batteries of tests of creative thinking and motivation. Some of these tests have been translated into at least ten different languages. His research and writings have made a significant impact, particularly in the area of creativity.

This present article, prepared especially for this book, is an excellent review of the research concerned with the identification of variables associated with the creative process in gifted children. The reader with research interests in this area will find the article invaluable.

In this review, creatively gifted children and youth will be defined as those who exhibit to an extraordinary degree the abilities and personality characteristics involved in the creative process. On the basis of an analysis of the diverse ways of viewing creativity, the author has defined creativity as a process which begins by becoming sensitive to problems, deficiencies, gaps in knowledge, missing elements, or disharmonies for which there are no learned or habitual responses. The process thus set in motion continues with efforts to identify the difficulty and a search for solutions, the making of guesses or formulating hypotheses about the deficiencies; the testing and retesting of these hypotheses and possibly their modification and retesting; and the communication of the results.

Strong human needs operate at each stage. If a person senses some incompleteness or disharmony, tension is aroused. He is aroused and wants to relieve the tension. Since habitual or learned ways of behaving are inadequate, he tries to get away from commonplace and obvious but incorrect or inadequate solutions by investigating, getting information, diagnosing, manipulating, and making guesses or estimates. Until the guesses or hypotheses have been tested, modified, and retested, he is still aroused. This arousal usually continues until he communicates what he has found out in some way.

The definition of creativity permits us to begin defining operationally the kinds of abilities, mental functioning, and personality characteristics that facilitate the process (Torrance, 1965a). It provides an approach for specifying the kinds of products that result from the process, the kinds of persons who can engage in the process with a high degree of success, and the conditions that facilitate the process. This definition is in harmony with historical usage and is equally applicable in scientific, literary, artistic, musical, dramatic, and interpersonal creativity.

Although the demands of the 1970s call for greater attention to the identification and cultivation of creative talent, many educators have long dreamed of being able to understand, identify, and cultivate the creative potentialities of all children. It is of obvious importance to society that creative talent be identified, developed, and utilized. Already, understandings derived from research concerning the creative thinking abilities have broadened concept of "giftedness" from that of the "child with the high IQ" to include also the highly creative child and perhaps other types. (Torrance, 1962, 1965b). It is becoming increasingly clear that nothing can contribute more to mental health and the general welfare of our nation and to the satisfactions of its people than a general raising of the level of creativity. There is little doubt that the stifling of creative thinking cuts at the very roots of satisfaction in living and eventually creates overwhelming tension and breakdown. It is important that creativity be energized and guided from birth. If stifled early, it will only become imitative, if it survives at all. It is true that vigorous creative imagination can survive early stifling and opposition; but if it learns only to act vigorously without direction, it becomes dangerous to society and to civilization.

The creative thinking abilities are important in the acquisition of even the traditionally measured kinds of achievement when children are permitted to achieve some of these goals in creative ways. Their importance in vocational success has also been mentioned. Goals become clearer and more urgent, however, when we look upon the creative thinking abilities as just one part of our expanded and expanding concept of the human mind and its functioning. An acceptance of this concept opens up new and tremendously exciting possibilities for counselors and teachers. It places a new emphasis upon consideration of what man may become. It suggests that we can educate to a higher degree many people whom we have not been very successful in educating. As we have begun to understand more deeply creative functioning, the case for learning creatively rather than just by authority has been strengthened.

For many years, common concepts of the human mind and its functioning were limited largely by the concepts embodied in intelligence tests. Developers of intelligence tests have not claimed that such tests assess all of a person's intellectual functioning. Yet an intelligence or scholastic aptitude test has almost always been used as the sole index of a person's intellectual potential. If his achievement in some area fell below the level which would be expected from his IQ, he was said to be underachieving. If he achieved at an age level higher than would be expected from his IQ, he was somehow supposed to be overachieving. Curriculums and methods of teaching generally have been designed to bring about the kinds of achievement related to the mental abilities involved in intelligence or scholastic aptitude tests. Tests of educational achievement likewise have been constructed along the same lines.

Educators have long talked about the necessity for individualizing instruction but we are only now beginning to realize how very different children are and finding out what some of the individual differences are that make a difference in the way they learn. Creative abilities and motivations are certainly among these individual differences. Recent research involving programmed instruction, for example, is showing that such instruction can bring into play different abilities and different strategies of learning. In some experiments (Stolurow, 1962), postprogram performance seems to be less related to mental age as assessed by an intelligence or scholastic aptitude test than to tests of originality. In other studies, with different programming strategies (Gotkin & Massa, 1963), there are negative relationships between measures of achievement and creativity. Several research findings suggest that we may be discovering clues that will enable us to educate to a higher degree many people whom we have not been very successful in educating, such as the vast army of dropouts and other poorly educated groups.

Creativity research of the 1960s has helped clear up many of the puzzling findings of earlier research concerning individual differences in learning. For example, we need no longer be puzzled by McConnell's (1934) finding that mental age as measured by an intelligence test is more highly related to achievement in second-grade arithmetic when taught by authoritative identification than when taught by the methods of discovery. Hutchinson (1963) in a study involving learning in junior high school social studies also found that, under traditional authoritarian teaching, there is a statistically significant positive correlation between mental age and achievement but not between measures of creative thinking and achievement. In experimental conditions offering considerable opportunities for learning in creative ways the reverse was true. In a study involving fifth-grade children using programmed instruction in language arts, Gotkin and Massa found significant negative relationships between measures of creative thinking and achievement. A year earlier, Stolurow had found higher positive correlations between measures of originality and achievement than between mental age and achievement with programmed materials in mathematics and statistics. The difference was that Gotkin and Massa used programmed materials that permitted only tiny mental leaps and gave little opportunity for making, identifying, and correcting errors, while Stolurow's programmed materials emphasized a trouble-shooting or hypothesizing approach that builds specific but multiple associations to a stimulus.

MacDonald and Raths (1964) found that highly creative children are more productive on frustrating tasks than are less creative children. Furthermore, they enjoy such tasks more than their less creative peers do. The least creative children are less productive in open tasks, and the most creative ones react less favorably to closed tasks. Thus, pupils of varying levels of creative thinking ability react differently to different kinds of curriculum tasks and are possibly best taught by varying procedures.

One of the most exciting insights from creativity research is that different kinds of children learn best when given opportunities to learn in ways best suited to their motivations and abilities. Whenever teachers change their ways of teaching in significant ways, a different group of learners become the stars or high achievers. This advance, it seems to me, has far-reaching implications for educating a larger number of people to a higher level and for achieving a higher level of dignity and mental health in our society.

In this paper the author will summarize what he regards as some of the most important research findings concerning the characteristics of creatively gifted children and youth.

PRESCHOOL STUDIES

One of the most important studies of creative imagination in the preschool child was published by Elizabeth G. Andrews of the University of Iowa in 1930. She concluded that while creative imagination exists in some degree in all healthy children, there are large individual differences and many types of creative imagination. She recognized quite clearly the difference between the mental abilities involved in creative imagination and those involved in intelligence tests and saw no reason why there should be a high relationship between them. She believed that it is the function of education to discover ways of fostering these special abilities and providing opportunities for their fullest development. She urged that vocational guidance begin in the nursery, not by forcing a vocation on the child, but by allowing him to develop along the lines of his strongest interests, with encouragement for his every creative act. She recognized that children must learn to distinguish between fact and fantasy but that this could be done without making children sacrifice their creative imagination. She believed that art, music, literature, and science offered special opportunities for this kind of education. She believed that it was through the "entering-in" of the adult in the child's "make-believe" world that he learned best to differentiate between fancy and reality.

Elizabeth Starkweather (1964a, 1964b, 1968) embarked upon her studies of creativity in preschool with more sophistication regarding creativity theory and research methods than most of her predecessors. She has accepted the concept that the word "creative" implies behavior that means a giving of one's self rather than behavior that is coerced or imitative. Finding many young children unable to do this, she sees the goal as being one of freeing the young child to live creatively and thereby preventing unnecessary loss of creative talent. In defining the nature of this freedom she has focused her attention on a number of motivational characteristics found to be important in creative behavior. She argues that the creative person is neither conforming nor nonconforming but rather is *free* to be conforming or nonconforming, depending upon which is most effective in the situation. He will not use either conforming or nonconforming behavior compulsively, but conforms when necessary and nonconforms when necessary. She also holds that the creative person is willing to try the difficult and prefers a calculated risk. Again, he is free. He does not pursue the difficult compulsively as though the easy task were beneath his dignity. He is free to pursue whichever is most effective. She also focuses on tolerance for chaos and ambiguity. Faced with ambiguous or disorganized situations, the creative child can rise above the chaos, disregard the irrelevant, and produce a new organization from the disorder. She has designed situations, games, play situations, toys, and the like that test the child's ability to manifest freedom in conforming or nonconforming, attempting difficult tasks, and making a new order from chaos. She finds that the highly creative children as identified by these means act purposively and are able to choose between courses of action. As she puts it, "He is not a machine or a mechanical toy that responds in predetermined ways when a key is turned" (1964a).

ELEMENTARY SCHOOL STUDIES

Perhaps one of the most illuminating and certainly the most intensive personality study of creative children thus far reported is by Weisberg and Springer (1961). Intellectually gifted children in the fourth grade were administered a battery of creative thinking tests developed by Torrance (1962, 1965a). Their personalities were studied on the basis of data derived from psychiatric interviews, the Rorschach ink blots, the Draw-a-Family technique, and the like. The characteristics of the children ranking in the upper half of the group were compared with those in the lower half. The more highly creative children were significantly higher than their peers on strength of self-image, ease of early recall, humor, and uneven ego development. Their Rorschach responses showed a tendency toward unconventional responses, unreal percepts, and fanciful and imaginative treatment. They were characterized as having a greater readiness to respond emotionally and spontaneously to the environment, and at the same time as more sensitive and more independent than less creative but equally intelligent children.

In a carefully conducted study involving 151 fifth-grade children in a suburban public school system in a middle-class region, Wallach and Kogan (1964, 1965) found some interesting characterizations of children with creative ability and varying levels of intelligence. Their criterion tests for creativity were five tasks each requiring the generation of different kinds of associates. The tests were administered individually in a game-like atmosphere without time limits. The associates generated were scored for uniqueness and number. Five measures of general intelligence were also used. These included verbal and performance subtests from the Wechsler Intelligence Scale for Children, the School and College Ability Tests (verbal and quantitative), and the Sequential Tests of Educational Progress. A single index of creativity and a single index of intelligence were derived for each child on the basis of these ten measures. Wallach and Kogan then composed four groups within each sex: those in the top half of the distribution on intelligence and also in the top half on creativity, those in the top half on intelligence and in the lower half on creativity, those in the lower half on intelligence and in the top half on creativity, and those in the lower half on both intelligence and creativity. The psychological characteristics of these children were ratings based on two weeks of observations in each classroom by two observers and a variety of other psychological measures such as Free Descriptions of Stick Figures, Thematic Integration, Equivalence Range, Emotive Connotations of Abstract Patterns, Emotive Attributions for Stick Figures, Free Descriptions of Paths, Self-report Measures, and a Fantasy Measure.

Among the girls high on both creativity and intelligence, Wallach and Kogan (1965) found the least doubt and hesitation; the highest level of self-confidence; the least self-deprecation; the highest levels of attention span, concentration, and interest in academic work; a high level of reciprocity in social relationships; and strong tendencies to disruptive, attention-seeking behavior apparently out of their eagerness to propose novel, divergent possibilities or out of their boredom. Girls high in creativity and low in intelligence seemed to be at the greatest disadvantage in the classroom. They are the most cautious and hesitant of all the groups, the least confident, and most self-deprecatory, and the least able to concentrate and maintain attention. They are also high in disruptive and attention-getting behavior but the nature of this behavior suggests an incoherent protest against their plight.

Even those who are low in both intelligence and creativity appear to fare better than those who are high in creativity but low in intelligence. Apparently they are more attuned to the nature of classroom activities. They are less hesitant, more confident, and more outgoing than their more creative peers. This low–low group apparently copes with academic failure by social activity, while the high creative–low intelligent group copes by social withdrawal and retreat within themselves.

Girls high in intelligence but low in creativity show a high degree of confidence and assurance; they are sought by others as companions but they tend not to seek companions themselves. Members of this group are least likely to seek attention in disruptive ways and are hesitant about expressing opinions. Their attention span, concentration, and interest for academic matters is quite high.

Wallach and Kogan (1965) found striking differences among their groups on conceptualizing and schematizing for boys. The creative boys seemed to be able to switch rather flexibly between thematizing and inferential-conceptual bases for grouping data. The high intelligent–low creative boys seem to be rather inflexibly fixated in inferential-conceptual categorizing and strongly avoided thematic-relational categorizing. Those low in both tend to stick with thematic modes of responding. Those who are lowest and highest in anxiety appear to be the most creative. Wallach and Kogan conclude on the basis of the anxiety data that creativity need not be "all sweetness and light," but may involve a tolerance for an understanding of sadness and pain. One of the lowest levels of anxiety is found among those high in intelligence but low in creativity. Defensiveness, however, operates differently from anxiety. Defensiveness seems to lower creativity; at least the more creative children appeared to be relatively lacking in defensiveness.

In summarizing their results, Wallach and Kogan (1964) concluded that whatever their measure of creativity assesses is different from intelligence as now measured and makes a big difference in the behavior of children. In general, they conclude that those high on both creativity and intelligence can exercise both control and freedom and engage in both adult-like and child-like behavior. Those high on creativity and low on intelligence appear to be in angry protest with their school environment and are bothered by feelings of unworthiness and inadequacy. In a stress-free context, as in the game-like tests of creativity, they can blossom forth cognitively. Wallach and Kogan describe those high in intelligence but low in creativity as "addicted to school achievement." They continually strive for academic excellence. Those low in both are basically bewildered and engage in various defensive strategies, ranging from intensive social activity to regressive behavior such as passivity and psychosomatic symptoms.

Several studies conducted by the author and his associates add information concerning the characteristics of creative children at the elementary school level. In one of these studies (Torrance, 1962), he analyzed the personality data of the most creative boy and girl in each of twenty-three classes in grades one through six in three elementary schools. The controls were matched for sex, intelligence quotient, race, class (teacher), and age with the highly creative subjects. In addition to the data from tests of intelligence, the author had available responses to the Draw-a-House-Tree-Person Test, a set of peer nominations on a variety of creativity criteria, and teacher nominations on a variety of creativity criteria, and teacher nominations on similar criteria.

From the statistical analysis of the comparison between the highly creative children and their less creative controls, three personality characteristics stand out as differentiators of the two groups. First, the highly creative children have a reputation for producing wild or silly ideas, especially the boys. Their teachers and peers agree on this point. Second, their drawings and other productions are characterized by originality. This emerges as a highly differentiating factor both when the author uses the number of unique or unusual details and when he uses the number of nonessential details as indices. This finding helps to explain why some of these highly creative children do not show up better than they do on traditional intelligence tests. Their ideas simply do not conform to the standardized dimensions, the behavioral norms, on which responses are evaluated. Third, their productions are characterized by humor, playfulness, and relative relaxation.

The three characteristics that emerge in this study would appear to be of considerable significance in guilding children with high creative abilities. In spite of the fact that these children have many excellent ideas, they have achieved reputations for having silly, wild, or naughty ideas. We can only guess from studies such as those of Wallach and Kogan already described and those of Dauw and Torrance to be described in the next section what effect this derogation of their ideas has on their personality development and the future development of their creative potentialities.

In another study the author and his associates (Torrance, 1963) studied some of the social-interaction characteristics of highly creative children. One class at each grade level from second through sixth grade was divided into five groups each and confronted with the task of discovering the intended and unintended uses of a box of science toys and discovering what principles can be demonstrated and explained with this collection of toys. Groups were composed on the basis of scores attained on a battery of tests of creative thinking ability administered earlier. One of the five most creative members of the class was placed in each group, one of the next five in each group, and so on. The focus of observation was on the techniques used by the group to control its most creative member and his method of counteraction. Groups were given twenty-five minutes in which to examine and manipulate the toys in an attempt to discover what can be done with them and why they work as they do. They were given five minutes in which to organize their demonstrations and twenty-five minutes for the demonstrations. A prize was awarded to the group in each class that demonstrated and explained the largest number of ideas.

In all the groups, there was observable evidence of pressure on the most creative member to reduce production and/or originality. Although a majority (68 percent) of the most creative group members produced more ideas than any other member of the group and many of the others came very close to this distinction, very few of them (24 percent) were credited by the other members with making the most valuable contribution to the success of the group.

From second through sixth grade there was a decreasing tendency for group members to work alone. The tendency for the most creative child of a group to work alone persisted rather strongly through the fifth grade, at which point the tendency for groups to organize emerged as an important technique for controlling the most creative member. By the sixth grade, the groups in this study had developed a varied repertoire of controlling techniques. The most creative members had in turn developed varied techniques of counteraction. Techniques of control included open aggression and hostility, criticism, rejection and/or indifference, the use of organizational machinery to limit scope of operations and to impose sanctions, and exaltation to a position of power involving paperwork and administrative responsibility. Counteraction techniques of the most creative members included compliance, counteraggressiveness, indomitable persistence, apparent ignoring of criticism, clowning, silence and apathy or preoccupation, inconsistent performance, and filling in the gaps when others falter.

HIGH-SCHOOL-LEVEL STUDIES

Studies of Creative Youths
Based on Achievement

Although secondary-level youth have manifested outstanding creative behavior in almost every field of endeavor, the group most frequently studied has been those who have manifested their creativeness in science. One of the most recent and productive of these is by Parloff and Datta (1965) of the National Institute of Mental Health. Their subjects were selected from the male high school seniors who competed in the 1963 Westinghouse Science Talent Search. This competitive program attempts to discover boys and girls whose scientific achievements, skills, and abilities indicate potential creative originality. From the more than 2,500 male applicants who completed successfully all entry requirements, Parloff and Datta selected the 573 who scored above the 80th percentile on a science aptitude examination developed by Science Service, Inc. Each of these subjects had also submitted to the Science Talent Search judges a report describing his independently conducted research report. This project was initiated and conducted by the contestant over as long a period as he felt necessary, ranging from a few weeks to three years. The judges scored the entries for "creativity and potential creativity."

Parloff and Datta regard this product criterion as a valid predictor because it is most comparable to the criterion used to assess the contribution of adult scientists. The norms and criteria for judging science projects have been refined over the period of 22 years of the Science Talent Search. Basically these include evidence that the applicant recognizes and formulates "novel" relationships and such formulations are plausible and/or effective. The judges were selected on the basis of their acknowledged eminence in one of five fields: chemistry, mathematics, biology, medicine, and physics. On the basis of the ratings of the judges, the sample was subdivided into three groups to reflect different levels of creative potential. Group I, High Potential Creativity, included 112 young men; Group II, Moderate Potential Creativity, included 140; and Group III, Low Potential Creativity, included 285. The groups were then compared on the basis of a variety of life experience and personality test variables.

The investigators found statistically significant differences on five scales of the California Psychological Inventory when the members of Groups I and III were compared. The young men in Group I were more ambitious and driving; more independent, autonomous, self-reliant, more efficient and perceptive; more rebellious toward rules and constraints and more imaginative.

Parloff and Datta found no meaningful differences among the three groups on age, intelligence, measured scientific aptitude, vocations of fathers, socioeconomic status, and intactness of family.

The investigators asked Gough, the author and developer of the California Personality Inventory, to provide clinical interpretations of five mean profiles without identification. The profile of Group I (High Potential Creativity) was described by Gough as follows: (1) a high level of intellectual ability, i.e., a level consistent with the group's being excellent students with a zest for independent effort and constructive endeavor; (2) a high level of resourcefulness, i.e., adeptness at coping with new and different situations and in evolving effective techniques for dealing with new problems; (3) the capacity for independent work, i.e., the ability to generate internal motivation without need for external props and reinforcements; and (4) a capacity for original and innovative work.

Group II was characterized by its complexity. This group was described by Gough on the basis of their profile as strong, resolute, and forceful and yet unsure of themselves, doubting, and pessimistic. They are characterized as valuing themselves and their work and seeking recognition and yet are dubious and even annoyed when recognition is forthcoming. They welcome change, uncertainty, and emotional expressiveness, and yet become anxious.

In contrast, the members of Group III were characterized as less concerned with individuality and freedom from external coercion and show less of the spontaneity that leads to creativity. They show less zest for counteracting complacency and inertia and less zest for innovation. They are described as insightful, intelligent, autonomous, constructively motivated, resourceful, and able to pursue meaningful goals.

Studies of Creative Youths Based on Test Criteria

Perhaps the best known and most penetrating of the studies of creative youths at the secondary school level identified as creative on the basis of ability tests is the one by Getzels and Jackson (1962). Although this study has been criticized rather widely (Burt, 1962; Vernon, 1964; McNemar, 1964; Wallach and Kogan, 1965), it is indisputable that Getzels and Jackson succeeded in differentiating by means of test criteria two distinctly different types of gifted secondary school students and differentiated their characteristics. They used the following battery of tests in determining their index of creative ability; Word Association, Unusual Uses, Hidden Shapes, Fables, and Make-up Problems. Their high creatives were defined as those whose creativity indices placed them in the upper 20 percent of students their age and sex but who were not in the upper 20 percent on intelligence or any other indicator of giftedness available to them. Their high intelligence group was similarly defined as those in the top 20 percent on IQ when compared with others in the sample of the same sex and age and who were not in the upper 20 percent on the index of creativity or other measures of giftedness. This meant that students high on both creativity and intelligence were excluded, as were those high on measures of psychological adjustment and morality. The total pool of subjects was 543 students in a private high school ranging from the sixth through twelfth grades. Twenty-six qualified for the high creative group and 28 for the high intelligence group. The mean IQ of the high-IQ group was 150 and for the high creativity group, 127. Thus, both groups are rather highly intelligent, even though there is a difference of 23 IQ points between them.

In this study it was found that the measured school achievement of the highly creative and highly intelligent groups was equally superior to that of the total population from which they were drawn. The high-IQ students were rated by their teachers as more desirable than the average student but the highly creative students were not. On their fantasy productions, the creatives made significantly greater use of stimulus-free themes, unexpected endings, and playfulness. On the basis of these findings, Getzels and Jackson have suggested that an essential difference between the two groups is the creative adolescent's ability to produce new forms and to risk joining together elements usually seen as independent and dissimilar. They also suggested that the creative adolescent seems to enjoy the risk and uncertainty of the unknown. The high-IQ adolescent prefers the anxieties of safety to those of growth. These differences are reflected in the occupational choices of the two groups. Sixty-two percent of the creatives chose unconventional occupations such as adventurer, inventor, writer, and the like. Only 16 percent of the high-intelligence subjects chose such occupations; 84 percent of them chose conventional occupations, such as doctor, lawyer, engineer, and the like.

Getzels and Jackson (1962) interviewed the parents of their two groups of subjects. The parents of the high-IQ students tended to recall greater financial difficulties during their childhoods and at the present time express greater real or imagined personal insecurity than those of the high creatives. The parents of the high-IQ adolescents also seem to be more "vigilant" with respect to their children's behavior and academic success. They are more critical of both their children and the school than are the parents of the highly creative students. The parents of the high-IQ youths focus their attention on immediately visible virtues such as cleanliness, good manners, and studiousness. The parents of the creative focus theirs on less-visible qualities such as the child's openness to experience, his values, and his interests and enthusiasms.

It should be noted that Getzels and Jackson's high creatives differ considerably in intelligence from Wallach and Kogan's high creative–low intelligence group. The latter were in the lower half of the total sample of 151 on the intelligence index. It should also be noted that many of the world's great creative achievements have come from people with estimated IQs in the range of Getzels and Jackson's high creatives. In the famous studies of Terman and his associates of historical geniuses (Cox, 1926), we find such notables as the following in the IQ range 100 to 110: Michael Faraday, Copernicus, James Cook, Robert Fulton, Jean de la Fontaine, and Miguel de Cervantes. In the 110 to 120 range, we find Martin Luther, Rembrandt, Oliver Goldsmith, William Hogarth, and Oliver

Cromwell. In the 120 to 130 range, there are Daniel DeFoe, William Harvey, Franz Joseph Haydn, Antoine Laurent Lavoisier, Robert Blake, Edward Jenner, Justus Leibig, John Locke, and Carolus Linneaus. Some of these men were also thought by their teachers to be of little promise and ranked at the bottom of their classes, failed in school, and became school dropouts.

A study by Gallagher and Jenné (1965) yields information about the classroom behavior of creative high school students. Using two tests similar to those employed by Getzels and Jackson, they identified three groups among high school students enrolled in a special program for gifted youngsters: (1) High IQ–Low Divergent, (2) Low IQ–High Divergent, and (3) High IQ–High Divergent. Among the boys, there were no differences among these three groups in classroom expressiveness. Among the girls, the High IQ–High Divergent subgroup was significantly more expressive than the High IQ–Low Divergent group on the categories of divergent thinking, convergent thinking, and evaluative thinking. The same trend emerged in the cognitive-memory dimension. Among the girls, the least expressive was the Low IQ–High Divergent group; they tended to be most expressive in the evaluative thinking area.

A study by Dauw (1965) differentiated between two types of highly creative high school seniors: highly original thinkers and good elaborators. Using the Torrance Tests of Creative Thinking (Torrance, 1966), six groups were identified within each sex: from a group of 712 seniors enrolled in a public high school (high 20 percent in all cases) on both originality and elaboration, high on elaboration but not on originality, high on originality but not on elaboration, low on both, low on originality but not elaboration, and low on elaboration but not on originality. Their characteristics were studied on the basis of responses to a life experience inventory, a creative personality self-description checklist, and the Minnesota Importance Questionnaire.

The high-original boys characteristically described themselves as adventurous, curious, independent in thinking, willing to take risks, and as having a sense of humor, and the opposite of timid, bored, conforming, and quiet. Their career aspirations tended to be creative and unconventional, such as anthropologist, actor, and the like. They expressed stronger vocational needs than any of the other groups of boys in creativity, recognition, and social service.

The high-elaborating boys perceived themselves as healthy, desiring to excel, considerate of others, willing to take risks, adventurous, and as having a sense of humor, and as not timid, bored, or fearful. They dislike working alone and do not regard themselves as being emotionally sensitive. Their school grades are higher than those of the high-original boys but their scholastic apitude scores (Minnesota Scholastic Aptitude Test) are slightly, though not significantly, lower. Their career aspirations are more conventional than those of the high originals. The strength of their expressed vocational needs is quite low.

Boys high on both originality and elaboration regarded themselves as willing to take risks, unwilling to accept things on other's say so, always asking questions, and having a sense of humor. They reject as self-descriptive such characteristics as timidity, good guessing ability, fearfulness, quietness, and a tendency to disrupt the procedures and organizations of groups. Their grades and scholastic aptitude test scores are higher than those of any of the other male groups. Their career aspirations are about as unconventional as those of the high-original boys, and their vocational needs are higher than the other male groups for variety, activity, and responsibility.

Among the female groups, the high originals are very much like the high-original boys. In addition, they tend to see themselves as desirous of excelling, emotionally sensitive, and often bored. Similarly, the high-elaborating girls are very much like the high-elaborating boys, except that they characteristically see themselves as affectionate, emotionally sensitive, and strongly emotional. Their career aspirations are focused on such occupations as teaching, direct services to others, psychology, and social work.

Girls highest on both originality and elaboration described themselves as characteristically desiring to excel, competitive, strongly emotional, emotionally sensitive, nonconforming, and as having a sense of humor. Their school grades and scholastic apitude test scores are higher than those of any of the other groups. Their career aspirations tend to be along such lines as biochemist, interior decorator, writer, and the like. Creativity and authority needs are higher among them than among any of the other groups of girls. They also express strong needs for variety, ability utilization, moral values, responsibility, achievement, and social service.

In their life experiences, the high elaborators among both girls and boys tend to be more perfectionistic than the high originals and do things over and over until satisfied with the results. The high originals—especially the girls—tend to set higher standards and goals for themselves more often than the high elaborators. Apparently, the parents and teachers of the high elaborators have very great expectations for them, and this group of young people seems to be desperately afraid that they will not be able to measure up to these expectations. The high originals seem "almost angry" because parents and teachers do not have higher expectations for them than they do and tend to restrain them in the high goals that they set for themselves. The highly original boys appear to prefer a more competitive work relationship while the high elaborators seem to prefer a more cooperative one.

In classes, the highly elaborating more frequently than the highly original girls volunteered answers "every time" and knew or thought they knew the answers. Among the boys, however, the high originals were more likely to volunteer answers. The "best" teachers, according to the high elaborators, are very strict, while the high originals preferred their teachers to be more permissive.

DO CREATIVE CHILDREN BECOME CREATIVE ADULTS?

Critics of creativity research have asked repeatedly, "Do creative children become creative adults?" This author has always argued that many highly creative children do not have a chance to become creative adults and that educators should be interested in identifying potentialities which, with opportunity and guidance, might become highly creative personalities and make important social contributions. Since it is extremely difficult to provide such opportunities and guidance and since considerable time must elapse before such hypotheses can be tested, the author and other creativity researchers have been slow to produce convincing evidence. Such evidence is now becoming available, however.

Perhaps one of the most significant experiments to test the author's hypothesis that creatively gifted children, if given opportunities to develop and guidance, will become creative persons was initiated by George Witt (1968) in the summer of 1965. Using only the results of a battery of creative thinking tests (Torrance, 1966) and one task that the investigator himself devised, Witt identified a group of highly creative, lower-class Negro children in a ghetto setting. Witt believed that highly creative children are injured more in such settings than are their less creative peers.

Twelve of the original 16 children have continued in the program for over three years and all of them have manifested high-level creative skills in such fields as music, art, science, and writing. Much work has been done with the families. In many instances, the high creative talents of siblings have been recognized and opportunities have been provided for them to have music, art, ballet, and other kinds of lessons from outstanding teachers. In a few instances, it has been possible to help parents of the children upgrade their job skills and acquire better jobs.

In fashioning a program for highly creative inner-city children, Witt attempted to incorporate the following major characteristics:

1. Be clearly structured but flexible.
2. Provide for opportunities to be rewarded for solving problems.
3. Be viewed by one and all in a positive light.
4. Be tangible; and have many activities conducted in the homes.
5. Have enough competent adults in charge to minimize the need for the ubiquitous instant jeering and quarreling.

6. Continue controls indefinitely.

7. Involve exciting people from the inner and non-inner city.

8. Design all learning experiences so that exciting perceptual-motor experiences precede, accompany, and follow cognitive growth.

9. Be intimately coordinated by a director expert in individual, group, and community dynamics.

10. Provide for the support, control, and involvement of the children's families, parents, and siblings.

Each year, Witt reports, new structural elements have been added to the program as the children, their families, and the programs have grown.

During the first part of the program the specialists who worked with the program began to doubt that the children who had been selected had any kind of creative potentialities. Witt encouraged them to keep working, however, and he continued working with the children and involving their families. Before the end of the first summer, all the children had exhibited outstanding promise in at least one creative field and many of them had shown unusual promise in two or more areas.

It would be hazardous to predict the adult futures of the twelve children who have continued in the program devised by Witt and called LEAP (Life Enrichment Activity Program). The present indication, however, are that these children are developing talents that are highly valued both in their own subcultures and in the dominant culture, and that their families are supporting their development and in most cases developing along with them.

The author has just completed a study initiated in a very different setting in 1959, but a setting in which there was a good chance for creative talent to flourish, the University of Minnesota High School (Torrance, 1966). Seven years after high school graduation, follow-up data were obtained from 46 of the 69 high school seniors administered the Torrance Tests of Creative Thinking in 1959 at the time they were entering their senior year. Although some of them were in Viet Nam and many of them were just completing their doctoral programs, their creative achievements were considerable. Twenty of the 23 high originals were in graduate programs and most of them were in the process of completing their doctoral dissertations at top-flight universities in the United States and Europe. None of the 23 low originals indicated that they had reached the dissertation-writing stage and only five of them were in graduate programs. The following creative achievements differentiated the high originals from the low originals; number of poems, stories, plays, songs, etc., written; number of such works published; number of books written; number of radio or television scripts and productions; number of original research designs developed; number of original suggestions for changes in their work situations; number who received research grants; and number of scientific papers published. Descriptions of their highest creative

Table 1 *Correlations between Predictors Established in 1959 as High School Seniors and Creative Achievement Criteria Established in 1966*

Predictors	Highest creative achievement	Quantity creative achievement	Future creative motivation
Intelligence test	.37[a]	.22	.32
High school achievement	.20	.09	.15
Peer nominations:			
creativity criteria	.13	.13	.18
Fluency (TTCT)	.39[a]	.44[a]	.34
Flexibility (TTCT)	.48[a]	.44[a]	.46[a]
Originality (TTCT)	.43[a]	.40[a]	.42[a]
Elaboration (TTCT)	.32	.37[a]	.25
Combined TTCT	.50[a]	.46[a]	.51[a]

[a] Significant at .01 level. N = 46.

achievements and their life aspirations were rated by a panel of experts on the basis of creativity criteria and these ratings differentiated the two groups quite sharply. The correlation data are presented in Table 1. It will be noted that only one of the nine coefficients of correlation for the noncreativity variables is statistically significant at the .01 level, while nine of the twelve creativity predictors reach this level of significance. If we lower the level of significance to the .05 level, two of the coefficients for the noncreativity predictors and eleven of the ones for the creativity predictors are significant.

CONCLUSION

Although it will take some time for creativity research to come to maturity, it seems clear that creatively gifted children and youth can be characterized and that they are different in important ways from their less creative peers. These differences create problems of adjustment between them and their peers and sometimes between them and their teachers. Evidence is beginning to accumulate to support the contention that children and young people identified as creatively gifted, if given opportunities and reasonable guidance, tend to become creative adults.

References

Andrews, E. G. The development of imagination in the pre-school child. *Univ. of Iowa Stud. of Character,* 1930, Vol. 3, No. 4.

Burt, C. Critical notice: *Creativity and intelligence* by J. W. Getzels and P. W. Jackson. *Brit. J. Educ. Psychol.*, 1962, *32*, 292–298.

Cox, C. M. *The early mental traits of 300 geniuses* (Vol. II, Genetic studies of genius). Stanford, Calif.: Stanford University Press, 1926.

Dauw, D. C. Life experiences, vocational needs and choices of original thinkers and good elaborators. Doctoral dissertation, University of Minnesota, 1965.

Gallagher, J. J., & Jenné, W. *Productive thinking of gifted children* (Cooperative Research Project 965). Urbana, Ill.: Institute for Research on Exceptional Children, University of Illinois, 1965.

Getzels, J. W., & Jackson, P. W. *Creativity and intelligence.* New York: Wiley, 1962.

Gotkin, L. G., & Massa, N. Programmed instruction and the academically gifted: The effects of creativity and teacher behavior on programmed instruction with young learners. New York: Center for Programmed Instruction, 1963. (Mimeographed)

Hutchinson, W. L. Creative and productive thinking in the classroom. Doctoral dissertation, University of Utah, 1963.

McConnell, T. R. Discovery vs. authoritative identification in the learning of children. *Univ. of Iowa Stud. in Education*, 1934, *9*(5), 13–62.

MacDonald, J. B., & Raths, J. D. Should we group by creative abilities? *Elementary School J.*, 1964, *65*, 137–142.

McNemar, Q. Lost: Our Intelligence? Why? *Amer. Psychologist*, 1964, *19*, 871–882.

Parloff, M. B., & Datta, L. E. Personality characteristics of the potentially creative scientist. *Science & Psychoanalysis*, 1965, *8*, 91–106.

Starkweather, E. K. Problems in the measurement of creativity in preschool children. *J. Educ. Measure.*, 1964, *1*, 109–114. (a)

Starkweather, E. K. *Conformity and nonconformity as indicators of creativity in preschool children* (Cooperative Research Project 1967). Stillwater, Okla.: Oklahoma State University, 1964. (b)

Starkweather, E. K. Studies of the creative potential of young children. In F. E. Williams (Ed.), *Creativity at home and in school.* St. Paul, Minn.: Macalester College, 1968, pp. 75–122.

Stolurow, L. M. Social impact of programmed instruction: Aptitudes and abilities revisited. Paper presented at the American Psychological Association Annual Convention, St. Louis, September 2, 1962.

Torrance, E. P. *Guiding creative talent.* Englewood Cliffs, N.J.: Prentice-Hall, 1962.

Torrance, E. P. *Education and the creative potential.* Minneapolis: University of Minnesota Press, 1963.

Torrance, E. P. *Rewarding creative behavior: Experiments in classroom creativity.* Englewood Cliffs, N.J.: Prentice-Hall, 1965. (a)

Torrance, E. P. *Gifted children in the classroom.* New York: Macmillan, 1965. (b)

Torrance, E. P. *Torrance tests of creative thinking: Norms-technical manual (Research Edition).* Princeton, N.J.: Personnel Press, 1966.

Vernon, P. E. Creativity and intelligence. *Educ. Res.* (England), 1964, *6*, 163–169.

Wallach, M. A., & Kogan, N. A new look at the creativity-intelligence distinction (*Research Memorandum RM-64-11*). Princeton, N.J.: Educational Testing Service, 1964.

Wallach, M. A., & Kogan, N. *Modes of thinking in young children: A study of the creativity-intelligence distinction*. New York: Holt, Rinehart and Winston, 1965.

Weisberg, P. S., & Springer, K. J. Environmental factors in creative function. *Arch. gen. Psychiat.,* 1961, *5,* 554–564.

Witt, G. The life enrichment program: A brief history. New Haven, Conn.: LEAP, Inc., 1968. (Mimeographed)

13

A Critique of
Research on the Gifted

T. Ernest Newland

Dr. Newland is Professor of Educational Psychology and Director of the School Psychology Program at the University of Illinois. His research interests and publications cut across many areas of exceptionality. Of particular note is his new test for blind children, The Blind Learning Aptitude Test. *He is advisory editor for* Exceptional Children *and for the* Journal of School Psychology. *He has also served as President of the Association for the Gifted.*

For the student interested in doing research in the area of the gifted, he should read very carefully the critical evaluations set forth by Dr. Newland in this paper. He sharply spells out many of the deficiencies in reported research and gives constructive suggestions for improvement.

This is a presumptuous statement, written by a person who wishes he were familiar with *all* the research in this area, by one who, for this purpose, would welcome some "absolutes" which could make communication simpler, by one who perceives the research on the gifted as being distressingly spotty. Even though the area of the gifted can boast of the only major truly longitudinal study of exceptional children, and a few other outstanding ones of lesser scope, the bulk of studies have resembled rifle

FROM *Exceptional Children*, April 1963. Reprinted by permission from The Council for Exceptional Children.

shots or ill-aimed shotgun blasts, rather than well-thought-out firing patterns.

Individual researchers and academic and public pressures being what they are, such spottiness is inevitable. Fundamental theory anchorage has been limited, or too often totally lacking. Even certain fundamental educational realities and psychometric concepts have been overlooked or ignored. Certain social realities, perhaps because of their complexity, subtlety, or elusiveness, have been disregarded. Many researchers in the area, because of geographic or conceptual provincialism, have realized less from their efforts than they should. But there are streaks of light in the east.

The teacher or administrator will find here few specifics which research has revealed about the gifted. There is an urgent need for a synthesized and integrated summary of research in this area which could provide that kind of information. But many "studies" cannot be interrelated meaningfully because of the incomparability of the measures obtained in them, the varying (and so-often unspecified) populations involved in them, and the absence of much significant social and educational information about the groups studied. Rather, this statement is devoted essentially to certain characteristics of research on the gifted, with the hope that the teacher and administrator, as consumers of research findings, may be caused to think twice when they read these findings.

Generally, communication continues to be a major problem in the reporting of research on the gifted. Underlying much of the research effort has been the usually implicit desire to *demonstrate* certain phenomena and practices—identification, grouping, and marking procedures. Those who have made such "studies" have sought to show local folk "what-happens-if," often duplicating or imitating (but seldom replicating) earlier studies which long have been a matter of record. The uninformed consumers of such research often have difficulty differentiating between such demonstration activities—not completely without value for local promotional purposes—and research which seeks to ascertain new facts. Fortunately, a few researchers who have carried out demonstration studies have, because of their research sensitivity and improvements recently made possible by more and better devices and by sharpened statisticizing, been able to explore facets formerly omitted, as in the case of self and social perceptions and other attitudinal milieu factors. The inadequately researched and/or reported backgrounds of both demonstration and exploration research unforunately has deprived the research consumer in this area of necessary fundamental orientation.

There is a high probability that the curious reader of research on the gifted will be frustrated when he seeks a clear picture of the populations which have been studied. He will experience difficulty if he seeks to relate the findings of one study on the "academically talented" to findings of other studies on the "gifted," or on the "precocious," or "bright," or "mentally superior." He will, understandably, confuse the "creative" with the "divergent thinkers." If he is sensitive to the large differences among "intelligence" tests, he will wonder how it could happen that the December 1959 periodic summary of research on the gifted and talented not once related the numbered IQs which were mentioned to the devices by means of which they were obtained. Further confusion regarding the population on which research was reported will result when the same term "gifted" will be used by the authors (or interpreters) to denote, on the one hand, those children above 120 (on Test X), on the other hand, those above 150 (on the same test), and, again, those above 180 (still on the same test). And dissertation writers add noise to the communication process when, having studied a well-identified superior population in Podunk, they draw conclusions and inferences which read as though they were applicable in Pittsburgh, Paducah, and Patagonia.

Convenience rather than conscientiousness or psychological conceptualization has determined the nature of much research on the gifted. The availability of data obtained by means of a widely sold (and even more widely criticized) test has played a major role in determining which children were studied. Conscientiousness and psychological conceptualization have yielded to impetuousness and pseudo-sophistication. Witness the implicit or explicit acceptance of the relationship—WISC V IQ; CTMM L IQ:: WISC P IQ: CTMM N-L IQ! Thesis and dissertation research, which has figured largely in the area of the gifted, has tended to be piecemeal rather than patterned. Educational gains, social adjustment, and other changing phenomena have been measured over only short periods of time, with inferences based upon extrapolations. As valuable as it is to find out what the facts about gifted children may be, care must be exercised in specifying what these children will be as adults; as necessary as it is to ascertain the characteristics of successful scientists, architects, mathematicians, any attempt at backward extrapolations to their (or others') childhoods must be most circumspect psychologically and socially.

SOME SPECIFICS

Certain areas of research involving or relating to the gifted warrant specific attention. Here, too, since this in no way constitutes a comprehensive survey of the field, the designation of specific studies and the customary bibliographic documentation will studiously be avoided (although they will be supplied the inquiring reader). As will be seen, some of these areas suggest hopeful and possibly fruitful beginnings in contrast with (happily) a few others which involve psychometric blundering. Some smack of near-saturation or stereotyping; others represent challenges and relatively unsensed opportunities; and still others suggest more the operation of unsophisticated enthusiasm than the presence of validated conceptualization.

Identification

Here research communication is hampered in large part by the ambiguity and abandon with which terms denoting different kinds of the gifted are used. Complete abandon is typified by the "you-know-what-I-mean-anyhow-so-I-don't-need-to-bother-with-defining-my-terms" attitude. Although such an attitude may be conducive to good missionary feeling, it muddies, if not precludes, meaningful research. The percentage pronouncers vary from those who hold, often psychologically blindly, to the top one, two, or three percent of the *generalized* population to those who, with equal lack of psychological reason, contend that the gifted constitute the top 15 to 20 percent of *any* population. Too often ignored are conceptualizations based on the psychological ways of learning and doing things which most fundamentally and uniquely delineate the gifted. Just as, 30 years ago, it was a shock to some to learn that "intelligence" tests then in use did not help in identifying salesmen, just so have some learned that that kind of test was not particularly effective in identifying "creative" thinkers. The discovery of the large number of factors of intellect—or the large variety of ways in which intellectual giftedness may manifest itself—has tremendously significant educational and social aspects. Much still needs to be found out about the preciseness with which factors of intellect identified with certain clarity in adults can be expected to exist with comparable clarity or differentiation among elementary school children. Whether, and how, the gifted should be identified in terms of what society needs in order to function has been little explored beyond the point of proclamations of needs in science, in mathematics, in some professions, and in a few technologies.

Dynamics

The slight shift in curiosity from what the relatively isolated personality traits of the gifted are to how these and other traits operate interactively is encouraging and challenging in terms of the potential yield, and intimidating in terms of the complexity of the problem. Particularly provocative have been findings regarding the impact on the gifted of the value systems of their fathers and mothers. As valuable and suggestive as such findings may be, and as impactful as extra-school social group, neighborhood and community values and tolerances yet may be found to be, research on how the school can capitalize upon some of them and must operate to compensate for or correct them, rather than just, perhaps, to profess an awareness of them, remains to be done on any major scale. The experimental verification, or other more objective ascertainment of the validity of many of the introspections and biographic interpretations is yet to be carried out. The increase in the amount and quality of research on self perceptions and social perceptions of and by the gifted and the interaction of the two have been encouraging. Still to be explored systematically are the effects which varying kinds of social milieu may have on these perceptions. In spite of the frustrations inherent in such research, much more such work is needed. Interestingly lacking have been any well-planned explorations of the validity of adults' claims regarding the nature and values of "peer" groups. For instance, considerable curiosity should be manifested by researchers on the gifted as to whether the "peerness" which is claimed to be beneficial is a phenomenon made up of adult (educator or parent) perceptions or of the perceptions of the children themselves, or in what combination these two types of perceptions operate. Only starting, and on a most limited scale, is the exploration of the role which mental level plays in the social interactions of children, the extent to which (and the situations in which) the conceptual complexity or simplicity in terms of which children interact (in games, classwork, committees, "just talking") in predisposing to social clusterings.

Underachievement

The resurgence, from the early 20's, of curiosity about the disparities between the school achievement levels and the mental levels of gifted children is understandable (although the lack of researchers' familiarity with that early work is unforgivable) because of the educational and social importance of the condition and because of the relative ease of exploring it. A recent research group rightly observed that near-saturation or actual saturation has been reached in this kind of exploration. The fact of bona fide underachievement of many gifted children has been re-established. The characteristics of the condition have been reasonably well re-demonstrated, although some dynamic factors in the condition can still be better delineated. But enough is known regarding the condition to warrant the next steps, still generally to be taken (or reported)—the experimental validation of appropriate remedial education techniques. Some of those who have been soundly motivated to study underachievement have unfortunately employed measuring devices having widely questioned validity, or have used devices the results of which were highly unrelatable, and have, therefore, contributed dubious data on a legitimate matter of concern. Some investigators have regarded "overachievement" as a valid, researchable phenomenon and have studied it without quotation marks; a few others retained the quotation marks, but still treated their data as though they were psychologically valid and logical.

There is one area, though, that invites research the execution of which would be quite difficult, but the results of which would be most significant socially and psychologically. Assume, for instance, that there has been identified—in some reasonably valid manner—a group of quite young children of superior learning potential. Assume their environments to be manipulable in such a manner that they can be treated in such a way as to prevent their becoming underachievers. Assuming that their treatment in school would be such at to follow through or supplement their preschool treatment, would their later school behavior be that of underachievers? If so, for how long? For how long would extra-school environmental manipulation (of a nurturant character) be needed? Fortunately, a few studies of the amelioration of cultural deprivation have been started. There is a risk, though, that, early gains having been discovered, extrapolations to continued nonunderachievement may not be supportable in fact. The necessity of truly longitudinal research planning and execution, of educational planning and efforts considerably beyond the confines of the school plant, and of objective information on adult performance in society is clearly indicated.

Creativity

With the factor of divergent thinking (as well as that of evaluative thinking) discovered in the intellect, it has now become possible to lend scientific support to the early philosophical admonitions that the schools encourage and nurture those kinds of behavior. Perhaps as a partial reaction to the impact of the "organizational man" thinking which started being so widely deplored a few years ago, much research has been published on creative behavior of school children—education's application of a psychological finding. Ignoring the matter of the relative educational values of knowing, remembering, evaluating, being able to arrive at specified solutions to problems, and of creating, and recognizing that educational practices may well have neglected the area of creativity, we find that many efforts in the study of creative behavior raise research questions.

Most of the studies of creative behavior have been and are being made by means of devices that have only face validity—the devices are perceived to measure such behavior because their creators say they do, not because they have been demonstrated objectively to do so. The criterion of creative behavior is a particularly sticky one. In view of the naming of the psychological factor "divergent thinking," it is understandable that a criterion of unusualness of response to some presumably standardized stimulus would be a statistical one, say a response that characterizes no more than three percent of a given group. Differentiating between the purely statistically infrequent response and the bizarre response of the individual who is essentially out of contact with his environment raises questions regarding the psychological connotation and ambiguity of data so obtained. Behaviorally related to this test-induced phenomenon in children is the "brainstorming" technique, used in industry since at least the 40's. But here the widely varying responses are evaluated in terms of the problem at hand, and major research on creative adults has been proceeding with the criterion that creative behavior in adults be oriented to the solution of problems in some way that will have social applicability. Here, again, longitudinal research is needed to ascertain whether those giving the purely statistically infrequent responses in childhood tend to be those who give socially applicable new responses as adults, and the extent to which the psychological processes underlying the divergent thinking at the two age levels are similar. From an *a priori* standpoint, a similarity could be presumed; but the history of research shows not a few such presumptions to have been false. Let it be clear: This is an expression of curiosity, not condemnation.

Two other aspects of the research on creative behavior in children merit consideration. Generally, the fact that divergent thinking is different from the other identified intellectual factors has tended to cause to be neglected the fact that there still remains a positive, though low, correlation between divergent thinking and the other factors. Playing up the unusualness and attractiveness of the one aspect can have the effect of playing down, if not completely obscuring, the importance of the others. Secondly, when it was discovered (!) that the most commonly used "intelligence" tests did not also identify well those children who were, by some other measure, believed to be creative, there developed a tendency to ignore or deny, nearly completely, the merits which such tests have had since their early use. Countering this influence is an attempt now being made to relate to the several identified factors of the intellect the various test items of the Binet. This effort awaits statistical validation, but does not seem devoid of promise.

Educational Provisions

In only a crude sense can the term research be applied to most attempts which have been made to find out how well gifted children have learned, what happened to their socio-emotional adjustments, and how they perceived themselves and/or each other when such children were put into different kinds of educational settings—interest groups, semi-special classes, or special sections or classes—or were "enriched," or accelerated. It is frightening to contemplate even the magnitude of the number of studies which resulted in conclusions that multiple track programs were found to be good (or bad); that a Colfax-type program resulted in better (or poorer) learning, or in greater (or less) social alienation; or that early admission had beneficial (or harmful) effects. The teacher or administrator who has said, "We tried homogeneous grouping (or special classes, or multiple tracking) and we found that it didn't (or did) work," differs from many researchers who have sought to study the effects of these same conditions only in that he lacks masses of data with which to buttress his statment. The naïveté of both such a teacher or administrator and the majority of those who have researched such matters resides in the fact that what happened educationally after the administrative provisions of special class, or multiple track, had been made most often has not been described, or has been described with gross inadequacy from an experimental point of view. It has so often been like running an experiment on the uses of different types of medication, putting the patients in private rooms, joint rooms, and wards, failing to describe just what the medication itself was, and then drawing conclusions with assumed constancies or comparability of medication but in terms of where the patients' beds were. Many researchers on the gifted have made tacit assumptions that certain kinds of educational treatment inevitably accompanied certain kinds of administrative shufflings of children. And yet, anyone with the slightest exposure to workaday or experimental classroom practices is acutely aware of the vast differences of teacher behavior under conditions which an outsider would regard as constant among those teachers. Even the provision of prescribed "experimental" curriculum materials does not assure experimentally comparable use of those materials, even on the part of teachers who may have been given some help or training in their use. All such studies should be evaluated in terms of the idea that research is a process of ascertaining well-described results of a well-described variable (variables) on a well-described population over a specified period of time.

All too many studies on what were assumed to be educational provisions were, rather, evaluations accompanied by administrative provisions, with insufficient sensitivity to the at least equally crucial variable of what happened educationally (what the teachers did with the children who were "grouped," or "tracked," or "accelerated," or "enriched"). The import of the criticism is not that research should be done only when and if all the variables are completely described and/or fully controlled, but rather that the researcher show greater sensitivity to the characteristics of the significant variables the effects of which he is trying to ascertain (not "enrichment" but what actually goes on under that label) and that he describe as fully as present sophistication permits such crucial variables as are under study. It is true that certain kinds of educational treatment are a bit more likely to occur in a special class than in a regular class, but we still are far from being able to say that there is an experimental constancy among the things that happen in special classes. This tends all the more to be a significant variable in school systems or buildings having "homogenous" grouping where administrative policy provides that teachers shall rotate among the fast, average, and slow classes on successive years, on the implied assumption that teacher competencies are constant for the three groups.

Some attempts are being made to develop ways of more precisely describing teacher and pupil behavior in the classroom, particularly with respect to divergent, evaluative, and inductive aspects of it. Even though, in large part, these efforts may have been motivated by or may have grown out of research on the gifted, they logically are less specifically integral aspects of research on the gifted than they are methodological developments which can be more generally useful.

Scholarships

Fortunately, major private scholarship-awarding organizations are sufficiently perceptive and research-conscious to conduct research on screening procedures, on characteristics of the recipients, and on postaward behavior of the recipients, so that some educationally and psychologically valuable information, even though on a limited segment of the gifted population, is building up. But it is important to keep in mind the fact that the scholarship movement resulted from findings (dating from at least the 30's) regarding the failure of a major portion of college-capable high school graduates to continue their schooling. At first the financial condition of the discontinuants was regarded as the primary cause. This being a relatively tangible kind of cause, it was more likely to catch the public eye (as well as 8-to-40-cent tax dollars) than was the more elusive contributive factor of motivation. However, even this has come to receive a limited amount of promising attention through the expanding "horizons" action research projects.

Related to this and, perhaps, capable of greater generality, is a potential scholarship area with respect to which curiosity is lacking and data apparently are unassembled. Questions such as these need to be answered: Among the 10 to 20 percent of students who drop out of high school before graduation, what percentage might have been of college caliber? In what percentage of such instances were finances the primary, or heavily contributive, determining factor? How much scholarship money would have been needed to enable such youngsters to complete their high school program? (Attitudinal and other motivational factors which would be amenable to manipulation in the form of guidance—broadly conceived—would constitute a valuable, and probably necessary, parallel study.) In other words, the concept of scholarships, particularly those made available by means of state funds, well could be extended to helping bright high school youngsters avoid becoming drop-outs and thus becoming the responsibility of the federal government in its completing the job the local schools failed to do in the first place—if we had facts which indicated the potential social and personal value of such action.

Another bit of curiosity exists with respect to the present scholarship picture. What would happen if society replaced the practice of granting scholarships and shifted to the practice of issuing partially repayable loans to bright students who wished to continue their education, thus creating a partial rotation of scholarship funds? This is not a problem for a master's thesis or a doctoral dissertation, but it is amenable to research.

SUMMARY

What major observations, then, can be made regarding research on the gifted? The following seem worthy of note.

1. Improvement is badly needed in the area of nomenclature. If researchers cannot agree upon uniform terminology, they have an even greater obligation to make unmistakably clear the nature of the group on which the research is reported.

2. The validity and reliability of the devices employed must be carefully considered before the research is carried out, and fully described in the report of any research.

3. The research should be based upon sound psychological theory and on well described educational practice.

4. The report of the research should be sufficiently precisely written that replication is possible on the basis of only the written report.

5. Even though studies involving successive level sampling can have considerable suggestive value, more truly longitudinal research is needed.

6. Patterned research involving a number of significant, interrelated variables, using contrasting samples where necessary, is sorely needed.

7. While descriptive research is valuable, research involving experimental manipulation of the variables identified by descriptive research must follow.

8. Along with the doing of all these things, there still is a significant place for highly intuitive, informal tinkering, either inductive or deductive in nature, for it is out of such manifestations of curiosity that more rigorous and precise study of the variables so identified can and must be carried out.

part III

Exceptional Sensory and Motor Processes

The Aurally and Visually Handicapped

14

Space Perception and Orientation in the Blind

Philip Worchel

Dr. Worchel is Professor of Psychology at the University of Texas. He has served as Chairman of the National Psychological Research Council for the Blind and Director of Clinical Training at the University of Texas.

This study, which has become a research classic in the field of the blind, was stimulated initially by Dr. Karl Dallenbach's research on obstacle perception in the blind as a way of determining the basic mental processes underlying space perception and orientation. The use of blind subjects and matched sighted subjects provides a means of assessing the importance of visual imagery and verbalization in space perception. In this study, differences were reported between sighted and blinded subjects, and between the congenitally and adventitiously blinded on such tasks as tactual form perception.

THE PROBLEMS

Centuries of controversy and speculation concerning the sensory basis of spatial perception have yielded no decisive solution. The problem as conceived is not a feasible one for experimental test. To deprive a subject

Reprinted and edited from *Psychological Monographs,* 1951, *65,* No. 15, with the permission of the publisher, American Psychological Association, and the author.

completely of tactile-kinesthetic sensitivity at birth, in order to determine its role in the development of spatial experience, is practically an impossibility. Furthermore, to deprive an adult organism of a sense is not a valid procedure for determining the role of a sense organ in perception. It neglects the possibility of sensory compensation which may follow after years of sensory loss. Adding or subtracting sense organs experimentally may involve intersensory influences which must be considered in the interpretation of the results. Finally, the inadequate and limited tests of space perception employed, and the lack of controls, preclude valid generalizations. The tests must take into consideration the complex and multiple nature of spatial perceptions. Extensity, spatial order (including figures, directions, positions, magnitudes, and distances) and spatial relations—all must be considered under the general term of space perception. The analysis of experience into simple elements based upon isolated stimulations can give an oversimplified and distorted picture of the qualitative importance of individual sense organs.

Space perception is of sufficient practical and theoretical interest to warrant further experimentation on fundamental problems. By a systematic and carefully controlled study of the spatial perceptions of the totally blind and sighted individuals, we may determine the basis of the interrelationship of postural and distance-receptor mechanisms in spatial experiences. An investigation of the effect of age at blindness on space perception may reveal the role, if any, of visual experiences in space development.

THE EXPERIMENTS

All the experiments reported here were performed at the Texas State School for the Blind, in Austin. The first two series of experiments on form perception and spatial relations were conducted in a large unused classroom in the basement. The third experiment on space orientation took place on a 40- by 80-ft. concrete skating rink located behind the main building.

Of the 196 blind students at the School, 33 were classified as totally blind. These 33 Ss participated in all three series of experiments. The control group consisted of 33 sighted students from the public schools of Austin. They were matched on the basis of sex and chronological age. The blind Ss had been given the Hayes-Binet Intelligence Test. None of the blind received an IQ score below 85 or above 120. The school level of the blind Ss ranged from the second to the eleventh grade.

The mean age of the blind and sighted Ss was 14.67 years and 14.42 years, respectively, and the range was 8 to 21 years. There were 19 males and 14 females in each group. Sixteen of the blind Ss were congenitally blinded, 7 lost their sight before the age of 6, and 10 became blind after the age of 6 years.

The sighted Ss were transported to the School for the Blind, where the experimental areas were located. All the Ss, both the sighted and the blind, were securely blindfolded in all three series of experiments.*

Three aspects of space perception were investigated in the present study: tactual form perception, tactual space relation, and space orientation.

EXPERIMENT A: TACTUAL FORM PERCEPTION

Statement of the Problem

This study attempts to evaluate the ability of the blind to perceive tactual form. The methods of reproduction, verbal description, and recognition are employed. The procedures in the present experiment isolated the form component from all other object components such as weight, texture, and size. By matching our blind Ss with sighted Ss of the same age and sex, and by using totally blind individuals with varying durations of blindness, we hoped to determine the role of visualization in tactual form perception.

The Method

The form perception experiments consist of three parts. In Part 1 small blocks of simple geometrical shapes are manipulated in one hand; in Part 2 larger blocks are used and both hands are permitted to explore the object. The methods of reproduction (drawing) and verbal report (description) are employed. In Part 3 the method of recognition is used in selecting the stimulus block from four choice blocks.

Small forms: reproductions and verbal report A set of nine blocks of three-ply wood was cut into the following shapes and dimensions: (1) square, 2 x 2 in., (2) circle, 1-in. radius, (3) equilateral triangle, 2-in. sides, (4) semicircle, 1-in. radius, (5) rectangle, 1 x 2 in., (6) quarter-circle, 2-in. radius, (7) parallelogram, 2-in. sides, (8) crescent, 2 in. from tip to tip, (9) ellipse, 1-in. and 2-in. radii.

These blocks were presented in the above order to the blindfolded S. The following instructions were given:

---

* The blind were blindfolded in order to eliminate any light perception that may have been present but not diagnosed by the oculist.

> I am going to hand you a number of objects one at a time. After I hand it to you, I want you to feel it with one hand so that you can remember the shape. When you lay it down, pick up the pencil which lies on your desk [*E* indicates pencil] and draw the shape to the best of your ability on the sheet of paper which lies in front of you.

The first object was then handed to *S*. When *S* placed the block on the desk, he picked up the pencil and drew the object (method of reproduction). He was then asked to name the form or describe it (method of verbal report). Then the second block was presented, and so on. The time between the presentation of the block to *S* and the return of the block to the desk was recorded. At no time, however, was *S* given any indication that speed was involved.

Large forms: reproduction and verbal report The nine blocks of this test duplicated the forms of the first part, but the area of each block was three times that of the ones in Part 1. The procedure of administration and scoring was repeated. After the completion of Part 1, the following instructions were read to the *S*:

> This time I am going to hand you a number of larger blocks, one at a time. After I hand one to you, I want you to feel it with both hands instead of one so that you can remember the shape. When you lay it down, pick up the pencil and draw the shape to the best of your ability on the sheet of paper.

After *S* had drawn the form, he was asked to name or describe that form.

Method of recognition In using the method of recognition, we had to construct two sets of blocks of identical forms but different sizes in order to isolate the form component from all other object components. The set of smaller blocks was used as the stimulus objects, and the second set (the larger blocks) was used as the response or choice forms. By this procedure, *S* could not use size and weight as cues for recognition. Texture and thickness were held constant by using .5-in. bakelite for all forms. The nine forms used in Part 3 were the same as those in Parts 1 and 2. The area of the choice blocks was twice that of the stimulus blocks.

The instructions for Part 3 were as follows:

> I am going to hand you a block. I want you to feel it so you can remember the shape. You may use one or both hands. When you lay the block down, I will hand you four blocks, one at a time. One of these four blocks has the same shape as the one you just felt. I want you to pick out the one of these four blocks that has the same shape as the first one. You may feel them as often as you like until you

are sure that you have the one that has the same shape. Do you understand?

Since recognition depends not only on the difficulty of the perception of the stimulus form but on the degree of similarity of the other choice forms, we presented in almost every case rounded forms as choice blocks when the stimulus form was rounded, and cornered forms when the stimulus form was cornered. For example, when the stimulus form was a square, we presented a triangle, trapezoid, diamond, and square. When the stimulus form was an ellipse, we presented a semicircle, ellipse, circle, and crescent. Also, in every presentation, we included a choice form that was similar in some respects to the stimulus object. Thus, when the circle was the stimulus form, an ellipse was included in the choice forms. When the diamond block was the stimulus object, a square was presented with the choice forms. Introspections were requested from each *S* at the end of each experiment.

Results

Standards for rating reproductions and verbal reports In order to rate the accuracy of the reproductions of the small and large forms in Parts 1 and 2, five standards were established. The letter grades, A to E, represented decreasing degrees of accuracy of the drawings. The size of the reproduction was ignored in the ratings. "A" was given for exact form reproduction. "B" denoted only one error; either the figure was not closed, or the lines crossed each other in one of the corners. When the corners of the form were rounded and either one of the errors listed for grade "B" was present, the reproduction received a grade of "C." "D" represented almost complete unrecognizability, and "E" showed no resemblance at all to the original form.

In evaluating the verbal reports or descriptions of the forms, three categories of accuracy were established. "Excellent" was assigned when the geometric form was named or when the angles and relationships of the individual parts were described. For example, in describing the square, *S* had to state that all the angles were right angles and all the sides were equal. "Fair" was given when one of the details was inaccurate. Thus, the right angles of the square might be mentioned, but the equality of the sides was omitted or the sides were described as unequal. When the description did not resemble the stimulus form, the report received the rating "poor."

No comments were made to *S* on the accuracy of the reproductions or verbal reports. All the ratings of the reproductions and verbal reports were made by *E* and his assistant. Strict adherence to the established criteria and standards was followed. At no time was there any serious conflict of rating or judgment. In making the ratings, care was taken to assure that E and asistant did not know to which group, blind or sighted, S belonged. In this way, experimental biases were minimized.

The results of the present experiment on form perception are shown in Tables I, II, and III. Gross results for both the sighted and the blind Ss and fractionation of the results according to age at blinding, chronological age, sex, and stimulus form are included.

The method of reproduction Table I shows the distribution of the ratings for each of the small forms for both the blind and the sighted Ss. Since the number of cases was the same for both groups ($N = 33$), direct comparisons can be made. The sighted obviously do much better than the blind.

Since the total ratings do not consist of independent observations (each S contributed nine ratings), the chi-square test cannot be applied directly to the totals for the blind and the sighted. The ratings on each of the nine forms, however, are independent. Since the theoretical cell frequencies of some of our five categories are less than 10, we combined the frequencies of the various categories for each form into two categories so that theoretical frequencies were all close to, or above, 10. The chi-square values for homogeneity of responses to each form were all greater than 12. The probabilities of obtaining such values by chance alone are all less than .001 ($df = 1$). For the individual forms, therefore, the sighted were consistently and significantly superior to the blind.

There were individual differences, however, in the accuracy of the reproductions for each form. The blind found the square and circle easier to reproduce than the other forms. The quarter-circle and parallelograms

Table I Distribution of the Ratings for the Reproductions of Each of the Small Forms of Part I for the Blind and the Sighted Ss

FORM	A Blind	A Sighted	B Blind	B Sighted	C Blind	C Sighted	D Blind	D Sighted	E Blind	E Sighted
Square	0	4	6	26	12	3	5	0	10	0
Circle	0	8	8	16	11	9	10	0	4	0
Triangle	0	4	4	22	7	3	7	2	15	2
Semicircle	0	4	5	22	4	1	11	4	13	2
Rectangle	0	2	4	24	8	5	8	1	13	1
Quarter-circle	0	0	1	20	3	10	7	1	22	2
Parallelogram	0	2	2	16	6	10	1	3	24	2
Crescent	0	2	3	12	3	16	13	1	14	2
Ellipse	0	0	3	22	5	6	12	3	13	2
Total	0	26	36	180	59	63	74	15	128	13

Table II Distribution of the Ratings for the Reproductions of Each of the Large Forms of Part 2 for the Blind and the Sighted Ss

FORM	A Blind	A Sighted	B Blind	B Sighted	C Blind	C Sighted	D Blind	D Sighted	E Blind	E Sighted
Square	1	8	4	20	11	5	8	0	9	0
Circle	0	8	6	18	17	7	7	0	3	0
Triangle	0	2	5	31	8	0	3	0	17	0
Semicircle	0	4	5	26	4	3	9	0	15	0
Rectangle	0	4	5	26	9	3	8	0	11	0
Quarter-circle	0	0	3	26	2	4	5	1	23	2
Parallelogram	0	0	0	16	4	12	7	5	22	0
Crescent	0	0	0	22	6	8	15	1	12	2
Ellipse	0	0	0	28	6	2	13	1	14	2
Total	1	26	28	213	67	44	75	8	126	6

were the most difficult. For the sighted, the square was the easiest, and the crescent, most difficult.

Table II presents a similar picture for the larger forms. The sighted were significantly better than the blind in the reproduction of each of the nine forms. The chi-square values (after combining categories) for each form are all above 12. The probability of obtaining this value by chance is above .001.

The difficulty of the reproductions was similar to that of the small forms in Part 1. The circle and square were the easiest for the blind,

Table III Distribution of the Ratings for the Verbal Reports of Each of the Forms on Parts 1 and 2 for the Blind and the Sighted Ss

FORM	Part 1 Excellent Blind	Part 1 Excellent Sighted	Part 1 Fair Blind	Part 1 Fair Sighted	Part 1 Poor Blind	Part 1 Poor Sighted	Part 2 Excellent Blind	Part 2 Excellent Sighted	Part 2 Fair Blind	Part 2 Fair Sighted	Part 2 Poor Blind	Part 2 Poor Sighted
Square	27	30	1	3	5	0	27	28	2	3	4	2
Circle	32	31	0	2	1	0	32	32	0	1	1	0
Triangle	23	30	5	1	5	2	24	32	3	1	6	0
Semicircle	26	28	4	1	3	4	27	33	1	0	5	0
Rectangle	26	28	5	3	2	2	26	32	2	1	5	0
Quarter-circle	15	22	11	8	7	3	13	26	15	4	5	3
Parallelogram	14	28	8	3	11	2	18	28	10	3	5	2
Crescent	16	26	11	3	6	4	18	28	9	2	6	3
Ellipse	24	30	3	1	6	2	26	28	2	3	5	2
Total	203	253	48	25	46	19	211	267	44	18	42	12

and the parallelogram, crescent, and ellipse were most difficult. For the sighted, the square, triangle, circle, semicircle, and rectangle were easier to reproduce than the ellipse, crescent, or parallelogram.

There was practically no difference between the reproduction scores for the smaller and larger forms for the blind. The distributions of ratings for each form are almost identical. For the sighted, however, there was a decided improvement when they were allowed to use both hands to manipulate the forms (Part 2). Table I shows that 206 reproductions of the small forms by the sighted Ss received B or better. For the larger forms (Table II), 239 reproductions were rated B or better. We cannot say whether this improvement was due to practice or to the use of two hands, inasmuch as we did not counterbalance the presentations of the smaller and larger forms. It is significant, however, that the blind did not show such improvement on the larger forms.

Method of verbal report The descriptions of the forms by the sighted are apparently superior to those by the blind. Table III gives for each form the frequency of the ratings "excellent," "fair," and "poor." In Part 1 (small forms), 203 of the 297 responses of the blind were rated excellent; 48, fair; and 46, poor. For the sighted, 253 responses were excellent; 25, fair; and 19, poor. The totals are misleading, however, since the superiority of the sighted appears only in the descriptions of the parallelogram and crescent in which the chi-square values (excellent *vs.* fair and poor) are greater than 8. The probability of obtaining this value by chance ($df = 1$) is less than .01. All other values for the remaining forms are not significant at the .01 level. The blind found it easier to describe the square and circle and more difficult to describe the parallelogram and quarter-circle. The sighted also found the quarter-circle more difficult to describe than the other forms.

The method of verbal report for the larger forms (Part 2) yields results similar to those of Part 1. Table III shows 211 ratings of excellent for the blind; 267 ratings of excellent for the sighted. The superiority of the sighted over the blind lies in their ability to describe more accurately the quarter-circle, the parallelogram, and the cresecent. The chi-square values for these forms are significant at less than the .01 level when we combine the frequencies of the fair and poor categories. The relative difficulty of the forms in Part 2 is the same as that in Part 1 (smaller forms) for both the blind and the sighted Ss. The quarter-circle again appeared to be most difficult to describe for both groups.

The distribution of the ratings of the verbal reports of the blind in Part 2 is almost identical with that in Part 1 (cf. Table III). The chi-square values (combining categories) for the individual forms of Parts 1 and 2 are all less than 1, and the p's are above .50. We can conclude that for the blind the use of two hands in manipulating the forms does not give any significantly better descriptions than those obtained in handling the forms with only one hand. For the sighted, however, there is slight improvement when both hands are used, but the improvement is not significant. All the p's of the chi-square values (with categories combined) for the ratings of the individual forms are above .20.

The time for the handling of the small forms by the blind is not significantly different from that taken by the sighted Ss. The mean for the blind was 9.9 ($SD = 8.52$) and for the sighted, 9.1 ($SD = 5.73$). The probability of obtaining a difference of .73 sec. by chance is between .40 and .50 ($t = .73$).

In Part 2, however, the sighted took much less time than the blind to handle the forms. The sighted required, on the average, 6.4 sec. ($SD = 2.85$ sec.) and the blind required 9.9 sec. ($SD = 8.52$ sec.). The difference of 3.5 sec. is significant at the .05 level. While the blind showed no improvement in time in Part 2 (9.9 sec.) over Part I (9.9 sec.), the sighted showed significant improvement. Their mean decreased from 9.1 sec. (Part 1) to 6.4 sec. (Part 2).

Method of recognition The results of the method of recognition show no difference between the blind and the sighted Ss in the tactual perception of form. Only two blind Ss made one error each, and no errors were made by the sighted. One blind S selected the triangle when the stimulus object was the trapezoid, and another selected the triangle when the stimulus object was the quarter-circle. These incorrect choices are not absurd since there is some similarity among the trapezoid, quarter-circle, and triangles.

Age at blinding and form perception The significant superiority of the sighted over the blind Ss in the reproduction and verbal report tests suggests the importance of visualization in these methods of testing tactual form perception. If this hypothesis is true, then the accidentally blinded should reproduce and describe their tactual form perceptions more accurately than the congenitally blinded. Tests of significance and relationship confirm this hypothesis. Reproduction ratings were converted into numerical scores: $A = 4$, $B = 3$, $C = 2$, $D = 1$, $E = 0$. Verbal report judgments were also converted: excellent $= 3$, fair $= 2$, poor $= 1$. The mean reproduction score of the congenitally blinded ($N = 16$) in Part 1 was $2.38 \pm .47$, and for the accidentally blinded ($N = 17$), $2.66 \pm .37$. The difference of .28 is significant at almost the .05 level ($t = 1.87$). On the reproduction test in Part 2, the congenitally blinded had a mean of $2.33 \pm .40$, whereas the accidentally blinded had a mean of $2.79 \pm .28$. The difference of .46 is significant at less than .001 ($t = 3.83$). On the verbal report test in Part 1, the mean for the congenitally blinded was $.63 \pm .52$, and for the accidentally blinded, $1.36 \pm .90$. The t of the difference is 2.81, which is significant at less than the .01 level. On the verbal report test in Part 2, the t of the difference was 3.33, which is significant at less than the .01 level.

The r's between age at blindness and the scores on the reproduction and verbal report tests of Parts 1 and 2 support the hypothesis that sight may be an important factor in tactual form perception. The r's between age at blindness and reproduction scores of Parts 1 and 2 are .61 and .76, respectively; between age at blindness and verbal report scores, .45 and .62, respectively. These coefficients are significant at less than the .01 level. Though vision may be important as a factor in the development of the ability to reproduce and describe tactual form, it apparently is of no importance in tactual form discrimination when tested by the method of recognition inasmuch as the congenitally blinded did as well as the accidentally blinded and the sighted Ss.

Chronological age and form perception All the r's between the chronological ages of the blind and the test scores indicate no significant relationship. The r's between age and the reproduction scores and between age and verbal report scores of Part 1 were .18 and .22, respectively, and between age and the reproduction scores and between age and the verbal report scores of Part 2 were .24 and .17, respectively.

Sex and form perception On the reproduction and verbal report tests of Parts 1 and 2, the differences in the means were in favor of the males, particularly on the reproduction tests, but the differences were not significant at the .05 level. The superiority of the males in the reproduction test, though not significant, suggests that drawing performance rather than form perception may be at the basis of this sex difference. On the tests of verbal report and recognition, the females did as well as the males.

Relationship between reproduction tests Comparison of the reproduction scores between Parts 1 and 2 showed almost no difference in the ratings of the individual forms for the blind. As we should expect, therefore, the r between these two tests is very high (.92). A score on either test represents the score on the other, and it may well be that the traits measured by these tests are identical even though movement is limited to one hand in Part 1.

Relationship between verbal report tests The homogeneity of the scores of the blind on the verbal report tests of Parts 1 and 2 should reduce the correlation coefficient. The r between these two sets of scores for the blind is .80. These correlation coefficients (reproduction and verbal report) indicate that more extensive kinesthetic activity in handling the blocks does not lead to better tactual form perception. It may be that with more difficult and complex forms, the use of two hands would lead to more accurate reproductions and descriptions.

Relationship between verbal and reproduction tests We should expect that Ss who excelled in form reproduction would give more accurate form descriptions. The r's of .64 and .76 between the reproduction scores and verbal report scores of Parts 1 and 2, respectively, confirm this hypothesis.

Reliability of the tests Split-half reliability was determined by correlating odd *vs.* even items on the form tests of our 33 blind Ss. The split-half correlation for the reproduction scores on the small form (Part 1) was .93. The Spearman–Brown formula for the reliability of the whole test gave a coefficient of .96. The split-half correlation for reproduction scores on the large forms (Part 2) was .90. The reliability coefficient of the whole test was .94. The split-half coefficients indicate that the two halves (odd *vs.* even) are equivalent, that is, they are measuring the same trait or traits. The high reliability coefficient of the whole test shows that the scores are a reliable index of the ability of our Ss at the time of testing.

Since the verbal report scores are much more homogeneous, smaller split-half correlation coefficients are expected. For Part 1 (small forms), the split-half coefficient was .70, and the reliability of the whole test was .82. For Part 2 (large forms), the split-half coefficient for the verbal report scores was .57, and the reliability of the whole test was .73.

Ss' comments During the various tests the blind Ss were encouraged to describe or tell how they knew the form. Their reports seemed to fall into a consistent pattern. Those who lost their sight later in life resorted to visual imagery when they were drawing, describing, or selecting the form. Typical comments of this group were: "You get a mental picture," or "I just get the shape down in my mind," or "I get a vivid picture." The congenitally blinded, on the other hand, either found it difficult to describe their mental processes, or vaguely mentioned, "I get the shape," or stressed the "feel of the shape." For example, JC said, "I remember the way it felt in my hand." HG stated, "I just feel the shape. It has a certain number of corners." On the recognition test, HG said, "If they were both the same size, they would fit. I think about what would fit what." WP mentioned, "I feel for the shape of it." On the recognition test, he added, "I think if figures had been more similar I would have had a hard time. We use raised figures in geometry."

The sighted invariably translated their tactile-kinesthetic impressions into visual imagery. Many of them just stated that they got a picture of the form as they felt it. The corners seemed much easier to distinguish. The rounded edge of the quarter-circle gave them trouble.

Discussion

The method of reproduction showed that the blind were far inferior to the sighted subjects and that almost half of the drawings of the blind were unrecognizable. With the method of verbal report, however, the blind did much better. Their descriptions indicated that they had perceived the forms fairly accurately. Their failures in reproducing the form, therefore, were not due to poor tactual perception but may have been due to lack of experience in drawing. Analysis of the results indicates, however, that the poor reproductions are probably due to the inability of the congenitally blinded *S*s to translate tactile impressions into visual imagery. The significant difference in the reproduction scores between the congenitally and the accidentally blinded and the high correlation between age at blinding and reproduction scores confirm this hypothesis. Also, though the blind showed better tactual form perception with the method of verbal report, the significant relationship between age at blindness and verbal report scores indicates again the importance of visualization. The introspective reports show the predominant use of visual imagery by the accidentally blinded. The congenitally blinded reported no such imagery. Stout contends that "those who have been blind in their fourth year translate their tactile impressions into visual imagery as we ourselves do in the dark" (*Stout, 1913*, p. 474). He finds support for this position in Heller's *Studien zur Blindenpsychologie (1904)*.

Sylvester, using a form board test on 85 blind *S*s, found that those who had no visual experience at all showed the least ability, and the longer *S* had retained his vision, the more successful he was in the test. He concluded that "those who have had visual experience retain their visual imagery and are assisted by it in the interpretation of their tactile impressions; and tactual imagery, even in those who have no other resource, is not as effective as a combination of tactual and visual imagery" (*Sylvester, 1913*, pp. 210 ff.).

The results on each of the forms show that the congenitally blinded had great difficulty in describing the quarter-circle, parallelogram, and crescent. It may be that visual imagery is particularly important in the synthesis of the individual tactile impressions of more complex forms. Most of the older writers have neglected the role of visual imagery in their conclusions that the remarkable feats of the blind are due to the extraordinary sensitivity of touch developed by compensatory functioning and attention. Identification of objects by the blind does not necessarily require a synthesis of tactile impressions into a composite whole. Identification may be due to a prominent feature of the object, such as odor, weight, texture, and size. Stout disregards visual imagery and emphasizes synthetic touch:

> In the case of simple and familiar things which they [the blind] have already often explored by active touch, they can at once recognize shape, size, etc., by merely passive contact. But when the objects are presented to them with which they are quite unfamiliar, it is found that for precise apprehension, analytic touch must be combined with synthetic. Synthetic touch alone without the aid of previous experience yields at most a general and schematic total impression. For instance, they can tell whether the object is round or angular, and whether it is regular or irregular, but for precise determination of its shape, analytic movements are required (*Stout, 1913*, p. 476).

Our results show that touch alone is not as efficient in the perception of, and response to, complex tactual form relationships as touch aided by visual images. Wundt reached the same conclusion that touch sensations alone could never suffice for the exact apprehension of spatial relations. Even though spatial properties of objects are apprehended by the movements of hands and fingers, "we always find that the blind do not apprehend even fairly simple relations with anything like the rapidity with which the perceptions of sight enable us to obtain an adequate idea of the most complicated figure. The sensations of touch and movement have to construct the object gradually for them out of its parts" (*Wundt, 1896,* pp. 157 ff.).

On the test of form recognition, the congenitally blinded did as well as the accidentally blinded and the sighted Ss. The method of testing form perception is, therefore, important in any conclusions concerning the relative superiority of the blind and the sighted Ss. If we had used only the method of reproduction, we should have concluded that the blind are far inferior to the sighted. The method of recognition showed, however, that there is no difference between the blind and the sighted.

The recognition test does not require visual imagery since the congenitally blinded did as well as the accidentally blinded. The method of testing form perception, therefore, is important in determining whether visualization will be utilized. Recently, aviation selection tests have been constructed for the purpose of testing visualization, but scoring convenience and the requirement of objectivity have resulted in multiple-choice responses. It may be that this type of response eliminates the need for visualization. A recall or reproduction test may be more suitable.

It is difficult in any recognition test to determine what cues are involved. Lowenfeld (*1945*) set out to construct tests to differentiate the visually minded from the haptic individual. He assumed that his test of visualization of kinesthetic experience, which involves the selection of one of five forms experienced tactually, detects the visually minded person. The congenitally blinded should do as well as his "visual" person if we may extrapolate from our results. Recognition may be due only to an awareness of the absence or presence of isolated prominent features. The similarity of the choice forms may determine the mental processes for correct identification. Discrimination rather than form apprehension may have been operating in our recognition test inasmuch as we dealt with simple geometric forms. More difficult tests with more similar choice forms may require visual imagery for correct recognition of form.

Summary and Conclusions

To determine the ability of the blind and the role of visualization in tactual form perception, three tests were administered individually to a matched group of 33 blind and sighted Ss. In Test 1, a series of simple geometrical blocks was presented to one hand of S. In Test 2, larger blocks were used, and S was allowed to manipulate the blocks with both hands. Reproduction (drawing) and description of the blocks were given by S immediately after presentation. Test 3 utilized the method of recognition. Four choice blocks were given to S after each stimulus presentation. These choice blocks were of the same texture, but all, including the correct choice block, were larger than the stimulus block. This procedure compelled S to depend on shape alone, apart from size, weight, and texture in his selection.

The results show that:

1. The sighted were significantly better than the blind in the reproduction and description of each of the blocks in Tests 1 and 2.

2. The accidentally blinded gave significantly better reproductions and descriptions than the congenitally blinded in Tests 1 and 2.

3. With the method of recognition, however, there was no significant difference between the blind and the sighted, and between the accidentally and the congenitally blinded. The scores for all the Ss indicated almost perfect tactual form perception.

4. There was a significant and high correlation between age at onset of blindness and the scores in Tests 1 and 2 for both reproduction and verbal report.

5. There was no significant relationship between the chronological age of the blind and the scores on Tests 1 and 2.

6. There was a slight but insignificant difference in favor of the male over the female blind with the method of reproduction in Parts 1 and 2, but no sex difference with the method of verbal report.

7. The introspective reports and the analysis of the results of age at blinding indicated that superior performance in tactual form reproduction and description was probably due to the translation of successive tactile impressions into a visual image of the total form. Visual imagery, however, did not result in superior performance in the recognition of tactual form.

EXPERIMENT B: TACTUAL SPACE RELATIONS

Statement of the Problem

Important to the spatial adjustment of the organism is its ability to manipulate spatial cues imaginally and to orient itself with respect to external objects and directions. The second experiment in the present series deals with the ability of the blind to solve a spatial problem requiring the perception of form and the imaginal manipulation of spatial cues, and attempts to determine the role of visualization in such problems.

Method

The spatial problems selected are similar to those in the Minnesota Paper Form Board except that our forms are presented tactually. Essentially, the problem consists of presenting one part of a form to one hand and the second part to the other hand, and asking S what form would result if the parts were placed together.

Apparatus The response blocks consisted of seven three-ply wood blocks of the following shapes: square, circle, equilateral triangle, semicircle, rectangle, trapezoid, and ellipse. The radii of the circle and semicircle were 1 in. and of the ellipse 1 and 2 in. The sides of the square and triangle were 2 in., and the rectangle and trapezoid measured 1 by 2 in.

The stimulus blocks consisted of two parts of a circle, semicircle, ellipse, square, rectangle, trapezoid, and triangle.

Instructions The following instructions were read to S:

> Now I am going to hand you two forms, one in each of your hands. I want you to imagine what form would result if these two blocks were placed together, that is, alongside each other. When you lay them down, I will hand you four different forms, one at a time. You are to give me the one which you think you would get if you had placed the two smaller forms together. Do you understand?

Procedure

The method of recognition was employed.

Two stimulus forms were handed to the blindfolded S. Without giving any indication that speed was involved, the time of handling the two forms was recorded. When the stimulus forms were laid down, the four response forms were handed to S and he was asked, "Which of these four forms do you think you would get if you had placed the two smaller ones side by side?"

At the completion of the experiment, S was asked to tell how he knew which was the correct form.

Results

The results of the present experiment on the manipulation of space relations are shown in Tables IV and V. The distribution of errors for the blind and sighted Ss appears in Table IV. A fractionation of the results according to errors on each of the seven forms is shown in Table V.

Blind versus sighted The significant superiority of the sighted over the blind Ss in the manipulation of space relations is evident from the distribution of errors in Table IV. The range of errors for the blind is

Table IV *Distribution of Errors on the Space Relations Test for the Blind and Sighted Ss*

ERRORS	Blind Ss	Sighted Ss
7	1	—
6	1	—
5	6	—
4	6	4
3	8	4
2	7	9
1	4	14
0	—	2
Mean	3.3	1.9
S.D.	1.61	1.40
t		3.8
P		< .001

from 1 to 7; for the sighted, the range is from 0 to 4 errors. Almost half of the sighted Ss and only 15 per cent of the blind made 1 or 0 errors. The mean number of errors for the blind Ss was 3.26 ± 1.61, and for the sighted, 1.85 ± 1.40. The difference of 1.42 errors yields a t of 3.8, which is significant at less than the .001 level. Since this test is one of recognition, we cannot argue that the superiority of the sighted Ss is due to experience. It seems more likely that the use of visual imagery by the sighted Ss leads to better performance. If this is true, then the accidentally blinded who possess visual imagery should do better than the congenitally blinded.

Though the blind made more errors than the sighted, there was no significant difference between the two groups in the mean time taken to handle the stimulus form. The mean time (sec.) for the blind was 15.7 ± 8.24, and for the sighted, 14.4 ± 9.04.

Age at blinding and space relations The results of the effect of age at blinding on the test scores confirm our hypothesis that visual imagery is a factor in our space relations test. The mean number of errors for the congenitally blinded was 4.00 ± 1.22, and for the accidentally blinded, 2.59 ± 1.61. The t of the difference is 2.76, which is significant at less than the .01 level. The superiority of the accidentally blinded, therefore, is probably not due to chance.

The relationship between age at blinding and the number of errors on the space relations test is significant also at the .01 level ($r = -.49$). This value is a conservative estimate of the correlation inasmuch as one of the variables, age at blinding, is quite homogeneous. Sixteen of our 33 blind Ss are congenitally blind. This inverse relationship indicates that the ability to deal with visual images in our accidentally blinded Ss leads to fewer errors on the spatial relations test. There was no difference, however, in the mean time for handling the stimulus forms between the congenitally blinded and the accidentally blinded. The mean time (sec.) for the congenitally blinded was 16.1 ± 8.1, and for the accidentally blinded, 15.3 ± 3.2. The t of the difference is .27, and p is between .70 and .80.

Chronological age and space relations The r between chronological age and the space relations score is .34. This coefficient is obtained in about 5 per cent of the cases and is thus indicative of a trend. The relationship, however, is positive, which means that the older the blind person, the poorer the score on the space relations test. In view of the negative correlation between age at blinding and space relations scores, and the positive correlation between chronological age and space relations scores, a more significant correlation would result between age at blinding and test scores if we eliminated the effect of chronological age. The partial correlation between age at blinding and test scores with chronological age "removed" is .57. The partial correlation coefficient between chronological age and test scores with age at blinding held constant is .47. Both coefficients are significant at less than the .01 level.

Sex and space relations The slight difference of .4 errors in favor of males was not significant. We can, therefore, conclude that sex is not a factor in our test of space relations. There was also no significant sex difference in time scores.

Table V Number of Errors for Each Form in the Space Relations Test for the Blind and the Sighted Ss

FORM	FREQUENCY OF RESPONSE ERRORS	
	Blind ($N = 33$)	*Sighted* ($N = 33$)
Square	17	4
Trapezium	12	5
Circle	3	0
Rectangle	22	9
Ellipse	5	1
Semicircle	31	30
Triangle	18	12
Total	108	61

Form and space relations The easiest forms for both the blind and the sighted Ss to recognize from the tactual perception of the two parts were the ellipse and the circle. Table V shows that only 3 blind and none of the sighted made errors on the circle; and 5 blind and 1 of the sighted made errors on the ellipse. The most difficult form for both groups to recognize was the semicircle. They usually selected the original stimulus form, the quarter-circle. Almost all the blind (31) Ss missed this form; and surprisingly, 30 sighted Ss also missed this form. The rectangle and square seemed best to differentiate the blind from the sighted. Only 4 of the sighted missed the square, whereas 17 of the blind missed it. On the rectangle, 22 of the blind made errors, whereas only 9 of the sighted made errors.

Reliability of the test Split-half reliability of the space relations test was determined by correlating odd *vs.* even items. The split-half correlation coefficient was .72. The two halves of the test are equivalent. The reliability of the whole test was .84. We can, therefore, conclude that the scores at the time of the administration of the test were a reliable measure of the ability of the blind and the sighted to manipulate spatial relations.

Ss' comments Very few Ss, blind or sighted alike, could give any description of the mental processes involved in deciding what form would result if the parts had been placed together. The most frequent response was, "I don't know." Many Ss simply said, "I just knew." A few of the responses indicated that visual imagery of the response form did not occur on the handling of the stimulus forms. Rather, the images of the stimulus parts were elicited when the response forms were selected. As one S said, "I tried to imagine whether the parts could make up this form." The images of the parts were retained but the total form could not be visualized from the parts themselves. This is understandable in view of the fact that the blocks could be placed side by side in various ways to form different total patterns. It was only when the response forms were presented that S actually could decide whether the parts could make up a particular form.

Discussion

A number of facts in the present experiment testify to the importance of visual imagery in the tactual recognition of form when only parts of the form are presented. The sighted group is significantly superior to the blind, and the accidentally blinded make fewer errors than the congenitally blinded. Not only do the accidentally blinded do better, but those whose blindness occurred later make fewer errors, as indicated by the r between age at blinding and test scores. The low but significant correlation of the chronological age of the blind with errors on the space relations test suggests that imagery becomes less vivid with increasing chronological age. This finding was originally reported by Galton, and later confirmed by Betts (*1900*). A more reasonable explanation, however, is that the longer the blind person is deprived of vision, the less does he depend on visual imagery. In other words, richness and vividness of imagery may require periodic visual stimulation. The longer a person is deprived of visual reinforcement, the less vivid becomes his visual imagery. This explanation is supported by the partial correlation between chronological age and test scores as age at blinding is held constant.

Cutsforth (*1933*) in an experiment on the relationship between tactual and visual perception, also showed the importance of visual imagery in tactual form perception. He concluded that tactual qualities provide "texture," "body," and subjective reference, but form, extent, position, and organization are visual.

Our present findings are not in agreement with the general conclusions of Czermak (*1855*), Gärttner (*1881*), and Brown and Stratton (*1925*) that the blind are superior to the seeing in the tactile discrimination of space. We might think that the blind, because of greater dependence on touch and attention to tactile cues, would be superior. The method of measuring tactile perceptions and the age at blinding must be considered in any such conclusions. The present test shows that the tactual advantage is actually on the side of those who could see or translate tactile impression into visual imagery.

An analysis of the results of the blind and the sighted Ss on each of the forms in the present test shows that the stimulus form, the quarter-circle, proved most difficult. It is easy to understand why the blind found it so inasmuch as in experiment A they made most errors in reproducing and describing the quarter-circle and parallelogram. With the small quarter-circle (Part 1), 22 of the blind gave unrecognizable reproductions, and with the large form (Part 2) 23 of the blind gave unrecognizable reproductions. With the method of verbal report, only 15 of the blind could describe the quarter-circle accurately. It is difficult to explain, however, why the sighted Ss had equal difficulty with this form. In experiment A, 20 and 26 sighted Ss, respectively, received a rating of B in Parts 1 and 2 with the method of reproduction. At least 22 Ss gave excellent descriptions of the quarter-circle with the method of verbal report.

Summary and Conclusions

The first experiment dealt with tactual form perception. The Ss were required to draw, describe, and recognize simple geometric forms that were presented to one and two hands. In the present series, the Ss not only had to perceive form tactually, but they were required to imagine what shape would result if two blocks were placed together. The response consisted in selecting the resulting shape from four blocks.

The results show that:

1. The sighted made significantly fewer errors than the blind.
2. The accidentally blinded were significantly superior to the congenitally blinded in the imaginal manipulation of space relations.
3. There is a definite relationship between age at blinding and accuracy on the space relations test.
4. There is a significant partial correlation coefficient between the chronological ages of the blind and error scores on the space relations test when the effect of age at blinding is held constant.
5. There is no significant sex difference on the space relations test.
6. Split-half reliability of the space relations test indicates that the scores are a fairly reliable index of the ability of the blind Ss at the time of the administration of the test.
7. The easiest forms for the blind and the sighted to recognize from the tactual perceptions of the individual parts were the ellipse and circle. The most difficult form to recognize was the semicircle when the stimulus forms were the two quarter-circles.
8. The few introspective reports that were given indicate that visual imagery in the sighted and in the accidentally blinded occurred during the process of handling the choice blocks. The Ss tried to imagine whether the individual parts previously experienced could make up a particular block.
9. The use of visual imagery is of definite aid to the sighted and to the accidentally blinded in imaginally manipulating tactual perceptions.

EXPERIMENT C: SPACE ORIENTATION

Statement of the Problem

It is the purpose of the present set of experiments to determine (a) the ability of the totally blind to orient themselves spatially, and (b) the role of visualization in spatial orientation.

Method

To make valid comparisons between the blind and sighted Ss and to determine the role of visualization, we set up a novel spatial task in which auditory cues would not give undue advantage to the blind, who are accustomed to using these cues. The procedure used by other Es of having Ss point to near and distant places, or point to compass directions, or indicate on maps certain prominent landmarks is not suitable inasmuch as interest and experience are heavily weighted in these tasks.

Our experiment took place on a large rectangular concrete area, 40 × 80 ft., located about 200 ft. behind the main building of the Texas

325   Philip Worchel

State School for the Blind. This area was used by some of the blind students for a skating rink. The nearest object to the rink was a large oak tree that stood about 150 ft. from the south side of the rink. On this area, we indicated in chalk the corners of eight right isosceles triangles with the following hypotenuse dimensions: 8, 10, 12, 14, 16, 18, 20, and 22 ft. Two series of spatial problems were presented to each of the blind and sighted Ss. Task 1 consisted in leading S along the two sides of the triangle. He was to return without guidance, via the hypotenuse path, to the starting point. In Task 2, S was led along the hypotenuse and he was to return to the starting point along the two paths which formed the legs of the triangle. In each task, the distance S stopped from the starting point was recorded to the nearest foot. At the beginning of the experiment we measured the angular deviation from the hypotenuse path. As these deviations correlated highly with the distance from the starting position, we eliminated the angular deviation measurements and recorded only the distance measurements.

The blindfolded S was brought to the experimental area and the following instructions for Part 1 were read by E:

> I am going to lead you by the arm in two directions on this concrete area. When I stop, I want you to turn around and walk back in a straight path to the place we started. I will again take you by the hand to another starting place and lead you once more in two directions. Again you are to return directly back to the starting place, and then stop. We will do this a number of times, and each time when we start I will tap you on the back so that you will know that this is the starting place. Do you understand? To make sure you know what we want you to do, we will show you the first time by leading you back to the starting point.

The S was then led along the two legs of the triangle, stopped, then told that this was the way he should walk back to the starting place. He was then led along the hypotenuse to the original starting position. For the following trials, after S had been led along the two paths, E said, "Now return to the starting place directly in a straight path like I showed you, and then stop."

The order of the trials according to the hypotenuse length was: 10, 14, 18, 20, 16, 12, 8, and 22 ft.

For Part 2, the instructions were:

> Now I am going to lead you in a straight line. When I stop, I want you to return to the starting point by such a path that you will make a right angle before you return. In other words, we will do the reverse of what we just did. Instead of my leading you in two directions and you return by a straight path, I will lead you along

326   The Aurally and Visually Handicapped

the straight path and you will now return by two paths. I will show you again what I want you to do. Remember I will tap you on the shoulder each time that we start from a new starting place.

The E then led S along the hypotenuse path, paused, then continued to lead him along the two legs back to the initial position. If at any time S indicated by his actions that he did not understand the directions, the instructions and demonstration were repeated. This was necessary only for a few of the younger Ss.

The order of trials in Part 2 was the same as in Part 1. Introspective reports were requested of each S, blind or sighted, at the end of the experiment.

Results

The results of the present experiment on space orientation are shown in Tables VI and VII. For both Parts 1 and 2, the means of the distances in feet between the starting position and the point where S stopped were calculated. The distribution of these mean distances for each S is given

Table VI   Distribution of the Mean Distances (in Feet) in Missing the Starting Position on the Space Orientation Tests of Parts 1 and 2 for the Blind and the Sighted Ss

MEAN DISTANCE	PART 1 Blind	PART 1 Sighted	PART 2 Blind	PART 2 Sighted
16	1		1	
14	—		—	
12	—		1	
10	3		1	
8	4	2	7	4
6	14	10	13	8
4	6	13	8	13
2	5	6	2	6
0	—	2	—	2
Mean	6.3	4.7	6.8	5.0
SD	2.76	1.71	2.61	2.11
t	2.88		3.03	
P	.001–.01		.001–.01	

Table VII *Mean Distances and Standard Deviations (in Feet) in Missing the Starting Positions on the Space Orientation Tests of Parts 1 and 2 for the Blind and the Sighted Ss on Every Hypotenuse Distance*

HYPOTENUSE DISTANCES (IN FEET)	Part 1 Blind Mean	Part 1 Blind SD	Part 1 Sighted Mean	Part 1 Sighted SD	Part 2 Blind Mean	Part 2 Blind SD	Part 2 Sighted Mean	Part 2 Sighted SD
8	4.1	4.15	2.4	1.11	4.0	2.66	2.6	1.53
10	3.6	1.74	2.6	2.27	4.1	2.07	2.6	2.08
12	5.8	4.99	4.4	1.79	5.9	3.58	4.1	2.95
14	4.7	2.81	3.7	1.86	5.8	3.62	5.6	3.34
16	7.0	4.48	4.2	2.03	7.6	3.68	4.5	2.37
18	6.7	3.36	5.6	3.02	8.3	3.75	5.3	2.91
20	8.5	4.45	6.9	3.43	9.3	4.16	6.4	3.60
22	9.9	6.88	7.4	4.29	10.2	4.84	8.2	4.46

in Table VI. In Table VII, the mean distances and standard deviations in feet between the "start" and "stop" positions for each hypotenuse distance are shown.

Blind versus sighted The significant superiority of the sighted over the blind Ss is evident from Table VI. For Part 1, in which S was required to return by way of the hypotenuse, the mean distance by which the blind Ss missed the starting position is 6.30 ± 2.76 ft. The sighted Ss in the same test missed the initial position by 4.66 ± 1.71 ft. The t of the difference is significant at less than the .01 level. On Part 2, where the Ss returned to the starting point via the right-angle path, the mean for the blind was 6.78 ± 2.61, and for the sighted, 4.99 ± 2.11 ft. The t of the difference (3.03) is significant at less than the .01 level. The range also shows some interesting differences. In both tests (Parts 1 and 2), two of the sighted Ss always returned within 2 ft. of the starting position. None of the blind could achieve this level of excellence. None of the sighted missed the starting position by more than a mean distance of 10 ft., whereas the blind ranged up to a mean distance of 18 ft.

Age at blinding and space orientation Both the t test of significance between the distance scores of the congenitally blinded and accidentally blinded, and the product-moment correlation between age at blindness and distance scores show that age at blinding is not a factor in our tests of space orientation.

In Part 1, the mean distance from the starting positions for the congenitally blinded was 6.48 ± 1.99 ft., and for the accidentally blinded,

6.16 ± 3.25 ft. The t of the difference in the means is .33 and the P is between .70 and .80. In Part 2, the mean for the congenitally blinded was 6.40 ± 1.35 ft., and for the accidentally blinded, 7.14 ± 3.37 ft. The probability of obtaining the t of .81 by chance is between .40 and .50.

The r between age at blinding and the distance scores in Part 1 was −.22. This negative correlation is not significant at the 5 per cent level. The correlation coefficient with the distance scores in Part 2 is .10 and, again, shows no significant relationship between age at blinding and the space orientation scores.

Chronological age and space orientation The r's of chronological age with the distance scores on the space orientation tests of Parts 1 and 2 are −.12 and .26, respectively. These coefficients are not significant at the 5 per cent level. We can therefore conclude that chronological age is not a factor in the present tests of space orientation.

Sex and space orientation The mean distance score for the female blind Ss ($N = 14$) was 7.49 ± 3.11 ft., and for the male blind Ss ($N = 19$), 5.44 ± 2.11 ft. The t of the difference is 2.05, and p is between .05 and .10. Though the difference is not significant enough to conclude that there is a real sex difference, it is suggestive of a trend in favor of the male Ss. On Part 2, however, the difference is too slight in favor of the male Ss, and we can be fairly certain that on this test there is no sex difference.

Distance and space orientation To determine whether any relationship exists between the distance S was removed from his starting position and his error in missing the initial position, the means and standard deviations in feet of the "error" or distance scores were calculated for every hypotenuse distance in Parts 1 and 2 for both the blind and the sighted Ss. The results are shown in Table VII. For every hypotenuse distance, the sighted did better than the blind; that is, the sighted returned closer to the starting position than did the blind. The performances of the sighted were also more consistent. In almost every case, the standard deviations of the means for every hypotenuse distance were smaller than those of the blind.

Table VII also shows that as the hypotenuse distance increased the mean "error" in missing the starting position increased for both the blind and the sighted Ss. For the blind, however, there was no noticeable increase in the distance for Parts 1 and 2 until after the 14-ft. hypotenuse distance. On the other hand, for the sighted Ss, there was no consistent increase until after the 16-ft. hypotenuse distance.

Relationship between space orientation tests It is surprising that in view of the almost identical means for the blind and the sighted in Parts 1 and 2 for each of the hypotenuse distances (Table VII), there is practically no relationship between the two space orientation tests. The product-moment correlation between distances of Tests 1 and 2 for our 33 blind Ss is only .13. We can be fairly certain, therefore, that we are not measuring the same traits in these two tests.

Reliability of the tests Since the space orientation tests contain items which differ in difficulty, that is, larger errors in missing the starting positions occur with the greater hypotenuse distances, we correlated the results of the 8-, 12-, 16-, and 20-ft. hypotenuse distances with the results of the 10-, 14-, 18-, and 22-ft. distances. The split-half correlation of the halves is .74. The reliability of the whole test is .85. For Test 2, the split-half coefficient of correlation is .71. The reliability of the whole test is .83. These coefficients indicate that the two halves of each test are equivalent, and that at the time of the administration of the tests, the scores were a fairly reliable measure of the ability of the blind to orient themselves spatially.

Ss' comments Most of the comments of the blind and the sighted Ss did not reveal the mental processes involved in the space orientation tests. Many Ss stated, "I don't know." Others said, "I just knew which way to walk and when to stop." A few of the comments, however, indicated that both the blind and the sighted Ss estimated the time it would require to return to the original starting position. None of the blind could tell how he knew the direction in which the starting point was located. A few of the sighted, however, mentioned that they had a vague picture of the location of the initial position. In the first test, their visual impressions became especially clear when E led them from the first leg to the second leg of the triangular path. It seemed when they started out from the initial position along a straight path, the direction of walking was important. As soon as they "turned off this straight path to follow along the second path," they "tried to keep in mind just about where the starting position was located." In the second orientation test, these few sighted Ss reported that after E had led them along the straight path, they had a "picture of the right-angular path which they were going to follow on returning to the initial position."

Discussion

The results of the first two experiments on tactual form perception and space relations demonstrated the important role of visual imagery. In the present tests of space orientation, however, though the sighted excelled the blind Ss, we found no difference between the accidentally and the congenitally blinded, and no correlation between age at blinding and test scores. What cues did the blind use, and why did the sighted do better than the blind?

An analysis of the errors of the blind shows that the "missing" of the initial position did not lie so much in the length of S's return path as it did in the angular deviations. They did not overshoot or undershoot the starting position, but their path deviated much more from the correct path than did that of the sighted. Their error, therefore, lay not so much in the estimation of the distance to the starting position as in direction. From the few introspective reports we received, apparently both the blind and the sighted estimated the distance by estimating the duration of walking. The sighted, however, probably translated the kinesthetic cues into visual images, and were better able to detect the correct direction. For some reason, the accidentally blinded, who in the first two experiments utilized visual imagery, did not do so in the present space orientation tests. It may be that in their movements about the environment, they have come to depend upon auditory cues or upon guidance by people or artificial aids (seeing-eye dog, cane, etc.) for directional orientation. In the present tests, reflected auditory cues were eliminated by selecting an experimental area free from objects. No guidance or other aids were given to the blind in their return to the initial position.

Investigators have concluded from the experiences and behavior of the blind in spatial orientation that the blind do not possess a spatial concept. Platner, in his *Philosophische aphorismen* (*1793*, p. 466), states that "in reality to the blind, time serves instead of space." Lotze (*1887*) mentions that the space of the blind may not be so much what is generally meant by space, as it is an artificial system of conceptions of movement, time, and effort.

Mellone and Drummond (*1907*) agree with Mill's statement regarding great distances of time, rather than space, serving the blind. The fact, however, that the blind may use time in space orientation does not necessarily signify that their conception of space is radically different from that of the sighted. Ordinarily, the blind utilize auditory cues. It may well be that if we had provided some objects in our experimental area, the blind would have done as well as, or perhaps better than, the sighted. Pillsbury states:

> ... for the blind, the auditory perception of space is much more important than for the seeing individual. They are more accurate in localizations of sound, and use sound to obtain an idea of the space in which they are walking, and of the distance of obstacles. It is said that the blind ordinarily refer their larger spaces to auditory qualities, as we refer them to vision. In all respects, perception of space by the ear follows the same law as the perception by the eye or skin (*Pillsbury, 1930,* pp. 23 ff.).

James also emphasizes audition in the space concept of the blind:

> In taking a walk through the country, the mutations of sound, far and near, constitute the chief delight of the blind. To a great extent, their imagination of distance and of objects moving from one distance to another seems to consist in thinking how a certain sonority would be modified by the change of place (*James, 1890,* p. 205).

331   Philip Worchel

Investigations of the space orientation of the deaf-blind may yield more basic clues to the sensory basis of the space perception and orientation.

Summary and Conclusions

To determine the cues involved and the ability of the blind to orient themselves spatially, two tests of orientation were administered to the blindfolded blind and blindfolded sighted Ss in an outdoor experimental area relatively free from objects in the near vicinity. In the first test, S was led by E along two legs of a right triangle. The S was instructed to return in a straight path to the starting position, that is, along the hypotenuse. In the second test, S was was led along a hypotenuse path by E, and S had to return to the starting position in a right-angle path. Seven different distances were used in each test. The results showed that:

1. The sighted were significantly better than the blind, that is, they returned closer to the starting position.

2. There was no difference between the congenitally blinded and the accidentally blinded on the space orientation tests.

3. There was no significant relationship between age at blinding and space orientation scores.

4. There was no significant relationship between the chronological ages of the blind and the space orientation scores.

5. There was no significant difference between the space orientation scores of the male and the female blind Ss.

6. The error in missing the starting position increased for both the blind and sighted Ss as the hypotenuse distance increased.

7. The few introspective reports given by the Ss indicated that both the blind and the sighted used *time* in estimating the distance from the starting position; but the sighted used visual imagery in determining the direction of the starting position and the returning path.

These results lead to the conclusion that in the absence of auditory cues, the blind rely primarily on *time* for distance estimation. Kinesthetic cues without the aid of visual imagery resulted in poor directional orientation. The sighted Ss, in the absence of visual cues, use both time and visual imagery for estimating distance and direction.

GENERAL SUMMARY AND CONCLUSIONS

The role of visualization in the ability of the blind to perceive and manipulate spatial relations tactually and to orient themselves spatially was investigated in the present series of three experiments. In the first experiment we employed the methods of reproduction, verbal report, and recognition in testing the tactual perception of simple geometric forms. The second experiment dealt with problems of imaginally constructing a total form from the tactual perception of two parts of the form. Space orientation was studied in the third series of experiments. The S was to return to an initial starting position via a straight path after having been led in a right-angle path, and via a right-angle path after having been led along a straight path.

Two groups of 33 totally blind and 33 sighted Ss matched on the basis of sex and chronological age were used in the investigation. The results were fractionated on the basis of age at blinding, chronological age, and sex. Reliability of all the tests was determined by the split-half technique. On the basis of the present results we can conclude that

1. The sighted Ss are superior to the blind in tactual form perception measured by reproduction and verbal report, in the imaginal manipulation of space relations, and in space orientation.

2. The blind do as well as the sighted in the recognition of tactual form.

3. The accidentally blinded surpass the congenitally blinded in tactual form perception (reproduction and verbal report) and in the space relations test, and equal the congenitally blinded in the recognition of tactual form and in space orientation.

4. There is a significant and high correlation between age at blinding and tactual form reproduction and description, and in the manipulation of space relations.

5. Sex differences are in favor of the males, but the differences were not significant in any of the tests.

6. For the blind Ss chronological age is significantly related to performance in the space relation test; in all the other tests, there is no relationship between chronological age and performance.

7. The ability to translate tactile-kinesthetic impressions into visual imagery gives significantly better scores in all of the tests of form perception except recognition and space orientation.

8. In the space orientation tests, visual imagery is important in directional orientation, but the estimation of time is fundamental in distance orientation for both the blind and the sighted Ss.

References

Betts, G. H. *The distribution and functions of mental imagery.* New York: Teachers Coll., Columbia Univ., 1900.

Brown, M. S., & Stratton, G. M. The spatial threshold of touch in blind and seeing children. *J. exp. Psychol.,* 1925, *8,* 434–442.

Cutsforth, T. D. An analysis of the relationship between tactual and visual perception. *Psychol. Monogr.,* 1933, *44,* No. 1 (whole no. 197), 125–152.

Czermak, J. Physiologische Studien: Beobachtungen über die Feinheit des Raumsinnes der Haut bei Blinden. *Akad. d. Wiss., Wien, Sitzungsber.,* 1855, *15,* 482–487.

Gärttner, O. Versuche über den Raumsinn der Haut an Blinden. *Z. Biol.,* 1881, *17,* 56–61.
Heller, T. *Studien zur Blindenpsychologie.* Leipzig: Wilhelm Engelmann, 1904.
James, W. *The principles of psychology.* New York: Holt, 1890. Vol. II.
Lotze, H. *Metaphysic.* Oxford: Clarendon Press, 1887. Vol. II.
Lowenfeld, V. Tests for visual and haptual aptitudes. *Amer. J. Psychol.,* 1945, *58,* 100–111.
Mellone, S. H., and Drummond, M. *Elements of psychology.* Edinburgh: Blackwood, 1907.
Pillsbury, W. B. *The essentials of psychology.* New York: Macmillan, 1930.
Platner, E. *Philosophische Aphorismen.* Leipzig, 1793.
Stout, G. F. *A manual of psychology.* London: Clive, 1913.
Sylvester, R. H. The mental imagery of the blind. *Psychol. Bull.,* 1913, *10,* 210–211.
Wundt, W. *Lectures on human and animal psychology.* New York: Macmillan, 1896.

15

Problems of Play and Mastery in the Blind Child

Doris M. Wills

> *Miss Wills is a clinical psychologist at the Hampstead Child Therapy Clinic in London, England. Anna Freud is Director of the clinic. For the past eight years Miss Wills has been working with the Research Group on Blind Children at the Hampstead Clinic. This has resulted in several publications and participation in a conference and symposium on blind children. The present paper was her Chairman's address to the Medical Section of the British Psychological Society in November 1965.*
>
> *The reader may note that this article departs somewhat from the format prescribed for this book. The editors feel there is ample justification for this. For some puzzling reason, experimentally based research on the blind child has been negligible in recent years. There is a great need to revive research interest in this important area of exceptionality. In her provocative address, Miss Wills generates a wealth of research ideas. She has collected convincing evidence that the psychological development of the blind child differs significantly from the normal child. Future research should be directed toward identifying and clarifying the interaction of these critical variables.*

Some explanation must be given for the fact that the Hampstead Clinic, directed by Anna Freud, has undertaken the study of blind children's early development at a time when the number of such children in this

FROM THE *British Journal of Medical Psychology*, 1968, *41*(3), 213–222. Reprinted by permission of The British Psychological Society.

country and in America is fortunately so small. The reasons for it were this: some disturbed blind children were referred to the Clinic a number of years ago and during their psychotherapeutic treatment it became apparent that their early development had followed a course different from that of sighted children; questions were raised that we could not answer. We found that sufficiently detailed accounts of the early development of blind children were not available, in spite of the extensive literature, and that adaptation of knowledge about sighted children's development would not suffice. There had been a tendency to assume that the blind child's development would follow the same course as that of a sighted child in all areas except vision, and, while in some cases this led to a healthier attitude in the adults handling the child (in that they were less tempted to overprotect him), it begged a major question: how does he circumvent his difficulty and how does his blindness modify the course of his development from babyhood onwards? In fact, the blind child can be regarded as unique in his development and worthy of close study in his own right. However, this lack of knowledge of the blind child's early development was not the only reason for undertaking further research. It was hoped that through the understanding of these children with the known, if major, sensory deficit of blindness, the understanding of children with unspecified, unknown, sensory deficits might be furthered; for instance, those which may be linked with psychosis and brain damage. (See, for example, Hermelin & O'Connor, 1955.) Again, since the pace of the blind child's early development could reasonably be expected to be uneven compared to that of a sighted child, namely slower in some areas, and faster in others, it was hoped that its study would illuminate certain phases of normal child development which had hitherto attracted little attention.

To provide material for this research, some years ago a day nursery school for blind children was set up. Clinic workers have followed the development of younger blind children and babies in their homes, and some further blind children have been taken into psychotherapeutic treatment. Many observations have been recorded from these various sources, and those concerning the blind children's play have presented a particular challenge. In a first attack on this subject a description was given of the curious imitative word play of some blind children, which in turn gives way to a form of role play (Sandler & Wills, 1965). The present paper is an attempt to provide a further chapter on the interesting problem of blind children's play and its many vicissitudes.

WITHDRAWAL FROM AGE-ADEQUATE PLAY

One of the most striking impressions one gains when observing a small group of blind nursery-school children is the ease with which they stop playing at an age-adequate level and withdraw into simple primitive activities unless an adult constantly stimulates and supports their interest. Why do they not play with the toys and other things in the room, and what does this mean in terms of their development? Reasons will be put forward for this tendency to withdraw unless supported by the adult, and an attempt will be made to examine what furthers and what holds up the blind child's play, an activity so necessary for the mastery of his inner and outer world. To this end, episodes from the play of a 4-yr.-old blind child, Sam, will be described, because the play showed, by its progress, his increase in mastery, and, by its hold-ups, the hurdles he had to surmount, hurdles that may be proving insurmountable to some blind children who, as a result, become withdrawn. Other clinic records will be used for purposes of additional illustration and discussion. With the exception of Sam, any children quoted are blind from birth. As to Sam, his eyes were enucleated because of retinoblastoma at 6 months, and there is no record of what he might have been able to see before this age. Our long contact with Sam (from 4 to 7 yr.) did not suggest that he had many memory traces from this first 6 months before his eyes were enucleated. He had great difficulty with many of the concepts of the sighted world; he was, however, very positive in his relationships to people, and some degree of sight in his first 6 months might well have played its part in this.

Since the play to be described is that of Sam in his fifth year, it is necessary to make some reference to the early development of blind children in order to explain why, by nursery-school age, they rely so much on the adult and are so little attracted by toys alone. It is not merely that lack of sight makes toys less attractive to the blind nursery-school child; in our experience children who lose their sight after the first year retain their interest in toys to a large extent, and do not need the adult for stimulation to anything like the same degree, though they may need her for other types of support. As Sandler (1963) has shown, it is that since babyhood the blind child's cathexis of the outside world, both people and the environment, has been following a different course from that of the sighted child. Without vision, the blind baby is not so readily attracted by the toys and other inanimate objects in his surroundings, and this means that he tends to revert to interest in his own body and that of his mother and the people and animals around him instead. These living creatures must stand out like beacons in a hazy world, since besides any relationship they may have with him, they present him with a more varied sensory impression and one that the blind baby can understand in terms of his own body. This attachment to bodily interests (which include body movement, body contact and so on) continues to provide a much-needed respite for the blind child in his task of coping with the world. However, their high cathexis carries all the dangers of a fixation point.

In the second year, when the sighted child cannot come into a room without seeing something with which he would like to play, it can be said of the blind child that 'for what the eye sees not, the heart grieves not'.

He is not attracted because he cannot see (sound does not exercise the same pull), and he may at first resist a new toy or new activity offered by the mother because, without the introduction that sight can give, its novelty frightens him. The mother must remain the mediator, and explain these new experiences to a far greater extent and for far longer than the mother of a sighted child. In addition, she continues to make a much more varied sensory impression on him than the inanimate objects that surround him. All this again increases her importance for the blind child. While the sighted child's cathexis also remains attached to the mother, much more of it attaches to, or is displaced from her on to, the surroundings. In the second year also, when the sighted child's developing motility brings him into contact with a wider range of inanimate objects, the blind child has, to some extent, to inhibit this in the interests of safety and is more restricted in his explorations. Again the mother must often help him in making them, both by guiding him, and by furthering his understanding of the inanimate objects he comes across. To some extent cathexis of sound appears to take the place of cathexis of sight for blind children, and, as speech develops, this redoubles the significance of the mother and other people to the child, since they can respond to him verbally. Caroline's behaviour at the seaside provides an example of this. At 3 yr. 2 mth. her favourite amusement was to talk to people on the esplanade. If they responded, as most of them did, she would settle down to finding out all about them, and recognize them when she met them again.

It appears therefore that people are cathected so heavily and to the detriment of things for two main reasons: they produce a varied and relatively understandable sensory impression, and they are necessary for the child as auxiliary egos, not only in the sense of providing for his physical needs, but also in the sense that they enable him to cope with and understand his world. Sighted children rely on their mothers for similar ego support, but to nothing like the same extent.

Dorothy Burlingham has described the behaviour of a small group of blind nursery-school children thus, when the teacher stops supporting them: 'Left to their own devices, the children tend to "play safe" by repeating the familiar, such as opening and shutting doors, turning switches on and off, playing with the water faucets . . . or filling and emptying containers . . . they cannot be coaxed away from repetition to constructive progress by a specific game or by offering them a toy; the achievement of this purpose has to rely on their personal attachment to the teaching adult. They do not progress without individual help . . . in an individual person-to-person relationship . . . they function surprisingly well' (Burlingham, 1965, p. 198). Such play with switches and so on is reminiscent of the play of 18-month-old sighted children. However, when the blind children are playing with the teacher not only to introduce a toy, but to further any activity with it and support their interest, there is a marked change in their behaviour and they present a much more age-adequate picture.

While the children certainly profit by the nursery-school group when it is actively led by the teacher, it was this striking discrepancy between the children's play when they are getting individual support, and when, in a group of blind children of the same age,* this degree of support cannot be given that led to the supplementing of the situation in the nursery school with an arrangement whereby each child spent the first hour of the morning four days a week with an adult alone, joining the group for the remainder of the morning. Sam, aged 4 yr. 4 mth., was allotted to me. My aim was to use the time not for psychotherapy in the ordinary sense, or for educational purposes as such, but to act as a kind of auxiliary ego, picking up any cues he gave as to his interests in people and in the world around and furthering them, and, as far as his inner world was concerned, helping him to understand his own drives and affects. My aim was also to deal with any anxieties that blocked his path as they arose, whether they were a response to inner tensions or outer reality (about which he was often confused).

Sam is the only child of parents in their 20s, who live with their many relatives on the different floors of a house in London. So there were always plenty of people to look after him, and when he came to us at 3¾ yr. he seemed to be much petted and carried around a great deal. He was rarely left alone, and slept in the same room as his parents.

According to the mother, Sam's birth was normal, and he was breast-fed for 6 months. As mentioned earlier, his eye condition was due to retinoblastoma, and both eyes had to be removed when he was 6 months old. The prognosis now is good.

Sam very quickly used the opportunities offered him during a term and a half of nursery-school attendance (mostly part-time) before coming to me, and his rate of learning and general behaviour suggested normal intelligence. (On a test given during Sam's seventh year he gained an IQ of 97 (Williams, 1956).) While it would be wrong to regard Sam's play as necessarily typical for a blind child, it showed many features that could be observed in our other blind children. Like most of them, Sam cathected people very highly. Unlike some of them, he was very outgoing. In addition, he remained very much himself, and he did not 'parrot' phrases that he did not understand. These special qualities meant that he demonstrated his thinking within the relationship to the adult in a way that could be understood.

* It is outside the scope of this paper to discuss the stimulating effect on the blind child of sighted siblings and of animals in the home. Reference here is to a group where the children are all blind.

SLOW DIFFERENTIATION OF SIMPLE REPETITIVE PLAY

The first aspect of Sam's play worthy of description was a certain type of simple and repetitive play he indulged in during his first weeks with me, which shifted as the affects behind it were put into words. I had purposely supplied only a few toys because I wanted Sam's interests to emerge, and to follow his lead. This resulted in his using very few modes of expression, and it seemed that both libidinal and aggressive drives were shown only in these, mostly very simple, undifferentiated, types of play. He enjoyed bodily games, he sometimes beat rhythms on the radiator with great precision, wanting me to accompany him by singing the right song, and, for much of the time, he was content to swing backwards and forwards from foot to foot, waving and rattling whatever musical toy I provided, until I introduced something else. But what he seemed to enjoy most was throwing a ball down with all the force he could muster (it was hard and had a rattle inside it, so it made a loud bang); following this he would rock to and fro wringing his hands in excitement. This ball-throwing probably had different meanings at different times, such as 'I enjoy a loud noise' or 'I am cross about something'. One day he did it after pulling the chain in the lavatory, which always excited and frightened him. I suggested he had to crash the ball because the noise of the chain had made him jump. He would ruminate on, and organize, such information, saying: "It made him * jump, and choo-choos made him jump"—another anxiety I had put into words for him—and he slowly became able to express these affects verbally and in more varied forms of play. As this happened the compulsive crashing of the ball stopped.

Such simple and repetitive play is to be seen from time to time in the nursery school when the situation is unstructured by the teacher, and, though most blind children slowly abandon it in favour of more differentiated ways of expressing themselves, this phase is expedited and the child's development furthered when the teacher or other adult can understand it. In some blind children, however, this repetitive play persists, and holds up the further development of their play, so posing a problem. The great disadvantage of such play is that its undifferentiated nature gives the child little or no insight and therefore leads to little or no mastery of the situation which has prompted it, and it is not easy for the adult to understand and so come to his help.

Such an arrest in play is often to be seen in the very withdrawn blind child, who may make little response to intervention, unlike Sam whose

---

* Sam used the third person to refer to himself during much of his fifth year.

response was more informative. Omwake & Solnit refer to such a problem in a withdrawn blind child, Ann, who used very few words spontaneously. Ann was 4 yr., and for 2 months 'used the play at the piano [of which the only verbalized theme was 'Leta * spank you'] to reveal the vague ideas and feelings which confused and often frightened her. With her voice and posture, and with a display of energy she attacked the piano, and in this way communicated her feelings of helplessness, anger, excitement, and dependency which she had been unable to express in a way that they could be dealt with. Through such piano play, strange as it was, she found her first medium for communication . . . The crescendo of laughter and hitting of the keys was interpreted as enjoyment of the excitement of spankings. As confirmation of the interpretation, her laughter which had been strident and harsh took on more normal modulations, and sometimes I detected the reassuring gleeful chuckle of a normally excited child engaged in mischief' (Omwake & Solnit, 1961, p. 364).

Much of this repetitive play is concerned with discharging affects, and modifies when the children are given words in which to verbalize them. Such clarification and its results recalls a point made by A. Katan that applies particularly to blind children. Katan emphasizes the great importance of giving the young child appropriate words for his affects, since without suitable words he will discharge them by acting them out in reality, or, it may be added, in repetitive play; with suitable words he can postpone and modify action in the real world, or, again it may be added, in the phantasy world of play. Katan goes on: 'If this process of acting upon feelings continues for a considerable time, the results will be fully evident. The child's ego will become fixated upon acting upon his feelings rather than attempting an adequate means of mastery. In such children the ego becomes weak, for it is repeatedly overwhelmed by affects' (Katan, 1961, p. 186).

PERSISTENCE OF SIMPLE ROLE PLAY

Another phase of Sam's play was the recapitulation of actual experience, often without any reversal of roles, and with little or no modification of the happening. This type of play was frequently to be observed in our other nursery-school children, some of them more intelligent than Sam. The adult was used as a playmate and assigned an exact role. Much of this play is to be seen in sighted children at a younger age. (Comparisons of the play of the blind child to that of the play of the sighted child at a younger age are made in order to give it a basis of reference, and not because it is precisely similar. Those who know the blind child will be aware that there is a qualitative difference, related to the blind child's

---

* Leta was Ann's nurse.

relative maturity in certain areas, which shows itself in rate of learning, memory and so on.)

Many were the mildly traumatic scenes that Sam re-enacted with me. He would say: 'You say, "Come out of that coal bucket" ' and next time add one word to my role, such as, "You say "Come out of that coal bucket quick" '. The scene had to be enacted a number of times in the very simple wording dictated, modifications of the role, making the mother's behavior less cross, or introducing more content, were not accepted until the scene had been repeated again and again, but they would then be incorporated and appear in later repetitions. The introduction of props to further the play often tended to deflect it at this stage. Such play demonstrates graphically what Greenacre describes as a neglected aspect of play: 'the necessity for repetition of experience in establishing a sense of reality . . . Any experience which is so strange that there is little in the individual's life to which he can relate it is felt as inimical, alien, and overwhelming. On the other hand, an experience which is only somewhat or a little bit new is pleasantly exciting. In the first instance, the individual is prompted to go back and take another look to verify reality again and again until familiarity is established. Then fear gives way to triumph of recognition' (Greenacre, 1959, p. 65). This exact recapitulation in play is strikingly observable in our blind children because much experience is strange to them, and they have greater difficulty in mastering it and the excitations it arouses in them.

The only way in which Sam modified his recapitulation of actual experience was by changing some endings to happy ones, and though our other blind nursery-school children do play imaginative games around tea parties, shopping, hospital, etc., they all show what appears to be a striking poverty of invention. It may be of course that we do not pick up the cues to such play or understand it properly, and so do not further it. Caroline (4 yr. 10 mth.) who was very intelligent and successful, would verbalize phantasies to herself as she played with her collection of Christmas and birthday cards (which she preferred to dolls), phantasies which neither her mother nor I could understand in more than a very general way, probably because the associations she made were strange to us. However, in some young blind children the lack of imaginative games may reflect their meagre understanding of the world at this stage; they have few ideas about it to manipulate. This raises the question as to what happens in these blind children to the phantasies which motivate such play in sighted children. In the absence of suitable decor and *dramatis personae*, the phantasies probably remain very primitive, and find discharge in simpler forms of play, as for instance in Sam's ball throwing and Ann's piano hitting, or in garbled talk, which is often a kind of play with words. The phantasies may even be discharged at a somatic level, and in some cases they may be inhibited or repressed.

MASSIVE INTERFERENCE OF ANXIETY

So far certain phases in Sam's play have been described and parallels have been drawn between them and the play of other blind children. Some outline has been given of the way in which the adult can help both by the clarification of inner and outer reality and as a co-operative playmate. But there is a further aspect which deserves more attention, since it narrows the field of the blind child's play, namely anxiety. While some anxiety was implicit in much of the play already described, when anxiety is excessive the child avoids altogether playing around the themes connected with it. The observer can only learn about the acute fears and the phobic anxieties which cause this avoidance in other contexts. ('Phobic' is used here in the broad psychiatric sense to cover all anxiety which is excessive in relation to the stimulus, and which must therefore contain some degree and kind of projection.) The anxiety has then to be reduced sufficiently for the child to be able to use in his play any theme connected with it. While excessive anxiety prevents play, once it is reduced, play is of great help in mastering any that remains. In psychotherapy with sighted children admittedly something of the same procedure is followed, but even the very anxious sighted child, because of his ability to displace and to symbolize, brings the anxiety-laden theme into his play far sooner.

It is an important topic since some blind children become extremely withdrawn because of their numerous anxieties, and many of our nursery-school children showed fears and anxieties of one kind and another. Sam's fears, though acute and varied, were still reversible.

It will be seen that his fears, and indeed his phobic anxieties, were based to some extent on a tie to an earlier highly cathected experience, and a failure to generalize from later experiences, probably because, without sight, meaningful experiences are so few and infrequent. When Sam started with me at 4 yr. 4 mth., his teacher reported that he was afraid of sand, plasticine, one special doll's blanket, doll's hair, teddy bears, and the words 'snack', 'nursery' and 'cut', the last because of its connexion with haircutting. Some of these anxieties were not altogether unreasonable and gave way to explanation, for instance that 'snack' did not mean 'smack'. However, the anxiety around haircutting took longer to clear up and its acuteness suggested that it had a phobic element. Sam avoided any theme of haircutting in his play. I first used the word 'cut' when I brought scissors to cut plaster to mend the ball, which had broken. 'Not cut, not cut!' said Sam. My primary task was clear; Sam had to be given more experiences of 'cut' in order to dilute its frightening association with haircutting, and to form a basis for generalization. The following week I introduced scissors and paper for him to use. He loved the scissors, but used them (with my help) while chorusing 'Not cut his hair!' every half-minute. Next week I offered a blunt knife and other things to cut. The chorus of 'Not go to the barber's, not cut his hair!' continued, but by this time he was able to add 'Sam likes to cut.' Games of cutting my hair followed this. Meanwhile his teacher and his mother had also been helping him by giving him the opportunity of cutting dolly's and mother's hair.

It may well be asked: Why attempt to explain away an anxiety which appears to be phobic? Why not try to interpret what has been projected, the unacceptable impulse, or the wish and the defence against it? But the way that such anxieties in the blind child respond to explanation and further experience suggests that he is going through a phase which the sighted child goes through at an earlier age, and which responds to similar handling; that is, explanation running alongside the child's developing ability to come to terms with his own impulses and wishes, so that less projection is needed. Interpretation at this stage in the child's development is not indicated because of his immaturity, though, as was the case with Sam, the adult can assist the child in coping with his impulses by verbalization and other means as they show themselves in other areas of his life. Some residue of phobic anxiety is probably left in each case (sighted and blind), which is then displaced on to other stimuli that are not understood, but this after all is the normal human lot. Interpretation is indicated only if the child, whether blind or sighted, has phobic anxieties which persist in some quantity and hold up his further development.

Sam's anxieties about the cat developed later and also had a phobic quality. He had a cat at home which may have scratched him unpredictably, but his anxiety was disproportionate, and, again, many cues set it off. One day a cat mewed from a wall while we were in the street going across to the nursery school. I told him what it was. It then jumped down and brushed his leg as it crossed our path. He panicked. Next day he announced an arrival: 'He's frightened of cats', and later, 'He fell over a pussy cat'. My attempt to explain what the cat had done, touching his trousers in the course of the explanation, made him panic again, and when I used a cushion to act as the cat, his fear spread to the cushion, and he said, "No cushion!" In fact, he lost his usual ability to pretend. The fear quickly became associated with the fur on my coat cuff, which he had always called pussy; almost every day that week he touched it and said, 'No pussy!' A week later we were crossing the road, Sam saying, 'No pussy!' as usual while we crossed it, when he stopped dead to listen to the whining noise of the dustcart, and then panicked, thinking it was a cat. However, subsequently his teacher brought a cat to the nursery school; she reported that by this time it made Sam more angry than frightened. A few months later he was able to enjoy acting a cat who scratched and bit, illustrating Greenacre's point that 'frequently some residue of the anxiety contributes to the fun and excitement of play' (Greenacre, 1959, p. 68).

The intensity of this phobic anxiety is to be expected in blind children, who have to control their impulses because of their reliance on their "objects"; they must often find a solution of a kind by repressing them and then projecting them in some way such as this. Parallels could be found amongst sighted children with a similar problem of control for other reasons. What is striking about this anxiety in the blind child, however, is the rate at which it sometimes spreads, as in this instance of the cat. This is due to the blind child's difficulty in assessing the reality situation. He is somewhat like a sighted child in the dark. Any use of the word 'cat', any sound or texture, may mean the feared cat. Avoidance is felt to be impossible, and without adult intervention, panic must ensue. Bruner (1961, p. 206) suggests that 'one of the prime sources of anxiety is a state in which one's conception or perception of the environment with which one must deal does not "fit" or predict that environment in a manner that makes action possible'. In contrast, the sighted child, with the help of vision, can avoid the object of his anxiety, leaving much of his life relatively anxiety-free, and leaving him a wide range of safe themes to play around.

Sam was phobic to a lesser degree about the teddy; he was not too sure it was not alive. This phase of his play is selected because the personification of inanimate objects is so necessary for phantasy play. There were hints that, with encouragement, Sam would have personified things that made more noise, but his play at home with sighted children made teddies also interesting for him. He introduced buying imaginary teddies into his shopping games. After a few sessions I produced a real one, and this did not at first disrupt his play. A few minutes later I tied a little bell around its neck, thinking it would make it more interesting; Sam at once dropped the teddy and became frightened. I took the bell off immediately, and he played with the bell, but he would not touch the teddy. During the remainder of the hour he referred to it as 'breathing' and 'squeaking'. I explained it was like the hood of his coat which was also fluffy and not alive like a cat, and the next day he was able to say, while on my lap, 'Got the bell off, eh?', adding 'like coat?'. I reintroduced teddy later, but one day when he had decided to wash it, he got frightened again; in fact, pretence easily broke down when teddy was personified.

This anxiety certainly held up his play, and if he had not been able to get over it and pretend that the teddy or some other inanimate object was a person, all the uses of such toys for displacement of aggressive and libidinal behaviour, and for the acting out of phantasies, would have been lost to him. Although Sam did slowly get over his anxiety that the teddy and doll were alive, and began to use them sometimes in his games, the next example shows that pretence was not fully and safely established. A game recurred in which he would insist that both the doll and I were Miss Wills; then Sam would throw the doll off my lap for crying. In other words, he could reject me in effigy but only if he made doubly sure of keeping me present in fact. Here the child's ego is struggling with a very important step, the differentiation of make-believe from reality, which was a characteristic problem for some of our less mature blind children. (In their Social Maturity Scale, Maxfield & Buchholz (1957) expect that the blind child by the age of 6 will usually differentiate between pretending and actual fact, and that he will know that animals do not really talk, etc. We should expect such understanding earlier in the sighted child.)

Though some of our disturbed blind children did take a very long time before they were able to use dolls or anything else for purposes of displacement and make-believe, most of the nursery-school children made this move. Loobiloo, a life-size rag doll in the nursery school, was a particularly useful character for a time; it was credited with all kinds of naughtiness by the children, although it was not actually handled very much. Some children preferred to personify things other than teddies or dolls, perhaps because, like Sam, they had feared teddies when they were first offered, perhaps because these other things had collected a suitable cathexis through sound and other associations. (It will be recalled that Caroline used to personify Christmas cards in her play.)

THE ENCOURAGEMENT OF DISPLACEMENT INTO PLAY

In *Beyond the Pleasure Principle* Freud (1922, p. 15) says: 'We see that children repeat in their play everything that has made a great impression on them in actual life, that they thereby abreact the strength of the impression and so to speak make themselves masters of the situation.' If we accept this, we can say that play is an essential part of normal development. We help sighted children by supplying them with models of all kinds—buildings, toy animals, dolls and teddies—all toys based largely on the visual aspect of the object. While watching a sighted child play, we will often make the play more real by what we say about it, and by the extra props we introduce, and we are able to do this because we are in close touch with his thinking. In this way we increase his ability to abreact to, and master, everyday experiences, and so we reduce his fears of external reality. As described earlier, sight enables the child to narrow down and pinpoint his phobic objects, so that he has a wide range of themes to play around where the anxiety is manageable. The fact that he can, through vision, separate make-believe from reality means that pretence in play is firmly established much sooner. This gives the sighted child a further means of playing out phantasies from his inner world of an aggressive or sexual kind without fear that he is really endangering his 'objects' or himself. This abreaction in play will, in its turn, lessen his need for projection and so his need for phobic objects.

The task of finding meaningful toys for the blind child is a difficult one not only because he cannot appreciate their visual aspect, but because he has difficulty in imitating actions he cannot see, so the constant identification with the physical activities (as distinct from language) of the adults around him is largely closed to him. Any cues the child gives as to what will lead him away from interest in his own and other people's bodies have to be followed. Since he cathects people so highly, it may be that we should first watch for any indication he gives as to what he will use as a substitute for them. Whatever he chooses, e.g. Christmas cards, pencils, robots, or even an imaginary character which Loobiloo, the doll, became for some children, it may be that we should foster this substitute, and further and fill out any pretend games around it as opportunity offers. This will allow for displacement and the externalization of aggressive and sexual phantasies which must otherwise be suppressed, with far-reaching consequences. In this way the child acquires an area of play around a theme he understands comparatively well, namely people. The blind child also gives cues as to what he will substitute for other things and experiences in the external world, but here to a greater degree he often lacks a basic understanding of the original experience, and needs ongoing support if he is to understand it and master it in play.

While the blind child should of course be given every opportunity for normal childhood experience with other children, he needs much adult support for the reasons described above if he is to cope with his outer and inner world, if he is to keep them separate so that he knows what is make-believe, what fact, and if he is to attempt their mastery in his play. If he receives this support, he will be well-launched on what Winnicott (1958, p. 230) describes as 'the perpetual human task of keeping inner and outer reality separate yet interrelated'—a task in which play has a major role.

SUMMARY

It is a common observation that young blind children easily withdraw from age-adequate play and revert to simple activities unless an adult stimulates their interest. This paper attempts to suggest reasons for this by tracing the different course that the early development of the blind child must follow and the degree to which his interest goes via his 'objects', that is, via people. Three aspects of the play of Sam, a 4-yr.-old blind child, are then described and discussed: (1) simple repetitive play that was helped by the verbalization of the affects involved; (2) simple role play concerned with the recapitulation of experience to which more content could slowly be given; (3) the part played by anxiety in narrowing the field of play, and its interference with the use of teddies, etc., in phantasy games, anxiety that was greatly diminished by the widening of experience, and the verbalization of impulses and affects which lessened projection.

Acknowledgements

The work with blind children is part of the Educational Unit of the Hampstead Child Therapy Course and Clinic and as such is maintained by the Grant Foundation, Inc., New York. The research work with the blind is assisted further by the National Institute of Mental Health, Bethesda, Maryland.

The research on blind children has been directed, since its inception, by Mrs Dorothy Burlingham. I am very grateful to Mrs Burlingham, Mrs A.-M. Sandler and Mrs H. Kennedy for many helpful suggestions and I am indebted to all members of the research group for making their records available.

References

Bruner, J. S. (1961). The cognitive consequences of early deprivation. In P. Solomon et al. (eds.), *Sensory Deprivation*, pp. 195–207. Cambridge: Harvard University Press.

Burlingham, D. (1965). Some problems of ego development in blind children. *Psychoanal. Study Child 20*, 194–208. London: Hogarth.

Fraiberg, S. H., & Freedman, D. A. (1964). Studies in the ego development of the congenitally blind child. *Psychoanal. Study Child 19*, 113–169.

Freud, S. (1922). *Beyond the Pleasure Principle*, p. 15. London: Hogarth.

Greenacre, P. (1959). Play in relation to creative imagination. *Psychoanal. Study Child 14*, 61–80.

Hermelin, B., & O'Connor, N. (1965). Visual imperception in psychotic children. *Br. J. Psychol. 56*, 455–460.

Katan, A. (1964). Some thoughts about the role of verbalization in early childhood. *Psychoanal. Study Child 16*, 184–188.

Maxfield, K. E., & Buchholz, S. (1957). *A Social Maturity Scale for Blind Pre-School Children*. New York: American Foundation for the Blind.

Omwake, E. B., & Solnit, A. J. (1961). It isn't fair: The treatment of a blind child. *Psychoanal. Study Child 16*, 352–404.

Peller, L. E. (1954). Libidinal phases, ego development and play. *Psychoanal. Study Child 9*, 178–198.

Sandler, A.-M. (1963). Aspects of passivity and ego development in the blind infant. *Psychoanal. Study Child, 18*, 343–360.

Sandler, A.-M., & Wills, D. M. (1965). Some notes on play and mastery in the blind child. *J. Child Psychother. 1*, no. 3, 7–19.

Williams, M. (1956). *Williams Intelligence Test for Children with Defective Vision.* Birmingham: University of Birmingham.

Wills, D. M. (1965). Some observations on blind nursery school children's understanding of their world. *Psychoanal. Study Child 20,* 344–364.

Winnicott, D. W. (1958). Transitional objects and transitional phenomena. In *Collected Papers,* pp. 229–242. London: Tavistock.

16

A Review of Recent Personality Research on Deaf Children

W. John Schuldt and Doris A. Schuldt

Dr. Schuldt is Associate Professor of Psychology and Director of the Psychological Clinic at the University of Arkansas. Mrs. Schuldt is a Certified Speech Pathologist and has taught the deaf-blind child.

In this review article the authors concentrate on empirical research that has been published over the past twenty years on the personality characteristics of deaf children. They point out methodological shortcomings and make the plea for experimental research in this area which is currently dominated by descriptive investigations.

Three excellent reviews (Barker, Wright, Meyerson, & Gonick, 1953; Berlinsky, 1952; Di Carlo & Dolphin, 1952 *) have summarized the personality research on deaf children which was published prior to 1950. As one evaluates this research and these reviews, various research trends can be noted. Deaf children seem to be somewhat more poorly adjusted, rigid, immature, and neurotic than their hearing peers. Better adjustment seems to be related to living within a nonresidential setting and having other deaf

---

* This article is also reprinted in the earlier edition of this book (Trapp and Himelstein, 1962).

members in the family. In addition, the deaf children who have less severe hearing losses and more intelligence appear better adjusted. However, one must be cautious in interpreting or attributing meaning to these findings because the reviewers indicate that most of the earlier research reflects methodological limitations such as inadequate controls, poor sampling, inadequate descriptions of samples, and questionable diagnostic tools with unstandardized measurement criteria.

The purpose of this paper is to continue these reviews by evaluating research published between 1950 and the present. The scope of the paper is limited to empirical personality research on deaf children and thus does not include publications, however meaningful, which were based on educational or clinical observations and opinions.

DIFFERENCES BETWEEN DEAF AND HEARING CHILDREN

Levine (1956) reported an investigation designed to "probe beneath the cumulative personality tests scores that have described the deaf as an emotionally unstable group and find out what actual dynamics and personality characteristics are present" (p. 129). She selected a group of 31 deaf girls who were in attendance at a residential school for the deaf. The girls were between 15 and 18 years old, had more than a 70-decibel loss in the better ear, had hearing parents, had become deaf before age 3, and were judged to be "normal" deaf individuals. The Rorschach records of these girls were compared with interpretive criteria previously established on hearing individuals. Levine interpreted the results as revealing a personality pattern within these deaf girls characterized by "(1) pronounced underdevelopment in conceptual forms of mental activity; (2) emotional underdevelopment; (3) a substantial lag in understanding the dynamics of interpersonal relationships as well as the world about; (4) a highly egocentric life perspective; (5) a markedly constricted life area; and (6) a rigid adherence to the book-of-etiquette code rather than inner sensibility as standards for behaving and even for feeling" (p. 146). Levine suggested that these findings do not have to be interpreted as evidence for maladjustment in that the concept of maladjustment implies a deviation from a normative criterion, which has not yet been established for deaf children.

Goetzinger, Ortiz, Bellerose, and Buchan (1966) also studied the deaf adolescent, with the use of the Rorschach. They selected 24 deaf adolescents (12 males and 12 females) who were between 16 and 20 years of age and who have been either congenitally deaf or lost their hearing before the acquisition of speech and language. In addition, a group of hearing adolesecnts of equal sex and age were selected. Both groups were administered the Structured Objective Rorschach Test as part of a larger test battery. The results revealed that the deaf and hearing adolescents differed on 12 of the 25 variables being assessed. On the personality variables measured, the deaf manifested more aggression, behavioral consistency and nonconformity, and less cooperation and anxiety. The authors indicated that, while group differences did exist, almost all of the performance of the deaf fell within the normal range.

A Rorschach study was also reported by Fiedler and Stone (1956) in which a group of 10 children with mild hearing losses were compared with 10 normal children matched on age, sex, and socioeconomic status. No statistical differences were found between these two groups. These negative differences are difficult to interpret because of the small number of subjects used in this study.

Many tests other than the Rorschach have been utilized to study possible differences in personality between deaf and normal children. Fiedler (1958) compared the performance of 110 7- and 8-year-old deaf children to 50 children with normal hearing on an adaptation of the World Test. The results showed that the deaf children scored significantly lower on integrative ability than the normal children and built more Worlds characterized by overinclusiveness. Moreover, the deaf children manifested more signs of possible psychological difficulties.

Rodda (1966) reported the results of a pilot study in which 26 15- and 16-year-old deaf children (16 in secondary school, 4 in grammar school, and 6 in special deaf schools) were evaluated on the Bristol Social Adjustment Guides. Their performance was compared to data obtained on a 15-year-old nondeaf group. Rodda stated that the two groups did not differ on social maladjustment. However, Rodda indicated that the grammar and special school students manifested poorer adjustment than did the secondary school students. The author also claimed that the girls seemed better adjusted than the boys. However, these last two conclusions were subjective evaluations as no statistical analyses were performed on the data.

Albright (1952) administered the Mental Health Analysis to 156 boys and 161 girls who were pupils in public, private day, and residential schools for the deaf. All these children were sixth-, seventh-, and eighth-grade students. The scores of these deaf children were compared to normative scores on the standardization group of the Mental Health Analysis. Albright concluded that the deaf children were "best with mental ill health more than others" (p. 124). However, the adequacy of her interpretation is again difficult to assess, owing to the lack of tests of statistical significance.

Reynolds (1955) studied the school adjustment of 36 children with mild hearing losses (i.e., a minimum loss in the better ear of 15 decibels) as compared to a group of children with normal hearing. The normal group was matched with the hearing impaired children on chronological age, sex, attendance at the same school, grade, nonlanguage mental age, race, and occupation. School adjustment was assessed by educational achievement, absences from school, teacher ratings, and personal and social adjustment as measured by the California Test of Personality. Statistical evaluation failed to demonstrate that the children with mild hearing loss differed significantly from their peers with normal hearing.

Vegely and Elliot (1968) designed a study to assess if the California Test of Personality, which was standardized on hearing children, could be used with severely hearing impaired children (i.e., median hearing level in the better ear was 98 decibels). A group of 53 hearing impaired children was given this test and their performance was compared to the normative sample of normal hearing children. The results indicated that all the subtest scores, except sense of personal worth, of the hearing impaired group were below the 50th percentile of the normative sample. In addition, the three summary scores—Personal Adjustment, Social Adjustment and Total Adjustment—were evaluated in terms of various characteristics of the hearing impaired sample. No significant differences were found between residential and day school children or between children with more and less severe hearing losses. Moreover, no differences were apparent between children in various divisions of the schools, between boys and girls, or between those with higher achievement and those with lower achievement. However, the post hoc analyses revealed that the older children manifested better performance on the Personal Adjustment index while not demonstrating such differences on the Social Adjustment or Total Adjustment indices.

Most of the studies reported thus far have been concerned with differences in personality structure or overall psychological adjustment between deaf and normal children. There have been three interesting studies reported which have focused on more specific differences between these two groups, i.e., perception of self and others, levels of aspiration, and conceptions of causality.

Blanton and Nunnally (1964) administered the Semantic Differential to 173 children and adolescents (81 males and 92 females who were enrolled in two schools for the deaf). All these subjects manifested severe hearing losses; i.e., no subject had less than an 80-decibel loss in the better ear. Their performance on the Semantic Differential was compared to the performance of a control group of 83 males and 95 females who had normal hearing and were enrolled in the public schools. The results, related to perceptions of self and others, indicated that the boys tended to see themselves, another handicapped group (i.e., blind), and their parents as being less well adjusted and less good than do normal boys. The deaf girls, in comparison, also saw themselves and their parents as less good while seeing themselves as less well adjusted. Other handicapped groups were evaluated by the girls more negatively, with the exception of the deaf, who were seen as relatively better adjusted. The control group of sighted children tended to evaluate the deaf children as less well adjusted but they did not tend to devalue them.

An interesting study was reported by Rutledge (1954) in which he attempted to assess deaf children's level of aspiration. Rutledge selected a deaf group composed of 52 adolescents who were 14 or 15 years old. This group had an equal number of boys and girls and an equal number of children having exogenous and endogenous etiology. He also selected a control group ($N = 52$) of normal hearing subjects who were matched on age, sex, father's occupation, and institutionalization. All children were administered the Heath Rail-Walking Test, a measure of locomotor coordination or balance, and the Rotter Aspiration Board, which the author felt would not handicap the deaf children. Rutledge found that the deaf group manifested significantly lower levels of aspiration on the Heath Test but did not manifest such differences on the Rotter Aspiration Test. However, deaf girls demonstrated lower level of aspiration than did normals on the Rotter test while no such differences were manifested between boys. To assess if there were characteristic levels of aspiration for these children, the aspiration measurements on the tests were correlated. The results revealed significant correlations on all but the deaf boys. Rutledge interpreted his findings as supporting the hypothesis that the two groups differed on the task which was considered to handicap the deaf child. However, the evidence did not strongly support the hypotheses that deaf children differed from hearing children in general aspiration level or that the deaf children manifested consistently reliable and thus characteristic aspiration level.

Nass (1964) also assessed one of the more specific personality variables, the child's conception of physical causality. He selected a deaf group composed of six girls and six boys who were congenitally deaf, attending a school for the deaf, and who demonstrated adequate verbal communication. He also selected two groups of hearing children—12 children who were evaluated as being emotionally adjusted and 12 children who were emotionally disturbed. All 36 children were asked a series of questions dealing with the operation of physical phenomena. Some of these questions concerned phenomena assessable to direct experience and others where the phenomena were inassessable to such experience. His results indicated that the deaf and emotionally disturbed groups differed significantly from the normals on questions where causal agents were inaccessible to direct experience. He reported that "The data suggest that deaf children of ages 8–10 years are not able to utilize a reasoning approach characterized by logical deduction where the agents of causality are not assessible to direct experience. Unlike the disturbed hearing group, however, they resort to more explanations of causality by contiguity (phenomenistic causality) and those of causality involving magical or animistic approaches" (p. 672). He did a follow-up study with a group of 18 deaf and 18 hearing children of an older age (10 to 12 years) and found no differences which suggest that these findings may only apply to younger deaf children.

The primary focus of the research reviewed thus far has been on differences between hearing impaired children and children with normal hearing. When one compares the samples selected for these studies, one can, of course, make inferences regarding variables which differentiate subgroups of deaf children. For example, children with more severe hearing losses seem to manifest more abnormal modes of adjustment than do children with less severe hearing losses. However, such conclusions must be based on uncontrolled comparisons rather than on controlled empirical studies of within deaf group differences. Thus, it is important to review studies within the last twenty years that have been designed specifically to assess personality and adjustment differences between subgroups of deaf children.

DIFFERENCES BETWEEN SUBGROUPS OF DEAF CHILDREN

Recent research on differences within the deaf population has been primarily concerned with a comparison of differences within children who attend various types of deaf schools, who have deaf versus hearing relatives and who differ in etiology.

Myklebust (1964) administered a projective test, The Drawing of the Human Figure Test, to 511 deaf children residing within residential schools, to 319 deaf children attending day schools, and to a control group of 274 hearing children. He concluded from this investigation that the body images, perceptions of self and others, and levels of maturity differ between deaf children and normal children. Moreover, he concluded that deafness affects the adequacy of identification in deaf boys. Myklebust reported that deaf children attending day schools manifested more emotional stress, conflict, frustration, and disturbed identification than did deaf children in residential schools or hearing children in public schools. However, the children in the day school concomitantly manifested more adequate self perceptions, more adequate body images, and demonstrated more accurate perceptions of others than did the children in the residential schools. Thus, Myklebust concluded that "no outstanding advantages emerged for either school" (p. 174).

Craig (1965) conducted a sociometric study of the self concepts of deaf children. She selected 48 children (16 per group) from a residential deaf school, a day school for the deaf, and a public school for hearing children. All the deaf children had a hearing loss greater than 65 decibels for the speech range in the better ear and lost their hearing previous to the acquisition of language. An attempt was made to control for acquaintance, age, class, sex, intelligence, and socioeconomic status. Sociometric tests, in which each subject had to rate others and to predict others ratings of themselves, were administered to every child. The results indicated that the deaf, as a whole, were less accurate in their ability to predict how others would rate them. The children in the deaf residential schools rated themselves as superior to the children in the other two groups and were highly accepting of their group. In comparison, the day school children were more rejecting of their group than they were of the children in the other groups.

Four studies have been reported on family variables and their relationship to the deaf child's adjustment. These studies, in general, evaluated the emotional adjustment of deaf children as a function of having deaf parents or relatives in the family and concomitantly of being exposed to early manual communication (i.e., signing), Brill (1960) compared the adjustment of three groups of deaf children—a group with deaf parents, a group with hearing parents but with deaf siblings, and a group with no deaf relatives. Brill utilized ratings by supervising teachers, classroom teachers, dormitory counselors, and supervising counselors as measures of adjustment. Brill found no significant differences between groups but found that boys with deaf parents had more extremes of adjustment, both positively and negatively. Deaf boys with hearing relatives had fewer extreme ratings, while boys with deaf siblings had more frequent ratings of poor adjustment.

Meadow (1968) compared a group of 59 children with deaf parents to 59 matched students whose parents were not deaf. An attempt was made to match the subjects on type of school, age, sex, IQ, degree of residual hearing, socioeconomic status, and family size. Rating scales, included as part of larger test battery, were utilized as measures of social adjustment. These scales were rated by classroom teachers, dormitory counselors, and either vocational arts teachers or other counselors depending upon the age of the child being rated. The ratings on all of the nine items selected as the criteria of emotional adjustment (e.g., maturity, sociability, sex-role behavior, etc.) were found to favor the children with deaf parents. Meadow attributed these differences to the deaf parents' relative ease of accepting deafness within their children or to the early communication existing between the deaf children and their parents through manual sign language.

Meadow (1969) also reported a similar study in which she hypothesized that deaf children with deaf parents would manifest more positive self-images than deaf children with hearing parents because of the presence of manual communication and more positive family climates. The performance of a group of deaf children ($N = 58$) with deaf parents, matched on the same variables as in the previous study, was compared with a group of deaf children with hearing parents on a rating instrument designed for the evaluation of self-images. In addition, the children's self-esteem, self-confidence, and adjustment were rated by a teacher and two counselors. Family climate was estimated by various indices of family stability and socioeconomic status. The results indicated that deaf children with deaf parents manifested more positive self-images than deaf children with hearing parents. Moreover, self-images of children with deaf parents seemed to vary as a positive function of the family climate while a medium family climate seemed to promote more positive self-images within the group of children with hearing parents. However, post hoc analyses also suggested that the self-images of the two groups tended to be influenced differentially by the children's level of school performance and communication skills.

Stuckless and Birch (1966) also studied the mode of communication in the home prior to entering school and its apparent effect on educational achievement and psychosocial adjustment. Thirty-six matched pairs of deaf children, who differed on their early exposure to oral or manual modes of communication, were compared on the Rating Scale for Pupil Adjustment. All the children had more than a 70-decibel hearing loss in the better ear and had become deaf before age two. The children in both groups were matched on sex, age ($M = 14$), age admitted to the sampled schools, severity of hearing loss, and IQ. No significant differences were found between these two groups.

The results of these four studies are inconclusive. Barker et al. (1953), in their review of earlier research, also noted the inconclusiveness associated with findings based on rating scales. Thus, one might question whether rating scales are reliable or valid means of measuring adjustment or if the adjustment of the parents also must be evaluated, as noted by Brill (1960), before meaningful results can be obtained on this interesting and important area of research.

The last area of current research involves personality differences between children whose deafness can be attributed to different etiologies. Vernon (1967a) compared a group of 40 educationally deaf children with an etiology of erythroblastosis fetalis (i.e., involving Rh-factor complications) with children having other common etiologies of hearing loss (e.g., rubella, prematurity, genetic, menigitic). All these children were evaluated by clinical interviews; nonverbal tests of personality,* perceptual motor functioning, and intelligence; and teachers' ratings of adjustment. The results suggested that children whose deafness resulted from Rh-factor complications had relative good adjustment when compared to children

* The specific tests utilized in this research are not mentioned in this article. However, the reader interested in these tests can refer to the original unpublished report (Vernon, 1966).

with other etiological determinants. Moreover, results of the teacher ratings indicated that children with genetic etiology were better adjusted than the Rh children.

Vernon (1967b) also reported a similar comparison between 129 post-rubella deaf children and children whose deafness resulted from other etiologies. Teachers' ratings and school records revealed that the post-rubella children manifested more psychological difficulties than other etiological groups (e.g., genetic, meningitic). In addition, psychological evaluations revealed that over 25 percent of his sample of postrubella deaf children were emotionally disturbed. A more thorough presentation of Vernon's findings regarding multiple handicaps in deaf children, including data on psychological adjustment, can be found in a recently published report (Vernon, 1969).

Bindon (1957a) noted that many people working with the deaf suggest that rubella deaf children behave differently from children whose deafness has been determined by other etiologies. However, she questioned these observations and conducted two investigations to evaluate these professional opinions. Bindon (1957a) compared three groups of 15-year-old adolescents on the Make-A-Picture Story Test (MAPS)—a group of 36 rubella deaf children (16 boys and 20 girls), a group of nonrubella deaf (7 boys and 8 girls), and a group of nondeaf children (13 boys and 17 girls). All groups were administered the MAPS test, which was altered to allow for nonverbal responses. The comparisons between the two deaf groups did not reveal significant differences nor did other analyses based on sample characteristics such as degree of deafness, sex, or institutional residence. However, the rubella group and the deaf group, as a whole, could be differentiated from the normal group on the basis of fewer normal signs and more schizophrenic signs.

Bindon (1957b) reported another study in which she selected three groups of 15-year-old adolescents—a group of ($N = 36$) rubella deaf, a group ($N = 15$) of nonrubella deaf or children who had gone deaf before age two, and a group ($N = 30$) of normally hearing children. The deaf groups had not acquired speech and language naturally and had hearing losses greater than 60 decibels. The Rorschach was individually administered to all these children. The administrative procedure was modified to reduce language handicap effect and was scored according to the Monroe Inspection Technique. To avoid the possibility of inflating chance differences produced by the multitude of possible comparison, which is not avoided in most of the studies on deaf children, she did not compare indivdual scores unless the composite scores were significantly different between groups. These composite scores did not differentiate between the two matched subgroups nor did they differentiate on further analyses based on degrees of deafness, sex, or residential factors. However, the composite scores differentiated between the rubella deaf and the normal children. She interpreted these findings as indicating that the two deaf groups have common behavioral patterns which are similar to emotionally disturbed children with normal hearing or to normal children of a younger age.

SUMMARY AND CONCLUSIONS

The basic findings in the research done since 1950 seem to be in general accord with earlier research. That is, the children with severe hearing losses seem to manifest more abnormal personality characteristics and less adequate adjustment when compared to hearing control groups or normative data on hearing children. However, as Levine (1956) has suggested, these findings do not necessarily indicate psychopathology resulting from deafness. Rather, these investigations can be interpreted as providing normative information on a minority group who live in a different educational and social environment and who do not have the language and other requisite skills necessary to develop personality characteristics or modes of adjustment similar to the majority of hearing children.

Certain changes in focus and quality can be noted in the current research. The major change in the focus of study is exemplified by the relative increase in research on specific personality variables which differentiate deaf and hearing children and with differences within the deaf population.

The research methodology seems to have generally improved. Many researchers have been more precise in defining samples and have utilized more appropriate experiment controls. However, some studies still contain data without appropriate statistical procedures and some without any statistical procedures at all. These studies, of course, do present information on the specific samples being studied but do not allow for generalization to any greater population of deaf children. Another common statistical error is the use of great numbers of post hoc analyses, based on various combinations of the same data, without any overall tests of significance. This procedure allows for the possibility of many apparently significant results which occur only as a function of chance due to the large number of statistical tests being calculated. Most of the studies reviewed in this paper are based on the method of systematic assessment in which the investigators attempt to describe personality or adjustment differences between deaf children or between deaf and normal children. These studies exemplify investigations "concerned with the *what* of behavior; with the disclosure of enumerative-descriptive facts concerning specific groups, problems, or situations; with status rather than cause" (Levine, 1963, p. 496). This can be differentiated from research in which the investigator "wants to know the *why* of behavior, and is fired with intense curiosity about cause" (Levine, 1963, p. 496).

There is a paucity of personality research on deaf children in which an experiment has been conducted utilizing measurable independent variables which can be manipulated and the effects of this manipulation can be evaluated. It is realized that research in most fields begins with the publications of observations and opinions—often brilliant—by professional workers in the field of study. This is frequently followed by carefully conducted descriptive investigations, as in the case of many of the studies reviewed in this paper, and eventually leads to actual experimental research in which the effects of the relevant variables can be identified and more fully understood. As one evaluates the data currently available on the relationship between personality and deafness, it becomes apparent that more researchers need to conduct such experiments.

References

Albright, M. A. Mental health of children with hearing impairments. *Except. Child.*, 1952, *19*, 107–124.

Barker, R. G., Wright, B. A., Meyerson, L., & Gonick, M. R. *Adjustment to physical handicap and illness: A survey of the social psychology of physique and disability* (2nd ed.). New York: Social Science Research Council, 1953.

Berlinsky, S. Measurement of the intelligence and personality of the deaf: A review of the literature. *J. speech hearing Dis.*, 1952, *17*, 39–54.

Bindon, D. M. Make-A-Picture Story (MAPS) Test findings for rubella deaf children. *J. abnorm. soc. Psychol.*, 1957, *55*, 38–42. (a)

Bindon, D. M. Rubella deaf children: A Rorschach study employing Monroe inspection technique. *Brit. J. Psychol.*, 1957, *48*, 249–258. (b)

Blanton, R. L., & Nunnally, J. C. Semantic habits and cognitive style processes in the deaf. *J. abnorm. soc. Psychol.*, 1964, *68*, 397–402.

Brill, R. C. A study in adjustment of 3 groups of deaf children. *Except. Child.*, 1960, *26*, 464–466, 470.

Craig, H. B. A sociometric investigation of the self-concept of the deaf child. *Amer. Ann. Deaf*, 1965, *10*, 456–474.

Di Carlo, L. M. & Dolphin, J. E. Social adjustment and personality of deaf children: A review of literature. *Except. Child.*, 1952, *8*, 111–118.

Fiedler, M. *Ninety-first annual report of the Clark School for the Deaf.* Northampton, Mass.: Metcalf Printing and Publishing Co., 1958, pp. 63–79.

Fiedler, M., & Stone, L. J. The Rorschachs of selected groups of children in comparison with published norms: 1. The effect of mild hearing defects on Rorschach performance. *J. proj. Tech.*, 1956, *20*, 273–275.

Goetzinger, C., Ortiz, J. D., Bellerose, B. & Buchan L. G. A study of the S. O. Rorschach with deaf and hearing adolescents. *Amer. Ann. Deaf*, 1966, *111*, 510–522.

Levine, E. S. *Youth in a soundless world.* New York: New York University Press, 1956.

Levine, E. S. Studies in psychological evaluation of the deaf. *Volta Rev.*, 1963, *65*, 496–512.

Meadow, K. P. Early manual communication in relation to the deaf child's intellectual, social and communicative functioning. *Amer. Ann. Deaf,* 1968, *113,* 29–41.

Meadow, K. P. Self-image, family climate, and deafness. *Soc. Forces,* 1969, *47,* 428–438.

Myklebust, H. R. *The psychology of deafness* (2nd ed.). New York: Grune & Stratton, 1964.

Nass, M. The deaf child's conception of physical causality. *J. abnorm. soc. Psychol.,* 1964, *69,* 669–673.

Reynolds, L. G. The school adjustment of children with minimal hearing loss. *J. speech hearing Dis.,* 1955, *20,* 380–384.

Rodda, M. Social adjustment of hearing impaired adolescents. *Volta Rev.,* 1966, *68,* 279–318.

Rutledge, L. Aspiration levels of deaf children as compared with those of hearing children. *J. speech hearing Dis.,* 1954, *19,* 375–380.

Stuckless, E. R., & Birch, J. W. The influence of early manual communication on the linguistic development of deaf children. *Amer. Ann. Deaf,* 1966, *111,* 452–460, 499–504.

Trapp, E. P., & Himelstein, P. (Eds.). *Readings on the exceptional child.* New York: Appleton-Century-Crofts, 1962.

Vegely, A. B., & Elliot, L. L. Applicability of a standardized personality to a hearing-impaired group. *Amer. Ann. Deaf,* 1968, *113,* 858–868.

Vernon, M. Multiply handicapped deaf children: A study of the significance and causes of the problem. Unpublished doctoral dissertation, Claremont Graduate School and University Center, 1966.

Vernon, M. Rh factor and deafness: The problem, its psychological, physical and educational manifestations. *Except. Child.,* 1967, *34,* 5–11. (a)

Vernon, M. Characteristics associated with post-rubella deaf children: Psychological, educational, and physical. *Volta Rev.,* 1967, *69,* 176–185. (b)

Vernon, M. *Multiply handicapped deaf children: Medical, educational and psychological considerations.* Washington, D.C.: Council of Exceptional Children, 1969.

17

Early Manual Communication in Relation to the Deaf Child's Intellectual, Social, and Communicative Functioning

Kathryn P. Meadow

Dr. Meadow is Research Sociologist at the Langley Porter Neuropsychiatric Institute, University of California Medical Center. She is associated with the Mental Health Services for the Deaf.

In the past several years Dr. Meadow has published extensively, contributing articles to nine major professional journals and presenting papers in a variety of conferences on the exceptional child. She is currently doing research with deaf children attending day schools in the San Francisco Bay Area to determine if the results of her study reported here may have to be restricted to deaf children attending residential schools.

This is a most significant article for those interested in the teaching and education of the deaf. The results show, contrary to popular opinion, that early exposure to manual communication does have a facilitating effect on the intellectual and social development of the deaf child. The most effective procedure would perhaps be a combination of oral and manual training at an early age.

The basic impoverishment of deafness is not lack of hearing, but lack of language. To illustrate this, we have only to compare the four-year-old

REPRINTED FROM THE *American Annals of the Deaf,* 1968, *113,* 29–41.

hearing child, with a working vocabulary of between two and three thousand words, to a child of the same age, profoundly deaf since infancy, who may have only a few words at his command. Even more important than vocabulary level, however, is the child's ability to use his language for expressing ideas, needs, and feelings. By the age of four, the hearing child in all cultures has already grasped the rules of grammar and syntax which enable him to combine words in meaningful ways.

There are those who feel that existing research points to the inability of the individual ever to recapture those phases of linguistic development which are by-passed (McNeill, 1965; Sigel, 1964). Data on the linguistic achievement of deaf adolescents and adults tend to confirm this notion. It is estimated that the average deaf adult reads at about the fifth grade level, or even below (Furth, 1966, p. 205). An investigation of language comprehension of deaf students in 73 schools in Canada and the United States showed that only 12 per cent of the sixteen-year-olds scored above the fifth grade level on the Metropolitan Achievement Tests Elementary Battery (Wrightstone, et al., 1962, pp. 13–14).

It has been suggested that the experiential deficiency resulting from communicative inadequacy influences the personality characteristics which have been noted among the deaf. One of the most consistent findings is that deaf persons are less "mature" than hearing individuals with whom they are compared. Levine, on the basis of a Rorschach study of normal deaf adolescent girls, described the complex which she summarized as "emotional immaturity" in terms of egocentricity, easy irritability, impulsiveness, and suggestibility (1956, p. 143). Neyhus characterized the deaf adults whom he studied (also using the Rorschach) as "restricted in breadth of experience, rigid and confused in thought processes, and characterized by an inability to integrate experiences meaningfully." He found that the "distorted perception" noted in younger persons was apparent in adulthood as well. However, this characteristic was diminished at the older age levels, "suggesting a delayed period of maturation in the deaf" (Neyhus, 1964, p. 325). Altshuler describes deaf persons as lacking in empathy, egocentric and dependent, handling tensions with "considerable impulsivity" and without much thoughtful introspection (1964, pp. 63–64).

On the one hand, deaf persons have been found to be noticeably deficient in their educational and intellectual functioning, compared to hearing persons, in spite of apparently normal capacities. On the other hand, findings have been presented which indicate many deaf persons to be less mature and more dependent than comparable groups of hearing persons. Since not all deaf persons exhibit these responses, we may assume that there is nothing inherent in early profound deafness which makes these deficiencies inevitable. Rather, we must look to environmental factors for explanations of developmental differences.

Because of the occasional genetic transmission of deafness, there are families in which both parents and children are deaf. "Nearly ten per cent of all children born to deaf subjects" in the survey of the deaf population in New York State, are also deaf (Rainer, et al., 1963, p. 27). The socialization experiences of these deaf children can be expected to differ markedly from those of deaf children with hearing parents. First, the emotional reaction of deaf parents to the birth of a deaf child is predicted to be less traumatic. Parental acceptance of and adjustment to the deaf child should be comparatively easier and more rapid. Secondly, most deaf children with deaf parents have a means of communication from earliest childhood, since most deaf adults utilize the manual language of signs as a matter of course.[1] These two basic differences in the family environments of deaf children with deaf parents and those with hearing parents provide the basis for a research design approximating a "natural experiment" for testing some hypotheses about the bases of differences in levels of social and intellectual functioning in deaf persons.

One reason for the presence of manual communication in deaf families and the absence of manual communication in hearing families with deaf children is related to a bitter controversy regarding the use of the language of signs with young deaf children. Most hearing parents are warned against the use of manual communication by the professionals with whom they come in contact. The reason for this proscription is the belief that if deaf children are not forced to rely exclusively on oral methods of communication, they will not be motivated to learn speech and speechreading: "the evidence is . . . impressive that speech seldom develops if signs come first" (DiCarlo, 1964, p. 115). Some social scientists, however, are not convinced that this statement is true. Furth, for instance, says that the insistence that the early use of signs is detrimental to the acquisition of speech *because* they are easier for the deaf to learn relies on "a mysterious doctrine of least effort." "Carried to its logical conclusion, this would mean that infants who are allowed to crawl would forever lack the motivation to learn to walk" (Furth, 1966). Kohl (1966) and Altshuler and Sarbin (1963) also believe that insistence on the exclusive use of oral communication with young deaf children has been carried to

[1] In the New York State study, almost half of the 493 deaf respondents stated that they used "mainly signs" for communicating, while another 18 per cent report the "equal use of speech and signs." This compares to 29 per cent who use "mainly speech" (Rainer, et al., 1963, computed from Table 6, p. 119). Of seventy-one deaf parents of deaf children responding to the Stuckless and Birch survey, only five stated that they did *not* use the language of signs with their deaf child. Sixty-four per cent stated that they had used the language of signs with the child when he was a baby (Stuckless and Birch, 1966, p. 458).

366   The Aurally and Visually Handicapped

extremes. A comparison of the communicative functioning of deaf children who were exposed to manual communication early in life, and those who had no exposure to it in the early years should provide parents and educators with additional evidence in this sensitive area.

The above discussion was designed to provide background for the rationale behind the selection of three crucial dependent variables examined in the research to be reported here: (1) the intellectual or academic functioning, (2) the social functioning, and (3) the communicative functioning of the deaf child. The major independent variable was defined as the parents' hearing status, since this factor was believed to affect (1) the socialization climate and (2) the existence of a system of early family communication. Four studies have been reported which have direct bearing on the present research. These are summarized briefly below.

PREVIOUS RESEARCH WITH SPECIFIC RELEVANCE FOR THIS INVESTIGATION

Stuckless and Birch (1966) used a matched-pair design very similar to the present one for comparing deaf children of deaf parents with deaf children of hearing parents. Of seventy-one deaf children with deaf parents in five different schools for the deaf, thirty-eight were selected who had been exposed to early manual communication as well as meeting other criteria. These were matched with deaf children of hearing parents on the basis of sex, age, age of admittance to present school, severity of hearing impairment and intelligence test scores. The authors found no significant differences between their two groups on scores for speech intelligibility, nor for "psychosocial adjustment" as measured by rating scales completed by teachers. Significant differences were found on reading scores, speechreading scores, and on written language scores. In all cases, higher scores were achieved by children with "early manual communication."

Stevenson (1964) compared the educational achievement of deaf children with deaf parents to the achievement of deaf children with hearing parents, using all children of deaf parents enrolled at the California School for the Deaf (Berkeley) between 1914 and 1961. "Of the 134 (children of deaf parents) only fourteen were found to be weaker, educationally, than the children of hearing parents with whom they were compared . . . This would mean that 90 per cent were better students and attained a higher educational level than the children of hearing parents (thus) invariably possessed a very strong command of language." He found that only nine per cent of the hearing parents "succeeded in going to college," compared to 38 per cent of deaf parents' children. In spite of some methodological questions which might be raised, we can agree with Stevenson that "the study is strong . . . enough to justify further study by other schools."

Brill (1960) compared the adjustment of 45 deaf children of deaf parents to that of the same number in two other categories: (1) deaf children with deaf siblings and hearing parents; (2) deaf children with no deaf relatives. The two comparison groups were equated with the children of deaf parents on the basis of sex, age, and IQ score. No significant differences were found for the group as a whole. However, when boys were compared separately, differences were significant, with the children of deaf parents showing "better adjustment." "Children with deaf parents and with deaf sibs have more ratings at both extremes, while those children who are the single deaf person in a family do not have as many extreme ratings" (Brill, 1960, p. 466). A subjective analysis of the 28 deaf families revealed "at least fifteen (who had 26 of the 45 children) were families that had given very definite evidence of social and/or psychological maladjustment." Brill suggests that the maladjustment in the homes of such a large number of deaf children of deaf parents might more than offset the advantage of communication between parent and child.

Quigley and Frisina (1961) compared day pupils to boarding pupils in residential schools. Although they did not set out to study children of deaf parents specifically, they did a separate analysis of this subgroup. Among the 120 day students studied, there were 16 who had deaf parents.

> Although the group with deaf parents had much poorer speech than the group with hearing parents, they had significantly higher scores in finger spelling and vocabulary . . . This group also had higher scores in educational achievement although not significantly so. The higher scores in finger spelling would be expected since this group with deaf parents would likely be exposed to much manual communication at home. Apparently, however, this use of manual communication also aided them in vocabulary development, although it hindered them in speech development. There was no significant difference between the two groups in speechreading (Quigley and Frisina, 1961, p. 33).

Two other studies have touched peripherally on the influence of the presence of "deaf relatives," in the deaf child's family, but the focus is somewhat removed from the central concerns of this paper (Titus, 1966; Pintner, 1920).

Research Hypotheses for the Present Study

On the basis of the theoretical considerations and results from previous research outlined above, the following hypotheses were formulated prior to the initiation of research procedures:

Hypothesis 1—Deaf children of deaf parents, compared to deaf children of hearing parents, are more likely to show a higher level of intellectual functioning.

Hypothesis 2—Deaf children of deaf parents, compared to deaf children of hearing parents, are more likely to show a higher level of social functioning, especially apparent in situations requiring "maturity" and "independence."

Hypothesis 3—Deaf children of deaf parents, compared to deaf children of hearing parents, are more likely to demonstrate a higher level of communicative competence, including competence in written and spoken, expressive and receptive language.

Research Population and Setting

All the children included in this study were enrolled at the California School for the Deaf in Berkeley between January and September, 1966. This is one of two residential schools for the deaf operated by the State. Minimum age for admission is five-and-one-half. Pupils either graduate or must leave the school by the age of twenty-one. School population is approximately 500. In January, 1966, sixty children (twelve per cent) were enrolled who had both a deaf father and deaf mother. One was eliminated because parents did not wish to participate. Thus, 59 deaf children with deaf parents formed the base of the study population. Each of these children was matched individually with a child whose father and mother both are hearing. Matching was done on the basis of sex, age, IQ test score, degree of residual hearing, and family size.[2] Some attempt was made to equate family socioeconomic status, using the father's occupation as a measure.

Before the matching procedure was begun, children of hearing parents were eliminated from consideration if they had any of the following characteristics:

1. deaf siblings
2. racial or ethnic minority group membership

[2] The aim of matching is to control or "hold constant" as many variables as possible other than the experimental variables. An attempt is made to make the two groups (*i.e.,* those with deaf parents and those with hearing parents) as nearly alike as possible. A random group of deaf children with hearing parents would, in all probability, not have the functional *potential* equal to that of the children with deaf parents because of the higher probability of additional neurological complications. In order to test the effect of parents' hearing status on the child's performance, we must start with groups who are "equivalent" in important ways. The most precise method of achieving this goal is by means of the matched-pair design.

3. secondary handicap (*e.g.,* physical condition in addition to deafness which interfered with functioning)

4. deafened after the age of two years

5. deafness resulted from maternal rubella, Rh incompatibility, or anoxia

After children with these characteristics had been eliminated, to the extent possible with the available records, there remained approximately 225 children with hearing parents who formed the pool from which matched pairs were formed.

The task of matching is an extremely laborious one, particularly when an attempt is made to control many variables simultaneously. Age and sex were the two variables on which most emphasis was placed in matching. The sex of the two members of the pair is the same in all cases: 34 pairs of boys, 25 pairs of girls. Fifty of the 59 pairs are matched within one year of age. Equating intellectual potential in the two groups was most difficult. The results of any intelligence test administered to a young child are of questionable reliability and validity; when the young child is also deaf, these difficulties are multiplied (Levine, 1960; Vernon and Brown, 1964). Every child who applies for admission to the school is given an intelligence test. The one used most often, and uniformly at the present time, is the performance scale of the Wechsler Intelligence Scale for Children. Forty-five pairs are matched within 10 points on IQ test score; 12 pairs show a discrepancy of between 11 and 15 IQ points; one pair has a 17-point discrepancy, another pair has a 20-point discrepancy. Mean IQ score for children of deaf parents is 111.5 while mean IQ score for children of hearing parents is 108.9. Eighty per cent of the children with deaf parents have a "profound" hearing impairment (greater than 80 decibels in the speech range of the better ear) as do 71 per cent of those with hearing parents (Flower, 1964).

The importance of family size to the socialization process has been summarized by Clausen (1966). An attempt was made to match children for this variable with the following success: 44 pairs were judged as having a "satisfactory" match (discrepancy of not more than one child); 11 pairs were "intermediate" in their match, with a discrepancy of two children; 4 pairs have an "unsatisfactory" match, with a discrepancy of more than two children.

Because of the skewed occupation distribution of deaf adults (Lunde and Bigman, 1959; Meadow, L., 1967), it is difficult to compare the deaf and hearing fathers. It was decided to equate deaf fathers who were skilled craftsmen with hearing fathers who were classified as professional, managerial, clerical and sales workers. On this basis, 40 pairs were judged to have a "satisfactory" match; ten pairs have an "unsatisfactory" match, and nine pairs cannot be evaluated because father's occupation was unknown for one pair member.

Research Instruments and Procedures

A rating scale was devised which included items dealing with intellectual, social, and communicative functioning (Meadow, K., 1967, pp. 336–340). Each student was rated *independently* by three separate raters. Of these, the first was the classroom teacher, and the second a dormitory counselor. Children in the fifth grade or above, who participate in the vocational training program, were rated by their vocational arts teacher. For the younger children, the third rating was completed by a different counselor. The three ratings were summed, scores ranked from highest to lowest and trichotomized for most of the analyses (referred to as "high," "medium," and "low" scores). To encourage raters to avoid the "halo effect" (Selltiz, et al., 1963), the positive and negative ends of the scale were shifted at random for different items.[3]

In addition to teacher-counselor ratings for intellectual functioning, Stanford Achievement Test scores, administered by the School in May, 1966, were utilized for evaluating students in this area. The Craig Lipreading Inventory (Craig, 1964) was administered to evaluate this area of communicative functioning.[4]

RESEARCH FINDINGS

Intellectual Functioning

There were thirty-two pairs of children for whom Stanford Achievement Test scores were available for both members. (These tests are administered only to children who are beyond the second grade in school.) The scores are expressed in terms of standardized "grade level" achievement, for "reading," "arithmetic," and "grade average." Table 1 shows the results of a pair-by-pair comparison, evaluated by means of a t test of differences. This table shows that differences in grade-level achievement, reading, and arithmetic, *favoring children with deaf parents* in each instance, were significant at the one per cent level of confidence or beyond. The average discrepancy in scores was greater than one year for grade level and arithmetic, and greater than two years for reading.

---

[3] The following persons gave a great deal of assistance in the development of the research instruments: Mr. Jacob Arcanin, Mr. Bernard Bragg, Mr. Ralph Jordan, Mr. Erwin Marshall, Mr. Hubert Summers.

[4] I am grateful to Mr. Hartley Koch for administering this test, and to Dr. William Craig, who loaned the films and test forms which he developed.

Table 1 *Matched-pair Comparisons of Stanford Achievement Test Scores: 1966 Grade Average, Reading, and Arithmetic*

	Mean difference	(N) (pairs)	t
Grade average	+ 1.28 years	(31)*	2.84**
Reading	+ 2.10 years	(31)*	2.56**
Arithmetic	+ 1.25 years	(32)	3.67**

*one tied observation dropped from the analysis.
**p $\leq$ .01

Three items included in the teacher-counselor rating scale are relevant to the assessment of intellectual functioning: apparent intellectual ability, use of intellectual ability, and apparent "achievement motivation." The results of the matched-pair comparisons on these three items are shown in Table 2. (Scores used in this comparison represent a summation of the ratings given by three raters, referred to as "Index Ratings.") Teachers' and counselors' judgments of the relative intellectual ability and use of ability show the same pattern as the Stanford Achievement Test comparisons: the children of deaf parents are judged to be of superior ability and performance (differences were significant beyond the one per cent level for both of these items). Fewer discrepancies in the predicted direction were found for the item describing the child's effort to achieve. While the comparisons favor children with deaf parents in 34 of 56 observations, this proportion could have been due to chance variation in seven of 100 samples.

Table 2 *Index Ratings of Intellectual Functioning for Matched Pairs of Children with Deaf or Hearing Parents*

Rating Scale Item	No. of Pairs	No. where Children with Deaf Parents Rated Higher	Wilcoxon T value	z
Intellectual ability	55	44 (80%)	255.5	4.31**
Use of intellectual ability	54	36 (67%)	326.0	3.58**
Works hard—strives to achieve	56	34 (61%)	619.0	1.46*

**p $\leq$ .01   *p = .07

Social Functioning

The areas of social and personal "adjustment" or behavior were evaluated by means of the Index of Teacher-Counselor Ratings. The pair-by-pair analysis of these items is shown in Table 3. Ratings for the nine items describing social functioning all favor the children with deaf parents, most beyond the one percent level of confidence.

In addition to the support which these findings give to the initial research hypothesis, they are of interest because of their relationship to previous comparisons of deaf and hearing subjects. As was stated earlier, a number of investigators have found deaf subjects to be "immature" compared to hearing subjects (Rainer, 1963; Neyhus, 1964; Levine, 1956). Several researchers have evaluated the "social maturity" of deaf children, using the Vineland Social Maturity Scale, designed to measure the "degree of independence or self-sufficiency." Streng and Kirk (1938), Avery (1938), Myklebust and Burchard (1945), and Myklebust (1960) all found that deaf children received lower scores on this Scale than did hearing children. Myklebust (1960, p. 215) reported that the discrepancy between the two groups increased with age. It has been suggested that the immaturity which seemingly characterizes deaf children and adults may result from the high proportion who attend residential schools, where the

Table 3 *Index Ratings of Social Adjustment Variables for Matched Pairs of Children with Deaf or Hearing Parents*

Rating Scale Item	No. of Pairs	No. where Children with Deaf Parents Rated Higher	Wilcoxon T value	z
Mature	56	39 (70%)	430.0	2.99**
Responsible	55	38 (69%)	432.5	2.83**
Independent	53	40 (75%)	281.0	3.85**
Enjoys new experiences	55	36 (65%)	501.0	2.25*
Friendly, Sociable	55	42 (76%)	405.0	3.06**
Popular with classmates	55	40 (73%)	434.0	2.82**
Popular with adults	52	34 (65%)	427.5	2.38**
Responds to situations with appropriate emotion	55	34 (62%)	535.5	1.97*
Shows appropriate sex-role behavior	54	33 (61%)	509.5	2.01*

**p $\leq$ .01   *p $\leq$ .05

development of independence and responsibility may be attenuated (Barker, 1953).

The results of the present study suggest that there is nothing inherent in the condition of deafness itself—that is, in the lack of auditory contact with the environment—which produces characteristics of immaturity which so many have noted. Since all subjects in the present study are students in a residential school for the deaf, and there are significant differences among them, the fact of residential living by itself would not seem to lead necessarily to immaturity. Rather, we should look to other conditions in the deaf child's environment to discover those which produce differences *within* the deaf population which may be as great as those between the deaf and hearing groups. (Of course, the hypothesized differences upon which the present study was designed relate to the presence or absence of early communication, and the quality of family relationships.)

Another similarly suggestive area is that represented by the item, "appropriate sex-role behavior," shown in Table 3 to be significantly more frequently rated higher among the children with deaf parents. Here differences are attributable almost entirely to higher ratings given to *boys* with deaf parents (Meadow, K., 1967, p. 193). The New York group found indications of a higher incidence of sexual maladjustment among their clinic patients than would be expected (Rainer, *et al.*, 1963, p. 148, 245).

The significance of differences found in these critical areas of "social adjustment" (maturity, sociability, sex-role behavior) is underscored by the *absence* of significant findings for a number of traits for which there is no evidence of deaf-hearing difference. These areas included traits summarized as "happy, calm, generous, obedient, kind, neat, mannerly, emphatic" (Meadow, K., 1967, p. 191). The absence of significant differences in these areas also provides support for the belief that the raters were not responding merely to a "halo effect" in scoring children with deaf and hearing parents.

Communicative Functioning

If the deaf child is to communicate effectively with the hearing world, he must acquire facility in speech, speechreading, and writing. If he is to communicate effectively within the deaf community, he must acquire both receptive and expressive facility in fingerspelling and the language of signs. In addition, he should feel comfortable about his own communicative skills, and be willing to use these skills to communicate with strangers, both deaf and hearing. All these items were included in the rating scale which teachers and counselors completed for this study. Table 4 shows the results of the matched-pair comparisons of children with deaf and with hearing parents on these items.

The critical communicative areas, for most parents and educators of

Table 4 Matched-pair Comparisons of Index Ratings for Communicative Functioning, Children with Deaf or Hearing Parents

Rating Scale Item	No. of Pairs	No. where Child w/Deaf Parents Rated Higher	Wilcoxon T value	z
Speechreading ability	46	22 (48%)	623.0	.10
Speech aptitude and performance	51	21 (41%)	758.0	.89
Facility in written language	49	35 (71%)	263.5	3.47**
Ability to fingerspell	54	50 (93%)	18.5	6.23**
Ability to read others' fingerspelling	52	49 (94%)	25.0	6.09**
Ability to use the language of signs	55	46 (87%)	117.0	5.47**
No apparent frustration from inability to communicate	56	39 (70%)	319.0	3.89**
Willingness to attempt communication with strangers	45	30 (67%)	335.5	2.06*

**p ≤ .01   *p ≤ .05

deaf children, are represented by *speechreading* and *speech*. Table 4 shows that the differences between children with deaf and hearing parents on these two variables are not significant. Twenty-two of 46 available score-comparisons favor children with deaf parents in ratings of speechreading ability; 21 of 51 comparisons favor children with deaf parents in ratings of speech aptitude and performance. The analysis of the additional six items dealing with communicative skills shows that children with deaf parents are given higher ratings in a significant proportion of the comparisons.

The results of the Craig Lipreading Inventory were essentially the same as those of the teacher-counselor ratings: no significant differences appeared in the scores of children with deaf parents and those with hearing parents. Of thirty-five pairs for whom a "Word Score" was available, differences favored children with deaf parents in eighteen instances. Of twenty-eight pairs for whom a "Sentence Score" was available, differences were in the predicted direction in eighteen instances (not statistically significant).

Because of the great interest in the relationship between proficiency in oral and in manual communicative skills, scores on the Lipreading Inventory were compared to Index Ratings for other aspects of communicative functioning. A significant positive relationship emerged between speechreading score and ratings for speech, expressive finger-spelling, and language of signs usage. (Relationships with written language facility and receptive fingerspelling were in the same direction but were not statistically significant at the five per cent level of confidence.) These findings fail to provide support for the notion that the knowledge and use of manual communication prevent the acquisition of speechreading skills. This contention is the heart of the oralist argument which forbids the use of manual communication with young deaf children. The findings of the present research agree substantially with those reported by Montgomery, who studied 59 prelinguistically deaf Scottish students and concluded that: "There are no negative correlations between any of the measures of oral skills and the manual communication rating: indeed there are no negative correlations at all. Positive significant correlations are recorded between the manual communication rating and the Donaldson Lipreading Test" (Montgomery, 1966, p. 562). Like the present author, Montgomery concludes that, "There . . . appears to be no statistical support for the currently popular opinion that manual communication is detrimental to or incompatible with the development of speech and lipreading" (*ibid.*).

Another variable which may well contribute to the deaf student's communicative functioning is the extent of the early oral training which he receives. From interviews with 34 deaf and 34 hearing families, it appears that the parents' hearing status is related to preschool training. About 40 per cent of the children with deaf parents had attended preschool classes for deaf children, compared to 80 per cent of those with hearing parents. Both children with deaf parents and those with hearing parents are more likely to score above the median on the lipreading inventory if they received some early oral training. (Approximately two-thirds of the groups with some early training scored above the median, compared to about one-third without early training. Because of the small numerical base, however, these differences were not statistically significant.)

SUMMARY AND CONCLUSIONS

The findings confirm the initial research hypotheses regarding the superior intellectual and social functioning of deaf children with deaf parents, compared to deaf children with hearing parents. Data from Stanford Achievement Tests (reading, arithmetic, and overall grade level), as well as teacher-counselor ratings for intellectual functioning, disclosed significant differences between the sets of matched pairs in the predicted direction. In the area of social functioning, differences favoring children with deaf parents were particularly impressive in areas of behavior which have often been cited as "characteristic" of deaf individuals. These include traits such as "maturity," "responsibility," "independence," "sociability," and "appropriate sex-role behavior."

The results of ratings and speechreading test, measuring communicative functioning, were less clear-cut. No differences were found between children with deaf parents and those with hearing parents on the ratings for speechreading and speech. Children with deaf parents received significantly higher ratings for facility with written language, receptive and expressive fingerspelling, and use of the language of signs. On the other hand, various measures of manual communication were positively related to facility in speechreading, as measured by the Craig Inventory. Early oral training seems to be related to later communicative functioning, and is less likely to have been experienced by children with deaf parents.

None of the evidence from the research reported above would seem to justify the strong injunctions placed by professional educators on the use of manual communication by parents of young deaf children. Children in this study who had been exposed to early manual communication performed at a higher level by almost every measure employed. This conclusion is not meant to discourage early oral training for deaf children. On the contrary, some evidence was reported to the effect that children who are most likely to be judged as having good communicative skills are those who were exposed to both oral and manual training at an early age.

References

Altshuler, K. Z., "Personality Traits and Depressive Symptoms in the Deaf," Wortis, J. (ed.), *Recent Advances in Biological Psychiatry*, Vol. VI, N.Y.: Plenum Press, 1964.

―――, and M. Bruce Sarbin, "Deafness and Schizophrenia: A Family Study," in John Rainer, et al. (eds.) *Family and Mental Health Problems in a Deaf Population*, N.Y.: Dept. of Medical Genetics, New York State Psychiatric Institute, 1963, pp. 204–213.

Avery, Charlotte B., "The Social Competence of Pre-school Acoustically Handicapped Children," *Journal of Exceptional Children*, 15, 1948, 71–73.

Barker, Roger G., in collaboration with Wright, Beatrice A., Myerson, Lee, and Gonick, Mollie R., *Adjustment to Physical Handicap and Illness: A Survey of the Social Psychology of Physique and Disability*, N.Y.: Social Science Research Council Bulletin 55 (rev.), 1953.

Brill, Richard G., "A Study in Adjustment of Three Groups of Deaf Children," *Exceptional Children*, 26, 1960, 464–466.

Clausen, John A., "Family Structure, Socialization and Personality," in Hoffman and Hoffman, *Review of Child Development Research*, Vol. II, N.Y.: Russell Sage Foundation, 1966, 1–53.

Craig, William N., "Effects of Preschool Training on the Development of Reading and Lipreading Skills of Deaf Children," *American Annals of the Deaf*, 109, 1964, 280–296.

DiCarlo, Louis M., *The Deaf*, Englewood Cliffs, N.J.: Prentice-Hall, 1964.

Flower, Richard M., "Fundamental Definitions of Hearing Impairment," in Godfrey, Beryl (ed.), *Orientation of Social Workers to Problems of Deaf Persons*, Washington, D.C.: U.S. Government Printing Office, 1964, 2–11.

Furth, Hans G., *Thinking Without Language, Psychological Implications of Deafness*, N.Y.: The Free Press, 1966.

Kohl, Herbert R., *Language and Education of the Deaf*, N.Y.: Center for Urban Education, 1966.

Levine, Edna S., *Youth in a Soundless World, A Search for Personality*, Washington Square, N.Y.: New York University Press, 1956.

———, *The Psychology of Deafness, Techniques of Appraisal for Rehabilitation*, N.Y.: Columbia University Press, 1960.

Lunde, Anders S., & Bigman, Stanley K., *Occupational Conditions Among the Deaf*, A Report on a National Survey Conducted by Gallaudet College and the National Association of the Deaf, Washington, D.C.: Gallaudet College, 1959.

McNeill, David, "The Capacity for Language Acquisition," in *Research on Behavioral Aspects of Deafness*, Proceedings of a National Research Conference on Behavioral Aspects of Deafness, New Orleans, May, 1965, Vocational Rehabilitation Administration.

Meadow, Kathryn Pendleton, *The Effect of Early Manual Communication and Family Climate on the Deaf Child's Development*, Unpublished Ph.D. Dissertation, University of California, Berkeley, 1967.

Meadow, Lloyd, "Implications of Technological Change for Employment Opportunities for the Deaf," Proceedings, University of Pittsburgh, Pennsylvania, 1967.

Montgomery, G. W., "The Relationship of Oral Skills to Manual Communication in Profoundly Deaf Students," *American Annals of the Deaf*, 111, 1966, 557–565.

Myklebust, H., & Burchard, E. M. L., "A Study of the Effects of Congenital and Adventitious Deafness on Intelligence, Personality, and Social Maturity of School Children," *Journal of Educational Psychology*, 34, 1945, 321.

Myklebust, H., *The Psychology of Deafness, Sensory Deprivation, Learning, and Adjustment*, N.Y.: Grune and Stratton, 1960.

Neyhus, Arthur I., "The Social and Emotional Adjustment of Deaf Adults," *The Volta Review*, 66, 1964, 319–325.

Pintner, R., & Reamer, J. F., "A Mental and Educational Survey of Schools for the Deaf," *American Annals of the Deaf*, 65, 1920, 451.

Quigley, Stephen P., & Frisina, D. Robert, *Institutionalization and Psycho-Educational Development of Deaf Children*, Council for Exceptional Children Research Monograph, Series A, No. 3, 1961.

Rainer, John D., Altshuler, Kenneth Z., Kallmann, Franz J. (eds.), *Family and Mental Health Problems in A Deaf Population*, N.Y.: Department of Medical Genetics, N.Y. State Psychiatric Institute, Columbia University, 1963.

Sellitz, Claire, Jahoda, Marie, Deutsch, Morton, Cook, Stuart W., *Research Methods in Social Relations* (rev. ed.) N.Y.: Holt, Rinehart and Winston, Inc., 1963.

Sigel, Irving E., "The Attainment of Concepts," in Hoffman, M., & Hoffman,

L. W. (eds.), *Review of Child Development Research,* Vol. 1, N.Y.: Russell Sage Foundation, 1964.

Stevenson, Elwood A., "A Study of the Educational Achievement of Deaf Children of Deaf Parents," *The California News, 80,* 1964, 1–3.

Streng, Alice, & Kirk, S. A., "The Social Competence of Deaf and Hard-of-Hearing Children in A Public Day School," *American Annals of the Deaf, 83,* 1938, 244–254.

Stuckless, E. Ross, & Birch, Jack W., "The Influence of Early Manual Communication on the Linguistic Development of Deaf Children," *American Annals of the Deaf, 111,* 1966, 452–460, 499–504.

Titus, Etha Sue, "The Self-Concept and Adjustment of Deaf Teenagers," unpublished Ph.D. dissertation, Columbia: The University of Missouri, 1965.

Vernon, McCay, & Brown, Donald W., "A Guide to Psychological Tests and Testing Procedures in the Evaluation of Deaf and Hard of Hearing Children," *Journal of Speech and Hearing Disorders, 29,* 1964, 414–423.

Wrightstone, J. W., Aronow, Miriam S., & Moskowitz, Sue, "Developing Reading Test Norms for Deaf Children," *Test Service Bulletin, No. 98,* New York: Harcourt, Brace and World, 1962.

18

Multiply Handicapped Deaf Children: Current Status

McCay Vernon

Dr. Vernon is Professor of Psychology at Western Maryland College and is currently editor of American Annals of Deaf. *A most active research worker, Dr. Vernon has published over 45 articles in a wide array of professional journals, has contributed five chapters in professional books, and in the past year authored the book,* Multiply Handicapped Deaf Children: Psychological, and Educational Considerations. *He has been a classroom teacher of the blind and deaf.*

In this excellent article, especially prepared for this book, Dr. Vernon describes and discusses the practical and theoretical implications of deaf children who have other serious handicaps. This is the one area in deafness, Dr. Vernon noted, that is most discussed and yet least acted upon.

Appropriate education and rehabilitation for multiply-handicapped deaf children represents the most discussed, yet least acted-upon problem in the area of deafness today. Evidence of this is that from 15 to 35 percent of deaf youth, the overwhelming majority with multiple disabilities, are either not accepted into educational programs for the deaf or else are dropped out at or before 16 years of age (Boatner, Stuckless, & Moores, 1964; Kronenberg & Blake, 1966; Vernon, 1969a).

When Dr. Tjerle Basilear, the noted Norwegian psychiatric authority, visited facilities in the United States, he inquired of educators how they served multiply handicapped deaf children. The answer given was that nothing was done for them. The irony of the United States spending millions of dollars on esoteric research projects in deafness while hundreds of these deaf children in need of education or treatment were literally being dumped back into the community was striking to Dr. Basilear. This is not to condemn research, but to indite the gross lack of service. Educators in schools for the deaf have the frequent and grisly responsibility of informing the parents of many of these young people that not only can their child not be accepted or kept in a regular school for deaf youth, but that there is absolutely no place for parents to go where they might get help for the multiply-handicapped deaf child. To fail to provide some sort of constructive program or opportunity for a child who already has the obstacles of deafness and other handicaps is to doom him to insurmountable odds in his struggle for even a chance at basic life satisfaction and human dignity.

CAUSES OF MULTIPLE DISABILITIES AMONG DEAF CHILDREN

To constructively approach the problem of multiple disabilities among deaf children, it is essential to know the causes of the problem. Such information forms the basis for prevention, it contributes to predictions about the number of such children to be expected, it leads to an understanding of the kinds of problems the children may have, and it yields clues to diagnoses and therapy.

The research to be reported here examines certain of the leading causes of deafness because it is known that these etiologies also result in other disabilities. By establishing the prevalences of deaf children with other disabilities in these large etiological groups and then determining the nature of their handicaps, some picture of the magnitude and types of problems multiply-handicapped deaf children have will result.

The etiologies to be studied are prenatal rubella, complications of Rh factor, meningitis, genetics, and premature birth. As indicated in Table 1, they cause a significant amount of the deafness which occurs in school-age children. With the exception of about 10 percent, the remaining deafness is of unknown etiology.

The point to be made from presenting these data is that the multiple handicaps associated with the five etiologies under study probably represent a major share of such handicaps which are to be found among deaf school-age children.

Nature of the Etiologies

Before presenting additional research data, cursory background information about the etiologies to be investigated will be provided. This is important in understanding their role as a cause of multiple handicaps.

Table 1 Prevalences of Major Etiologies of Deafness[a]
(1,468 Cases)

	Range of prevalence (%)	
Etiology	From	To
Five etiologies studied in this research		
Genetics	5.4	26.0
Maternal rubella	8.8	9.5
Meningitis	8.1	8.7
Prematurity	11.9	17.4
Rh factor	3.1	3.7
Total	37.3	65.3
Other etiologies		
Unknown	30.4	30.4
Other	9.4	32.3
Total	39.8	62.7

[a] This table is presented primarily to illustrate the prevalence of the five etiologies presented in this chapter. For a more complete report of etiological factors in 1,468 cases, refer to the original report (Vernon, 1969a, pp. 42–50).

Maternal rubella As a result of the 1963–1965 rubella epidemic and the one projected for 1970, there is going to be a huge increase in the number of postrubella children in schools for the future. Estimates vary, but based on available statistics, the best guess is that there will be at least 4,500 children (Vernon, 1967a) from 1963–1965 alone. Miss Kent (1969) reports two thirds the entering class of 1969 had prenatal rubella, and of 30 preschoolers in Chicago's Xavier College's preschool deaf program, 25 are postrubella cases. Fragmented though these data may be, they clearly indicate an influx of rubella children of far greater numbers than has ever occurred before—even in the epidemic of 1943 when rubella had approximately a 20 percent incidence among the causes of deafness (Vernon, 1969a). With this evidence illustrating the huge number of postrubella children entering schools, the question of the effects of rubella assumes major importance.

Rubella is a viral infection which when contracted by a mother during pregnancy is often passed on to the fetus. The pathogenic organisms then attack developing organs of the embryo, rendering them defective. The major sequela are eye defects, heart disease, deafness, microcephaly, mental retardation, abnormal behavior patterns, motor disabilities, and failure to thrive (Campbell, 1961; Jackson & Fisch, 1958; Lunstrom, 1962;

Manson, Logan, & Roy, 1960, 1961; Montagu, 1962, p. 282; Signurjonsson, 1963; Skinner, 1961). Estimates of the percentage of postrubella children having at least one serious congenital defect vary from as low as 4.5 percent (Lunstrom, 1962; Manson et al., 1961) to as high as 80 percent (Berger & Melnick, 1961, pp. 314–315), with the consensus being that from 12 to 19 percent of these children have major anomalies (Silverman, 1961, p. 277) (see Table 2). Preliminary reports from Johns Hopkins (Hardy, 1965; Monif, Hardy, & Sever, 1966; Hardy, Monif, & Sever, 1966) may cause an upward revision of these figures. Of all defects, hearing loss is probably the greatest risk (Campbell, 1961; Jackson & Fisch, 1958).

Recent medical advances have resulted in a rubella vaccine which should eliminate this disease just as polio has been. However, the huge number of youth infected and deafened in the 1963–1965 and 1970 epidemics will remain an educational and rehabilitative challenge for many years to come (Buynak, et al., 1969).

Complications of Rh factor   Certain combinations of parental blood type which involve Rh factor can result in the mother's blood destroying the Rh blood cells of the fetus. As a consequence, the brain and central nervous system are often damaged. Eighty percent of children who survive kernicterus, a major complication of Rh-factor incompatability, have complete or partial deafness (Cohen, 1956; Flower, Viehweg, & Ruzicka, 1966a, 1966b). Cerebral palsy, mental retardation, epilepsy, and behavior disorders are other prominent sequela (Blakely, 1959; Brain, 1960, p. 216;

Table 2   Major Sequelae and Their Causes in Postrubella Children

Causes	Sequelae	
Viral infections and damage to tissue during embryonic development. Anoxia	Brain damage	
	Cerebral palsy	
	Epilepsy	
	Mental retardation and/or lowered intelligence level	
	Behavior disorders	
	Psychoses	Strauss syndrome (hyperactivity, etc., with emphasis on impulse disorders)
	Learning disability	
	Physical disabilities	Dental pathology
	Microcephaly	Premature birth
	Microphthalmus	Failure to thrive
	Deafness	Orthopedic defect
	Visual pathology (cataract, chorioretinitis, nystagmus, etc.)	

Clarke & Clarke, 1958, pp. 143–144; Cook & Odell, 1957, p. 605; Grinker, Bucy, & Sahs, 1960, p. 1153; Vernon, 1967d) (see Table 3). Perhaps the most important factor about deafness and Rh factor is that aphasoid disorders and central nervous system lesions are often present in addition to hearing loss (Cohen, 1956; Hannigan, 1956; Myklebust, 1956; Rosen, 1956; Vernon, 1967d).

Complications of Rh factor are now preventable with good prenatal care. Soon this condition may also cease to be a major cause of deafness (Clarke, 1968).

Meningitis Meningitis has long been the leading postnatal cause of deafness (Robinson, 1964; Vernon, 1967c). Other sequelae which result from the disease are hydrocephalus, paralysis, deafness, cortical blindness, mental retardation, epilepsy, cranial nerve palsy, learning disorders, and psychiatric symptoms (DeGraff & Creger, 1963, pp. 249–255; Ford, 1960, pp. 544–550; Kelley, 1964, p. 36; Nelson, 1959, p. 428; Swartz & Dodge, 1965). Estimates of the percent of cases having major neurological sequelae range from 15 to 71 (DeGraff & Creger, 1963, p. 243; Kelley, 1964, p. 36; Mackay, 1964, pp. 38–39; Swartz & Dodge, 1965) (see Table 4).

The important new consideration with regard to meningitis is that it responds favorably to the antimicrobal therapies developed in recent years. Consequently, a great change has occurred in the nature of the postmeningitic deaf population. Today those who contract the disease after the age of three or four generally recover with no loss of hearing (Vernon, 1967c, 1969a).

The premature and newborn, who are especially susceptible to the

Table 3 Major Sequelae and Their Causes in Children Born with Complications of Rh Factor

Causes	Sequelae
Actual causality is not clear. Factors involved are	Brain damage
	Cerebral palsy (very common)
	Epilepsy
	Mental retardation and/or a lowered intelligence level
	Behavior disorders
Anoxia	Learning disability, especially aphasia
Jaundice	Strauss syndrome and chronic brain syndrome
Nuclear masses of the brain and central nervous system	Physical disability
	Deafness
	Visual pathology
	Orthopedic defect

Table 4 *Major Sequelae and Their Causes in Postmeningitic Deaf Children*

Causes	Sequelae
Inflammation of tissue around the brain	Brain damage
	Hydrocephalus
	Paralysis (hemiplegia, diplegia, etc.)
Intracranial pressure	Cortical blindness
	Epilepsy
Hematomas	Mental retardation and/or lowered intelligence level
Rupturing of cranial blood vessels	
	Behavior disorders
General hemorrhaging	Learning disability, especially aphasia
Accumulation of exudate	Psychoses
	Strauss syndrome (hyperactivity, distractibility, etc., with an emphasis in some cases of difficulty controlling hostile impulses)
Cortical abscess	
Abnormalities in body physiology and biochemistry	Physical disability
	Deafness
	Cranial nerve palsy

disease and in whom it is most difficult to diagnose and treat, are now surviving, whereas in past years they almost invariably died (Ford, 1960, p. 537; Kelley, 1964; Nelson, 1959, p. 344). This means that today's postmeningitic deaf child is likely to be both prelingually deafened and to have other sequelae of the disease.

In years past postmeningitic deaf children generally had naturally acquired language and no other disabilities. They comprised about one third of the deaf youth who went to college and from this group were drawn many of the academically capable students who were able to function successfully in day schools and classes and in competition with the normally hearing. Now that postmeningitic children are primarily a prelingually deafened group and have a high prevalence of multiple handicaps, programs of higher education and programs that expect deaf children to compete in educational settings with hearing children are going to find that there will be fewer qualified students unless the educational level of present-day students is raised.

Prematurity Prematurity is approximately four times more prevalent in the deaf school-age population than among hearing children (DeHirsch, Jansky, & Langford, 1966; Vernon, 1967b). Related to this is the fact that more infants born prematurely are now surviving, but often with severe physical and psychological residua (Hardy & Pauls, 1959;

Kelley, 1964, p. 42; Nesbitt, 1959; Lubcheno et al., 1963; Vernon, 1967b).

Conditions of prematurity which lead to these sequelae are numerous. One is that the weaker blood vessel walls of the premature infant lead to intracranial hemorrhage caused by mechanical trauma and/or the fragility of the tiny blood vessels (Brennemann, 1937, p. 40; Silverman, 1961, p. 301). Another condition is anoxia which, apart from the condition of the cranial blood vessels, is relatively frequent among prematures and can cause serious brain destruction (Montagu, 1962, p. 369). Oxygen deficits of as brief as 90 seconds result in irreversible brain damage which may not become apparent for several years (Montagu, 1962, pp. 370–386).

Consequently, cerebral palsy, epilepsy, mental deficiency, reading problems, degenerative brain conditions, visual pathology, other physical defects, and behavioral anomalies are more prevalent among prematurely born children (Douglas, 1956a, 1956b, 1960; Kelley, 1964, p. 42; Knobloch et al., 1956; Weiner, 1962). Those prematures who are also deaf have especially high prevalences of these conditions (Vernon, 1969a) (see Table 5).

Genetic deafness As a group, children deafened by heredity seem to be relatively free of other disabilities. However, one third of genetic deafness is associated with some other trait, the Waardenburg syndrome and Usher's syndrome being the most common (Vernon, 1969b). The latter is particularly disabling as it involves congenital hearing loss, pro-

Table 5 Major Sequelae and Their Causes in Children Born Prematurely

Causes	Sequelae	
Intracranial hemorrhage	Brain damage	
	Cerebral palsy	
	Epilepsy	
	Degenerative conditions of the brain	
	Mental retardation and/or lowered intelligence level	
	Behavior disorders	
	Schizophrenia	
Anoxia	Learning disability (aphasia, reading problems, and others)	
Mechanical trauma	Strauss syndrome (hyperactivity, distractibility, restlessness, etc.)	
	Physical disabilities	
	Visual pathology	Liver and kidney defects
	Deafness	Stomach ruptures
	Hernia	Failure to thrive
	Cryptic orchidism	

gressive blindness, and central nervous system lesions (Vernon, 1969b). All told there are some 30 known syndromes involving deafness, 10 of which have ear, eye, and central nervous system pathology.

It is clear from this cursory medical picture of these five etiologies of deafness that among children having these causes of hearing loss are many who are multiply handicapped. The balance of the chapter will address itself to the prevalence and nature of these multiple disabilities as they were distributed among the 1,468 children who entered or applied for admission to the California School for the Deaf at Riverside over the 11-year span following the school's opening in 1953. Although other etiologies, such as polio, maternal flu, head injury, mumps, etc., are also associated with multiple handicaps, this report restricts itself to the five already discussed because it is felt they account for the major share.

Prevalence of Physical and Psychological Anomalies

Table 6 presents the prevalence of major types of physical and psychological anomalies in the deaf children of the five etiological groups under consideration. It is these groups which cause most major disabilities. The data will be discussed in terms of the categories of Table 6.

Cerebral palsy and/or hemiplegia Cerebral palsy has a prevalence rate of from .1 to .6 percent in the general population (Nelson, 1959, p. 1138). Among this sample of deaf children, the rate is 15.8 percent, or about 100 times greater. Of particular note is the fact that over half of the children deafened by Rh factor are cerebral palsied. This figure is approximately 80 percent if marginal cases are included which involve clear problems of motor coordination but not gross palsy. A prevalence of almost one in five prematures with cerebral palsy also deserves attention in view of the increasing prominence this etiology is playing in deafness (Vernon, 1967a). With prematures, it is among those of the lowest birthweight categories that there is the most cerebral palsy. Hemiplegia rather than what is generally considered cerebral palsy accounts for the cases in the meningitic group. Fortunately, in view of the recent rubella epidemic, the prevalence of cerebral palsy among those children was low. Recent medical advances reducing the main causes of the clinical phenomena of deafness and cerebral palsy will result in fewer children with this double handicap in the future (Vernon, 1970).

Mental retardation Approximately 2.2 percent of the general population is mentally retarded (IQ below 70). The rate for this sample of deaf children was about six times greater (12.2 percent). The highest prevalence was among the premature (16.5 percent) and the meningitic (14.1 percent) samples. The existence of about four times the normally expected rate of mental retardation among the postrubella children is an

Table 6 Prevalence of Physical Anomalies in Four Etiologies of Deafness[a]

Physical anomaly	Rubella Total sample	Rubella Percent handicapped	Prematurity Total sample	Prematurity Percent handicapped	Meningitis Total sample	Meningitis Percent handicapped	Rh Factor Total sample	Rh Factor Percent handicapped	Total Total sample	Total Percent handicapped
Cerebral palsy and/or hemiplegia	104	3.8	113	17.6	92	9.7	45	51.1	354	15.8
Mental retardation (IQ below 70)	98	8.1	115	16.5	92	14.1	39	5.1	344	12.2
Aphasoid disorders	105	21.9	113	36.2	92	16.3	35	22.8	345	25.2
Visual defects	104	29.8	113	28.3	87	5.7	45	24.4	349	22.6
Orthopedic defects	104	4.8	101	8.9	92	5.4	45	2.2	342	5.8
Seizures	104	—	113	1.7	92	3.2	45	6.6	354	1.9

[a] Differences in sample sizes for the various etiological groups, depending on the handicap reported, exist because it was not always possible to obtain valid diagnoses of the presence or absence of each of the six physical anomalies on every child.

ominous sign in view of the expected influx of these children into schools within the next few years.

Aphasoid disorders The presence of aphasia or aphasoid disorders among the deaf is a rarely mentioned and little understood subject, probably because of the difficulty of making the diagnosis. However, it is logical to assume that etiological conditions resulting in nerve deafness and a higher than average prevalence of chronic brain syndromes, such as cerebral palsy and exogenous mental retardation, would frequently cause lesions to the brain tissues involved in language functions. This would be especially true of cases of so-called central deafness; because the areas of the brain where auditory and linguistic operations occur are close together, damage to one increases the probability of lesions to the other.

The obvious conclusion from this medical knowledge is that a significant amount of the language difficulty experienced by many deaf children is in all probability due not only to the absence of hearing but is, in part, the result of brain lesions affecting language development. The problem of establishing this prevalence is tremendously difficult diagnostically. This research did not solve the problem but approached it by using the best method available.

Classroom teachers and departmental supervising teachers were given the age, IQ, hearing loss, age of onset of deafness, and chronological age of the children in their class or, in the case of supervising teachers, their departments. Using the criterion for aphasia of "a marked difficulty with language greater than that expected due to deafness or level of intelligence," the school faculty were asked to indicate those children they thought to be aphasic. Only in cases where both the classroom teacher and the supervising teacher agreed on the diagnosis was a child classified aphasic. On behalf of this technique, it should be pointed out that the faculty of the California School for the Deaf at Riverside is outstanding, the classes are small, and many of the staff have had training or experience at C.I.D. and other centers specializing in aphasia.

The results as shown in Table 6 indicate that one fourth of the children were judged to be aphasic using this criterion. Among the prematures, it was over one third and among rubella and Rh children more than one out of five had the involvement. If these figures seem to be spuriously high due to the criterion used, it should be noted that when the same criterion was applied to the genetically deaf where there is relatively little basis for suspecting brain damage, only 1.5 percent were judged aphasic (Vernon, 1969a).

The professional literature has referred to aphasoid disorders associated with Rh-factor complications (Cohen, 1956; Myklebust, 1956; Rosen, 1956; Vernon, 1967d), but actual prevalences have not previously been established. However, until recent publications on rubella (Vernon, 1967a), prematurity (Vernon, 1967b), and meningitis (Vernon, 1967c), neither the presence of aphasia nor its prevalence had previously been reported among deaf children having these etiologies of hearing loss.

Extensive effort has been devoted to the discussion of aphasia as a second handicap in deafness for several reasons. First, language is the crucial educational variable in the life of a deaf child. Any condition affecting it must be diagnosed and therapies developed if the deaf child is to progress satisfactorily educationally and psychologically. Second, aphasoid involvements are almost invisible in deaf children despite their extreme importance. Greater attention must be focused upon their recognition, prevention, and treatment.

Visual defects The number of cases having visual defects (Table 6) includes all children who had refractory errors requiring glasses or who had other medically diagnosed pathology of the visual system. Among the 113 prematures, 28 percent wore glasses, 4 were legally blind, and 6 had strabismus (Vernon, 1967b). The only other cases of blindness were postrubella children. Strabismus was found among them and those with complications of Rh factor. The meningitic represented primarily refractory problems.

These findings on vision are based on the number of children recommended by the school ophthamologist for glasses and on visual defects noted in the child's general physical examination. They, therefore, reflect only a cursory survey of the visual anomalies of the sample.

Orthopedic defects Orthopedically, it is the premature infant who exhibited the greatest amount of pathology. Most conditions were congenital and included a case of only two toes on each foot, one bilateral dislocation of the hips, missing fingers and arm bones, rib cage anomaly, etc. Among the postrubella children were found spine curvatures, missing appendages, and structural defects of the legs, chest, and arms.

Seizures Seizures were not a major problem in any group except those deaf due to complications of Rh factor, where the prevalence was 6.6 percent. These cases involved a combination of marked athetoid cerebral palsy, abnormal EEGs, along with the seizures. Worthy of comment is the fact that of the 104 postrubella cases none were known to have seizures.

Psychological adjustment Not contained in Table 6 but a part of the original report (Vernon, 1969a, pp. 69–74) are data on the amount and degree of emotional disorder present. Highest prevalences of psychological disturbance were noted among prematures and postrubella children. Here the rates of psychosis were 5 to 7 percent and emotional disturbance was present in from 25 to 30 percent of cases. The postmeningitic group had slightly less disturbance and among the cases of complications of Rh factor only 12 percent were behavior disorders.

Bender–Gestalt responses and administration of the Diagnostic Screening Forms for the Detection of Brain Injury in Deaf Children (Vernon,

1961) indicate extensive brain damage among all four of the etiological groups (Vernon, 1969a, pp. 102–117). It is felt that this accounts for a lot of the mental illnesses found, particularly the impulse disorders noted in this sample and reported in other deaf populations by Rainer & Altshuler (1966, p. 142).

Educational achievement A number of approaches were taken to determine the relationship of various aspects of educational achievement to the four etiologies, or, more specifically, to the central nervous system pathology associated with them. Written language skill, achievement test scores, academic records, etc., were all examined, with the conclusion that as a group children having maternal rubella, complications of Rh factor, meningitis, or premature birth as a cause of deafness did more poorly than deaf children having a genetic etiology where brain damage was not suspected (Vernon, 1969a, pp. 85–89). The postrubella children had the greatest prevalence of educational failures and had an overall below-average academic achievement. They were followed in this respect by the prematures and those having complications of Rh factor. The meningitic group having a number of cases of postlingual deafness showed great variability in academic achievement.

Multiple Handicaps

Previously, the nature and prevalence of various physical anomalies were given (Table 6). This section approaches the same basic problem somewhat differently by examining the prevalence of multiply handicapped deaf children and the number and type of disabilities in addition to deafness which they have.

The data of Table 7 are rather striking in that over two thirds of deaf children having prematurity complications of Rh factor as etiologies have at least one other major disability in addition to deafness as do over half of postrubella cases. Among the postmeningitic, more than one third had secondary disabilities.

To place these data in some perspective, it is helpful to recognize that among genetically deaf children are very few multiply handicaps. For example, those of deaf parents have only a 6.5 percent prevalence of other disabilities. Most of this is accounted for by a single genetic syndrome (Vernon, 1969a, pp. 90–98). Incidentally, the same criteria of multiply handicapped were applied to this genetic sample as had been used in establishing the prevalences for the other five etiological groups.

It is important to know the types as well as the number of secondary disabilities associated with the various causes of deafness. Those multiply handicapped with an etiology of complications of Rh factor generally have cerebral palsy or aphasoid disorders alone, in combination with each other, or in combination with mental retardation and emotional distur-

Table 7 Distribution of Multiple Handicaps among the Four Etiological Groups[a]

Multiple handicaps: (cerebral palsy, mental retardation, aphasia, blindness or strabismus, orthopedic defect, or emotional disturbance)	Rubella (104 cases) Handi-capped	%	Prematurity (115 cases) Handi-capped	%	Meningitis (92 cases) Handi-capped	%	Rh factor (45 cases) Handi-capped	%	Total (356 cases) Handi-capped	%
Deafness and one other handicap	31	29.8	38	33.0	26	28.3	16	35.6	111	31.1
Deafness and two other handicaps	18	17.3	31	27.0	4	4.3	12	26.7	65	18.2
Deafness and three other handicaps	4	3.8	9	7.9	4	4.3	4	8.9	21	5.8
Deafness and four other handicaps	3	2.9	—	—	1	1.1	—	—	4	1.1
Totals	56	53.8	78	67.8	35	38.0	32	71.1	201	56.4

[a] In order to present these data in a two-dimensional table, it was necessary to use a constant N for each etiological group in computing the percentages. As noted from Table 6, data with regard to some disabilities were not available on all cases. Consequently, certain prevalences stated in percentages are slightly higher than Table 3 indicates (Vernon, 1969a, pp. 167–168).

bance. Of the Rh children having four or more major handicaps, cerebral palsy and aphasia are almost always present (Vernon, 1969a, pp. 109–110).

The premature children, in contrast to the Rh-factor cases, have a broad spectrum of disabilities. Aphasia, cerebral palsy, mental retardation, visual pathology, and emotional disturbance all occur frequently as the second handicap. Cerebral palsy and mental retardation are almost always present among the prematurely born children who had four or more disabilities.

Postrubella children have a 53.8 percent prevalence of multiple handicaps. Aphasia and emotional disturbance are the most common conditions. Heart defects, cataracts, cerebral palsy, and orthopedic conditions are noted in severely disabled cases, and a high rate of psychoses is found (Vernon, 1969a, pp. 90–98).

Postmeningitic children have a 38.0 percent rate of secondary disabilities. Only 8.6 percent have more than one handicap in addition to deafness. This second handicap is generally aphasia followed in frequency by mental retardation, emotional disturbance, and cerebral palsy. When the age of onset of meningitis is early, the danger of multiple involvements is much higher (Vernon, 1969a, pp. 107–109).

CONCLUSIONS

The data reported here provide factual information about the magnitude and nature of the problem of the multiply handicapped deaf child. This information has great theoretical and practical importance.

Theoretically, it is now apparent that behavior noted as characteristic of deaf children cannot be explained primarily as a reaction to deafness as has been done in the past (Vernon & Rothstein, 1968). It is instead often an interactional effect of both the loss of hearing and of other central nervous system lesions associated with the condition causing the deafness. For example, a significant amount of the language disability found among deaf children is due, in part, to organically caused aphasoid disorders, not just deafness. The same is true of other types of learning disabilities.

The impulse disorders, psychoses, and general behavioral disorders found in the deaf population can also be accounted for in part by the central nervous system pathology present. For example, Rainer and Altshuler (1966; Rainer et al., 1963) report symptoms among some deaf mentally ill that are similar to the "Strauss syndrome" found to characterize brain-injured people.

From a practical viewpoint, an understanding of the kinds of disabilities and their prevalences provides a description of the educational, vocational, and mental health problem which is to be met. With the increasing complexity of our society, the greater productivity demands being made upon workers and the fewer simple manual tasks available on the job market, the past educational policy in the United States of eliminating multiply handicapped deaf children from school at an early age or else not admitting them at all is no longer tenable. Whereas there used to be agricultural or other routine tasks that offered these persons job opportunities, this is no longer true. Today uneducated multiply handicapped deaf adults and children are forced to stay at home unemployed and out of school living with their parents until the parents will not or cannot provide for them any longer. At this time, these individuals frequently are sent to state hospitals for the mentally ill or the retarded or, in some instances, they get into difficulty with the law and are placed in penal institutions. The tendency to custodial institutionalization is further accentuated by the current lack of emphasis on strong family ties in our society, a trend contingent in part on the increase in mobility of our population and its greater urbanization.

This kind of management of the multiply handicapped deaf is morally wrong and grossly inexpedient. What is needed are educational-training programs for these individuals when they are young and vocational services for them as adults. The schools serving them would have to offer flexible experimental approaches to teaching because the answers about how to educate these youths are not available. Certainly, efforts to adapt existing materials developed in the area of learning disabilities to the deaf children would be a minimal first step. Vocational services should consist not only of the existing programs of the Division of Vocational Administration, but terminal workshops (Chouinard & Garrett, 1956, p. 7) and transitional workshops (Gellman & Friedman, 1965; Usdane, 1959).

The multiply handicapped deaf person's dilemma today is that he faces a high probability of receiving little or absolutely no educational opportunity. Following this, he is asked to compete as a worker in the contemporary job market in spite of his being functionally illiterate and deaf with one or more other major disabilities. When he fails to do this successfully, he faces either institutionalization as mentally ill or mentally retarded or else custodial dependency upon his family. This is an inditement of public education, vocational services, and the rights of multiply handicapped deaf persons to a fair opportunity in our society.

References

Berger, E., & Melnick, J. L. (Eds.). *Progress in medical virology.* New York: Hafner, 1961.

Blakely, R. W. Erythroblastosis and perceptive hearing loss: Response of athetoids to tests of cochlear function. *J. speech hearing Dis.,* 1959, 2, 5–15.

Boatner, E. B., Stuckless, E. R., & Moores, D. F. *Occupational status of the* young adult deaf of New England and demand for a regional Technical-Vocational Training Center. West Hartford, Conn.: American School for the Deaf, 1964.

Brain, R. *Clinical neurology.* New York: Oxford University Press, 1960.

Brennemann, J. *Brennemann's practice of pediatrics.* Hagerstown, Md.: W. F. Prior, 1937.

Buynak, E. B., Weibel, R. E., Stokes, J., & Hilleman, M. R. Combined live measles, mumps, and rubella virus vaccines. *Science,* 1969, *207,* 2259–2262.

Campbell, M. Place of maternal rubella in the aetiology of congenital heart disease. *Brit. med. J.,* 1961, *1,* 691–696.

Chouinard, E. L., & Garrett, J. F. (Eds.) *Workshops for the disabled: A vocational rehabilitation resource,* U.S. Office of Vocational Rehabilitation. Washington, D.C.: U.S. Government Printing Office, 1956.

Clarke, A. M., & Clarke, A. D. B. *Mental deficiency: The changing outlook.* New York: Free Press, 1958.

Clarke, C. A. The prevention of "rhesus" babies. *Science,* 1968, *219,* 46–48.

Cohen, P. Rh child: Deaf or "aphasic?" 2. "Aphasia" in kernicterus. *J. speech hearing Dis.,* 1956, *21,* 411–412.

Cook, R. E., & Odell, G. B. Perinatal factors in the prevention of handicaps. *Pediat. Clin. N. Amer., 1957,* 595–609.

DeGraff, A. C., & Creger, W. P. (Eds.) *Ann. Rev. Med.* Palo Alto: Annual Reviews, 1963.

DeHirsch, K., Jansky, J., & Langford, W. S. Comparisons between prematurely and maturely born children at three age levels. *J. Orthopsychiat.,* 1966, *36,* 616–628.

Douglas, J. W. B. The age at which premature children walk. *Med. Officer,* 1956, *95,* 33–35. (a)

Douglas, J. W. B. Mental ability and school achievement of premature children of eight years of age. *Brit. med. J.,* 1956, *1,* 1210–1214. (b)

Douglas, J. W. B. Premature children of primary school. *Brit. med. J.,* 1960, *1,* 1008–1013.

Flower, R. M., Viehweg, R., & Ruzicka, W. R. The communicative disorders of children with kernicteric athetosis, Part I. Auditory disorders. *J. speech hearing Dis.,* 1966, *31,* 41–59. (a)

Flower, R. M., Viehweg, R., & Ruzicka, W. R. The communicative disorders of children with kernicteric athetosis, Part II. Problems in language in comprehension and use. *J. speech hearing Dis.,* 1966, *31,* 60–68. (b)

Ford, F. R. *Diseases of the nervous system in infancy, childhood & adolescence* (4th ed.). Springfield, Ill.: Charles C Thomas, 1960.

Gellman, W., & Friedman, S. B. The workshop as a clinical rehabilitation tool. *Rehab. Lit.,* 1965, *26,* 34–38.

Grinker, R. R., Sr., Bucy, P. C., & Sahs, A. L. *Neurology* (5th ed.). Springfield, Ill.: Charles C Thomas, 1960.

Hannigan, H. Rh child: Deaf or "aphasic?" 3. Language and behavior problems of the Rh "aphasic" child. *J. speech hearing Dis.,* 1956, *21,* 413–417.

Hardy, J. B. Viral infections in pregnancy: A review. *Amer. J. Obst. & Gynec.,* 1965, *93,* 1052–1065.

Hardy, J. B., Monif, G. R. G., & Sever, J. L. Studies in congenital rubella, Baltimore, 1964–1965, II. Clinic and virologic. *Bull. Johns Hopkins Hosp.,* 1966, *118,* 97–108.

Hardy, W. G., & Pauls, M. D. Atypical children with communication disorders. *Children,* 1959, *6,* 13–16.

Jackson, A. D. M., & Fisch, L. Deafness following maternal rubella. *Lancet,* 1958, *2,* 124–144.

Kelley, V. C. (Ed.) *Practice of pediatrics* Vol. IV. Hagerstown, Md.: W. F. Prior, 1964.

Kent, M. Personal communication, 1969.

Knobloch, H., Rider, R., Harper, P., & Pasamanick, B. Neuropsychiatric sequelae of prematurity. *J. Amer. med. Assoc.,* 1956, *161,* 581–585.

Kronenberg, H. H., & Blake, G. D. *Young deaf adults: An occupational survey.* Washington, D.C.: Vocational Rehabilitation Administration, Department of Health, Education, and Welfare, 1966.

Lunstrom, R. Rubella during pregnancy. *Acta Pediat.,* 1962, *51,* Suppl., 133.

Mackay, R. P. (Ed.) *The yearbook of neurology, psychiatry, & neurology.* Chicago: Yearbook Medical Publishers, 1964.

Manson, M. M., Logan, W. P. D., & Roy, R. M. Rubella and other virus infections during pregnancy. Reports on Public Health and Medical Subjects No. 101. London: H. M. Stationery Office, 1960.

Manson, M. M., Logan, W. P. D., & Roy, R. M. Rubella and other virus infections during pregnancy. *Quart. Rev. Pediat.,* 1961, *16,* 57–59.

Monif, G. R. G., Hardy, J. B., & Sever, J. L. Studies in congenital rubella, Baltimore 1964–1965, I. Epidemiologic and virologic. *Bull. Johns Hopkins Hosp.,* 1966, *118,* 85–96.

Montagu, A. M. F. *Prenatal influences.* Springfield, Ill.: Charles C Thomas, 1962.

Myklebust, H. R. Rh child: Deaf or "aphasic?" 5. Some psychological considerations of the Rh child. *J. speech hearing Dis.,* 1956, *21,* 423–425.

Nelson, W. E. *Textbook of pediatrics.* Philadelphia: Saunders, 1959.

Nesbitt, R. E. L., Jr. *Perinatal casualties. Children,* 1959, *6,* 123–128.

Propp, G. Chaff. *Deaf American,* 1966, *20.*

Rainer, J. D., & Altshuler, K. Z. *Comprehensive mental health services for the deaf.* New York: Columbia University, 1966.

Rainer, J. D., Altshuler, K. Z., Kallmann, F. J., & Demings, W. E. (Eds.). *Family and mental health problems in a deaf population.* New York: New York State Psychiatric Institute, 1963.

Robinson, G. C. Pediatrics and disorders in communication. I. Hearing loss in infants & young preschool children. *Volta Rev.,* 1964, *66,* 314–318.

Rosen, J. Rh child: Deaf or "aphasic?" 4. Variations in auditory disorders of the Rh child. *J. speech. hearing Dis.,* 1956, *21,* 418–422.

Signurjonsson, J. Rubella and congenital deafness. *Amer. J. med. Sci.,* 1963, *242,* 712–720.

Silverman, W. A. *Dunham's premature infants* (3rd ed.). Springfield, Ill.: Charles C Thomas, 1961.

Skinner, C. W. The rubella problem. *J. Dis. Child.,* 1961, *101,* 78–86.

Swartz, M. N., & Dodge, P. R. Bacterial meningitis—a review of selected aspects. II. Special neurologic problems, postmeningitic complications and clinopathical correlations. *New England J. Med.*, 1965, *272*, 954–962.

Usdane, W. Employability of the multiply handicapped. *Rehab. Lit.*, 1959, *20*, 3–9.

Vernon, M. The brain-injured (neurologically impaired) child: A discussion of the significance of the problem, its symptoms and causes in deaf children. *Amer. Ann. Deaf*, 1961, *106*, 239–250.

Vernon, M. Psychological, educational & physical characteristics associated with post-rubella deaf children. *Volta Rev.*, 1967, *69*, 176–185. (a)

Vernon, M. Prematurity and deafness: The magnitude & nature of the problem among deaf children. *Except. Child.*, 1967, *38*, 289–298. (b)

Vernon, M. Meningitis & Deafness. *Laryngoscope*, 1967, *77*, 1856–1874. (c)

Vernon, M. Rh factor & deafness: The problem, its psychological, physical, & educational manifestations. *Except. Child.*, 1967, *38*, 5–10. (d)

Vernon, M., & Rothstein, D. A. Prelingual deafness: An experiment of nature. *Arch. gen. Psychiat.*, 1968, *19*, 361–369.

Vernon, M. *Multiply handicapped deaf children: Medical, educational and psychological considerations.* Washington, D.C.: Council of Exceptional Children, 1969. (a)

Vernon, M. Usher's syndrome—Deafness and progressive blindness. *J. Chronic Dis.*, 1969, *22*, 133–151. (b)

Vernon, M. The clinical phenomenon of cerebral palsy and deafness. *Except. Child.*, 1970, *36*, 743–751.

Weiner, G. Psychologic correlates of premature birth: A review. *J. nerv. & ment. Dis.*, 1962, 129–144.

The Speech Handicapped

19

A Survey of the Literature on Functional Speech Disorders and Personality: Forty Years of Research

Leonard D. Goodstein and Ellin L. Block

> *Dr. Goodstein is Professor of Psychology and Director of Professional Training in the Department of Psychology at the University of Cincinnati. Mrs. Block is a Counselor, University Counseling Service, at the University of Cincinnati.*
>
> *In the area of exceptionality, Dr. Goodstein has published articles on functional speech disorders, children with cleft palates, and parents of children who are emotionally disturbed. He is also one of the authors of the book* The Onset of Stuttering, *which appeared in 1959.*
>
> *This present article, written especially for this book, is an extension and elaboration of Dr. Goodstein's article that appeared in the first edition. The authors review the literature over the past forty years that pertains to personality variables in functional speech disorders. Among other things, the reader should become sensitive to the scope of the methodological problems in this complex area and the caution that must be exercised in interpreting findings.*

Clinical case reports in speech pathology are almost always concerned with the personality of the speech-handicapped individual as an important factor in formulating the etiology of the problem and in evaluating the assets of the person for therapeutic planning. Since speech-handicapped individuals seen by speech pathologists are frequently children under the influence of their parents, the personality of the parents becomes a matter of interest as an etiological factor in the development of the disorder and in the utilization of the parents as therapeutic agents. Yet despite the importance placed upon the personality and adjustment of speech-handicapped individuals and their parents in both diagnostic and therapeutic work, the research evidence relating pathology of speech and personality is widely scattered and there have been few attempts at any systematic survey of this evidence. Furthermore, much of this evidence is difficult for those speech pathologists without considerable formal training in psychometrics, particularly personality measurement, to evaluate and utilize. This paper is an attempt to summarize and evaluate those investigations in which the personality and adjustment of individuals with functional speech disorders and their parents were measured and some comparison with a control group was made.

The present paper is based upon a survey of the literature of the past 40 years (through December, 1968) abstracted in the *Journal of Speech and Hearing Disorders,* the *Psychological Abstracts,* and the *Speech Monographs.* Included are all studies of an investigative nature reporting on the relationship between functional speech problems and measured personality and adjustment. Not included are those studies dealing with organic speech disorders, with disorders of hearing,* with disorders of speech resulting from severe psychopathology, with stage fright, or with the relationship between expressive speech and personality in normal persons.

The scope of this paper is further limited by the exclusion of those reports, which are essentially clinical case studies, in which some relationship between a functional pathology of speech and some aspect of the patient's personality or adjustment is reported. The published literature in speech pathology, psychiatry, and psychology is replete with such clinical papers reporting that the author has a number of patients. typically a small number, and in each case it was "immediately obvious" that the pathology of speech was definitely related to some etiological condition, such as an Oedipus complex or an acute state of anxiety. Perhaps one example might serve to illuminate this point: Stein (1949) reported from his experience with a "small number of male stammering cases seen in the Tavistock Clinic . . . (that) in the background of more than half the cases studied we find the male stammerer identifying himself with the mother in the presence of a monstrous, violent, overpowering father. Homosexuality of an infantile narcissistic kind, usually strongly suppressed, is a frequent phenomenon." It should be clear that such reports,

---

* See Berlinsky (1952) for an excellent summary of this literature.

regardless of the author's clinical acumen or sagacity, can scarcely be considered as meeting the usual methodological criteria in scientific inquiry. Further, since typically these personality factors can be uncovered only by specially trained psychiatrists or clinical psychologists, such findings are of little practical use for most speech pathologists.

Excluded also, because of limitations of space, were those studies in which the major concern was an evaluation of the reactions to a functional speech disorder, for example the reactions of stutterers to their impediment. Also excluded from this report are those theoretical papers in which the need for personality research was stressed, although no actual research data were included. Speech pathologists are all too frequently exhorted to study personality, develop more and better clinical skills in this area, use the Rorschach and other personality tests; but all of this without any direct suggestions or, even more importantly, without any evidence as to how this can be realistically done in typical clinical practice. The present report includes only those investigations in which some empirical relationships have been reported between personality variables and the major functional disorders of speech: articulation disorders, delayed speech, voice disorders, and stuttering.*

Articulation Disorders

Functional disorders of articulation—the omission, substitution, or distortion of speech sounds—are typically explained (Johnson et al., 1956) in terms of a disruption of the normal learning process in speech development. Such disruption may be a function of inadequate speech models, of a lack of stimulation in and motivation for adequate speech, or of some more basic emotional disturbance. Since such etiological factors are seen as operating in the home environment in the typical development sequence, the area of parent–child interactions must be investigated.

PERSONALITY AND ADJUSTMENT OF THE PARENTS

The reference study by Wood (1946a, 1946b) represents the earliest and most comprehensive investigation of the relationship between parental adjustment and the presence of functional articulatory defects in chil-

---

* Seven studies (Dike, 1953; Elliott, 1951; Marge, 1966; Shank, 1954; Templin, 1938; Woods and Carrow, 1959; Wright, 1939) were not included because the authors studied heterogeneous groups of speech-defective individuals without further specifying the composition of the group. Such investigations may obscure significant differences within the group, producing results that may be misinterpreted.

dren. Psychological tests,* including the California Test of Personality (CTP), the Bernreuter Personality Inventory, and the Thematic Apperception Test (TAT), were administered to parents of 50 articulatory-disordered children and their scores compared with the test norms. The results indicated considerable emotional maladjustment of one or both parents, with more maladjustment found for the mothers than for the fathers. Case histories revealed disruptions in the home, including both parents working, both parents away from home frequently, or the parents separated or divorced. The data also showed that these parents were ignorant of good child-rearing practices and used overly severe techniques of child discipline.

The 50 children were later divided into two matched groups for a program of therapeutic procedures. For one group of 25 children, ordinary remedial articulation procedures were followed; for the other 25, extensive parental counseling was carried on in addition to the speech training. Children of this second group were found to improve more rapidly in their speech than did those whose mothers were untreated. Wood concluded that parental emotional factors are important not only in the etiology of articulation defects but also in any corrective treatment.

Berlin (1958) and Moll and Darley (1960) utilized parental attitude scales in comparing one or both parents of articulatory-defective children ($N = 86$ and 26, respectively), of normal-speaking children, and of a second speech-defective group. In agreement with Wood, both studies indicated poorer attitudes toward child rearing and development among parents of children with articulation problems. Moll and Darley reported that the mothers of children with articulation disorders set higher standards of behavior for their children and were more critical of their activities. These two attitudes appear to be the significant ones that distinguish these mothers from mothers of normal-speaking children and mothers of a second speech-defective group of children.

Wood's conclusions appear to be partially supported in a study by Andersland (1961), who investigated the relationship between the effects of a kindergarten speech-improvement program and maternal personality and attitudes. Unlike Wood's study, a control group of mothers of normal-speaking children was utilized. In agreement with Wood, it was found that mothers of children with articulation problems resistant to treatment ($N = 10$) scored lowest on a personality adjustment scale.

Andersland reported, however, that mothers of children with articulation problems were not more maladjusted than mothers of children

---

* It is beyond the scope of the present paper to discuss either the basic issues involved in personality measurement or the typical instruments utilized in such measurement. The interested reader will find the texts by Anastasi (1968) and Cronbach (1960) useful introductions to these areas.

with superior speech. Mothers of children who did not receive improvement lessons, but who later achieved errorless articulation, were reported to have provided an atmosphere of acceptance with regard to home and family. Similar findings have been reported by Dickson (1962). Using the Minnesota Multiphasic Personality Inventory (MMPI), this investigator compared the emotional adjustment of parents of children who spontaneously outgrew articulation errors with parents of children who retained such errors. No significant differences in adjustment were found between either group of parents and the adult "normal" standardization group. Although there was a tendency among mothers of children who retained articulation errors to exhibit a greater degree of neuroticism than mothers of spontaneously recovered children, no evidence was available for the existence of severe maladjustment within this group.

PERSONALITY AND ADJUSTMENT OF THE CHILDREN

There is extensive research, extending over a period of years, dealing with the child with articulatory disorders and his personality and adjustment. Unlike earlier studies, more recent research has supplemented the simple differentiation of articulatory-defective and normal-speaking children with investigation of the relationship between severity of articulation disorder and level of severity of personality maladjustment.

Of seven studies reporting a positive relationship between functional articulation disorders and personality, Butler (1965), using the Bender–Gestalt Visual Motor Test ($N = 15$); Greenberg (1952), using the Rosenzweig Picture Frustration Test and the Brown Personality Inventory ($N = 36$); Kennedy (1951), using the personality rating scale of the American Council of Education ($N = 27$); and Bjermeland (1951), using the TAT ($N = 21$)—all reported emotional disturbances in their speech-defective subjects. Solomon (1961) reported greater tension and anxiety and poorer overall adjustment among articulatory-defective children ($N = 49$), concluding nevertheless that "this was by no means typical of every child in the experimental group," and that the "slight" problems that did exist within this group were unrelated to the severity of articulatory disorder.

Perrin (1954), in an important sociometric study, found that more of the isolates came from the speech-defective group ($N = 37$) and that the speech-defective child is not readily accepted into the classroom group. In addition, Lerea and Ward (1966) reported that children with articulation problems ($N = 20$) indicated greater reluctance to interact with others. In contrast, Freeman and Sonnega (1956) and Sherrill (1967) reported internally contradictory results in studies dealing with the social and self perceptions of children with articulation problems. These children were perceived by others and by themselves as less effective in verbal communication skills, but as similar to their normal-speaking peers in social acceptance characteristics. Sherrill noted, however, that degree of social acceptance appeared to decline with increasing severity of articulation disorder.

Four studies (Anders, 1945; McKee, 1949; McAllister, 1948; Reid, 1947), using the children's form of the CTP, have reported no relationship between personality and articulation disorders in children ($N = 53$, 100, 100, and 38, respectively). Wylie, Feranchak, and McWilliams (1965), in a comparison of several speech-defective groups of children, found that children with articulation problems ($N = 11$) resembled most closely the normal-speaking population. Trapp and Evans (1960) suggested that studies yielding inconclusive findings with regard to personality differences between articulatory-defective and normal-speaking children may exist in part because level of severity was not a variable. They investigated the severity of articulation disorder as a function of anxiety level. Using the Wechsler Digit-Symbol Test, it was found that normal-speaking children perform less well (i.e., exhibit greater anxiety) than children with mild articulation disorders but perform better than those whose disorder is severe. Trapp and Evans stress the point that had the scores of the mildly and severely disordered children been combined and compared to the scores of the normal-speaking children, no differences between the groups would have been demonstrable.

PERSONALITY AND ADJUSTMENT OF THE ADULT

There is only a single study reporting upon the personality characteristics of adults with articulation disorders. Sergeant (1962) used a test battery, consisting in part of the Bell Adjustment Inventory and the Bernreuter Personality Inventory, to compare the personality traits and emotional adjustment of each of five groups of speech-defective adults with a group of normal-speaking adults. In comparison with normal speakers, the articulation group ($N = 45$) exhibited less self-confidence and a less satisfactory social adjustment. However, no significant differences between the two groups were found in terms of anxiety level or degree of emotional stability. The results of this study remain somewhat obscure because the several measures yielded inconsistent findings.

EVALUATION OF THE STUDIES WITH ARTICULATORY DISORDERS

Any generalization about these studies as a whole is rather difficult in view of the inconsistent nature of the reported results. There appears to be some evidence indicating the etiological importance of parental personality, and even stronger evidence pointing to the role of parental personality and adjustment in children's speech improvement.

Studies of articulatory-disordered children yield largely contradictory findings with regard to personality traits and emotional adjustment. Some, but by no means all, of these inconsistencies may be partially resolved when level of severity is considered as a variable. Nevertheless, the basic need for studies utilizing larger N and better standardized and validated personality measures is obvious. The validity of newly devised rating scales and questionnaires (Solomon, 1961; Wylie, Feranchak, & McWilliams, 1965; Sherrill, 1967), as well as the validity and reliability of the more widely used Bell Adjustment Inventory, CTP, and Wiley Attitude Scale, is questionable. Caution is required in the clinical interpretation of these tests.

At present, the only possible conclusion is that the relationship between personality factors and articulation disorders has not been clearly demonstrated and much additional research is required.

Delayed Speech

Many cases of retarded speech development are referred to speech therapists when the retardation is not directly related to general mental retardation, to impairment of hearing, to motor defects, or to anomalies of the speech mechanism. Explanations of such disturbances often stress the importance of parental influence and personality (Johnson et al., 1956; McCarthy, 1954), and presumably research on parent–child interactions should provide clues about the etiological bases of this disorder and should also provide information useful in planning therapeutic work with these children.

Parental personality and attitudes have been studied by Beckey (1942), Peckarsky (1953), and Moll and Darley (1960). Beckey reported that mothers of speech-retarded children ($N = 50$) regarded their children with more anxiety than did a group of parents of normal-speaking children, and anticipated their needs without verbal request. Mothers of the speech-retarded group ($N = 52$) in Peckarsky's study were evaluated on the Fels Rating Scales as overprotective, rigid individuals who outwardly seem devoted to their children but were actually very critical of them. On the other hand, Moll and Darley, using the Parental Attitude Research Instrument and Wiley's Attitude Scale, found that mothers of speech-delayed children ($N = 30$) differed from mothers of normal-speaking children and of articulatory-disordered children only in terms of offering their children less encouragement to talk. Because of the low reliability and uncertain validity of these personality measures and in consideration of the fact that the retarded group also included children with deviant articulation, parental personality and attitudinal differences may have been obscured.

Personality disturbances in the speech-retarded children themselves have been reported by Wylie, Feranchak, and McWilliams (1965) in the single study of personality factors and adjustment in these children. Children with delayed speech ($N = 11$), of five speech-defective groups studied, least resembled the control group of normal-speaking children, exhibiting particularly the symptoms of temper tantrums and bed-wetting to a greater degree than any of the other groups. These symptoms might be interpreted as indicative of emotional disorder.

While these studies are intriguing and suggestive, it seems clear that much additional work needs to be done on the relationship between delayed speech and personality variables, particularly parental personality variables, as factors in therapeutic planning. No research has been reported on personality and the child without speech, but since the problem of psychogenically delayed speech typically disappears before an age when adequate measures for personality and adjustment are available, this finding should not be surprising.

Voice Disorders

Functional voice disorders, characterized by marked deviations in loudness, pitch, quality, or flexibility, are also frequently explained as a result of psychological disturbance or maladjustment (Johnson et al., 1956). Voice disorders, in contrast to both articulatory disorders and delayed speech, are frequently found in both adolescents and adults. Since good voice quality is an important factor in communication and, consequently, in adjustment, as Sanford (1948) states in a discussion of this relationship, there should be a clearly established relationship between voice disorders and personality factors. Further, it may be presumed that personality factors would play an important role in effective therapy with such disorders.

Aronson et al. (1964, 1966, 1968) have reported a series of studies examining the personality characteristics of female patients with voice symptoms. These patients ($N = 25$) obtained MMPI profiles more like those of psychiatric patients than like those of general medical patients (1966). In the 1968 study, however, a greater incidence of abnormal profiles was found among general medical patients than among voice-disordered patients ($N = 49$). The disproportionate size of comparison groups, unmatched controls, and conclusions drawn largely from visual inspection of percentages, however, render these findings extremely dubious.

Personality inventories have been utilized in three additional studies. Using the Bernreuter Personality Inventory, Moore (1939) reported that whiney and breathy speakers ($N = 61$) were significantly more submissive and emotionally unstable than the harsh and metallic speakers, who were not different from the superior speakers. Duncan (1947) and Sergeant

(1962) have reported divergent results on the Bell Adjustment Inventory. Duncan found that home maladjustment was more characteristic of his functional hoarseness cases ($N = 22$) than of subjects in a matched control group. In contrast, Sergeant reported that, in comparison to four other speech-defective groups and a group of normal controls, subjects with voice disorders ($N = 29$) obtained scores indicating the most satisfactory home adjustment. In addition, voice-disordered subjects were found to be superior to all other groups in overall social adjustment.

In the single study utilizing projective techniques, Brice (1950) obtained the TAT responses of eight college cases with severe voice disorders and concluded that her TAT measures of anxiety were inversely related to her independent, voice-quality ratings.

The research investigating the relationship between voice disorders and personality is necessarily limited by the small number of cases, the generally inadequate composition of control groups, and a recurrent failure to base conclusions upon the statistical tests used. In addition, these studies have relied upon personality measures of somewhat dubious validity; in particular, the validity of the Bell Adjustment Inventory is open to question (Ferguson, 1952). The number of studies in this area is very few, and little remains known about personality as an etiological, consequential, or therapeutic factor in voice disorders.

Stuttering

Of all the functional pathologies of speech, none has excited more speculation or research than the phenomenon of stuttering, the severely hesitant, stumbling attempt at speech with spasmodic repetitions and pauses. Stuttering is often explained (Johnson et al., 1956; Stein, 1949) in terms of psychological or personality factors either in the stutterer himself or in his background. Even those theorists who believe in the importance of organic factors will frequently also include psychological factors in their formulations of the etiology of stuttering. Certainly there is no one concerned about the problem of the stutterer who denies the importance of stuttering as a factor in the consequent development of personality and adjustment or as a factor in therapeutic planning.

The severity and frequently bizarre nature of the stutterer's deviant speech behavior seemingly have led many to the extreme formulation that stuttering either is essentially neurotic or is a symptom of some underlying personality disturbance; for example (Despert, 1946), stuttering " . . . is only one aspect of the neurotic personality and there are always other neurotic traits present." Bender (1939, 1942), as a demonstration of how widely such beliefs were held, asked 50 authorities in speech pathology to list the most common personal characteristics of stutterers. Most frequently reported as the most common were inferiority feelings (listed by 13 of the experts), self-consciousness (listed by 12), neuroticism (listed by 9), shyness and introversion (each listed by 8 of these experts), and anxiety (listed by 6). Bender himself (1939) stated that stutterers are insecure, have extremely strong needs for affection, and are inadequately socialized.

PERSONALITY AND ADJUSTMENT OF THE PARENTS

Since all theories of stuttering, excluding those based exclusively upon organic factors, are essentially acquisitional or environmental theories (this would be true even for those theories which regard stuttering as neurotic in origin), and since the parental influence is most pervasive prior to and during the years of the onset of stuttering, studies of the stutterer's parents and the home environment should cast much light on the development of the stuttering phenomenon. Five such studies have assessed parental personality and attitudes through psychological inventories. Berlin (1958), using the Wiley Inventory of Parent Attitudes, and Thile (1967), using the Research Inquiry Form, reported no significant differences between parents of stuttering ($N = 67$ and 90, respectively) and nonstuttering children. Berlin, however, found a conflict in attitudes between stutterers' parents that was not present between parents of normal-speaking children. Goodstein and Dahlstrom (1956) also found no significant differences on the MMPI between parents of young, nonchronic stutterers and a matched control group ($N = 100$ in each group). Goodstein (1956) has cross-validated these findings with the parents of a typical group ($N = 50$) of clinic stutterers. Kinstler (1961), in the only inventory study reporting parental intergroup differences, compared the responses of mothers of stuttering and nonstuttering children ($N = 30$ in each group) on the U.S.C. Maternal Attitude Scale. Unlike the control group, mothers of stutterers appeared to be outwardly accepting of their children, while implicitly conveying a great deal of rejection.

Three studies have attempted to assess parental attitudes through standardized clinical interviews, which were then compared with the results obtained from a matched control group of parents. Moncur (1951, 1952) concluded on the basis of his results ($N = 48$ in each group) that the stutterers' parents had exceptionally high standards, were overprotective, overcritical, and particularly overdominant—attitudes which Moncur concluded precipitated and aggravated the stuttering. Overprotection by stutterers' mothers has been independently concluded by Abbott (1957) from direct observation of experimental and control mother–child pairs ($N = 30$ in each group) in a free-play situation. Johnson (1942, 1955) and Darley (1955), on the other hand, reported few striking differences between the two groups of parents ($N = 46$ and $N = 50$ in each group, respectively). Darley (1955), in partial agreement with Moncur, found that stutterer's parents had somewhat higher standards than non-stutterer's parents, but both groups appeared well within the normal range of adjustment. The differences between Johnson's parent groups were more circumscribed, centering primarily around the stutterer's parents' concern about the adequacy of the child's speech.

Robbins (1962, 1964), utilizing clinical interview material, has investigated parental attitudes as part of a uniquely comprehensive study of 1,056 child and adult stutterers. Few parents of the child stutterers suggested that they themselves played a role in the onset of stuttering, attributing this onset to a bad fall, severe fright, or hospitalization of the child. Yet a greater percentage of the adult nonstutterers reported these "trauma" occurring in their childhood than did the stutterers. Unfortunately, this interesting study did not use a parent control group or any statistical analysis of data.

The assessment procedures utilized in the foregoing studies—personality inventories and clinical interview data—involve the subject's personal report of a wide range of feelings, ideas, and experiences. Still another method available to the investigator of parental attitudes is the observation of the subject under somewhat more artificial but experimentally manipulatable conditions. Goldman and Shames (1964a, 1964b) have examined the manner in which parents of stuttering and nonstuttering children establish goals both for themselves and for their children. Goal-setting behavior was assessed by observing subjects' estimates of their own performance on a motor task ($N = 30$ in each group) and of their children's performance on the same task and in telling a story ($N = 48$ in each group). Estimates were given after each of a number of predetermined "successes" and "failures" experienced by the subjects. While parents of stutterers and nonstutterers did not differ significantly in setting goals for themselves, parents of stutterers were found to set higher standards for their children than parents of nonstutterers. These results were highly task-specific and varied under the conditions of either "success" or "failure"; nevertheless, it was concluded that stutterer's parents, especially the fathers, set more unrealistic goals for their children generally, and higher speech goals specifically, than parents of nonstutterers.

In summary, the majority of studies of parental adjustment report few or no differences between parents of stutterers and nonstutterers. Those differences that have been reported tend to center around subtle attitudes of parental aspirations and protectiveness, and there is evidence that these attitudes may be specifically related to the speech area. There was no evidence in these studies that would support the contention that the parents of stuttering children are severely maladjusted or have a particularly aberrant personality pattern. One important aspect of this problem, the relationship of parental personality to therapy with the child, has not yet been examined by research.

PERSONALITY AND ADJUSTMENT OF THE CHILD STUTTERER

Considerable research has been reported on the personality and adjustment of both the child and the adult stutterer. A number of personality tests, including the Rogers Test of Personality Adjustment (Darley, 1955), the Bender–Gestalt Visual Motor Test (Burleson, 1949), and the Kent–Rosanoff Free Association Test (McDowell, 1928), have yielded no significant personality differences between groups of stuttering children ($N =$ 28, 36, and 46, respectively) and matched controls. Robbins (1962, 1964), examining case histories, found that hypersensitivity and shyness were outstanding traits shared by child stutterers ($N = 556$); but when these children were compared with nonstutterers previously studied by Johnson (1959), more similarities than differences in personality and adjustment were noted. Moncur's (1951) clinical data, however, revealed that the stutterers ($N = 42$) showed more symptoms of nervousness and maladjustment than did a matched control group of nonstutterers.

The Blacky Pictures Test has been used by Eastman (1960) to test a psychoanalytic hypothesis that stutterers will show greater emotional disturbance related to the anal-sadistic phase of psychosexual development than to any other phase of development. The expectation that repressed hostility would be most characteristic of child stutterers ($N = 30$) was only partially confirmed No control group of normal-speaking children was employed for purposes of comparison, and no reliability coefficients were reported for the scoring of this projective test.

The Rorschach Test has been utilized by a number of investigators to measure the personality of the child stutterer. Meltzer (1935, 1944), in two Rorschach studies involving a control group ($N = 50$ in each group) of normal-speaking children, and Krugman (1946), using a control group ($N = 50$ in each group) of children with severe emotional problems, both found their child stutterers to be emotionally unstable, with predominantly obsessive–compulsive personality traits. It is noteworthy that the same conclusion was reached in spite of the diametrically opposite findings of response productivity by Meltzer's stutterers and response underproductivity by Krugman's subjects.

Several investigators have employed a battery of projective tests to study the personalities of stuttering children in comparison to matched controls. Wilson (1950) and Christensen (1951) used the Rorschach, the TAT, and the Travis–Johnson Projective Test with the same 30 stuttering children, their nonstuttering siblings, and the parents. While some differences in Rorschach responses were reported, neither of the findings was suggestive that the stutterers were more neurotic or maladjusted than their nonstuttering siblings. Wyatt (1958), using a story-telling test battery, compared the mother–child relationship of 20 stuttering children in both initial and advanced stages of stuttering with 20 normal-speaking children. Of major interest was the finding that stutterers, more than nonstutterers, experienced "distance anxiety," an intense fear of losing physical and emotional closeness to the mother. Möller (1960) has analyzed eight variables on both the Rorschach and the Wechsler Intelligence Scale for Children (WISC) in a comparison of child stutterers, predelinquents, and adjusted boys ($N = 20$ in each group). Adjusted boys showed the most favorable scores on the Rorschach, while contrary to expectation stutterers had many more indications of maladjustment than predelinquent boys, including less self-awareness and empathic ability, poorer interpersonal relationships, and greater anxiety. On the WISC, a more structured test, fewer such intergroup differences were reported.

Motor performance of the stuttering child has been examined by Kopp (1946), in a study comparing 50 stuttering and 50 problem children on the Ozeretsky Tests of Motor Proficiency. Kopp concluded that the stutterers had a global uniform deficiency in motor functioning despite the fact that there were no quantitative differences. There was no indication of this uniform deficiency in a subsequent cross-validation study (Finkelstein and Weisberger, 1954). Martin (1962), in an evaluation of perseverative behavior, compared mild, moderate, and severe stuttering cases ($N = 52$) with a group of normal-speaking children ($N = 109$) on four motor tasks. No significant differences in behavior rigidity were found either between stutterers and nonstutterers, or among mild, moderate, or severe stutterers.

In general there is little evidence that the stuttering child has a particular pattern of personality or is severely maladjusted. Greater anxiety in interpersonal relationships, with attendant symptoms of oversensitivity or compulsivity, has been noted in stutterers; but when considering the premium placed on early and effective verbal communication in our culture, it is unclear whether these findings relate more to etiological or to expected consequential factors in stuttering. As yet, the effect of stuttering upon the child's self-perceptions, his peer relationships, and his choice of activities and interests has not been closely examined, as factors relevant particularly to therapeutic planning.

PERSONALITY AND ADJUSTMENT OF THE ADULT STUTTERER

Stuttering is the only functional disorder of speech to afflict a significant number of adults. Since the personality and adjustment problems of adults, as well as the measurement techniques sometimes used to assess such problems, tend to be different from those of children, the adult stutterer deserves special attention.

The personality and adjustment of the adult stutterer have also frequently been assessed by means of the Rorschach. Haney (1950), Ingebregtsen (1936), and Pitrelli (1948) all used the Rorschach and have generally concluded that the stutterers' responses were symptomatic of a neurotic disorder, although none of these three studies involved a control group. Haney's study also involved stutterers' responses to the TAT from which he inferred that stutterers are "spatially disoriented, structurally confused" and have contradictory self-concepts. On the other hand, Richardson (1944a, 1944b) reported no important significant differences on either the Rorschach or the TAT between a group of 30 stutterers and a matched control group.

Diverse results with a variety of projective tests have been reported in the literature. Emerick (1966), for example, reported no differences among tonic stutterers, clonic stutterers, and nonstutterers ($N = 20$ in each group) in responses to frustration as measured by the Rosenzweig P-F Test. Font (1955) also reported no significant personality differences between stutterers ($N = 9$) and normal speakers ($N = 49$) on the Kent–Rosanoff Word Association Test. Tuper and Chambers (1962), using the Picture Identification Test, concluded that stutterers ($N = 48$), in contrast to a group of normal-speaking college students, were overly sensitive to blame and criticism and exhibited quite negative attitudes toward affiliation needs. In a pilot study (Rieber, 1962) of stutterers and clutterers ($N = 20$ in each group), the low scores of stutterers on a figure drawing test were interpreted as indicating their greater dependency, introversion, and withdrawal.

Six studies have utilized projective techniques in order to test psychoanalytic hypotheses related to stuttering. Bernhardt (1954), Carp (1962), and Eastman (1960) all reported areas of psychosexual conflict significantly related to stuttering ($N = 44, 20,$ and 30, respectively), as revealed by the Blacky Test. There was no general agreement, however, as to the phase of psychosexual development—oral, anal, or phallic—most likely to be involved in the disorder. According to the psychoanalytic model, stutterers have difficulty expressing their aggressive impulses, tending to turn the aggression against themselves or to express it in subtle ways. Madison and Norman (1952), using the Rosenzweig P-F Test, found evidence of strong tendencies toward self-aggression among stutterers ($N = 25$); but Quarrington (1953), in a later cross-validation study ($N = 30$), was unable to confirm these findings. In an analysis of both written and oral responses to the TAT, Solomon (1963) concluded that while stutterers and nonstutterers ($N = 35$ in each group) did not differ in terms of broad categories of aggression (e.g., "strong aggression"), stutterers expressed more themes involving a particular kind of aggression, more subtle and less physically violent aggression. This carefully designed study tested quite specific hypotheses and, unlike other studies, included a second speech-defective group as an additional control measure. The findings, while sometimes difficult to interpret, are nevertheless interesting and point up the need for examining more specific variables in stuttering research. Projective studies designed to examine gross personality differences between stutterers and nonstutterers have thus far yielded such inconsistent results that no generalizations about the personality or adjustment of the adult stutterer are possible.

The outcome of therapy with adult stutterers has been successfully predicted by selected projective and inventory test variables. Both Shames (1952) and Sheehan (1954; Sheehan et al., 1954) concluded that certain of the Rorschach variables were related to the outcome of therapy, but their statistics were not entirely conclusive. Lanyon (1966) correlated the MMPI scores of 25 severe stutterers at the beginning of therapy with independent speech-improvement ratings. The speech improvers were reported to resemble improvers in psychotherapy in terms of ego strength and nondeviancy in personality and thinking patterns; unlike the improvement therapy group, however, improvers in stuttering therapy were found to be more energetic, less pessimistic, and less socially alienated.

The clinical interview as an assessment technique has been utilized by Glasner (1949), Whitman (1942), and Robbins (1962, 1964)—all reported some maladjustive traits among stutterers ($N = 70$, 15, and 490, respectively) in uncontrolled and nonstatistical studies. Martyn (1968) and Wingate (1964), in clinical studies of recovered stutterers ($N = 48$ and 50, respectively), reported high spontaneous recovery and a tendency for recovery to occur during adolescence, a period of development ordinarily considered one of increased psychological stress. Investigation of the hypothesis of a "critical" or optimum period for changes in stuttering behavior and a comparison of the personality of recovered stutterers with improvers and nonimprovers in therapy would appear to be promising avenues of research.

Several investigators have found no differences between stutterers and nonstutterers on personality inventories. Bearss (1950), Brutten (1951), and Berlinsky (1954), using inventories including the Rotter Incomplete Sentences Blank, the Saslow Screening Test, and the Maslow Security Index, reported no significant differences between a group of stutterers and a matched control group ($N = 26$, 16, and 14, respectively). From an analysis of responses to the Guilford–Zimmerman Temperament Survey and the Gordon Personal Profile, Anderson (1967) concluded that his two groups ($N = 50$ in each group) were highly similar in terms of general emotional stability.

On the other hand, a number of inventory studies have reported evidence of serious maladjustment in stutterers. Bender (1939, 1942), using the Bernreuter Personality Inventory, reported that male college stutterers were more emotional and introverted, less dominant and confident than nonstutterers ($N = 249$ in each group). These results led Bender to conclude that there was a particular kind of stuttering personality and that stuttering is "definitely associated with personality maladjustment." Schultz (1947) and Perkins (1946), using the California Test of Personality, reached much the same conclusion ($N = 20$ and 75, respectively); neither of these investigators, however, used a control group but, rather, the published test norms. Duncan (1949) reported that stutterers were more maladjusted at home than nonstutterers ($N = 62$ in each group) as revealed by scores on the Bell Adjustment Inventory. This finding has been confirmed in a recent cross-validation study by Sergeant (1962), in which stutterers ($N = 60$) were compared to several other speech-defective groups and to normal-speaking adults. In addition, Sergeant reported poorer social adjustment, less self-confidence, and greater emotional instability among stutterers, as determined both by the Bell and Bernreuter inventories. It is to be noted, however, that while these characteristics were found significantly less often among normal speakers, they were shared to a large extent by all the speech-defective groups studied.

The association between stuttering and anxiety has been investigated with a number of quite different experimental and personality assessment techniques. Agnello (1962) found no differences between stutterers and nonstutterers ($N = 50$ and 450, respectively) in scores on the Taylor Manifest Anxiety Scale. Brutten (1957) and Gray and Karmen (1967) used a measurement of palmar perspiration (PSI) as an anxiety index with a group of stutterers and a matched control group ($N = 33$ in each group), with quite contradictory results. Unlike Brutten, who reported intergroup differences in anxiety in a verbal situation, Gray and Karmen found no differences under either verbal or nonverbal conditions. Further, they were able to demonstrate a relationship between anxiety and severity of the disorder, with high and low nonfluency groups exhibiting less anxiety than a moderately dysfluent group of subjects. Santostefano (1960), using both the Rorschach Content Test (RCT) and laboratory-induced stress, concluded that stutterers are more anxious and hostile than nonstutterers ($N = 26$ in each group). The conclusion of stutterers' hostility from their poorer recall of a learning task after experienced stress, as well as the validity of the RCT and the usefulness of measuring anxiety in stutterers with a complex verbal task, all raise serious doubts about the credence to be placed in the results reported.

There is a series of five investigations of the personality and adjustment of adult stutterers which deserves special attention. These investigations utilize the MMPI, the only one of the inventories used in research with speech-handicapped groups which was empirically derived and which has been shown to have more than face validity. Boland (1952), Dahlstrom and Craven (1952), Pizzat (1949), Thomas (1951), and Walnut (1954) all have reported that the mean MMPI profile for their groups of stutterers ($N = 24$, 100, 53, 29, and 38, respectively) was somewhat elevated as compared either with the test norms or with a matched control group. However, the higher means for the stutterers were still well within the normal range of adjustment as defined by the MMPI norms. Dahlstrom and Craven compared college stutterers with normal-speaking college freshmen, with psychiatric patients, and with college students who had sought counseling help on their personal problems. The authors concluded that, while the stutterers did differ from the control students, they were not as severely disturbed as the psychiatric patients and most closely resembled the college students with other kinds of problems. This study further reported no significant relationship between the MMPI scores and the severity of stuttering.

Several investigators, rather than assessing the overall personality or relative adjustment of the stutterer, have sought to tap what might be considered more basic personality variables such as level of aspiration (Emerick, 1966; Mast, 1951; Sheehan & Zelen, 1951, 1955), achievement motivation (Goodstein, Martire, & Spielberger, 1955), perseverative tendencies or rigidity (Diamond, 1953; King, 1953, 1961; Solomon, 1951; Kapos & Standlee, 1958; Wingate, 1966), self-concept (Staats, 1955; Zelen, Sheehan, & Bugental, 1954; Gildston, 1967; Wallen, 1959), and the social-interaction characteristics of stutterers (Buscaglia, 1962; Sheehan, Hadley, & Gould, 1967). Earlier studies suggested that stutterers set a somewhat lower level of aspiration than nonstutterers, that stutterers are somewhat more perseverative than nonstutterers, and that stutterers do not have a different self-concept from nonstutterers. Several studies done more recently have reported quite different results—that stutterers are not unlike nonstutterers in terms of level of aspiration (Emerick, 1966) and perseverative factors (Kapos & Standlee, 1958; King, 1961; Wingate, 1966); in addition, it has been found that stutterers may indeed exhibit significantly less self-acceptance and degree of personality integration than normal speakers (Gildston, 1967; Wallen, 1959). Recent research on social-role perception and interpersonal interaction (Buscaglia, 1962; Sheehan, Hadley, & Gould, 1967) has suggested that stutterers experience some difficulty in accurately appraising the role of others, and that the frequency of stuttering behavior directly varies with the gap between perceived status of the self and that of a listener. While no generalizations may be safely drawn from what appear to be quite inconsistent results, the studies of basic personality variables have yielded provocative findings which require considerable additional work before the implications of such data for either clinical or research data can be clearly seen.

In summary, the most general conclusion to be drawn from these studies of adult stutterers is that while stutterers appear to exhibit more personality problems than normal speakers, there is little evidence to support the contention that they are neurotic or severely maladjusted. Although there is evidence that adult stutterers are somewhat more anxious, less self-confident, and more socially withdrawn than nonstutterers, there is additional evidence that efforts to differentiate stutterers from nonstutterers in terms of a particular syndrome of maladjustive traits have proved unfruitful.

The inconsistencies in reported results—present both among studies using identical test instruments and among studies utilizing different personality measures—have been due in part to a preference on the part of most researchers to examine gross personality differences between broadly defined subject groups which may, in fact, be quite heterogeneous in composition. The necessity for studying more specific personality variables has already been noted. Additionally, it is important to recognize an implicit assumption in the majority of the studies reviewed—that stuttering is a single entity and that therefore the stuttering population is a homogeneous one. In fact, there appears to be no general agreement at the present time as to a standard definition of stuttering and its possible variants (St. Onge, 1963; St. Onge & Calvert, 1964; Wingate, 1962). Thus the criteria for inclusion in a stuttering group have ranged from "any auditorially perceived failure in fluency" (Gray & Karmen, 1967) to the diagnosis of stuttering by a speech therapist or lay person (Wallen, 1959). Few studies have carefully specified and operationally defined their criteria for subject selection, thus obscuring possible differences in dynamic patterns both among the stutterers themselves, and among stutterers, normal-speaking adults, and other speech-defective individuals. A small number of studies have examined "subtypes" of stutterers, in relationship to the personality characteristics of nonstutterers and other speech-defective populations, but a great deal more research is required before the implications of these studies become meaningful both for the prevention and treatment of stuttering problems.

EVALUATION OF THE STUDIES OF STUTTERING

While a large number of investigators have studied the personality and adjustment of stutterers and their parents, areas of agreement in reported results have been quite limited. Because of such inconsistencies, and due to methodological limitations such as inadequate control measures, small N, and the use of unvalidated instruments, few trustworthy generalizations are evident. There is some evidence to support the conclusion that stutterers' parents, while not maladjusted themselves, do tend to play a role in the development of stuttering, primarily through attitudes of criticalness and overprotection which may be implicitly conveyed to the child. There tends to be no consistent evidence that either the child or the adult stutterer has a consistent personality pattern which is different from that of nonstutterers. Greater anxiety, hypersensitivity, and lack of self-confidence have been reported among stutterers, but there is little evidence of neuroticism or severe maladjustment within this population. One important problem—the relationship between personality and therapeutic progress—remains relatively unexamined by research workers.

SUMMARY

The purpose of this paper was to survey the literature reporting some empirical relationships between measured personality and the major functional disorders of speech—articulation disorders, delayed speech, voice disorders, and stuttering. In each of these four areas, the published literature of the past 40 years was categorized according to parental personality and adjustment and according to personality and adjustment of the speech-disordered individual himself, first as a child and then as an adult. Where appropriate, the methodological and conceptual limitations of the studies were pointed out and suggestions for additional research made. While some studies have utilized careful procedures and have yielded provocative findings, their number has been small. The methodological and conceptual inadequacies of the greater proportion of studies were so important that few generalizations were clearly suggested, emphasizing the need for more and better research.

References

Abbott, T. B. A study of observable mother-child relationships in stuttering and nonstuttering groups. Ph.D. thesis, University of Florida, 1957.

Agnello, J. The effects of manifest anxiety and stuttering adaptation: Implications for treatment. *Amer. speech hearing Assoc.*, 1962, *4*, 377 (abstract).

Anastasi, A., *Psychological testing* (3rd ed.). New York: Macmillan, 1968.

Anders, Q. M. A study of the personal and social adjustment of children with functional articulatory defects. Ph.D. thesis, University of Wisconsin, 1945.

Andersland, P. B. Maternal and environmental factors related to success in speech improvement training. *J. speech hearing Res.*, 1961, *4*, 79–90.

Anderson, E. G. A comparison of emotional stability in stutterers and non-stutterers. Ph.D. thesis, Wayne State University, 1967.

Aronson, A. E., Peterson, H. W., & Litin, E. M. Voice symptomatology in functional dysphonia and aphonia. *J. speech hearing Dis.*, 1964, *29*, 367–380.

Aronson, A. E., Peterson, H. W., & Litin, E. M. Psychiatric symptomatology in functional dysphonia and aphonia. *J. speech hearing Dis.*, 1966, *31*, 115–127.

Aronson, A. E., et al. Spastic dysphonia: I. Voice, neurologic, and psychiatric aspects. *J. speech hearing Dis.*, 1968, *33*, 203–218.

Bearss, L. M. An investigation of conflict in stutterers and non-stutterers. M.S. thesis, Purdue University, 1950.

Beckey, R. E. A study of certain factors related to retardation of speech. *J. speech Dis.*, 1942, *7*, 223–249.

Bender, J. F. *The personality structure of stuttering.* New York: Pitman, 1939.
Bender, J. F. The stuttering personality. *Amer. J. Orthopsychiat.*, 1942, *12*, 140–146.
Bender, J. F. *The personality structure of stuttering.* New York: Pitman, 1939.
Berlin, C. I. A study of attitudes towards the non-fluences of childhood of parents of stutterers, parents of articulatory defectives, and parents of normal-speaking children. Ph.D. thesis, University of Pittsburgh, 1958.
Berlinsky, S. Measurement of the intelligence and personality of the deaf: A review of the literature. *J. speech hearing Dis.*, 1952, *17*, 39–54.
Berlinsky, S. L. A comparison of stutterers and nonstutterers in four conditions of induced anxiety. Ph.D. thesis, University of Michigan, 1954.
Bernhardt, R. B. Personality and conflict and the act of stuttering. Ph.D. thesis, University of Michigan, 1954.
Bjermeland, Y. B. A comparative study of personality factors of children with functional articulatory defects. M.A. thesis, Whittier College, 1951.
Boland, J. L., Jr. A comparison of stutterers and nonstutterers on several measures of anxiety. Ph.D. thesis, University of Michigan, 1952.
Brice, B. C. A pilot study of the relationship of selected voice quality deviations and anxiety level as determined by the Thematic Apperception Test. M.A. thesis, Florida State University, 1950.
Brutten, E. Anxiety as a personality factor among stutterers. M.A. thesis, Brooklyn College, 1951.
Brutten, E. J. A colorimetric anxiety measure of stuttering and expectancy adaptation. Ph.D. thesis, University of Illinois, 1957.
Burleson, D. E. A personality study of fourth, fifth, and sixth grade stutterers and nonstutterers based on the Bender Visual Motor Gestalt Test. M.S. thesis, University of Pittsburgh, 1949.
Buscaglia, L. F. An experimental study of the Sarbin-Hardyck Test as indexes of role perception for adolescent stutterers. Ph.D. thesis, University of Southern California, 1962.
Butler, K. G. The Bender-Gestalt Visual Motor Test as a diagnostic instrument with children exhibiting articulation disorders. *Amer. speech hearing Assoc.*, 1965, *7*, 380–381 (abstract).
Carp, F. M. Psychosexual development of stutterers. *J. proj. Tech.*, 1962, *26*, 388–391.
Christensen, A. H. A quantitative study of personality dynamics in stuttering and non-stuttering siblings. Ph.D. thesis, University of Southern California, 1951.
Cronbach, L. J. *Essentials of psychological testing* (2nd ed.). New York: Harper & Row, 1960.
Dahlstrom, W. G., & Craven, D. D. The Minnesota Multiphasic Personality Inventory and stuttering phenomena in young adults. *Amer. Psychol.*, 1952, *7*, 341 (abstract).
Darley, F. L. The relationship of parental attitudes and adjustments to the development of stuttering. In W. Johnson (Ed.), *Stuttering in children and adults.* Minneapolis: University of Minnesota Press, 1955.
Despert, J. L. Psychosomatic study of fifty stuttering children. I. Social, physical and psychiatric findings. *Amer. J. Orthopsychiat.*, 1946, *16*, 100–113.

Diamond, M. An investigation of some personality differences between predominantly tonic stutterers and predominantly clonic stutterers. Ph.D. thesis, Syracuse University, 1953.

Dickson, S. Differences between children who spontaneously outgrow and children who retain functional articulation errors. *J. speech hearing Res.*, 1962, 5, 263–271.

Dike, G. W. A study of the personal and social adjustment of speech defective children. M.A. thesis, Kent State University, 1953.

Duncan, M. H. Personality adjustment techniques in voice therapy. *J. speech Dis.*, 1947, 12, 161–167.

Duncan, M. H. Home adjustment of stutterers versus non-stutterers. *J. speech hearing Dis.*, 1949, 14, 255–259.

Eastman, D. F. An exploratory investigation of the psychoanalytic theory of stuttering by means of the Blacky Pictures Test. Ph.D. thesis, University of Nebraska, 1960.

Elliott, J. Personality traits of 199 school children with speech deviations as indicated by the California Test of Personality, Primary and Elementary Series, Form A. M.A. thesis, University of Michigan, 1951.

Emerick, L. L. An evaluation of three psychological variables in tonic and clonic stutterers and in non-stutterers. Ph.D. thesis, Michigan State University, 1966.

Ferguson, L. W. *Personality measurement.* New York: McGraw-Hill, 1952.

Finkelstein, P., & Weisberger, S. E. The motor proficiency of stutterers. *J. speech hearing Dis.*, 1954, 19, 52–58.

Font, M. M. A comparison of the free associations of stutterers and nonstutterers. In W. Johnson (Ed.), *Stuttering in children and adults.* Minneapolis: University of Minnesota Press, 1955.

Freeman, G. G., & Sonnega, J. A. Peer evaluation of children in speech correction class. *J. speech hearing Dis.*, 1956, 21, 179–182.

Gildston, P. Stutterers' self-acceptance and perceived parental acceptance. *J. abnorm. Psychol.*, 1967, 72, 59–64.

Glasner, P. J. Personality characteristics and emotional problems in stutterers under the age of five. *J. speech hearing Dis.*, 1949, 14, 135–138.

Goldman, R., & Shames, G. H. A study of the goal-setting behavior of parents of stutterers and parents of nonstutterers. *J. speech hearing Dis.*, 1964, 29, 192–194. (a)

Goldman, R., & Shames, G. H. Comparisons of the goals that parents of stutterers, and parents of nonstutterers set for their children. *J. speech hearing Dis.*, 1964, 29, 381–389. (b)

Goodstein, L. D. MMPI Profile of stutterers' parents: A follow-up study. *J. speech hearing Dis.*, 1956, 21, 430–435.

Goodstein, L. D., & Dahlstrom, W. G. MMPI differences between the parents of stuttering and non-stuttering children. *J. consult. Psychol.*, 1956, 20, 365–370.

Goodstein, L. D., Martire, J. G., & Spielberger, C. D. The relationship between 'achievement imagery' and stuttering behavior in college males. *Proc. Iowa Acad. Sci.*, 1955, 62, 399–404.

Gray, B. B., & Karmen, J. L. The relationship between nonverbal anxiety and stuttering adaptation. *J. commun. Dis.*, 1967, *1*, 141–151.

Greenberg, K. R. A study of the relationship between articulatory disorders and personality in the intermediate grades. M.A. thesis, Ohio State University, 1952.

Haney, H. R. Motives implied by the act of stuttering as revealed by prolonged experimental projection. Ph.D. thesis, University of Southern California 1950.

Ingebregtsen, E. Some experimental contributions to the psychology and psychopathology of stutterers. *Amer. J. Orthopsychiat.*, 1936, *6*, 630–650.

Johnson, W. A study of the onset and development of stuttering. *J. speech Dis.*, 1942, *7*, 251–257.

Johnson, W. A study of the onset and development of stuttering. In W. Johnson (Ed.), *Stuttering in children and adults.* Minneapolis: University of Minnesota Press, 1955.

Johnson, W. (Ed.) *The onset of stuttering.* Minneapolis: University of Minnesota Press, 1959.

Johnson, W., et al. *Speech handicapped school children* (rev. ed.). New York: Harper & Row, 1956.

Kapos, E., & Standlee, L. S. Behavioral rigidity in adult stutterers. *J. speech hearing Res.*, 1958, *1*, 294–296.

Kennedy, G. M. The relationships among articulatory speech defects, personality maladjustments, educational retardation, and physical deviations. M.A. thesis, Emerson College, 1951.

King, P. T. A study of perseveration in stutterers and normal speakers. Ph.D. thesis, Pennsylvania State University, 1953.

King, P. T. Perseveration in stutterers and nonstutterers. *J. speech hearing Res.*, 1961, *4*, 346–357.

Kinstler, D. B. Covert and overt maternal rejection in stuttering. *J. speech hearing Dis.*, 1961, *26*, 145–155.

Kopp, H. Psychosomatic study of fifty stuttering children: II. Ozeretsky Tests. *Amer. J. Orthopsychiat.*, 1946, *16*, 114–119.

Krugman, M. Psychosomatic study of fifty stuttering children: IV. Rorschach study. *Amer. J. Orthopsychiat.*, 1946, *16*, 127–133.

Lanyon, R. I. The MMPI and prognosis in stuttering therapy. *J. speech hearing Dis.*, 1966, *31*, 186–191.

Lerea, L., & Ward, B. The social schema of normal and speech-defective children. *J. soc. Psychol.*, 1966, *69*, 87–94.

Madison, L. R., & Norman, R. D. A comparison of the performance of stutterers and non-stutterers on the Rosenzweig Picture-Frustration Test. *J. clin. Psychol.*, 1952, *8*, 179–183.

Marge, D. K. The social status of speech-handicapped children. *J. speech hearing Res.*, 1966, *9*, 165–177.

Martin, R. Stuttering and perseveration in children. *J. speech hearing Res.*, 1962, *5*, 332–339.

Martyn, M. Onset of stuttering and recovery. *Behav. Res. & Therapy*, 1968, *6*, 295–307.

Mast, V. R. Level of aspiration as a method of studying the personality of adult stutterers. M.A. thesis, University of Michigan, 1951.

McAllister, M. G. A study of the relationship between defects of articulation in speech and emotional instability in elementary school children. M.A. thesis, University of Washington, 1948.

McCarthy, D. Language disorders and parent-child relationships. *J. speech hearing Dis.*, 1954, *19*, 514–523.

McDowell, E. D. *Educational and emotional adjustments of stuttering children.* New York: Teachers College, Columbia University, 1928.

McKee, M. M. A study of the relationship between defects of articulation in speech and emotional instability in elementary school children. M.A. thesis, University of Washington, 1949.

Meltzer, H. Talkativeness in stuttering and non-stuttering children. *J. genet. Psychol.*, 1935, *46*, 371–390.

Meltzer, H. Personality differences between stuttering and nonstuttering children as indicated by the Rorschach Test. *J. Psychol.*, 1944, *17*, 39–59.

Moll, K. L., & Darley, F. L. Attitudes of mothers of articulatory-impaired and speech-retarded children. *J. speech hearing Dis.*, 1960, *25*, 377–384.

Möller, H. Stuttering, predelinquent, and adjusted boys: A comparative analysis of personality characteristics as measured by the WISC and the Rorschach test. Ph.D. thesis, Boston University, 1960.

Moncur, J. P. Environmental factors differentiating stuttering children from non-stuttering children. *Speech Monogr.*, 1951, *18*, 312–325.

Moncur, J. P. Parental domination in stuttering. *J. speech hearing Dis.*, 1952, *17*, 155–165.

Moore, W. E. Personality traits and voice quality deficiencies. *J. speech Dis.*, 1939, *4*, 33–36.

Peckarsky, A. K. Maternal attitudes towards children with psychogenically delayed speech. Ph.D. thesis, New York University, 1953.

Perkins, D. W. An item by item compilation and comparison of the scores of seventy-five young adult stutterers on the California Test of Personality—adult form A. M.A. thesis, University of Michigan, 1946.

Perrin, E. H. The social position of the speech defective child. *J. speech hearing Dis.*, 1954, *19*, 250–252.

Pitrelli, F. R. Psychosomatic and Rorschach aspects of stuttering. *Psychiat. Quart.*, 1948, *22*, 175–194.

Pizzat, F. J. A personality study of college stutterers. M.S. thesis, University of Pittsburgh, 1949.

Quarrington, B. The performance of stutterers on the Rosenzweig Picture-Frustration Test. *J. clin. Psychol.*, 1953, *9*, 189–192.

Reid, G. The etiology and nature of functional articulatory defects in elementary school children. *J. speech Dis.*, 1947, *12*, 143–150.

Richardson, L. H. The personality of stutterers. *Psychol. Monogr.*, 1944, *56*, No. 7 (whole no. 260). (a)

Richardson, L. H. A personality study of stutterers and non-stutterers. *J. speech Dis.*, 1944, *9*, 152–160. (b)

Rieber, R. W. An investigation of dependent and independent characteristics of stutterers and clutterers. *International Assoc. Logoped. and Phoniat.*, 1962.

Robbins, S. D. Relation between insecurity and onset of stuttering. Unpublished report, 1962.

Robbins, S. D. 1000 stutterers: A personal report of clinical experience and research with recommendations for therapy. *J. speech hearing Dis.*, 1964, *29*, 178–186.

St. Onge, K. R. The stuttering syndrome. *J. speech hearing Res.*, 1963, *6*, 195–197.

St. Onge, K. R., & Calvert, J. J. Stuttering research. *Quart. J. Speech*, 1964, *50*, 159–165.

Sanford, F. H. Speech and personality. In L. A. Pennington and I. A. Berg (Eds.), *An introduction to clinical psychology*. New York: Ronald Press, 1948.

Santostefano, S. Anxiety and hostility in stuttering. *J. speech hearing Res.*, 1960, *3*, 337–347.

Schultz, D. A. A study of nondirective counseling as applied to adult stutterers. *J. speech Dis.*, 1947, *12*, 421–427.

Sergeant, R. L. An investigation of responses of speech defective adults on personality inventories. Ph.D. thesis, Ohio State University, 1962.

Shames, G. H. An investigation of prognosis and evaluation in speech therapy. *J. speech hearing Dis.*, 1952, *17*, 386–392.

Shank, K. H. An analysis of the degree of relationship between the Thematic Apperception Test and an original projective test in measuring symptoms of personality dynamics of speech handicapped children. Ph.D. thesis, University of Denver, 1954.

Sheehan, J. G. Rorschach prognosis in psychotherapy and speech therapy. *J. speech hearing Dis.*, 1954, *19*, 217–219.

Sheehan, J. G., et al. A validity study of the Rorschach Prognostic Rating Scale. *J. proj. Tech.*, 1954, *18*, 233–239.

Sheehan, J., Hadley, R., & Gould, E. Impact of authority on stuttering. *J. abnorm. Psychol.*, 1967, *72*, 290–293.

Sheehan, J. G., & Zelen, S. L. A level of aspiration study of stutterers. *Amer. Psychologist*, 1951, *6*, 500 (abstract).

Sheehan, J. G., & Zelen, S. L. Level of aspiration in stutterers and nonstutterers. *J. abnorm. soc. Psychol.*, 1955, *51*, 83–86.

Sherrill, D. D. Peer, teacher, and self-perceptions of children with severe functional articulation disorders. Ph.D. thesis, University of Nebraska, Teachers College, 1967.

Solomon, A. L. Personality and behavior patterns of children with functional defects of articulation. *Child Develop.*, 1961, *32*, 731–737.

Solomon, I. L. Aggression and stuttering: an experimental study of the psychoanalytic model of stuttering. Ph.D. thesis, Yeshiva University, 1963.

Solomon, N. D. A comparison of rigidity of behavior manifested by a group of stutterers compared with 'fluent' speakers in oral and other performances as measured by the Einstellung-Effect. M.A. thesis, University of Michigan, 1951.

Staats, L. C., Jr. Sense of humor in stutterers and nonstutterers. In W. Johnson (Ed.), *Stuttering in children and adults*. Minneapolis: University of Minnesota Press, 1955.

Stein, L. The emotional background of stammering. *Brit. J. Med. Psychol.*, 1949, *22*, 189–193.

Templin, M. Study of aggressiveness in normal and defective speaking college students. *J. speech Dis.*, 1938, *3*, 43–49.

Thile, E. L. An investigation of attitude differences in parents of stutterers and parents of non-stutterers. Ph.D. thesis, University of Southern California, 1967.

Thomas, L. A personality study of a group of stutterers based on the Minnesota Multiphasic Personality Inventory. M.A. thesis, University of Oregon, 1951.

Trapp, E. P., & Evans, J. Functional articulatory defect and performance on a non-verbal task. *J. speech hearing Dis.*, 1960, *25*, 176–180.

Tuper, H. L., & Chambers, J. L. An analysis of stutterers' responses to the Picture Identification Test. *Amer. speech hearing Assoc.*, 1962, *4*, 377 (abstract).

Wallen, V. A Q-technique study of the self-concepts of adolescent stutterers and nonstutterers. Ph.D. thesis, Boston University, 1959.

Walnut, F. A personality inventory item analysis of individuals who stutter and individuals who have other handicaps. *J. speech hearing Dis.*, 1954, *19*, 220–227.

Whitman, E. C. The role of the father in the development of the personality of the stutterer. *Psychol. Bull.*, 1942, *39*, 476 (abstract).

Wilson, R. G. A study of expressive movement in three groups of adolescent boys, stutterers, nonstutterers, maladjusted and normals, by means of three measures of personality, Mira's Myokinetic Psychodiagnosis, the Bender-Gestalt and Figure Drawing. Ph.D. thesis, Western Reserve University, 1950.

Wingate, M. E. Evaluation and stuttering: I. Speech characteristics of young children. *J. speech hearing Dis.*, 1962, *27*, 106–115.

Wingate, M. E. Recovery from stuttering. *J. speech hearing Dis.*, 1964, *29*, 312–321.

Wingate, M. E. Behavioral rigidity in stutterers. *J. speech hearing Res.*, 1966, *9*, 626–629.

Wood, K. S. Parental maladjustment and functional articulatory defects in children. Ph.D. thesis, University of Southern California, 1946. (a)

Wood, K. S. Parental maladjustment and functional articulatory defects in children. *J. speech Dis.*, 1946, *11*, 255–275. (b)

Woods, F. J., & Carrow, M. A. Choice-rejection status of speech-defective children. *Except. Child.*, 1959, *25*, 279–283.

Wright, A. K. The effect of maternal attitudes on the outcome of treatment of children's speech defects. *Smith Coll. Stud. Soc. Work*, 1939, *10*, 123–124 (abstract).

Wyatt, G. L. Mother-child relationship and stuttering in children. Ph.D. thesis, Boston University, 1958.

Wylie, H. L., Feranchak, P. B., & McWilliams, B. J. Characteristics of children with speech disorders seen in a child guidance center. *Percept. & Motor Skills*, 1965, *20*, 1101–1107.

Zelen, S. L., Sheehan, J. G., & Bugental, J. F. T. Self-perceptions in stuttering. *J. clin. Psychol.*, 1954, *10*, 70–72.

20

Stuttering and Its Disappearance

Joseph G. Sheehan and Margaret M. Martyn

Dr. Martyn is Clinical Psychologist at Olive View Hospital in Los Angeles. The reader is referred to Article 21, The Modification of Stuttering Through Nonreinforcement, *for a brief description of Dr. Sheehan's duties and research activities.*

Dr. Martyn's research interests and publications involve factors related to recovery from stuttering, speech disorders in retardation, and speech disorders in psychosis.

This interesting paper reports new research on factors related to the onset of stuttering and eventual recovery from it. Those readers concerned with the psychopathology and prognosis of stuttering should find the article particularly useful.

In the absence of any therapy, or sometimes in spite of it, spontaneous recovery is believed to occur in a significant number of cases. Each variety of disordered behavior must have its own incidence rates for such recoveries, yet we do not know what they are.

Knowledge of spontaneous recovery rates becomes important both to psychopathology and to psychotherapy. To psychopathology, because

> From the *Journal of Speech & Hearing Research,* Vol. 13, 1970. Reprinted by permission. This study was made possible by grants from the Faculty Research Committee, University of California, Los Angeles. Data for this and previous related studies were gathered through the cooperation of Dr. Donald MacKinnon, Director of the Student Health Service, University of California, Los Angeles, and Dr. Henry Bruyn, Director of the Student Health Service, Cowell Memorial Hospital, University of California, Berkeley.

426   The Speech Handicapped

those who remain in a symptom category may not be representative of the problem as originally seen, so that research knowledge may become based on stragglers not representative of the class as a whole. To psychotherapy, because spontaneous recoveries may provide keys to essential variables in psychotherapeutic change, and because spontaneous recoveries in control groups comprise one of many complexities in the evaluation of outcome.

This paper focuses on spontaneous recovery from the problem called stuttering, which is known to begin in childhood and to persist in a number of cases into adult life. Since the sizable literature on stuttering has been built upon study of the adult, it becomes salient to learn what slice of the original population the adult represents. Moreover, factors associated with recovery become important leads for therapy with any disorder based on anxiety—which Freud (1936) called the central problem of neurosis.

Those who seek treatment for a problem probably differ in important respects from those who do not, so those who come to clinics to find us may be a special breed. Data reported in this paper were derived from University of California student health examinations for incoming students, so the subjects were not a group of treatment seekers.

Fresh data from a recent UCLA survey have not been combined with data from two Berkeley samples previously analyzed in part (Sheehan & Martyn, 1966; Martyn & Sheehan, 1968). The new analysis has been based on a sufficient quantity of data so that the addition of an active clinic sample for comparison purposes became unnecessary. Therefore, differences between recovered and active cases may be reported without possible intrusion of the variable of treatment seeking. The latter has proved to be of sufficient importance so that it has become the subject of a separate paper (Sheehan & Martyn, 1970).

Other recent studies, differing from the design indicated above, are those of Dickson (1968), Shearer and Williams (1965), and Wingate (1964).

METHOD

Three general speech surveys of all new students, both undergraduate and graduate, were undertaken on two different campuses of the University of California, Berkeley and Los Angeles. These surveys were a part of the 1964, 1965, and 1967 registration student health examinations, during which four speech clinicians asked each student the following questions:

SPEECH SURVEY

Name _____ Date _____

Date of birth _____

1. How do you rate yourself as a (conversational) speaker?
   Excellent _____; Good _____; Poor _____; Inferior _____.
2. Have you ever had any special speech training? Yes _____; No _____.
3. Have you ever had a speech problem? Yes _____; No _____.
4. Do you consider that you now have a speech problem?
   Yes _____; No _____.
5. Have you ever had a hearing problem? Yes _____; No _____.

Students then read individually all or part of the speech screening passage called "My Grandfather" (Van Riper, 1963).

The nature of the interview easily evoked stuttering and identification of the active stutterers. By the same token the interview produced the self-identification of the recovered stutterers, who were asked (1) to describe their previous speech behavior, (2) to imitate it, (3) whether or not they anticipated blocks, (4) whether they feared words and situations, (5) whether they avoided specific words by substituting others, and (6) and whether they had in the past believed themselves to be stutterers.

In this way students were divided into three groups: (1) active stutterers, (2) recovered stutterers, and (3) normal speakers.

SUBJECTS

Of the 5,138 students examined during the three University of California surveys, 116 were found to be recovered stutterers and 31 were found to be active stutterers—a ratio of 4 to 1.

It was possible to obtain full interview data on the great majority of these subjects. However, because of the time pressure of student health examinations, a very few interviews were incomplete. Such responses as were obtained were tabulated and total Ns from table to table vary accordingly.

Recovered stutterers, including 79 males and 22 females, ranged in age from 17 to 56 with a mean of 23.7. The active stutterers, including 26 males and 5 females, ranged in age from 17 to 32 with a mean of 22.6.

PROCEDURE

As the survey questionaire suggests, the initial judgment of stutterer, recovered stutterer, or normal speaker was made by the students themselves. The active stutterers and the self-identified recovered stutterers were then directed to the two investigators, who conducted a second speech evaluation as a check on the results of the first. The two investigators then administered the following structured individual interview to the recovered and the active stutterers:

RECOVERY INTERVIEW FORM

Name _____

Date _____

1. At what age did you begin to stutter? 3–6 _____ 7–10 _____ 11–14 _____ 15–18 _____
2. How did your stuttering begin? Repetitions _____ Hesitations _____ Blockings _____
3. What was the level of your stuttering at its worst? Mild _____ Moderate _____ Severe _____
4. Who first noticed your stuttering? Parents _____ Teacher or speech therapist _____ Self _____ Other _____
5. What was the atmosphere in your home at the onset of your stuttering? Parent conflict _____ Tension _____ Good _____ Other _____
6. What has been your belief as to the cause of your stuttering? Something within self _____ Something outside self _____
7. Have you received any formal speech therapy? Yes _____ No _____
8. Was the therapy beneficial? Yes _____ No _____
9. How much have you improved? Complete _____ Partial _____ None _____
10. At what age did you improve (or recover)? 3–6 _____ 7–10 _____ 11–14 _____ 15–18 _____ 19–22 _____ 23–26 _____ 27 and over _____
11. What was the nature of your improvement (or recovery)? Sudden _____ Gradual _____
12. Is stuttering a part of your self-concept (or do you consider yourself a stutterer)? Yes _____ No _____
13. Was stuttering ever a part of your self-concept (or did you ever consider yourself a stutterer)? Yes _____ No _____
14. To what do you attribute your improvement (or recovery)? Speech therapy _____ Self-therapy (taking some action) _____ Don't know _____ Other _____
15. Based on your experience as a stutterer, what advice would you give to a stutterer? Self-therapy _____ Seek therapy _____ Can't advise _____ Other _____
16. Are there other stutterers in your family? Yes _____ No _____
17. Which is your own preferred hand? Right _____ Left _____
18. Are there left-handed persons in your family? Yes _____ No _____
19. How much fear of stuttering do you have at the present time? None _____ Some _____ Great _____
20. Do you presently consider yourself recovered from stuttering? Yes _____ No _____

Findings reported in this paper result from a chi-square analysis of six pairs of questions, which produced a bivariate frequency table for each pair as follows: (1) severity and recovery, (2) receiving public school speech therapy and recovery, (3) severity and receiving public school speech therapy, (4) who first noticed stuttering and receiving therapy, (5) how stuttering began and recovery, and (6) stuttering in the family and recovery.

The term "spontaneous recovery" as used in this study (and in Sheehan & Martyn, 1966; Martyn & Sheehan, 1968) refers to recoveries which take place in the absence of any ongoing therapy, or any previous therapy to which recovery could be reasonably attributed. Included in the latter category are formal enrollments in therapy of too brief and superficial a nature or too far removed in time from the period of improvement or recovery. For example, an adult who had recovered at age 13 may have been enrolled in three voice lessons at age 6, but recalls them very vaguely and does not attribute any effect. In the absence of any other therapy, such recovery would be counted as spontaneous.

RESULTS AND DISCUSSIONS

Ratio of Recovery to Continuation

As a first finding, about four out of five of those who had ever become stutterers recovered spontaneously, as depicted graphically in Figure 1. Ratios found in the UCLA sample and in the earlier Berkeley samples were not significantly different, although the new sample mean was arithmetically lower within fluctuations expected of different samples from the same population.

The finding that nearly 80 percent of those who ever become stutterers recover spontaneously is most challenging in implications for the nature of stuttering, for research, and treatment. The present extensive literature on stuttering is based largely on information gleaned from adults who persist as active stutterers—a slim minority of the problem as it develops and exists in childhood and adolescence.

To the puzzle of the persistence of stuttering—that the behavior continues despite being apparently more punishing than rewarding—must be added the puzzle of its predominant failure to persist in four fifths of the cases. In terms of conflict and reinforcement theory (Sheehan, 1962), why does stuttering actually drop out in most of the cases? And why does it drop out when it does? And how do those who have recovered differ from those who did not? These are some of the basic questions to be considered in this section.

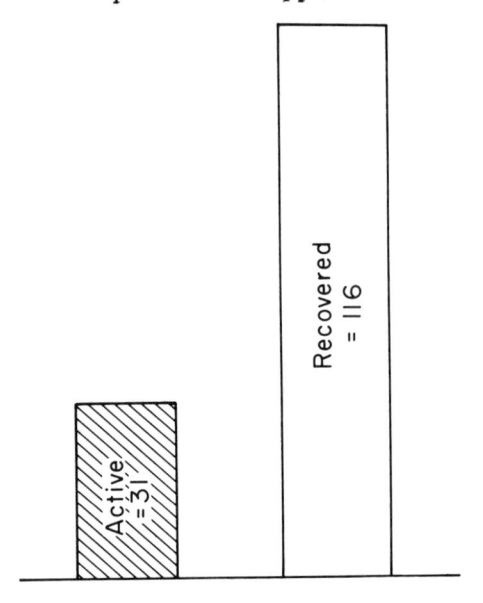

Fig. 1 *Ratio of disappearance of stuttering to continuation.*

Severity and Recovery

Although four fifths recover spontaneously, it should not be assumed that the 80 percent prospect holds for every child who becomes enmeshed in the problem called stuttering. Severity modifies the recovery ratio materially. For mild stutterers the ratio is even higher, but for severe stutterers the ratio is lower. Table 1 presents this relationship in terms of a breakdown into categories of mild, moderate, and severe, as judged by stuttering at its worst.

Figure 2 presents graphically the proportion of recoveries among the mild, the moderate, and the severe, as judged by how the stuttering was at its worst. It may be seen that a mild stutterer had an 87 percent chance

Table 1 *Probability of Recovery in Relation to Level of Severity:*
$X^2 = 10.40$; df $= 2$; p $= .01$

Severity of stuttering at worst	Recovered Yes	Recovered No	Total
Mild	53 (+52.0)	9 (−14.94)	67
Moderate	35 (−36.51)	12 (+10.48)	47
Severe	8 (−12.43)	8 (+3.56)	16
Total	101	29	130

MILD	87% RECOVERED
MODERATE	75% RECOVERED
SEVERE	50% RECOVERED

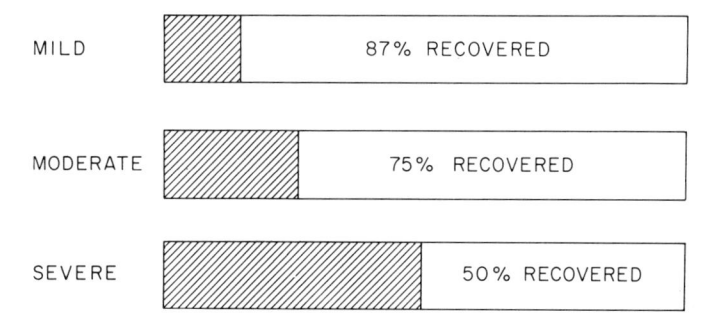

Fig. 2 Ratio of continuation of stuttering to its disappearance in relation to levels of severity.

of recovering, and a moderate stutterer had a 75 percent chance, while a severe stutterer's chances were only 50:50.

Severity, Recovery, and Public School Therapy

For the first time, we now have sufficient survey-based data, without any addition of clinic stutterers, so we may more precisely assess the influence of severity on some of the other results, particularly the receiving of public school therapy.

The previously reported finding that a negative relationship exists between receiving public school therapy and recovery failed the test of cross-validation in our new UCLA sample. This result may be seen in Table 2.

When the results of all three samples are combined, as in Table 3, the significance reappears, primarily because the earlier Berkeley sample results were so very negative. With the addition of the data from UCLA, we are now able to separate out more clearly the contribution of severity to the finding that fewer of those who received public school therapy re-

Table 2 Relation of Recovery to Receiving Public School Speech Therapy; Data from New UCLA Sample Only: $X^2 = .143$; df $= 1$; p $= .50$; Not Significant

Received speech therapy	Recovered Yes	No	Total
Yes	14 (−14.6)	5 (+4.4)	19
No	39 (+38.4)	11 (−11.6)	50
Total	53	16	69

Table 3 Relationship of Recovery to Receiving Public School Therapy; Data from Combined Berkeley and UCLA Samples: $X^2 = 5.315$; df = 1; p = .05

Received speech therapy	Recovered Yes	Recovered No	Total
Yes	35 (−39.81)	14 (+9.18)	49
No	56 (+51.18)	7 (−11.81)	63
Total	91	21	114

covered. When either the mild or the severe were considered separately, no effect of public school therapy was observed, either positive or negative. With severity held constant as our new data permitted, enrollment in public school therapy had no effect upon the probability of eventual recovery.

Diagnosis, Therapy, and Severity

Moreover, as Table 4 clearly shows, the more severe, who were in any case less likely to recover, were more likely to be assigned to public school therapy. Since there is a coexistence of severity and public school therapy, either (1) the more severe are more likely to be assigned to public school therapy, or (2) those assigned to public school therapy are more likely to become severe. Although we prefer the first interpretation, the latter dire possibility cannot be ruled out, and even received indirect support from the data in Table 5. Those who were first diagnosed by others were more likely to be sent into public school therapy. Those who were self-diagnosed were less inclined to choose therapy. Did the diagnosis from important authority figures (parent, teacher, speech therapist) plus the experience of being put in a special class contribute to the development of

Table 4 Relationship between Level of Severity and Probability of Receiving Public School Speech Therapy: $X^2 = 9.07$; df = 2; p = .02

Severity of stuttering at worst	Received therapy Yes	Received therapy No	Total
Mild	16 (−24.0)	51 (+43.0)	67
Moderate	21 (+15.0)	21 (−27.0)	42
Severe	8 (+6.1)	8 (−10.3)	16
Total	45	80	125

Table 5 Person Who First Noticed Stuttering in Relation to Assignment to Public School Therapy: $X^2 = 24.35$; df $= 3$; p $= 0.001$

Who first noticed stuttering	Received therapy Yes	Received therapy No	Total
Self	5 (−15.34)	40 (+29.65)	45
Parents	24 (+18.41)	30 (−35.58)	54
Teacher or speech therapist	13 (+6.48)	6 (−12.51)	19
Other	2 (−2.75)	9 (+7.24)	11
Total	44	85	129

greater severity? Those who did not follow the same path more often remained mild. An impressive number of those who had recovered noted that therapy had been offered them while in the schools but that they had turned it down. Our clinical impression was that the independence reflected in this decision appeared to be an important asset contributing to their eventual recovery.

Among those who had received the therapy, the attitudes were even more negative. By their accounts, the therapy was woefully inadequate, amounting in some instances to a sham. In our two Berkeley samples, no recipient of public school therapy for stuttering attributed any positive effects to it or recommended it for any other stutterer. In the UCLA sample, two recipients reported improvement and recommended the therapy—although neither had recovered.

Speech Behaviors at the Onset

Some mitigation of the situation for the public school clinician is provided by the data in Table 6, which shows differences in speech behaviors at the onset. Those who became severe more often began in a different way (with blockings rather than with syllable repetitions) from the mild stutterers. Apparently the type or subtype of stutterer matters greatly; and the public school clinician had more of the subtype who began with blocking.

Severity at periods of worst stuttering and beginning to stutter with complete blocking involves some circularity. However, what emerges from the data in Table 6 are two more or less distinct developmental patterns. An important developmental sequence leading to persistence and chronicity involves beginning with blockings, experiencing strong fear, and developing into a severe rather than mild case. On the other hand, beginning with easy repetitions and hesitations, experiencing moderate fear, and developing mild or moderate stuttering appears to lead to a pathway to-

Table 6 Relationship between Recovery and Manner in Which Stuttering Began: $X^2 = 9.287$; $df = 2$; $p = .01$

How stuttering began	Recovered Yes	Recovered No	Total
Repitions	57 (−57.81)	17 (+16.18)	74
Hestitations	30 (+25.0)	2 (−7.00)	32
Blockings	13 (−17.18)	9 (+4.81)	22
Total	100	28	128

ward recovery. The most conservative conclusion is that our data show that public school therapy of the kind represented in these studies definitely does not facilitate recovery and possibly retards it.

Even the result of nonsignificance as to the effects of public school therapy is fairly negative. Being enrolled in therapy raises hopes, and when nothing results, hopes are dashed and future motivation is diminished. The already complex therapy necessary for adult stutterers is further complicated when the clinician has to overcome a heritage of distrust from previous therapy. Moreover, many stutterers acquire an attitude of hopelessness, give up the search, and deny themselves the possibility of future therapy that might really help them.

Stuttering in the Family

Familial incidence of stuttering did not differentiate active stutterers from recovered stutterers. In other words, stuttering appeared in the families of those who recovered just as often as in those who did not (Table 7).

Although familial incidence did not distinguish those who recovered from those who continued, familial incidence did distinguish stutterers

Table 7 Familial Incidence of Stuttering in Those Who Recovered and Those Who Did Not: $X^2 = 2.735$; $df = 1$; $p = 10$; Not Significant

Stuttering in family	Recovered Yes	Recovered No	Total
Yes	19 (−22.3)	10 (+6.69)	29
No	81 (+77.6)	20 (−23.3)	101
Total	100	30	130

from normal-speaking controls (Sheehan & Martyn, 1967; Martyn & Sheehan, 1968). This finding is in agreement with Andrews and Harris (1964) and many previous reports.

The result that proportionately as many recovered stutterers as active stutterers reported the problem in their families may be cited as evidence against genetic or physiological interpretations of the etiology of the disorder. This finding is in line with the view that stuttering is based upon learned behaviors which can be unlearned, or replaced with new learned behaviors.

Relationship to Other Studies on Recovery

One of the methodological problems of a study of this kind is that it is based on recall data, for subjects may distort their own histories to some extent. We have noted this problem in these words: "The most substantive methodological limitation . . . (is that) all of these are *ex post facto* studies and are based upon recall data . . . What we need most for the future, however, are long-term follow up and longitudinal studies" (Sheehan & Martyn, 1967).

In his recent book, *Principles of Behavior Modification,* Bandura (1969) referred to our first paper on spontaneous recovery (Sheehan & Martyn, 1966) as a retrospective study. However, both for that study and this one, crucial portions of the data are based upon current observation of subject behavior rather than recall. In particular, the decision as to whether a person had been a stutterer was based in part on his present mode of behavior at the time of interview and did not hinge entirely upon his memory for precise events. Some lesser findings, of course, did depend upon recall data, as we have noted. But the crucial questions that related to whether an individual had been a stutterer did not depend upon his ability to recall exact dates, but whether he showed at the time of interview that he knew the "inside of stuttering." Anyone who had ever been a secondary stutterer readily recognized during interview the concealment behaviors typically found only in stuttering, and could demonstrate them from his own experience. Independent judgments of the investigators in the UCLA and Berkeley samples produced no instances of disagreement as to who had been a stutterer.

Further indication of the reliability and validity of the method employed here is provided by an independent study by Dickson (1968) using an entirely different approach.

Interviewing parents rather than stutterers themselves, Dickson obtained data in close agreement with our own on such factors as age of onset, relation of severity at onset to persistence of stuttering, relation of speech behaviors at onset to persistence, and relation of persistence to involvement in therapy.

Moreover, our data are congruent with those of Johnson's studies of the onset and development of stuttering in relation to such factors as age of onset, familial incidence, and other findings (Johnson et al., 1959; Johnson, Darley, & Spriestersbach, 1962).

On the important observation that recoveries occur gradually (Sheehan et al., 1957), our results are in agreement with those of Wingate (1964), Shearer and Williams (1965), Sheehan and Martyn (1966), Martyn and Sheehan (1968), and Dickson (1968). Dickson's corroboration is particularly important, since his data were independently derived via parent interviews yet check so closely with out own findings on stuttering and its disappearance.

References

Andrews, G., & Harris, M. *The Syndrome of Stuttering.* London: Heinemann Medical Books, 1964.

Bandura, A. *Principles of Behavior Modification.* New York: Holt, Rinehart and Winston, 1969.

Dickson, S. Spontaneous remission and retention of incipient stuttering symptoms. Paper read at ASHA Convention, Denver, Colorado, 1968.

Freud, S. *The Problem of Anxiety.* New York: Norton, 1936.

Johnson, W., et al. *The Onset of Stuttering: Research findings and implications.* Minneapolis: University of Minnesota Press, 1959.

Johnson, W., Darley, F., & Spriestersbach, D. C. *Diagnostic Methods in Speech Pathology and Audiology.* New York: Harper & Row, 1962.

Martyn, M. M., & Sheehan, J. G. Onset of stuttering and recovery. *Behav. Res. & Therapy,* 1968, *6,* 295–307.

Shearer, W., & Williams, J. D. Self-recovery from stuttering. *J. speech hearing Dis.,* 1965, *30,* 288–290.

Sheehan, J. G. Stuttering as a self-role conflict. In H. H. Gregory (Ed.). *Learning Theory and Stuttering Therapy.* Evanston, Ill.: Northwestern University Press, 1968, pp. 72–83.

Sheehan, J. G. (Chairman), Bluemel, C., Clancy, J., Coleman, W., Frick, J., Johnson, W., Van Riper, C., & Williams, D. A symposium of recovered stutterers. ASHA Convention, Cincinnati, 1957.

Sheehan, J. G., & Martyn, M. M. Spontaneous recovery from stuttering. *J. speech hearing Res.,* 1966, *17,* 121–135.

Sheehan, J. G., & Martyn, M. M. Methodology in studies of recovery from stuttering. *J. speech hearing Res.,* 1967, *10,* 296–400.

Sheehan, J. G., & Martyn, M. M. Treatment seeking as a personality variable. Psychology Speech Clinic, UCLA 1970. (Mimeographed)

Van Riper, C. *Speech correction: Principles and methods,* 4th ed. Englewood Cliffs, N.J.: Prentice-Hall, 1963.

Wingate, M. E. Recovery from stuttering. *J. speech hearing Dis.,* 1964, *29,* 312–321.

21

The Modification of Stuttering Through Nonreinforcement

Joseph G. Sheehan

Dr. Sheehan is Professor of Psychology at the University of California, Los Angeles. He is one of the most prominent and productive scholars doing psychological research on stuttering. He has published over fifty scientific articles and has served as Associate Editor for both the Journal of Speech and Hearing Disorders *and the* Journal of the American Speech and Hearing Association.

Among other things, he is currently doing research on status as a factor in stuttering, spontaneous recovery from stuttering, and stuttering as a self-role conflict.

With behavior-modification techniques based on reinforcement principles so common today, the experiment in this article, which first appeared in 1951, anticipated to a remarkable extent the present interest in modifying stuttering behavior through reinforcement methods. In addition, the paper also contains the first formalized statement of the theory of stuttering as an approach–avoidance conflict.

From the *Journal of Abnormal & Social Psychology,* 1951, 46, 51–63. Reprinted by permission of American Psychological Association. From a doctoral dissertation submitted at the University of Michigan in August, 1949. The author is indebted to the late Dr. Edward L. Walker for his guidance, and he is grateful to Dr. Wendell Johnson and Dr. C. Van Riper for making subjects available from their clinics and for stimulating counsel in the initial stages of the study.

438   The Speech Handicapped

In a follow-up study on the original paper, prepared especially for this book, Dr. Sheehan presents new data reporting a successful replication. Special attention is given to a new dimension of concern, what happens when a nonreinforcement technique is removed. The results also raise questions as to the ultimate effects of reinforcement procedures.

Stuttering is of special interest to the psychologist in that it involves non-integrative or persistently maladaptive behavior. The challenge in stuttering behavior lies in the explanation of its reinforcement, the problem of why the behavior continues despite its unserviceability. That speech pathologists have been concerned with this problem and are aware of its crucial role in the understanding of stuttering is apparent from the writings of Dunlap (4), Van Riper (14), and Johnson (8). However, the exact nature of reinforcement in stuttering has never been formulated and subjected to experimental test.

In the past the problem of stuttering has been approached from a variety of disciplines, including the physiological, the neurological, the psychoanalytic, the personality, the semantic, and the developmental. Frequently, two or three approaches overlap within a single explanation. Different investigators have addressed themselves to different aspects of the problem, some to nature and cause, some to treatment, and some entirely to personality variables. Too often there has been scant relation between an authority's theoretical and therapeutic treatment of the problem. For example, many of the older workers in the field who ascribe stuttering to physiological causes are still advocating for its treatment phonetic drills and breathing exercises which bear no relation to the assumed physiological bases.

Although nearly all authorities have observed the presence of a "habit pattern" in stuttering, many of them make no provision for dealing directly with it in their systems of treatment. Some seem to imply that purely verbal procedures, e.g., nondirective counseling, will cause the habit pattern to disappear automatically. Even among those who do work on the habit pattern, few have made an effective application of scientific principles of learning. This lack has been characteristic of speech correction practices in general.

It is with an awareness of this lack that the present study has attacked the problem of stuttering within the framework of modern learning theory. That habit plays an important role in stuttering has, of course, long been recognized. It may be worth while to trace briefly the work of those who have treated stuttering within a learning framework and to examine their contributions. They include references both to the origin of stuttering and to the growth of the stuttering pattern through a building-up of new habits.

A generation ago the educational theory, which regarded stuttering as a bad habit arising out of the natural hesitancies of childhood speech, enjoyed a wide following. Among those who have propounded this view are Stoddard (13) and Russell (11).

Bluemel (2), who utilized Pavlovian concepts, considered speech to be a conditioned response and stuttering to result from the inhibition of this conditioned response through traumatic experiences.

In applying his beta hypothesis, Dunlap treated stuttering essentially as a form of learned behavior, in which unlearning of the stuttering habit could be facilitated by "negative practice."

An important early study by Van Riper (14) bears closely upon the reinforcement problem in stuttering. Van Riper investigated the effect of punishment on the stuttering response, finding that the frequency of stuttering was increased by the administration of electric shock following the response.

The acquisition of new responses in stuttering, described by Van Riper (15), may be expressed in learning terms as follows:

In attempting to say a difficult word the stutterer finds that employing a novel response, such as a sudden intake of breath, releases the word more quickly due to the disinhibiting effect of response-produced stimuli. With continued use the device loses its disinhibitory properties and becomes incorporated into the characteristics pattern of the stuttering. The response loses its voluntary characteristics along with its effectiveness, and the stutterer soon finds himself gasping automatically with every stuttered word. This cycle is repeated as he seeks relief in other novel responses.

The *Iowa Studies in the Psychology of Stuttering*, directed by Wendell Johnson, have investigated various stimulus variables of which the stuttering response is a function. They have included studies of the adaptation effect—the reduction in frequency of stutterings with repeated readings of the same passage—and of the consistency effect—the degree to which the same words appear as stutterings from earlier to later readings. An excellent summary of these studies, along with other investigations of the cues and conditions under which stuttering is increased or diminished, may be found in Bloodstein (1).

In one of the series directed by Johnson, Harris (5) concluded his discussion with this provocative statement:

> . . . Is the adaptation effect to be regarded as a type of experimental extinction? This last question serves to raise the more general and theoretically very important question as to the degree to which and in what particular stuttering is to be interpreted as learned behavior.

Speech pathologists could hardly find a more crucial issue for investigation in the further study of stuttering.

Johnson has concluded, from the results of the *Iowa Studies,* from the Davis study (3), and from his own investigation of the onset and development of stuttering (7), that stuttering as a speech disorder develops *after* diagnosis, i.e., it is a learned anxiety system resulting from the evaluative behavior of parents, teachers, and others close to the stutterer. A child becomes a stutterer *after* he has been labeled one. Johnson has spoken of stutterers as having "tongues that learn to stumble," not because they are innately deviant but because of the nature of their semantic environment.

Again illustrating that approaches to stuttering do not necessarily exclude each other, Johnson's semantic approach is at the same time avowedly a learning theory. One of Johnson's students, Shulman (12), concluded in summarizing his study of the adaptation and consistency effects that "stuttering is primarily a form of learned behavior." Another of Johnson's students, Wischner (17), attempted systematically to interpret stuttering data in conditioning terms such as generalization, extinction, and spontaneous recovery, and suggested further study of stuttering as learned behavior.

Somewhat earlier, Hill (6) had independently worked out a stimulus-response interpretation of stuttering behavior within the "interbehavioral analysis" of J. R. Kantor.

Harris' suggestion, quoted above that adaptation may be a form of experimental extinction, has been elaborated by Wischner, who has drawn up points of similarity between the two. The seeming parallel is furthered by earlier findings, such as Shulman's that "relative massing of the oral reading periods is conducive to greater adaptation than would be attained under conditions of distributed practice" (12).

In the standard adaptation situation, the stutterer reads the same passage over, and, during the successive readings, there is a reduction in the amount of stuttering. The words "experimental extinction" should not be applied to this treatment, however, since the decrease in stuttering takes place in spite of the fact that the stuttering behavior is being continually reinforced. The word "extinction" ought to be reserved for the decrement of a response under non-reinforcement.

Within a learning approach to stuttering, there are of course many possibilities other than those related above. For instance, stuttering could be investigated (1) in terms of the effect of non-reinforcement on the stuttering response; (2) as conflict behavior; (3) in terms of the functioning of preparatory sets or expectancies; (4) in terms of the fractional anticipatory goal response; (5) in terms of maladaptive anticipatory startle responses involved; (6) in terms of the role of configurations or disorders of perceptual organization; (7) in terms of alteration of the stuttering pattern—the acquisition and dropping out of specific movements within the stuttering response; (8) in terms of the cues which determine the form of the stuttering block and the moment of its release; (9) in terms of a possible decrease in the discriminability of instrumental acts under increased motivation. It can thus be seen that the selection of the present problem is arbitrary—others could have been employed within a learning approach.

The present study is concerned primarily with stuttering's reinforcement aspect and secondarily with its conflict aspect. Reinforcement has been made the focus of attack here because the persistence of stuttering behavior is one of its principal mysteries and because it is felt that utilization of non-reinforcement techniques has been one of stuttering therapy's greatest needs.

STATEMENT OF THE PROBLEM

Since stuttering involves behavior which is apparently more punishing than rewarding, why does the behavior persist? Why doesn't the stuttering response extinguish?

One answer which can be given is that, under ordinary conditions, the stuttering response is reinforced. As the instrumental act by means of which the stutterer is attempting to produce the difficult word, it eventually does lead to the production of the word and so to the termination of the anxiety which the word has elicited. The situation might be diagrammed as follows:

$$S_{word} \text{---} R_{anx.} \text{---} S_{anx.} \searrow$$
$$R_{stutt.} \text{---} G_{term.\ seq.}$$

S_{word} can be taken to be a printed word on a page which has cue value in terms of the stutterer's past experience with similar words in similar situations. The word is a stimulus to anxiety, which in turn elicits the avoidant behavior we call "stuttering." The goal, G, is here defined as the termination of the sequence, the point at which the stutterer is able to go on to the next word.

In the case of the normal speaker, however, and in the case of the stutterer when he has no trouble on the word:

$$S_{word} \searrow$$
$$R_{normal\ sp.\ attempt} \text{---} G_{term.\ seq.}$$

Here a normal speech attempt, rather than the stuttering response, is the instrumental act leading to reinforcement. The assumption is made that the termination of the sequence, the point at which the stutterer is able to go on to the next word, is the point of reinforcement, and that the instrumental act which terminates the sequence is reinforced.

There are times when a stutterer makes a normal speech attempt even in the presence of anxiety (15). This is what may under favorable conditions happen in therapy.

$$S_{word} \text{---} R_{anx.} \text{---} S_{anx.} \searrow$$
$$R_{normal\ sp.\ att.} \text{---} G_{term.\ seq.}$$

Here there is no reinforcement of the stuttering response, but the introduction of a set which operates in the presence of anxiety-producing cues to elicit normal speech attempt. This is the kind of training that can reduce stuttering on a permanent basis. Older forms of treatment failed to achieve this because they merely tried to increase the number of normal speech attempts by preventing anxiety through "confidence" measures, but gave the stutterer nothing to help him deal with anxiety when it was elicited.

The crucial feature of the above chain of events is that the instrumental act leading to the termination of the sequence is the normal speech attempt. However, a stutterer ordinarily does not respond to anxiety with a normal speech attempt. Usually, stuttering is the response which gets reinforced. In the present study the experimental group is given a set which does not permit the termination of the sequence until a normal speech attempt has taken place. Ordinarily, the goal would be simply to speak and be understood; the stuttering would be incidental, in fact, necessary, to the attainment of that goal. The experimental set here changes the goals so that the stutterer is no longer rewarded just to speak and be understood. The new goal involves making a normal speech attempt before leaving the word, no matter how much stuttering takes place prior to that point.

$$S_{word} \text{---} R_{anx.} \text{---} S_{anx.} \searrow$$
$$R_{stutt.} \text{---} S_{exper.\ set} \text{---} R_{norm.\ sp.\ att.} \text{---} G_{term.\ seq.}$$

If we can succeed in giving the stutterer a set which will permit nonreinforcement of the stuttering, it will be a tremendous lead for therapy. The set in this experiment is something which the inexperienced therapist, or even the child or the outpatient, could utilize. Many cases of adult stuttering are believed to be on a self-maintaining or functionally autonomous level. For these cases, finding a means for preventing continued reinforcement of the stuttering response should be especially helpful.

The reinforcement implications of our experiment may be further developed by a brief sketching of its conflict aspect.

Stuttering may be considered a resultant of opposed urges to speak and to retreat from the speaking of the word feared. This conflict aspect of stuttering, which is discussed more fully below, may be included in our diagram:

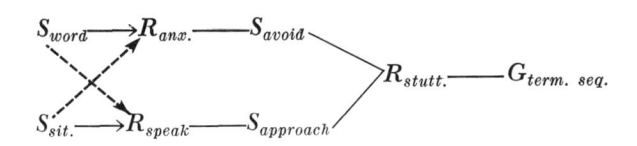

$$S_{word} \rightarrow R_{anx.} \text{------} S_{avoid}$$
$$\phantom{S_{word}} \times R_{stutt.} \text{------} G_{term.\ seq.}$$
$$S_{sit.} \rightarrow R_{speak} \text{------} S_{approach}$$

Following first the solid arrows, we have again S_{word}, an anxiety-arousing cue which leads to an avoidance drive, and opposing this we have $S_{sit.}$, the stimulus of the situation which calls for the response of speaking and leads to an approach drive. The resultant response, stuttering, terminates the sequence and is reinforced. This is the nature of the conflict in word-fear.

By following the broken arrows, it will be noted that S_{word} and $S_{sit.}$ now have exchanged places in terms of cue value, so that S_{word} becomes a stimulus to speak and $S_{sit.}$ becomes a stimulus to anxiety and avoidance. The resultant response, stuttering, gets reinforcement as before. This is the nature of the conflict in situation-fear.

It should be noted further that S_{word} by itself can evoke conflicting responses. Ordinarily a word is a stimulus to speak; but when word-fear is present, the same word can also be a stimulus to anxiety and avoidance. $S_{sit.}$, too, can in itself evoke conflicting responses. As every stutterer knows, a situation can demand speech but at the same time hold enough threat so that there is a competing drive to hold back from speaking. The resultant between the opposed urges to speak and not to speak is in each instance the response of stuttering, and in each instance it gets reinforcement.

Suppose we insert in this sequence, by means of an experimental set, a normal speaking of the word at a point between the stuttering and the termination of the sequence. Now the approach response, that of speaking the word normally, is strengthened, while the avoidant response is moved farther away from the point of reinforcement and is correspondingly weakened. We would predict from our formulation that such a technique would lead to more normal speech and less stuttering.

The general hypothesis of this study is that stuttering is reduced most rapidly under conditions which permit least reinforcement of the stuttering response.

Specific hypotheses may be stated as follows:

1. There will be greater decrements in the frequency of stuttering for the experimental than for the control conditions described: (1) *Control:* each subject reads the passage six times in his characteristic way; (2) *Experimental:* the subject reads the passage five consecutive times, repeating each stuttered word until he has said it once successfully, without stuttering, before he goes on to the next word and then reads it a sixth time as he normally would.

2. The difference between the experimental and control conditions will persist during a 30-minute interval.

3. The experimental treatment will reduce the "consistency effect," i.e,. the particular words stuttered on in the first reading will be stuttered on less during subsequent readings in the experimental or non-reinforcement condition than in the control condition.

METHOD

Subjects

The subjects (Ss) used were 20 adult stutterers ranging in age from 18 to 35. Thirteen were undergoing treatment in the Speech Clinic of the University of Iowa and three in the Speech Clinic of Western Michigan College, Kalamazoo. Four who were residents of Ann Arbor, Michigan, were not and had not been undergoing treatment. Six of the 20 subjects were females. In addition, five Ss were lost as cases for this study when the wire recorder broke down during their readings.

In accordance with Shulman's (12) criterion, subjects were eliminated from this study if they did not stutter on at least 2 per cent of the words on the first passage which they read. Since in a 200-word passage any normal speaker might easily bobble on three or four words, the 2 per cent criterion is fairly conservative. Stuttering cannot be studied except when it occurs, and this study was designed to investigate stuttering rather than "stutterers" as such. Four potential Ss were eliminated in this manner.

Table 1 Experimental Design

Subject no.	First day	Second day
1	Experimental "Iron"	Control "Heredity"
2	Control "Iron"	Experimental "Heredity"
3	Control "Heredity"	Experimental "Iron"
4	Experimental "Heredity"	Control "Iron"

Apparatus and Materials

Apparatus used consisted of a Silvertone wire recorder. Two comparable 200-word passages were selected from those available for experimental purposes at the University of Iowa Speech Clinic. Each passage was edited where necessary for length and difficulty of material. One passage described the history of the making of iron and will be referred to as the "Iron" passage; the other described views on heredity and will be referred to as the "Heredity" passage.

Experimental Design

Twenty stutterers participated. Each served as his own control. The order of passages, days, and experimental conditions within each block of four subjects followed the design shown in Table 1. There were five such blocks.

Thus 10 performed under experimental conditions on their first day and under control conditions on their second. For the other 10 the order was reversed. Each passage appeared equally often under the two conditions. Although the passages were approximately equivalent in length and difficulty, the design insures that variance arising from any differences between them was held to a minimum.

Experimental Procedure

The subject sat facing a wire recorder with the mike resting on a desk about two feet away. The experimenter (E) sat behind the desk, somewhat to the side of the subject, so that he observed S directly when necessary and still operated the recorder. In practice, E usually followed a printed copy of the passage before him and depended on auditory cues for judging moments of stuttering.

At the beginning of the instructions S was handed a copy of the passage, face down, and was asked not to turn it over until E nodded to him as a signal to begin. E then recorded S's code letters, testing the wire-recorder in the process. Next, E read the instructions, turned on the recorder, and nodded to S, who began reading.

As S read, E followed an identical copy of the passage, underlining each word on which observable stuttering occurred. In order to minimize the influence that judgments on one reading might have on the next, a separate copy was used by E for each of the seven readings. This had the additional advantage of reducing chances of error in the tabulation of results.

The seven readings may be summarized as follows: In both conditions the first five readings were consecutive with S returning immediately to the beginning of the passage after each reading. The experimental and control conditions differed only in the nature of the experimental set. There was in each instance an interval of 10 to 15 seconds between the fifth and sixth repetitions of the passage for the reading of instructions. Thirty minutes intervened between the sixth and seventh readings.

Instructions

Instructions for the experimental readings were as follows:

[*Before Readings 1–5.*] You are to read this passage aloud, five times in succession. I would like you to read for me at your normal rate, as well as you can, and in the way that is most natural for you at this time. When you stutter on a word, repeat the whole word until you can say it without stuttering. Do this before going on to the next word, but do not interrupt yourself in the middle of a block. That is, be sure to finish the word first before repeating it, and be sure to repeat it until you can say it without stuttering before going on to the next word. Do not "fake" any stuttering that would not otherwise occur. Read the passage through in the manner that is most natural for you, repeating every stuttered word until you have said it once normally. [*Pause*.]

For instance, if the sentence were, "Once upon a time there was a young rat named Arthur," and you stuttered on "once" and "time" it would be like this: "On-On-Once On-Once upon a ti-ti-ti-time ti-ti-ti-time ti-time time etc." [*E tests S to see whether he can carry out the instructions.*]

[*Before Reading 6.*] Now just read the passage as you ordinarily would, without the special instructions.

[*After Reading 6, S was told to return in 30 minutes for a short session, meanwhile to refrain from engaging in conversations and to spend the period studying.*]

[*Before Reading 7.*] Read the passage as you did the last time, without the special instructions.

Instructions for the control-reading were:

[*Before Readings 1–5.*] You are to read this passage aloud, five times in succession. I would like you to read for me at your normal rate, as well as you can, and in the way that is most natural for you at this time. Do not 'fake' any stuttering that would not otherwise occur. Just read the passage through in the manner that is most natural for you.

[*Before reading 6.*] Now read the passage once more just as you have been doing.

[*After Reading 6, subject is told to return in 30 minutes for a short session, meanwhile to refrain from engaging in conversations and to spend the period studying.*]

[*Before Reading 7.*] Read the passage as you did the last time.

Method of Tabulating Adaptation and Consistency Effects

The frequency of stuttering in each reading was tabulated by counting the number of underlined words on each copy of the passage. Seven sheets were used per S for each condition.

In tabulating the consistency effect, carbons were inserted between each of the pages for the seven readings. Since the first reading was to be used as a base, all words which had been stuttered on in the first reading were marked again, using a stylus, which marked these words on all remaining sheets. The second markings could be distinguished from the original judgments because they appeared in a different color and because a diagonal stroke was used.

For each reading, the number of words which had been marked twice was counted. The twice-marked words for any passage represented the particular words stuttered on in that reading which were also stuttered on originally in the first reading. The frequencies were then converted into percentages, using the frequency in the first reading as a base of 100. Thus 45 per cent on the fourth reading for the control condition would mean that, of the words stuttered in the first reading, 45 per cent had also been stuttered in the fourth reading.

Check on Observer Reliability and Experimenter Bias

To handle the problems of observer reliability and experimenter bias, each S was assigned code letters which were recorded along with his readings, e.g., "AFB," "BRL." Thus on the playback of the sixth and seventh readings, it was impossible for a listener to tell whether a control or experimental reading was being played.

Observer reliability was checked in this manner: During the playback of all the seventh readings, E made second judgments using fresh copies of the passages. A qualified speech correctionist, who acted as an observer, made independent judgments in the same manner.

Pearson product-moment correlations were calculated with these results: the r between the second judgments of E and the observer listening to the playback was $+.96$, while that between E's two sets of judgments was $+.93$. The highest obtained coefficient was $+.98$, that between the observer's judgments and E's original judgments. The latter represent first listenings for each. Table 2 summarizes these results. These correlations were sufficiently high so that E's original judgments could be used

Table 2 Observer Reliability Coefficients

Listener	Judgment	Correlation between judgments
Experimenter (original)	1st	
Experimenter (from playback)	2nd	r .93
		r .96 → r .98
Observer (from playback)	1st	

throughout without appreciable danger of influencing results through experimenter bias.

RESULTS

A comparison of the frequency of stuttering for all seven readings is presented in Figure 1.

The effect of the experimental variable is clearly in evidence in the first reading. By the third, the t for the difference between experimental

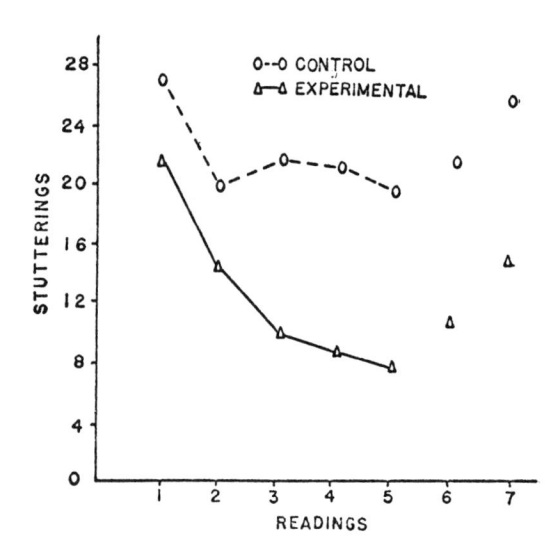

Fig. 1 Frequency of stuttering through successive readings in experimental condition and control condition. Differences between the two conditions for Readings 3 and 4 were significant at the 5 per cent level.

and control conditions is 2.44, which with 19 degrees of freedom is significant beyond the .05 level. Further statistical comparisons of the differences between experimental and control groups are summarized in Table 3.[1]

The hypothesis of no difference between the experimental and control conditions, which is the null form of the first specific hypothesis given above, may be rejected at the .05 level. This finding is in accord with our prediction, viz., that substituting an attempt at normal speech for the stuttering response at the point of reinforcement would lead to a greater decrement of stuttering in the experimental condition.

From Tables 4 and 5 it can be seen that stuttering decreased significantly with successive readings for both experimental and control treatments. Differences between Readings 1–3 and 1–5 were significant beyond the .01 level. It may be noted that these t-values are higher even though the actual differences are smaller than those between experimental and control treatments for the same readings. This result is a function of the comparatively high σ_D's in Table 3 and the comparatively low σ_D's in Tables 4 and 5. This, in turn, is a function of higher correlation between readings of the same material on the same day than between readings of different material on different days.

The difference between experimental and control Ss on the first reading is not statistically significant ($P < .20$). For those who raise the possibility that with a greater N it might have been significant, the following interpretation is offered. An attempt was made to demonstrate the possible operation of the experimental set within the first reading.

Table 3 Significance Levels of Differences in Frequency of Stuttering between Experimental and Control Conditions

	Reading						
	1	2	3	4	5	6	7
M_C*	26.70	19.90	21.65	21.15	19.60	21.25	25.50
M_E*	21.70	14.40	10.10	8.85	7.95	10.40	14.65
D_M	5.00	5.50	11.55	12.30	11.65	10.85	10.85
σ_D	3.893	4.276	4.729	5.849	5.990	6.135	5.850
t	1.28	1.29	2.44	2.10	1.95	1.78	1.85
P†	.20	.20	.05	.05	.10	.10	.10

* M_C and M_E refer to means for control and for experimental readings.
† Degrees of freedom = 19.

[1] The t's in this table were obtained by setting up a distribution of differences and applying McNemar's formula 92(19) for small samples involving means based on the same individuals.

450   The Speech Handicapped

Table 4 *Significance Levels of Differences between Readings within the Control Condition*

	Readings 1–3	Readings 1–5	Readings 1–7	Readings 7–5
M	26.70 21.65	26.70 19.60	26.70 25.50	25.50 19.60
D_M	5.05	7.10	1.20	5.90
σ_D	1.717	1.410	1.170	1.010
t	2.94	4.85	1.02	5.84
P*	.01	.01	.30	.01

* Degrees of freedom = 19.

The first reading for each condition was divided into four 50-word quadrants. The frequencies were tallied in each quadrant, and the results seem to show a faster drop *within* the passage for the experimental than for the control data. This difference, which may be seen in Figure 2, was not, however, statistically significant.

It should be noted that there was no control of the relative difficulty of different quadrants, an effect only partly alleviated by summing data from two different passages. It seems reasonable, however, that if there is a differential drop in Figure 2, it is largely a function of the operation of the experimental set, and that the small differences in the first quadrant might also be attributed to this condition.

The second specific hypothesis concerned persistence of effect. An estimation of the relative persistence of the effect of the experimental and control conditions may be had by reference to the initial and final levels of stuttering for each group. The reduction in stutterings between the first and seventh readings in the experimental group was significant be-

Table 5 *Significance Levels of Differences between Readings within the Experimental Condition*

	Readings 1–3	Readings 1–5	Readings 1–7	Readings 7–5
M	21.70 10.10	21.70 7.95	21.70 14.65	14.65 7.95
D_M	11.60	13.75	7.05	6.70
σ_D	2.170	2.479	1.630	2.498
t	5.35	5.555	4.11	2.68
P*	.01	.01	.01	.02

* Degrees of freedom = 19.

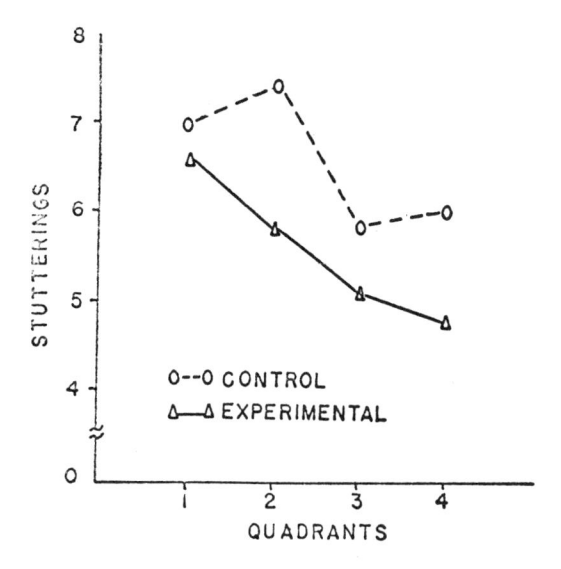

Fig. 2 Intra-passage decrements for the first reading. Numbers 1, 2, 3, 4 refer to successive 50-word quadrants. The faster drop in the experimental group is interpreted as being due to the operation of the experimental set within the first reading.

yond the .01 level ($t = 4.11$), while the corresponding difference for the control group was not statistically significant ($t = 1.02$). The difference between the two conditions on the seventh reading was significant beyond the 10 per cent level. That these differences could occur, despite the fact that the experimental set was operating within the first reading and so reduced the mean difference between the first and last readings, strongly suggests the decrement in stuttering under the nonreinforcement (experimental) set has relatively persistent effects. Extinction of the stuttering response under the experimental set, in other words, was not only faster but more lasting in its effects.

The third specific hypothesis referred to the differences in consistency between experimental and control treatments when words stuttered upon during the first reading were used as a base. These results are presented graphically in Figure 3.

An extremely large number of cases would be required to demonstrate the statistical significance of a difference between one pair of obtained percentages. However, since the design of the experiment virtually rules out any consistent difference between experimental and control data other than the operation of the experimental set, persistence of a differ-

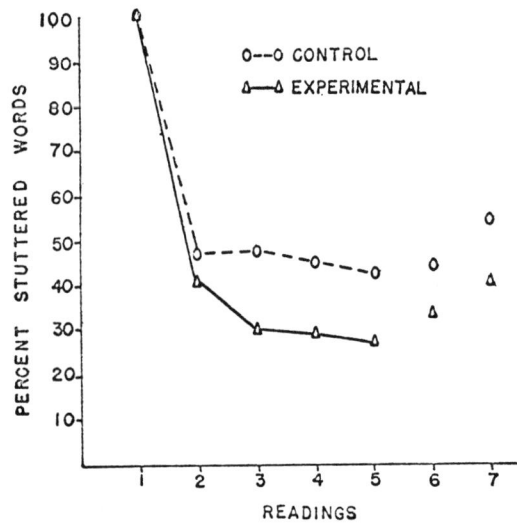

Fig. 3 *Differences in consistency between the two conditions. Each point of reading 2 through 7 represents the percentage of stuttering words in the first reading also stuttered on in that reading. Significant at 2 per cent level.*

ence can become a criterion of significance. If the difference between the points on the two curves in Figure 3 were attributable to chance alone, we would expect the percentage for the experimental condition to be lower in all six tests after the first, only once in 64 times. Thus the null form of the third hypothesis can be rejected beyond the 2 per cent level of confidence.

It should be noted that since spontaneous recovery was tested under control conditions for the experimental group, the experimental effect had to compete against the S's established cues in a straight reading situation. A greater difference would be demonstrated if recovery were tested under experimental conditions.

DISCUSSION

Stuttering has sometimes been described as a hodgepodge, a maze of contradictory behavior, unpredictable by its very nature. In terms of general theoretical significance, the finding that stuttering behavior can be modified in accordance with principles of learning supports the thesis that it is not qualitatively different from adaptive behavior, that no different laws of behavior are involved.

It is obvious from the results that the experimental technique employed leads to a reduction in stuttering behavior. Not only did the experimental condition show a greater decrease in total stuttering through successive readings, but a greater reduction of stuttering on the particular words stuttered on in the initial reading. In addition, the reduction in stuttering was more lasting in the experimental condition.

Of other possible interpretations, certain ones are excluded by the nature of the design. The idea that distraction was really the agent responsible for the improvement is excluded by the nature of the results.

Two positive interpretations have already been developed in the statement of the problem. First, less stuttering and more normal speech appeared in the experimental condition because the non-reinforcement technique made the normal speech attempt rather than the stuttering response the instrumental act leading to reinforcement. Second, the experimental technique was effective because it substituted the approach response of speaking for the avoidance response of holding back at the point of reinforcement. It thus reduced the source of conflict for the stutterer and made it easier for him to "go ahead and speak."

The interpretation of stuttering as conflict behavior may be developed more fully at this point. Johnson has described stuttering as an avoidance reaction, a view which is fairly logical since it is a response to painful stimulation. Normal speech, of course, involves approach behavior in that the speaker "approaches" or attacks directly the word which he is to say. Stuttering is manifested by a fear of or an avoidance of the act of speaking. The stutterer is in a conflict situation because he has a tendency to approach the word, i.e., he needs to say it, but he has a competing tendency to avoid the word because of fear that he may stutter on it. Stuttering can in this fashion be looked upon as approach-avoidance conflict, the resultant of the opposing urges to speak the word and to hold back from speaking it. We know from Miller's (10) investigations that since the avoidance gradient is steeper than the approach gradient, an organism put into an approach-avoidance conflict situation characteristically *approaches part way and then stops.* This is exactly what the stutterer does on a word; he goes part way and then stops and goes back—he say "K-K-K-Katy."

If the foregoing formulation may be regarded as essentially correct, then we can more fully interpret the function of our experimental variable. The approach response, that of a direct normal speech attempt on a word, is reinforced, but the avoidance response, that of stuttering or holding back, is not. The experimental set forces the stutterer to attack a feared word until he has "conquered" it; in other words the approach tendency is so strengthened and the avoidance tendency so weakened that he no longer stops part way through the word. He can, therefore, say it fluently, is rewarded for doing this, and is able to read the passage next time with significantly fewer stutterings. The formulation is entirely consonant with the "instrumental act" interpretation and would involve identical predictions, since modification of reinforcement is the essential feature of each.

It should be emphasized that the important contribution of this study is not the specific technique which is involved—although this has been shown to have definite possibilities—but the finding that stuttering can be systematically reduced through modification of the conditions which ordinarily lead to its continued reinforcement. Further modification of techniques in speech correction in accordance with predictions of learning theory now appears feasible.

From the standpoint of planning stuttering therapy, it appears from this study that the point of reinforcement of the stuttering response should become a foremost area for attack on the problem. Instead of contenting himself with speech drills or distraction rituals, which by their nature give only temporary fluency, the progressive therapist of the future can put at the stutterer's disposal techniques which will prevent further reinforcement of the stuttering response and lead to improvement on a more permanent basis.

Other techniques which would seem to hold potentialities in terms of nonreinforcement may be mentioned: (1) Use of a smooth prolongation or "slide" at the point of reinforcement. (2) Use of a "bounce" provided it is carried beyond the moment of release. The author does not feel that a "bounce," or voluntary repetition, is helpful when it simply becomes a device for helping the stutterer say the word. (3) Any system which encourages the stutterer to attack feared words and situations and which decreases avoidance tendencies should be effective, since it would reduce conflict behavior.

While, in terms of preventing reinforcement of the stuttering response, the experimental set used here is only one possibility, the relative simplicity of this technique and its demonstrated value recommend it as a valuable clinical tool.

It should be emphasized that non-reinforcement involves direct work on the stuttering block itself. It involves a direct attack by the stutterer on his problem and on his fears. The non-reinforcement technique should never be confused with distraction devices which encourage the stutterer's avoidance tendencies and depend upon the necessarily temporary effects of disinhibition for their usefulness. That the results of this study could not possibly be due to distraction is shown by the fact that successive trials are necessary in order that the non-reinforcement take effect. Distractors or disinhibitors, on the other hand, would produce their greatest effect initially.

As a therapeutic technique in stuttering, non-reinforcement must be fitted into a certain context without which its proper role in treatment cannot be understood. Probably the most suitable context would involve a general program of training in non-avoidance and a direct attack on the stuttering block, within a general program of personality readjustment.

No implication should be drawn from the foregoing discussion of the applicability of non-reinforcement to the treatment of stuttering, that psychotherapy should be slighted, nor that individual personality factors should be ignored, nor that all cases should be treated in the same way. The application is to only one phase, but a very crucial phase, of stuttering treatment. Nearly all therapists working extensively with stutterers find it necessary at some stage in treatment to work on the symptoms themselves, namely, on that part of the disorder which presents itself as a self-perpetuating habit. In this aspect of stuttering treatment, non-reinforcement would appear to be far superior to techniques currently used. In short, to those who treat stutterers and find it necessary to work on the habit—here is a more effective means for doing it.

The particular non-reinforcement technique employed in this experiment was chosen for several reasons:

1. It involved a clear-cut case of substituting a normal speech attempt for the stuttering response as the instrumental act leading to reinforcement.

2. It could be carried out without difficulty by naive subjects; thus, if it demonstrated therapeutic possibilities, it would be available to outpatients, children, and others unable to undergo intensive treatment.

3. It involved a specific test of the effect of the much-maligned parental technique of telling the child to "stop and say it over."

For years we have been telling parents that it was wrong to stop Johnny and have him repeat the word. We have always thought this undesirable, because it meant calling attention to the stuttering and aggravating it by putting a penalty on it (16); and, indeed, studies of such practice have tended to conclude that it makes the victim worse (3). Yet in apparent contradiction to this, we occasionally see people who relate that at one time they stuttered, but their parents broke them of the habit by making them "say it over until they got it right." In such cases it has always been easier to account for stuttering than for its disappearance. The present results suggest a possible clear explanation as well as a testable hypothesis. Those children who continued to stutter were those who *did not follow out the instructions* but simply experienced them as a penalty; while those who "outgrew" or "overcame" stuttering were those who altered their stuttering behavior, however uninsightfully, in accordance with the extinction principle demonstrated in this study.

SUMMARY

Stuttering persists even though it is more punishing than rewarding in the long run, because under ordinary conditions the stuttering response is continually reinforced. The assumption was made that the point at which the stutterer is able to go on to the next word is the point of reinforcement, and that stuttering is the instrumental act receiving reinforcement.

This experiment was designed under the general hypothesis that stuttering is reduced most rapidly under conditions which permit least reinforcement of the stuttering response and most reinforcement of the normal speech attempt.

Twenty adult stutterers read two 200-word passages on two different days and acted as their own controls. Under the control condition each S read the passage six times in his characteristic way. Under the experimental (non-reinforcement) condition S read the passage five consecutive times, repeating each stuttered word until he had said it once without stuttering before he went on to the next word, and then read it a sixth time as he ordinarily would. Under both conditions, a seventh reading followed a 30-minute rest interval.

The experimental set did not permit termination of the sequence until a normal speech attempt had been made. Since in this case stuttering as an instrumental act for producing the word is farther removed from the point of reinforcement than the normal speech attempt, we have produced non-reinforcement of the stuttering behavior.

The specific hypotheses being tested were supported by these findings:

1. Stuttering was found to decrease more rapidly through successive readings in the non-reinforcement condition.

2. The experimental set resulted in a more rapid decrease in stuttering on the particular words subjected to the non-reinforcement treatment.

3. The greater reduction in stuttering behavior under nonreinforcement conditions was more lasting over a 30-minute rest interval.

The non-reinforcement technique was held to be more effective in reducing total stuttering behavior because it substituted the normal speaking of the word for the stuttering response at the point of reinforcement. The approach response of speaking was thereby strengthened while the avoidant response of stuttering was correspondingly weakened. As was predicted, the experimental set led to more normal speech and less stuttering.

The finding that stuttering can be modified in accordance with principles of learning supports the thesis that it is not qualitatively different from adjustive processes and that it involves the same laws of behavior.

The modification of stuttering through non-reinforcement should become an area of first importance in therapeutic attacks on the problem. The experimental set employed here commends itself to the clinician, not only because of its simplicity but because of its demonstrated effectiveness in the systematic elimination of stuttering behavior.

References

1. Bloodstein, O. A study of the conditions under which stuttering is reduced or absent. Unpublished Doctor's dissertation, Univ. of Iowa, 1948.
2. Bluemel, C. S. *Stammering and allied disorders.* New York: Macmillan, 1935.
3. Davis, Dorothy M. The relation of repetitions in the speech of young children to certain measures of language maturity and situational factors. Parts II and III. *J. Speech Disorders,* 1940, 5, 235–246.
4. Dunlap, K. *Habits: Their making and unmaking.* New York: Liveright, 1932.
5. Harris, H. E. Studies in the psychology of stuttering: XVII. A study of the transfer of the adaptation effect in stuttering. *J. Speech Disorders,* 1942, 7, 209–221.
6. Hill, H. An interbehavioral analysis of several aspects of stuttering. *J. gen. Psychol.,* 1945, 32, 289–316.
7. Johnson, W., et al. A study of the onset and development of stuttering. *J. Speech Disorders,* 1942, 7, 251–257.
8. Johnson, W. *People in quandaries.* New York: Harper, 1946.
9. McNemar, Q. *Psychological statistics.* New York: Wiley, 1949.
10. Miller, N. E. Experimental studies of conflict. In Hunt, J. McV. (Ed.), *Personality and the behavior disorders.* New York: Ronald Press, 1944. Vol. I, pp. 431–465.
11. Russell, G. O. Neuro-pedogogical process of treating stammerers and stutterers at Ohio State University. In West, Robert (Ed.), *A symposium on stuttering.* Madison, Wis.: College Typing Co., 1931.
12. Shulman, E. A study of certain factors influencing the variability of stuttering. Unpublished Doctor's dissertation, State Univ. of Iowa, 1944.
13. Stoddard, Clara B. The correction of stammering in Detroit. In West, Robert (Ed.), *A symposium on stuttering.* Madison, Wis.: College Typing Co., 1931.
14. Van Riper, C. The effect of penalty upon frequency of stuttering. *J. genet. Psychol.,* 1937, 50, 193–195.
15. Van Riper, C. The growth of the stuttering spasm. *Quart. J. Speech,* 1937, 23, 70–73.
16. Van Riper, C. *Speech correction: Principles and methods.* (Rev. Ed.) New York: Prentice-Hall, 1947.
17. Wischner, G. J. Stuttering and learning: A program of research. Unpublished Doctor's dissertation, Univ. of Iowa, 1947.

Part II: A New Venture into the Nonreinforcement of Stuttering

PROBLEM

Although the burgeoning literature on behavior modification is replete with accounts of the effect of reinforcement and nonreinforcement procedures, follow-up data are seldom offered. What happens when the experiment is complete and the reinforcement technique is removed? New data (Biggs and Sheehan, 1969) recently gathered under the same design and procedure employed in our original study (Sheehan, 1951) throw new light on these questions.

We were intrigued by the appearance of the control curve (Figure 1 of the nonreinforcement study just reported). It seemed to show unusual resistance to extinction and provided less rapid drop than control curves typically found in studies involving the adaptation effect (Johnson and Knott, 1937; Van Riper and Hull, 1955; Sheehan and Voas, 1957).

We started out with a reanalysis of data from the original study (Sheehan, 1951). Controls who had run first under the control condition were compared with the controls who had reversed this sequence. They were shown to differ markedly. The E-First Controls did not do nearly so well as did the C-First Controls. Their adaptation was dramatically slower.

Why should this be? Was it just an ad hoc result, or was an important unanticipated order effect happening here? Would the effect hold on a new sample run under the same design and procedure?

To answer this question, we undertook what might be termed a minireplication: a new study utilizing a smaller number of subjects than the original study, but which still serves to rule out the possibility of an ad hoc result.

METHOD

Subjects
The subjects (S's) were eight college age adult stutterers attending the speech clinic at UCLA. Two of the eight were females. Subjects were eliminated from the study if they did not stutter on at least 2 percent of the words in the first passage they read. As it happened, the first eight run were usable, so no S's were eliminated by this criterion.

Apparatus and Materials
Apparatus consisted of a Revere tape recorder. Two comparable 200-word passages used in previous experimentation (Sheehan, 1951) were employed. One passage described the history of the making of iron and will be referred to as the "Iron" passage; the other described views on heredity and will be referred to as the "Heredity" passage.

Experimental Design
Utilizing the same design as in the original non-reinforcement study, two new blocks of subjects were run, four in each block. This provided data on four new E-First Controls which could be compared to four new C-First Controls. Data from these new subjects were analyzed separately and in combination with the data from the original study. Thus, four performed under experimental conditions their first day and under control conditions their second day. This group is called the E-First Controls. The other four performed under control conditions the first day and under experimental conditions their second day. These are called the C-First Controls. Each passage appeared equally often under the two conditions. The experimental design in Table 1 is presented to clarify the differences between the E-First Controls and the C-First Controls (see Table 1, p. 444).

Experimental Procedure
The procedure was identical to that of the previous experiment in which the experimenter followed a printed copy of the passage while the subject read the passage. Other procedure details were also identical.

Instructions
As detailed in the original nonreinforcement study (Sheehan, 1951), the experimental condition consisted of repeating the whole word stuttered

until it could be spoken once to a criterion of fluency. The control condition consisted of repeated reading of a comparable passage without the specific instruction to repeat. Readings Six and Seven under both conditions were normal readings with no special instructions. Methods of tabulating data were as in the original study.

RESULTS

As a main result, the new data yielded comparison of the experimental and control conditions, with curves strikingly similar to those of the original study. This result may be seen in Figure 1, based upon the eight new subjects only, and in Figure 2, combining all twenty-eight subjects from the two studies.

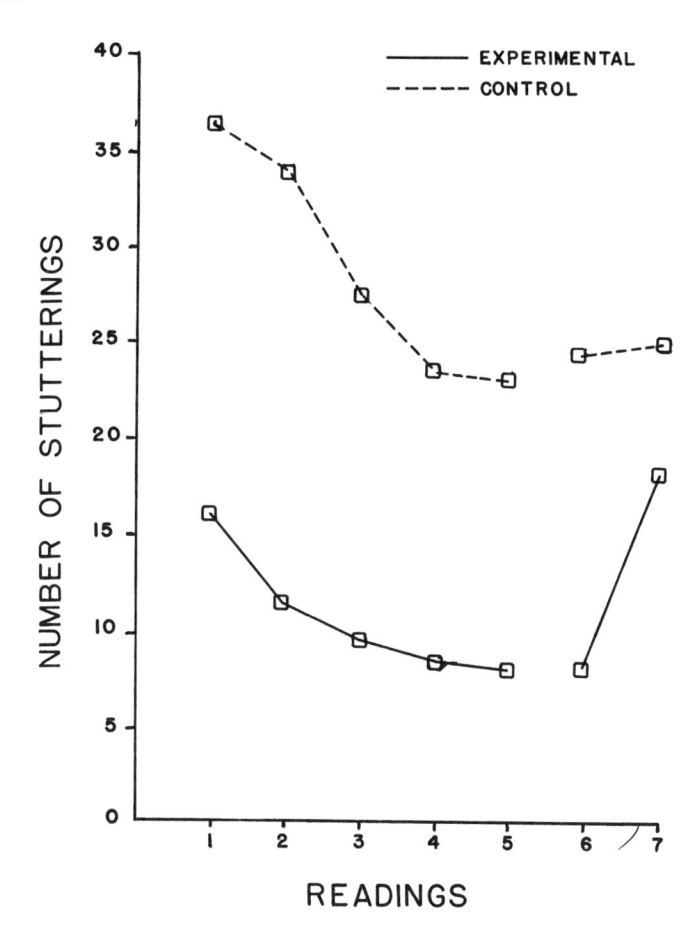

Fig. 1 Frequency of stuttering through successive readings under experimental and control conditions (new sample only: N = 8).

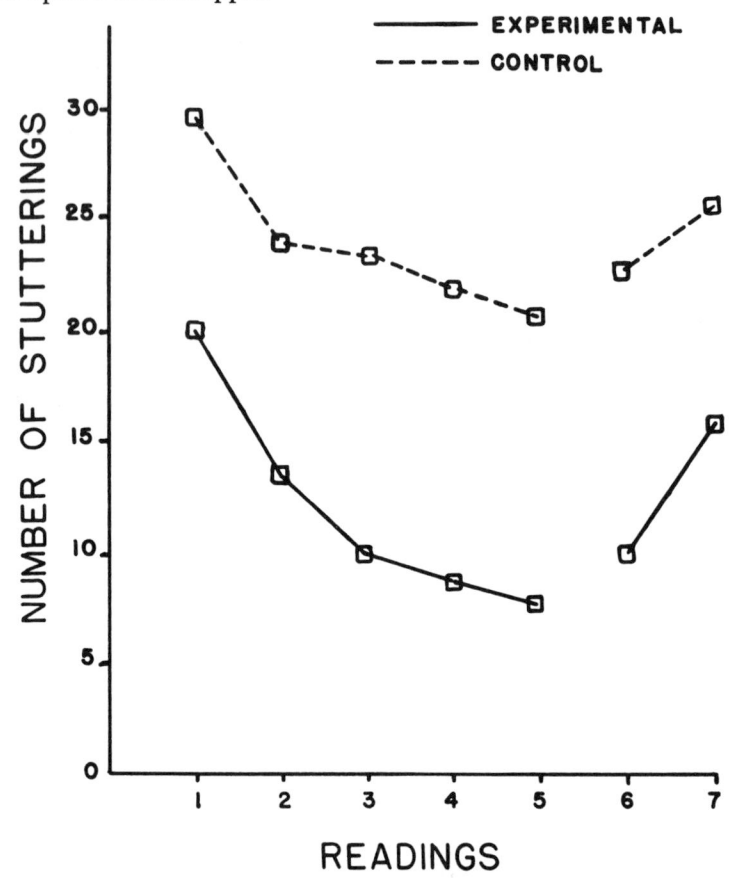

Fig. 2 Frequency of stuttering through successive readings under experimental and control conditions (combined sample: N = 28).

The comparison of E-First Controls with C-First Controls provided most dramatic results of our mini-replication. It is shown in Figure 3. Those who had used the non-reinforcement technique of repeating the word over and over until they could speak it fluently seemed to benefit from this method as long as they were under the experimental set. However, once they were deprived of this previously helpful set through reverting to control instructions, they did dramatically worse. In fact, they showed a greater frequency of stuttering than those who had never performed under the experimental set.

Possibly one reason for the sometimes discouraging results of stuttering therapy is that techniques or new instructional sets are effective only as long as the set is operating. Once the set is relinquished, stuttering

△----△ E–FIRST CONTROL
○----○ C–FIRST CONTROL

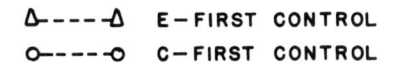

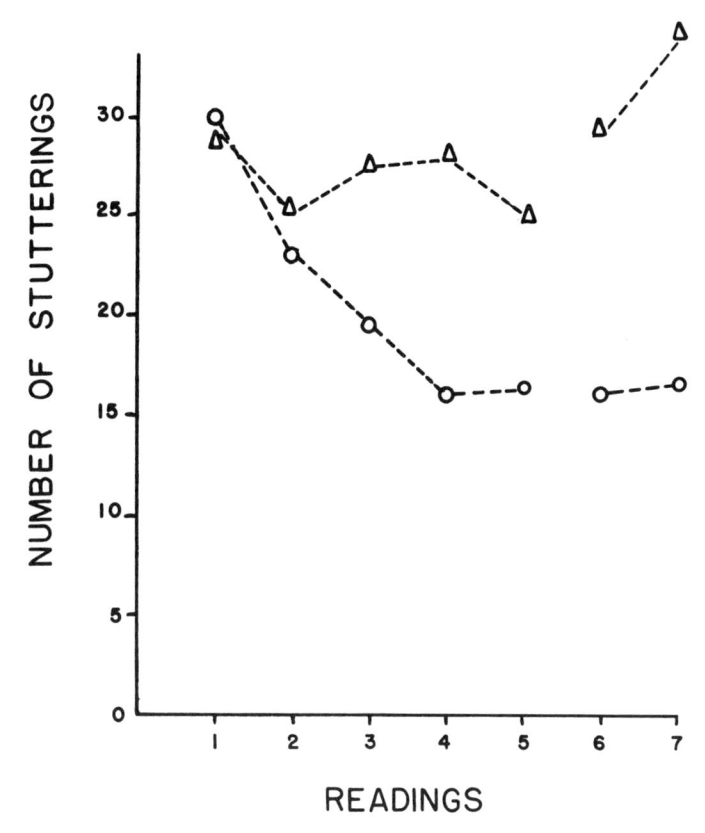

Fig. 3 Frequency of stuttering for control readings which had been preceded by experimental readings compared with those which had not (combined sample: $N = 28$). Similar curves were obtained separately for the original and for the new samples.

which has previously been suppressed by means of the technique rises again above the surface.

Figure 4 portrays an analogous comparison for the Experimental condition. The finding just reported for the Control condition finds no parallel with the Experimental condition, as the similarity of the curves in Figure 4 clearly shows. When the stutterer repeats each stuttered word until he has said it once fluently, he achieves a faster reduction of stuttering frequency. Previous servitude under the Control condition does not change performance under the Experimental set.

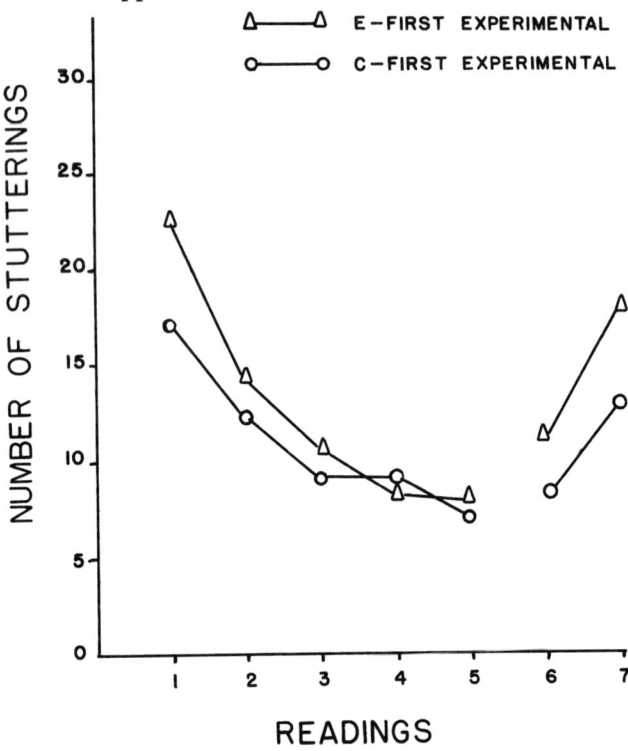

Fig. 4 *Frequency of stuttering for experimental readings which had been preceded by control readings compared with those who had not (combined sample: N = 28). Similar curves were obtained separately for the original and for the new samples.*

A comparison of frequencies of stuttering on the First Day with those on the Second Day revealed no significant differences.

Perhaps asking a stutterer to repeat the stuttered word until he has spoken it once fluently involves a kind of behavioral suppression that leads to future trouble. Possibly there is a recovery from the reactive inhibition due to massed adaptation trials on single words. In any case, what are the implications of this finding on the behavioral modification of stuttering or, for that matter, for other disorders?

Perhaps the path toward response suppression leads but to the experience of grave later consequences. Perhaps there is an artificiality in some "reinforcement" techniques that is inconsistent with the ongoing conceptions of the self. Perhaps we have here a false-role enactment which pays the price of later difficulty. Such effects are easily identifiable in experiment based upon distraction or novelty; but we carefully considered and attempted to rule out these elements. Indeed, there is still some evidence of the lastingness of the improvement under the Experimental condition, as readings Six and Seven in Figures 1 and 2 demonstrate.

We are still of the view that stuttering may be modified by reinforcement principles and reduced by systematic non-reinforcement. What our new data do show, however, is that we still have much to learn about the ultimate effects of behavior modification, however impressive the curves when only the conveniently proximate data are accorded diplomatic recognition.

We would still counsel against the procedure of having Johnny "say it over and say it right," not only because it may serve as a penalty, but because the ultimate effects may be the opposite of those immediately obtained. Perhaps all behavior therapies involve some possibility of some immediate "dramatic improvement" at the cost of ultimate exacerbation of the problem. In particular, what happens to the child or adult when he is no longer under special instructions? This is one of the great questions which remains unanswered—though not unanswerable.

References

Biggs, B. E., and Sheehan, J. G. Punishment or distraction? Operant stuttering revisited. *J. abnorm. Psychol.,* 1969, *74,* 256–262.

Johnson, W., and Knott, J. R. Studies in the psychology of stuttering. I. The distribution of moments of stuttering in successive readings of the same material. *J. speech dis.,* 1937, *2,* 17–19.

Sheehan, J. G. The modification of stuttering through nonreinforcement. *J. abnorm. soc. Psychol.,* 1951, *46,* 51–63.

Sheehan, J. G., & Voas, R. B. Stuttering as conflict: I. Comparison of therapy techniques involving approach and avoidance. *J. speech Dis.,* 1957, *22,* 714–723.

Van Riper, C., & Hull, C. J. The quantitative measurement of the effect of certain situations on stuttering. In Johnson, W., and Leutenegger, R. R. (Eds.), *Stuttering in Children and Adults.* Minneapolis: University of Minnesota Press, 1955.

*Brain-Damaged and
Physically Handicapped Persons
and Learning Disabilities*

22

The Problems and Promises of Psychological Research in Rehabilitation

Franklin C. Shontz

> *Dr. Shontz is Professor of Psychology at the University of Kansas and Director of Program in Somatopsychology-Rehabilitation. A most productive scholar, Dr. Shontz has written three books, contributed to several others, and has published research studies in sixteen different journals.*
>
> *Through the years Dr. Shontz has maintained strong interest and active research in the area of rehabilitation. In this article, prepared especially for this book, Dr. Shontz explores extensively the many facets and problems involved in research in this area. It is an indispensable article for all students concerned with research in rehabilitation.*

In 1958 a group of distinguished psychologists met in Princeton, New Jersey, to discuss the role of psychology in rehabilitation. The report of their meeting (Wright, 1959) notes that expressions of the need for research, more research, and better research arose in every discussion of every aspect of the rehabilitation process. Awareness of the need for research was consistently coupled with the belief that research in rehabilitation not only produces information about the disabled but also contributes to basic psychological knowledge and theory. Members of the group that met at Princeton went on record to recommend the organization of a subsequent conference, devoted solely to the discussion of the matter of research.

The recommended conference was held in November 1960 at Miami Beach, Florida. It included representatives from the field of rehabilitation and a group of psychologists who were not identified with the field of rehabilitation but who had gained prominence because of their theoretical and empirical contributions to the study of perception, cognition, learning, individual differences, personality, and social psychology. The report of this conference (Lofquist, 1960) reflects the consistency with which participants found that the field of rehabilitation raises new theoretical problems and provides facilities for testing hypotheses that cannot be critically evaluated in any other setting. Indeed, the conference might be well summarized as a concrete demonstration of the correctness of the belief of those who participated in the 1958 gathering that the scope of rehabilitation is broad enough to encompass sound research on any subject of psychological interest.

Since research in rehabilitation can cover virtually all the subject matter of psychology, it is not easy to point to specific features of rehabilitation research that make it either especially difficult or especially inviting for students of human behavior. However, rehabilitation agencies do have certain characteristics that pose challenges for scientist and therapist alike. In the following sections, some of these characteristics are examined as sources of both the problems and the promises of rehabilitation research.

VALUES IN REHABILITATION RESEARCH

Perhaps the most universal feature of rehabilitation research is that every investigation that claims relevance for rehabilitation derives from and reflects an implicit or explicit set of value judgments about people and what is good for them. Whatever else rehabilitation may be, it is always identified with attempts to make clients better in some ways than they were before.

The laboratory scientist may feel that he operates outside the realm of personal values. His scientific duty, as he sees it, is to test hypotheses, to examine his data objectively, and to serve as an unbiased reporter of the relationships revealed by nature in his experiments. Of course, no scientist is totally immune to values. Even the decision to test one hypothesis instead of another implies a value judgment. What the laboratory scientist means when he says that he eliminates value judgments from his work is that he does everything he can to prevent anyone's personal wishes about the outcome of research from influencing the events he observes and the conclusions he draws. That is exactly why such a scientist chooses to work in a laboratory. There he can control conditions so thoroughly and effectively that personal bias, prejudice, and other uncontrolled factors can be virtually eliminated. It is almost impossible to eliminate such factors from a rehabilitation setting, and for this reason the laboratory scientist often feels that rehabilitation agencies are not very promising places in which to work.

In the 1960 Miami conference on psychological research in rehabilitation, the laboratory approach to research was recognized as a legitimate expression of interest in "science for its own sake." But conference participants felt that the laboratory scientist too often disregards the standpoints of other parties directly involved in his research. For example, he rarely takes the trouble to consider the possible practical implications of his findings. Consequently, much of the potential usefulnes of research conducted in the laboratory is lost to rehabilitation workers who have a vital interest in it, and separation, if not actual conflict, of interests develops between rehabilitation worker and scientific investigator.

Value Conflicts

The investigator who decides to conduct research in a rehabilitation setting often faces frankly contradictory alternatives. Consider the problems of research in a typical agency for children with disabilities. No investigator will find it easy to enter such a setting and announce that he is going to conduct research on, say, the body image of children with disabilities. The staff will doubtless be willing to concede the general merits of the proposed project. But they will surely have several searching questions to ask about the proposal. They value the time they spend in therapeutic activities and will want to know how great the demands on them will be for tasks such as data collection or rating of patients. They will also want to know how much client time is involved (i.e., how much regular therapy or classroom time their clients will miss) because they feel that time spent by clients in research is time lost to the more vital activity: progressing through the rehabilitation program. If the investigator proposes a new form of therapy, the staff will almost certainly be distressed by the prospect that the research will have to include a nontreated control group. They will feel that it is unjust to withhold a possibly beneficial treatment from children who need it. At the same time they will wonder where room for the new therapy is to be found in treatment schedules that are already overloaded. Further, if the research employs procedures that result in evaluations of the effectiveness of existing treatment methods, they may feel threatened by the presence of an outsider who might criticize their work.

Often, the investigator finds himself on the horns of a dilemma. He has a project he does not wish to give up, but he is blocked in his efforts by established values and practices of the agency that make proper execution of the project impossible. If he does not fit his procedures into the ongoing activities of the agency, he cannot conduct his research.

Should he accede to agency demands, he must sacrifice the controls he needs for his research to lead to a clearcut result.

In such situations, the only solution possible is compromise. The staff of the agency agrees to make some necessary sacrifices so that the research may proceed.

For his part, the investigator softens some of his demands for time, labor, facilities, and control groups. Somehow, the data are collected and the research is completed.

There are no hard and fast rules by which value problems can be solved. Each case of conflict between investigator and agency must be resolved in terms of the specific problems it raises. But the general question of values cannot be ignored in rehabilitation research; all participants must be prepared at the outset to deal with such problems and solve them as best they can.

THE ASSUMPTION OF INCOMPATIBILITY

An implicit belief underlies most of the value conflicts encountered in rehabilitation research. Simply stated, it is the belief that the conduct of research and the proper provision of services to clients make incompatible demands on agency resources.

In the final analysis, specific problems of the sort described in the preceding section can usually be traced to acceptance of this assumption. Scientific investigator and rehabilitation worker alike seem to take it for granted that there is something inherent in the research process which requires that the effectiveness of rehabilitation activities be reduced. No one can deny that some forms of research do require significant alteration of agency routines and may effect temporary reductions in service efficiency. However, there is nothing in the nature of research, per se, to demand that such be the case.

If a sound basis can be found for discarding the assumption of incompatibility, most of the problems of research in rehabilitation will disappear along with it. Therefore, the task of the balance of this discussion is to show that the problems of rehabilitation research can be overcome and that practical models exist which can successfully solve the problem of integrating research and service in mutually beneficial ways. Before presenting these models, it is helpful to examine the types of research that are commonly undertaken in rehabilitation settings.

TYPES OF RESEARCH IN REHABILITATION

It is useful to think of research in rehabilitation as representing two methodological types, the *informational* and the *criterion-oriented*. The types differ in the way each approaches the problems of research design and data evaluation. Although a single study often incorporates features of both types, these can usually be distinguished by procedural criteria. One has only to examine what the investigator did to determine which approach he used at any stage of his work.

Informational Research

The fundamental question asked by an informational research is: What traits or characteristics are exhibited by the behavior of a specific group of people? An investigator may wish to answer this question for theoretical reasons, or his intentions may be to provide solutions to purely practical problems. An example of informational research conducted mainly for theoretical purposes is Davis's (1963) intensive longitudinal study of the social-psychological impact of serious illness (spinal paralytic poliomyelitis) on fourteen children and their families. The purpose of this study was to discover how family units handle the crisis that occurs when one of their members (specifically, one of the children) becomes dangerously ill. The study sought information about the process of adaptation, because very little is yet know about this process, and it is highly desirable to learn as much as possible about it in a fairly systematic, yet comprehensive and reasonably objective way. The data from such a study provide a foundation upon which theories of reactions to crisis may be built.

Another example of an informational research, conducted for theoretical purposes, is the study by Wright and Shontz (1968) of the hopes and wishes of parents for their children with disabilities. This research used structured interviews and rating scales to study parents' feelings about the futures of their children, as well as the aspirations of the children themselves. The purpose of the study was to provide data from which a theory of the structure and function of hopes in the lives of persons who have experienced misfortune or value loss could be constructed.

Informational research conducted for applied purposes usually consists of studies which determine the sheer frequency of occurrence of particular problems in a certain population. Often, such studies have strictly local relevance, as, for example, when the director of an agency for the physically disabled asks for a determination of the incidence of personality disturbance among his clients so that he can decide whether to add psychiatric consultation to the services already available in his agency.

Since it is purely descriptive, informational research contains no explicit standard by which data are evaluated. As suggested by the examples cited above, the tools of pure informational research are the survey, the case study, and naturalistic observation. Such research is often called *exploratory* or *inductive;* these terms convey its essential characteristics reasonably accurately.

Criterion-oriented Research

Criterion-oriented research is designed at the outset to evaluate the validity of a specific proposition or to answer a specific question, preferably with a single word, "yes" or "no." To be effective, such research must ask its question in a form that can be answered by the data; it must contain data that are clearly relevant to the question asked; and it must specify the outcomes that lead automatically, as it were, to an answer to the question posed by the investigator.

In some instances it is obvious that a criterion-oriented research has exclusively theoretical implications, as, for example, when an investigator studies how children with disabilities perceive leg length and angle of adduction (Wight and Moed, 1963). In other instances, criterion-oriented research is conducted exclusively for practical purposes. In the so-called actuarial approach (Meehl, 1954; Shontz, 1965, Chap. 5), the purpose of research is solely to improve the prediction of behavior, and no attempt is made to understand or explain the relationship between predictor and outcome.

An example of a criterion-oriented research which combines theoretical and practical purposes is Holden's study (1962) of the effect of summer-camp experience on the body images of children with physical disabilities. Holden obtained drawings of the human figure from two groups of children with physical disabilities. One group attended a two-week summer day camp; the other attended a two-week residential camp. A comparison group was made up of children without disabilities, tested over a two-week period during the regular school year. Additional comparison data were obtained from one of the groups of children with disabilities by asking them to draw the human figure two weeks before going to camp.

Changes in body image were assessed by having six judges evaluate drawings from each child. It was found that improvement in body image was not evident in drawings from the children without disabilities or in drawings from the children with disabilities who had been tested two weeks before going to camp and just before going to camp. However, statistically significant evidence of improvement in body image was present for children with disabilities who attended summer camp. (In criterion-oriented research, statistical significance is the conventional standard by which results are evaluated and research questions are answered.)

Clearly, the question asked in this research was whether summer-camp experience alters the body image of children with physical disabilities. Clearly, too, the investigator felt that the answer to his question was "yes." The research makes a contribution to theories about the body image. It also suggests that summer camp is a beneficial experience for children with disabilities.

When used to answer purely practical questions, such as "what are the characteristics of successful and unsuccessful clients?", criterion-oriented research may encounter few methodological problems. Apparently, all the investigator needs to do is collect information about clients, find out which clients are successful, and correlate the two. But research of this type sets a special snare for the unwary investigator. The difficulty is that no one can yet specify precisely or objectively the standards by which rehabilitation success may be assessed. What is "successful" by one set of criteria may be "unsuccessful" by another. For example, a rehabilitation center may train a child to manage the activities of daily living so that he is fully prepared in this respect to return to his parental home. However, the agency may fail either to alter parental attitudes of guilt and hostility toward the child or to prepare the child psychologically to cope with these parental attitudes. In this situation, a physical therapist may well decide that rehabilitation has been successful, whereas a social worker will judge that one of the main goals of rehabilitation has not been met.

Where the complex phenomena of rehabilitation are involved, it is no simple matter to evaluate outcomes in any objective, universally acceptable way.

Uses of the Two Orientations

Informational research suffers certain weaknesses as a decision-making device, because it does not state the rules by which its results will be evaluated. Nevertheless, informational research is useful in rehabilitation because there are, in reality, many questions that do not require precise, clearcut answers. It is perfectly legitimate for an investigator simply to want to know what is going on or how frequently a particular event occurs. The ultimate value of such knowledge may become apparent only when it is integrated with facts, theories, or judgments from a variety of sources other than the specific investigation itself. Knowledge of how clients handle the crisis of physical disability may not lead to important theoretical assertions until the investigator discovers essential similarities between the behavior he has observed and descriptions by other scientists of the reactions of people without disabilities to crises such as tornadoes, bombings, floods, and accidents. Information about the incidence of psychological disturbance among clients may not lead to an immediate administrative decision to hire a psychologist or psychiatrist, but it may serve a useful purpose by alerting the staff to such disturbances and by making them more sensitive to the psychological characteristics of their clients.

Criterion-oriented research provides clearcut decisions but is difficult to conduct properly in many institutional settings. One way to conduct criterion-oriented research is to compromise the need for rigid controls.

When this is done, it implies that answers to research questions will be imprecise. Lack of precision offends the scientific mind, but, if a question is really important, any scientist ought to accept an imprecise but empirical answer when the only alternatives available are sheer speculation or no answer at all.

Another way to conduct criterion-oriented research is to take advantage of the naturally occurring events that occur in all rehabilitation settings. Holden's research on the influence of summer-camp experience on the body images of children with disabilities exemplifies this solution to the problem, since it is likely that the children who went to camp would have done so whether or not they participated as subjects in Holden's investigation. Actuarial research, which predicts rehabilitation outcomes from data routinely available on all clients, also exemplifies this solution.

Natural-process research necessarily relies more heavily than laboratory studies on probabilistic controls, such as randomization of extraneous variables, subject matching, and statistical adjustments of data through the use of covariance analysis or partial correlation (Shontz, 1965, Chap. 8). Although the use of such devices implies some loss of precision, they are gaining increasing acceptance in psychological research on complex natural processes. Some investigators actually prefer them because they reduce the extent of the investigator's disturbance of real-life processes and still minimize interference with the outcome of the research by irrelevant factors.

INTEGRATION OF RESEARCH AND SERVICE

The scientific literature provides few examples of prolonged, close collaboration between research and service in rehabilitation settings. Consequently, the discussion from here on is somewhat hypothetical. Three methods recommend themselves as particularly promising. Of these, the first and third are criterion-oriented; the second is informational and descriptive. All possibilities are not exhausted by these alternatives, but each has something distinctive to offer and each therefore deserves separate summarization.

Operant Techniques

"Operant methodology" is a term used to describe a set of techniques for modifying a subject's behavior by controlling its consequences. Some stimuli have the property of increasing the probability of future occurrence of the behavior that was taking place immediately prior to the administration of stimulation. Thus, giving a child a piece of candy just when he says "please" increases the probability that he will say "please" in the future. Other stimuli have the property of decreasing the probability of future occurrence of the behavior taking place immediately prior to the administration of the stimulation. Thus, slapping a child's hand as he reaches for the steaming kettle on the stove reduces the likelihood that he will reach for objects on the stove in the future.

By arranging the "contingencies of behavior" (the relationships between the subject's actions and the consequences of his actions) the operant technician attempts to shape the subject's behavior so that it meets criteria that have been specified in advance. Behavior modification often takes place most effectively when only a certain number of emitted actions are reinforced. Consequently, the operant technician must incorporate consideration of reinforcement schedules into his plan of behavior contingencies.

The techniques of operant conditioning are summarized in an article by Michael (1969), who shows as well how these techniques have been used, with apparent success, in rehabilitation settings. Michael's presentation provides more than just a summarization of principles and findings. It is a veritable fount of hypotheses, all of which can be tested in rehabilitation settings and all of which have important implications for the provision of rehabilitation services. A few examples will show how these hypotheses can be applied in work with children with disabilities.

Michael notes that many problems of behavior management occur because staff members reinforce the wrong behavior from clients and do not reinforce desired behavior when it is exhibited. In an agency for children, for example, the child who whines and cries often gains sympathy and attention from concerned professional personnel. He is thereby reinforced for whining and crying and is likely to continue this behavior. By contrast, the child who is cooperative, attentive, and quiet may be given no special praise or attention. If he is not, his good behavior will tend to diminish and he will begin to engage in other behavior, like whining and crying, which he finds has a greater probability of bringing about reinforcement.

This proposal can easily be tested. To establish a base line for the evaluation of later data, one must first observe and count the frequency of occurrence of desirable and undesirable behaviors. A program of systematic reinforcement of desirable behaviors and systematic extinction (non-reinforcement) of undesirable behaviors can then be instituted. Plotting frequency of occurrence of both kinds of behavior against time produces an objective record of the effectiveness of the program as well as a test of reinforcement theory.

Michael also suggests that a patient's tolerance for therapy can be increased by proper management of rest periods. He notes that rest periods are typically reinforcing but are provided only when the patient shows signs of fatigue. This procedure encourages fatigue rather than work. It is better, perhaps, to grant rest periods when the patient is working hardest and doing his best. Thus, reinforcement will be provided for desirable behavior, which should then increase. Likewise, complaints of pain should be reduced if patients were given more reinforcements for pain-free behavior than for exhibiting signs of discomfort (which usually brings someone running with attention and a pill). Both of these propositions could be tested by means similar to those described above.

Finally, it is possible to organize a whole institution according to operant principles. The result is a "token economy" in which children earn tokens for active participation in rehabilitation and have the privilege of exchanging these tokens for desired reinforcements, such as candy, television, movies, or trips to interesting places. The proposal of a token economy system is probably too radical to be accepted by many agencies at present, but it has been tried in several places and it is worth mentioning, for it provides a device that can integrate service and research functions in an especially comprehensive way. Like all proposals that emerge from operant methodology, the idea of the token economy offers unparalleled opportunities for the collection of objective scientific data within the context of ongoing therapeutic activities.

Psychological Ecology

The *ecological approach* in psychology developed from the methodological tradition of naturalism. *Ecology* is the study of the interrelationships of organisms and their natural environments. Psychological ecology studies the reciprocal linkages between persons and naturally occurring, extrapersonal phenomena. Generally, it tends to emphasize the importance of environmental determinants of behavior and to minimize intrapsychic determinants (Barker, 1962). The need for ecological study was recognized in 1943 by Kurt Lewin (1951a, 1951b), but it was not until Barker and his colleagues worked on the problem that the concepts and methods of ecological psychology were developed into generally usable research tools (Barker, 1963; Barker, 1968; Barker & Wright, 1955; Wright, 1967).

Psychological ecologists use several techniques to study naturally occurring events. One of these is the *specimen record,* a detailed, sequential account of a long segment of a single person's behavior and situation as seen and described by a skilled observer. The best available example of such an account is the day-long record reported by Barker and Wright in the book *One Boy's Day* (1951).

Another frequently used technique is the *behavior-setting survey.* A behavior setting is a naturally occurring unit of the psychological environment. It is not simply a physical arrangement of objects, but includes social and behavioral influences. It is "a cluster of activity and interrelated behavior occurring at a given place and time" (Willems, 1965). An example of a behavior setting in rehabilitation is the "planning conference" or "team meeting" at which the professional team discusses clients and sets up programs for their rehabilitation. Shontz (1967) described planning conference at one agency and expressed the opinion that some behavior settings coerce undesirable responses (dependency, passivity, apathy) from the clients who are exposed to them.

A behavior-setting *survey* is essentially a list of "ecological possibilities" that describes the actual living habitat of people. Such a survey shows the range of ecological opportunities available. When combined with observation of the behavior of specific inhabitants of a given environment the survey enables the investigator to specify the range and mode of participation of individuals in their environment and to identify variables, such as setting size and population density, that determine degree and type of activity of the participants.

Since the methods of ecological psychology are naturalistic and noninterfering, it is obvious that they lend themselves well to use in rehabilitation agencies. The investigator does everything he can *not* to change existing procedures or to influence the actions of the people he observes, for it is precisely the ordinary course of events that he wishes to study. His goal is to describe what goes on and to expose in systematic fashion the relationships between people's behavior and the environmental forces brought to bear on people. Once these relationships are known, it becomes possible to make specific recommendations. Suppose, for example, that the particular setting in which parents of a child with a disability are introduced to the agency where their child will live or go to school has characteristics that tend to coerce nonparticipation and noninvolvement on the part of the parents. The principles of ecological psychology can be applied to suggest changes in the setting which will induce parents to become more actively engaged in the rehabilitation process. Because the methods of ecology are objective, criterion-oriented tests of the effectiveness of these changes can easily follow (see Shontz & Wright, 1968).

Perhaps because they are so new, the methods and concepts of ecological psychology have not yet been extensively applied in rehabilitation settings. However, the approach has considerable promise and could make a major contribution to the improvement of rehabilitation practice.

Predictive Research

A final example of criterion-oriented research will serve to show how rehabilitation research can be effectively integrated with the provision of rehabilitation services. Although this example is drawn from the study of adults, its procedures can easily be adapted to agencies that work only with children.

Beginning with data routinely available in agency files, Eber (1966,

1967a, 1967b) correlated descriptive data about clients witth evaluations of rehabilitation outcomes (success of vocational placement). One result of this procedure is the production of a *multiple regression equation,* which specifies (1) the overall success with which descriptive data can be used to predict the outcome of rehabilitation, and (2) the relative contribution of each bit of descriptive data to the overall success of prediction. Thus, it might be found that knowledge of a person's age, sex, and marital status leads to a better-than-chance prediction about vocational placement, while knowledge of his hair color, weight, and height does not.

What is interesting about Eber's approach is not its routine solution of the problem of prediction, but the use to which he then puts the results of his statistical manipulations of data. These results are fed back to the vocational counselors so that they may assess their functioning and modify their behavior. Suppose, for instance, that the data show that young, married men are generally successfully placed. On the basis of this knowledge, counselors may decide that this group of clients needs their professional services least and could therefore be processed much more routinely and efficiently in the future than in the past.

Another feature of this approach to the problem of prediction is that the process of research never ends. After the results have been transmitted to the counselors, new data are collected and fed into the computer. Because the research process is continuous and data are constantly accumulating, the investigator can tap into the computer at any time for an up-to-date analysis of the agency's operations.

Not the least of the incidental benefits of this approach is that it provides complete and current information on the characteristics of the client population of the agency. Thus it lends itself to descriptive as well as to predictive uses.

CONCLUSIONS

The thesis of this discussion can be quickly summarized. All types and varieties of psychological research can be undertaken in rehabilitation settings. Informational and criterion-oriented investigations, as well as research that combines the two methodologies, can be made to serve valuable theoretical and applied purposes.

The problems that hinder the conduct of effective research are problems that arise from accepting the assumption that research and service are intrinsically incompatible processes. The promise for the future of psychological research in rehabilitation can be realized only if this assumption is discarded. Means exist by which research and service cannot only be carried on simultaneously but can be of mutual benefit to basic science and applied technology. The task that faces workers in rehabilitation is to apply these means for solving problems, answering questions, and improving rehabilitation services.

References

Barker, R. G. The psychology of the absent organism. Paper read at Dept. of Psychology Colloquium. University of Kansas, Fall, 1962.

Barker, R. G. *The stream of behavior.* New York: Appleton-Century-Crofts, 1963.

Barker, R. G. *Ecological psychology.* Stanford, Calif.: Stanford University Press, 1968.

Barker, R. G., & Wright, H. F. *One boy's day.* New York: Harper & Row, 1951.

Barker, R. G., & Wright, H. F. *Midwest and its children.* Evanston, Ill.: Row, Peterson, 1955.

Davis, F. *Passage through crisis.* Indianapolis: Bobbs-Merrill, 1963.

Eber, H. W. Multivariate analysis of a vocational rehabilitation system. *Multivariate Behav. Res. Monogr.,* 1966, No. 66-1.

Eber, H. W. Multivariate analysis of a rehabilitation system: Cross validation and extension. *Multivariate Behav. Res.,* 1967, *2,* 477–484. (a)

Eber, H. W. Economic-managerial influences on counselor behavior. Paper read at seminar on Decision-Making Processes in Vocational Rehabilitation. University of Texas, July 1967. (b)

Holden, R. H. Changes in body image of physically handicapped children due to summer camp experience. *Merrill-Palmer Quart.,* 1962, *8,* 19–26.

Lewin, K. Defining the "field at a given time" (1943). In K. Lewin, *Field theory in social science.* New York: Harper & Row, 1951, pp. 43–59. (a)

Lewin, K. Psychological ecology (1943). In K. Lewin, *Field theory in social science.* New York: Harper & Row, 1951, pp. 170–187. (b)

Lofquist, L. H. (Ed.), *Psychological research and rehabilitation.* Washington, D.C.: American Psychological Association, 1960.

Meehl, P. E. *Clinical versus statistical prediction.* Minneapolis: University of Minnesota Press, 1954.

Michael, J. L. Rehabilitation. In C. Neuringer & J. L. Michael (Eds.), *Behavior modification in clinical psychology.* New York: Appleton-Century-Crofts, 1969.

Shontz, F. C. *Research methods in personality.* New York: Appleton-Century-Crofts, 1965.

Shontz, F. C. Behavior settings may affect rehabilitation client. *Rehab. Rec.,* 1967, *8,* (2), 37–40.

Shontz, F. C., & Wright, B. A. Parent-staff agreement in evaluations of children in rehabilitation. *Rehab. Lit.,* 1968, *29,* 166–168.

Wight, B. W., & Moed, G. Perception of lower limb position and extension in physically disabled children. *Percept. & motor Skills,* 1963, *17,* 667–676.

Willems, E. P. An ecological orientation in psychology. *Merrill-Palmer Quart.,* 1965, *11,* 317–343.

Wright, B. A. (Ed.), *Psychology and rehabilitation.* Washington, D.C.: American Psychological Association, 1959.

Wright, B. A., & Shontz, F. C. Process and tasks in hoping. *Rehab. Lit.,* 1968, *29,* 322–331.

Wright, H. F. *Recording and analyzing child behavior.* New York: Harper & Row, 1967.

23

Disorders of Conceptual Thinking in the Brain-injured Child

Alfred A. Strauss and Heinz Werner

The late Dr. Strauss was Director of Cove Schools, Evanston, Illinois. At the time of his death, Dr. Werner was Director of the Institute of Human Development, Clark University, Worcester, Massachusetts.

Dr. Strauss and Dr. Werner were pioneers in the psychological investigation of perceptual and conceptual processes of the brain-injured child. Their many published studies in this area laid the foundation for much of the current attitude toward the brain-injured child. Hence, the student's introduction to the topic would appear to us to be incomplete without at least a sample of their work. One of their frequently cited studies, now considered a classic, is the one presented below dealing with the nature of conceptual thinking in the brain-injured child. The issue is very much a live one today.

Psychopathological investigations concerning brain-injured children have dealt almost exclusively with their motor and behavior disturbances. A full understanding of the mental organization of the brain-injured child, however, demands also an examination of the various psychological functions and their specific disturbances (*Strauss* and *Werner, 1941*). This goal may be reached by comparative studies of brain-injured and non-brain-injured children.

REPRINTED AND EDITED from the *Journal of Nervous and Mental Disease*, 1942, *96*, 153–172, with the permission of the Williams & Wilkins Co., and Dr. Werner.

Previous studies in this series of investigations have been concerned with behavior and with sensorimotor disturbances (*Strauss* and *Werner, 1941*). These studies have indicated that brain-injured mentally defective children are impaired in sensorimotor integration, i.e., visuo-motor, tactual-motor and auditory-motor performances.

The group of brain-injured children employed in these studies includes only children in whose histories there is an indication of an early brain lesion (birth injury, inflammatory processes, etc.); and for whom it may be assumed that the existing mental impairment is a consequence of the brain damage; children with gross motor disturbances, aphasia, agnosia, etc., were excluded.

The present study is concerned with certain phases of the intellectual behavior of brain-injured children. Experimental situations have been devised to analyze behavior involving the grasp of concrete relations. It is to be expected that the child's manner of attacking a problem of concrete relationship will furnish cues as to his manner of perceiving and conceptualizing the environmental material.

Two groups of 20 children have been selected. The first group were mentally retarded children of the so-called endogenous, familial, or hereditary type (*Strauss, 1939*); they are children whose developmental histories and neurological examination give no evidence of a lesion in the central nervous system. The average mental age of this group was 9.0 years, with a quartile deviation of eleven months, the average IQ was 73.

The second group consisted of mentally retarded children who showed evidence of brain lesion (so-called exogenous type of mental defectives). The average IQ and mental age were almost identical with that of the endogenous group, the average mental age being 8 years, 11 months, with a quartile deviation of 9 months, the average IQ 70.

Two types of tests have been used; the first two involving the grouping of objects, the third the adequate selection of objects with reference to pictured situations.

SORTING TESTS

Halstead constructed a grouping test which he used with adult patients with cerebral injury. We have employed this test for an introductory investigation of the forms of behavior typical of brain-injured children.

Our materials consisted of fifty-six objects selected from the sixty-two objects of Halstead's Test. Some of Halstead's objects, particularly those which appeared twice, were exchanged for new ones or were omitted. Our list includes the following objects:

1. Glass bottle
2. Multicolored cube
3. Sunglass lens
4. Wax crayon
5. Pink candle-holder for cakes
6. Glass stopper

7. Hair pin
8. Colored picture of a bell
9. Metal whistle
10. Bookmatches
11. Rubber grummet
12. Razor blade
13. Wooden pulley
14. House key
15. Blue poker-chip
16. Piece of red wool cloth
17. Small metal key
18. Playing card
19. Thin roundish stick
20. Red paper stock
21. Cancelled foreign-postage stamp
22. Colored picture of a rooster
23. Metal jar lid
24. Electric bulb
25. Silver-colored wooden pulley
26. Small paste brush
27. Cork
28. Padlock
29. Cylindrical wooden piece
30. Abstract design
31. Electric socket
32. Pipe bowl
33. Small round red button
34. Paper clip
35. Pink yarn
36. White Xmas-tree bulb
37. Toy metal knife
38. Small wax candle
39. Picture of a key
40. Red poker-chip
41. Card labeled "ball"
42. Metal spring
43. Piece of cord
44. Card labeled "pipe"
45. Thick round stick
46. Metal thimble
47. Rubber band
48. Coarse sandpaper
49. Lipstick
50. Rubber covered wire
51. Fine sandpaper
52. Ping-Pong ball
53. Colored picture of a rabbit
54. Round metal box lid
55. Round metal box
56. Black wooden cube

The objects were presented in a prescribed arrangement similar to that of Halstead. The child was first asked to name the objects placed before him; thus the examiner was assured that he understood the meaning of each object. The child was then asked to "Place those things together which go together, which fit together." The minimum number of groups requested was ten. After the completion of ten groups, the child was interrupted for a short pause before the grouping procedure was continued. No social pressure was exerted; the task was considered finished if the child showed no desire to continue. After completion of the experiment the child was asked for each grouping, "Why did you put these things together?"

The results indicate that there was a considerable difference in total number of objects selected by the two types of children. The brain-injured group chose a total of 450 objects as compared with 328 objects selected by the endogenous group. Thus, of the possible total of 560 choices (ten times fifty-six objects) 59 per cent of the objects were chosen by the endogenous group and 80 per cent by the brain-injured group. If, however, one considers only the first ten groups made by each child the number of objects chosen is about the same (242 in the brain-injured group, 241 in the endogenous group) indicating that the average size of a combination or grouping is 2.4 objects for each child.

In addition to the difference in the percentage of objects chosen by each type of children, there was a difference in the "commonness" of the combinations formed. Combinations which appeared only once during the experiment were considered "infrequent." The endogenous group as a whole showed only eleven of such combinations whereas thirty uncommon combinations occurred with the brain-injured group. Every child in the brain-injured group showed at least one uncommon response, whereas only half of the endogenous children so responded.

The following conclusions may be drawn from this preliminary study:

1. The brain-injured children tend to form more groups than the non-injured children.

2. Uncommon responses are far more frequent, absolutely and relatively, among brain-injured children than among the members of the endogenous group.

The results suggest that in grouping objects brain-injured children grasp or use more relationships than do endogenous children; they obviously achieve this by the perception of singular and unusual combinations. An appraisal of these results in the light of qualitative characteristics of the conceptual thinking of brain-injured children will be discussed later.

The need for more careful control of the experimental situation has led us to the construction of a second sorting test based on the preliminary one. Sorting test II differs from test I in the limitation of the number of objects to be grouped. The task consisted in matching one object with any one of three other objects. The instructions given were: "Look at this object. (*Examiner* points to the key object.) Which of the three objects goes best with the object (the key object) here?" After his choice had been made the child was asked: "Why do you think these objects go together?"

There were eighteen problems, thus fifty-four different relationships were possible. Of these, twenty-nine different relations appeared among the choices of the endogenous group, whereas fifty-two appeared among those of the brain-injured group.

The following computation is intended to demonstrate the difference between the two groups with respect to the commonness and uncommonness of combinations. After the fifty-four combinations had been marked according to the frequency of their occurrence in the total group of children, these combinations were divided into three sections: one section contains the 25 per cent of the combinations showing the greatest frequency of occurrence, another section the 25 per cent occurring least frequently, and a middle section the other 50 per cent. Seventy-nine per cent of all responses of the endogenous group deal with the most common combinations, whereas only 47 per cent of the responses of the exogenous group deal with these combinations. Conversely, no combinations of lowest frequency occur among the endogenous group, whereas 13 per cent of the combinations made by the brain-injured group belong to this category. (The difference of these percentages is statistically significant.)

The quantitative differences between the two groups are only part of the picture. Equally important for the understanding of these differences is the qualitative aspect of grouping behavior. Frequent combinations include objects such as a red chip and blue chip, thimble and thread, candle and match; these objects have been grouped together because they have something essential or typical in common; they have identical or similar features, or belong together functionally. Almost all of the combinations which strike the adult as being unusual or off the point belong to the less frequent responses. Most of these unusual combinations, according to the explanations given by the children, seem to have been formed on the basis of one of the following principles:

1. Selection on the basis of singular, unspecific, or vaguely conceived qualities (sunglass-silver wheel: both are round).

2. Selection on the basis of an unessential or accidental detail (sandpaper–match: because of the stripe of sandpaper glued on the matchcover).

3. Selection on the basis of an unessential or accidental functional relationship (metal cover-knife: because the knife can be used as an opener).

4. Selection on the basis of an *ad hoc* construed situation comprising both objects (whistle-sunglass lens: you find both in the face of a policeman).

Almost all uncommon responses given by children of the endogenous group belong to category "1"; i.e., their unusual combinations occur mostly because of unspecificity and vagueness of perception. Relationships based on the singling out of unessential, accidental, or functional details appear to be characteristic for brain-injured children.

These facts may be observed also in the preliminary experiment, although under less strict conditions.

Without going into detailed analysis in many instances we may say that the observer is struck by the marked peculiarity of the point of view upon which the brain-injured children relate the objects.

The psychopathological significance of the difference found between brain-injured children and those without brain injury will be discussed later, in connection with the results obtained from the third test.

THE PICTURE–OBJECT TEST

The first two tests were concerned with the grouping of relatively abstract single objects. In order to observe the intellectual behavior of brain-injured children under experimental conditions which permit greater freedom of mental activity and which are closer to the exigencies of reality, the present test was constructed.

This test involves the relationship between life situations as represented in pictures and small objects. Two pictures (both black and white reproductions taken from *Life* magazine) were used. Picture I (D picture) represents a drowning situation—a boy completely surrounded by waves is about to drown. Picture II (F picture) presents a fire situation—a large building is on fire at night; firemen are shown attempting to rescue the house.

The following is a list of the eighty-six toy objects used:

Human and animal figures: doctor, male nurse, female nurse, boy running, boy carrying milk can, boy with wheelcart, Negro porter with bags, woman, peasant, stewardess, Santa Claus, black dog, white dog, pink pigeon, chicken.

Cars: fire engines, big and small, ambulance, red bus, red coupé, blue coupé, yellow car, luggage car, tanker, towing car, racer, locomotive.

Furniture: table, chest, two chairs, two garden benches.

Domestic utensils and tools: two pieces of rubber hose, electric bulb, key, piece of rope, wrench, chisel, screwdriver, pliers, scissors, hammer, nails, cork, soap, screw, piece of wire, spoon, fork, tea-set, cup of water.

Out-of-door objects: three traffic signs (Stop, Slow, Turn), bridge, boat, two trees, stone, sand.

Miscellaneous objects: life-saver, matches, medical supply (first aid, bandage, cotton, tongue-plate, cotton stick), sticks of burned wood, pill, bottle, cigarette, small book, letter, paper and pencil, two doll dresses, broken wheel, wheel, piece of red cloth, yellow yarn, hairpin, red poker-chip, playing ball, airplane.

The two pictures (picture I, $3\frac{1}{2}'' \times 3\frac{1}{2}''$, picture II, $6\frac{1}{2}'' \times 5\frac{1}{2}''$) were pasted on pieces of white cardboard, $12'' \times 9''$, and these were mounted on wooden blocks. They thus stood upright on the table, 16" in front of the child, the fire picture on the right, the drowning picture on the left. The objects were arranged in random order to the left of the drowning picture. The instructions were as follows: "Do you see this picture? It is a picture of a drowning boy. Do you see how he struggles in the water, looking for help?—Now, this other picture shows a building on fire. Do you see the fire and smoke coming out of the house?" The child was then led to the objects and told—"There you see a number of objects.

Now you put before this picture (I) those objects which go with the picture of the drowning boy; those objects which you think go with the picture of the building on fire you put over there (picture II); and those objects which you are sure do not fit either the picture of the drowning boy or the picture of the building on fire, you put away here (to the right of the fire picture)."

The test was finished when the child had taken all objects from the left side and placed them in front of one of the pictures or laid them aside. If the child, after selecting a number of objects, hesitated to handle the remaining objects according to instructions, the *Examiner* said: "Take each object into your hand; if you are sure it does not fit, put it away." After he had completed the task, the child was asked to state the reasons for the placement of the objects.

For convenience of presentation the results will be discussed under the following headings:
1. Uncommon choices.
2. Deviation from the standard meaning of objects.
3. Organization of the objects in circumscribed small units.
4. Conspicuous formalistic behavior.
5. Dynamic–concrete grasp of relationship.

Uncommon Choices

There is very little difference between the two groups in the frequency of selection of the most common objects. There are certain objects whose relationships to one of the pictures is obvious. Such most frequently chosen objects for the fire situation are: the two fire engines, the two rubber hoses, matches, the "ambulance complex" (ambulance, doctor, nurses, first aid, bandage, cotton), the half-burned wooden sticks. For the drowning situation the most frequently chosen objects are: the life-saver, boat, rope, cup of water. However, there are many objects seldom or never used by the endogenous group which were used frequently by the brain-injured group. For example, the human figures aside from their representing medical personnel were seldom used by the endogenous children whereas they comprise 49 per cent of the selections of the brain-injured children. None of the paper and the cloth objects were used by the endogenous children whereas, surprisingly enough, brain-injured children made this choice quite frequently (31 per cent). Such strange placements, as putting dwelling furniture before the drowning picture, appear only in the arrangements of the brain-injured children.

The genuine tendency of the brain-injured child to choose uncommon objects comes to the fore if we consider the total number of objects used by the two groups. The brain-injured children placed about twice as many objects to the pictures; as a group they employed also about twice as many different objects as the endogenous children. It may be, however, noted that the average child even in the brain-injured group used less than half of all objects.

Here the question arises whether the brain-injured children select the uncommon objects more frequently simply because they use a greater number of objects than the endogenous children. This question may be answered by an analysis of the commonness of the initial choices of the brain-injured and the non-brain-injured children. In defining initial responses we arbitrarily chose the first three objects placed before the D picture and the first seven placed before the F picture.

These represent the minimum number of objects placed before the two pictures by any child and equals about half the average number of responses made by endogenous children and about one-fourth the average number made by the brain-injured children.

In order to define most common and least common objects we ranked the objects according to the total number of children who used them for each picture individually. Beginning at the top of each list we then selected the group of objects which had elicited one-fourth of the total number of responses (93 responses to the D picture and 141 responses to the F picture). For each picture we then selected the least commonly used objects. We considered as least common those objects which appeared in the lowest quartile. For the D picture most common objects were: the life-saver, the boat, the cup of water, etc.: for the F picture: the big fire-engine, small fire-engine, big hose, small hose, ambulance, matches, male nurse, etc. Least common objects were for the D picture: the Negro porter, the stewardess, the yellow car, etc.; for the F picture: the tea-set, chest, paper and pencil, small book, etc.

The average percentages of most common responses among the initial choices of the two groups were: 86 per cent in the D picture and 59 per cent in the F picture in the endogenous group and 55 per cent and 36 per cent in the brain-injured group, respectively; the difference between the percentages is statistically significant. We may, therefore, conclude in their initial responses, brain-injured children chose the common objects less frequently than endogenous children.

On the other hand, among the first three objects placed by the brain-injured group before the drowning picture 10 per cent are least common. Eleven per cent of their first seven selections for the fire picture belong to this class of least common objects. Such uncommon choices did not occur in the initial placements of the endogenous children.

These results demonstrate that the selection and use of less common objects among brain-injured children cannot be reduced to the greater total number of objects which they placed before the picture. These results corroborate those of the Sorting Tests.

Deviation from the Standard Meaning of Objects

One of the principal causes of the differences of the behavior of the two groups on the Sorting Tests was demonstrated to be a peculiarity in abstracting the properties of objects. Similarly, in selecting objects for the two pictures brain-injured children frequently deviated from the standard meaning of these objects. As in the Sorting Test certain objects were selected because they were perceived through qualities of a secondary order. For example, one child places a wire before the fire picture saying, "That's a hose." The wire can represent a hose to this child because essential qualities of the object have been neglected while less significant characteristics have been considered. Other examples are the placement of the following objects. A child explains his placement of the wire before the drowning picture by saying: "This is to save the boy." The small cork is placed before the drowning picture: "For helping the boy in the water." A small stone is selected for the drowning picture because, "This goes on the edges of the walk." (Stones are placed along the borders of the sidewalks on the Training School terrain.)

Other objects were perceived through unusual stress of unessential or accidental physical properties. For instance, one child laid a bulb before the fire picture and remarked: "This is the bulb which blew out the fuse and started the fire." The bulb was blackened on one side and this had proved sufficient for its selection. The engraved ornament of the poker-chip was perceived as a picture and the chip was selected with the remark: "To hang it on the wall of the house so that it looks pretty." Another child took the poker-chip as a "rug on the table." Still other objects were selected because they were perceived in terms of accidental or unessential functional properties. A child placed the pliers close to the doctor, explaining: "This is for bad teeth." Another child laid the electric bulb near the ambulance, saying: "In case they get a sore mouth." The broken wheel of a carriage was laid before the fire picture with the statement: "To put the water hose around it."

The last principle of selection of objects, on the basis of an *ad hoc* construed situation, is much more frequent in the Picture than in the Sorting Tests. Some of the examples just mentioned might perhaps be classified under this category also. The following examples are chosen because they demonstrate clearly the pliability of the meaning of objects with respect to situations of which they are made a part. A child placed the boy with wheelcart and the piece of a rubber hose before the fire picture, saying: "This man has to carry the babies out of the house," and pointing to the hose: "This is for the babies to suck milk." Another child placed the stop-sign in front of the cars and the red poker chip in front of the stop-sign, saying: "This (the chip) is the red light." In rare cases such pliability may even lead to double meanings; the character of a previously selected object may be changed during the test. One child placed the cup with water before the fire picture, explaining: "Water for putting out the fire"; later he picked up the cotton-stick and placed it on the top of the cup, saying: "This is medicine for the sick people."

Organization of the Objects in Circumscribed Small Units

In addition to the objects they selected, the two clinical groups differed in their method of organizing the material before the pictures. Usually the endogenous child solved the task by simply placing the objects he considered appropriate in front of the respective pictures. He took no pains to place the objects in a particular order, and their arrangement did not indicate a link between objects. The brain-injured children, on the contrary, frequently arranged the materials to indicate a linking of certain objects. These objects were apparently closely interrelated, but were less related to the picture. For instance, one child put the rubber hose into the steamer of the fire-engine, placed the matches and the wrench on top of it, and explained that these objects should be there because they put the fire-engine into operation.

In analyzing these data two criteria were assumed to indicate that the child perceived certain objects as part of a closely knit group: (1) The objects were physically connected. For instance, the figure of the woman was clothed with one of the doll-dresses. (2) The objects, though not physically connected, were placed close to each other and the child stated that these objects were part of a unit. For instance, the child put one of the doll-dresses beside the woman, declaring that this dress belonged to the woman.

We have computed for each group the occurrence of this type of arrangement. Very few such small circumscribed units occurred among the endogenous children whereas almost half of the objects placed before the drowning picture and almost one-fourth of the objects placed before the fire picture were united in closely knit groups by the brain-injured children. Only two of the twenty brain-injured children did not form at least one unit before one of the two pictures.

The physical connection was apparently suggested, in many cases, by certain properties of the objects, such as openings, holes, etc. One child, for instance, noticed the hollow tube of the boiler of the fire-engine and decided to stick the piece of rubber hose into it. As many as eight of the brain-injured children placed objects such as human and animal figures, life-saver, rope, etc., on the bridge. Other examples of such combinations are: placing the cotton-stick into the bottle; putting the boy and dog on the sailboat; fastening the hairpin onto the woman's head (there was a small hole in the woman's head); setting the knife and fork on the tray of the teaset; putting the bottle on the chest; placing the little pink pigeon on the limb of the tree; stacking the nails, tools, etc., in the boy's wheelcart; placing medical utensils, such as cotton, bandages, scissors, etc., under the bent arm of the nurse.

Illustrations of the second, less frequent, type of combination are: adjoining the rope and piece of red cloth, since "This is the clothes line with laundry"; placing the stop-sign near the fire-engine, because "This sign is here to stop the fire-engine"; setting the bench near the ambulance, so that they can "Put the bench into the ambulance"; grouping the teacup, matches, cigarette and chair, saying the "chair is for the fire-chief to sit on; matches, teacup, cigarette belong to the fire-chief."

There was great variation in the number of objects combined in one unit. Sometimes these units were enlarged into loosely connected object complexes. One child conceived of a part of the space before the drowning picture as a "garden," expressing this idea by making the man with the wheelcart a gardener carrying garden tools, stone, small sticks, sand, trees, etc.

Conspicuous Formalistic Behavior

Any task of grouping or relating objects requires execution and systematic arrangement of material; the overstressing, however, of orderliness, a pedantic systematization of attack not warranted by the task was an abnormal feature of behavior exhibited by some of the brain-injured children. This type of behavior may be termed "formalistic" behavior.

One feature found only with brain-injured children was the formal-geometrical arrangement of objects in front of the picture. For instance, four children placed the objects in a half circle around the picture. The bridge was placed at a right angle or parallel to the picture with several figures placed rigidly one behind the other; such an arrangement occurred five times. Nine of the twenty brain-injured children show some formalistic behavior in arranging the objects.

Another characteristic was the meticulosity exhibited in selecting and discarding the objects. The usual natural procedure in placing the objects makes no reference to a particular temporal order: the endogenous child, as soon as he finds that an object is related to one of the pictures, immediately places it there. The brain-injured child may see the relation of an object to the picture, but does not place it at once because it does not fit into his present performance scheme. One child placed a car on the bridge and took it away immediately. When asked why he did not want to use it, he said, "Not now."

Dynamic-Concrete Grasp of Relationship

It should be borne in mind that the picture-object test is essentially a problem of grouping. The endogenous child apparently conceives the problem that way; he selects and places the objects which in his opinion are directly related to the general concept represented in the picture. For him the task is a sober logical problem. As we shall attempt to demonstrate the brain-injured child approaches the task from a different point of view. Neither the pictures nor the objects are simply representatives of generalized situations or concepts. The pictures are conceived, as, in a sense, three-dimensional realities; they are not still pictures representing an immediate event; the child sees in them a series of actions taking place not only in the present but in the past and future as well. The dynamic, functional properties of the objects are stressed; they are not so much representatives of rather abstract concepts as concrete elements of a situation.

A striking visual evidence of the way the brain-injured child dramatizes the picture-object situation is the fact that human and animal figures are frequently turned with faces toward the picture; the endogenous child usually simply places such figures somewhere in front of the picture without regard to position.

A second type of response demonstrating the intimate dynamic relationship between object and picture is the *identification* of the human figures as the persons appearing in the picture or as persons related to them. All such identifications occurred with the picture of the drowning boy. Forty per cent, or 8 of 20 brain-injured children placed a figure representing the drowning boy or his father or mother before the picture, whereas such identification occurred only once among the endogenous children.

This peculiar dynamic grasp of objects and relationships which distinguishes the brain-injured children from the endogenous children has a definite bearing on the previously discussed differences in the number and quality of objects selected. A child who conceives the picture as a three-dimensional reality extended into the past and the future will naturally see more objects appropriate to the situation than one who conceives the task as a logical problem of selecting objects related to a static situation.

GROUPING BEHAVIOR OF HEALTHY CHILDREN

A further control experiment employing a group of 10 healthy children [1] (chronological ages 8 to 10 years, IQ 100 to 119) has been conducted. The

[1] We acknowledge the generous co-operation of the administration of the University Elementary School, Ann Arbor, Michigan.

It must be noted that utmost care has to be used in this sort of com-

purpose of this investigation was to inquire whether or not there is a similarity in the responses of normal, and of non-brain-injured but mentally retarded children. The pathological characteristics found in brain-injured children are absent. The same result is obtained in the picture-object test. Though it is true that, compared with non-brain-injured mentally retarded children, there is a wider range in the variety of responses to the picture, deviations from the main problem, so frequently found with the brain-injured children, are not noted. The dynamic-concrete grasp of relationship, typical for the brain-injured child, is also absent; the normal children conceive the task in terms of a rather abstract detached relationship.

Summary

Before beginning the discussion we may first recapitulate the principal results of the three tests. The main feature common to all three tests is the selection of objects on the basis of their belongingness either to another object or to a pictorial situation. All tests, then, involve the grasp of conceptual relationship. In all three test situations characteristic phenomena, differentiating the brain-injured mentally defective child from the non-brain-injured normal and mentally retarded child, have been found. These differences are:

1. The brain-injured children selected more objects than the children in the two control groups.

2. There was a significantly higher percentage of uncommon responses in the brain-injured group than in the control groups.

3. A principle of selection of objects made by brain-injured children seemed to be based particularly upon unusual or accidental or apparently insignificant details.

4. The brain-injured children were markedly attracted by properties of objects apt to elicit motor responses.

Some further differences between the brain-injured and the control groups were found in the picture-object test only. That these differences did not appear in the sorting tests is probably a consequence of the peculiarity of the third test which includes such special features as arrangements in terms of life-situation, space-time relation, etc. Such forms of response found in the brain-injured group were:

1. Arrangements of objects in circumscribed units.

2. Formalistic behavior. (Viz., meticulosity, organic pedantry, arbitrary patterning, etc.)

---

parative study for the selection of healthy children. Children whose developmental histories gave even a slight indication that they were exposed to a possible affliction of the brain were discarded. Children with marked psychopathic behavior were also excluded.

3. Dynamic-concrete grasp of relationship. (E.g., dramatization, animation of the situation.)

Discussion

One can assume that the behavior deviations of brain-injured children found in the various tests are a result of the functional changes which are known to occur as the result of brain lesions in the child. Clinical experience as well as previous experimental studies have demonstrated general characteristics of so-called organic behavior disturbance of which the following seem to have a definite bearing on our findings:

Forced responsiveness to stimuli It is known that children with severe brain-injuries are handicapped in their performances in that they may easily be distracted by extraneous stimuli. Since the child cannot help turning his attention to such stimuli, any noise, brilliant object, moving object, etc., may be a source of interference. This abnormal distractability has been described as "hypervigilance" (exaggerated vigilance) of postencephalitic children by Homburger (*1926*). Goldstein (*1939*) includes this phenomenon under the term "forced responsiveness" or "stimulus bond" in cases of brain-injured adults. In a previous experiment in which certain drawings were presented by short time exposure, we have demonstrated that brain-injured children in contradistinction to non-brain-injured children will react more readily to a large background configuration than to a small figure in the foreground.

Pathological fixation It would be incorrect to define the abnormal distractability as lack of attention. Opposite behavior can be observed in the seemingly inattentive brain-injured child, i.e., an exaggerated attentiveness often occurs. The type of reaction with which we are concerned here has been described as "pathological fixation" by Goldstein (*1939*). There are two aspects of this phenomenon. One aspect is related to the forced responsiveness to external stimuli. It is the long endurance of the stimulation exhibiting itself in such phenomena as prolonged after-effect, etc. The other aspect is internal in nature. It exhibits itself in the inertia of the organism, the inability to shift from one nervous activity to another, for instance, in such phenomena as perseveration in spontaneous activity. In our clinical experience and in several experiments we have found perseverative tendencies conspicuously present in brain-injured children. Werner (*1940*) observed this phenomenon clearly in an experiment where the task involved the performance on an optical Knox-Cube test. A further confirmation can be found in a recent experimental investigation by Cotton (*1941*). Spastic and physically normal children, both of average intelligence, were requested to repeat a sequence of colored lights. Perseverative tendencies were found to be frequent in the spastic children and absent in the physically normal.

Disinhibition Motor disinhibition has been found to be a characteristic behavior trait in brain-injured children (*Kasanin, 1929; Schroeder, 1929*). Kahn and Cohn (*1934*) have even defined "driveness" as a brain-stem syndrome. Part of the picture of motor disinhibition is the often noticed hyperactivity and restlessness; this may lead to an exaggerated attention for those qualities of the objects which particularly elicit motor response. For instance, the brain-injured children cannot restrain themselves from manipulating handles of doors, turning knobs, rolling round objects, etc., which are within their reach.

Dissociation Dissociation (lack of integration of elements into more comprehensive configuration) has been shown to characterize sensorimotor performance of brain-injured children (*Werner* and *Strauss, 1941*). They are, for instance, disturbed in tests which require the construction of mosaic-like patterns: they construct those patterns predominantly in an incoherent rather than a sequential manner. The brain-injured child jumps from one part of the figure to another quite unrelated one. Since he cannot comprehend the pattern as a whole the results are frequently disorganized forms lacking connection. This type of procedure is uncommon in non-brain-injured normal and mentally defective children. Lack of organization appears to be a disturbance of a general nature since it has been found in various performances involving entirely different sensory fields (visual, auditory, tactual) (*Strauss* and *Werner, 1941; Werner* and *Strauss, 1939*). It is to be expected, therefore, that a child with these behavior deviations should perform a task of grouping objects differently from the normal or mentally retarded non-brain-injured child. It could, of course, be argued that the peculiarities of responses of our brain-injured children are a direct consequence of their intellectual impairment. It must be emphasized, however, that mentally retarded children which are not brain-injured show little sign of these disorders. There are brain-injured children with relatively high IQs who exhibit responses strongly deviating from those of non-brain-injured children even of lower intelligence level. Since our investigations employed two control groups of non-brain-injured normal and non-brain-injured mentally defective children the results can be related only to the functional change due to brain injury.

We may now discuss our results in the light of the general disturbances enumerated above.

One of the outstanding differences found in all three tests was the strong reaction of the brain-injured child to unessential details of the objects or situations. One general factor responsible for such a reaction is probably the forced responsiveness to stimuli. Such a pathological responsiveness causes the child to turn to any detail of the situation because of its impressiveness, its intensity, or extensity. But, why does the child not discard the unessential detail once perceived and proceed to a more comprehensive relationship? Probably he fails to do this because of the existence of two other disturbing factors: the first is the abnormal fixation which makes it difficult for the child to shift. The second factor is dissociation (a disregard for the more complex units of which such a detail forms only an element). A child who relates the card with the word "ball" to the picture of the bell has made his choice by isolating an element; he points to the pellet of the clapper as a ball, a relationship which a normal child, seeing the bell as a whole, would hardly perceive. An interesting illustration of this point has been furnished by Cotton (*1941*) in the experiments with physically normal and spastic children of normal intelligence. In a sorting test where objects presented were predominantly edible or not edible, all the normal children so classified the objects, whereas the spastic children classified according to single properties like shape, color, and size.

One of the reasons why brain-injured children selected more objects or combinations in all tests is due to this tendency of the brain-injured child to abstract many details; seeing more details enables the child to form more relationships. Disinhibition is probably another reason. The child feels forced to use up all the material within his reach.

Furthermore, this factor, disinhibition, may cause the brain-injured child to select objects stimulating motor responses. To illustrate: objects were frequently chosen which fitted into holes, like the rubber hose into the fire engine, a wooden stick into the hole of the silver button, etc.

There are certain peculiarities of the performance of brain-injured children which appeared predominantly or exclusively in the picture-object test. One is the frequent arrangement of objects in circumscribed units. We suggest that this is a phenomenon somewhat related to the detail-reaction discussed before. The only difference seems to be that here one is dealing with a detailed part of a complex situation instead of a detailed property of an object. The child attracted by an object, its function, or its relationship with other objects may be sidetracked for the moment, losing sight of the main idea because of his fixation.

Two seemingly opposed features encountered in this test are the exaggerated formalism and the dynamic concretism. Exaggerated formalism is clinically known as meticulosity or pedantry in organic brain disturbances. Some strange repudiations of quite obvious combinations can be understood only by such meticulosity. A brain-injured child, for instance, refuses to accept the Ping-Pong ball as a ball because of a dent disturbing its roundness. The organic pedantry is probably a complex trait; it may be interpreted in two ways. The one interpretation is causal, the other teleological. Pedantry may be the outcome of certain behavior characteristics like the tendency of the child to select the detail and to stay with it. But, it may also be the child's compensatory reaction to his disinhibitory and dissociative tendencies, his only way out from potential chaos into orderly procedure.

It may be finally suggested that affective-motor disinhibition ("drivenness") might be partially responsible for the particular form of concrete behavior called dynamic concretism. An organism governed by uncontrolled drives, confined within a concrete pictorial situation like the picture-object test, might easily be given to such phenomena as dramatization and animation of the objects and the situation.

References

Cotton, C. B. A study of the reactions of spastic children to certain test situations. *J. genet. Psychol.,* 1941, *58,* 27.

Goldstein, K. *The Organism.* New York: American Book Co., 1939.

Halstead, W. C. Preliminary analysis of grouping behavior in patients with cerebral injury by the method of equivalent and non-equivalent stimuli. *Amer. J. Psychiat.,* 1940, *96,* 1263.

Homburger, A. *Vorlesungen ueber Psychopathologie des Kindesalters.* Berlin: Julius Springer, 1926.

Kahn, E., & Cohn, L. C. Organic driveness, a brain-stem syndrome and an experience. *New England J. Med.,* 1934, *210,* 748.

Kasanin, J. Personality changes in children following cerebral trauma. *J. nerv. ment. Dis.,* 1929, *69,* 385.

Schroeder, P. L. Behavior difficulties in children associated with the results of birth trauma. *J. Amer. Med. Assoc.,* 1929, *92,* 100.

Strauss, A. A. Typology in mental deficiency. *Proc. Amer. Assoc. ment. Def.,* 1939, *44,* 85.

Strauss, A. A., & Werner, Heinz. The mental organization of the brain-injured mentally defective child. *Amer. J. Psychiat.,* 1941, *97,* 1194.

Werner, Heinz. Perception of spatial relationship in mentally deficient children. *J. genet. Psychol.,* 1949, *57,* 93.

Werner, H., & Strauss, A. A. Types of visuo-motor activity in their relation to low and high performance ages. *Proc. Amer. Assoc. ment. Def.,* 1939, *44,* 163.

Werner, H., & Strauss, A. A. Casual factors in low performance. *Amer. J. ment. Def.,* 1940, *45,* 213.

Werner, H., & Strauss, A. A. Pathology of figure-background relation in the child. *J. abnorm. soc. Psychol.,* 1941, *36,* 236.

24

Neurological Abnormality in Infancy, Intelligence, and Social Class

Raymond H. Holden and Lee Willerman

Dr. Holden is Associate Professor in the Department of Psychology and director of the Learning Center at Rhode Island College and Dr. Willerman is Research Psychologist, Perinatal Research Branch, National Institute of Neurological Diseases and Stroke, National Institute of Health.

Dr. Holden's active research program on exceptional children, particularly the cerebral palsy and mentally retarded, has resulted in over thirty major publications in a variety of professional journals. Dr. Willerman, also actively involved in research, is currently contributing papers on the role of brain injury as an etiological agent in mental retardation.

In this excellent study, prepared for this book, the authors demonstrate the importance of environmental factors on the intellectual development of neurologically damaged infants. Past research had tended to ignore social factors and the assumption seemed to be that the course of development was predominately a function of the area, degree, and time of the neurological damage. The results of this study clearly invalidates this assumption.

The following institutions participated in this research: Boston Lying-in Hospital; Brown University; Charity Hospital, New Orleans; Children's Hospital of Buffalo; Children's Hospital of Philadelphia; Children's Medical Center, Boston; Columbia University; Johns Hopkins University; Medical College of Virginia; New York Medical College; Pennsylvania Hospital; University of Minnesota;

University of Oregon; University of Tennessee; Yale University; and the Perinatal Research Branch, N.I.N.D.S.

This paper must be regarded as a preliminary exploration of Collaborative Study data. Possibilities remain that differences observed in the present study may be due to as-yet-unanalyzed factors which will be disclosed in the course of a comprehensive analysis of Collaborative Study data now underway.

One assumption about early neurological damage is that the behavioral adaptation to the insult tends to follow a predestined course, dependent on the site, severity, and time of the damage. Social factors in the past have largely been ignored. This study attempts to show that neurologically damaged infants from the lower class, when compared with similarly damaged infants from the higher social class, will perform more poorly on psychological tests at 4 years of age.

Recent investigations have shown that prematures, those subjected to perinatal stress, and developmentally retarded infants are more vulnerable to the adverse effects of a poor social environment than the normal child.

Drillien (1964) found that among full-term infants, social class differences in developmental quotient were approximately of the same magnitude at 4 years of age as they had been at 6 months of age. However, among premature infants, differences in developmental quotient between the higher- and lower-class children were far greater at 4 years than they had been at 6 months.

Werner et al. (1967), testing children at 20 months of age, found that social class produced only small differences in IQ if the delivery was uncomplicated, but that social class was strongly related to IQ among deliveries with severe complications.

Willerman, Broman, and Fiedler (1970) demonstrated that the incidence of IQs < 80 at 4 years of age for infants originally in the lowest quartiles of mental and motor development at 8 months of age was strongly related to the social class of their parents. Retarded infants from the lowest social class were seven times more likely to have 4-year IQs below 80 than similarly retarded infants from the highest social class. Conversely, infants in the highest quartiles of mental and motor development display no social-class effect in the incidence of low 4-year IQs.

PROCEDURE

Subjects

Subjects were 192 infants with a neurological diagnosis made by a physician immediately after administering a one-year neurological examination. These examinations are routinely performed on all children born into the Collaborative Study on Cerebral Palsy, Mental Retardation and Other Neurological and Sensory Disorders of Infancy and Childhood, sponsored by the National Institute of Neurological Diseases and Stroke, National Institutes of Health.

The project, still in progress, has included gravidae who have delivered over 48,000 infants at 12 collaborating hospitals throughout the country. The children are now being followed through 8 years of age with batteries of neurological, psychological, and speech, language, and hearing tests. All children in the present study, in addition to having a single neurological diagnosis, were required to have had 8-month and 4-year psychological examinations.

The subjects were chosen because they had only one of the following diagnoses: spastic hemiplegia, right or left; tetraplegia; paraplegia; hypotonia with deep tendon reflexes; dyskinesia; microcephaly, hydrocephaly; or mongolism. Cases having more than one of the above diagnoses were excluded, since our aim was to study relatively pure cases and thus be able to make more definitive statements about prognoses in individual disorders. The subjects, identified by computer, were individually matched with controls of like sex, race, hospital of birth, and socioeconomic status. None of the control subjects were diagnosed as having any neurological abnormality at 1 year of age.

On the basis of a socioeconomic index (SEI), a modification of the Bureau of the Census socioeconomic index adapted for the Collaborative Study by Myrianthopoulos and French (1968), all children were classified into one of three socioeconomic groups: low, middle or high. The SEI is multidimensional, based on the average of a set of rankings of head of household, education and occupation, and family income, and was assigned to the family around the time of delivery. The modal low-SEI member (values 0 to 39) might be characterized as an unskilled worker with no more than two years of high school and a family income of less than $3,500 per year ($n = 101$). The middle-SEI member (values 40 to 69) might be a skilled worker who graduated from high school with a family income of less than $5,000 per year ($n = 73$). The high-SEI member (70 to 98) might be a clerical worker, proprietor, or manager who would have completed at least one year of college and have a family income of at least $6,000 per year ($n = 18$).

As part of the Collaborative Study design, all children were administered the COLR Research Form of the Bayley Scales of Mental and Motor Development at age 8 months (Bayley, 1961). At 4 years of age all children were given either the abbreviated form of the Revised Stanford-Binet, Form L-M (1960), or in the event that their IQ could not be determined on the Binet, because of mental retardation preventing the establishment of a basal age, the children were given either the Cattell Infant Intelligence Scale or the Bayley Mental and Motor Scales.

Table 1 *Diagnosis by Social Class*

Diagnosis	Mean IQ	High	Middle	Low	N Total
Spastic hemiplegia right	99.2	1	3	2	6
Spastic hemiplegia left	81.3	0	1	2	3
Tetraplegia	86.8	1	9	8	18
Paraplegia	89.7	1	2	10	13
Hypotonia with deep tendon reflexes	89.8	11	45	60	116
Dyskinesia	76.5	2	2	3	7
Microcephaly	79.7	1	5	6	12
Hydrocephaly	83.8	1	6	8	15
Mongolism	39.0	0	0	2	2
Total		18	73	101	192

Table 1 gives the type of diagnosis by social class for all the neurologically damaged infants in the present study and mean 4-year IQs for each of the diagnostic categories. With the exception of the hypotonias, there are relatively few cases in most cells.

Mean IQs for each of the diagnostic categories rank from a high of 99.2 for the spastic right hemiplegias to a low of 39 for mongolism. However, most of these means are based on so few subjects that their statistical reliability is low.

Table 2 *Diagnosis by Race and Sex*

Diagnosis	White M	White F	Negro M	Negro F	Puerto Rican M	Puerto Rican F
Spastic hemiplegia right	0	1	2	2	0	1
Spastic hemiplegia left	0	0	3	0	0	0
Tetraplegia	2	2	8	6	0	0
Paraplegia	1	0	5	7	0	0
Hypotonia with deep tendon reflexes	45	36	17	15	3	0
Dyskinesia	4	1	1	1	0	0
Microcephaly	0	4	3	5	0	0
Hydrocephaly	3	5	2	1	2	2
Mongolism	0	0	0	2	0	0
Total	55	49	41	39	5	3
	104		80		8	

Table 2 presents diagnoses by race and sex. There appear to be differences in diagnosis as a function of race. In the combined categories of spasticity (right and left hemiplegia, tetraplegia, and paraplegia) there are only 6 whites as compared to 33 Negroes. Conversely, there were 81 whites diagnosed as hypotonic as compared to only 32 Negroes. The reasons for these differences are unclear.

RESULTS

Since there were only 18 cases in the "high" socioeconomic group, it was decided that for statistical purposes they be combined with the "middle" socioeconomic group, making a combined $n = 91$. Also, the eight Puerto Rican children are combined with the Negro sample in all subsequent analyses since their socioeconomic characteristics and mean IQs are very similar.

Table 3 gives mean Bayley Mental Scores at age 8 months for the neurologically damaged children and controls by race and social class. In all comparisons, as expected, the damaged children performed significantly more poorly than their controls regardless of race or social class. Looking at the damaged children separately it can be seen that there are no significant differences in Bayley Mental Scores between social classes at this age, and the same is true for the comparisons of the controls on Mental scores.

Table 4 gives mean Bayley Motor Scores at age 8 months. Again as expected, the damaged children performed significantly more poorly than their controls regardless of race or social class. Looking at the damaged children separately, once more there are no significant differences in Bayley Motor Scores between social classes at this age. The same holds true for the control Motor comparisons between social classes.

Table 5 gives mean Binet IQ scores at age 4. Among whites, the damaged children perform significantly more poorly than their controls regardless of social class. However, among the Negroes, the differences between the damaged children and their controls are not significant in either social class, although the trend is in the same direction.

For whites, there is a clear social-class effect, with middle-class damaged children performing significantly better than damaged lower-class children. This also occurs for the white controls. For Negroes, only the controls show a significant social-class effect. The damaged Negroes only show a nonsignificant trend in the expected direction. However, when the Negro and white samples are combined, there are clear social-class effects, with middle-class children performing significantly better than lower-class children.

Because of the increased variance among some of the neurologically damaged groups, as indicated by a significantly larger standard deviation

Table 3 Mean Bayley Mental Scores at Age 8 Months by Race and Social Class

	Race	N	$\overline{X}$ Middle	S.D.	N	$\overline{X}$ Low	S.D.	Between social classes t
White	Damage	62	74.9	(10.0)	43	72.2	(13.0)	1.2
	Control	62	80.7	(4.6)	43	81.2	(4.1)	−0.6
	Between damage and control t		4.6a		t	4.4a		
Negro	Damage	29	71.7	(13.0)	58	72.2	(11.1)	0.6
	Control	29	79.9	(3.7)	58	79.2	(4.3)	0.7
	Between damage and control t		3.4b		t	5.5a		
Total	Damage	91	73.9	(11.1)	101	71.0	(11.9)	1.7
	Control	91	80.5	(4.3)	101	80.0	(4.3)	0.8
	Between damage and control t		5.7a		t	7.1a		

a $p < .001$.
b $p < .01$.

for the damaged lower-class children, it seemed worthwhile to examine the number and percent of cases from *each* social class with IQs 79 and below, and this is done in Table 6. For illustrative purposes, we return to our threefold classification of social class. The proportion of damaged children with IQ ≤ 79 increases sevenfold (from 5 to 35 percent) from high to low social class. There are no retarded children among the higher class controls and only 14 percent retarded among the lower-class controls. Looking now within each of the social classes, the incidence of retardation (IQ ≤ 79) in the higher-class damaged cases is only 5 percent greater than their controls, whereas the incidence of retardation is 18 and 21 percent greater in the middle and lower classes, respectively. Thus, it

Table 4 *Mean Bayley Motor Scores at Age 8 Months by Race and Social Class*

	Race		Middle			Low		Between social classes
		N	$\overline{X}$	S.D.	N	$\overline{X}$	S.D.	t
White	Damage	62	26.6	(5.6)	43	25.4	(5.6)	1.1
	Control	62	32.7	(4.7)	43	33.8	(4.1)	1.2
	Between damage and control t		7.0[a]		t	7.4[a]		
Negro	Damage	29	25.4	(5.8)	58	26.1	(6.2)	−0.5
	Control	29	34.0	(3.9)	58	33.0	(3.7)	1.2
	Between damage and control t		6.9[a]		t	7.1[a]		
Total	Damage	91	26.2	(5.7)	101	25.8	(5.9)	0.5
	Control	91	33.1	(4.5)	101	33.3	(4.0)	0.3
	Between damage and control t		9.6[a]		t	10.2[a]		

[a] $p < .001$.

appears that with decreasing social class there is an increasing difference in the incidence of mental retardation between the damaged children and their controls. It suggests that low social class potentiates the likelihood of an unfavorable outcome for these neurologically damaged infants.

The objection may be raised that the phenomenon described may be due to the fact that the severity of the damage is greater in the lower-class population. Assuming greater severity of damage in the lower classes, one would expect larger differences between the subjects and their controls. Although this question cannot be answered directly from the present data, there are sufficient numbers of cases having the diagnosis "hypotonia with deep tendon reflexes" to compare hypotonics with their con-

Table 5 *Mean Binet IQ at Age 4 Years by Race and Social Class*

	Race		Middle N	Middle $\overline{X}$	Middle S.D.	Low N	Low $\overline{X}$	Low S.D.	Between social classes t
White	Damage		62	94.6	18.4	43	83.9	21.6	2.7[a]
	Control		62	106.1	14.7	43	99.9	10.6	2.4[a]
	Between damage and control	t		4.5[b]		t	4.4[b]		
Negro	Damage		29	89.2	18.2	58	82.2	17.5	1.7
	Control		28	96.6	16.5	58	87.1	12.9	2.5[c]
	Between damage and control	t		1.9		t	1.7		
Total	Damage		91	92.9	18.4	101	82.9	19.3	3.7[b]
	Control		91	103.0	15.8	101	92.6	13.0	5.0[b]
	Between damage and control	t		4.8[b]		t	4.2[b]		

[a] $p < .01$.
[b] $p < .001$.
[c] $p < .05$.

Table 6 *Frequency and Percent of Neurologically Damaged and Control Children with IQ ≤ 79 by Social Class*

SEI	N (pairs)	Damaged	Control	Diff.	X^2	P
High	18	1 (5%)	0 (0%)	5%	—[a]	—
Middle	73	18 (25%)	5 (7%)	18%	8.7	.01
Low	101	36 (35%)	14 (14%)	21%	12.9	.001
Total	192	55 (29%)	19 (10%)	19%	21.7	.001

[a] Expected values too small for X^2.

Table 7 *Frequency and Percent of Children Diagnosed "Hypotonic with Deep Tendon Reflexes" and Controls with IQ ≦ 79 by Social Class*

SEI	N (pairs)	Damaged	Control	Diff.	X^2	P
High	11	1 (9%)	0 (0%)	9%	—	—
Middle	45	10 (22%)	3 (7%)	15%	3.2[a]	.01
Low	60	19 (32%)	9 (15%)	17%	4.7	.05
Total	116	30 (26%)	12 (10%)	16%	9.4	.01

[a] Corrected for continuity.

trols by social class. This group as a whole may be considered among the least damaged of all the neurologically damaged cases, and the mean IQ of these children (89.8) is exceeded only by the mean IQ of the spastic right hemiplegias (IQ = 99.2).

Table 7 gives the number and percent of hypotonic cases with IQ ≦ 79 as a function of social class. The incidence of retardation in the higher-class hypotonics is 9 percent greater than their controls, whereas the incidence of retardation is 15 and 17 percent greater in the middle and lower classes, respectively. This suggests that severity of damage is *not* the variable responsible for the differential effects of damage between higher and lower classes.

DISCUSSION

The results show that neurologically damaged infants from the lower social class, when compared with similarly damaged infants from a higher social class, perform poorer on psychological tests at 4 years of age but not in infancy. We can assume that we are dealing with an originally homogeneous group of children in terms of developmental levels, since no significant differences were found between middle and low socioeconomic indices on mental *or* motor scores at age 8 months.[1] The 4-year findings are strikingly similar to those of Willerman, Broman, and Fied-

---

[1] Another question of bias can be raised that neurologically abnormal infants from higher social classes are institutionalized at a higher rate and therefore lost to follow-up. A comparison of the distributions of SEIs of the 110 institutionalized children in the Study and in the present report failed to reveal statistically significant differences in the distribution of SEIs in the two groups. Thus there does not appear to be a bias in terms of institutionalization rates for the different social classes.

ler (1970). Both that and the present report (Table 6) found a sevenfold greater likelihood of intellectual retardation in infants from the lower social class when they were developmentally retarded at age 8 months or neurologically abnormal at age 1 year, respectively.

The question also arises as to whether neurological diagnoses as well will change as a function of social class. The present report sheds no light on that particular issue, but there are a few relevant studies in the literature which prospectively followed the neurologically damaged child and investigated changes in neurological status over time. In a follow-up of 177 cases, Paine (1962) found considerable improvement in cerebral-palsied children, both spastics and athetoids, even in those cases with no therapy. The mild cases improved more than the moderates or severes, and the spastics improved more than the athetoids. Solomons, Holden, and Denhoff (1963) studied 36 children diagnosed as cerebral palsied between 4 and 12 months of life and followed until 3 years of age. They found that half the group improved so much that on reexamination they could be classified as "Normal." A reanalysis of these 18 improved cases suggested that the common factors in all were average intelligence of the child and an accepting attitude on the part of the mother. Social class was not studied. Neither of these studies employed any measures of social class, but it would be interesting to learn whether a relationship between neurological improvement and social class existed.

An aspect of the variable of social class operates via parental behavior toward the child and the question could be asked: What are the parental behaviors associated with differential outcomes in infancy and early childhood? Some efforts have been made to study this problem. For example, Williams and Scott (1953) found that developmental quotients of Negro infants were significantly higher for those whose mothers were classified as permissive-accepting as compared to those classified as rigid-rejecting. These mean differences were greater than those found when these same families were dichotomized as middle or lower class. Caldwell and Richmond (1967) found significant correlations ranging from $r = .30$ to $r = .75$ between certain components of mothers' affective and achievement behavior and the child's developmental quotient in the second year of life.

In conclusion, our results are interpreted as indicating a depressing effect of neurological damage and low social class on intelligence at 4 years. At 8 months of age there are no social-class differences in Bayley Mental or Motor Scores within the damaged or control children regardless of race. However, damaged white children show a stronger social class–IQ relationship at 4 years than damaged Negro children. The results are interpreted as suggesting that an enriched environment can favorably affect the intellectual fate of the neurologically damaged infant.

References

Bayley, N. *Manual for COLR research form of the Bayley Scales of Mental and Motor Development.* Collaborative Study, Perinatal Research Branch, NINDS, 1961.

Caldwell, B. M., & Richmond, J. B. Social class level and stimulation potential of the home. In J. Helmuth (Ed.), *Exceptional infant.* Seattle: Special Child Publications, 1967, pp. 453–466.

Drillien, C. M. *The growth and development of the prematurely born infant.* Baltimore: Williams & Wilkins, 1964.

Myrianthopoulos, N. C., & French, K. S. An application of the U.S. Bureau of the Census socioeconomic index to a large diversified population. *Soc. Sci. & Med.,* 1968, *2,* 293–299.

Paine, R. S. On the treatment of cerebral palsy. *Pediatrics,* 1962, *29,* 605–616.

Solomons, G., Holden, R. H., & Denhoff, E. The changing picture cerebral dysfunction in early childhood. *J. Pediat.,* 1963, *63,* 113–120.

Terman, L. M., & Merrill, M. A. *Stanford-Binet Intelligence Scale.* Boston: Houghton Mifflin, 1960.

Werner, E., Simonian, K., Bierman, J. M., & French, F. E. Cumulative effect of perinatal complications and deprived environment on physical, intellectual and social development of preschool children. *Pediatrics,* 1967, *39,* 490–505.

Willerman, L., Broman, S. H., & Fiedler, M. Infant development, preschool IQ and social class. *Child Develpm.,* 1970, *41,* 69–78.

Williams, J. R., & Scott, R. B. Growth of Negro infants: IV. Motor development and its relation to child rearing practices in two groups of Negro infants. *Child Develpm.,* 1953, *24,* 103–121.

25

Methods of Rehabilitation in Children with Neuromuscular Disorders

Herman Weiss and Henry B. Betts

> *Dr. Weiss is at the Rehabilitation Institute of Chicago and Dr. Betts is Professor in the Department of Physical Medicine and Rehabilitation at Northwestern University Medical School.*
>
> *This is an excellent article for the reader who wishes to get an overview of the management of the cerebral palsy child. The authors describe clearly the traditional approaches to cerebral palsy with the strong concentration on physical therapy and conclude with the multidisciplinary approach which characterizes their therapeutic program.*
>
> *One definite trend that can be noted in the literature on children with physical disorders is to tie in the child, family, and community in a global, total effort. The reader will see how this is effectively accomplished in the treatment program at the Rehabilitation Institute in Chicago.*

In discussing the treatment of such neuromuscular disorders as muscular dystrophy, polydermatomyositis, or polio, there is a general consensus of opinion among physicians. The principles of muscle reeducation and strengthening, prevention of deformities and the use of bracing are universally accepted. In contrast, great controversy arises when discussing the rehabilitation of the child with cerebral palsy.

FROM WEISS AND BETTS in *Pediatric Clinics of North America*, Vol. 14, No. 4, Nov. 1967. Reprinted by permission of W. B. Saunders Company, Philadelphia.

Articles on the subject of the rehabilitation of cerebral palsy patients have almost invariably begun or ended with an overt or subtle apology for the inadequacies of the treatment available. We propose to review the existing methods of treatment and to offer a more positive approach to the therapy of cerebral palsy, by far the most complex and difficult of neuromuscular disorders.[18] Our method of diagnosis, treatment and follow-up of the child with cerebral palsy is a global, comprehensive method which includes the parents and the community and capitalizes on assets to offset deficiencies.[2]

To describe the syndrome of cerebral palsy as dysfunction related to and resulting from a cerebral lesion implies a philosophy of total treatment of the individual child.[17] Because this dysfunction appears not only in the area of motor activity but also in the realms of perception, learning and emotion, authors writing on the subject unanimously acknowledge a need for total treatment. Concentration, however, has been directed toward physical therapy, for it is here that different methods may be proposed as "the optimal" procedure.

Methods of management are based on several assumptions. (1) Fine movement develops from crude movements. (2) Fine movements are controlled by cerebral cortical function. (3) Growth and development require progressive refinement of movement with the necessary assimilation of primitive, infantile reflex activity. (4) Poor development is due to the lack of assimilation, suppression and coordination of these primitive, postural reflex activities by higher levels of primarily cerebral cortical control.

The developmental sequential patterns of the central nervous system are in the cephalad fashion. The child's central nervous system learns to integrate the segmental and supraspinal postural tone reflexes into a meaningful experience that we then call funciton. The child learns to support his head and neck and orient himself to his environment in a vertical manner. He progresses from control of proximal activities, such as those of the head, neck and trunk, to distal ones, such as fine coordination of the fingers, and lastly to the use of his legs in a coordinated fashion.

The earliest manifestation of cerebral palsy is poor head-neck-trunk control, asymmetric tonic reflexes or persistence of abnormal pathologic reflexes. Unassimilated postural reflex tone promotes activities which resist cerebral cortical control, resulting in disturbance of muscle tone and movement.

Types of Cerebral Palsy

Traditionally, children with cerebral palsy are described according to disturbance of muscle tone and measured by a reaction to the myotatic (stretch) reflex. A child will be categorized as having spasticity if the stretch reflex is hyperactive and muscle tone constantly exaggerated. The "athetoid," mainly identified by rigidity and choreoathetoid movements, is characterized by bursts of hyper- or hypotonus and an inability of the cortex to suppress segmental and brain stem reflex activities when movement is initiated. The child with ataxia represents the last category of cerebral palsy, which is by far the smallest in number; traditionally, however, the clinician is impressed by the hypotonia apparent in this disability.

METHODS OF TREATMENT

In general, the procedures advocated by different groups have certain areas of agreement but many more points of almost contradiction. The need for controlled evaluations of all methods is apparent. They agree on a proximal-distal chronology in treatment and also on a gross to fine continuum. However, they disagree on the use of bracing, the decision to use or resist "natural" lesion-produced peculiarities of motion, the importance and function of residual reflex activity and the significance of sensory feedback. These disagreements, it must be explained, seem to be related more to a question of emphasis than to the exclusive use of particular methods of therapy.

Phelps proceeds generally from passive range of motion through active assistive to active motion for all joints, also relying on reciprocal motion of pairs of joints.[19] For the athetoid child he adds preliminary training in conscious relaxation. Motion is begun after this is achieved, and movement is encouraged in the least involved segments or limb. For ataxics he emphasizes the use of combined motions and development of balance and position sense. The use of extensive bracing to prevent and correct deformities and of special exercise equipment is advocated. During the exercise phase of the program, music is used to promote rhythm of movement. Reciprocal motion is started in the proximal joints and progresses distally. Massage is advocated to overcome spasticity and slow stretch is advocated so as not to cause stretch reflex induced spasticity.

The popular use of weights on shoes, wrists, and crutches is advocated by Phelps. These reduce extraneous movements and promote coordination. In effect it promotes more proprioceptive sensory feedback which is so vital for coordinated activities. Primitive movement patterns, as described in reptilian stages of phylogeny, are seen when cortical control suppressor and coordinator centers are destroyed or released by decerebration phenomena. The midbrain and lower centers then respond to proprioceptive sensory feedback. Thus postural attitudes and reflex activities can be facilitated.

Doman and associates [4] have promoted Fay's techniques and added various sensory stimulation, body image training and breathing techniques in an effort to upgrade the functional abilities of the child. In direct opposition to this is the approach employed by the Bobaths.[1] It is their contention that the ultimate functional problems of the child with cerebral palsy are due primarily to the uninhibited firing of these same reflex chains that Fay encouraged.

Two systems of treatment emphasize the importance of the reflex activity of the body. In one it is utilized and maximized and in the other it is inhibited and extinguished. Followers of Fay[6] use reflexes as the initiators of movement patterns. Exercise programs consist of eliciting various combinations and sequences of reflex chains to produce, for example, automatic "walking" movements. Continued repetition is believed to yield an increase in functional muscle activity. Bobath refers to paresis as arising from a disturbance of the normal postural reflex mechanism. Normal muscle tone results from integration of postural reflex activities at all levels: spinal, brain stem, midbrain and cerebral cortex. Normally, spinal and tonic reflexes are inhibited by adaptive movements such as the righting reflex and equilibrium reflexes. When a patient is spastic, increase in muscle tone occurs and co-contraction of groups arises, agonist and antagonist, more confined to proximal groups than distal. Co-contraction is energy-consuming and deranges movement. The "athetoid" shows the postural reflex patterns very strongly with asymmetrical and symmetrical tonic neck reflex and tonic labyrinthine reflexes. The distinguishing disturbance is the lack of co-contraction and the lack of fixed postural tone. This is apparent by a fluctuating type of muscle tone. The Bobath method concentrates on the learning of body postures which are directly resistant to the particular abnormal reflex pattern, and it is in the independent assumption of such postures that the child is able to control his body. Their method is somewhat more limited than Fay's in application since it cannot be used with children who have deformities, low intelligence or severe spasticity.

A method which is founded upon a specific theory of proprioceptive neuromuscular facilitation patterns (that of Herman Kabat)[10] is that practiced by two physical therapists (Knott and Voss).[15] It emphasizes progressing from a position of extreme stretch in a muscle group to extreme flexion and employs both isometric and isotonic forms of exercise. The individual exercises maximize mass movement patterns in a spiral and diagonal system. They emphasize the value of concomitant sensory stimulation, direct and indirect, in the generalization and facilitation of activities. They employ no bracing or assistive devices and utilize and reinforce reflex patterns. Reinforcement of the exercise pattern is aided by oral commands. The neurophysiologic rationale was based on Sherrington's work on the spinal process or irradiation or spread of excitation with increasing strength of peripheral muscle contraction.[21] This is further substantiated by Gellhorn's work demonstrating that the excitability of the motor cerebral cortex is increased by muscle stretch and resistance to movement, causing greater sensory feedback to the cortex (proprioceptive stimulation primarily).[7, 8] Thus the term "P.N.F.," or proprioceptive neuromuscular facilitation, has been coined. However, if the sensory feedback mechanism is impaired, then posture, tone, and reflex activity are concomitantly diminished. This same rationale may be applied to methods of therapy previously discussed.

One might pause to reflect a bit on what has been read so far. The methods described focus on the quality and manner of muscle tone, either utilizing or encouraging postural tone reflex, increasing muscle tone or inhibiting or suppressing abnormal tone. Not only do these systems call for appropriate sensory motor reflex arcs with emphasis on intact sensation, but they also require a considerable degree of conscious awareness: the ability of the child to supply conscious movements and to assimilate and coordinate them into meaningful actions. This degree of cortical awareness implies that the patient is nearly intact intellectually, but this is not always the case. Any child who has poor sensory feedback mechanisms, either through peripheral impairment, touch, proprioceptive or higher cortical defects which impair kinesthesia,[22] will have an intellectual deficit. A multiply handicapped child functions in a sensory vacuum.[9, 24] There are different degrees of impairment depending on the degree of disability, intellect or learning ability.[23] This is dependent upon the sensory feedback; that is, if the child has some deficient sensory feedback and has been placed in a nonfunctional wheelchair, he has no opportunity to explore his environment, and with poor postural attitudes he fails to gain the upright position and develop vertical visual relationships. He has no sense of space, texture or depth, which are the building blocks of learning. This child is called paretic.

The measure of paresis is, of course, the amount of functional ability. If function in a particular muscle group is hampered by antagonistic spasticity, by a lack of sensory feedback or awareness, or by lack of functional mobility in the performance of meaningful activities, the child is termed paretic. In many instances, however, this is aggravated by "disuse weakness." Problems of function, or rather the lack of function, require a global, total therapy approach and a sensorimotor, intellectual and emotionally oriented treatment program. Without this effort all systems of therapy break down. No one isolated therapist can practice a system of therapy and achieve any degree of success in terms of the functional goals that the child is entitled to have.

Another approach which capitalizes on a theory of sensorimotor interfacilitation is that of Rood.[20] The goal is to stimulate cutaneous receptors and proprioceptors and thereby to induce contraction in a particular muscle group. Rood utilizes ice, as an anesthetic, and light stroking or brushing, as stimuli, to inhibit or stimulate the cutaneous receptors. Proprioception is elicited by stretching the muscle and tendon, thereby facilitating contraction. Her technique is based on neurophysiologic observations confirmed by Eldred and Hagbath.[5]

The last specific method to be described is one which approaches most closely our own procedures, that espoused by Deaver.[3] His emphasis is on improvement of functional activities, and to this end he concentrates upon the extremity involved in the particular function. This is then restricted until it is capable of only two types of movement. Extensive bracing, if necessary, is employed at first and gradually removed as the child gains greater control over the parts of his body. Deaver also advocates the use of a period of inpatient care for most children. During this time, accurate inventories of skill and problem areas can be made. He utilizes, besides bracing, any and all assistive devices necessary for establishing maximal independence for the child in activities of daily living, with particular emphasis on bed and wheelchair activities. Higher levels of performance are encouraged where they are considered practical.

Review

There is a preoccupation with the status of paresis and muscle tone in the treatment of cerebral palsy. Evolutionary thinking in neurophysiology has generated diagnostic categories based on hypotonus, hypertonus and fluctuating tone—spastic, athetoid, ataxic. The Bobaths encouraged cortical control and suppression of more premature postural reflex activities. They think of co-contraction of agonist and antagonist as characteristic of spastic patients and are articulate in their description of the abnormalities present in postural reflex activities. In effect, the emphasis of therapy is conscious effort and control of the pathologic sequelae of abnormal central nerve lesions. Equally as rational are Fay's efforts at utilizing and referring these abnormal reflex patterns into generating tone where a deficit exists or reinforcing postural tone reflex activity to "induce" a lower threshold of central nervous system excitability and mature higher levels of functioning in a "cephalad fashion." The method of Doman et al. is termed an effort at total management but unfortunately is totally patient-oriented and not really global. Kabat's [11] rationale of proprioceptive sensorimotor feedback is productive of gross movement but produces little discrete functional carryover. The one practical method that begins to focus mainly on function is that of Deaver. He is more concerned about functional abilities and disregards the cosmetic appearance of the athetoid. He pays less attention to tone, paresis or reflex activities and more to practical problems of how movement can be facilitated, and patterns of movement helped by bracing and splinting, to accomplish activities such as feeding, wheeling a chair or transferring to a bed.

The description of how the Children's Division of the Rehabilitation Institute of Chicago functions must necessarily lean heavily on exposition of treatment philosophy. To try to be inclusive with respect to technique or devices employed would be useless, for ours is essentially an eclectic approach and uses whatever seems most appropriate for the individual child at a particular time and in a particular activity. This flexibility is one of the advantages of a multidisciplinary approach and of a center with enough staff so that different treatment orientations are represented within each field.

CAPITALIZATION METHOD

Our approach considers the child, family and community in a global, total effort. We consider describing a child's muscle tone and anatomic deficit and the severity of his disease to be only the first phase in diagnosis. A comprehensive assay of deficits, physical, intellectual and emotional, is not sufficient. It is just as important, if not more so, to have a similar evaluation of assets and strengths. It is from the total knowledge of assets that we can capitalize and substitute in areas where there is complete loss of function and compensate where there is deficiency. The goal is to capitalize on muscle, sensory and intellectual assets to offset deficits and achieve function. The chief goal is more efficient function; cosmesis is secondary.

Before beginning our diagnostic evaluation we must relate the child in a vertical position to his environment. The child must have adequate eye, head and neck control to have appropriate visual coordinates. Too often the drooling, hypotonic youngster with no head and neck control is "tested out" [16] unjustly, with poor results, because his chin rests on his chest; the "aphasoid" qualities are so apparent that only rough, inadequate estimates are made of intellectual and physical developmental abilities. In addition to establishing visual coordinates and encouraging head and neck control, recognition must be given to figure ground relationships as part of the visual sensory feedback mechanism. Care is taken to insure foot-ground contact when in the wheelchair. To accomplish this, blocks of wood may have to be added.

When adequate visual and emotional rapport is established, our diagnostic assay has begun. It is acknowledged that a child with multiple handicaps of intellectual, motor, sensory and emotional development may have functioned in a sensory vacuum. It has been our clinical experience that a controlled environment with subdued and structured stimulation is necessary for accurate diagnostic work-up. Generally an inpatient stay is required at this time.

The overall philosophy of the program is a principle of capitalizing on and emphasizing strengths over weaknesses in areas of function. This permeates all three phases of our program: diagnosis, treatment and follow-up. The listing of diagnosis as the first phase rather than as a preliminary step is based on the belief that it is only by extensive and intensive evaluation that the complete child can be adequately known. This, in practice, means that all medical and paramedical facilities of the Institute are utilized for evaluation of each child under the coordination of the physiatrist. Each is asked to emphasize strengths and to suggest whatever is deemed helpful in each particular area. All specialties are represented at a staff conference with the physiatrist, where a coordinated plan of procedure is drawn up for the child, delineating both long-term goals and explicit proximate aims, substitution for absolute loss and compensations for poor levels of function.

The emphasis in the treatment phase is on optimal functioning in daily living. For the child this would also include learning activities, so that special education classes are as much a part of the program as are physical therapy, occupational therapy and speech therapy. In treatment we start with fundamental orientation of the child in his environment. Practically this means head-neck control, head-eye coordination and eye-hand coordination. All are given major emphasis and must be established before any further training is attempted. Both bracing and assistive devices are used to implement each step of the treatment program. Substitute motions which serve functional purposes are encouraged and reinforced as are the adaptive uses of reflex patterns.

Khalili's work [12-14] on peripheral nerve blocks has added a valuable new dimension in the management of the spastic child. By his use of dilute phenol solutions he can effectively relieve spasticity of a particular muscle and facilitate overall functional upgrading. Phenol, at 2 to 3 per cent dilutions, injected into a nerve will have a selective affinity for gamma fibers of the proprioceptive nerve system. This will relieve muscle tone, spasticity particularly, for a year or more. If antagonistic muscles which are spastic can be relieved of involuntary spasm, the agonist and synergistic groups may be permitted to function. The evaluation and selection for a nerve block procedure places a high priority on functional results.

The social and emotional development of the child and his integration into both the family unit and the community are dealt with directly by psychology and social service and indirectly by all other staff. This includes the parents as well as the child himself. It is acknowledged by all who work with children with cerebral palsy that they are slow in maturation, physically, emotionally and intellectually, and because of this fact, it is imperative that an active follow-up program be maintained for each child. New problems arise and new abilities emerge with growth, and each must be taken into consideration. This is done at our Institute by frequent periodic recheck appointments with the physiatrist and, at his discretion, re-evaluations by the various disciplines. It is our policy, when feasible, to follow the child until he reaches adulthood and has found his own particular niche in his family and the society at large.

In an effort to develop appropriate community attitudes, an enormous amount of energy has been put into organizing "community auxiliaries." The purpose of these groups is to pursue the follow-up phase of our program. Under the guidance of the Social Service Department, home visits are made and pertinent information obtained. The auxiliaries become more acquainted with the handicapped child's needs, and architectural projects are undertaken to remove barriers. Sheltered workshops, educational programs and other areas of need are being filled and with the gradual change of community attitudes, the handicapped will find meaning and purpose in their existence.

SUMMARY AND CONCLUSIONS

Over the past several years a wealth of knowledge of the neurophysiology of the central nervous system has accrued. The application of this knowledge has served to spawn many methods of treatment of the child with cerebral palsy. The authors have here attempted a review of the most prominent of these methods and have offered their own view.

It is our opinion that the problem of children with cerebral palsy is most complex in its diagnosis, treatment and follow-up to productive living. It has been our clinical experience that only by means of a comprehensive method of management can the best results be obtained. We advocate a shift in the thinking of the medical community. Total management requires the multidisciplinary approach in determining assets, capitalizing on these in therapy and reaching out past the patient into the community to give him realistic, productive functioning.

References

1. Bobath, K., & Bobath, B.: A treatment of cerebral palsy. *Brit. J. Phys. Med.*, 1952, *15*, 105.
2. Cruickshank, W. M., & Raus, G. M.: *Cerebral Palsy: Its Individual and Community Problems.* Syracuse, Syracuse University Press, 1955.
3. Deaver, G. G.: Cerebral palsy: Methods of treating the neuro-muscular disabilities. *Arch. Phys. Med. Rehab.*, 1956, *37*, 363–367.
4. Doman, R. J., et al.: Children with severe brain injuries: Neurological organization in terms of mobility. *J.A.M.A.*, 1960, *174*, 257–262.
5. Eldred, E., & Hagbath, K. E.: Facilitation and inhibition of gamma efferents by stimulation of certain skin areas. *J. Neuropsychiat.*, 1955, *3*, 644–652.
6. Fay, T.: The use of pathological unlocking reflexes in the rehabilitation of spastics. *Amer. J. Phys. Med.*, 1954, *33*, 347.
7. Gellhorn, E.: Proprioception and the motor cortex. *Brain*, 1949, *72*, 35.

8. Gellhorn, E.: Validity of the concept of multiplicity of representation in the motor cortex under conditions of threshold stimulation. *Brain*, 1950, *73*, 268.
9. Jones, M. H.: The management of hemiplegic children with peripheral sensory loss. *Pediat. Clin. N. Amer.*, 1960, *7*, 765–775.
10. Kabat, H., & Knott, M.: Proprioceptive facilitation techniques for treatment of paralysis. *Physical Ther. Review.*, 1953, *33*, 53–64.
11. Kabat, H.: Studies on neuromuscular dysfunction. XV: Role of central facilitation of motor function in paralysis. *Arch. Phys. Med.*, 1952, *33*, 521.
12. Khalili, A., & Benton, J. G.: A physiologic approach to the evaluation and the management of spasticity with procaine and phenol nerve block. *Clin. Ortho.*, 1966, *47*, 97–103.
13. Khalili, A. A., et al.: Management of spasticity by selective peripheral nerve block with dilute phenol solutions in clinical rehabilitation. *Arch. Phys. Med.*, 1964, *45*, 513–519.
14. Khalili, A. A., & Betts, H. B.: Peripheral nerve block with phenol in management of spasticity: Indications and complications. *J.A.M.A.*, 1967, *200*, 1155.
15. Knott, M., & Voss, D. E.: *Proprioceptive Neuromuscular Facilitation*. New York, Paul B. Hoeber, 1956.
16. Myklbust, H. R., & Boshes, B.: Psychoneurological learning disorders in children. *Arch. Pediat.*, 1960, *77*, 247–256.
17. Paine, R. S.: On the treatment of cerebral palsy. *Pediatrics*, 1962, *29*, 605.
18. Perlstein, M. A., & Hood, P. N.: Infantile spastic hemiplegia: Incidence. *Pediatrics*, 1954, *14*, 436–454.
19. Phelps, W. M.: Birth injuries. *Practitioners* (The Library of Medicine and Surgery, New York), 1936, *9*, 935.
20. Rood, M. S.: Neurophysiological mechanisms utilized in the treatment of neuromuscular dysfunction. *Amer. J. Occup. Ther.*, 1956, *10*, 220.
21. Sherrington, C. S.: *Selected Writings* (D. Denny-Brown, Ed.) New York, Paul B. Hoeber, 1940.
22. Tachdjian, M. O., and Minear, W. L.: Sensory disturbances in the hands of children with cerebral palsy. *J. Bone Joint Surg.*, 1958, *40A*, 85–90.
23. Tizard, J. P. M., Paine, R. S., & Crothers, C.: Disturbances of sensation in children with hemiplegia. *J.A.M.A.*, 1954, *155*, 628–632.
24. Twitchell, T. E.: Sensory factors in purposive movement. *J. Neurophysiol.*, 1954, *17*, 239–252.

26

Some Aspects of Specific Learning Disabilities in Children

Sidney Rosenblum

Dr. Rosenblum is Professor of Psychology at the University of New Mexico. His research interests in addition to learning disabilities in children and adolescents are on activity levels in children, cognitive and personality development in the mentally subnormal, and antecedents of behavioral abnormalities in children. A very active psychologist, he has held many consultantships, participated in many workshops and conferences, and has published over twenty major articles.

Children with learning disabilities have become a topic of major interest in recent years. Dr. Rosenblum does an excellent job of presenting the reader with an overview of the problem, sparing him of unnecessary jargon, and providing him with a useful glossary at the end. For the student wishing to pursue the topic in more depth, he will find the bibliography most helpful.

This paper focuses on the elementary school child who fails to learn one or more of the basic academic skills necessary for school and community success and whose lack of achievement cannot be explained by such commonly accepted causes of learning problems as mental retardation, gross sensory impairment, emotional disturbance, lack of motivation, environmental disadvantage, or poor pedagogy. In years past these children were quite often considered either the dunces or recalcitrants of the class or possessed of a "learning block" and were left mostly to their own devices until, frequently, they chose to drop out of school. Today, they are viewed more realistically as individuals with identifiable learning disabilities for whom systematic remedial help is not only available but usually highly salutary.

Although wide individual differences abound among these children (virtually every child with a learning problem presents a singularly unique case), as a group they have been characterized as experiencing difficulties in one or more of the basic psychological processes involved in understanding or using spoken or written languages. Stated another way, there apparently is disruption of some sort in the processing of information received by the child, manifesting itself typically as difficulty in listening, thinking, reading, writing, spelling, or arithmetic, either in isolation or some combination. (The reader is referred to the glossary at the end of this section for a sample of terms used to describe these problems.)

INCIDENCE

The number of children with learning disabilities of this type can be only roughly estimated. Denhoff et al. (1968) have stated that these disorders are reaching "epidemic proportions" among children of normal intelligence. Ellingson (1967) estimates there are close to 6 million such "shadow children," as she calls them, which constitutes about 17 percent of the total school-aged population (between 6 and 18). More commonly cited figures range between 3 and 5 percent of children in this age group, or around 1 to 1½ million (Myklebust & Boshes, 1960).

Part of the difficulty in reliably assessing the exact scope of the problem lies in the fact that most of these children are not grouped in easily identifiable units, such as special classes. They have typically remained in a regular classroom setting, pursuing the standard curriculum as best they can, and have achieved identification as disabled learners only after repeated and progressive failure. Other blocks to the accumulation of more precise figures are the lack of refined techniques for identification of the problem and the confusing and repetitious terminology used in its description. For example, the Public Health Service recently published 38 different terms employed by professionals in describing children with learning disabilities caused by presumed damage to the brain (Clements, 1966).

Whatever the exact figures may be, the fact remains that each year sizable numbers of children fail to acquire and/or retain specific school-related skills in spite of average or better intelligence, an absence of gross defects in vision or hearing, adequate motivation, and exposure to and practice with modes of classroom instruction that profit their peers. These children are typically free of neurotic disorders, although repeated failure in school may lead either to major disturbances in conduct, such as temper tantrums and aggressive behavior, or to withdrawal tendencies with accompanying depression and anxiety.

CAUSES

In the absence of the above commonly cited causes of learning disabilities, researchers have alternatively stressed two other factors in the etiology of children's failure to learn: (1) malfunctions or lesions in the brain, and (2) maturational lags.

The role of brain damage in the etiology of learning disorders is certainly not a new concept. Historically, Broadbent in 1872 (Westman, Arthur, & Scheidler, 1965) was among the first to document a learning problem (in this case a reading disability) due to cerebral impairment, and since his time literally hundreds of articles have cited organic deficits as the major cause of learning failure. When damage is severe, as is true, for example, in cases of profound retardation, cerebral palsy, cortical blindness, deafness, or epilepsy, the subsequent interference with learning is most usually dramatic and extensive. However, the learning problems manifested by most children are not the consequence of involved neurological impairment but are due to cortical malfunctions of a less severe and often more subtle nature.

The latter group has increasingly become identified as manifesting "minimal brain dysfunction" (MBD), a condition that involves close to 100 observable behavioral signs according to Clements (1966). Although they cluster differentially for each child, the most commonly cited behavioral consequents of MBD include the following: impairment of muscle movements or coordination; deviations in attention, activity levels, impulse control, and effect; specific perceptual, intellectual, and memory deficits; and disorders of speech, hearing, and language.

Unfortunately, since "MBD" describes both a condition and its presumed cause, the label appears to be circular and lacking in precision. Recently, Boshes and Myklebust (1964) have embarked upon an ambitious long-range research project aimed at eliminating the vagueness of the concept through improved analyses of detailed diagnostic information and the testing of programs designed for remediation of specific disabilities. These researchers hypothesize that learning problems are caused primarily, but not exclusively, by disturbances in the occipital–parietal area of the brain, and they use the term *"psychoneurological* learning disability" to describe the psychological consequences of these neurological deficits. Stevens and Birch (1957), recognizing the problems inherent in the concept MBD, have suggested that the term be eliminated entirely, and that children of average or better intelligence with perceptual, motor, and attentional difficulties be labeled as manifesting the "Strauss syndrome," in honor of a pioneer researcher and practitioner in the field of children's learning difficulties (Strauss & Lehtinen, 1947). Although the term may have heuristic as well as sentimental value, it would appear that "minimal brain dysfunction" remains the preferred etiological label of authorities, as judged by references in the literature. Indeed, Dunn (1967) suggests that even the "Strauss syndrome" is too much of a catch-all phrase, needing subcategories for more precise communication among professionals.

A second factor cited as a cause of learning disabilities is that of "maturational lag." Adherents of this point of view (e.g., Ames, 1968; Bender, 1957) imply that there may be genetically determined variations in the appearance of different functions controlled by the brain. In other words, there may be irregularities in the developmental time clock which result in imbalances in the child's total level of skill development or delay the appearance of abilities normatively viewed in his age mates. Often, family investigations reveal adult relatives with histories of maturational delays similar to those of the child (Glaser & Clemmens, 1965).

In discussing children with developmental lags, Bender (1956) suggests they typically reveal "soft" neurological signs upon examination. For example, they tend to be clumsy, show left–right confusion, lack orientation involving their bodies, and demonstrate distortions in form perception. Observations of this kind have led some to speculate that these children would profit most from a program of "therapeutic neglect," that is, time to catch up with themselves. Others (Ames, 1968) believe special education attention is needed while maturation progresses. Bender (1957) states that many of these children have the potential for accelerating their academic development, particularly since they maintain their ability to think abstractly, a characteristic that significantly differentiates them from their brain-damaged peers.

IDENTIFICATION AND ANALYSIS OF LEARNING DISABILITIES

Children with potential learning disabilities often present behavioral signs at an early age that portend future school difficulties. A parent may recognize in his preschool child the awkward movements, slow speech development, failure to understand the language of others, highly changeable emotions, and low frustration tolerance that are predictive of later school problems. A family physician, pediatrician, or neurologist may be asked to examine the child at that time, particularly for vision and hearing, and may also require an electroencephalograph (EEG) test to spot abnormal brain patternings. Depending on the nature of the case, medications or drugs may be prescribed in an effort to help remediate whatever behavioral problems are extant.

Nearly all these children will begin a regular school program, and it is here that specific learning problems are most likely to be evinced and identified. Indeed, a sensitive and knowledgeable teacher trained to recognize and describe learning problems can play a major role in the early diagnosis and subsequent remediation of such difficulties. By spotting visual and hearing defects, perceptual and motor weaknesses, maturational immaturities, and inadequate responses to instruction the teacher can begin the diagnostic–remedial process that incorporates the expertise of a variety of professionals interested in the problem.

Although there is growing encouragement for teachers themselves to administer and score specific evaluation techniques aimed at identifying the scope and nature of a child's learning problems (Kephart, 1968; McCarthy, 1969), it is often not possible for this to be done in light of other, more pressing classroom commitments. It is here that the psychologist, preferably one with interests in the learning process of children, can play a helpful diagnostic role. A variety of techniques are available to the psychologist, among which the following representative examples have been found to be particularly useful in contributing to precise diagnostic formulations:

Illinois Test of Psycholinguistic Abilities (Kirk, McCarthy, & Kirk, 1968): an individually administered test designed for the detection of abilities and disabilities of psycholinguistic functions in children between the ages of 2 and 10.

Wepman Auditory Discrimination Test (Wepman, 1958): an individual test for children between the ages of 5 and 8 which identifies auditory deficits by presenting oral word pairs for the child to discriminate.

The Purdue Perceptual–Motor Survey (Roach & Kephart, 1966): a screening test for perceptual–motor deficits in children through the performance of tasks involving gross and fine motor movements.

Marianne Frostig Developmental Test of Visual Perception (Frostig, 1961): a test of the perceptual adequacy of children between the ages of 3 and 8, using tasks of eye–motor coordination, figure–ground discrimination, form consistency, position in space, and spatial relations.

Bender Visual–Motor Gestalt Test (Bender, 1938): a measure of perception and visual–motor coordination based on performance in copying designs.

Wechsler Intelligence Scale for Children (Wechsler, 1949): an individual test of general and specific intellectual functioning of children based on a minimum of five verbal and five performance subtests.

Certainly, the diagnostic skills of the neurologist, pediatrician, ophthalmologist, and psychiatrist are as valuable for children of school age as they are for preschoolers, and any complete diagnostic procedure should include data obtained from examinations provided by these specialists. In addition, the diagnostic services of a speech therapist, audiologist, and reading specialist may contribute significantly to the complete understanding of the child's learning difficulties.

Some general principles involving the total diagnosis of children with learning disabilities have been discussed in comprehensive fashion by Bateman (1964, 1967) and Wood (1960), among others. On the whole, there is general agreement among authorities that a diagnostic evaluation must result not merely in a global classification of the child's difficulties but a precise formulation of the specific disability involved. Thus, "directionality disturbances underlying reversals in reading" is to be preferred to the more general diagnostic label, "reading retardation" or "dyslexia."

REMEDIATION: GENERAL PROCEDURES

Once all the evaluation data are in, remedial procedures geared to aid the child's specific problem(s) must begin. Kephart (1968) suggests three general frameworks within which remediation may be implemented: (1) the regular classroom teacher aids the child in his own setting; (2) regularly scheduled, adjunctive procedures are provided outside the regular classroom; and (3) separate classes are established.

Regular Classroom Setting

When a child's learning problems interfere with relatively few classroom-oriented activities, working on the difficulty within the context of the class setting is preferred to treating the child in isolation from his customary peers. Kephart (1968) states that this would be the recommendation of choice for a variety of reasons, not the least of which is that "retention within the classroom maintains the basic relationship to education represented by these difficulties and encourages an attack upon them which is educationally based" (1968, p. 125). There is also tentative evidence coming from the work of Kirk and McCarthy that children with minimal difficulties who are removed from their regular classes demonstrate less progress overall and tend to have greater difficulty returning to the mainstream of their normal academic setting than is true for comparison groups receiving aid in their own classrooms (McCarthy, 1969).

Adjunctive Programs

When children present the more involved learning problems that substantially interfere with classroom progress (e.g., reading, writing, spelling), and to which the teacher cannot attend adequately, special adjunctive programs may be needed. Kephart (1968) suggests that the model for such programs may be found in provisions made by school systems for children with speech difficulties. Such children are typically removed from their regular activities for routinely scheduled periods of group or individual therapy and instruction, returning to the classroom afterward.

Services for disabled learners may be similarly scheduled, utilizing the services of specialists who come to the child's own school, a central psychological clinic run by the school system, or the facilities of community child development or university-based centers. Whatever the locus of these programs, their goal is to help the child achieve within the framework of his natural classroom setting by offering remedial help in those areas that are interfering with academic progress.

Special Classes

Some children (relatively few of the kind described in this paper) manifest learning difficulties so extensive as to preclude normal classroom participation. These are the "hard-core" learning cases who have little to gain from the curricular experiences that profit their peers, and whose problems are likely to intensify significantly in the regular classroom. Special classes are needed for such children, where remedial personnel and programs can focus on the difficulties involved. In most cases, this intensive, segregated form of treatment must be thought of as a long-term experience for the children involved, often buttressed by psychotherapeutic sessions geared for ameliorating accompanying emotional difficulties. Every effort must be made, however, to return these students ultimately to their regular classrooms and the mainstream of academic life.

REMEDIATION: SPECIFIC TECHNIQUES

Specific remedial techniques are formulated after a thorough diagnostic picture of the learning problem has evolved. Since remediation involves the learning process per se, it is preferable that teachers or educational psychologists interested and trained in learning disabilities be responsible for the bulk of the remedial effort. There currently exists, however, a shortage of qualified personnel, and until larger numbers of such professionals appear on the scene, it is highly likely that the classroom teacher herself will need to implement the recommendations emanating from the diagnostic evaluation.

The following procedures are offered as a representative sample of the sorts of activities from which children with learning disabilities have profited, and are drawn heavily from the recommendations made by Kephart (1968) in his very pragmatic guide to the remediation of learning problems. The reader is also referred to Frierson and Barbe (1967) and Godfrey and Kephart (1969) for additional, practical aid in formulating specific remedial programs. It should be noted that although certain general procedures are described in all resources, in actual practice the remedial program for any given child with a learning problem must be highly individualized. As Kephart states: "No technique is 'good' for all children, and by the same token, no technique is 'bad' for all children. Techniques are but suggestions of possible ways to approach certain types of problems" (1968, p. 82). He further suggests that the primary goal of any remedial program should be to teach the child generalizable responses rather than specific skills. To that end, constant variations of any basic activity or procedure must be presented and practiced.

In many cases the *gross motor responses* of disabled learners are deficient, particularly in the areas of balance, laterality, locomotion, and coordination, and retraining programs are needed to improve them. Ideally, such activities are centered in specially oriented programs of physical education departments, but when such facilities are unavailable or limited, the teacher may be able to foster these skills within the classroom. Practice in walking either upright or in a squatting position on a log or "T"-beam can improve the child's balance, coordination, and notions of left and right. Goal-oriented jumping, hopping, crawling, and rolling activities move the child's body through space in ways that are probably less familiar to him than walking and running. Jumping activities may be combined with orientation tasks, such as asking a child to jump up and make a half-turn while in the air after first describing how he will be facing when he completes the task successfully. Hopping on one foot involves a balance problem for the child; rolling on a mat teaches the concepts of forward and backward, and left and right. Children can also be taught "pacing," either by having music introduced into the performance of their motor activities or by simply having them clap their hands rhythmically while moving about. Insofar as possible, all these activities should be presented as problem-solving tasks of one sort or another, with interest focused on the learning that is taking place rather than the final quality of the performance.

Activities involving *fine motor responses* include coloring, paper-cutting, pasting, tracing, finger painting, modeling with clay and paper-mache, and copying figures or designs on the blackboard. As the reader realizes, most of these activities are more typical of the skills required in routine academic endeavors than is true of gross motor responses, and therefore have greater generalization value to actual learning situations in the classroom. In practicing such activities, perceptual "feedback" is generated which guides the child's subsequent movements. Such visual monitoring of motor responses is mandatory for the achievement of a variety of academic skills, particularly writing.

If the child is experiencing primary difficulty with *perceptual relationships*, a variety of procedures may be utilized to improve whatever deficiencies exist. Materials developed by Marianne Frostig and her associates (Frostig & Horne, 1964) have proved effective. They involve, among other activities, paper and pencil exercises designed to foster visual–motor coordination, figure–ground perception, perceptual constancy, position in space, and spatial relationships. Through such activities children are helped to develop skills in shifting from concrete experiences to symbolic representations and back. Another program, similar in intent to Frostig's, is Vallet's (1967) handbook of psychoeducational exercises, which involve instructional materials for improving sensory–motor, conceptual, perceptual, social, and language skills.

A variety of remedial techniques have been suggested when children encounter difficulties with *specific school subjects* during exposure to a regular academic curriculum. Approaches for nonreaders of average or better intelligence have been discussed by Bookbinder and Flierl (1968), Bryant (1965), Campbell (1965), Fletcher (1967), Frierson (1967), Money (1962), and Rabinovitch et al. (1954, 1962), among many others, and merit the attention of the interested reader. Suggested procedures for children with spelling difficulties are presented by Brueckner and Bond (1967), while Kaliski (1962) summarizes her techniques in teaching arithmetic and Enstrom (1968) discusses poor handwriting and its remediation.

Implicit in all these presentations is the underlying notion that any technique utilized must be geared for the dominant sense modality on which the disabled learner depends for processing informational input. Although vision is most commonly relied upon, a large number of children find auditory presentations of material more beneficial. Still others rely on their tactual or kinesthetic senses and learn most profitably when they are permitted to manipulate materials.

A more general implication of this point for educators is that classroom subject matter should be *routinely* presented in multiple forms, permitting children to use whichever sensory avenue is most efficient for them. Indeed, it is highly likely that typical reliance on visually presented textbook materials contributes significantly to the spiraling academic failure of children for whom some other sense modality is more efficient. As Kephart has stated,

> . . . classroom presentations need to be much more flexible than is currently the rule. Not only must a much wider range of materials be made available but it must be recognized that not all children in the class need to have the same routine. Children should be permitted freedom to use those materials which are most adequate for them. For the normal child, such freedom of learning method will increase learning efficiency. For the child with learning disorders, it may well spell the difference between success and failure (1968, p. 133).

OUTCOME STUDIES

There is almost universal agreement among professionals that children with learning disabilities find themselves in a cumulatively worsening academic position unless they experience some form of psychoeducational program aimed at remediating their problems (Ross, 1967). When such aid is provided, reports of improvement during the course of the program and shortly afterward are generally positive. Balow (1965), for example, cites remarkable progress among fifth and sixth grade disabled readers of average or better intelligence while participating in special remedial programs at the University of Minnesota. However, follow-up data, collected 9 to 36 months later, revealed a significant erosion of these gains once formal remedial aid had terminated.

Schiffman (1964) presents essentially the same findings in reviewing a four-year survey of the progress of 10,000 children who had been referred for remedial-reading instruction. The gains demonstrated by many of these subjects during their participation in special programs and shortly afterward faded when a return to regular classroom routines transpired.

Silver and Hagin (1964), in a well-controlled and innovative study, retested 24 subjects of an original group of 41 who had received remedial-reading instruction at Bellevue Hospital's Mental Hygiene Clinic during the period 1949–1951. The battery of tests was the same one used 10 to 12 years earlier when initial contact with the child was made. A control group of subjects, referred to the clinic for problems other than reading disability, was also retested as adults. Neurological and perceptual assessment of the disabled readers as adults (median age, 19 years) showed that in spite of maturation in some areas, problems persisted in visual–motor coordination, figure–ground perception, auditory discrimination, and tactile responses. Nine of the 24 originally disabled readers remained poor readers as adults. The other 15 demonstrated some improvement in reading skills but did not match the performance of the control group.

Although outcome studies of this kind are rare, their implications are clear, at least for severely disabled readers: continuing progress for the child depends upon continuing attention to the problem. The upper limits of time for such support will vary for each child and the type of problem he presents. As a general philosophy, however, it is probably the most realistic to assume that learning disabilities of whatever kind are merely ameliorated rather than permanently corrected by short-term episodic treatment, and that continuing attention is mandatory to ensure the permanence of whatever gains are achieved during remediation.

FUTURE NEEDS

The significant progress made within the past decade in understanding and teaching children with learning disabilities of the type discussed in this paper is heartening, but much remains to be done. In many instances, research reports on diagnostic and therapeutic procedures suffer from poor controls, subjective criteria of improved performance in the classroom, contaminated ratings, mixed diagnostic groups, and/or inappropriate statistical analyses of results. Until such shortcomings are corrected, the status of our knowledge may have to remain at the level of interesting hunches, or, at best, educated guesses.

Perhaps the area needing most systematic and rigorous research attention is that involving specific teaching methodologies and their effects. There are literally dozens of remedial approaches to reading, for example, but controlled comparisons of these instructional strategies are rare. A related question involves the role of other variables in improved performance. Although the remedial approach itself might be the major contributor to demonstrated gains in learning, the effects of teacher expectancies, individual instruction and attention, diminished parental concern in the face of positive programming, and changes in the child's self-concept are among the factors that need to be systematically defined and manipulated.

There is also a need for the preparation of screening techniques designed to identify potential learning problems in preschool children. It would be of major interest to chart in elementary school the progress of these children, in an effort to differentiate between those who subsequently fulfilled the prediction of academic difficulty or failure and those who did not.

Coexisting with the above is the necessity to solve some of the more pragmatic problems abounding in the field, among which are the following:

1. Elimination of the confusing terminology employed in discussions of learning disabilities and the development of concepts (preferably behaviorally anchored) that clarify communication efforts among different professional groups.

2. More realistic coordination of community and professional services now providing for this population of children.

3. Additional emphasis on the topic of learning disabilities in curricular offerings to elementary and secondary teachers.

4. Provisions of continuing in-service programs for classroom teachers designed to upgrade their skills in dealing with the problem.

5. Establishment of adjunctive programs of counseling for parents and siblings of disabled learners, with particular attention to remedial efforts in the home provided by the family (see, e.g., Golick, 1968).

GLOSSARY OF TERMS ASSOCIATED WITH LEARNING DISABILITIES IN CHILDREN

The following terms appear consistently in the literature dealing with learning disabilities in children, and although their use is often as confusing as heuristic, those listed below have commonly agreed upon behavioral referents. For additional glossaries, the reader is referred to those compiled by Bannatyne (1968), Coleman (1968), and Staffen and Frierson (1967).

acalculia: the inability to perform mathematical exercises.

agitographia: a writing disturbance characterized by rapid motor movements and the omission or distortion of letters or words.

agnosia: the inability to identify familiar persons or objects; may be restricted to a particular sense modality, as, for example, *visual agnosia* (inability to recognize persons or objects by sight) or *tactile agnosia* (inability to recognize objects by touch).

agraphia: the inability to recall the motor responses necessary for writing; a type of apraxia.

alexia: also known as "word-blindness"; the inability to receive, interpret and understand visual language symbols; reflected most commonly in reading and writing disabilities.

aphasia: impaired ability to understand or use language meaningfully, most usually due to brain injury or defect; common examples are *auditory aphasia* (inability to comprehend spoken words), *expressive aphasia* (inability to speak even though words are well known), and *formulation aphasia* (confusion in grammar, syntax, and word tense).

apraxia: the inability to perform purposeful movements in the absence of muscular paralysis.

ataxia: a loss of normal muscular coordination, often reflected in illegible handwriting.

brain damage: a general term referring to injury to the brain by trauma, disease, or surgery.

dyscalculia: the inability to perform simple arithmetic skills.

dysgraphia: a partial inability to communicate through writing; a type of apraxia.

dyslalia: impaired speech due to defects in articulatory organs.

dyslexia: restricted ability to comprehend the written or printed word; one form of visual agnosia.

dysnomia: the inability to recall at will sounds or words that have been mastered at some previous time.

laterality: awareness and use of either side of the body, with a recognition of the difference.

organicity: central nervous system impairment.

perception: the process by which sensory information is recognized and interpreted; the association of present sensory input with past experience.

strephosymbolia: a perceptual disorder in which symbols are reversed or twisted and reflected in reading and writing: for example, "dab" for "bad."

References

Ames, L. B. Learning disabilities: The developmental point of view. In H. R. Myklebust (Ed.), *Progress in Learning Disabilities,* Vol. 1. New York: Grune & Stratton, 1968, pp. 39–74.

Balow, B. The long-term effect of remedial reading instruction. *Reading Teacher,* 1965, *18,* 581–586.

Bannatyne, A. Diagnosing learning disabilities and writing remedial prescriptions. *J. Learning Disabilities,* 1968, *1,* 242–249.

Bateman, B. Learning disabilities—An overview. Paper read at CEC 42nd Annual Convention, Chicago, April 1964.

Bateman, B. Learning disabilities—Yesterday, today and tomorrow. In E. C. Frierson and W. B. Barbe (Eds.), *Educating children with learning disabilities: Selected readings.* New York: Appleton-Century-Crofts, 1967, pp. 10–25.

Bender, L. *A visual-motor Gestalt test and its clinical use.* New York: American Orthopsychiatric Association, 1938.

Bender, L. *Psychopathology of children with organic brain disorders.* Springfield, Ill.: Charles C Thomas, 1956.

Bender, L. Specific reading disability as a maturational lag. *Bull. Orton Soc.,* 1957, *7,* 9–18.

Bookbinder, K. F., & Flierl, N. E. A plan for teaching pupils with severe reading disability. *J. Learning Disabilities,* 1968, *1,* 140–147.

Boshes, B., & Myklebust, H. R. A neurological and behavioral study of children with learning disorders. *Neurology,* 1964, *14,* 7–12.

Broadbent, E. On cerebral mechanisms of thought and speech. Cited in J. C. Westman et al., Reading retardation: An overview. *Amer. J. Dis. Child.,* 1965, *109,* 359–369.

Brueckner, L. J., & Bond, G. L. Diagnosis and treatment of spelling difficulties. In E. C. Frierson and W. B. Barbe (Eds.), *Educating children with learning disabilities: Selected readings.* New York: Appleton-Century-Crofts, 1967, pp. 442–457.

Bryant, N. D. Some principles of remedial instruction for dyslexia. *Reading Teacher,* 1965, *18,* 567–572.

Campbell, Sister St. Francis. Neurological approach to reading problems. *Catholic Educ. Rev.,* 1965, *43,* 28–34.

Clements, S. D. *Minimal brain dysfunction in children.* Washington, D.C.: National Institute of Neurological Diseases and Blindness, Monograph No. 3, 1966.

Coleman, H. M. Visual perception and reading dysfunction. *J. Learning Disabilities,* 1968, *1,* 116–123.

Denhoff, E., Siqueland, M. L., Komich, M. P., & Hainsworth, P. K. Developmental and predictive characteristics of items from the Meeting Street School Screening Test. *Develpm. Med. & Child Neurol.,* 1968, *10,* 220–232.

Dunn, L. Minimal brain dysfunction: A dilemma for educators. In E. C. Frierson and W. B. Barbe (Eds.), *Educating children with learning disabilities: Selected readings.* New York: Appleton-Century-Crofts, 1967, pp. 177–132.

Ellingson, C. *The shadow children: A book about children's learning disorders.* Chicago: Topaz Books, 1967.

Enstrom, E. A. Left-handedness: A cause for disability in writing. *J. Learning Disabilities,* 1968, *1,* 410–414.

Fletcher, L. G. Methods and materials for teaching word perception in corrective and remedial classes. In E. C. Frierson and W. B. Barbe (Eds.), *Educating children with learning disabilities: Selected readings.* New York: Appleton-Century-Crofts, 1967, pp. 467–471.

Frierson, E. C. Clinical education procedures in the treatment of learning disabilities. In E. C. Frierson and W. B. Barbe (Eds.), *Educating children with learning disabilities: Selected readings.* New York: Appleton-Century-Crofts, 1967, pp. 478–488.

Frierson, E. C., & Barbe, W. B. *Educating children with learning disabilities: Selected readings.* New York: Appleton-Century-Crofts, 1967.

Frostig, M. *Marianne Frostig Developmental Test of Visual Perception.* Palo Alto, Calif.: Consulting Psychologists Press, 1961.

Frostig, M., & Horne, D. *The Frostig program for the development of visual perception.* Chicago: Follett, 1964.

Glaser, K., & Clemmens, R. L. School failure. *Pediatrics,* 1965, *35,* 128–141.

Godfrey, B. B., & Kephart, N. C. *Movement patterns and motor education.* New York: Appleton-Century-Crofts, 1969.

Golick, M. A parents' guide to learning problems *J. Learning Disabilities,* 1968, *1,* 366–377.

Kaliski, L. Arithmetic and the brain-injured child. *Arithmetic Teacher,* 1962, *9,* 245–251.

Kephart, N. C. *Learning disability: An educational adventure.* West Lafayette, Ind.: Kappa Delta Pi Press, 1968.

Kirk, S. A., McCarthy, J. J., & Kirk, W. D. *The Illinois Test of Psycholinguistic Abilities.* Urbana, Ill.: University of Illinois Press, 1968.

McCarthy, J. Learning disabilities in children. Paper presented at Conference on Learning Disabilities, Albuquerque, New Mexico, May 1969.

Money, J. (Ed.). *Reading disability: Progress and research needs in dyslexia.* Baltimore: Johns Hopkins Press, 1962.

Myklebust, H. R., & Boshes, B. Psychoneurological learning disorders in children. *Arch. Pediat.,* 1960, *77,* 247–256.

Rabinovitch, R. D., Drew, A. L., De Jong, R. N., Ingram, W., & Withey, L. A research approach to reading retardation. *Res. Publ. Assoc. Res. nerv. ment. Dis.,* 1954, *34,* 363–396.

Rabinovitch, R. D., & Ingram, W. Neuropsychiatric considerations in reading retardation. *Reading Teacher,* 1962, *15,* 433–438.

Roach, E. G., & Kephart, N. C. *The Purdue perceptual-motor survey.* Columbus: Chas. E. Merrill, 1966.

Ross, A. O. Learning difficulties in children: Dysfunction, disorders, disabilities. *J. School Psychol.,* 1967, *5,* 82–92.

Schiffman, G. Early identification of reading disabilities: the responsibility of the public school. *Bull. Orton Soc.,* 1964, *14,* 42–44.

Silver, A. A., & Hagin, R. A. Specific reading disability: Follow-up studies. *Amer. J. Orthopsychiat.,* 1964, *34,* 95–102.

Staffen, P. M., & Frierson, E. C. Glossary: Terms associated with learning disabilities. In E. C. Frierson and W. B. Barbe (Eds.), *Educating children with learning disabilities: Selected readings.* New York: Appleton-Century-Crofts, 1967, pp. 489–493.

Stevens, G. D., & Birch, J. W. A proposal for clarification of the terminology used to describe brain-injured children. *Except. Child.,* 1957, *23,* 346–349.

Strauss, A. A., & Lehtinen, L. E. *Psychopathology and education of the brain-injured child.* New York: Grune & Stratton, 1947.

Vallet, R. S. *The remediation of learning disabilities.* Palo Alto, Calif.: Fearon Publishers, 1967.

Wechsler, D. *Wechsler Intelligence Scale for Children.* New York: Psychological Corporation, 1949.

Wepman, J. *Auditory Discrimination Test.* Chicago: Language Research Associates, 1958.

Westman, J. C., Arthur, B., & Scheidler, E. P. Reading retardation. An overview. *Amer. J. Dis. Child.*, 1965, *109*, 359–369.

Wood, N. Language disorders in children. *Monogr. Soc. Res. Child Developm.*, 1960, *25*, 15–23.

part IV

Exceptional Emotional Processes

27

Slicing the Mystique of Prevention with Occam's Razor

Eli M. Bower

> *Dr. Bower is Professor of Education and Head of the Joint Doctorate in Special Education at the University of California at Berkeley. He is a most active research worker who has already published over fifty major articles, primarily on the mentally retarded child and the emotionally disturbed child.*
>
> *In this delightfully readable article Dr. Bower takes to task the traditional view that only the "professional" can effectively cope with the problems of prevention and identification of emotionally disturbed children. The article is particularly timely in view of the growing interest and developments in community psychology.*

Prevention is a word with many shades and ranges of meaning. I have read somewhere that in colonial days Philadelphia health officials sought to prevent an epidemic of yellow fever by repeatedly firing a cannon from the steps of City Hall. This was certainly an unique preventive approach; however, it lacked any evaluation, since no one really knows how many mosquitoes were killed by this procedure.

> FROM *The American Journal of Public Health, 59,* 3, 478–484 (March) 1969. Reprinted by permission of the author and The American Public Health Association. This paper was presented before a Joint Session of the American School Health Association and the Maternal and Child Health, Mental Health, Public Health Nursing, and School Health Sections of the American Public Health Association at the Ninety-Fifth Annual Meeting in Miami Beach, Fla., October 25, 1967.

Occam's Razor turns out to be a more formidable preventive weapon than Philadelphia cannon. Occam's Razor was tempered by a few cutting remarks about human functioning which, loosely translated and brought up to date, could be stated thus: "Don't complicate simple things." For those who prefer a more literal translation, Occam's words were: "Assumptions introduced to explain something should not be multiplied beyond necessity."

The focus in this paper is not so much on the hard-nosed data about early identification of children with potential problems, but the mythologics and encrustations about mental health and education which have kept this kind of an attempt feeble and ineffective. We will need to change blades in Occam's Razor more than once, before we get any program of real significance and impact operating in this area. Now what is the mystique which needs slicing and why?

The state of a child's mental health or ill health is best known and judged by a mental health professional (psychiatrist, clinical psychologist or psychiatric social worker) rather than by less "sophisticated" professional persons who live with the child on a day-to-day basis.

About ten years ago, the State of California decided to invest a sizable amount of money and some of my time to find out whether emotionally disturbed children could be identified early in their school life and, if so, could something be done to immobilize, interrupt, or intercept this kind of development. We found we could identify children with beginning learning and behavior problems, if we effectively and economically used perceptual ratings of students by teachers, peers, and the students themselves. Not surprisingly, we found our measures of the state of emotional development of students to be highly reliable and, on the basis of what good sense and little research we had, to be valid. At this point, however, some of our mental health colleagues began to shake their heads. Remember, they said, the old Wickman study [7] in which considerable doubt was raised about the ability of teachers and schools to recognize the symptoms of serious emotional problems. How do we know that the children you have identified are *really and truly* the mental health problems of our society? Are children identified by teachers (and peers and themselves) really emotionally disturbed? And what is more important, how do you know that these are the children who will eventually become mentally ill? The last question was always posed with the all-knowing scowl of the pipe-smoking scholar searching for the first star in the night sky.

Let me resurrect Wickman's study for those too young to have been exposed or too old to remember. Wickman asked a group of 511 teachers and a group of 30 mental hygienists to rate the seriousness of 50 behavior traits of children. What set the fulminating cap sizzling was the finding that ratings made by the mental hygienists and those made by the teachers had zero correlation. Wickman himself was not at all dismayed by this result, and was most emphatic in pointing out that the directions to each group had been significantly different. The teachers had been asked to rate the behavior as problems in the present reality of the classroom, while the mental hygienists were directed to rate the behavior on the basis of its effect on the future life of the child. Teachers were also told to define the seriousness of a problem by the amount of difficulty it produced in the classroom. The mental health group was asked to rate problem behavior in relation to its importance to a child's mental health. When the smoke cleared and the ratings of the two groups were compared, it became obvious that teachers were concerned with behavior that related to classroom disruption; mental health people, on the other hand, focused attention on behavior that was disturbing the child's inner psyche. Each group was looking at the problem in terms of their own professional biases and from their job-related firing lines.

Although Wickman was careful to point out the limitations of his study, this did not prevent many alexic professionals from jumping to unwarranted conclusions. Two educators [5] examined 12 texts in psychology and educational psychology which mentioned Wickman's study, and found only two which gave a clear and concise statement of the study and its findings. Most discussed the study as indicating that, as judges of the mental health status of children, teachers were way off base. The basic assumption, of course, was that the mental health experts were right and that teachers were wrong.

The myth still exists that someone, somewhere, somehow, knows how to assess behavior and/or mental health as positive or negative, good or bad, healthy or nonhealthy, and independent of the social context wherein the individual is living and functioning. It is possible that the teacher who focuses on the child's observable behavior in school is closer to an operational reality of mental health than can be determined in an office examination. What a teacher is judging is how a specific behavior affects him as a key professional person in a primary social system and how well a child can play the role of student in a school. Similarly, when a child in a play group cannot play the play role (adhere to the rules of the game), the nursery school supervisor will find his behavior a problem in that setting. In both instances, the lack of these role skills isolates the child from his peers. A child with an absence of emotional responsiveness to a parent will be a problem in a family setting where such responsiveness is one of the expected behaviors of children and of satisfaction to parents. But each behavior can only be judged as positive or negative in relation to the social system in which feelings or behavior are expected and prescribed.

Each of the social contexts in which children function has specific goals, rules, and competencies that act as guides for assessing prescribed and expected behavior. A school is a system which demands learning competence; a play group requires rule-abiding behavior; a family should provide an opportunity for some interchange of healthy hostility and affection. Life is lived by children within primary humanizing institutions, each of which requires specific functioning skills and behavior appropriate to its goals. I have no idea what mental health is in the abstract, but I would like to define it as comprising the kinds of competence and reality-testing which allow a child to function effectively in the humanizing institutions where he is asked to live. Specifically, these are the home, the peer or play group, and the school.

The fact is that teachers gather enough information about children in their routine operations to make highly accurate professional predictions about the course of a child's school life. However, there is little or no magic in such predictive data unless, in the process of gathering such data, the key professional person in the system is moved to act. For example, there is very good evidence that it is possible to detect potential delinquents at an early age if the Social Prediction Scale, developed by the Gluecks, is used.[2] Why is it not used as a preventive tool? By and large, I would guess because the process of prediction requires operations not consistent with the goals and processes of the institution. In addition, the prediction itself has little curriculum implication or program consequences for the key professional worker in the school—the teacher. Prediction processes must lead to positive action by someone in the system, and this is especially critical in the case of problems which have not as yet become major crises to the teacher. How often one hears a kindergarten or first-grade teacher in a teachers' room react to a fifth- or sixth-grade teacher's description of the gory adventures of a problem child. "Oh, him —he was somewhat of a problem in the first grade," is the likely comment. "I thought he might get over it." The upper-grade teacher sadly shakes her head, indicating a less optimistic state of affairs.

But can teachers and schools be effective screeners of children with beginning mental health problems? In a 1963 study,[3] teachers were asked to rate children on five steps, ranging from the first which was: the child has no problems and is obviously extremely well adjusted; there is absolutely no need for referral, to the last: the child has problems of sufficient severity to require referral. Following this, a sample of children were seen by psychiatrists in privately conducted interviews of, predictively enough, about 50 minutes each. There was a marked lack of agreement between professional groups in classifying children who had severe adjustment problems and needed referral. The investigator thereupon concluded that teachers cannot adequately serve as case finders in mental health screening.

In discussing this research with the investigator, two questions were posed: (1) to what extent do you feel that a 50-minute appraisal by a psychiatrist to be a more valid assessment of a child's functioning capabilities and liabilities in a school setting than a teacher's day-in-day-out experience; (2) how, exactly, do teachers react to the concept and meaning of the term "adjustment" and "referral?" One teacher explained her meaning of adjustment: "I guess it means how well a student gets along in school and with others. Now I have this one student who gets along pretty well and I guess is well adjusted, but can't seem to learn anything." While the concept of adjustment is understood by teachers, its operational implementation is somewhat out of the frame of reference and functioning of teachers. Most feel that in rating "adjustment," they are attempting to fill the role of a psychiatrist; somehow, they rate the degrees of intrapsychic conflict and chaos in the minds of their students. Whatever rating adjustment means, teachers should stick to school-related behaviors and roles which can be operationally defined and observed. Does the child get into fights? Can he pay attention when necessary? Does he learn to read? Is he always in a blue funk? Does he get sick? Does he get hurt? Can he express an idea?

To put the shoe on the other foot, another study compared the predictive skill of a teacher, psychologist, and child psychiatrist in judging which kindergarten children would learn up to their IQ potential in first grade.[1] A total of 56 kindergarten children were included in the study. Each professional person related to the children as they would normally. The teacher taught and observed, the psychologist tested, and the child psychiatrist used a standard play situation. All three did a good job of predicting the achievement, but the teacher's was best. The psychiatrist had a tendency to predict underachievement more frequently than it occurred. He suggested that the reason may be that some of the clinical anxiety which the psychiatrist picked up in the children—and which he expected to lead to underachievement—actually produced overachievement. This is, of course, the nub of the problem. Only when the teacher observes how a child may use different aspects of his personality and self can he assess the nuances of how the child mediates what he has, be it anxiety, IQ, shyness, or aggressivity. The investigation confirms Robins' study (discussed later) that (1) raters in general are better at spotting potential positive achievers than the negative ones; (2) teacher judgments provide the most economical and efficient guides to predictions of school success.

THE NONMAGIC OF TEACHER REFERRALS

Another wicked slice with Occam's Razor needs to be taken at the notion and concept of "the referral." In the past, teachers have been so convinced of their lack of mental health expertise and so impressed with the competence of their mental health colleagues that the only significant help for problems which they could verbalize was: "If we only had adequate referral resources." We have invested this process, at least for teachers, with a penicillin-like magic which, unfortunately, is dissipated in the realities of limited knowledge and manpower. The referral concept of the majority of teachers is one where the child is taken elsewhere, where something magical is done to straighten him out, and then returned to school a healthy, well-motivated student. This rarely turns out to be the case. Occasionally, referrals are consummated to the satisfaction of the teacher. When this happens, it is evident that some mental health expert has learned to translate what he knows clinically and psychodynamically into the frame of reference of the teacher and into educational processes and objectives. Unfortunately, there are only a few referral agencies that have the competence to do this or know how to begin to do this. Most teachers have high regard for mental health persons and their professional competence. When the secrets of a problem are revealed to a teacher, she often stands aghast at the marvels of modern psychiatry, psychology, or casework. Indeed, she is thrilled to be a partner to such mighty revelations. She may reenter the class with a better understanding of the "why" and "what" of the student's difficulty, but with her major problem still unanswered: "How do I teach this child?"

There is another assumption about teachers and referrals which needs slicing. If, in a hypothetical community, there were available immediate, convenient, and useful referral services (each of these will affect the process significantly) and teachers were encouraged to refer children who needed help, one would not get the most serious or the most difficult problems. A referral is the result of a dyadic relationship between a teacher and a child in the context of a class and a school. One psychologist who attempted to help teachers in an inner city school wanted to know why he got so few referrals. The teachers laughed at the question, and pointed out that if he were serious they would be happy to send him three-fourths of their class. There is also the phenomenon that when a teacher refers a child, she does so because *she* is puzzled or anxious about his behavior. Many teachers will not refer students with serious problems if they feel they understand some of the background and causes of the problems, but will refer less serious problems when the behavior or learning difficulty is puzzling or anxiety-provoking to them.

It is no longer possible in this day and age to think of referral services as desirable or necessary, if one is concerned with the basic preventive question: how do you increase the ecological competence of a humanizing institution to serve more children more effectively? One way would be to develop mental health professions (clinical behavioral workers) who would not be walled off from the primary institutions by having to deal with its casualties, but could become an active partner with the teacher, principal, and parents in monitoring and enhancing the behavior of all children in the school.

THE OBJECT OF EARLY IDENTIFICATION IS TO IDENTIFY CASES EARLY

It took me quite a while to realize that the notion of early identification meant different things to different professional groups. One of my psychiatric colleagues used to puzzle me by his lack of enthusiasm for research in this field. Once, when I confronted him with this, he replied: "I don't see why you get worked up about this early identification of emotionally disturbed children. We've got more cases than we can handle right now without finding some more."

His notion of early discovery had to do with what is known in the profession as "cases." My notion of early discovery has to do with the discovery of a child in a primary institution, such as a school, who is having beginning trouble in coping with the demands and processes of that institution. The essential assumption is that, left alone, a beginning problem either finds a wise and highly competent teacher or it continues to grow. In our California studies, children identified as emotionally handicapped fell further and further behind in reading and arithmetic achievement, and were increasingly deemed by their peers to be negative or inadequate students. After five years, they were seen in child guidance clinics and appeared in the Juvenile Index for vehicle code and penal code violations in stark contrast to a randomly selected group of their classmates. This was replicated and amplified by the Minnesota Study [6] which confirmed the fact that children identified by the California materials as emotionally handicapped fall further and further behind their classmates in achievement, and get stuck on a track which leads to severe educational embarrassment and incompetence.

The humanizing institutions to which children are mandated are unfortunately social systems that tend to reward those who succeed in it and punish those who fail. Programs of early identification in schools must therefore not only find failing and problem children early; but, in the process of finding them, must provide for the institutional changes which will make the discovery worth while. This means that processes of early identification must be carried out by key persons in specific humanizing institutions in the context of the goals and processes of that institution, and in such a way that alternative possibilities for action are natural outcomes of the process. Programs of early identification which require teachers to do nonteacher-like jobs will not last and cannot be effective. Moreover, such programs cannot enlist mental health workers to visit homes to make clinical appraisals of how a child is disciplined at home, the degree of affection shown to him by his parents, and so on, critical as this kind of information may be. Early identification processes which solely aim at identifying children with "mental health" problems are no more than exercises. They must lead to and be conceptualized in a program framework, and must be translatable into valid interventions within the humanizing institution where the child is living and is attempting to function.

Nobody believes it is possible for all children to experience our humanly constructed humanizing institutions in a positive and ego-enhancing way.

If one can remove one's home-grown complexities and professional blinkers about this sordid world and its people, it is possible to conceptualize humanizing institutions which can carry out their goals and processes for greater ranges of children and eventually for all children. Either we do this or pay the cost in lives and money for remedial or rehabilitative institutions such as prisons, mental hospitals, welfare programs, alcoholic and drug wards. It is also well to remember that when children cannot function in institutions devised for their benefit, they hurt and they bleed. One does not have to ask whether they have broken a leg or cut an artery before administering first aid. It is questionable whether the children identified as emotionally disturbed in school are really and truly disturbed or if they represent the group who will later become mentally ill. I suspect more of them later become antisocial, inadequate, dependent, alcoholic, drug-addicted, and physically ill than a random group of adults. This conclusion is supported by an interesting study of 524 adults who were seen as children in a child guidance clinic and 100 controls of the same age, sex, neighborhood, race and IQ.[4] The purpose of the study was to describe, through a longitudinal natural history, the kinds of childhood behavior problems that present serious danger signals and those that do not. Robins's study is interesting in that there was an unexpected dividend in the data on the control group.

Let us first look at what happened to the 524 adults who had been seen as children in the child guidance clinic. Robins divided them into two categories, antisocial and non-antisocial, on the basis of behavior which led to referral. She found that antisocial children by and large became antisocial adults. Not only were these adults more often arrested and imprisoned than expected, but they were more mobile, had more marital difficulties, poorer occupational and armed service histories, used alcohol and drugs excessively, and had poorer physical health. "But," Robins adds, "from one point of view . . . what we have found is not so much a pathological patient group as an extraordinary well-adjusted control group."

Such a control group was selected from the files of the St. Louis public schools by setting quotas for year of birth, sex, census tract, no clinic visit, IQ above 80, no grade repeats, and no record of expulsion or transfer. Microfilm reels were spun and selection made in the Las Vegas tradition, This, however, turned out to be a winner. Using these four not high standard criteria (IQ over 80, not seen at the municipal psychiatric clinic, no grade repeated, and no expulsion from school), Robins had selected a group of 100 adults of whom only two ever appeared in juvenile court and who, as adults, had good psychiatric adjustment and social competence. She concludes that while having repeated grades in elementary school certainly does not efficiently predict serious adult problems, having not had serious school difficulties may be a rather efficient predictor of the absence of gross maladjustment as adults. Perhaps we have been so concerned with the prediction of deviant behavior that we were not aware how well we could do in predicting effective behavior.

In light of our earlier comment about predicting eventual mental illness, Robins found no clear connection between type of deviance in childhood and type of problem in adulthood. For example, those adults with antisocial behavior in childhood not only showed antisocial adult behavior, but also showed a greater degree of social alienation and more psychiatric and physical disabilities. As a result, Robins found that children referred for antisocial behavior have a less promising prediction than children referred for other reasons. This is a group that vitally needs mental health services, as teachers have repeatedly pointed out to their principals and mental health consultants.

CONCLUSION

Don't complicate simple things. Prevention is getting children through our health, family, and school institutions "smelling like a rose." A little soap, a little affection, and a little learning are the holy trinity of prevention. If we can send rockets to the moon, we certainly can do these three little things for the human condition on earth.

References

1. Cohen, T. B. Prediction of Underachievement in Kindergarten Children. *Arch. Gen. Psychiat.*, 1963, *9*, 444–449.
2. Glueck, S., & Glueck, E. *Unraveling Juvenile Delinquency.* New York, N.Y.: Commonwealth Fund, 1950.
3. Goldfarb, Allan. Teacher Ratings in Psychiatric Case-Findings. *A.J.P.H.*, 1963, *53*, 1919–1927.
4. Robins, Lee. *Deviant Children Grown Up.* Baltimore, Md.: Williams & Wilkins (1966), p. 70.
5. Schrupp, M., & Gjerde, C. Teacher Growth in Attitudes Toward Behavior Problems of Children. *J. Ed. Psych.*, 1953, *44*, 203–214.
6. Stennett, R. G. Emotional Handicap in the Elementary Years: Phase or Disease. *Am. J. Orthopsychiat.*, 1966, *36*, 444–449.
7. Wickman, E. K. *Children's Behavior and Teachers' Attitudes.* New York, N.Y.: Commonwealth Fund, 1928.

28

Psychiatric Syndromes in Children and Their Relation to Family Background

Richard L. Jenkins

Dr. Jenkins is Professor of Child Psychiatry and Chief of the Child Psychiatry Service at the University of Iowa. He has published extensively on emotionally disturbed children and is author or coauthor of three books. In recent years he has been concerned with background factors in types of delinquent behavior and in classifying behavior problems of children.

In this present article, Dr. Jenkins demonstrates the effectiveness of the computer as a research tool. With the aid of the computer, he was able to ferret out the significant variables from the massive amount of data made available. This study is particularly significant in that the second edition of the Diagnostic and Statistical Manual *of the American Psychiatric Association recognized and made official his groupings of diagnostic categories of behavior disorders of childhood and adolescence. In the revised manual his categories of shy-seclusive children, overanxious children, hyperactive children, undomesticated children, and socialized delinquents were labeled, respectively, as withdrawing reaction, overanxious reaction, hyperkinetic reaction, unsocialized aggressive reaction, and group delinquent reaction.*

FROM THE *American Journal of Orthopsychiatry,* Vol. 36, No. 3, April, 1966, pp. 450–457. Reprinted by permission of Journal and author.

The development of high-speed computers does not offer any substitute for thinking, but once data have been assembled, it does facilitate routine comparisons which otherwise would not be possible. Our diagnostic understanding evolved largely from the slow process of case comparisons. In the field of child psychiatry, in which our diagnostic understanding leaves so much to be desired, it seems appropriate that computer techniques should be employed to facilitate such comparisons and the resulting development of understanding.

The basis for this study is 500 cases on which IBM cards were carefully prepared by a former associate, Dr. Lester Hewitt, some years ago at the Michigan Child Guidance Institute. Each card represents a case examined at the Institute, and the case records were unusually complete. On each card each of 90 symptoms was checked if it was noted in the case record.

This material was the basis for two articles in this Journal [1, 2] and a monograph [3] which contrasted the three most prominent syndromes. The findings of the study have been confirmed.[4, 5, 6]

The present study is a reexamination of this material by computer techniques which were not available at the time of the original study. Its purpose was to determine what background factors might be associated with any clusters so determined. From this material the existence of five clusters of symptoms was established by computer.* The symptoms most

* The procedure was to take the 500 cards in four groups of 125 cards each. (This division into smaller groups was occasioned by the finite memory of our computer.) Each card in a group was compared successively with every other card in the group. Let us suppose that card one and card two had five entries in common, and card one had a total of ten and card two a total of fifteen entries. Then card one shared 50 per cent of its entries with card two, and card two shared 33.3 per cent of its entries with card one. These two values were summed to provide a convenient index (.833) of the resemblance between card one and card two. (An average of these two values would accomplish the same thing but presented no advantage.) If card one and card three shared two entries and card three had sixteen entries in all, then card one shared 20 per cent of its entries with card three, and card three shared 12.5 per cent of its entries with card one. The resemblance between card one and card three is represented by sum of these values, .325. Thus, card one resembles card two more than it resembles card three.

All possible comparisons were made in this way within each group of 125 cards. Each card was then placed with the card it resembled most. This process formed clusters and these were our initial clusters.

The fact that a card was placed with the card it resembled most did not insure that it was in the cluster it resembled most. Proceeding from initial groupings, the average value of the resemblance of each card to all the other cards in each cluster was calculated. Those cards with a greater

Table 1 *Two Inhibited Groups (Each child showed at least 3 of the traits listed)*

Shy-seclusive group	Overanxious-neurotic group
Seclusive	Sleep disturbances
Shyness, timidity	Fears
Absence of close friendships	Cries easily
Apathy, underactivity	Fantastic thinking (overimaginative)
Depressed or discouraged attitude	Marked inferiority feeling
Sensitiveness	Nervousness
N = 61 21 per cent girls	N = 43 37 per cent girls
Typical age 9–14	Typical age 9–12

characteristic of each of these clusters were used to assign the cluster membership of cases. The first two groups are illustrated in Table 1.

Table 1 lists six symptoms selected as most characteristic of what I shall call the shy-seclusive group. Sixty-one cases in the 500 had at least three of these symptoms and also had more symptoms characteristic of this group than of any other group. Of these 61 cases, 21 per cent were girls. The interquartile age range, which contains at least half of the cases, was 9 to 14.

Table 1 also lists the symptoms characteristic of the overanxious-neurotic group. There were 43 cases with three or more of these symptoms and in which the symptoms falling in this group were more numerous than the symptoms falling in any other group. These 43 cases were 37 per cent girls, the highest percentage of girls appearing in any of our groups. The interquartile age range was 9 to 12.

As might be expected, there was some overlap between these two groups. Both these groups were classified as inhibited. The next three groups to be described we classified as aggressive.

Table 2 lists the characteristic symptoms of a hyperactive group char-

---

average resemblance to the cards of another cluster than to the cards of their own cluster were reassigned to the cluster they resembled most closely. Then the process of calculating average resemblances was repeated and reassignments were made again until the groups stabilized. Some clusters disappeared in this process.

At this point, a card was made out for each cluster. If an item were present in 50 per cent or more of the members of a cluster, it was considered characteristic of that cluster and punched on the cluster card. The cluster cards were then treated in a matrix just as the original cards had been treated. The result was five clusters of clusters or "super-clusters."

Table 2 *Three Aggressive Groups (Each child showed at least 3 of the traits listed)*

Hyperactive-distractible group	Undomesticated group	Socialized delinquent group
Hyperactive	Negativistic	Furtive stealing
Lack of concentration	Defiance of authority	Cooperative stealing
Mischieviousness	Vengefulness	Running away from home overnight
Inability to get along with other children	Sullenness	Habitual truancy from school
Overdependent	Malicious mischief	Association with undesirable companions
Boastfulness	Temper outbursts	Petty stealing
N = 76 16 per cent girls Typical age 9–11	N = 58 24 per cent girls Typical age 11–14	N = 53 9 per cent girls Typical age 12–15

acterized by poor concentration. Seventy-six cases, 16 per cent girls, had at least three of these symptoms, and more of these than of the symptoms of any other group. This is our youngest group, with an interquartile age range of 9 to 11 years. Of the aggressive groups, this is the one with the most in common with the overanxious-neurotic children. These are immature, poorly organized children.

Table 2 next presents an older group which I call the undomesticated children. This group tends to overlap with the hyperactive group but presents a more serious picture. There are 58 children in this group, 24 per cent girls. The interquartile age range is 11 to 14. The extreme of this group is the antisocial or psychopathic personality.

Our last and oldest group, consisting of the socialized delinquents, is also included in Table 2. The interquartile age range is 12 to 15 years. There are 53 cases, of which only 9 per cent are girls. The extreme of this group is the dyssocial reaction. By contrast with the undomesticated group, these individuals are not basically unsocialized. Rather they are more or less socialized with the narrow but exacting limits of a predatory and fighting group. They depend on each other.

We regard the discovery of five groups as significant in disclosing or confirming the existence of five differentiable core types of behavioral deviations. Too much significance should not be ascribed to the *size* of the groups obtained, as it is possible to vary the size by narrowing or widening the definition. For example our hyperactive-distractible group is our largest group. It is possible to define this group so narrowly and extremely as to restrict it largely to brain-damaged children who can be diagnosed chronic brain syndrome, or to define it so broadly (as we do) that it includes many functionally immature children.

Table 3 *Inhibited Children*

Typical Traits	
Worrying	Staying out late at night
Daydreaming	Deceptive (lying, cheating, crafty, sly)
Often submissive	Often obscene and profane language
Often finicky food habits	Sometimes cruel
Often speech defect	Often projects blame

School Adjustment	
Seldom dislike teacher	Often dislike teacher
Disturbing behavior rare	Disturbing behavior frequent

Specific Talents or Interests	
Art	Sports

Special Deficiencies	
Lack of physical coordination or dexterity	

Mother Person	
Natural mother	Often substitute mother
Rarely openly hostile	Often openly hostile
Child does not feel rejected by mother	Child sometimes feels rejected by mother

Father Person	
Natural father	Often substitute father

Guilt Feeling	
Adequate	Often inadequate

If now we compare our two groups of inhibited children, the shy-seclusive group and the overanxious group with the three groups of aggressive children, the hyperactive children, the undomesticated children and the socialized delinquents, certain statistically significant * contrasts are evident. The inhibited children are prone to worrying and to daydreaming. They are often submissive, often have finicky food habits and often show a speech defect. I suspect that this last is true because having a speech defect tends to inhibit a child rather than because either of these symptom groups tends to produce a speech defect.

The aggressive children, on the other hand, differ from the inhibited children in that they are prone to stay out late at night and to be deceptive. They often use profane or obscene language, are sometimes cruel and often project blame on others.

* A difference which would be expected to occur on a chance basis less than once in 20 times was accepted as significant. Calculations were based on a Chi-square with $P < .05$ for a two-tailed distribution.

The inhibited children seldom dislike their schoolteachers, and disturbing behavior in school is rare. The aggressive children often dislike their schoolteachers, and disturbing behavior in school is frequent.

A further significant difference is that the aggressive children are disposed to have a particular talent for or interest in sports, while the inhibited children are prone to have a particular talent for or interest in art. The inhibited children are prone to lack physical coordination or dexterity. It does not seem surprising that a child lacking physical coordination and dexterity is less likely to be interested in sports or to be aggressive.

When we look for elements of family background which distinguish these groups and are presumably related to these differences, we find the inhibited children nearly always with both natural parents, the aggressive children less likely to be with both natural parents. The mother person of the inhibited child was rarely openly hostile toward the child, and in none of our cases was the child recorded as feeling rejected by the mother person. In the case of the aggressive children, the mother person was often openly hostile, and in each group of aggressive children we not infrequently find the entry that the child sometimes feels rejected by the mother. The association strongly indicates that change of parent figures (which is often interpreted by the child as rejection) and maternal hostility stimulate hostile, rebellious, aggressive responses in the child. The last entry indicates also that these experiences often are related to an inadequate development of conscience and of guilt feeling. The overdeveloped conscience of the inhibited child may present a problem, but typically it is less disturbing or threatening to others than the underdeveloped conscience of the aggressive child.

If we compare our two groups of inhibited children, we find most of the overanxious children hyperactive, while this symptom is much less prominent in the shy-exclusive group. This fact relates to the overlap of the overanxious group and the hyperactive group of aggressive children.

A majority of our overanxious-neurotic group have a history of prolonged, serious or repeated illness. These children frequently come from educated middle-class homes as is indicated by the fact that more than a quarter of the fathers have had some college training.

It is the characteristics of the mother persons, however, which most clearly distinguish these groups. Nearly half of the overanxious-neurotic children have mothers who were described as neurotic because of extreme nervousness, compulsions or evident emotional complexes. A close and sometimes morbid bond between the natural mother and the child is common enough so that, as compared with the shy-seclusive children, it is much more frequently recorded that the overanxious child prefers the natural mother to the other parent.

Chronic illness, serious crippling or physical impairment occur in a quarter of the mothers of the shy-seclusive children, and one in six was

Richard L. Jenkins

Table 4

	Shy-seclusive children	Over-anxious-neurotic children
Hyperactive (restless)	16%	65%
History of prolonged, serious or repeated illness	31%	54%
Father: some college training	8%	26%
Mother person neurotic (extreme nervousness, compulsions, etc.)	23%	44%
Mother person preferred by child over other parent(s)	2%	12%
Mother person: chronic illness, serious crippling or physical impairment*	25%	12%
Mother person mentally inadequate*	15%	5%

* Reaches only 0.1 level of probability with a two-tailed distribution. (All other contrasts are beyond the .05 level.)

considered mentally inadequate. Neither one of these two comparisons reaches the conventionally accepted .05 level of significance. Neither one of these contrasts, however, would occur on a chance basis as often as once in ten times, and because of their consistency and the fact that they seem to make sense, we have included them.

The overanxious-neurotic child appears more frequently in more educated families (which are prone to set higher standards) and with neurotic mothers, who are themselves anxious, and the more discouraged shy-seclusive child more frequently has an ill, handicapped or inadequate mother.

Table 5 gives us a comparison of some symptom entries in our three aggressive groups of children. Nervousness, which was one of the symp-

Table 5

	Hyperactive group	Un-domesticated group	Socialized delinquent group
Nervousness	49%	38%	13%
Quarrelsomeness	54%	55%	9%
Rudeness to person in authority	38%	48%	17%
Staying out late nights	15%	29%	47%
Gang activities	1%	12%	19%

toms used in defining the overanxious-neurotic group, is recorded in nearly half of our hyperactive group, in nearly two-fifths of our undomesticated group and in only about an eighth of the socialized delinquent group. This underlines the closeness of our hyperactive group to our overanxious group. Quarrelsomeness and rudeness toward persons in authority are high in the hyperactive group and particularly in the undomesticated group, and are much less frequent among the socialized delinquents who are, in their own way, more socialized. On the other hand, staying out late at night and gang activities are relatively infrequent in the younger hyperactive group, and most frequent among the socialized delinquents.

Table 6 indicates that the backgrounds of the undomesticated children characteristically include an unstable mother unable to relate herself to responsibility, and either a pregnancy unwanted by the mother or maternal rejection occurring after birth but while the child is still in infancy. Frequently, the child is openly hostile to the natural mother, and rarely does he prefer the natural mother to the other parent or parents. Lack of sufficient maternal love and acceptance early in life is a significant factor in this reaction.

Table 7 indicates that the socialized delinquent is, as we might expect, selectively a product of the uneducated family, the large family with the working mother whose children are unsupervised, the unkempt irregular household. If a mother has eight or more children and is working, to take the extreme, it is difficult to see how she could supervise the children's activities.

The socialized delinquent is a product not of maternal rejection but of neglect (which may be unavoidable lack of supervision) and a bad neighborhood. In this group, paternal deficiencies are much more prominent than maternal deficiencies. In more than half of our cases the natural father is not regularly at home. In nearly a quarter of the cases he is

Table 6

	Hyperactive group	Un-domesticated group	Socialized delinquent group
Unstable mother unable to relate self to responsibility	13%	38%	15%
Maternal rejection in infancy	37%	55%	25%
Child openly hostile to natural mother	7%	24%	17%
Child prefers natural mother to other parent(s)	15%	2%	8%

Table 7

	Hyperactive group	Un-domesticated group	Socialized delinquent group
Mother completed high school	25%	16%	2%
Father had some college training	16%	10%	6%
Working mother	12%	17%	32%
Eight or more children in the home	0%	5%	21%
Unkempt dwelling interior	12%	19%	32%
Irregularity of meals, work, retiring	10%	12%	38%
Lack of supervision of children's activities	24%	21%	42%

Table 8

	Hyperactive group	Un-domesticated group	Socialized delinquent group
Natural father not regularly in home	34%	38%	53%
Father dead	7%	10%	23%
Alcoholic father person	16%	19%	42%

dead, and in more than two-fifths of our cases the present father person is described in the record as alcoholic. Here the problem is not one of the child's primary socialization. This was accomplished in the home and particularly by the mother early in his life. Here the problem is one of the direction, training and control particularly of the preadolescent and the adolescent boy and the lack of an adequate masculine pattern for identification. Under these circumstances, he may find his emotional security and identification with the delinquent gang. I do not believe that this represents psychopathology so much as social pathology.

SUMMARY

In summary, a purely symptomatic grouping of 500 child guidance clinic cases brings out five symptomatic clusters. The shy-seclusive children and the overanxious-neurotic children are inhibited groups. The hyperactive children, the undomesticated children and the socialized delinquents are aggressive groups.

These symptomatic groups are very significantly related to background factors which may be presumed to have substantial etiological importance.

Anxiety in children is accentuated by illness and by maternal anxiety. Hostility is generated by hostile treatment and the feeling of being rejected. The hyperactive syndrome appears to be relatively more age-limited than the others, and under favorable conditions children probably more often outgrow it spontaneously than is the case with the other symptom groups. Maternal rejection early in life and the child's reaction to it appear to be a central factor in the development of the undomesticated child, who is hostile, defiant and vengeful. The socialized delinquent, on the other hand, is typically the product of a combination of poverty, parental neglect, the lack of an adequate father figure, and the delinquent associates of the bad neighborhood. Since his delinquency is typically adaptive, it represents social pathology rather than psychiatric pathology.

References

1. Jenkins, R. L., & L. Hewitt. Types of personality encountered in child guidance clinics. *Amer. J. Orthopsychiat.,* 1944, *14,* 84–94.
2. Jenkins, R. L. Motivation and frustration in delinquency. *Amer. J. Orthopsychiat.,* 1957, *17,* 528–537.
3. Hewitt, L., & R. L. Jenkins. *Fundamental patterns of maladjustment: The dynamics of their origin.* State of Illinois, 1964.
4. Lewis, H. *Deprived children.* Oxford University Press, London, 1954.
5. Saksida, S. Motivation mechanisms and frustration stereotypes. *Amer. J. Orthopsychiat.,* 1959, *29,* 599–611.
6. Jenkins, R. L. *Diagnoses, dynamics and treatment in child psychiatry.* Psychiatric Research Report, American Psychiatric Association, 1964, *18,* 91–120.

29

School Phobia:
A Study in the Communication of Anxiety

Leon Eisenberg

Dr. Eisenberg is Psychiatrist-in-Chief of the Department of Psychiatry at Massachusetts General Hospital. He has published extensively on the brain-damaged child, infantile autism, and treatment procedures with the emotionally disturbed child. Dr. Eisenberg has also been editor of the American Journal of Orthopsychiatry.

This article on school phobia, first appearing in 1958, has been so frequently cited that it must now be considered a classic.

In the editors' correspondence with the author, he states that the clinical validity of the therapeutic emphasis on early return to school in the treatment of school phobia has been supported in a follow-up study of 41 cases. The results indicate that percentage of success varied inversely with the age of the child and the severity of the psychopathology. The author concludes that on the basis of his subsequent research and related studies in the field there now seems to be general agreement that the outlook for the young child is uniformly good with appropriate psychiatric help; the problem of the adolescent with school phobia is considerably more difficult, although successful resolution of the syndrome can be attained with good psychiatric care in many instances.

In recent years the literature has reported much success in the treatment of school phobia with behavior modifications techniques.

FROM THE *American Journal of Psychiatry*, Volume 114, pages 712–718, 1958. Copyright 1958 the American Psychiatric Association.

The reader is referred to Leff's article, Behavior Modification with Emotionally Disturbed Children.

Psychiatric efforts to understand the meaning and genesis of neurotic behavior begin with the painstaking task of reconstructing a reliable version of the patient's previous life history from the accounts he and his relatives provide. We soon learn—as Freud disconcertingly discovered—that the emotional involvement of the participants distorts the very process of anamnesis. This leads us to attend to the behavior of the patient and his relatives toward the psychiatrist. The sample of behavior in the office, termed transference or parataxis, is presumed to be representative of other interpersonal transactions, though it is clearly a very special kind of interpersonal relationship, not immediately equivalent to any other. Both of these sources, case history and interview, valuable though they are, fail to provide the direct data of observation that might verify or contradict the dynamic hypotheses we erect to account for the origin of disturbed behavior. We are in search of the specific patterns of verbal and nonverbal communication *within the family unit* that give rise to the patient's symptoms.

It may be of interest, therefore, to report direct observations of parent-child interaction that bear directly upon the source of a particular syndrome of neurotic behavior: school phobia. The mode of relationship was available to study at the very juncture when the symptoms were *in statu nascendi:* the moment of separation. The drama could be seen as it unfolded rather than having to be reconstructed from the incomplete and colored versions offered by the actors in terms of their experience of it and their attitudes toward the auditor. In this way recurrent psychotherapeutic encounters with parental ambivalence were thrown into bold relief by observation of the critical role it played in the interaction between parent and child. The communication patterns that could be significantly related to the onset and perseverance of this specific syndrome may be pertinent to an understanding of the origins of neurotic behavior in children.

THE CLINICAL PROBLEM

Children with school phobia are coming to psychiatric attention with increasing frequency. In a survey of the last 4,000 admissions to our clinic, the incidence was noted to have risen from 3 cases per 1,000 to 17 cases per 1,000 over the last 8 years. It is difficult to ascertain whether this reflects a real change in incidence or merely in recognition and referral from physicians and school authorities, the latter hypothesis representing the more likely explanation. Presumably, in former years such problems were handled by the truant officer or the children were made invalids at home by certificate of the family physician.

At the outset of this discussion, it is essential that school phobia be distinguished from the far more common problem of truancy. The truant, as a rule, has been an indifferent student. He cuts classes on the sly and spends his time *away from home,* frequently for antisocial purposes. He is likely to be a rebel against authority and usually stems from the lower socioeconomic strata of the community.

The phobic child, on the other hand, urgently communicates to his parents his inability to go to school and is usually unwilling to leave home at all during school hours. Most commonly, he is of average or better intellectual endowment and has done well academically prior to the onset of his neurotic symptoms. His difficulty may present itself frankly as fear of attending school or may be thinly disguised as abdominal pain, nausea and vomiting, syncope—or the fear of nausea or syncope in school. Frequently the child is unable to specify what he fears. At times, if pressed, he may offer a rationalization of his behavior in terms of a strict teacher or principal, unfriendly classmates or the danger of failing. The incidents that may be blamed for provoking the reaction do not differ in kind or intensity from those most children experience at some time during the course of schooling. Moreover, the correction of the apparent difficulty by change of classroom, reassurance of passing, etc., is conspicuously unsuccessful in resolving the problem. In general, the longer the period of absence from school before therapeutic intervention is attempted, the more difficult treatment becomes.

Systematic study of these children reveals that, almost without exception, the basic fear is not of attending school, but of leaving mother or, less commonly, father. Johnson and her collaborators *(1941* and *1956)* have suggested, therefore, that these cases be classified as separation anxiety and that the term school phobia be discarded. We have no argument with the contention that this group of cases constitutes a clinical variant of separation anxiety *(Kanner, 1957).* The older term, however, has not only the merits of historical priority and wide clinical usage, but as well the useful function of serving to emphasize clinical symptomatology that must be the first target of therapeutic efforts. That is, the key to successful treatment lies in insistence on an early return to school for older children or the introduction to a therapeutic nursery school for the younger; left at home, the patient is further isolated from his peers, multiplies his anxiety about returning, is trapped in the vortex of family pathology, and is reinforced to persist in infantile maneuvering by the "success" of his efforts.

Sources of the Clinical Data

The findings to be summarized are based upon 2 groups of patients, totaling 26 cases. The first group comprised 11 children, 6 boys and 5 girls, of preschool age, who were treated for separation problems at the Children's Guild, a specialized nursery school for emotionally disturbed children. The second group, 7 boys and 3 girls in elementary and 3 boys and 2 girls in junior high or high school, were studied in outpatient therapy, mostly at the Children's Psychiatric Service. On each of the patients, a thorough initial psychiatric evaluation was performed; in most cases, supplementary information was obtained during the course of psychotherapy. In the children attending nursery, careful observations were made of the behavior of child and mother during the initial period when mother was invited to be present and particularly during the transitional period when separation was accomplished. As we became aware of the significance of the interaction patterns that were noted in the younger group, we were alerted to waiting room behavior before and after therapeutic interviews and inquired more closely about parental actions during efforts to get children to school.

While the specific problems in no two families were identical nor were precisely the same behavior patterns exhibited during the moments of separation, an intense ambivalent relationship between parent and child was present in every case, with separation as difficult for the parent as for the child. In 24 of the cases, the nuclear problem for the child lay in his relationship to his mother, in 2 to his father. There would seem to be little purpose in statistical enumeration; rather, illustrative case synopses and representative anecdotes of separation behavior will be presented as exemplary of the dynamic factors evident in each case, but in varying intensity.

Parent–Child Interaction during Separation

During his first days at the Guild, the typical child remained in close physical proximity to his mother. Attracted to group activities despite himself, he could be seen oscillating toward and away from the play area. As he began to look less and less in his mother's direction and to enter tentatively into the nursery program, his mother was noted to move from her now peripheral position in order to occupy a seat closer to her child. The umbilical cord evidently pulled at both ends! Periodically the mother intruded herself into the child's awareness on the pretext of wiping his nose, checking his toilet needs, etc., each such venture being followed by his temporary withdrawal from the group—much to her dismay.

As trial separations were begun by having the mother move into an adjacent room after telling her child goodbye, several mothers jeopardized a previously successful transition by finding it "necessary" to return to the play area. When the director suggested actual departure, the mothers responded with an admixture of indecisiveness, apprehension, and resentment. One anguished mother, literally led out by the hand, commented, "The least I can do is keep my feet moving." Another bid her twins goodbye with many reassurances of her early return. They played on unconcerned. She stopped again at the door to assure them they had nothing to fear. They glanced up but played on. Having gotten her coat, she made a third curtain speech in a tremulous voice, "Don't be afraid. Mommy will be back. Please don't cry." This time one of the twins got the cue and cried till she left. Another mother, after two farewells without responsive anguish in her daughter, turned to the teacher bitterly, "How do you like that! She doesn't even seem to care!" A fourth mother, tearing herself away from a whining daughter, took her departure with this parting shot, *"Miss Sally* (the teacher) says I *have* to go." Once gone, the mothers spent an unhappy hour or two, returned almost invariably before the time agreed upon and greeted their children effusively with unsolicited reassurances and anxious questioning about how they had fared.

In dealing with the school-aged children, similar, though usually more subtle, phenomena were evident. On the first clinic visit, the psychiatrist might be told in the child's presence "you won't be able to get him to leave me." At that very moment, mother would tighten her grip on the child's hand or about his shoulder. During the interview, she was constantly on the alert for the sound of his voice or footsteps. If he did enter to ascertain her whereabouts, she was conspicuously ineffectual in getting him to leave. When mother and child had to be seen together, she answered for him and constantly catered to his demands, although in an exasperated fashion. A Binet under these circumstances would likely result in a composite I.Q. for the two!

We, of course, were not able to observe the actual school-going behavior but obtained accounts dynamically equivalent to what had been observed in the nursery setting. One father reported during the course of treatment that, on the day his son had agreed to begin his return to school, his mother wondered aloud whether it might not be wiser to wait a day since it was raining and he might catch cold. When the youngster insisted he should keep to his agreement, the mother suggested she consult his father. Called at his office, the father responded with an exasperated "of course he should go!" Whereupon, the mother turned to the patient and stated, "Your father thinks it's raining too hard." Another mother reported that her son, who had finally been gotten back to school for a week, had been absent the 3 days prior to the clinic visit because he lacked rubbers and there had been a heavy snow. This seemed not unreasonable until we learned from the patient that he had been out sledding each of those 3 days!

In one of the two cases where the father played the cardinal role, the following description was offered by his wife. When the morning for return to school arrived, the patient responded with his customary complaints of nausea and abdominal pain. After a few incoherent attempts to insist that his son must go, his father broke into tears, shouted "My God, I can't do it" and tore off to the bathroom to vomit. When the mother called me at 7:30 a.m., in a state of considerable agitation herself, I could hear the lamentation of the men in the family in the background. In the second case, the father was so distressed by his son's morning behavior that he had to be excused from his legal duties, couldn't eat and spent an agitated day—all this at a time when the patient was contentedly watching television at home.

The Parents

Without exception, the mothers were anxious and ambivalent. Each gave a history of a poor relationship with her own mother; most were currently in the throes of a struggle to escape the overprotective domination of a mother or mother-in-law who visited daily, insisted on frequent phone calls, and was constantly critical. Pregnancy had usually been regarded as a mixed blessing; childbirth was feared. The infant had been surrounded by apprehensive oversolicitude and had never been trusted to babysitters, at least outside the immediate family. As the child ventured forth from his home, he was constantly warned of hazards. As one mother phrased it, "I thought it was better to frighten my Joey than to lose him."

The dynamic forces in the mother-child relationship were quite complex. Several of the mothers had responded with primary overprotection to a child who had been a late arrival after many sterile years. Others saw the child in terms of their own pathetically unhappy childhood and re-experienced with each of the child's tears remembered moments of loneliness and misunderstanding. But, inevitably, the children's strivings for independence and self-gratification led to feelings of personal rejection and reactive hostility. "After all I've given her! How can she treat me like this?" was a typical expression.

Lacking emotional fulfillment in their marital relationships, many of these mothers turned to their children. On the one hand, the marriage yielding little, the child had to be both child and lover. On the other, he was resented as the hostage by whose presence the mother felt trapped. This anger, prominent in most cases, led to reactive guilt and secondary overprotection. These mothers could not let themselves experience the resentment normally aroused by difficult behavior and consequently had difficulty in setting limits. As the child, accustomed to having every whim gratified, finally drove her to exasperation, her explosion, disproportionate to the precipitating incident, would lead via guilt to another cycle of overindulgence and latent resentment.

Dependent and anxious as these mothers were, they found little support from their husbands. We found no instances of overt infidelity, but many of the fathers were more strongly wedded to occupational interests than to their wives. They tended to be more effective with the children when they troubled to take an interest, but usually confined themselves to disgruntled criticisms of their wives' inadequacies. Of the two fathers mentioned earlier, one had suffered from an unusually sadistic relationship with his own father and was attempting to provide and, at the same time, experience vicariously through his son the kind of fathering he had missed and still searched for. His efforts to spare his son any unhappiness had been accelerated by a mild attack of poliomyelitis in the boy. The other father, as far as could be determined from a brief contact, had been tremendously affected by the sudden death of his own brother at 17, for which he felt responsible.

Parental attitudes toward therapy The ambivalent attitudes so evident between parent and child overflowed into relationships with the psychiatrist, the case worker and the teachers. One unusually blatant example may serve to dramatize the ever-present rivalry between these mothers and those to whom they appealed for help to wean their children away from them.

> Mrs. L., "devoted" to her own hypochondriacal mother whom she feared to leave lest "something happen to her," married late in life a pleasant but ineffectual husband whom she completely dominated. Successful as a career woman, she commented, "I never thought I wanted marriage or children. Now I can't even think of leaving them." She reported her daughter's lack of interest in the nursery with evident satisfaction and did her best to insure that the school would have little special to offer by duplicating games and equipment at home. She told the nursery director one day, "You know my daughter really doesn't like you very much. In fact, the only nice thing she says is that you have a nice complexion." At this point, she leaned over, scrutinized the director's face, and added, "And I don't see what's so nice about *that!*"

Whereas advice was sought with an imploring and almost desperate air, it was usually received with, "and what do I do when that doesn't work?" There can be little doubt that this anticipation of failure effectively undercut whatever measures might have been taken. That the overdependence of the child had positive values for the mother was often pointed up by the disappointment and even resentment shown to the therapist when the child made strides out on his own.

The Children
Without exception, these children were of normal or superior intelligence. Those with prior school attendance had not been singled out by school authorities as deviant in any way. Their parents described them as

having been sensitive to change, even as infants, and as fearful of new situations. Yet, pathetic and frightened as they might appear on arrival when separation was first attempted, they became remarkably free from anxiety once the therapist had won their confidence, usually in the first interview. In the younger children, intrinsic psychiatric disturbance was far less prominent than neurosis in their parents. The one significant exception was a child who conformed to Mahler's description of a symbiotic psychosis (*1952*). In the adolescents, intrafamilial pathology had been translated into intrapsychic.

An element of infantile manipulation, at times more prominent than anxiety, was evident in the child's behavior. Richard, at 3½, had so successfully trained his mother that the merest cloud of dissatisfaction lowering over his face would send her into frantic activity to offset an impending tantrum. Eddie, at 10, needed only to whine and his father would purchase gifts beyond his means. Lisa, 6, was clearly involved in a vendetta of punishment for her mother's sin of leaving her for a vacation. Wendy, 3, had learned to arouse guilt and anxiety in her mother, who had been hospitalized twice, once postpartum, with the deliberate comment "you like to go to the hospital" whenever mother attempted to leave. Arlene, 8, went to school without a murmur when staying at her grandmother's house but couldn't be budged from her mother's.

There would seem to be a line of demarcation, however, at about the junior high school level. The 5 adolescents were, as a group, far more disturbed. In this we agree with Suttenfield (*1954*). Kathy, 15, tied to a chronically anxious mother, developed a fear of fainting at school or in crowds and retreated to a symbiotic relationship essential to both; interestingly, her mother had quit high school herself for the very same reason. Fear so strong as to overcome the need for conformity and the striving for independence in the adolescent implies a greater degree of illness than it does in the younger child who is normally more dependent. One might suppose that the chronic action of the forces we have identified in the families of the younger children had ultimately warped personality growth beyond the hope of ready change.

The pattern of symptom formation The configuration of psychic forces that generates separation anxiety has the following attributes. There is a background of overdependence on the mother (or father) almost consciously fostered by the parent in response to her needs rather than the child's. At the same time, the child's parasitic clinging is resented by the mother as it impinges on her own freedom of movement. Superimposed is hostility toward the child stemming from sources not in immediate awareness: the child as an image of a resented husband, as bond to an unwanted marriage, as symbol of a hated sibling, etc. Secondary to this is guilt and compensatory overprotection. The child responds as well to the rejection he can sense as to the indulgence in which he luxuriates.

This supersaturated atmosphere is precipitated out by some transitory situation which arouses anxiety: illness, change of school, harsh word from a teacher, etc. At a time when the support of firm handling is needed, the child's anxiety is multiplied by the sight of a distraught and decompensated parent. Maternal apprehension makes quavering the voice and tremulous the gestures that accompany empty verbal assurance. It is as if the children are told by nonverbal communication that what lies ahead is even more frightening than they had dared think—a kind of *folie à deux*.

The child's symptoms are comprehensible as the response to contradictory verbal and behavioral clues. He is told that he must go at the same time that he is shown he dare not; he is told that he is loved at the same time that his needs are lost in the morass of his mother's. The mother is unwittingly sabotaging her own ostensible goals as she struggles in the relentless grip of ambivalent feelings. The child, in response to felt hostility, strikes back by displaying the behavior that he senses will be most disconcerting to her. Anxiety is aroused when the latent (behavioral) cue to the child is rejection or fear; manipulation is activated when the latent cue is the possibility of gratification. The contradiction between words and behavior in the transactions between mother and child is the catalytic agent in generating separation anxiety. The history of early sensitivity to change in these children as infants suggests that an intrinsic anxiety proneness may exist which renders them more susceptible to the acquisition of these patterns. Certainly, they are not exhibited by all children who may grow up in dynamically similar family situations.

Treatment

The therapeutic corollary to this conception of the genesis of symptom formation is an insistence on early return to school. At the initial psychiatric consultation—made if necessary on an emergency basis for the school-aged child—an attempt is made to identify the etiologic factors and to assess the degree of sickness in family members. The parents are given the reassurance that the prognosis is relatively good and the main dynamic features they are deemed capable of assimilating are pointed out. A program for rapid return to school is outlined. Often this can be negotiated with the child once it is made clear to him that school attendance is prescribed by law and that the issue is not whether he will return but how and when. If necessary, he may be permitted to begin by spending his day in the principal's or counsellor's office or by having his mother attend class with him, but he must in any event be in the school building (*Klein, 1945*). We have, on occasion, when a thorough trial of other methods has failed, gone so far as to schedule a hearing in juvenile court—which did not have to take place—in order to shore up ineffectual parents. One father, indeed, decided on his own to call in police officers to convince his son (and himself) that he meant business. Once return has been achieved, therapy continues with the family in order to eradicate underlying pathological attitudes. Obviously, these strictures do not apply to the preschool child for whom a nursery program can be introduced gradually on an elective basis.

Our results confirm the practicability of this plan. Not one child has been precipitated into panic or has gone into psychic decompensation as some might have expected. Ten of the 11 preschool children and 10 of the 10 elementary school children have returned to and are still in school. Results have been far less impressive in the junior high and high school groups. Only 1 or possibly 2 are now attending school regularly; the remaining 2 have been in and out and as of this moment have a questionable outlook; 1 is definitely a therapeutic failure.

These results contrast with a situation uncovered in a recent survey of children in Baltimore on home teaching for medical reasons (*Hardy, 1957*). Of 108 children taught by visiting teachers, 8 elementary school pupils were discovered to be on medical certificates for school phobia. Consequently, no effort had been made to insist on attendance. All had been out for at least 1 year and one as long as 3 years. This points to the unwisdom of recommending home teaching which makes the situation far too comfortable for the whole family and removes a major motivation for change. By accepting the apparent inability of the child to attend as a real inability, it reinforces his regression. The insistence on attendance, on the other hand, conveys to the child our confident expectation that he can accept and carry through a responsibility appropriate to his age.

The objection may be raised that we have produced a symptomatic cure but have not touched the basic issues. It is essential that the paralyzing force of the school phobia on the child's whole life be recognized. The symptom itself serves to isolate him from normal experience and makes further psychological growth almost impossible. If we do no more than check this central symptom, we have nonetheless done a great deal. Furthermore, we have been impressed with the liberating role of this accomplishment in opening avenues for rapid progress in both child and parents in subsequent treatment. The psychiatric task is, of course, not complete when return is accomplished, though it is sometimes so regarded by the parents. Every effort should be made to follow through with family-oriented treatment.

SUMMARY

School phobia has been shown to be a variant of separation anxiety. Direct observations of transactions between parents and children at the time of separation have been presented. Key dynamic factors have been identified and the mode of symptom formation has been outlined as a paradigm for the genesis of neurotic behavior. The outcome of a treatment program has been reported in validation of the theoretical conception of the nature and genesis of the disorder.

References

Estes, H. R., Haylett, C. H., & Johnson, A. M. Separation anxiety. *Amer. J. Psychother.*, 1956, *10*, 682.

Hardy, J. B. *Personal communication*, 1957.

Johnson, A. M., et al. School phobia. *Amer. J. Orthopsychiat.*, 1941, *2*, 702.

Kanner, L. *Child psychiatry*. (3rd ed.). Springfield: C. C Thomas, 1957.

Klein, E. The reluctance to go to school. *Psychoanalyt. Stud. Child.*, 1945, *1*, 263.

Mahler, M. S. Autistic and symbiotic infantile psychoses. *Psychoanalyt. Stud. Child.*, 1952, *7*, 286.

Suttenfield, V. School phobia: A study of five cases. *Amer. J. Orthopsychiat.*, 1954, *24*, 368.

30

Operant Conditioning: Breakthrough in the Treatment of Mentally Ill Children

Bernard Rimland

Dr. Rimland is Director of the Institute for Child Behavior Research in San Diego, California. He is one of the leading scholars today in the field of the autistic child. His book Infantile Autism won the Appleton-Century-Crofts Prize for the Distinguished Contribution to Psychology in 1964. He has published over fifty professional articles and founded the National Society for Autistic Children.

In New York City, in 1965, at the founding of the National Society for Autistic Children, Dr. Rimland presented a paper on operant conditioning, which was one of the first attempts to explain operant conditioning in lay language. It was intended to be, and succeeded in being, a summons to parents to come forward and insist upon the abandonment of Freudian theory and the adoption of a totally new and different concept in the treatment of autistic-type children. The success of his effort is reflected, in part, by requests of copies of his paper in virtually all English-speaking countries, and in translation in half a dozen other countries.

The present paper is a slightly revised and updated version of his talk, still retaining its speech-like flavor. The most significant change is his emphasis on the role of operant conditioning as a precursor to the next step for the child—placing him in a purposeful, firmly structured educational environment with other children.

The reader should find this article, together with Dr. Leff's, most instructive in clarifying the role of operant conditioning in the treatment of emotionally disturbed children.

In each of the years that has passed since my book *Infantile Autism* (Rimland, 1964) was published, it has been read by hundreds of parents of mentally ill children who have then written to me for help. Some of these parents have children afflicted with infantile autism itself; others have children with childhood schizophrenia or one of the other baffling and severe disturbances of behavior which resemble autism and are often confused with autism, even by professional workers. The parents write with a sense of despair and anguish that can easily be felt: "Is there *anything* we can do to help our child? Is there any hope? We will come anywhere, do anything, to save our child. Please help us." Many of these people have invested small fortunes in psychoanalytic or other kinds of psychotherapeutic treatment for their children and often themselves. As the years slip by they grow increasingly desperate.

For the first year or two my letters of reply to these painfully burdened people contained little that would allay their anguish: sympathy, hope that research might provide a breakthrough, and not much else. To face the bleak facts squarely, we must admit that the present, traditional methods of treating such children are simply not satisfactory (Levitt, 1963; Lewis, 1965). If they were satisfactory, we would not be here tonight.

My own belief is that the ultimate answer to the problem of severe behavior disturbances in children—and adults—will come from the biochemistry laboratory, in the form of a drug or a special diet, like the one for phenylketonuria (PKU). Few appreciate the fact that PKU is a good illustration of successful treatment of a mental disorder with a special diet. Most of us do know that there is a special diet which, if started early enough, will allow children with PKU to grow up to be essentially normal. What is not appreciated is that the behavior of children with PKU is seriously *disordered,* not just retarded, and that many such children would ordinarily be classified as "mentally ill" or "emotionally disturbed" in the absence of awareness of the biochemical defect. As a matter of fact, there are hints of a biochemical relationship between PKU and infantile autism, just as there are certain behavioral similarities. Research on this problem is just getting underway (Friedman, 1969; Boullin, Coleman, & O'Brien, 1970).

Since it may be some time before drugs or diets can be developed to the point of usefulness for other behavior disorders, why am I implying that I now am able to hold out some hope—to send a more optimistic message—to the parents who have written to me? I want to make it clear that it is far too early to become jubilant, but I do feel that there is a recent development which will dramatically change the outlook for many, perhaps most, mentally ill children. This development, which in its present form is just a few years old, is called "operant conditioning."

Simply stated, operant conditioning consists of making sure the child is motivated, somehow inducing him to perform the behavior that is desired, then instantly rewarding him for his performance. Once it has been decided what behaviors are to be taught, and what the reward will be, the process itself becomes so clearcut and explicit that it can sometimes be done by a machine. Indeed, there are people who have done this kind of training of mentally ill children with machines. First, let me tell you more about the process itself and about some of the results that have been achieved with it.

Here is a very simple example: I will decide to condition a child to close the door when asked to. I start by closing the door myself, saying each time, "Close the door." After each closing, I quickly give the child a small piece of candy or potato chip, and say "Good!" After several closings, I guide the child through the motions of closing the door while I say, "Close the door." Again he gets candy after each closing, followed by the word "Good!" Next the child is weaned so he gets the food and verbal reward only by closing the door himself. And finally, by giving the food reward less and less often, I have a child who will close the door when asked. I may also have a fringe benefit: very often, in later training the word "Good!" may be enough. This is a very primitive example but it illustrates the process.

When I describe operant conditioning a listener will often comment, "That is how I trained my dog," or, "That is exactly how Helen Keller was taught." Very true. It is not so much the *method,* but the systematic application of the method to children who were misleadingly labeled "emotionally disturbed" which is new. Also new is our realization that the result of this kind of training—the payoff—is far greater than most of us imagined just a few years ago.

I was aware of the research underway on operant conditioning of mentally ill children in the early 1960s while working on my book. I was skeptical then, as I should have been at that stage, and referred to the matter only indirectly in my chapter on needed research. I said, ". . . since *meaning* cannot serve its usual role in guiding the learning of autistic children, it may be necessary to rely on lavish praise and other forms of overt reward to provide direction as well as incentive to the child's efforts" (p. 138). My skepticism was due in part to my belief that even if the children could be trained to do certain things—perform certain acts—it would make so little difference in the long run as to scarcely be worth the effort. It seemed to me that we would be accomplishing something akin to training a dog to walk on his hind legs. After he's trained, so what? One child psychiatrist said something like this to a mother I know who was considering operant conditioning for her child: "If you want to turn your child into a terrified trained seal, go ahead."

Actually, the analogy with a trained dog or trained seal is not a good one—at least in the case of most of the children I know who have been trained with operant conditioning. The outcome of operant conditioning is much more comparable to the pattern followed when normal children learn to talk. In a normal child acquiring speech, there is at first a long and tedious word-at-a-time start, then comes a sudden second stage: rapid acceleration with the production of new thoughts and sentences that were *not* specifically taught. In operant conditioning, as it happens, there is also a slow start, then a rapid acquisition of acts not specifically taught. Furthermore, operant conditioning is a technique that parents themselves can apply with demonstrable success.

Let me at this point give you some of the background that is required for an understanding of the method. What is operant conditioning? First, look at the word "operant." It implies "action," "behavior," "performance," as in "operate" or "operator." This is one of the sharpest distinctions between the new kinds of psychological treatment and the old, for both adults and children. The new *behavior therapies,* which include "operant conditioning," are classified as "action therapies," in contrast to the old psychoanalytic and psychotherapeutic methods, which have been called "insight" therapies. The older therapies depend on "insight," "understanding," and similar concepts. They assume there are emotional blocks, conflicts, subtle aggressions, and guilt feelings which are at the root of the behavior disorder and which somehow must be expressed, "worked out," or "understood" before the problem can really be resolved. These therapies are based on the assumption—*and it is merely an assumption,* tenaciously believed though it is—that personality disorders are caused by faulty interpersonal relations, such as between the child and his mother (Rimland, 1964, Chap. 3; 1969).

The action therapies, on the other hand, make no such assumptions about cause. Contrary to what many people believe, they do not even make the assumption that the patient is *physically* intact—that he has nothing physically or chemically wrong with his brain. The method has been shown to work on pigeons, cats, rats, dogs (even with half their brain cut away), mongoloid children, blind deaf-mutes like Helen Keller, and even sleeping normal people, so why need it be assumed that an autistic child who responds to operant conditioning must *really* be intact and have no biochemical or neurological defect?

So much for "operant." The word "conditioning" takes us back to the turn of the century and the work of the great Russian physiologist Ivan Pavlov. It started when Pavlov wanted to collect some saliva from his laboratory dogs for use in his experiments on digestion. In a "by-the-way" observation which turned out to be a real landmark in science, Pavlov noticed that his dogs salivated simply when he approached, even before he showed them the meat intended to stimulate their saliva. By experimentation, he learned that a dog could be trained to react to almost any signal, like a bell, if the dog were given the signal often enough at just about the same time the dog was going to respond to perform an act. As every psychology student has since had to learn, this process is called "conditioning." The dog is said to be conditioned to respond to the sound of the bell.

It is important to understand that the conditioned dog was not simply a dog who had learned to "expect" food at the sound of the bell. In the first place, the conditioning depended on a near-immediate timing of the bell and the salivation. A delay of a few seconds could prevent conditioning. Second, other researchers showed that even a decorticate dog, a dog deprived of the use of much of his brain by surgery, could be conditioned. Even a simple planarian, a flatworm, it was found, can be conditioned if we are patient enough. For these and other reasons it seems safe to say that conditioning can take place without "awareness" or "understanding." Conditioning seems to be a universal, very primitive law of behavior. This raises the interesting question: Can a child who is largely unaware of his surroundings and has very poor understanding be conditioned?

Let me tell you, as an aside, that I have been advised by several people to soft-pedal animal research, because parents and students may be offended at the idea that children, mentally ill or normal, bear any resemblance to animals. I'm going to ignore that sound advice, at the risk of offending you, because I think it is critically important to encourage an objective reappraisal of the prevailing permissive philosophy of handling children. Whether or not the child is normal, it has been found that his *behavior can usually be modified by making the child's rewards contingent on his behavior.* The widely prevalent and very naive view that a child will grow up to be just wonderful if his parents will only love, understand, and accept him without imposing our old-fashioned ideas on what constitutes acceptable behavior has led to a stress on permissiveness and indulgence which in my view constitutes one of the most dismal, near-catastrophic failures of the twentieth century. I hope my heavy stress on animal research, although it may disturb you, will help you to gain a fresh and objective perspective about your power and your responsibility for managing the behavior of your own children, normal and otherwise.

While Pavlov was making his discoveries in Russia, an American psychologist, E. L. Thorndike, was experimenting with the ways in which cats could learn to pull wires or press levers to escape from a "puzzle box." Although his cats learned quickly when their *own* struggling brought them into contact with the release lever, they failed to benefit at all from watching another cat escape from the same box, or even from having the psychologist deliberately press the cat's own paw against the release lever so he could see how it worked. Thorndike's cats, like Pavlov's dogs, learned their own *reward-related actions,* and understanding or awareness was of little or no consequence. (Notice that I am not denying that understanding can help—in normal humans it certainly does. I am merely saying learning *can* take place without it.)

Let's skip 40 years of history and look in at the lab of psychologist B. F. Skinner (see Skinner, 1960). Just before World War II, Skinner reported that you could, with sufficiently clever timing of food or other "rewards," use conditioning to "shape" a laboratory animal's behavior in amazingly intricate ways. By watching a caged pigeon and punching the button that gives it a grain of corn *only* when it raises its head, you will quickly have a "superstitious" pigeon that repeatedly jerks his head upward. Or you can have pigeons that continuously circle to the left (or right) by first rewarding with corn *any* move to the left, then holding off until you see a rather large move to the left, then holding off until you get a half turn to the left, and so on. The trick is to start with some action that resembles the one you want, then selectively reward only those actions which progressively approach the behavior you have in mind for the animal. Surprisingly complex things can be taught in this way.

During World War II Skinner trained a number of pigeons to act as self-contained guidance systems for missiles. The pigeons were taught that they would get food only when they pecked at the very center of a certain "target" projected on a screen in front of them. Some were trained to peck at top-view outlines of battleships, and others were trained to peck at radar-scope maps of certain cities. The pigeons were to be installed in the nose cones of missiles which were to be launched near the target. If the missile began to deviate, sensitive switches under the pecking plate would detect the change in the pigeon's pecking, and a correction would be made in the missile's course.

Incredible though it may seem, Skinner was able to amass a body of evidence strongly supporting the reliability and accuracy of his pigeon-controlled missile guidance system. The War Department decided this was merely another "crackpot" idea (I must confess I had the same reaction, originally) and, despite Skinner's stature as a scientist, his idea was never put to use. More recently, of course, the idea of having a machine quickly reward a learner for responding correctly is seen in devices for programmed learning. If I ever meet Skinner, I will apologize for thinking his operant research on pigeons was just "for the birds"!

Let's skip another ten years or so and consider the so-called verbal conditioning studies of the 1950s. Psychologists learned that by giving a person some sign of approval—a smile, a "yes," an affirmative nod, or an "un-hunh"—they could manipulate or "shape" his speech, apparently without his being aware of it. For example, the psychologist might decide he would reward (or "reinforce") only words relating to food, or to buildings, and, if he did, before long the speaker would be talking about food or buildings. The speaker had been conditioned to produce the desired kind of speech. (Incidentally, it has been suggested that Freud found so many of his patients to be interested in sex because *he* became more alert and interested when their talk related to sex. If his interest flagged when the patients droned on and on about other matters and heightened when they mentioned sex, no wonder they soon devoted full time to talking about sex!)

Finally, let me tell you about an invention of the 1960s. College students have discovered they can condition or "shape" the behavior of their professors, and there are many stories of how they do it. One class decided it would rather hear the professor talk ad lib than read from his notes, so they paid rapt attention each time he looked up to say something. When he read from his lecture notes, there was whispering, foot shuffling, giggling, and other annoying noises. You can guess the result. Another class decided they wanted to have the professor stand before them and lecture rather than pace the floor or write on the blackboard. Again the technique of rewards and punishments successfully shaped the professor's behavior. I've talked to professors who have had this done to them, and they swear they didn't realize they were being manipulated. (Maybe I'm being shaped right now!)

Actually, I shouldn't have used the words "rewards" and "punishments." Conditioners especially dislike the word "punishment" because it carries all kinds of surplus meanings. It implies that the organism willfully decides to avoid punishment—as you or I might decide to answer our tax forms honestly to avoid jail. Instead they talk about "positive" and "negative" "reinforcement" for actions designed to encourage or discourage a certain act. Food, or some sign of social approval, are typical positive reinforcers. Failure to provide food, and electric shock, are examples of "aversive" or negative reinforcements. Social reinforcement, such as paying attention to someone, has proved to be a powerful reinforcer, even on very severely disordered children and adults.

Credit for first systematic use of conditioning methods with autistic children seems to belong to a Dutch nun, Sister Gaudia, who used bits of chocolate and other rewards several decades ago to teach autistic children and induce them to attend to their environment (Gaudia, 1954).

Let me give you a few illustrations of how the method works with the kinds of children we are interested in. A highly instructive study was performed some years ago at the University of Washington. Psychologists Montrose Wolf, Todd Risley, and Hayden Mees (1964) teamed up to combat an imposing list of behavior problems in a $3\frac{1}{2}$-year-old psychotic and retarded boy whose parents had been advised to institutionalize him as hopeless. Dicky was without speech. He did not eat or sleep normally.

Despite the use of tranquilizers, sedatives, and restraints, he would not sleep at night, thus forcing his parents to maintain night-long vigils at his bedside. As a result of an earlier operation for cataracts, he needed glasses, but he would not wear them. Without the glasses, his vision would soon be permanently impaired. Dicky engaged in a great deal of self-destructive behavior, which is common in these children. He engaged in temper tantrums which included slapping and scratching his own face, pulling his own hair, and banging his head on hard objects. These tantrums left him "a mess, all black and blue and bleeding," according to his mother.

The psychologists' report, covering the six-month period from the beginning of Dicky's treatment until his discharge from the hospital, is neatly summarized in five graphs. Four of the graphs depict very clearly the "extinction" of four undesirable behaviors—tantrums, self-destructive acts, bedtime disturbances, and "glasses thrown." Each of these graphs starts by showing the steady day-after-day rate of occurrence of the untreated acts, then an initial leveling off of the curve as the acts are brought under control, and a final straightening and leveling off of the curve which shows that the problems have been overcome and the unwanted acts have not recurred for weeks at a time. The fifth curve, "Hours per day glasses worn," starts at zero hours per day, stays near zero for a time, then skyrockets to 12 hours a day. The experimenters tell us that at the time of his discharge from the hospital, Dicky had worn his glasses over 600 hours and was continuing to wear them at the 12-hour-a-day rate. At the beginning of treatment, he had never worn them more than a few seconds.

In these dramatic graphs may be found some of the secrets of the operant method. Perhaps most important is the concentration upon specific, observable, countable *behaviors*. Unlike previous methods, there are no assumptions made about hypothetical emotional blocks, concealed conflicts, or covert hostilities which must be "worked out" or "understood." Instead, on the assumption that the child has a *deficiency* in his behavior repertoire, new behaviors are systematically built in a series of carefully planned and rewarded small steps (Ferster, 1961).

The usual response of a psychoanalyst or other "insight" therapist at this point is a gasp of pity or dismay: "You are concentrating on the symptom, not the disease. The conflict will only reappear in perhaps a worse symptom." To this the behavior therapist answers, "Nonsense."

The idea that the underlying "cause" will produce another symptom (symptom substitution or "psychohydraulic reaction") is simply an inference from the theory, supported by impressionistic rather than objective evidence, and is by no means a scientifically demonstrated fact. Actually, research shows that both with neurotic adults (for whom psychoanalysis was devised) and for the more severely disturbed psychotic children and adults on whom psychoanalysis is often practiced, symptom substitution rarely if ever occurs—psychoanalytic theory notwithstanding.

A second point that can be learned from inspection of the graphs in the University of Washington study is that the change generally takes place only a little bit at a time, and for extended periods there may be no *detectable* change at all. Nevertheless, over a period of time change *does* take place, and despite what seem like infinitely small steps, it takes place much more swiftly and surely than under any other form of treatment. To persons used to seeing the sudden changes brought about by the more familiar, nonconditioning way of learning through understanding, the smallness of the steps may cause abandonment of the method—this would be unfortunate!

A third principle that may be learned from the study of Dicky's case is that despite what may look like very limited goals (why concentrate on five types of behavior out of possibly hundreds?), a very significant improvement in *total behavior* was achieved. While we still don't know how he will turn out in the long run, we do know that he was discharged from the institution—vastly improved—only six months after entering with a "hopeless" outlook.

This last point—magnification of effect of small therapeutic change—is even more clearly illustrated in the case of Nelson, which also has several additional interesting angles. Nelson's case was reported some years ago by psychiatrist I. H. Weiland and psychologist Robert Rudnick (1961). Nelson was a severely withdrawn 8-year-old child who had never developed a meaningful relationship with anyone, despite three years of psychotherapy, and still had not developed speech. As an experiment, nonprofessional volunteer workers were directed to take Nelson's favorite toy (a ball) and return it to him *only* if he would say "ball." This was the only change made in the routine of working with him. It took twelve weeks of several-times-a-day "teasing" of this sort before Nelson first repeated "ball," but shortly afterward he began to ask for the ball even when it was not being shown to him. The method was repeated with doughnuts, another favorite of Nelson's. This time it took only eleven days to teach him the word. Let me quote Weiland and Rudnick's report directly at this point:

> Within another week he began adding an average of one or two words a day, and by the end of this week Nelson had taken the lead and was eagerly learning words to communicate his wants to the child-care worker. At the present writing, Nelson has use of several dozen nouns and verbs to indicate his desires to the staff and eagerly plays games of identifying objects as a pleasurable activity in itself. He even enjoys singing simple songs (p. 562).

Frankly, I must admit that when I originally read this case report I simply reserved judgment—I couldn't really accept it at face value. It was only after evidence from other sources began to mount that I recognized that Nelson's improvement might be more than a freak occurrence. It is not often that you will find a case which shows such dramatic improvement in the space of four months. Remember that Nelson had received three years of psychotherapy without much if any change.

As I learned more about how effective operant conditioning techniques could be, and as letters from parents continued to pour in pleading for help, I decided to see first hand what was being done. One of the first places I visited was UCLA. I had heard of the unusually successful work being done there by psychologist Ivar Lovaas (see Lovaas, 1966). I talked with Lovaas, his staff, and his students, who were excited and enthusiastic about what they were learning and accomplishing. I also talked with some of his patients—the children who were later shown in the *LIFE* magazine article on Lovaas's work (May 7, 1965). I was very impressed with both Lovaas and what he was achieving.

As it happened, five Los Angeles families with autistic-type children were among the people who had written to me. On the evening of my visit to UCLA there was to be a dinner party at which I would meet these parents. I brought Lovaas to that party. It turned out to be a very important meeting—for those parents, for their children, for Lovaas, for me, and for many other people. It was the beginning of a worldwide movement for active and vigorous parent participation in their children's training.

As a result of that meeting, Dr. Lovaas set up an experimental workshop at UCLA in which the mothers were taught to use operant methods to teach their children speech, simple arithmetic, imitation, and other things. Before the one-hour daily sessions got underway the parents' letters to me were full of misgivings. Professionals had advised them for years to be permissive and loving and to accept anything the children did, in the hope that they would someday, somehow, realize that they were *really* loved and accepted. "Permissiveness" and "reassurance" were the official doctrine with psychotic kids, as with normals. Now the parents were told, in effect, to "crack down." "Reinforcement," even food, was to be made contingent on behavior. Some children were brought to the clinic without breakfast. If you want a child—even a child with autism— to repeat a speech sound, or to move a card with the word "blue" on it to its place under a blue square, there is nothing like a pancake dripping with syrup to direct the child's attention to where you want it. This was no general "cracking down." It was a carefully planned program, aimed at teaching the child certain highly specific acts. But there was to be no retreat. Those acts *would* be learned.

The results were spectacular. I began to get glowing reports in my mail. Mothers reported more progress in weeks than they had seen in years. A child who was being trained to speak not only began to speak—at home as well as at the clinic—but suddenly added four new foods to his hamburgers-only diet. A destructive boy whose home (to quote his father) looked like Hell's Angels had been camping there and who had been biting the back of his hand bloody for years suddenly improved remarkably in these things. A boy who had never said a word in his eleven years was trained to speak a sentence—meaningfully. All the parents were thrilled and delighted, and so was Lovaas. He was so impressed and pleased at the skill and determination the mothers showed in their work that he invited several of the mothers to lecture to his classes at UCLA. He and other operant conditioners have since made parent workshops a routine part of their instructional programs.

One day at UCLA I watched a mother being taught to work with her 10-year-old boy. The boy was hungry and his mother was shown how to pop a grape into his mouth, if he imitated a speech sound correctly.

She didn't just *give* him a grape, she *popped* it into his mouth. (Remember, there must be nearly instant reward if behavior is to be conditioned.) It was hard work and the boy grew angry and lashed out at his mother. A Lovaas assistant instantly shouted "No!" and grabbed the boy's hands. He held the boy's hands at his sides for five seconds, then let go. This happened several times, and each time the boy met an immediate and firm response. Quickly the *negatively* reinforced hitting dropped out and the verbal imitation—which was getting positive rewards (grapes)— grew stronger.

Although there are cases of remarkable improvement, no child has been made normal—yet. Perhaps no child ever will become completely normal. There may be children for whom this method will not work, but so far no child has failed to improve. (Later: Experience has shown that one of the most important uses of operant conditioning is to bring the child to the point of being teachable in a structured, purposeful classroom environment with other children. Such school placement seems to be *essential* to the child's further progress.)

One interesting finding is that true cases of infantile autism, as objectively diagnosed by the diagnostic check list which appears in my book, seem to respond especially well to operant conditioning (see Gelfand & Hartman, 1968; Leff, 1968). Among children who are not true cases of autism, some do well and some do not.

At this point I would like to dispose of several serious and common misconceptions about operant conditioning. The first was mentioned in my discussion of psychological versus biological causation. Let me emphasize that the need to be firm with the children does not imply in any way that their problems are willful or voluntary, nor that there is nothing "really" (biologically) wrong with them. As I noted earlier, people and animals with known neurological damage can be conditioned—central nervous system intactness is not required. A related misconception: "The fact that the child's behavior can be *treated* by controlling psychological stimulation means it must have been *caused* by a failure in stimulation; for instance, by the mother's failing to reward the child's early social responses." Nonsense! This is no more logical than claiming that the success of asprin in *treating* headaches means that headaches are *caused* by a lack of aspirin. The usefulness of operant conditioning implies *nothing* about causation.

Another misconception that requires correction concerns the occasional need to use aversive or punishing stimulation. Many readers of popularized accounts—including Bruno Bettelheim's (1967) gross distortion of the method—come away with the impression that striking or shocking the child is commonly or casually done. This is simply not true. Ideally and actually, the program is heavily loaded with smiles, pats, bits of candy and cornflakes, and expressions of praise and approval. Rarely, and only when it is in the child's best interest, do operant conditioners shout at or slap the child or use the startling but highly effective electric "shock stick," which is completely harmless. Many operant conditioners *never* use aversive stimulation, but I consider such a taboo to represent mere conformity to a currently popular dogma, and prefer a policy of basing action on the child's welfare rather than on the professional's ideological position.

If anyone protests this method, let him consider the far greater risk and more enduring pain that we subject a child to without hesitation when it is necessary to remove his tonsils or appendix. It would be much *more* cruel *not* to use a shout or a slap, if that is what is needed. Helen Keller was lucky her teacher didn't insist on using only hugs and kisses. If she had, Helen would assuredly have ended up as a living vegetable—a hopeless, institutionalized blind deaf-mute. It's time we became more pragmatic and less dogmatic.

No one knows why operant conditioning works nor why the changes in behavior generalize and apply to so many new behaviors. My own theory is that the operant training, in addition to teaching the specific behaviors, also teaches the child *how to direct and focus his attention.* Turning in our attention—learning how to focus our attention and deciding what to pay attention to—comes so naturally to us that we take it for granted. But *you can't learn unless you can pay attention.* You may have heard the expression, "You can teach a mule anything—if you can get him to pay attention." And paying attention is a sensitive biochemical process. Have you ever fought off sleep when tired and fatigued? Even while driving a car, and your life depends on it, it is hard to fight sleep—such is the power of the biochemistry of the body. But psychological motivation is powerful too—if someone were chasing you with a flame thrower, you'd stay awake! Psychotic children, I suggest, need to learn how to concentrate, focus, and direct their attention. Without specific *immediate* motivation—not long-range motivation such as a college degree—without a specially designed program which allows them to proceed in small steps, many will never learn. With operant training, the autistic child not only learns, he learns how to learn. It is disquieting to consider what damage may have been caused in decades past by the well-intentioned professionals who in the name of "treatment" lavished affection on such children and so rewarded their drifting, uncontrolled attention. Today it seems obvious that we should instead constantly insist that the child marshal his resources and learn as well as possible how to adapt.

Emotionally disturbed? Yes, these children are emotionally disturbed. So would you be if you couldn't make sense of the world. The use of terms like "emotionally disturbed," by focusing attention on the *effect* rather than the *cause* of behavior disorders, has, I believe, set us back many years, even decades, in the task of working out constructive ways of teaching mentally ill children how to cope with the world.

Lovaas has told me that he has seen the movie *The Miracle Worker* many times, and each time he is amazed at how long the methods have been at hand for breaking down the barriers of behavior disorder: you feed order to the patient—bits of meaning—a tiny piece at a time. He must be motivated to pay attention to this input, and his responses to it must be guided by immediate consequences.

Let me extend for a moment my hunch as to why operant conditioning works. Consider the 1-year-old child who touches a hot stove. Once is enough—you couldn't persuade him to touch it again. The pain—the consequence of his act—is immediate. Learning, as it happens, took place with awareness, but the awareness was incidental. It is the *immediacy* of the consequence which was important. He appears to have a virtually conditioned aversive response to the hot stove. Now take a child who plays with something you want him to let alone. "If you do that again I'll spank you." Ha! Most parents soon learn how futile *that* is, and put fragile things out of reach. What is the difference between the first (burned fingers) incident and the second? Immediacy. You don't depend on understanding—on self-discipline—in a child with limited understanding. What you want is to manage the behavior. Meaning comes later. I suspect that the effectiveness of operant conditioning stems from the same principle: a quick reward, which teaches the child how to concentrate his attention. But that is just my theory.

A very important contribution made by operant conditioning is its ability to provide control over the behavior of deviant children to the point where they can be managed in a firm, structured classroom situation (see Hewett, 1964). The value of placing children in such a classroom situation with other children—similar to themselves, retarded, or normal—cannot be overstated. Once the child's behavior and attention is under control, the family and teachers can take over his further training and socialization. From many conversations and letters from delighted parents it has become clear that the children who have been entered into firmly structured and directive school programs are those who make the most progress. If the child's teachers and his family are insistent that the child conform and improve, and they employ the principles described above, his improvement will often be remarkable.

References

Bettelheim, B. *The empty fortress.* New York: Basic Books, 1967.

Boullin, D. J., Coleman, M., & O'Brien, R. A. Abnormalities in platelet 5-hyroxytrptamine efflux in patients with infantile autism. *Nature,* 1970, *226,* 371–372.

Ferster, C. B. Positive reinforcement and behavioral deficits of autistic children. *Child Develpm.,* 1961, *32,* 437–456.

Friedman, E. The "autistic syndrome" and phenylketonia. *Schizophrenia,* 1969, *1,* 249–261.

Gaudia, Sister. Handling of children with an autistic condition. In F. Grewel and J. Muuses Purmerend (Eds.), *Infantiel Autisme,* 1954, pp. 72–87. (I am grateful to Professor Gerard Baerends for translating this symposium for me from the Dutch.)

Gelfand, D. M., & Hartman, D. P. Behavior therapy with children: A review and evaluation of research method methodology. *Psychol. Bull.,* 1968, *69,* 204–215.

Hewett, F. M. Teaching reading to an autistic child through operant conditioning. *Reading Teacher,* 1964, *17,* 613–618.

Leff, R. Behavior modification and the psychoses of childhood: A review. *Psychol. Bull.,* 1968, *69,* 396–409.

Levitt, E. E. Psychotherapy with children: A further evaluation. *Behav. Res. & Therapy,* 1963, *1,* 45–51.

Lewis, W. W. Continuity and intervention in emotional disturbance: A review. *Except. Child.,* 1965, *31,* 466–475.

Lovaas, O. I. A program for the establishment of speech in psychotic children. In J. K. Wing (Ed.), *Early childhood autism.* New York: Pergamon Press, 1966.

Rimland, B. *Infantile autism: The syndrome and its implications for a neural theory of behavior.* New York: Appleton-Century-Crofts, 1964.

Rimland, B. Psychogenesis vs. biogenesis: The issues and the evidence. In S. C. Plog and R. B. Edgerton (Eds.), *Changing perspectives in mental illness.* New York: Holt, Rinehart and Winston, 1969, pp. 702–735.

Skinner, B. F. Pigeons in a pelican. *Amer. Psychologist,* 1960, *15,* 28–37.

Weiland, I. H., & Rudnick, R. Considerations of the development and treatment of autistic childhood psychoses. *Psychoanal. Study Child,* 1961, *16,* 549–563.

Wolf, M. M., Risley, T. R., & Mees, H. L. Application of operant conditioning procedures to the behaviour problems of an autistic child. *Behav. Res. & Therapy,* 1964, *1,* 305–312.

31

Stimulation-level Preferences of Autistic Children

J. Richard Metz

Dr. Metz is a Staff Psychologist at the Permanent Medical Group San Francisco, California. His research interest and publications have been primarily in the area of the autistic child. One of his major concerns has been the adaptation of behavior-modification techniques in the treatment of the autistic child.

In this well-controlled and interesting research study, Dr. Metz has demonstrated that there is a difference in stimulation-level preference between autistic children and successful children. Contrary to a popular theory that stimulation is painful to autistic children, Dr. Metz found that the autistic children actually preferred higher than normal levels of stimulation. The autistic children also showed preferences for higher stimulation levels than matched schizophrenic children.

FROM THE *Journal of Abnormal Psychology*, 1967, 72, 529–535. Reprinted by permission of American Psychological Association. Supported in part by Research Grant No. 61-5-24 (A-111) from the State of California, Department of Mental Hygiene. The support and cooperation of Norbert I. Rieger, assistant superintendent, Children's Division, is gratefully acknowledged, as is the assistance of Antioch College students, Vicki Levine and Barry Singer. Domingo Martinez of Harrington School, Oxford, California, and Carol James of the Community Methodist Church Nursery School, Camarillo, California, very kindly made available facilities and subjects.

588   Exceptional Emotional Processes

> *In personal communication with the author, he stated that 2½ years following the testing of these children, six of the ten schizophrenic subjects had been discharged as improved from the hospital, while only one of the autistic subjects had been so discharged. Discharge from the hospital was significantly related to stimulation-level preference. However, 2 years later, or 4 years from original testing, the relationship no longer obtained.*

In 1949 Bergman and Escalona (1949) published some clinical observations of five psychotic children whom they felt were similar to those described by Kanner (1944). These children were reported to possess unusual sensitivity to stimulation of several if not all sensory modalities. According to Bergman and Escalona (1949):

> Colors, bright lights, noises, unusual sounds, qualities of material, experiences of equilibrium, of taste, of smell, of temperature, seemed to have an extraordinarily intensive impact upon the children at a very early age. They were "sensitive" in both meanings of the word: easily hurt, and easily stimulated to enjoyment [p. 333].

The authors speculated that such children may have been overwhelmed by stimulation at an early age, whereupon they developed "defenses" against such stimulation, resulting eventually in the appearance of autistic and/or psychotic symptoms.

Bergman and Escalona reported unusual responsiveness to or interest in music in four of their five cases. They also reported that "only one of the more than thirty such children observed by Kanner did not show deep interest in music [p. 334]." Relevant also is an observation reported by Pearson (1947):

> I have noticed, in the two cases with which I have really worked very hard, and a third case with which a friend of mine worked, that these [psychotic] children have a history of having very acute hearing. They are able to hear acutely as babies and are disturbed by noises to a tremendous extent. A little later on they put up a defense against their acuteness of hearing by seeming to be deaf. The two cases of which I spoke later developed an interest in music, which was almost the only interest they had [p. 178].

In a recent textbook on child psychiatry Finch (1960) wrote, concerning infantile autism: "Children with this syndrome react so inadequately to noises and voices that they have often been considered deaf. They try to shut out all stimuli from the external world in order to remain more comfortable in their own world [p. 182]."

Studies of autistic children have, until recently, been restricted to such clinical observations of the patient, or to studies of his family background. More recently, operant conditioning studies such as those of Lindsley (1956, 1960, 1962); Ferster and DeMyer (1961); Wolf, Risley, and Mees (1964); Lovaas, Freitag, Kinder, Rubenstein, Schaeffer, and Simmons (1964); and Metz (1965) have suggested the usefulness of behavioral concepts and methods in the study and treatment of autistic children. These studies, however, have typically been arranged so as to demonstrate S's ability to learn or perform, given appropriate conditions. The S's *interest* in various forms and levels of stimulation has not been the primary focus of investigation. Yet, as suggested by the clinical observations noted above, a basic abnormality may lie in this area.

What relative level or volume of auditory stimulation do autistic children actually prefer, when given free choice and the means of control? The purpose of the present study was to examine this question under controlled laboratory conditions. For the sake of clarity it should be emphasized that *preference* for a particular level of volume within the audible range was the object of this study, rather than stimulus response thresholds. It was assumed that the act of selecting a particular level of volume would reflect a preference for that level.

METHOD

Two separate experiments were conducted. In Experiment I the response to auditory stimulation of three exceptional groups was studied. In Experiment II the response to auditory stimulation of three age groups from a normal population was studied, to help interpret the results of Experiment I.

Subjects

Exceptional subjects ($N = 30$). Two groups of 10 boys each were drawn from the Children's Division of Camarillo State Hospital. A third group of 10 boys was drawn from a nearby public elementary school. No at-

Table 1 Mean Age and Length of Hospitalization (in years) of the Three Exceptional Groups

Group	N	Mean age	Age range	Length of hospitalization
A (Autistic)	10	8.4	6.5–10.1	1.4
B (Schizophrenic)	10	8.4	5.8–10.2	1.3
C (Successful)	10	7.6	5.3–10.1	—
C1 (Successful)[a]	7	8.4	6.6–10.1	—

[a] C1 is Group C with the three youngest members dropped, to bring the mean age up to 8.4 yr.

tempt was made to equate these groups for socioeconomic level, but obvious differences between the groups in this respect were not observed. Descriptive statistics for these groups are given in Table 1. The three groups were composed as follows:

Group A (autistic) consisted of 10 institutionalized children diagnosed by the psychiatric team as "schizophrenia, childhood type," and whose clinical history strongly revealed behavioral characteristics resembling those of early infantile autism (Kanner, 1944). The essential characteristics looked for included profound withdrawal from contact with other people occurring or observed during the first 2 yr. of life; an intense need to preserve the status quo; at least average physical dexterity; appearance of alertness despite possible low intellectual functioning; severe disturbance of language and verbal communication. In addition, the children usually showed autoerotic and stereotyped behavior and mannerisms (rocking, toe walking) and distorted relationships with toys. None of these children carried a diagnosis of organic brain injury.

Group B (schizophrenic) consisted of 10 institutionalized children diagnosed "schizophrenia, childhood type," whose clinical history did *not* show early profound withdrawal of contact with other people. These children may have shown evidence of emotional disturbance at an early age, but all had shown interest in relating to people, and sufficient language development to communicate verbally some of their simpler needs. None of these children carried a diagnosis of organic brain injury.

Group C (successful children) consisted of 10 public school children selected by their teachers as examples of outstanding overall adjustment, including especially a position of leadership and respect among their peers, ability to adjust and cope with new situations, and ease of communication with others. The outstandingly successful nature of this group places it in the "exceptional" category, and distinguishes it from the normal sample described below.

Normal subjects (N = 30). Two groups (10 each) of 5-yr.-old and 8-yr.-old boys were drawn from the public school described above. A third group of 10 four-yr.-old boys was drawn from a nearby church-sponsored nursery school. All the normal Ss were selected at random from class lists. None of the children so selected had serious behavior or academic problems.

Apparatus

The apparatus was designed to permit S to make a continuous adjustment of the volume of tape-recorded sound coming from a loudspeaker, presumably to suit his preference, just as one might adjust the volume control of a radio to a desired level.

The S's apparatus consisted of a wooden box, approximately 1 ft. ×

1 ft. × 2 ft. One side of the box, facing S, displayed a speaker, broomstick control lever, and signal lights. The lever could be moved by S horizontally back and forth to any position along a slot in the front of the box. A light-tension spring inside the box kept the lever to the extreme left when not held in some other position by S. Signal lights at each end of the lever slot were alternately lit. Recorded material was fed to the speaker through a connection from a tape recorder in an adjoining room. Moving the lever toward the signal light, which was on, gradually increased the volume of sound to the maximum obtainable from the tape recorder, while moving it toward the unlit signal light gradually reduced the volume to a just-audible level. The level of volume thus selected was continuously monitored and permanently traced on the moving chart of a Varian graphic recorder.

The presumed advantages of the broomstick lever over the more usual rotating volume control knob were as follows: first, the lever action seemed simpler to execute than turning a knob; second, the spring feature required a continual response from S in order to maintain a desired volume level (except when resting position of the lever and desired level coincided). This is unlike the usual radio volume which remains where it is set; third, the relationship between direction of lever movement, signal lights, and volume level appeared to be more obvious with a horizontal lever movement than with a rotating knob.

To control for factors other than volume level preference possibly influencing lever settings (such as handedness, directional preference, indifference, propensity to manipulate, etc.), the position of the illuminated signal light and corresponding direction of volume control were simultaneously changed back and forth from left to right, automatically, once every 1½ min. throughout the 15-min. session. Thus, during the first 1½-min. period the right-hand signal was lit, volume was near zero at the normal left-hand lever position, and volume increased with movement of the lever toward the right (increase condition). During the second 1½-min. period the left-hand signal was lit, volume was maximum at the normal left-hand lever position, and volume decreased with movement of the lever toward the right (decrease condition). Each such reversal produced an abrupt change in the volume of sound unless the lever was being held in the center position, in which case the volume of sound simply continued at the same level. For example, when the right signal was lit and with the lever in its resting position (at the extreme left) the auditory stimulus was barely audible. Presumably, a lever movement under this (increase) condition would indicate a desire for greater volume. On the other hand, when the direction of volume control changed automatically (indicated by illumination of the left signal light) and with the lever still in its resting position (left) the auditory stimulus suddenly became very loud (quite aversive to the average adult, as observed in pretests). Presumably, then, a movement of the lever under this condition would indicate a desire to reduce the volume level. The reversals continued each 1½ min. throughout the session. At the end of the session the sound was cut out entirely and both signal lights went off.

Subject Testability

One reason for alternating the direction of the volume control from increase to decrease throughout the session was to determine whether extreme volume settings, when they occurred, were by S's choice or by default, through lack of participation by S. The rule was adopted that, for inclusion in the study, S had to make some movement of the lever in at least four of the ten 1½-min. sections of a session. Seven potential autistic Ss and three schizophrenic Ss initially failed to meet this criterion. In such cases one or two special demonstration sessions were administered for the purpose of teaching S the function of the lever. After the special demonstration sessions, three of the autistic Ss were still unresponsive to the apparatus, and had to be replaced.

Stimulus Material

The tape-recorded material which was played through the external speaker (built into S's box) consisted of the following series of 3-min. segments (the first three were taken from commercial phonograph recordings):

1. Children's folk songs sung by Burl Ives with instrumental accompaniment.
2. Instrumental march music.
3. Selections from *A Child's Garden of Verses,* read by Judith Anderson.
4. Relatively unorganized variety of percussion instrument sounds.
5. Human breathing accompanied by simulated human heart beat.

These 3-min. segments were all recorded in series on a single magnetic tape in the above order. No attempt was made to equate these selections for loudness. The five selections were intended to provide a wide variety of sounds to which Ss could respond.

Procedure

The same E, a young woman, tested all Ss. The E picked up S at the ward or classroom, greeted him in a pleasant way, but remained noncommittal regarding what would occur, except for saying, "I have something interesting to show you." In the experimental room, which was relatively isolated and free from distractions, S was seated before the apparatus, and instructed as follows:

When one of these lights goes on you can hear things from the box. See this handle? You can make the box play loud or soft by moving this handle. [*E* demonstrated the mechanical movement.] You can make it as loud or as soft as you want. When both lights go out we'll be finished. From now on just pretend I'm not here. Wait 'til the light goes on and then make it as loud or as soft as you want.

The *E* sat behind *S* and avoided as much as possible any response to the auditory stimulus. Once the experiment proper had begun (light on) there was no attempt to interfere with *S*'s leaving his seat, and no further encouragement was given regarding his response to the apparatus. If he chose to ignore the box completely and occupy himself with something else this was permitted. (However, *S* was not permitted to bring toys into the room with him.) The *E* only interfered to prevent damage or injury. If *S* became too disturbed and insisted upon leaving, the testing was discontinued. After both signal lights went out *E* announced, "That's all for today. Thank you for coming," and returned *S* to his group.

One week later each *S* was tested again using the same stimuli and procedure.

Independent Variables

The variables under study as possibly related to volume settings were (*a*) age, (*b*) exceptional group membership, and (*c*) direction of volume control. It was not possible to study the effect of stimulus material (e.g., vocal versus instrumental music) because of the possible confounding effects of serial position and recording volume level.

Dependent Measures

The permanent record of volume level permitted or selected by *S* consisted of a continuous, variable line drawn on a strip chart, with values (corresponding to volume levels) ranging from 0 to 100. Each 1½-min. period (an increase or decrease condition) was divided into 10 time samples, each being scored for "high" and "low" volume settings. Thus each record yielded a total of 100 pairs of high and low scores representing volume of sound. Four scores were derived from these basic data:

Mean volume. The mean of the high and low points for each of the 100 time samples was found. Possible range of scores was 0–100.

Fast variability in level of volume. Differences between high and low points for each of 100 nine-sec. time samples were found. Possible range of scores was 0–100.

Slow variability in level of volume. Differences between high and low points for each of the ten 1½-min. time samples were found. Possible range of scores was 0–100. There was no theoretical significance to the choice of two variability scores. Both were based upon arbitrary units or time samples. In one, the time sample was simply longer than the other.

Responsiveness to the apparatus. The number of 1½-min. periods in which the lever was held away from the resting position for any length of time was tallied. This score was used only to determine "subject testability" as described earlier.

RESULTS

Reliability

Product-moment correlation coefficients calculated between scores from the first and second sessions for two groups are shown in Table 2. Not all children were available for repeat testing, hence the reduced N. Of particular importance is the fact that mean volume scores were fairly reliable in both the normal and the exceptional groups. Fast variability scores were the least reliable and failed to yield significant findings.

Analyses of Variance and Comparison of Means

For the sample of exceptional children (Experiment I), a two-way analysis of variance was carried out for each of the three scores. The variables studied were group membership and direction of control. For the sample of normal children (Experiment II), three comparable analyses were carried out. The statistical method used for the analyses of variance was that for Type I designs, described by Lindquist (1953, p. 267ff). Significant Fs ($p < .05$) were followed up with t tests or, in cases of more than two means, Duncan range tests (Edwards, 1960, p. 136ff) to determine the significance of differences between the individual means involved. Analysis of variance of the fast variability scores yielded no significant result, although the pattern of the differences among means in both experiments for this measure was the same as that obtained with slow variability scores. Accordingly, nothing further will be reported for the fast variability data. In the following paragraphs the results of the remaining two

Table 2 Test-Retest Product-moment Correlation Coefficients

Group	N	Mean volume	Fast variability	Slow variability
Normal	28	.61**	.44*	.68**
Exceptional	23	.69**	.39	.51*

* $p < .05$.
** $p < .01$.

analyses are summarized. The reader may assume that any effect mentioned is significant at the .05 level of confidence or better (two-tailed tests). Table 3 shows mean scores and standard deviations for each of the groups in Experiments I and II. Tables 4 and 5 display the analyses of variance which yielded significant *F*s.

Effect of age and direction of volume control From this analysis there were two major findings, both related to mean volume scores. (The variables had no effect upon the two variability scores.) First, under the increase, but not the decrease, condition the older group selected higher volume settings than did the two younger groups. Second, when the younger *S*s had to act to diminish the sound (decrease condition), they selected higher levels. But when they had to act to increase sound (increase condition), they selected lower levels. Like a thermostat with wide tolerance, the younger children were less likely to maintain a constant level of stimulation.

To rule out the possibility that these differences might merely reflect differences in lever moving activity (regardless of sound level) the records were scored for the number of 9-sec. intervals during which the lever was at rest. These scores were determined separately for the increase and decrease conditions. Kilmogorov-Smirnov two-sample tests (chosen because most of the scores were zero) showed no significant differences on this score between any of the relevant groups, in both experiments, under either condition (Siegel, 1956). Thus, an interpretation of the above findings in terms of motor activity or active lever manipulation alone would not seem justified.

Effect of exceptional group membership and direction of control
Autistic children selected higher volume settings than did schizophrenic or successful children. The latter two groups did not differ from each other in this respect.

Since the mean age of the autistic children was slightly above that of the successful children, but not statistically significant by the Mann-

Table 3 Auditory Stimulation Scores

Group	N	Mean volume $\bar{X}$	SD	Slow variability $\bar{X}$	SD
Exceptional					
Successful	10	49	3.8	18	13.9
Schizophrenic	10	50	18.6	51	29.6
Autistic	10	70	21.6	34	27.7
Normal					
Age 4	10	46	8.0	45	30.1
Age 5	10	49	3.1	45	29.4
Age 8	10	59	13.6	53	27.9

Whitney U test (Siegel, 1956), and since higher volume settings were found to be associated with increased age, it was possible that the above differences might be accounted for on the basis of age differences alone. Consequently, the three youngest Ss were dropped from the successful group in order to match the groups more closely for mean age (see Table 1). A t test then showed that the difference between the autistic and successful groups remained significant, confirming the above finding.

The second finding from this analysis, based upon the slow variability score (Table 3), was that schizophrenic Ss varied their volume settings more than did the successful Ss.

Thus, the autistic and schizophrenic groups each differed from the

Table 4 Analyses of Variance of Mean Volume Scores

Source	SS	df	MS	F
Between subjects	2,220,584	29		
Exceptional groups	569,643	2	284,322	4.650*
Error	1,650,941	27	61,146	
Within subjects	1,280,677	30		
Direction of control	235,376	1	235,376	6.862*
Interaction	119,211	2	59,606	1.738
Error	926,090	27	34,300	
Total	3,501,261			
Between subjects	723,022	29		
Age groups	188,174	2	94,087	4.786*
Error	534,848	27	19,809	
Within subjects	869,488	30		
Direction of control	137,761	1	137,761	7.041*
Interaction	203,476	2	101,738	5.200*
Error	528,251	27	19,565	
Total	1,592,510			

* $p < .05$.

Table 5 Analyses of Variance of Slow Variability Scores

Source	SS	df	MS	F
Between subjects	1,182,248	29		
Exceptional groups	262,453	2	131,227	3.852*
Error	919,795	27	34,066	
Within subjects	93,925	30		
Direction of control	9,126	1	9,126	3.139
Interaction	6,317	2	3,159	1.087
Error	78,482	27	2,907	
Total	1,276,173			
Between subjects	1,295,785	29		
Age groups	21,880	2	10,687	—
Error	1,264,825	27	46,845	
Within subjects	52,100	30		
Direction of control	1,041	1	1,041	—
Interaction	764	2	382	—
Error	50,295	27	1,863	
Total	1,337,485			

* $p < .05$.

successful group in a unique way: contrasted with the successful Ss, the autistic Ss chose higher volume settings, whereas the schizophrenic Ss chose more variable settings.

Finally, as with the normal groups, the direction of volume control affected volume selection. In this instance, however, *all* exceptional groups selected higher volume settings under the increase as compared with the decrease condition.

Observations

During the course of working with the autistic and schizophrenic children, several observations were made which seem worth reporting. To the average person, including the normal children in our sample, the operation of the apparatus seemed to be a relatively simple matter. One had only to move a large lever to produce changes in volume. Furthermore, verbal instructions and a demonstration were given.

Even so, as reported above, a number of the hospitalized Ss were initially unwilling or unable to move the lever in order to adjust the volume. Observations of the children's reactions suggested that this failure was in most cases not due to indifference. On the contrary, most of the children showed either pleasure or fear in response to the auditory stimulus. (The autistic children mainly showed pleasure rather than fear reactions.) Some tried to get E to move the lever. Others engaged in various ineffectual behaviors, such as temper tantrums, hitting the box, touching the lights, etc., in an apparent attempt to control the stimulus. Some hid during one volume control condition, then approached the lever smiling and rocking when the volume automatically changed. Thus, the children were not indifferent to the stimuli. However, some did lack the instrumental skills necessary to control the sound.

DISCUSSION

With the exception of the younger, normal children, there was a general tendency to select higher volumes of sound under the increase as compared with the decrease condition. Of particular interest is the fact that differences between exceptional groups were obtained under both the increase and decrease conditions. That is, no significant interaction was observed between exceptional group membership and direction of volume control, as they affected mean volume or variability scores. This helps to rule out the possibility of such differences appearing as a result of factors other than volume level.

The main results of this study suggest that autistic children prefer, and will act to maintain, higher levels of auditory stimulation, as compared with successful and schizophrenic children. In the following paragraphs some ways of viewing this phenomenon are considered, followed by implications for treatment of autistic children.

The possibility of a peripheral hearing impairment should, perhaps, be mentioned. Only 1 of the 10 autistic Ss had a formal hearing test, which was negative, but there were no gross clinical indications of a hearing loss in any S.

While autistic children function at a regressed or immature level in many realms of behavior, *immaturity* would not seem to account for their higher volume selections. On the contrary, this study showed that *older* children selected higher volume settings.

A widely held theory is that autistic children avoid external stimulation because it is in some way painful to them. The reader may recall Finch's (1960) statement, quoted earlier, that autistic children ". . . try to shut out all stimuli from the external world. . . ." This statement seems to be contradicted by our finding that autistic children acted to maintain a relatively high level of external stimulation. In order to reconcile such a position with the finding of the present study, it would be necessary to postulate an unconscious attempt to reduce stimulation existing side by side with a conscious attempt to overcome this by abnormally increasing stimulation. Without supportive evidence (such as might be provided by longitudinal studies) this theory would seem to lack the virtue of parsimony.

Another viewpoint has been expressed by Rimland (1964). He reviewed evidence that ordinary levels of stimulation are insufficient to arouse children with "infantile autism" to a level of efficient cortical activity. He suggested that such insensitivity could interfere with abstract thought and hence normal social behavior. The findings of this study are not inconsistent with this point of view.

Regardless of the underlying reasons for the phenomenon, the present findings, especially if confirmed for other sensory modalities, would suggest a direction for treatment of the autistic child: either change his physiology to increase his reactivity to stimulation, or increase the level of environmental stimulation so as to create a greater impact upon him. A step in the latter direction has been reported by Schopler (1964), who increased tactile stimulation in his treatment of an autistic child. He felt that as a result of increased stimulation through bodily contact, communication with the child was facilitated. A more systematic effort to determine the therapeutic effects of increased stimulation upon autistic children would seem warranted.

References

Bergman, P., & Escalona, S. Unusual sensitivities in very young children. *Psychoanalytic Study of the Child*, 1949, *3–4*, 333–352.

Edwards, A. L. *Experimental design in psychological research.* (Rev. ed.) New York: Holt, Rinehart & Winston, 1960.

Ferster, C. B., & DeMyer, M. The development of performances in autistic children in an automatically controlled environment. *Journal of Chronic Diseases,* 1961, *13,* 312–345.

Finch, S. M. *Fundamentals of child psychiatry.* New York: Norton, 1960.

Kanner, L. Early infantile autism. *Journal of Pediatrics,* 1944, *25,* 211–217.

Lindquist, E. *Design and analysis of experiments in psychology and education.* Boston: Houghton Mifflin, 1953.

Lindsley, O. Operant conditioning methods applied to research in chronic schizophrenia. *Psychiatric Research Reports,* 1956, No. 5, 118–139.

Lindsley, O. Characteristics of the behavior of chronic psychotics as revealed by free operant conditioning methods. *Diseases of the Nervous System,* 1960, *21,* 3–15.

Lindsley, O. Operant conditioning methods in diagnosis. *Sixth Hahnemann symposium on psychosomatic medicine.* Philadelphia: Lea and Febiger, 1962. Pp. 41–54.

Lovaas, I., Freitag, G., Kinder, M., Rubenstein, B., Schaeffer, B., & Simmons, J. Developing social behaviors in autistic children using electric shock. In H. Work (Chm.), Experimental studies in childhood schizophrenia. Symposium presented at the American Psychological Association, Los Angeles, September 1964.

Metz, J. R. Conditioning generalized imitation in autistic children. *Journal of Experimental Child Psychology,* 1965, *2,* 389–399.

Pearson, G. H. J. Discussion of paper of H. M. Little on "The psychotic child." *Pennsylvania Medical Journal,* 1947, *51,* 178.

Rimland, B. *Infantile autism.* New York: Appleton-Century-Crofts, 1964.

Schopler, E. The development of body image and symbol formation through bodily contact with an autistic child. *American Journal of Orthopsychiatry,* 1964, *34,* 399–340.

Siegel, S. *Nonparametric statistics for the behavioral sciences.* New York: McGraw-Hill, 1956.

Wolf, M., Risley, T., & Mees, H. Application of operant conditioning procedures to the behavior problems of an autistic child. *Behavior Research and Therapy,* 1964, *1,* 305–312.

32

Behavior Modification with Emotionally Disturbed Children

Robert M. Leff

Dr. Leff is Clinical-Research Psychologist at the Children's Treatment Center in Madison, Wisconsin.

One of the major developments in the past ten years has been the marked increase of research and application of behavior-modification techniques to emotionally disturbed children. During his tenure as a United States Public Health Service predoctoral fellow at the University of Pennsylvania, Dr. Leff wrote an excellent review on behavior modification and psychoses of childhood which appeared in Psychological Bulletin, *1968, 69, 396–410. In the present article, written especially for this book, Dr. Leff reformulated, updated, and expanded his review to include other categories of emotionally disturbed children. The net result is the most comprehensive survey yet published on behavior modification with emotionally disturbed children. It is an invaluable article for the serious student in this area.*

In our personal communication with Dr. Leff he said that he did not wish to leave the impression that he is offering a potential panacea. In his own words: "It's not a cure . . . it's only the best we have today. We're working on to make it better." And, incidentally, Dr. Leff is working on. He is currently working in behavior modification research relating to generality of adaptive change and classroom-behavior-control techniques in a research facility for severely emotionally disturbed children.

Late in the 1950s some unprecedented experimental-clinical studies were carried out with emotionally disturbed children. The work was an outgrowth of earlier pioneering contributions by men such as I. V. Pavlov and B. F. Skinner, whose efforts had illuminated the basic mechanisms of learning. It was the later handful of experimental investigations, however, that was to have such tremendous impact on the evolution of psychotherapeutic methods for emotionally disturbed children. For the first time in more than a half century, disturbed behavior was being seriously conceptualized in a new way—one that explained it in terms of explicit, immediate, behavioral antecedents and consequences, rather than vague, historically determined "complexes" of thoughts and feelings.

The crucial issue was not the metaphysical one of the existence or nonexistence of such cognitive and affective complexes, but rather was one of methodological efficiency and power. Many years invested in the psychodynamic approach to treatment had yielded relatively little in the way of successful application; the "new" work, on the other hand, soon to become known as "behavior modification," was producing remarkable results. Ignoring the possible symbolic significance of psychopathological symptomatology, and focusing instead on the relationships between behavior and environmental stimuli, behavior modifiers were learning to control previously intractable deviant behavior, and in some instances, were replacing it with totally new, adaptive modes of living.

How was this being accomplished. What is behavior modification? To paraphrase Ullmann and Krasner's (1965, p. 29) succinct definition, behavior modification is simply the systematic use of environmental and intrapersonal contingencies to alter a subject's responses to certain stimuli. A straightforward, but nonetheless revolutionary approach, this therapeutic model grew out of a relatively novel view of psychopathology as a learned set or pattern of deviant behaviors that follows the same principles of learning as more adaptive, or "normal" behaviors. The behavioristic view recognizes the importance of genetic and physiological factors as predisposing conditions for emotional and behavioral disturbance, but it focuses attention on those aspects of psychological disorder which have been learned and those which can be modified by training techniques.

An instructive contrast between behavioral and psychodynamic approaches is provided by an examination of the syndrome of autism, a rare, but fascinating form of childhood disturbance. Early infantile autism is a diagnostic entity first described by Kanner (1943) and eventually recognized by him and his coworker (Eisenberg, 1957, p. 79) as "the earliest possible manifestation of childhood schizophrenia." Autistic children, whose basic characteristic was described as a fundamental "disturbance of effective contact" with other persons, typically show definite early onset of the syndrome, before the age of 2, early preference for "self-isolation" or "aloneness," and an obsessive insistence on the preservation of "sameness" in the environment—move a toy or article of clothing even slightly from its customary position and the autistic child will tantrum violently.

Generally accepted, but scientifically unvalidated psychodynamic explanations of this peculiar syndrome typically place emphasis on the victim's emotional reactions to callous, unloving, and indifferent parents, and stress the qualitative uniqueness of the strange cluster of symptoms shown by the autistic child. Behavior analysts take a different view. While it is an extreme and no longer tenable position (in the light of subsequently compiled evidence), C. B. Ferster's early formulation (Ferster, 1961; Ferster & DeMyer, 1961a) of autism is a dramatic case in point. Ferster's major contribution was his presentation of the relatively simple and, most important, the *testable* thesis that autism, like any other behavioral phenomenon, is best understood and treated within the framework of a social-learning theory. In this context, the autistic child is not seen as qualitatively different from the normal one; rather, he is distinguished from the normal organism only by the relative frequency of occurrence of all the performances in his repertoire. Thus, for example, the autistic child engages in a great deal less behavior which influences his social environment and a great deal more behavior intended to influence only the physical environment than does the normal child.

The value of reconceptualizing psychopathology in these terms lies in the implication that deviant behavior can be treated using the basic principles of learning. These principles are formulations of ways in which well-learned or habitual behaviors may be reduced in strength, or *decelerated,* and in which desirable (but weak) behaviors may be strengthened, or *accelerated.* Briefly summarized, the primary methods of deceleration are *extinction* and *punishment training,* while acceleration may be accomplished through reward or *reinforcement* of desired behaviors, or through *avoidance training.* Since an understanding of basic behavior-modification procedures and related experimental designs is essential to an appreciation of their application to the problems of emotionally disturbed children, they will be described in greater detail in the following section.

TREATMENT AND RESEARCH METHODOLOGY

Among the most common problems presented by disturbed children are deviant behaviors, which, if eliminated, would do much to improve the child's and his family's situation. The basic method for eliminating any behavior is extinction. Extinction of a behavior, or more specifically, of a response, is accomplished by preventing the occurrence of the rewarding or reinforcing consequence which has established and/or is maintaining the response. When reinforcement is no longer forthcoming, an organism will gradually cease to make the response in question. If one wishes to "hurry" extinction, which is often a gradual process of response "disappearance," a useful procedure is "punishment," defined as the contingency of an unpleasant or *aversive* event (stimulus) on the response to be eliminated. If the "aversive" stimulus that is chosen is truly aversive, punishment will usually weaken an unwanted response very quickly.

When, on the other hand, one wishes to strengthen a response, or to establish a "new" behavior, the usual procedure is to reward or reinforce it. Difficulties arise, however, when the behavior to be established occurs so infrequently as to rule out simple reinforcement as a practical method of strengthening it. In this event (more common among psychotic children, with their extremely limited behavioral repertoires), several alternatives can be used. A valuable class of procedures are the modeling techniques (Bandura, 1965), in which the subject learns a new response or set of responses through observing a model who carefully demonstrates the behavior to be acquired. In cases where this method is insufficient or difficult to employ because of practical considerations, the child's drive level can be increased, by depriving it of food, or perhaps social attention, in the hope of stimulating the occurrence of the target behavior as part of the generally increased activation associated with many high-drive states. Another alternative is the *method of successive approximations,* which is informally called *shaping*. This method involves the reinforcement of behaviors that are similar to, but more frequently occurring than the ultimately desired behavior. As the shaping procedure continues, the therapist gradually requires behavior that is progressively more like the target behavior, until the target behavior has finally been closely approximated. In this last stage the child is rewarded only for the originally desired response, which is then strengthened by continuing reinforcement. A technique which combines two of the above procedures is *counterconditioning,* in which the behavior modifier extinguishes a previously learned response to certain stimuli while he simultaneously reinforces and thereby strengthens a desirable, alternative response to the same stimuli.

Avoidance training is yet another procedure that produces heightened motivation to perform the desired act and that yields immediate strong reinforcement for appropriate learning. In this paradigm, the organism is placed in an aversive situation from which he can escape, or which in later stages he can *avoid,* only by making a response specified by the modifier. When the organism does so, he can be reinforced doubly —first, by the cessation of aversive stimulation, and second by whatever positive contingency the behavior modifier chooses to place on the avoidance response.

Before a behavior modifier can select an appropriate technique or set of techniques for the problems of any particular client, he must specify those problems in fairly precise terms. His major interest is usually in the subject's *current* behavior and the entire set of circumstances that contributes to it. As Ferster and DeMyer (1961a, p. 344), referring to the autistic child's weak behavioral repertoire, put it, "all of the basic processes by which new performances are generated, strengthened, maintained, eliminated, punished, suppressed, or controlled by special aspects of the environment are relevant . . ." to an analysis of the child's disturbance.

The "operant model" of behavior, which deals with behavior maintained largely by its consequences, has been of great use in carrying out these analyses. In the operant approach, the domain of interest is usually a *set of behaviors* exhibited by an *individual*. This contrasts markedly with traditional statistical-experimental approaches, which study a particular behavior as it appears in large groups of subjects. In order to evaluate the effect of some variable upon behavior, psychological researchers have traditionally compared the results of their manipulation on an "experimental" group with the results of "no manipulation" on a control group. The use of groups was devised as an experimental procedure to minimize the influence of intersubject variability, i.e., differences among subjects in the way they react to external forces, so that the results could be said to have general applicability across populations. A statistic such as the mean or median is typically chosen as the fairest representation of all the combined reactions of the subjects in that group. This, of course, tends to do some injustice to individual members of the group who react quite differently from the response described by the mean. Further scientific violence results from comparisons of the experimental group's mean with the mean of a "control" group of subjects, who, though usually matched on certain characteristics with members of the experimental group, are nevertheless inevitably quite different with respect to a myriad of other personality and cultural variables. It is easy to understand the clinician's long-standing dissatisfaction with research of this type, which attempts to establish general laws of behavior based on group averages. The clinician, with his primary concern for the individual, is far more interested in idiographic research, which, taking one subject as its universe, exhaustively studies the functional relationships between behavior and the environmental stimuli that influence it.

The tremendous contribution of the operant model, which has been most thoroughly explicated by Sidman (1960), is its provision of an experimental methodology and technology for the evaluation of experimental effects *on one subject*. Such evaluation is accomplished by means of successive experimentation with the same organism—the subject becomes his own control. Typically, his "base-rate" or *baseline* behavior before introduction of the experimental independent variable is compared with behavior measures taken after its application. Evidence of change from baseline to treatment periods is suggestive of the independent variable's potency. Such evidence of experimental efficacy, however, is not completely convincing, since the modification may have been brought about by uncontrolled variables acting coincidentally with the experimental variable. In order to clarify evaluation of results, several control procedures (Baer, Wolf, & Risley, 1968) have been designed and are currently in wide use in operant experimentation. Most popular is the "ABAB" method, where "A" stands for baseline and "B" for treatment. After suggestive evidence of experimental efficacy has been obtained, i.e., after the first A-B sequence, the experimental variable is temporarily discontinued in order to effect a "return to baseline" conditions (AB-A). Then the experimental procedure is reinstated (ABA-B) and the effects of the ABAB progression evaluated. Systematic variation of behavior in accordance with the changing experimental conditions provides conclusive evidence of efficacy. When it is patently impossible or clinically unwise to return to baseline conditions, an alternative control procedure, called the *multiple baseline method*, may be employed. Here, baseline measures are taken on a variety of target behaviors which are treated successively rather than together. If maximal change for each treated behavior is associated with its respective treatment phase, efficacy has again been demonstrated.

Using one or more of the above-described operant experimental paradigms, it is possible to analyze a subject's deviant behavior and to isolate effective treatment procedures. Once this kind of analysis has been made, the next logical step in the construction of an appropriate behavior-modification program is the systematic rearrangement of reinforcement (and/or punishment) contingencies in the child's everyday environment so as to bring about maximal adaptive change. It is important to note that the primary goal of any therapeutic modification, whether it be predominantly accomplished through the use of positive reinforcement or avoidance-learning techniques, is to render other human beings "meaningful in the sense of becoming rewarding to the child (Lovaas, Schaeffer, Benson, & Simmons, 1965b, p. 108)," and to develop *positive,* adaptive behavior. The goal of therapy is to establish the patient in a normal social environment where most desirable behaviors are maintained through positive social interactions and their associated positive social and material reinforcements.

In line with the above statement of therapeutic purpose, it is particularly important to recognize that "punishment" programs, which may be primarily designed to do away with undesirable operant behavior, are likely to be successfully therapeutic *only* if provision is made for the strengthening, preferably through positive reinforcement, of substitute, or alternative behaviors which can "replace" the eliminated maladaptive behavior. The replacement referred to is a functional one—while the substituted behavior must be more acceptable to the patient's social environment, it must also gain for him a measure of gratification, or reinforcement, as did the old deviant behavior. Otherwise, the effect of the punishment program is likely to be a temporary suppression of undesirable behavior with a return to the old habit shortly after discontinuance of punishment, since the child in such a situation has learned no alternative way of obtaining gratification. If, however, an alternative was provided, and was appropriately reinforced during the course of the punishment program, the child will have already learned a new way to achieve his end, and will not find it too difficult, as the substitute response grows stronger, to permanently give up the old deviant behavior.

APPLICATION: NONPSYCHOTIC CHILDREN

Although behavior modification can be said to have its roots in the basic empirical investigations of I. Pavlov and E. Thorndike early in the twentieth century, we will begin our consideration of this work with the 1960s, when therapeutic behavior modification began to receive concerted attention. Much of this earlier work was carried out with nonpsychotic children, who typically showed a delimited problem or set of problems. At this time, the operant model as applied to human therapeutic work had not yet achieved its present popularity, but another area of learning theory was proving useful in treating psychological disturbance. It became evident that one of the commonest and most troublesome adjustment difficulties of childhood—"phobias," or phobia-like fears—was quite amenable to learning-theory-derived treatments. The technique employed was a variant of the *desensitization* procedure developed by Wolpe (1958) for use in treating a wide range of adult anxieties. Lazarus (1960, p. 115) summarized the rationale of the method as follows: "If a response antagonistic to anxiety can be made to occur in the presence of anxiety-evoking stimuli so that it is accompanied by a complete or partial suppression of the anxiety responses, the bond between these stimuli and the anxiety responses will be weakened." Basic to this "reciprocal inhibition" technique, which is a form of counterconditioning, is the "piecemeal" reduction of anxiety by gradual, successive exposure of the patient to anxiety-provoking stimuli in the presence of incompatible (nonanxious) response states. In practice, a hierarchy of fear-arousing stimuli is usually constructed, based on the individual's particular sensitivities, and one by one, the hierarchy items are presented to the patient (either physically, or in terms of the patient's visual imagery) while he is kept in a pleasurable state, through simultaneous presentation of appetitive stimuli, such as food, or through drug- or suggestion-induced relaxation. When the highest (most fearsome) item in the hierarchy has finally been presented and the old anxiety reaction to it extinguished, the patient is typically "cured" or "desensitized" to his original fear hierarchy—including many of the *actual* fear stimuli as well as the imaginary ones used during the therapy.

Lazarus (1960), using a variety of methods to counteract anxiety arousal, ranging from relaxation and the presentation of food to drug administration, treated a variety of childhood phobias (of autos, dogs, and sleeping alone). His success rate was high, as measured against objective criteria of improvement, and therapeutic effects were long lasting. In a subsequent paper, Lazarus and Abramovitz (1962) presented still another reciprocal inhibition technique which used "emotive imagery," that is, positive-affect-arousing, imagined stimuli (Walter Mitty–type fantasies), to combat anxiety arousal. Of nine phobic children treated by this method, seven improved significantly in a mean of 3.3 sessions, without evidence of relapse in later 12-month follow-ups.

Using a mother as therapist, Bentler (1962) treated a water-phobic 1-year-old via *in vivo* desensitization. The infant, who was gradually exposed to water in more and more concentrated and massive form in the presence of food, toys, and physical warmth and comfort from his mother, recovered from his excessive fear in 1 month.

An interesting study by Patterson (1965b) used an essentially operant approach to countercondition separation anxiety and to establish classroom approach responses in a "school-phobic" child. Toward the end of the treatment, as the child's originally high anxiety diminished, it was possible to treat the school-phobic behavior directly by reinforcing approaches to the actual classroom setting. It is Patterson's initial method, however, that deserves special comment. The therapist exposed the child to a graded course of reinforced doll-play separations of "boy" from "mother" doll in order to reduce the child's extremely high anticipatory anxiety levels. This adaptation of the standard "imagined-scene" stimulus presentation is important because it extends the desensitization method's applicability to a variety of highly anxious children with whom the use of unaided imagination or visual imagery is precluded.

The last childhood-phobia study to be discussed here was carried out by Lazarus, Davison, and Polefka (1965). Also reporting successful treatment of a serious aversion to school attendance, these workers noted interestingly the interchangeability of the two graduate-student therapists who carried out the therapy by exposing the child to situations that progressively approximated the actual school setting. The authors concluded reasonably that both classical and operant training can often be useful in phobia treatment. They suggest that classical reciprocal-inhibition procedures are called for in cases of extremely high anxiety, while operant techniques, such as reward of alternative positive behavior, can be immediately applied in cases of minimal anxiety where the avoidance behavior appears to be maintained largely by "secondary gains," i.e., reinforcers such as social attention.

The body of evidence in support of behavior-modification's success in decelerating negative behavior extends beyond the elimination of phobias. Baer (1962) reduced a 5-year-old's thumbsucking via a laboratory punishment technique, and Wolf, Birnbrauer, Williams, and Lawler (1965) extinguished the operant vomiting of a retarded child by removing what the authors guessed had been the reinforcing contingency, i.e., being sent to her room for each vomit. Both studies demonstrated the effectiveness of their manipulations by temporary restoration of baseline reinforcement conditions, which temporarily restored the negative behaviors. Less well controlled, but nevertheless strongly suggestive case studies were carried out by Brown and Elliott (1965), Patterson, Jones, Whittier, and Wright (1965), and Wetzel (1966), who, respectively, reduced classroom aggressiveness in nursery-school boys, classroom hyperactivity in a brain-damaged child, and the "compulsive" stealing of a 10-year-old boy in a residential treatment center.

Other workers have directed attentions primarily to the acceleration of prosocial behaviors. Employing social reinforcement and candy for successes, Hundziak, Mauer, and Watson (1965) toilet trained severely mentally retarded boys. In an ABAB reversal paradigm, Allen, Hart, Buell, Harris, and Wolf (1964) successfully used teacher attention to reinforce only peer interactions, thereby developing adequate social play in a previously isolated nursery-school child. A controlled study by Johnston, Kelley, Harris, and Wolf (1966) helped a young child in an ordinary preschool program to develop important motor skills solely through contingent social attention from his teachers. The authors describe in informative detail their application of the *method of successive approximations:*

> The reinforcing teacher, stationed near the climbing frame, smiled and spoke to him when he approached or walked by, terminating her attention to him when he moved away. As he came closer, and stayed longer, she narrowed her criteria for reinforcement; that is, at first she gave attention to him when he came within about six feet of the climber, then not until five feet, and so on. Eventually, he touched the frame and was soon climbing on it. From this point on, the teacher gave him attention only for climbing-frame behavior as previously defined (p. 381).

Equally as instructive as the foregoing material is the author's account of the "thinning" of the reinforcement schedule from a *continuous schedule* (where *every* appropriate response is reinforced) to an *intermittent* one, where responses are reinforced on a schedule approximating that of the normal social environment:

> On a schedule of continuous reinforcement, the teacher gave Mark attention every time for as long as he played on the climbing frame. . . . When an intermittent schedule was instituted, the teacher first attempted to reinforce approximately every other incidence of this behavior for as long as it continued. Next, she gradually reduced the duration of the reinforcement by staying only a few minutes. Slowly then, the teacher increased the number of responses required

for reinforcement and varied the duration of reinforcement in the direction of shorter periods, flexibly adjusting her two-way leaning of the schedule so that the child's climbing-frame behavior was maintained. In the final stages of this phase, teachers reinforced Mark on an intermittent schedule consistent with that given to any child in the group (p. 382).

Further suggestive evidence for the effectiveness of relatively uncomplicated behavior-modification procedures comes from studies by Homme, de Baca, Devine, Steinhorst, and Rickert (1963) and Patterson (1965a), who increased appropriate classroom behaviors in nursery-school subjects and in an older, minimally brain-damaged child, respectively. White (1959) reported a case study involving the development of a variety of helpful and cooperative behaviors in a young girl who had previously been a poor eater and generally out of parental control. Another case study by Gittelman (1965) describes the development of self-control in previously highly reactive (belligerent) preadolescents through the use of a group role-playing technique in which socially acceptable, alternative responses to provocation were reinforced according to a point system.

Other investigators have amply demonstrated the power of optimal behavior-modification methodology. By withdrawing attention to, or by punishing deviant behavior, while stressing positive reinforcement of adaptive behavior, these workers have replaced operant crying with appropriate classroom activity (Hart, Allen, Buell, Harris, & Wolf, 1964), and have used a mother as therapist for her 4-year-old child to decrease his aggressive behavior and increase his obedience (Zeilberger, Sampen, & Sloane, 1968). Doubros and Daniels (1966), investigating the power of a token-reinforcement system under strict controls for external (i.e., social, such as peer) reinforcement, found that the tokens (exchangeable for, or "backed up" by, material reinforcement) were effective in eliminating hyperactive behavior and in fostering the growth of constructive activity. It should be noted, however, that in the complex, special classroom situation (where token systems are especially applicable) tokens alone are not likely to be the answer to all the behavior problems of emotionally disturbed children. As Kuypers, Becker, and O'Leary (1968) have aptly pointed out in an article entitled, "How to make a token system fail," it is probably of at least equal importance that teachers have adequate training in applied behavior theory and that they make systematic use of differential social reinforcement at all times.

In the area of language development, Gray and Fygetakis (1968) have recently completed an exploratory study with far-reaching implications. Their results suggest that dysphasic children, those with basic speech difficulties, can be efficiently taught syntactic structure and grammatical usage via preplanned operant programming, or what the authors call "programmed conditioning." The method provides a program logic which tells the teacher precisely what move to make in the event of a setback at any point in the program. Advantageous is the simplicity of the system, which was largely implemented in this study by minimally trained housewives under the supervision of an experienced special teacher. Most important, however, is the finding that children who successfully negotiated the operant teaching program not only learned to use functional language, but also spontaneously generated structurally correct *variations* of target responses. Similar results have been reported by Hewett (1964, 1965) and Risley and Wolf (1967), who used similar, but not formally programmed techniques with several echolalic, autistic children. Spontaneous language growth like that achieved in these studies after short operant training experiences suggests that, contrary to the position of some linguists, it *is* possible to build a "base structure" from which new compositions can be correctly formed through simple reinforcement of increasingly complex combinations of language units. Further research is necessary to establish the applicability and efficiency of this technique, but the results of this pilot study are promising for the development of a technology for remediation of serious language disabilities.

A number of other papers (case studies, rather than rigorously controlled experiments) have reported successful modification of children who showed a wide range of deviant behaviors. Common to all these studies (Allen & Harris, 1966; Hawkins, Peterson, Schweid, & Bijou, 1966; Patterson & Brodsky, 1966; Russo, 1964; Wahler, Winkel, Peterson, & Morrison, 1965; Wetzel, Baker, Roney, & Martin, 1966) was their involvement of parents as therapists to facilitate transfer of therapeutic effects to home environments and other natural settings. Such work will hopefully be the cornerstone of future behavior modification directed at general adaptive change in disturbed children, but it is important to recognize that its implementation presupposes strong parental motivation to help the child. Although behavior-modification techniques are relatively easy to understand and to correctly apply, they require a consistent, sustained effort that is usually a departure from the parents' previous child-handling procedures. Thus, it should be noted that the investigators who have reported successful therapeutic modification using parents in the therapeutic role have generally been working with a selected sample of cooperative, highly motivated parents—a sample that does not appear to be representative of parents of emotionally disturbed children in general. That families can be involved, however, even in the treatment of psychotic children, will be further documented and discussed in the following sections.

PSYCHOTIC CHILDREN

The childhood psychoses are the group of profound personality and behavior disturbances—including early infantile autism—that affect children.

612   Exceptional Emotional Processes

The broadest subcategory of this general classification is childhood schizophrenia, which, according to Bender and Helme (1953), is a disorder of the entire organization and maturation of behavior processes. Manifest in such primary disturbances of function is a "global instability and poor integration of the control and direction of behavior at all levels" (p. 415). Also typical of these cases are pan-anxiety and secondary disturbances in the basic perception of the self as an object in the psychological world, including perturbations in body image, identity, and orientation to the objects and forces of the external world. On the more specific level of symptomatology, the schizophrenic child is often subject to somatic complaints, shows abnormal EEG activity, and indulges in bizarre, regressive behavior, repetitive motor actions, and tantrums. Also noted are speech and thinking disturbances.

In behavioral terms, many psychotic children present symptomatology that may be loosely thought of as a "lack of behavior," that is, deficiency in a great many of the most elementary developmental skills. Thus, psychotic children frequently need grounding in fundamental behavior systems that are taken for granted in most other children. A particularly difficult problem in working with such children arises from their unresponsiveness or, in many cases, their perverted responsiveness to social attention. Beyond the common practical experience of many clinicians, Levin and Simmons (1962a, 1962b) have reported experimental evidence for ineffectiveness, and actual aversiveness for some emotionally disturbed boys of what is normally considered positive social reinforcement. Browning and Stover (1971) provide extensive experimental evidence for a phenomenon that they have labeled "reversed polarity of reinforcers," a term that refers to the frequently noted tendency of severely disturbed children to respond to social stimuli according to an incentive or motivational system that is diametrically opposed to that of the normal child. Whereas most normal children's behavior is accelerated by adult positive social attention, such as physical affection or praise, and decelerated by negative social attention (e.g., anger, withdrawal of affection), the behavior of disturbed, and especially psychotic children often seems to follow a reversed pattern. In operant terminology, such children will "work" for social punishment, i.e., engage in activities likely to elicit negative social reactions, while they typically seek to avoid, show no reaction to, or decelerate behavior in response to positive social stimuli. What is "positive," pleasurable, or reinforcing for the normal child seems often to be neutral or aversive to the psychotic child, and what is normally aversive is likewise apparently attractive to many psychotic children.*

> * Informal observations by D. O. Stover (1969) suggest that preadolescent emotionally disturbed boys who appear to experience teachers' social reinforcement for on-task performance as neutral or aversive may never-

As a result of this reversed polarity of reinforcers, the therapist attempting to work with psychotic children is faced with more than the need to rearrange social-behavioral contingencies in order to change behavior patterns. Indeed, he is faced with the far larger, preliminary task of *modifying the incentive values* of various social stimuli. If the child is eventually to be integrated into the extratherapeutic environment, it is essential that he react generally within the expectations of that environment. It is thus necessary to make customary social reinforcers reinforcing to the child, and similarly, to render ordinary aversive social events aversive to him. This process of reversal is typically accomplished through a classical conditioning paradigm. For example, a known positive reinforcer, such as food, may be presented repeatedly in combination with, or just before, the social stimulus (e.g., a hug) that is to become reinforcing. The result of many such pairings is the hug's gradual acquisition of "secondary" reinforcing value. By virtue of its programmed, close association with an already-reinforcing stimulus, the hug tends to become reinforcing, itself, and can later be used to shape desirable new behaviors. Through the application of such procedures to a variety of "normal" social reinforcers, the behavior modifier accomplishes two missions—he enlarges the range of reinforcers available to him in his subsequent shaping programs (where reinforcer "satiation," i.e., loss of attractiveness due to prolonged, repeated use, is often a serious problem) *and* he readies the child for a more adaptive reactivity to the various motivational contingencies that predominate in the natural social environment.

Again, since much of the work reviewed in this section has been reported in preliminary and case studies, complete demonstrations of experimental control were not often incorporated. The outcomes, then, of a good deal of this work must be evaluated with respect to the degree to which the results reflect dramatic changes in behavior that appeared to be reasonably permanent and to contribute substantially to the adaptation of the children so treated. The studies are grouped accordingly to the type of basic procedure—positive reinforcement, avoidance, or punishment—that was used.

---

theless experience teacher-controlled desk lights, which are illuminated only as long as the student attends to his work, as reinforcing. It is interesting to speculate that while relatively affect-free cognitive feedback, or positive evaluation, or even knowedge of adult approval may be reinforcing to disturbed children, the verbal and/or expressive components of such reinforcement (e.g., a smile and a hearty "good" or "nice work") may be, for a variety of reasons, aversive to some of them. Current research being conducted by the author and R. E. Shores is experimentally investigating this issue.

Positive Reinforcement

It should be recognized, of course, that the great majority of these experiments with psychotic children incorporated *some* positive-reinforcement contingencies in their procedures, but those that are grouped here are distinguished by their sole reliance upon positive reinforcement. Ferster and DeMyer (1961a) showed that the response patterns emitted by two schizophrenic children who were nonverbally reinforced under various schedules of reinforcement approximated the characteristic functions obtained with animals and normal humans under such schedules. In addition, a conditioned, or "generalized" reinforcer (coin) was established. The children failed to learn on a complex "multiple" (combination) schedule and had great difficulty in a relatively simple transfer-of-training task, where learned discriminative control could not be maintained upon introduction of a new, slightly different apparatus. Nevertheless, both subjects exhibited more experimentally controlled behavior and less tantrum activity with increasing exposure to the automatic environment.

In 1962 Ferster and DeMyer further demonstrated the practicability of controlling key-press behavior in two autistic children through nonverbal intermittent-reinforcement schedules. The children, who eventually performed discriminative acts quite well for intermittent food reward, nevertheless exhibited very restricted behavioral repertoires, in that their operant activity was largely uninfluenced by a wide variety of available stimuli which are reinforcers for normal children. Both these demonstration experiments were informative because they showed that conventional learning technology is adequate for the experimental analysis of childhood psychosis—a disorder that had been refractory to previous efforts at precise analysis.

Metz (1965) obtained "generalized imitation" in two schizophrenic children using conditioned verbal and nonverbal reinforcers ("good" and tokens) in a gradual shaping procedure which began with the experimenter passively "putting the subject through" the action he was to imitate later and rewarding him with food and verbal praise ("good") after each passive demonstration. The experimenter's guidance was progressively withdrawn (*"fading"* technique) until eventually only an occasional verbal reinforcement was necessary to maintain imitative performances. The problems encountered in this program involved slow learning rates and strong tendencies toward "superstitious" responding. In this latter form of inappropriate learning, the subject responds in accordance with a contingency that is not actually in effect but which he has been led to believe is operative by accidental reinforcements of irrelevant behavior. Everyday examples of this common phenomenon are found in the dozens of so-called "compulsive" acts that most of us perform routinely without knowing exactly why we do.

Additional problems encountered in Metz's (1965) study were occasional "regressive" behaviors, that is, previously appropriate responses that were emitted in subsequent situations where they were inappropriate. More than balancing the effects of these setbacks, however, were Metz's observations that (1) many imitative responses "persisted and increased, in a context of reward for imitation, *without specifically being rewarded*" (p. 397, italics added); (2) the frequency of inappropriate, ritualistic, and emotional behavior (tantrums) decreased as appropriate activity increased; and (3) these withdrawn, autistic children eventually "expressed joy or delight upon 'solving' a problem . . . sought the model out whenever he appeared on the ward . . . etc." (p. 398).

Two comments are in order here: First, this investigator enjoyed a greater degree of control over the motivational states of the subjects than is usually possible, since the subjects were deprived of their breakfast daily, and their lunch consisted solely of the reinforcements earned in the experiment. The second point, this one made by the author, limits the interpretation of the results somewhat since no control subjects or procedures were run, and, in the light of the diverse extraexperimental experiences undergone daily by these institutionalized children, no strong inference can be made that the increased generalized imitative performance was the specific result of the operant-training procedures.

In an interesting experiment by DeMyer and Ferster (1962) that was conducted on the ward, rather than in a laboratory, new social behaviors were taught to eight schizophrenic children (aged 2 to 10) by the regular hospital staff of nurses and attendants, who had received explanatory lectures on the basics of operant learning. Each worker spent a great deal of time with the child according to regular hospital routine, but, in addition, each of these "experimenters" had the task of discovering those particular adult behaviors which were especially reinforcing to each of the children involved. Such reinforcers ranged from verbal praise and reassurance to holding the child, playing music, and dancing. When the worker to whom the child seemed most responsive was found, he began the shaping program that constituted the "therapy" of this study. The authors, in conjunction with each worker, decided what sort of behavior was to be shaped with each child, and the worker spent ½ hour a day, three or four times a week, engaged in these activities. Since most of the workers relied heavily on bodily contacts, such as holding and rocking the children, the therapy was more practicable with the younger children, and, indeed, the children under 6 showed the greatest positive effects. Results were reported in terms of individual improvements for each child, with the general conclusion that "there were classes of behavior which definitely seemed to improve as a result of this therapy and other, more general behavior changes, not directly attributable to the specific procedures employed" (DeMyer & Ferster, 1962, p. 460). The authors did not fail to mention the inherent difficulty of evaluating these results due to the subjects' numerous uncontrolled contacts with other institutional personnel during the course of the study. But it is noteworthy that untrained, nonprofessional workers probably did accomplish some important behavioral changes in the appropriate direction.

That the strategy of employing inexperienced nonprofessionals in operant-training programs for severely disturbed children can be successful has been further demonstrated in a study by Davison (1965). Here, four college undergraduates were given one month of classroom training in the basic concepts of social reinforcement and operant learning. The undergraduate "therapists," working in teams of two, then applied their newly learned techniques to modifying the behaviors of two autistic children. They returned daily reports to the author-supervisor, and he in turn made suggestions and changes during the course of the program. Working conditions in the day-care center at which this experiment was performed were far from ideal. The psychotic children were exposed to the student therapist for less than 15 percent of their waking hours for a total of only four weeks. Also, as a result of unanticipated situational problems with the children, the author was prevented from carrying out his postmeasure of behavioral change as originally planned. Since the pre- and postmeasurements were quite dissimilar, the only firm conclusion that was warranted was that "the therapists *probably* were able to control the child better after the treatment" (Davison, 1965, p. 148). (The more successful team achieved an average increase of about 40 percent in the number of commands obeyed.) Of course, the failure in experimental rigor involving measures and the limitations imposed by uncontrolled institutional settings limit interpretation of these results. But one highly significant implication of this work is that intelligent, highly motivated students may be trained in a very short time to execute a behavior-control program that requires the application of learning principles to the manipulation of psychotic behavior in children.

Perhaps most universally characteristic of children who are labeled schizophrenic is their withdrawal from interpersonal relationships. It has become a classically noted feature of childhood schizophrenia that very little physical contact occurs between afflicted children. Yet, Hingtgen, Sanders, and DeMyer (1965) observed that their six schizophrenic subjects did eventually engage in such behavior, despite the fact that reinforcement was never made directly contingent upon social contacts. The children were seen experimentally for one session per day, five days a week. They were first taught to press a lever to obtain coins on a fixed-ratio (FR) schedule of reinforcement. Then the six subjects were paired into three teams, the members being taught, through nonverbal shaping procedures, to emit cooperative responses. That is, they were eventually required to alternate their bar presses to obtain rewards, one subject's response allowing the other subject to obtain reinforcement. The results indicated that it was possible to shape these alternative cooperative responses in early childhood schizophrenics within an average of 23 sessions. It must be noted that the achievement was probably facilitated by the several months of preexperimental operant training experienced by each of these subjects. Their specific, cooperative behavior, however, was clearly attributable to the training program employed.

As mentioned above, it was also noted that other, more general behavior changes occurred as the experiment progressed. The increase in physical contact activity between the children was one of the most striking of these changes. Children who typically behaved as if they were unaware of the presence of other humans were now seen to direct a good deal of their attention and their activity toward another child, within the confines of an experimental setting. As the experimenters have noted, their subjects were exposed, during the remainder of each experimental day, to play therapy, psychotherapy, occupational therapy, music therapy, and so forth. Yet it seems likely that the observed increase in forms of social interaction which were not directly reinforced was also primarily due to the experimental manipulations, since the behavior referred to increased in the experimental room, but not on the ward.

If it is accepted that the experimental manipulations incidentally established certain situation-specific social interactions, a critical evaluation of this result becomes necessary. Such an evaluation depends partly on a closer examination of the types of interpersonal behavior which occurred. While some of the contact actions involved one subject's guiding the hand of the other to the lever, there were other "cooperative" interactions of a less passive nature, in which one subject would slap or otherwise attack the other in order to rouse him to action. It is obvious that behavior such as this may be called "cooperative" only within the context of this experiment—a subject who forces his teammate to act in order to render his own actions effective in securing reinforcement is not cooperating, or "operating jointly with another," in the usual sense of that definition. Rather, he is coercing another in order to further his own ends—in this case, the acquisition of material rewards.

The above analysis is not meant to imply that the so-called cooperative behavior is of no potential value in an operant-learning approach to a therapeutic training program for psychotic children. Though the physical prompting of a teammate cannot be classified as true cooperative behavior, it does entail reality testing and the tacit recognition of other human beings as significant mediators of desired ends. Action taken with reference to the instrumental value of others is indicative of an adaptiveness that is characteristically absent in the autistic or schizophrenic behavioral repertoire. Thus, the elicitation here of such adaptiveness through the use of reinforcement-contingency techniques suggests that these operant-training methods are fruitful approaches to the problems of the primary behavior disorders of childhood.

Indeed, a follow-up study by Hingtgen and Trost (1964) provides added support for this inference. In an attempt to induce more general behavioral changes, the authors made provision for the direct reinforcement of vocal and physical interactions between four young nonverbal schizophrenic children. After an average of 46 sessions, the two pairs of children (who had all had approximately one year of previous experience in operant-learning procedures) exhibited a low but stable rate of interactive behavior. This level of contact action was significantly greater than that measured in a series of preexperimental toy-play observations in which the subjects participated. Moreover, in line with the authors' expectations, physical contact and vocal behavior were observed to increase in the ward setting, as well as in the home.

Further evidence for the power of operant-training methods is provided by the work of Hewett (1964, 1965). This author has been able to engineer and maintain a consistently enforced training program with his hospitalized subject population. In the course of one year of daily individual training, a 13-year-old autistic boy who had not developed useful speech was taught a 55-word sight vocabulary (Hewett, 1964). This was accomplished by using gumdrop reinforcers for correct matching of visually presented words with corresponding pictures. Eventually, picture cues became unnecessary, and the child could select any word card on the verbal command of the teacher. Finally, the subject was taught the alphabet and was required to write out any requests that he wished to make of the hospital personnel.

In connection with the modifier's long-term goal—the socialization of this psychotic child—there were other behavioral changes which accompanied those mentioned above. The author described the subject's growing interest in his education and his increasing conformity to his teacher's instructions, even under conditions of decreasing reinforcement. The child showed enjoyment of his work by emitting laughter and other vocalizations. He also frequently initiated new learning tasks by bringing the teacher pictures whose symbolic designation he was eager to master. Finally, the subject gave definite indications that the teacher had acquired secondary reinforcement value for him. The child began to look directly at the teacher's face, rather than only at his hand (the immediate reinforcement-delivery mechanism), and drew simple sketches which symbolized events of great importance in his life.

All these changes, especially the latter ones, which represent the definite attempts of a previously intractable, autistic child to communicate with his adult teacher, are behavior modifications which were not directly reinforced in this child's educational program. In the absence of even rudimentary control procedures, it would be unwarranted to attribute these changes solely to the operant-reinforcement program per se. The author, for instance, did not describe the extraexperimental daily activities engaged in by the subject. Nor did he characterize in any detail the nature of the teacher's behavior toward the child. For example, it cannot be ascertained from this report whether the relationship between the teacher and child was warm and solicitous or mechanically impersonal. These variables could conceivably play an important role in the behavior-modification program. Such deficiencies in descriptive information notwithstanding, it seems likely that the dramatic general improvements shown by this child were largely the outgrowth of the experimental manipulations. In strong support of this statement is the fact that the subject had remained virtually inaccessible to all previous socialization attempts during the first 13 years of his life. Only when reinforcement became reliably contingent, through human mediation, upon certain goal-directed behaviors did the child acquire elementary communication skills. And it would seem that in large measure the acquisition of these skills facilitated the further socialization of this autistic boy.

Several other papers which describe therapeutic programs for psychotic children are of direct relevance here. Though the practitioners involved are psychodynamically oriented, they have explicitly incorporated basic tenets of reinforcement theory in their therapies. Weiland and Rudnik (1961), for example, made an 8-year-old autistic boy's receipt of his favorite toy contingent upon his verbalization of the word "ball," thus widening the child's vocabulary until he was eventually singing songs. The authors stated:

> In the ideal therapeutic program, the total environment of the child should be organized to allow all of his gratifications to be offered by some single person who could erect such barriers as to make it impossible for the child to achieve these gratifications by himself (autistically) . . . Gratification without asking for the assistance of his specific worker(s) would not be permitted, while withdrawal would be obstructed by the persistent efforts of the worker. The child would be offered certain activities or objects which were known to be of high desirability to him. These would be given, however, only if the youngster specifically asked the worker for them (p. 560).

Thus would these workers establish the secondary or generalized reinforcing power of other human beings for the schizophrenic child.

Dubnoff (1965), who successfully treated a child who had been diagnosed as "early infantile autistic" by Kanner, similarly mentioned that such a child in her therapeutic program "is expected to verbalize his demands before they are gratified . . . Only appropriate behavior is gratified" (p. 386). This kind of therapy seems a long conceptual way from the all-accepting, permissive, and indiscriminately rewarding type of treatment advocated by some psychoanalysts (e.g., Bettelheim, 1952, 1965). However, despite this apparent gulf between behavior-modification approaches to therapy and more traditional psychodynamic models, it seems likely that the most successful therapeutic strategies will evolve from judicious use of the insights of both approaches.

An example of such a collaborative effort is provided in two papers by Ferster (1965a, 1965b), who described a program in which he cooperated with the clinical director of a treatment center for autistic children. Ferster stated that in the course of their work together, he was continuously impressed by the underlying similarity of their two superficially disparate approaches. In describing his previous investigations of the phenomena of operant learning, Ferster (1965a) stated that his "customary approach to an experiment is essentially clinical." That is, procedures in his animal and human experiments "are carefully designed to meet the repertoire of each individual subject; there is a day-by-day interaction with the experiment in which each procedure derives from the results of previous procedures" (p. 14). Conversely, emphasized Ferster, careful observation of the clinical director's therapeutic activity revealed that

> Many of her procedures consisted of direct and forceful manipulation of the milieu directly contingent upon the child's behavior (1965b, p. 3). She places limits on the child's behavior, gives or withholds food, attention and automobile rides and toys (1965a, p. 14).

It is in practices such as these that many therapists, either wittingly or unwittingly, often make effective use of the basic principles of operant learning. The evidence suggests that therapeutic potency is a direct function of the degree to which these principles are *systematically* applied.

Positive Reinforcement and Punishment Training

Lovaas et al. (1965b) performed a series of well-controlled experiments, the results of which supported many of the implications about children's psychotic behavior derived from the findings of earlier studies. In their first study, Lovaas and his coworkers increased the "appropriate music behavior" and simultaneously decreased the seriously self-destructive behavior of a 9-year-old schizophrenic girl. In acquisition periods, music was played and social reinforcements (smile and "good") were delivered only following appropriate behaviors, such as clapping in rhythm. Significantly, control or extinction periods were also run, during which music was again played, but no social rewards were forthcoming. Appropriate changes in the subject's behavior from acquisition to extinction periods revealed that the behaviors in question had come under experimental control.

A second study, this time using a bar-press response, confirmed the finding of the first study; that is, frequency of self-destructive behavior is a function of the presentation and withdrawal of reinforcement for other behaviors in the same situation. The third study reported in this article demonstrated the tremendous importance of the parental or adult "attention" variable. The authors showed that delivery of sympathetic comments ("I don't think you're bad") contingent upon the occurrence of self-destructive behavior *increased* the frequency and magnitude of such undesirable behavior over levels of performance obtained in baseline control sessions, which were interspersed among experimental sessions. Furthermore, a reduction in tantrum and destructive behaviors was observed in sessions in which the experimenter was nurturant and attentive to the subject *except* when the subject indulged in tantrum or destructive behavior, at which times he was ignored. Such results make it difficult to escape the authors' conclusion that the types of self-destructive acts they examined are best understood "as learned, operant, or instrumental behavior" (Lovaas, Freitag, Gold, & Kassorla, 1965a, p. 79).

Wolf, Risley, and Mees (1964) described their rather dramatic therapeutic intervention into a case which had proved intractable to conventional therapies. They used shaping procedures with a food-deprived hospitalized schizophrenic boy of 3½, who was characterized by severe self-destructive behavior and refusal to wear eyeglasses (which were necessary to save his sight) and to sleep at night. Using bits of food as reinforcement, and isolation from all social contacts as punishment (the "time-out" procedure), these therapists were highly successful in decreasing the child's tantrums and increasing his eyeglass wearing to an acceptable level. When the child began to throw the glasses, isolation, made contingent upon such throwing, effectively reduced this unwanted behavior. Subsequent eating-habit problems were similarly eliminated. The child (who had complex but noncommunicative verbal habits at the outset) was trained to imitatively name pictures and use pronouns correctly in social speech. Verbal stimuli such as "no" came to suppress undesirable nonverbal behavior, probably as a result of frequent pairing with the experience of being sent into isolation. Perhaps most impressive is the authors' account of the mother's report, six months after the child's return home: "Dicky continues to wear his glasses, does not have tantrums, has no sleeping problems, is becoming increasingly verbal, and is a new source of joy to the members of his family" (Wolf et al., 1964, p. 312). A later study by Risley and Wolf (1967) reported Dicky's continuing social and academic progress, and described in instructive detail similar speech-development work being done with several other autistic children.

Risley and Wolf (1964) also used shaping based on ice-cream-bite rewards, and incorporated prompting and fading procedures in a program of therapy with a 6-year-old autistic child. They succeeded in enlarging the child's verbal repertoire from echolalic speech to appropriate picture naming and eventually to appropriate answers to questions such as, "What's your name?" and "Where are you going?" Of special interest in this study was the follow-up procedure conducted with the child's parents. The mother, who had observed several laboratory sessions, was instructed and supervised in basic operant techniques so that she could continue the therapy at home. Although she manifested an early tendency to urge and prompt the child too frequently, she soon came to understand the necessity for strict adherence to a schedule of contingent rewards and in this manner was able to make remarkable progress with the boy. Praise became an effective reinforcer, though not quite as effective as food, in motivating learning. Tantrum screaming, formerly a serious problem, was reduced greatly by sending the child to his room whenever he engaged in such "atavistic" behavior. Chanting, repetitious verbalizations were converted, through gradual shaping and imitative learning, into meaningful sentences. The authors concluded on an optimistic note, stating that seven other sets of parents were effectively working with their disturbed children in this way. (As mentioned earlier in connection with less disturbed children, the factors affecting procurement of intensive parental involvement have yet to be systematically investigated.)

A talkative (but uncommunicative) schizophrenic child who met criteria of (1) being in no individual therapy, (2) having no known physiological damage, (3) receiving no medication, and (4) accepting a candy when offered to her was chosen by Davison (1964) as the subject in an experiment which used previously inexperienced undergraduates as behavior modifiers. The students received training similar to that described in Davison (1965). They saw the psychotic child in the uncontrolled environment of a day-care center where they occupied only 8 of the child's 25 weekly institutional hours. According to the author, "the crux of this therapy was to utilize play situations for the differential reinforcement and extinction of various behaviors" (p. 150). The extinction referred to, as in other studies, was a sort of time-out procedure, in which the positively reinforcing therapists withdrew a certain distance from the subject if the subject misbehaved. The results of the short "therapy" indicated that both therapists had achieved a markedly greater degree of control over the subject than they had had at the outset in terms of the number of commands issued to the child that were obeyed.

But, in addition, and somewhat to the author's surprise, the child also obeyed an equally high percentage of the standard commands given by both a nonprofessional worker who spent a great deal of time with the child and a college student never before seen by the child. The author tentatively concluded that the child had become, as a result of the behavior therapy, more responsive to adults in general. Other positive features of the results were the incidental apparent desensitization of several phobic fears, and the fact that adults seemed to have acquired the status of generalized reinforcers to whom the child was attracted. Finally, the "extinction" procedures evidently eliminated at least two deviant behaviors—kicking and pouring sand on others. It is tempting to conclude that the behavior-modification program was responsible for all these changes, but there was obviously insufficient control of the child's activities to warrant any strong conclusions of this nature.

Ferster and DeMyer (1961b) described the salutary effects of prochlorperizine administered to an autistic child who was required to perform a matching-to-sample discrimination task. Correct matches enabled the child to get a wide variety of reinforcers; incorrect matches were followed by short time outs from positive reinforcement. Analysis of results indicated that matching to sample was significantly better under drug than under placebo conditions. However, since the authors' only statement about the effects of the drug was that it "increased the amount of his behavior," it is difficult to tell whether the improved matching performance was due specifically to the drug's psychological effects or whether it was merely a function of the child's hyperactivity.

Positive Reinforcement and Avoidance Learning

Hewett (1965) reported teaching a mute autistic child 32 words over a six-month period using a paradigm that combined both reinforcement and avoidance procedures. The 4-year-old subject, sitting in a special teaching booth, was exposed to a variety of reinforcing stimuli when he responded correctly, but was subjected to isolation in the darkened booth if he failed to respond correctly on cue. In preliminary training, the child was required to perform a series of imitative acts, such as touching appropriate facial features. Subsequently, an undifferentiated vowel sound that was frequently uttered by the child was used as the basis for the verbal learning program. The method of shaping, using successive approximations and the fading technique that was previously described in connection with Metz's (1965) paper, was employed. Ward personnel and the child's parents observed many of these procedures and continued to require the newly learned words from the child, reinforcing him only at appropriate times. Although the subject's acquired speech did not approach normal language, Hewett (1965, p. 935) was justified in stating that the child "generalized an experimentally acquired vocabulary to the larger environment and uses it to verbally express his needs (e.g., 'I want toilet.')." The successful training given to this child is particularly impressive in view of the extremely poor prognosis that is typical for the psychotic child who fails to develop language by the age of 4 or 5.

Lovaas, Schaeffer, Benson, and Simmons (1965b) conducted a major study in which electric shock was used to motivate learning. Schizophrenic twins were given escape-avoidance training in a room with an electrified-grid floor. The children were first physically guided, then more and more required to initiate the approach response when they heard the experimenter's command, "Come here!" At first they responded in order to escape painful shock, but they soon learned that a rapid, low-latency (less than five seconds) response would enable them to avoid shock. In addition, the children were shocked (punished) whenever they began to emit tantrum behavior. These procedures resulted in a long-lasting response tendency to the "come here" command (9 to 10 months passed before extinction began to occur) and good suppression of the tantrums. Pairing the word "no" with shock gave it the status of a conditioned suppressor, demonstrated by its reduction of the frequency of a child's bar press for positive reinforcement.

In a second part of this study, the subjects received further shock-avoidance training with a portable subject-mounted shock apparatus. The children, who were required to hug and kiss the experimenter, showed increased affection-like behavior as a result of training. Nurses who rated the subjects immediately after the avoidance sessions, but who were unaware of the purpose of the experiment, described the children as more dependent upon adults, more responsive and affection-seeking, and more anxious and fearsome. They saw the children as less happy and content, but emitting less pathological behavior. It is well known that professional raters of such general classes of behavior as those preceding often have difficulty in agreeing upon what they observe. Relatedly, it has been explicitly pointed out by Harris, Wolf, and Baer (1964), Brown and Elliot (1965), and others that teachers, nurses, and attendants who are direct participants in shaping procedures, as well as relatively uninvolved research observers, often produce completely fallacious subjective estimates of behavior change resulting from such procedures. Though the nurses in the present study were not involved in the therapy procedures nor, say the authors, did they know about them, it is appropriate to use caution in accepting such nonitemized behavior ratings of impressions.

The last experiment reported in this article by Lovaas et al. described children's learning to press a bar for candy and the sight of the experimenter's face. Accompanying shock-escape training required the subjects to go to the experimenter. Eventually, the subjects pressed the bar for the sight of the experimenter alone, without showing any generalized increase in activity resulting from the shock sessions. Here again, one has the nurses' informal observation of a perhaps generalized tendency resulting from his training. The children, who previously showed only immobility when hurt, now sought out other human beings when hurt in a variety of extraexperimental situations.

IS CONTROLLING BEHAVIOR ETHICAL?

The almost explosive growth of experimental research in behavior modification has not been paralleled by a corresponding spread of the clinical practice of behavior therapy. While the popularity of clinical behavior therapy is undoubtedly increasing, it has not kept pace with the expansion of scientific interest in and knowledge of this field. Although some of the reluctance of practitioners to embrace this new methodology may be ascribed to an understandable professional conservatism, it would appear that another factor, an ethical one, may be influential in retarding widespread acceptance of behavior therapy.

In general, the feeling that there are ethical problems inherent in the practice of behavior therapy seems to revolve around a concern for the client's "humanity." Critics of this approach point to the "dehumanization" of the client, whose individuality and free will they feel is ignored and/or perverted in the therapist's frenzy to control his "subject," whom he views as an object to manipulate—a common laboratory animal without higher human values and spiritual qualities.

Nothing, of course, could be further from the truth. Behavior modification is the most individualized of treatment, entailing a complete and objectively detailed study of the client's behavior and a tailoring of therapy to his unique problems, without the distortion introduced by preconceived notions of personality structure and various types of mental "illnesses." Instead of lumping a client in a traditional psychodiagnostic category with millions of other disturbed people, and thereby obliterating much of his individual identity, the competent behavior therapist makes a careful, idiographic study of each client in order to specify key behaviors and the personal and environmental parameters which maintain them. While this is hopefully a precise process which yields accurate data, it in no way need be "mechanized" or impersonal. In fact, the recognition of critical problem behaviors and the design of clinically appropriate treatment programs probably demand as much sensitivity, empathy, and general clinical acuity of the behavior modifier as ever is the case in other types of therapy.

The behavior therapist's ominous-sounding, alleged "control" of his client is a related, important issue which probably arises out of the traditional psychotherapist's ambivalence about accepting responsibility for his influence on the client. Psychodynamic therapies have emphasized the role of the *client's* insight. They have allowed, and even encouraged, therapists to avoid personal responsibility, the dogma being that the therapist's duty is somehow to "set the stage" for beneficial change, but to avoid active participation in, or direction of, the process of change. In spite of this credo, it seems likely that all good psychotherapists have always influenced behavior, however subtly, through advice-giving, but that few have publicly acknowledged or privately admitted how large a part such directiveness plays in their work.

Psychotherapeutic control is a complex issue, and the traditional therapist's ambivalence about it should not be criticized as willful irresponsibility or negligence, but rather should be seen as the outcome of the therapist's conflict between his desire to help his client and his moral concern with the client's ultimate welfare. The problem can be reduced to the question of the propriety of the therapist making "value judgements"—that is, his deciding, on the basis of his analysis of each case, what his client ought specifically to do to attain a more satisfactory equilibrium, a better level of functioning, and, in many cases, what would constitute a "better level of functioning" for that person.

"Therapy" is a word that means "doing something to change a disordered state of affairs," and since a therapist is supposed to be an expert in accomplishing this end, it is difficult to understand objections to his assumption of an active role in doing so. Whether the patient, himself, or his society has decided that he is in a disordered state is irrelevant to this issue—the therapist is explicitly part of a system that routinely evaluates people and decides whether or not, and to what extent a person is disordered, i.e., unfit to adaptively get along in his environment. By arriving in the therapist's domain, the patient openly expresses a need for help—he needs help to change. If, at any time, the therapist disagrees with society's evaluation of disorder in a particular person that comes to his professional attention (on a nonvoluntary basis, for instance), the therapist is confronted with a personal decision about the ethics of seeking to change this person *at all*. But, once it is established that the client *does* require aid in changing some aspect of himself, it is clearly the therapist's job to change what needs changing, or, more specifically, to equip his patient with the skills he needs to get along reasonably well in his lifespace. As long as the behavior-modifier's goal is the client's goal—the client's achievement of appropriate self-control—his work as a therapist is morally irreprehensible.

The concept of psychotherapy being advanced here places a heavy burden on the behavior therapist. He must exert utmost vigilance in determining exactly what changes ought be made and how he ought go about helping the client to make them. While such decision-making will inevitably involve what we commonly call "value judgements," it is the core of the present position that these judgements are legitimately a part of the psychotherapist's expected area of expertise. If the layman-client could successfully do these things for himself, he obviously would not require the therapist's services. But, given the need for therapists, it seems equally obvious that their task should be the prescription of treatment regimens designed to accomplish appropriate remediation. Interestingly, this philosophy seems to dominate at least a substantial segment of current Soviet psychotherapy. Summarizing his observations of Russian psychiatry over the course of a year at the Bechtyerev Institute in Leningrad, Ziferstein (1966) described the Soviet therapist as "highly active, freely dispensing advice and manipulating the patient's social environment, if necessary" (p. 440). The current position holds that without such a commitment to straightforward prescription and active guidance of the client, psychotherapy is doomed to effete inefficiency.

Krasner and Ullmann (1965, p. 107) have said that the goal of learning approaches to therapy is "to develop a new, more responsible role for the patient . . ." who is helped to come to an often completely new idea—the realization "that he can have a major influence on his own environment," and that he can do so through *adaptive* behavior. According to these authors, the behavior therapist's over-riding "purpose is to assist the patient to greater responsibility and less dependency on the therapist. Thus, there is a genuine partnership with the patient and respect for his ability to control his environment. . . ." And, say these authors, "from the patient's point of view, therapy changes from a vague, often inexplicable process, with a superior, all-knowing therapist, to an understandable process between equals." It is not difficult to see why the behavior modifier's overt and unself-conscious acceptance of his responsibility to change behavior has been described as heretical "controlling" by some of the devotees of other, more mystical forms of therapy. Nevertheless, their argument is not compelling, and it fails to establish a credible ethical problem for behavior modification.

THE FUTURE OF BEHAVIOR MODIFICATION

At this time behavior modification is no longer a "toy." The number of those who view it as an overnight sensation, destined to plummet into obscurity as precipitously as it rose to notoriety, is dwindling. Its claim to serious consideration has become steadily more legitimate with the amassment of scientific testimony to its effectiveness. Still, if behavior modification is to mature fully into a viable psychotherapy, it needs to go beyond individual behavior changes to modification that produces general adaptive change. The course that behavior modification is likely to follow in its quest for general effectiveness, and some of the obstacles that it will have to overcome along the way, are the topics of this concluding section.

A brief review of what has been accomplished thus far is in order. The results of these studies indicate that behavior-modification techniques may be extremely useful tools in the education and rehabilitation of emotionally disturbed and, especially, of psychotic children. Few of the investigators whose work has been reviewed here would claim that they have cured their subjects, but many can justifiably state that they have equipped them with several of the basic skills and habits necessary for elementary adjustments to their social environments. Furthermore, behavior "therapists," guided by social-learning models which are more parsimonious than traditional psychodynamic theories, have been able to effectively control, and in several cases eliminate, much of the undesirable and maladaptive behavior of these children.

A consideration of the potential advantages of behavior-modification methods invariably focuses on the speed or relative efficiency with which these procedures seem to work. Davison (1964), for example, working under the poorest of nonlaboratory conditions and seeing the subject for only a short time each day, achieved significant control over the child in four weeks. Other studies reviewed here which have reported remarkably short treatment periods are those by Allen and Harris (1966), Lazarus (1960), and Lazarus and Abramovitz (1962). The direct, objective, and specifically prescriptive nature of behavior therapy would seem to be factors working in favor of its relative efficiency.

Exemplified also in Davison's (1964, 1965) work, as well as that of others (e.g., DeMyer & Ferster, 1962; Risley & Wolf, 1964), is the fact that such programs can apparently be executed by rapidly trained non- or semiprofessional workers and continued in the home by parents. The studies which involved parents as major therapists (Allen & Harris, 1966; Bentler, 1962; Hawkins et al., 1966; Patterson, 1965b; Patterson & Brodsky, 1966; Russo, 1964; Wahler et al., 1965; Wetzel et al., 1966; Zeilberger et al., 1968) further confirm the potential widespread applicability of this body of techniques. To the extent that such paraprofessionals can be efficiently trained and used, it will eventually be feasible for a small core of professional therapists to supervise simultaneously many therapeutic workers in behavior-modification programs with large numbers of clients.

An instructive outcome of this behavior-modification research has been the demonstration that certain types of behavior, previously conceptualized by psychodynamic theories of psychopathology as complex reactions to internal states, are more realistically and profitably conceived as socially learned and maintained acts. An example of the rapidly achieved benefits of such reanalysis was the above-described virtual elimination of self-destructive tantrums without recourse to harsh, suppressive punishment. Such tantrum behavior was found to be maintained by adult attentiveness to it and was eliminated by withdrawing attention or merely by occupying the child with incompatible behavior (Davison, 1964; Lovaas et al., 1965).

The foregoing discussion of the potential assets of learning-theory-derived therapeutic models is based on evidence from a variety of both experimental and essentially clinical studies. It is obvious that further demonstration of the adequacy and efficacy of behavior modification with disturbed children is necessary. Future investigations must employ better controlled procedures and long-term follow-ups with more varied subject populations in order to relate general as well as specific enduring results to the techniques used. Additionally, in anticipation of widespread application, it will be increasingly important that negative side effects of treatment procedures be recognized and evaluated by competent observers. The following section is addressed more specifically to the problematic issues that loom largest on the behavior-modification horizon.

Challenges

The problems that behavior modifiers must confront squarely in the coming years are numerous and diverse. Bijou, Peterson, and Ault (1968) have pointed to a strong need for planned compatibility between general, descriptive "field" studies, which ideally would stimulate the experimental investigation of specific hypotheses, and experimental studies themselves. Recognizing the value of descriptive information about social and cultural processes to our ultimate understanding of human behavior, these authors emphasize the importance of bringing to the descriptive study the basic, scientific principles of data collection and organization that have been so useful in experimental behavior modification. They call attention to the present difficulty of integrating descriptive field studies, which usually present data that is either insufficiently specific, detailed, and/or objective, with experimental studies that yield precise, functional analyses of limited segments of behavioral events. Bijou et al.'s discussion of this problem considers in detail the need for "(1) specifications of the situation in which a study is conducted, (2) definitions of behavioral and environmental events in observable terms, (3) measurements of observer reliability, and (4) procedures for collecting, analyzing, and interpreting the data" (p. 177). Descriptive field studies phrased in such empirically verifiable terms would no doubt contribute much to the progress of scientific understanding of behavior and its functional interrelationships.

The above-proposed technical criteria for scientifically acceptable investigations constitute a basic outline of desirable goals for the immediate future of behavior modification. Clinical studies and partially controlled experiments have produced ample suggestive evidence of the potency of behavior modification—needed now is extended basic research as well as more sophisticated behavior-definition and measurement techniques for applied research. The latter need requires further investigation of the apparent extreme short-term, intrasubject variability of much disturbed behavior (e.g., Doubros & Daniels, 1966; Patterson, Jones, Whittier, & Wright, 1965; Werry & Quay, 1969), and requires the development and application of statistical analyses that will adequately take account of such variability. Experimental paradigms with as complete control as possible must become the rule rather than the exception and high reliability of experimental observers must be universally required. Where relevant, observer influence on data must be minimized or eliminated by complete removal of observers from experimental environments, as well as through experimental "blinding" procedures that guard against inadvertent but demonstrably powerful effects of observer knowledge of experimental design (see, e.g., Rosenthal, 1964, 1966, 1967).

The foregoing demand for a new era of advance in behavior modification does not arise from a sterile or bleak landscape of the present. The recent appearance of several studies exemplifying many of the just-described virtues is an encouraging sign for the future. In the area of basic research, Hingtgen and Coulter (1967) carried out investigations designed to answer a fundamental question about the capacities of autistic children. The question was: Can mute, autistic children learn to respond to auditory stimuli in the absence of other cues? This study demonstrated, under appropriate experimental control, that some mute, autistic children are indeed capable of simple discriminative learning involving auditory-motor association. Knowledge gained here of the specific nature of the childrens' difficulties in this task, and of the stimulus conditions that seemed to facilitate their learning, may be of great value to our growing understanding of autism, in general. A similar, welcome contribution to this field has been made by Metz (1967), who determined experimentally that autistic children show a preference for higher levels of certain auditory stimulation than do normal or schizophrenic children. Again, this seemingly isolated finding might be instrumental in leading to research into important autistic sensory processes, about which little is now known.

Birnbrauer (1968) reported a study of the effects of severe electric-shock punishment on the suppression of various aggressive and destructive behaviors in a psychotic boy. Tightly controlled laboratory, as well as clinical, ward procedures were used in this intensive investigation of the effects of punishment. The author examined the establishment of conditioned suppressive value of verbal stimuli, as well as the generality of such secondary suppressive stimuli across nontreated, but similar (e.g., destructive) behaviors, and across different agents of punishment. The study demonstrated the power of such punishment procedures, while also presenting their limitations—the effects of the relatively short (60 to 90 minutes daily) laboratory sessions were not surprisingly highly specific to the behaviors treated, indicating that the subject discriminated well among various responses, situations, schedules of punishment, and disciplinary agents. These results call attention to the strong need for developing punishment procedures with more general effectiveness, and especially those which will increase the spread of power of related verbal stimuli. At present, the best available method appears to be intensive, long-term, repetitive treatment by several individuals on a trans-situational basis (see, e.g., the case study of "Heidi" in Browning & Stover, 1971).

A study by Charlesworth and Hartup (1967) serves as a model for the sort of descriptive field work called for earlier. These investigators devised an observational method for obtaining normative information on the amount and kinds of positive social reinforcement dispensed by preschool-age children to each other in a nursery-school setting. The authors collected informative data which provides qualitative and quantitative descriptions of the childrens' typical interactions, and which points to an interesting developmental trend toward higher output rates of positive reinforcement to peers with increasing age.

In another basic research area, Bandura and Menlove (1968) have been investigating "vicarious extinction" phenomena, with special attention to the relevance of their findings for desensitization treatment of fears and phobias. These authors and other members of their research group have found that various fears can be eliminated in young children by exposing them to relatively "fearless" models, who either in person, or in movie-film presentations, are involved in progressively more intimate interaction with feared objects. This work continues to provide fascinating new insight into the mechanics of desensitization, and it offers numerous implications for future applied work, which will probably be increasingly automated, or independently client controlled.

Measurement is the last area to be covered in this brief review of literature that represents needed behavior-modification progress. Many researchers, working independently of each other, have developed a variety of measurement instruments for the recording and analysis of children's disturbed behavior. A consolidation of the best of these efforts will probably be useful in the eventual construction of standardized scales for the accurate, replicable description of more varied and, in some instances, more complex behaviors. Efforts like those of Werry and Quay (1969), who developed a technique for measurement of classroom interactions between children, as well as between children and their teachers, and of Scherer and Nakamura (1968), who produced a fear-survey schedule for the evaluation of children's verbally reported fears, seem destined to stimulate the constructive growth of behavior modification.

Formulation and Speculation

How and why does behavior modification work? At present, the key to its effectiveness is still a matter for speculation. For simplicity's sake, the model that will be offered is derived from a consideration of the basic deficits of psychotic disturbance, but there is nothing to prevent its extension, with appropriate adaptation, to other, more complex areas of application. This hypothetical explanation for the unique success of behavior modification specifies that much of psychotic (and especially autistic) deficit is due to the disturbed child's *inability to learn under ordinary circumstances*. Whether it is due to organic malfunction, parental influence, or the more likely interaction of both, early failure to solve extremely simple problems would be expected to interfere with subsequent learning. Such interference would, in turn, be expected to increase exponentially, with successive failures producing progressively greater decrements in learning skills.

It follows, then, that the infant with such a developmental history would be for the most part helpless to organize or adapt to his environment and would therefore tend to withdraw from interaction with his surroundings. If this sort of etiological conception is accepted, then it may be hypothesized that behavior-modification methods achieve their striking effects simply because they order the environment sufficiently so that even the most severely impaired child can successfully manipulate it. Once the subject begins to experience manipulative success, it is possible that a facilitation process begins, whereby an eventual approximation to normal intellectual growth can occur.

The crux, then, of successful behavior modification may lie in the cumulative capacity of novel, positive experience to effect substantial reorganization of personality. In many relatively "intact" individuals, cognitive feedback and the reinforcement associated with knowledge of positive achievement probably provide much of the motivation for continued change, even after the therapist's discontinuance of extrinsic reinforcement. Summarizing this process, Leitenberg, Agras, and Thomson (1968) have said,

> A characteristic feature of behavioral therapies is to make the behavior to be changed overt and observable to experimenter and patient alike. Throughout therapy, the patient receives constant feedback from his own observation that the desired behavior is being more and more closely approximated or that the desired behavior is gradually increasing in frequency or that 'deviant' behavior is becoming less frequent. The patient thus perceives that he is being successful and is on the road to recovery (p. 217).

Although such positive self-perceptions are no doubt instrumental to a good deal of successful behavior modification, especially in cases of relatively circumscribed initial problems, there remains a broader problem— that of the promotion of *general adaptive change*—which has yet to be adequately defined and explored.*

---

* For clarity of communication, as well as scientific precision, it is important, in the present context, to avoid the use of the term "generaliza-

That most of the studies reviewed here reported only restricted behavior changes is not surprising. In this early developmental phase in the history of behavior modification, most investigators have been interested mainly in exploring the power of their technology in various problem areas. When behavior-modification programs were planned, they were designed with a carefully specified goal or set of goals in mind. Certain undesirable behavior was to be eliminated; adaptive skills and habits were to be imparted. The aims of these sorts of procedures contrast sharply with those of various orthodox therapies which direct their efforts at more molar goals such as attitude change and the modification of personality traits. Yet, some of the first empirical clues that behavior modification could eventually aim at the latter sort of goals appeared in a number of studies (Hawkins et al., 1966; Lazarus, 1960; Lovaas et al., 1965a; Metz, 1965; O'Leary, O'Leary, and Becker, 1967; Risley and Wolf, 1964; Wolf, Risley, & Mees, 1964). These authors reported that positive, "generalized" changes did accompany the more circumscribed changes resulting from their experimental manipulations. Lazarus (1960), for example, wrote, "Once the improvement occurred, the dynamics of Bryan's situation altered markedly in directions which served to consolidate the gain." Phenomena like these raise important questions concerning their determinants, for it seems clear that the task of greatest ultimate significance will be the development of those procedures that have maximal catalytic effects in appropriate or adaptive directions.

The modification or establishment of certain key behaviors is expected to play a central role in preparing the child for such change. The specification of key behaviors—those likely to trigger the growth of related, adaptive behaviors—may therefore be of primary importance. More basically, the underlying organizations of behaviors, that is, the connections and patterning of processes that link overt behavior systems, must be illuminated. Casting such light is an interesting experimental analysis of verbal imitation in normal preschool children by Brigham & Sherman (1968). These authors found that the accuracy of pronunciation of *never reinforced* responses varied directly with the reinforcement dispensed for accuracy of certain other responses. Children consistently and accurately reproduced unfamiliar Russian words for which they were not reinforced as long as they *were* reinforced for alternately presented English words.

---

tion" to describe nonspecific, adaptive change, since the phenomenon under discussion has little in common, structurally, with stimulus or response generalization. That is, the broader behavior and attitude changes that may result from behavior-modification procedures cannot properly be described in terms of their location on any true generalization gradient, except insofar as one refers to a continuum of "adaptiveness" or "improvement" to describe the nature of the change.

While the design of this study does not permit a clear choice from among several alternative explanations for the observed control of one type of verbal production by the reinforcement of another, it does suggest that the further sophistication of our knowledge of behavioral control will depend upon the experimental investigation of interacting response systems.

A valuable study by Buell et al. (1968) was one of the first addressed to this issue of interrelationship of various response tendencies. These authors report a behavioral analysis of a three-year-old, preschool girl with both motor- and social-repertoire deficits. Working on the premise that an increase in certain outdoor motor-play skills would be likely to positively affect the girl's almost nonexistent peer-interaction, the investigators instructed the girl's teacher to systematically socially reinforce outdoor play *only on certain equipment*. As expected, as play with the outdoor equipment increased, so did a variety of never-directly reinforced *but adequately monitored and measured social interactions with peers*. This documented "collateral social development" which accompanied a very specific behavior-modification program is empirical evidence for the value of a "key-behavior" concept in applied behavior modification, and should stimulate further basic research designed to identify other types of "core" behaviors.

At this point, it may be helpful to grossly outline the course of an "ideal" behavior-modification program for a generalized case of severe disturbance. Basic modification procedures would normally be followed by what Ferster and Simons (1966) call the "transfer of reinforcers," in which secondary, social reinforcers are gradually substituted for initially invaluable primary reinforcers, such as food. This process brings the abnormal child a major step closer to his eventual approximation of normal adaptation. Throughout and beyond such early retraining, progress may depend heavily upon the teacher's ability to modify the child's typical attentional behavior. That is, it may be of central importance to first teach the child to orient toward a variety of potential reinforcement sources and "reinforceable" types of behavior that are appropriate and adaptive in character, but toward which he was generally indifferent prior to training. Once this crucial reorientation phase is negotiated, the child is ready for rapid, global change and for a gradual reintegration into his family.

In their recent discussion of the role of behavior modification in producing generality of adaptive change, Baer and Wolf (1967) have conceptualized this therapeutic process as one in which initial modification of certain of the subject's key behaviors promotes his "entry into natural communities of reinforcement" that were hitherto unavailable to him or ineffective in influencing his behavior. Thus, for example, after having received appropriate language or motor training, a socially isolated or immobile psychotic child might suddenly "discover" the reinforcement potential of his age-mates or of activities that are available to him. The "characterologically" disordered child whose only previous method of obtaining social gratification was through anti-social acts might learn that prosocial activity can lead to the same ends, and without the unpleasant consequences. And the neurotically phobic child, freed from his central irrational fear, and from a host of related defensive behaviors which had generally alienated his parents, might quickly become aware of a freshly responsive and affectionate family. Behavior emitted with reference to such channels of gratification would be expected to be instrumental in the consolidation of earlier changes and the amplification and extension of therapeutic gains.

The Family

The seriously disturbed child is a partially closed behavior system that is caught, along with other partially closed systems, in a longstanding, negative cycle of interpersonal events. The child customarily does little to elicit positive attention, and the significant others in his life return the favor by dispensing few rewarding stimuli in his direction. Now pluck the child from the home environment and introduce a behavior-modification program that punishes undesirable behavior and rewards alternative, positive behavior. In all likelihood, the child will change in accordance with the contingencies of the new (therapeutic) environment. He is "cured." If, however, upon his return to the old (home) setting, he is greeted by the old set of contingencies—doled out by still closed behavior systems that react not in terms of his current behavior, but according to overlearned biases against him—then the child is fated to a rapid reintegration into the hopeless cycle from which therapy temporarily extricated him.

If on the other hand, the various significant elements of the "old" social environment—parents, siblings, and school personnel—are adequately trained in positively modified child-handling techniques, then therapeutic intervention has the greatest likelihood of leading to a generally improved adaptation. In this case, family and community provide continuation and extension of the therapeutic environment, and thereby maximize the potential for enduring change and growth.

It is becoming increasingly clear that general adaptive change in children will be reliably and efficiently achieved only when it becomes possible to involve important aspects of the child's social environment in the therapeutic process. Patterson and Brodsky (1966) have said that the future of child behavior modification lies in the development of methods for "reprogramming the social environment." These authors, pointing to the child's tremendous dependence on his social environment, emphasize the need for behavior therapy to invade traditional bastions of privacy such as the home, and secondarily, the school. They suggest that behavior modification can and must find ways to modify not only the principal "patient," but also the members of his immediate and extended family who share in the maintenance of his disturbance. While this principle may have limited relevance for adult treatment, it is more and more the consensus that it should be the *sine qua non* of child treatment. The study by Patterson and Brodsky (1966), as well as other recent ones by Hawkins et al. (1966); O'Leary, O'Leary, & Becker (1967); Patterson (1965b); and Wetzel et al. (1966), has pioneered the involvement of parents, teachers, and other educational personnel in various aspects of outpatient treatment, much of which was carried out in the childrens' homes and/or schools. Hawkins et al. (1966) say, "Since . . . many of the child's problems originate in the home environment, direct modification of this environment (including the behavior of other family members) may arrest the difficulty at its source." On the more specific, procedural level, Bandura (1962) stated,

> If a child's deviant patterns are to be altered to any significant degree, the parents must be informed, in one way or another, about (a) the cues eliciting the child's undesired behavior, (b) the response-reinforcement contingencies maintaining that behavior, and (c) the manner in which the reinforcement contingencies must be modified if clearly specified therapeutic objectives are to be achieved. . . . In any event, it is the parents who must create and sustain the necessary learning conditions, and serve as the therapeutic agents (p. 301).

Innovative work that incorporates these principles in residential treatment is the experimental-clinical treatment program described by Browning and Stover (1971) who demand regular and active family participation in their milieu behavior modification of even the most severely disturbed, institutionalized youngsters. As mentioned earlier, an important field of applied research stemming from this approach concerns the development of methods for integrating poorly motivated parental figures into treatment efforts. The search for effective methods of involving and retraining the caretakers and educators of emotionally disturbed children will be one of the most challenging aspects of future child behavior modification.

The concluding message of this concluding section, then, is a reiteration of the necessity for modification of more than the child. The child's disturbance does not develop in a vacuum, but in a system composed of repeated interactions with a limited segment of the general social environment. Treatment effects cannot be expected to persevere and thereby to facilitate further adaptive growth if that social environment fails to play a suitably complementary role in accommodating itself to the initially modified element—the child.

References

Allen, K. E., & Harris, F. R. Elimination of a child's excessive scratching by training the mother in reinforcement procedures. *Behav. Res. & Therapy,* 1966, *4,* 79–84.

Allen, K. E., Hart, B., Buell, J. S., Harris, F. R., & Wolf, M. M. Effects of social reinforcement on isolate behavior of a nursery school child. *Child Develpm.,* 1964, *35,* 511–518.

Baer, D. M. Laboratory control of thumbsucking by withdrawal and representation of reinforcement. *J. Exp. Anal. Behav.,* 1962, *5,* 525–528.

Baer, D. M., & Wolf, M. M. The entry into natural communities of reinforcement. Paper presented at the meeting of the American Psychological Association, Washington, D.C., September 1967.

Baer, D. M., Wolf, M. M., & Risley, T. R. Some current dimensions of applied behavior analysis. *J. appl. Behav. Anal.,* 1968, *1,* 91–97.

Bandura, A. Punishment revisited. *J. consult. Psychol.,* 1962, *26,* 298–301.

Bandura, A. Behavioral modifications through modeling procedures. In L. Krasner & L. P. Ullmann (Eds.), *Research in behavior modification.* New York: Holt, Rinehart and Winston, 1965.

Bandura, A., & Menlove, F. L. Factors determining vicarious extinction of avoidance behavior through symbolic modeling. *J. Pers. & Soc. Psychol.,* 1968, *8,* 99–108.

Bender, L., & Helme, W. H. A qualitative test of theory and diagnostic indicators of childhood schizophrenia. *Arch. Neurol. & Psychiat.,* 1953, *70,* 413–427.

Bentler, P. M. An infant's phobia treated with reciprocal inhibition therapy. *J. Child Psychol. & Psychiat.,* 1962, *3,* 185–189.

Bettelheim, B. Schizophrenic art: A case study. *Sci. Amer.,* 1952, *186* (4), 30–34.

Bettelheim, B. Early ego development in a mute, autistic child. Freud lecture presented at the meeting of the Philadelphia Association for Psychoanalysis, University of Pennsylvania, May 1965.

Bijou, S. W., Peterson, R. F., & Ault, M. H. A method to integrate descriptive and experimental field studies at the level of data and empirical concepts. *J. appl. Behav. Anal.,* 1968, *1,* 175–191.

Birnbrauer, J. S. Generalization of punishment effects—A case study. *J. appl. Behav. Anal.,* 1968, *1,* 201–211.

Brigham, T. A., & Sherman, J. A. An experimental analysis of verbal imitation in preschool children. *J. appl. Behav. Anal.,* 1968, *1,* 151–158.

Brown, P., & Elliott, R. Control of aggression in a nursery school class. *J. exp. Child Psychol.,* 1965, *3,* 102–107.

Browning, R. M., & Stover, D. O. *Behavior modification in child treatment: An experimental-clinical approach.* Chicago: Aldine-Atherton, 1971.

Buell, J., Stoddard, P., Harris, F., & Baer, D. M. Collateral social development accompanying reinforcement of outdoor play in a preschool child. *J. appl. Behav. Anal.,* 1968, *1,* 167–173.

Charlesworth, R., & Hartup, W. W. Positive social reinforcement in the nursery school peer group. *Child Develpm.,* 1967, *38,* 993–1002.

Davison, G. C. A social learning therapy programme with an autistic child. *Behav. Res. & Therapy,* 1964, *2,* 149–159.

Davison, G. C. The training of undergraduates as social reinforcers for autistic children. In L. P. Ullmann & L. Krasner (Eds.), *Case studies in behavior modification.* New York: Holt, Rinehart and Winston, 1965.

DeMyer, M. K., & Ferster, C. B. Teaching new social behavior to schizophrenic children. *J. Amer. Acad. Child Psychiat.,* 1962, *1,* 443–461.

Doubros, S. G., & Daniels, G. J. An experimental approach to the reduction of overactive behavior. *Behav. Res. & Therapy,* 1966, *4,* 251–258.

Dubnoff, B. The habituation and education of the autistic child in a therapeutic day school. *Amer. J. Orthopsychiat.,* 1965, *35,* 385–386.

Eisenberg, L. The course of childhood schizophrenia. *Arch. Neurol. & Psychiat.,* 1957, *78,* 69–83.

Ferster, C. B. Positive reinforcement and behavioral deficits of autistic children. *Child Develpm.,* 1961, *32,* 437–456.

Ferster, C. B. An operant reinforcement analysis of infantile autism. Unpublished manuscript, Institute for Behavioral Research, Silver Spring, Md., 1965. (a)

Ferster, C. B. Operant reinforcement in the natural milieu. Paper presented at the meeting of the Council for Exceptional Children, Portland, Ore., April 1965. (b)

Ferster, C. B., & DeMyer, M. K. The development of performances in autistic children in an automatically controlled environment. *J. chronic Dis.,* 1961, *13,* 312–345. (a)

Ferster, C. B., & DeMyer, M. K. Increased performances of an autistic child with prochlorperizine administration. *J. exp. Anal. Behav.,* 1961, *4,* 84. (b)

Ferster, C. B., & DeMyer, M. K. A method for the experimental analysis of the behavior of autistic children. *Amer. J. Orthopsychiat.,* 1962, *32,* 89–98.

Ferster, C. B., & Simons, J. Behavior therapy with children. *Psychol. Rec.,* 1966, *16,* 65–71.

Gittelman, M. Behavior rehearsal as a technique in child treatment. *J. Child Psychol. & Psychiat.,* 1965, *6,* 251–255.

Gray, B. B., & Fygetakis, L. Medicated language acquisition for dysphasic children. *Behav. Res. & Therapy,* 1968, *6,* 263–280.

Harris, F., Wolf, M. M., & Baer, D. M. Effects of adult social reinforcement on child behavior. *Young Child.,* 1964, *20,* 8–17.

Hart, B. M., Allen, K. E., Buell, J. S., Harris, F. R., & Wolf, M. M. Effects of social reinforcement on operant crying. *J. exp. Child Psychol.,* 1964, *1,* 145–153.

Hawkins, R. P., Peterson, R. F., Schweid, E. R., & Bijou, S. W. Behavior therapy in the home: Amelioration of problem parent-child relations with the parent in a therapeutic role. *J. exp. Child Psychol.,* 1966, *4,* 99–107.

Hewett, F. M. Teaching reading to autistic children through operant conditioning. *Reading Teacher,* 1964, *17,* 613–618.

Hewett, F. M. Teaching speech to autistic children through operant conditioning. *Amer. J. Orthopsychiat.*, 1965, *35*, 927–936.

Hingtgen, J. N., & Coulter, S. K. Auditory control of operant behavior in mute autistic children. *Percept. & motor Skills*, 1967, *25*, 561–565.

Hingtgen, J. N., Sanders, B., & DeMyer, M. K. Shaping cooperative responses in early childhood schizophrenics. In L. P. Ullmann & L. Krasner (Eds.), *Case studies in behavior modification*. New York: Holt, Rinehart and Winston, 1965.

Hingtgen, J. N., & Trost, F. C., Jr. Shaping cooperative responses in early childhood schizophrenics: II. Reinforcement of mutual physical contact and vocal responses. Paper presented at the meeting of the American Psychological Association, Los Angeles, September 1964.

Homme, L. E., de Baca, P. C., Devine, J. V., Steinhorst, R., & Rickert, E. J. Use of the Premack principle in controlling the behavior of nursery school children. *J. exp. Anal. Behav.*, 1963, *6*, 544.

Hundziak, M., Mauer, R. A., & Watson, L. S., Jr. Operant conditioning and toilet training of severely mentally retarded boys. *Amer. J. ment. Def.*, 1965, *70*, 120–124.

Johnston, M. K., Kelley, C. S., Harris, F. R., & Wolf, M. M. An application of reinforcement principles to development of motor skills of a young child. *Child Develpm.*, 1966, *37*, 379–387.

Kanner, L. Autistic disturbances of affective contact. *Nerv. Child*, 1943, *2*, 217–250.

Krasner, L., & Ullmann, L. P. *Research in behavior modification*. New York: Holt, Rinehart and Winston, 1965.

Kuypers, D. S., Becker, W. C., & O'Leary, K. D. How to make a token system fail. *Except. Child.*, 1968, *35*, 101–109.

Lazarus, A. A. The elimination of children's phobias by deconditioning. In H. J. Eysenck (Ed.), *Behaviour therapy and the neuroses*. London: Pergamon Press, 1960, pp. 114–122.

Lazarus, A. A., & Abramovitz, A. The use of emotive therapy in the treatment of children's phobias. *J. ment. Sci.*, 1962, *108*, 191–195.

Lazarus, A. A., Davison, G. C., & Polefka, D. A. Classical and operant factors in the treatment of a school phobia. *J. abnorm. Psychol.*, 1965, *70*, 225–229.

Leitenberg, H., Agras, W. S., & Thomson, L. E. A sequential analysis of the effect of selective positive reinforcement in modifying anorexia nervosa. *Behav. Res. & Therapy*, 1968, *6*, 211–218.

Levin, G. R., & Simmons, J. J. Response to praise by emotionally disturbed boys. *Psychol. Rep.*, 1962, *11*, 10. (a)

Levin, G. R., & Simmons, J. J. Response to food and praise by emotionally disturbed boys. *Psychol. Rep.*, 1962, *11*, 539–546. (b)

Lovaas, O. I., Freitag, G., Gold, V., & Kassorla, I. Experimental studies in childhood schizophrenia: Analysis of self-destructive behavior. *J. exp. Child Psychol.*, 1965, *2*, 67–84. (a)

Lovaas, O. I., Schaeffer, B., Benson, R., & Simmons, J. Q. Experimental studies in childhood schizophrenia: Building social behaviors in autistic children by use of electric shock. *J. exp. Res. Pers.*, 1965, *1*, 99–109. (b)

Metz, J. R. Conditioning generalized imitation in autistic children. *J. exp. Child Psychol.*, 1965, *2*, 389–399.

Metz, J. R. Stimulation level preferences of autistic children. *J. abnorm. Psychol.*, 1967, *72*, 529–535.

O'Leary, K. D., O'Leary, S., & Becker, W. C. Modification of a deviant sibling interaction pattern in the home. *Behav. Res. & Therapy*, 1967, *5*, 113–120.

Patterson, G. R. An application of conditioning techniques to the control of a hyperactive child. In L. P. Ullmann & L. Krasner (Eds.), *Case studies in behavior modification.* New York: Holt, Rinehart and Winston, 1965, pp. 370–375. (a)

Patterson, G. R. A learning theory approach to the treatment of the school phobic child. In L. P. Ullmann & L. Krasner (Eds.), *Case studies in behavior modification.* New York: Holt, Rinehart and Winston, 1965, pp. 279–285. (b)

Patterson, G. R., & Brodsky, G. A behaviour modification programme for a child with multiple problem behaviours. *J. Child Psychol. & Psychiat.*, 1966, *7*, 277–295.

Patterson, G. R., Jones, R., Whittier, J., & Wright, M. A. A behaviour modification technique for the hyperactive child. *Behav. Res. & Therapy*, 1965, *2*, 217–226.

Risley, T., & Wolf, M. Experimental manipulation of autistic behaviors and generalization into the home. Paper presented at the meeting of the American Psychological Association, Los Angeles, September 1964.

Risley, T., & Wolf, M. Establishing functional speech in echolalic children. *Behav. Res. & Therapy*, 1967, *5*, 73–88.

Rosenthal, R. Experimenter-outcome orientation and the results of the psychological experiment. *Psychol. Bull.*, 1964, *61*, 405–412.

Rosenthal, R. *Experimenter effects in behavioral research.* New York: Appleton-Century-Crofts, 1966.

Rosenthal, R. Covert communication in the psychological experiment. *Psychol. Bull.*, 1967, *67*, 356–367.

Russo, S. Adaptations in behavioural therapy with children. *Behav. Res. & Therapy*, 1964, *2*, 43–47.

Scherer, M. W., & Nakamura, C. Y. A fear survey schedule for children (FSS-FC): A factor analytic comparison with manifest anxiety (EMAS). *Behav. Res. & Therapy*, 1968, *6*, 173–182.

Sidman, M. *Tactics of scientific research.* New York: Basic Books, 1960.

Stover, D. O. Personal communication, 1969.

Ullmann, L. P., & Krasner, L. *Case studies in behavior modification.* New York: Holt, Rinehart and Winston, 1965.

Wahler, R. G., Winkel, G. H., Peterson, R. F., & Morrison, D. C. Mothers as behaviour therapists for their own children. *Behav. Res. & Therapy*, 1965, *3*, 113–124.

Weiland, I. H., & Rudnik, R. Considerations of the development and treatment of autistic childhood psychosis. *Psychoanal. Study Child*, 1961, *16*, 549–563.

Werry, J. S., & Quay, H. C. Observing the classroom behavior of elementary school children. *Except. Child.*, 1969, *35*, 461–470.

Wetzel, R. Use of behavioral techniques in a case of compulsive stealing. *J. consult. Psychol.*, 1966, *30*, 367–374.

Wetzel, R. J., Baker, J., Roney, M., & Martin, M. Outpatient treatment of autistic behaviour. *Behav. Res. & Therapy*, 1966, *4*, 169–177.

White, J. G. The use of learning theory in the psychological treatment of children. *J. clin. Psychol.*, 1959, *16*, 227–229.

Wolf, M. M., Birnbrauer, J. S., Williams, T., & Lawler, J. A note on apparent extinction of the vomiting behavior of a retarded child. In L. P. Ullmann & L. Krasner (Eds.), *Case studies in behavior modification*. New York: Holt, Rinehart and Winston, 1965, pp. 364–366.

Wolf, M., Risley, T., & Mees, H. Application of operant conditioning procedures to the behaviour problems of an autistic child. *Behav. Res. & Therapy*, 1964, *1*, 305–312.

Wolpe, J. *Psychotherapy by reciprocal inhibition*. Stanford: Stanford University Press, 1968.

Zeilberger, J., Sampen, S. E., & Sloane, H. N., Jr. Modification of a child's problem behaviors in the home with the mother as therapist. *J. appl. Behav. Anal.*, 1968, *1*, 47–53.

Ziferstein, I. The Soviet psychiatrist: His relationship to his patients and to his society. *Amer. J. Psychiat.*, 1966, *123*, 440–446.

33

The Santa Monica Project: Evaluation of an Engineered Classroom Design with Emotionally Disturbed Children

Frank M. Hewett, Frank D. Taylor, and Alfred A. Artuso

Dr. Hewett is Associate Professor of Education and Psychiatry and Chairman of the Area of Special Education at the University of California, Los Angeles. Dr. Taylor is Director of Special Services of Santa Monica Unified School District, and Dr. Artuso is Superintendent of Schools.

Dr. Hewett's research interests and publications are in the areas of learning disorders, remedial reading, autistic children, behavior modification, and the emotionally disturbed. Dr. Taylor and Dr. Artuso's research interest has been primarily with emotionally handicapped children.

In the present study the authors have applied behavior modification methodology in a thoughtfully worked out teaching program for emotionally disturbed children. The encouraging results support further research in this area and hold the promise that the emotionally disturbed child can be "reached" in the public schools.

Application of behavior modification methodology in educational programs for children with emotional disturbance has provided evidence that systematic manipulation of stimuli and consequences in the class-

FROM *Exceptional Children*, reprinted by permission of The Council for Exceptional Children and the author.

room often results in significant behavioral and academic improvement (Patterson & Ebner, 1965; Quay, Werry, McQueen, & Sprague, 1966; Whelan, 1966; Nolen, Kunzelmann, & Haring, 1967). The teacher approaches the disturbed child as a behavior and learning problem rather than as "ill" or "impaired," and while demands which the child cannot handle emotionally or which call for competencies he lacks are not arbitrarily made, appropriate and reasonable behavioral and academic goals are established. In general, selection of these goals is based on a desire to aid the child in changing maladaptive behavior to adaptive behavior. At best, these concepts of "maladaptive" and "adaptive" provide only the broadest of guidelines for selection of specific behavioral goals. In this sense the powerful methodology of the behavior modification approach is not matched by concern with goals in learning. Teachers are provided with an efficient means of taking emotionally disturbed children someplace but are not substantially aided in the selection of where to go.

It is this lack of balanced emphasis on goals and methods that may preclude the acceptance of behavior modification in the field of education, particularly in the public school, and thereby may greatly limit its usefulness. An interesting parallel to this state of affairs can be drawn with reference to psychoanalytic theory and psychodynamic psychology. These approaches have had an important influence on special education for the emotionally disturbed over the past several decades, but their preoccupation with therapeutic goals to the almost complete exclusion of concern with educational methodology has restricted their acceptance and effectiveness in public school programs for these children.

ENGINEERED CLASSROOM DESIGN

The engineered classroom design attempts to approach education of the emotionally disturbed with a balanced emphasis on goals and methods. The disturbed child is viewed as a socialization failure and assessed in terms of his development learning deficiencies. These deficiencies are determined with reference to a developmental sequence of educational goals (Hewett, 1968) which postulates that in order for the child to learn successfully he must pay *attention,* make a *response, order* his behavior, accurately and thoroughly engage in multisensory *exploratory* behavior, gain *social* approval, and require *mastery* of self care and cognitive skills. Finally he must function on a self motivated basis with *achievement* in learning providing its own reward.

The room arrangement, teacher pupil ratio, schedule, and operations of the engineered classroom support attainment of these goals, and manipulation of stimuli and consequences in the program is done in accord with the behavior modification methodology. The room is divided into three major centers: (a) the mastery and achievement center including the students' desks and two study booths where academic assignments are given; (b) the exploratory-social center where science, art, and communication activities take place; and (c) the attention-response-order center which provides simple direction following tasks. There are nine students, a teacher, and an aide in each classroom. The 4 hour class day is divided into 2 hours of reading, written language, and arithmetic; one hour of exploratory activities; and a total of one hour of physical education and recesses. Each child carries a Work Record Card with him throughout the day, and earns a possible 10 checkmarks every 15 minutes. Checkmarks are given for starting and working on tasks and for behavior related to the levels on the developmental sequence which are most critical for each individual child. Completed Work Record Cards may be exchanged weekly for tangible rewards in Phase I of the program, for time to pursue self selected activities in Phase II, and for daily graphing of total checkmarks earned in Phase III. The Santa Monica Project as reported here utilized only the Phase I approach. Throughout the day, a given child may be assigned tasks relating to any level on the developmental sequence in an effort to keep him learning and earning checkmarks as a successful student. A complete description of the program and the planned interventions directed toward assuring students success have been reported elsewhere (Hewett, 1966, 1967, 1968a, 1968b).

The Santa Monica Project was undertaken by the authors to assess the effectiveness of the engineered classroom design in maintaining student attention to tasks and in improving academic achievement level. It was done in the Santa Monica Unified School District, Santa Monica, California, during 1966–1967. Santa Monica is a coastal community near the city of Los Angeles with a broad range of socioeconomic levels similar in proportion to the greater Los Angeles county area.

SUBJECTS

Fifty-four children with learning and behavior problems, the majority of which were considered "emotionally disturbed," were assigned to six project classrooms with nine students in each. These children ranged in age from 8–0 to 11–11 years and ranged in Full Scale IQ score from 85 to 113 as determined by the Wechsler Intelligence Scale for Children. Academically the children were functioning in reading from 0 to 6.2 grade levels and in arithmetic fundamentals from 0 to 5.2 grade levels, as measured by the California Achievement Test (elementary level). With the exception of five children, all students were 2 or more years below their expected grade level in reading and all but seven were 2 or more years below in arithmetic fundamentals.

In the assignment of individual children to project classrooms, an attempt was made to arrive at comparable class groupings with respect to

IQ, age, and reading and arithmetic achievement. Since so few girls were located, control could not be exerted over the variable of sex. Table 1 reports the mean values for IQ, age, and achievement level in each of the six project classrooms.

TEACHERS

Six female elementary school teachers were selected from teaching applicants to the Santa Monica District prior to the 1966–1967 school year. None had taught previously in the district, one had never taught before, and the teaching experience of the others ranged from 3 to 8 years. Only one teacher had worked before with emotionally disturbed children. Their final selection was made by the Santa Monica School District personnel office on the basis of strong qualifications and an expression of willingness to participate in the project. Six female teacher aides (without prior teaching experience) were also selected from a group of housewives and graduate students who applied.

A 2 week training program was conducted prior to the beginning of the school year to acquaint all of the teachers and aides with the goals and methods of the engineered classroom design. This training program included lectures, group discussions, and demonstrations conducted by the authors. Following this training program each teacher and aide was randomly assigned to a project classroom which had previously been designated as either experimental or control.

PROCEDURE

The experimental condition of the project involved rigid adherence to the engineered classroom design and systematic reliance on the giving of

Table 1 Mean Values for IQ, Age and Achievement Level for the Six Project Classrooms

Class	Mean IQ	Mean age	Mean total reading grade equivalent	Mean total arithmetic grade equivalent
1	93	10-4	3.0	3.9
2	95	10-6	2.9	3.4
3	92	10-8	2.5	3.0
4	96	10-1	3.2	3.3
5	98	9-9	3.0	3.4
6	93	10-4	2.3	3.0

checkmarks. The control condition of the project consisted of any approach the teacher chose to follow, including aspects of the engineered design except use of tangible or token rewards. Conventional grading, verbal praise, complimentary written comments on completed assignments, and awarding privileges for good work were all acceptable. To facilitate assessment of the effect of introducing and withdrawing the experimental and control condition, the project classes were assigned as shown in Table 2.

Class E maintained the experimental condition for the entire project year while Class C maintained the control condition during that time. Classes CE began as control, but abruptly introduced the experimental condition at midyear. The reverse was true for classes EC which started as experimental and then abruptly shifted to control at the project's midpoint.

As has been stated, the independent variable in the project was rigid adherence to the engineered design and use of the checkmark system. The dependent variables also were briefly mentioned—student task attention and academic functioning level in reading and arithmetic.

Two observers sat in front of each project classroom for 2½ hours daily during the 34 week project period. These observers were undergraduate college students recruited and trained for this assignment. Each observer held a stopwatch and was assigned four or five children to observe regularly. The children were observed for 5 minute segments throughout the observation period in random order so that at least five separate samples of task attention were obtained on each student each day. Observers recorded the number of seconds the student's eyes (or in some cases his head and body) were appropriately oriented toward an assigned task. Specific criteria for crediting a student for "task attention" were established. The project observers were trained by two graduate students who had reached a 90 percent or better agreement between themselves for task attention measurement. Each observer was then paired with one of the graduate students until reliability was established at a level of 90 percent or better. Every 2 weeks the graduate students rotated through the classrooms rechecking reliability and at no point in the

Table 2   *Assignment of Project Classes to Experimental and Control Conditions*

Class	Fall semester	Spring semester
1 (E)	Experimental	Experimental
2 (C)	Control	Control
3 and 4 (CE)	Control	Experimental
5 and 6 (EC)	Experimental	Control

project was agreement found to be below the 85 percent level. Daily individual task attention percentages were obtained on each child, these percentages were totalled for all the children in a class, and a weekly task attention percentage mean was obtained for each project class.

All students were retested twice with parallel forms of the California Achievement Test used in the initial screening—once at midyear and once at the close of the project.

The six project classrooms were visited each week by the authors and the project coordinator. Weekly meetings were held with the teachers, at which time problems with individual students were taken up with the project coordinator. In general he continually referred to the engineered design and its resources for handling problems presented by experimental teachers. With the control teachers he made similar suggestions (without reference to the giving of tangible or token rewards) but usually offered several alternatives. Separate meetings of the project staff and the parents of children enrolled in each class were held near the start of the project. The class program was presented and questions brought up by the parents were discussed at this time. There was no other systematic attempt to meet or work with the parents during the project.

On the first Monday morning of the spring semester the teachers in Classes CE introduced the engineered design to their students. At the same time, the teachers in Classes EC announced that checkmarks would not be used any more. These teachers had altered the room arrangement and were free to conduct the program from that point on any way they wished but without the previous reward system. Class E continued as a year long experimental class and Class C continued using the control condition for the remainder of the year.

RESULTS

The results of the Santa Monica Project evaluation will be discussed in reference to three main questions:

1. What was the effect on task attention and achievement level of introducing the experimental condition to emotionally disturbed children who had previously been in a regular class?

2. What was the effect on task attention and achievement level of introducing the experimental condition to emotionally disturbed children who had previously been in a small, individualized class under the control condition?

3. What was the effect on task attention and achievement level of abruptly withdrawing the experimental condition from a class of emotionally disturbed children who had become accustomed to it over a semester?

Table 3 presents the mean task attention percentages for all project

Table 3 *Mean Task Attention Percentages for All Classes, Averaged for 4-Week Intervals during Fall and Spring Semesters*

	Fall semester				Spring semester			
Class	1 weeks 2–5	2 weeks 6–9	3 weeks 10–13	4 weeks 14–17	5 weeks 2–5	6 weeks 6–9	7 weeks 10–13	8 weeks 14–17
E	82.3	87.6	94.2	93.8	92.0	93.9	94.8	94.0
C	90.7	84.5	81.1	89.0	86.7	86.3	86.7	84.4
EC	85.5	85.8	87.7	86.6	85.6	90.0	91.8	91.3
CE	76.2	78.0	84.3	81.6	84.5	91.0	92.0	90.5

classrooms, averaged for 4 week intervals during the fall and spring semesters. The mean task attention percentages are based on five daily 5 minute observations made on each child in a given class; in most cases at least 100 such observations were made on every child during each 4 week interval. Figure 1 shows these 4 week interval mean task attention percentages.

Table 4 reports the achievement data obtained during initial screening, at the midyear point, and at the end of the project year.

In the discussion which follows a difference reported as "significant"

Fig. 1 *Mean task attention of Class E, Class C, Classes EC, and Classes CE averaged for 4-week intervals during the fall and spring semesters.*

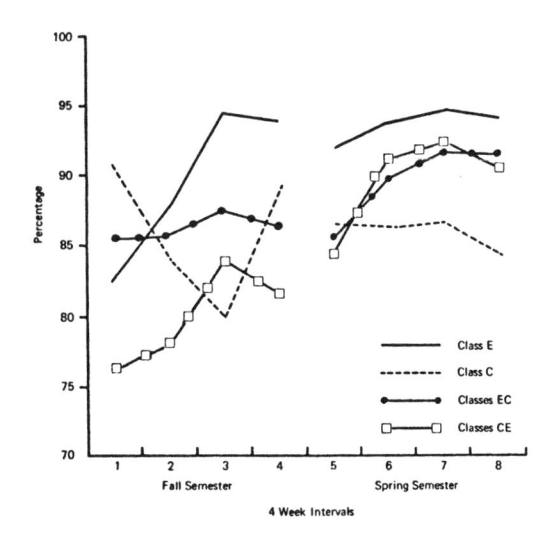

Table 4 Mean Raw Scores and Grade Equivalents in Reading and Arithmetic for All Project Classes

Test	Initial screening			Midyear			End of year		
	E	C	EC	CE	E	C	EC	CE	E	C	EC	CE
CAT Total Reading	31.4 (3.2)[a]	23.1 (2.8)	28.1 (3.1)	24.8 (2.9)	33.1 (3.3)	34.4 (3.4)	32.9 (3.3)	33.4 (3.3)	38.0 (3.6)	30.6 (3.2)	35.9 (3.5)	37.8 (3.6)
CAT Arithmetic Fundamentals	15.1 (3.9)	10.5 (3.4)	10.7 (3.4)	11.1 (3.5)	20.7 (4.6)	13.9 (3.8)	15.2 (3.9)	13.5 (3.8)	24.9 (5.0)	11.7 (3.6)	19.8 (4.5)	19.7 (4.5)

[a] Figures in parentheses represent grade equivalents.

represents the .05 level of confidence or better. Specific reference to the statistical method used to evaluate project data (analysis of variance, covariance, and t test) will not be made nor will the complete data from the evaluation be presented. However, this has been reported elsewhere (Hewett, Taylor, & Artuso, 1967).

Classes E and C provide information with reference to question one cited earlier. While Class C enjoyed a significant task attention advantage over Class E during interval 1 in Figure 1, this disappeared in interval 2. Beginning with interval 3 Class E maintained superiority in task attention for the remainder of the project year.

Achievement data in Table 4 reveal no significant difference in reading between the classes, but a significant difference in arithmetic fundamentals in favor of Class E is seen. Class E showed a 1.2 year gain while Class C gained only 0.4 year during the project. The experimental condition, then, was related to significantly higher task attention among students coming from regular classes from interval 3 on, and was also related to a significant gain in arithmetic over the year.

Question 2 may be considered by comparing Class C and Classes CE. During the fall semester, all three classes utilized the control condition. At midyear Classes CE shifted to the experimental condition, thus providing evidence regarding the effect of this condition on children already enrolled in a small class group. Class C maintained a significantly higher task attention percentage during intervals 1, 3, and 4 during the control phase over Classes CE. But by interval 5 when Classes CE introduced the experimental condition there was no such difference, and during intervals 6, 7, and 8 these classes attained a significantly higher task attention level than Class C. While no significant differences emerged in reading, Classes CE made a significant gain over Class C in arithmetic fundamentals during the spring semester when they utilized the experimental condition. Therefore both task attention and arithmetic gains were related to the introduction of the experimental condition.

In relation to question 3, Class E and Classes EC provided information. All three classes utilized the experimental condition during the fall semester but at midyear Classes EC eliminated rigid adherence to the experimental condition and use of checkmarks and tangible rewards. Evidence was then obtained regarding the effect of abrupt withdrawal of the experimental condition on a small class that had become accustomed to it. Except for intervals 1 and 2, Class E achieved a significantly higher task attention level during the fall semester than Classes EC when all were using the experimental condition. This continued during intervals 5 and 6 but ceased to exist during the last half of the spring semester. During these intervals Classes EC attained their highest task attention level, indicating with respect to task attention that removal of the experimental condition had a facilitating effect. There were no significant differences in reading or arithmetic between Class E and Classes EC either semester. Class E and Classes EC made their gain in arithmetic consistently over the entire year. In summary, removal of the experimental condition resulted in improved task attention in Classes EC but did not affect achievement levels in reading or arithmetic.

DISCUSSION AND CONCLUSIONS

The major findings of the Santa Monica project can be summarized as follows: task attention of students was significantly facilitated by the experimental condition when that condition was introduced to emotionally disturbed children following placement in either a regular or control condition class. Task attention was also facilitated by removal of the experimental condition from classes which had become accustomed to it over a one semester period. Reading achievement was not significantly affected by either the experimental or control condition but gains in arithmetic fundamentals were significantly correlated with the presence of the experimental condition.

The facilitating effect of the experimental condition on student task attention is seen as related to the emphasis in the engineered design on building *attention, response,* and *order* behaviors. The planned routine of the classroom, the provision for systematic acknowledgment of functioning level by means of the checkmark system, and continual reassignment to tasks promoting success undoubtedly contributed to students becoming more willing, efficient, and consistent in paying attention. The teacher in Class C, which enjoyed a significant task attention advantage over Class E during interval 1, was concerned with maintaining her students at a high task attention level since she, as did all the other teachers, knew this was being measured by the observers. Without the checkmark system she had to use considerable verbalization and social reinforcement in controlling student behavior. While this technique made her initially more effective in orienting them toward assigned tasks, its effectiveness quickly diminished following the first 4 weeks. This may be related to the questionable responsiveness of emotionally disturbed children to social reinforcement, which has been reported by Levin and Simmons (1962) and Quay and Hunt (1965). The more objective and neutral checkmark system, while admittedly providing reinforcement on a more primitive level, may be better suited for initiating contact with disturbed students and starting them toward success in school.

The correlation between arithmetic improvement and presence of the experimental condition is also probably a reflection of the emphasis on attention, response, and order behavior present in classes utilizing this condition. The building of these basic learning competencies may more directly and immediately apply to arithmetic than to language arts subjects such as reading.

Perhaps the most interesting and somewhat surprising finding was that Classes EC actually improved in task attention following removal of the experimental condition. This change was apparently not just due to time in a special class alone since Class E and Class C showed no such improvement during the second half of the year. Another hypothesis to explain Classes EC improvement under the control condition might center on a novelty effect; any major innovation, even the taking away of something supposedly desirable such as tangible rewards, might be expected to bring about an initial change in student behavior. This hypothesis is rejected because of the long period of time covered in the evaluation. A novelty effect might exert influence over the first several weeks but it is doubtful it would be maintained over a 17 week period. A more logical explanation is to view the improvement of Classes EC in task attention under the control condition as resulting from (a) the increased effectiveness of the teachers in these classes to function as secondary social reinforcers due to their semester long association with a success oriented approach using a primary reward system, and (b) the investment made in building competencies at the attention, response, and order levels during the experimental condition which readied the students for participation in a teacher centered, more traditional educational program utilizing exploratory, social, and mastery tasks and rewards.

Certainly evidence was provided that the use of tangible rewards on a temporary basis does not doom children to dependence on them. On the contrary, it appears such rewards may be extremely useful in launching children with behavior and learning problems into successful learning in school.

The engineered classroom design as evaluated in the Santa Monica Project appears basically a launching approach. Its provision for increasing the teacher's effectiveness as a social reinforcer through systematic association with student success and primary rewards and for building fundamental learning competencies often forgotten about in education past the primary grades may greatly aid the disturbed child in taking the first step toward achieving success in school.

References

Hewett, F. The Tulare experimental class for educationally handicapped children. *California Education,* 1966, *3,* 6–8.

Hewett, F. Educational engineering with emotionally disturbed children. *Exceptional Children,* 1967, *33,* 459–467.

Hewett, F. An engineered classroom design for emotionally disturbed children.

In J. Hellmuth (Ed.), *Educational therapy*. Vol. 2. Seattle: Special Child Publications, 1968. (a)

Hewett, F. *The emotionally disturbed child in the classroom: A developmental strategy for educating children with maladaptive behavior*. Boston: Allyn and Bacon, 1968. (b)

Hewett, F., Taylor, F., & Artuso, A. *The Santa Monica Project: Demonstration and evaluation of an engineered classroom design for emotionally disturbed children in the public school, phase 1: Elementary level*. Final Report. Project No. 62893, Demonstration Grant No. OEG-4-7-062893-0377, Office of Education, Bureau of Research, U.S. Department of Health, Education and Welfare, 1967.

Levin, G., & Simmons, J. Response to praise by emotionally disturbed boys. *Psychological Reports*, 1962, *11*, 10.

Nolen, P., Kunzelmann, H., & Haring, N. Behavioral modification in a junior high learning disabilities classroom. *Exceptional Children*, 1967, *34*, 163–169.

Patterson, G., & Ebner, M. Application of learning principles to the treatment of deviant children. Paper presented at the meeting of the American Psychological Association, Chicago, September 1965.

Quay, H., & Hunt, W. Psychopathy, neuroticism and verbal conditioning: A replication and extension. *Journal of Consulting Psychology*, 1965, *29*, 283.

Quay, H., Werry, J. S., McQueen, M., & Sprague, R. L. Remediation of the conduct problem child in the special class setting. *Exceptional Children*, 1966, *32*, 509–515.

Whelan, R. J. The relevance of behavior modification procedures for teachers of emotionally disturbed children. In P. Knoblock (Ed.), *Intervention approaches in educating emotionally disturbed children*. Syracuse: Syracuse University Press, 1966.

part V
Exceptional Environments

34

Characteristics of Socially Disadvantaged Children

Edmund W. Gordon

Dr. Gordon is Professor of Education and Chairman of the Department of Guidance at Teachers College, Columbia University. His productive research activities have led to over twenty-five major articles which have appeared in more than a dozen journals. His primary research interest is on the socially disadvantaged, although he has published papers on the mentally retarded, the emotionally disturbed, and infant behavior.

In the past decade society has shown strong interest in the economically and socially deprived. The amount of national legislation passed to cope with this segment of the population is one major indication of the rising concern. The growing body of research in this area is another indicator.

In his article, Dr. Gordon summarizes the research that has been concerned with identifying the characteristics of socially disadvantaged children. It is evident on examining his bibliography that this aspect of the problem has drawn considerable attention. This article should serve as an excellent starting point for the reader not too familiar with the area.

A review of research related to the education of socially disadvantaged children reveals no aspect of this investigative problem that has received

FROM *Review of Educational Research*, 1965, *35*, pp. 377–389. Reprinted by permission of the American Educational Research Association.

more attention than the study of the characteristics of this population. There are few studies reported since 1950 which have not devoted some attention to the enumeration, identification, or confirmation of those behaviors or circumstances which are assumed to set these children apart from their more privileged peers. These investigations have focused on home environment and family status, on language, cognition, and intelligence, on perceptual styles and patterns of intellectual function, and on motivation and aspiration.

HOME ENVIRONMENT AND FAMILY STATUS

The home environment has received considerable attention from investigators concerned with identifying characteristics of the socially disadvantaged child. This environment has been described as noisy, disorganized, overcrowded, and austere. It has generally been seen as lacking many of the cultural artifacts often associated with the development of school readiness, such as books, art work, variety of toys, and self-instructional equipment. Adult models in the environment have been seen as being incongruous with the demands of the school or the broader community, and the parents of these children often have been reported as failing to support their children's academic pursuits. This environment has been described largely in negative terms, and little attention has been directed toward those aspects of the environment which have positive implications or which could be utilized to the educational advantage of these children.

Keller (1963) described the lower class Negro homes in her study as more crowded than homes of similar white families. She found that one out of every six breadwinners was currently unemployed, and she reported that only one half of the children in this study regularly ate a meal with their parents. Fifty percent of the Negro parents and all white parents of a similar socioeconomic status were satisfied with their children's progress in school. Riessman (1963) pointed out the crowded conditions in lower class homes but stressed also the more positive aspects of such environments. These included cooperativeness and mutual aid of extended families; lack of strain accompanying competition, individualism, and equalitarianism; lessened sibling rivalry; and the security of a large family.

Milner (1951) found the environment of the lower class home to be much less verbal than that of the upper class home. Not only were there fewer books in lower class homes but lower class children were read to less frequently, spoke less with their parents, and received more physical punishment more often than did children from higher socioeconomic backgrounds. Riessman (1963) described the anti-intellectualism of the disadvantaged, but Hofstadter (1963) pointed out that anti-intellectualism is pervasive in present-day America. Considerable evidence is available, however, to show that parents of disadvantaged children are interested in and concerned about education for their children, even though these parents share our society's less-than-enthusiastic viewpoint toward intellectualism (Durkin, 1961; Cloward and Jones, 1963; Lewis, 1963; Harlem Youth Opportunities Unlimited, 1964).

Maas (1951) found what he described as closed and rigid relationships between lower class parents and their children. Socially disadvantaged children were found to exhibit a fear of parental authority and a dependence on siblings and peers greater than that found in middle class children. Their parents were reported to be closed or inaccessible to these children's communications. Bronfenbrenner (1961) noted that overprotection of girls and inadequate discipline of boys were more likely to occur in lower class than in middle class homes. Similarly, according to Gill and Spilka (1962) underachieving boys and achieving girls appeared to come from strong mother-dominated environments, which were thought to be more prevalent in lower class than middle class homes. Deutsch (1963) concluded that in the lower class home the lack of systematic visual stimulation plus the presence of much noise fostered inattention and poor concentration. Dave (1963) indicated that parents with low levels of educational or occupational skills can still provide very stimulating home environments for their children. He found parental behavior, rather than parental status, to be the powerful determiner of academic performance.

Working class parents were reported by Kohn (1959) to be more likely to react to the child's misbehavior in terms of the immediate consequences of the action, while middle class parents tended to respond in terms of their interpretation of the child's intent. Kohn and Carroll (1960) found that while the middle class mother expected the father to be as supportive of the child as she was and saw his role of disciplinarian as secondary, working class mothers wanted their husbands to be more directive in their relationship with the child and considered the husband's major responsibility to be that of imposing restraints. Working class fathers felt that child rearing was the responsibility of the wife. Leshan (1952) described lower class families as tending to train their children with immediate punishments and rewards. Upper class parents were seen as tending to stress the future, with punishment and reward often deferred. MacDonald, McGuire, and Havighurst (1949) found systematic differences in leisure-time family activity according to social class, with the higher socioeconomic strata participating most frequently in family activity.

These environmental studies provide some insight into the home experiences of disadvantaged children, but few represent systematic long-term investigations conducted in naturalistic settings. Too much of this work tends to be speculative and is based on relatively small and unrepresentative samples. The findings, nonetheless, point to the importance of environmental studies. Interpretation of such findings, however, will be greatly limited until simple enumeration and description of environmental factors are replaced by ecological investigations designed to show the relationship between certain features of the environment and certain behavioral characteristics.

LANGUAGE, COGNITION, AND INTELLIGENCE

Nowhere is this relationship between environmental encounters and subsequent behavior in greater need of study than in the area of the development of language and cognitive function. Although much effort has been directed at identifying patterns of function in these areas, little of the work leads to meaningful concepts of causation or to clear directions for remediation. Data from several studies suggest that children from disadvantaged backgrounds show weaknesses in the utilization of normative abstract symbols to represent and interpret their feelings, their experiences, and the phenomena of their environment. In a discussion of the cognitive and motivational effects of disadvantaged status, Ausubel (1964) concluded that a delay in the acquisition of certain formal language forms resulted in difficulty in the transition from concrete to abstract modes of thought. Deutsch (1964) observed lower class children to be inferior in abstract conceptualization and categorization of visual stimuli. Bean (1942) found Negroes to be relatively poor in visual imagery. Deutsch (1963) studied the tasks performed at home by disadvantaged children and found that they tended to be motoric, required short time spans, and related primarily to concrete objects and services. In another study, Deutsch and others (1964) indicated certain functions underlying measures for which race is associated with poor performance. These were reported to be abstraction, verbalization, and "experientially dependent enumeration." Siller (1957) investigated the greater tendency toward abstraction in children from higher social classes. When his subjects were matched on nonverbal scores with low status children, the higher status children were superior on tests of verbal concepts. The socially disadvantaged child, according to McCandless (1952), tended to be more concrete and inflexible in his intellectual functioning than did the more privileged child.

Comparing Negro and Caucasian children, Anastasi and D'Angelo (1952) found among the latter a greater frequency of mature sentence types and complex constructions and better elaborated concepts. Comparing by parental occupational status, Irwin (1948) found significant differences in the mastery of speech sounds after age one and one half, favoring the children from higher occupational groups. Investigating fifth graders, Deutsch and Brown (1964) determined a relationship between race and measures of intelligence, reading, and sound discrimination, with nonwhites trailing white children. Deutsch and Brown (1964) also found a relationship between range of oral vocabulary and social class level. Parents of adequate readers were significantly higher in occupational status, according to Newton (1959), than were parents of retarded readers. Hilliard and Troxell (1937) found children with rich information backgrounds to be better equipped for reading than were children of meager backgrounds. The latter finding was substantiated by Bernstein (1960), who reported the higher intellectual development of the middle class child to be a cultural function of linguistic advantage and not a matter of genetic superiority. Jensen (1963) and John (1963), working independently, concluded that the lower class child's use of language as a cognitive tool is deficient, and noted that the acquisition of more abstract and integrative language forms seems to be hampered by lower class living conditions. Olim, Hess, and Shipman (1965) found that the child's ability to handle abstractions was related to maternal language style. These investigators concluded further that the mother's tendency to use abstract language was a better predictor of the child's abstract function on a cognitive task than was either the mother's verbal IQ or the child's own IQ. The retarded language development of the lower class child was described by Cohn (1959) as contributing to his dislike of and difficulty in public school. This author felt lower class language to be a separate dialect, related to but distinct from standard English. As a result of this widely held view, many educational planners are concerned with the feasibility of changing linguistic function through training.

These several inferential conclusions about deficits in symbolic representation and language development are reflected in studies of concept development in disadvantaged children, whose concept formation has been described as content-centered rather than form-centered and whose reasoning has been described as more inductive than deductive (Riessman, 1963). This conceptual style was reported by Gordon (1964) to limit the child's ability to make accurate generalizations from the specific to the universal and to transfer knowledge utilizing previously learned concepts. Deutsch (1963) and Hilliard and Troxell (1937) have noted that differences in the quality of language between classes increase with age. As Deutsch suggested, if a high level of language development is a prerequisite to advanced concept formation and problem solving, the lower class deficit in conceptual function can only be tremendous. These postulates and conclusions result from a growing body of data relevant to the cognitive development of low-income children.

In a cross-cultural study of the acquisition of arithmetic concepts by kindergarten children, Montague (1964) found significant differences between social class groups in favor of the higher group. Deutsch (1960) found arithmetic scores to be higher than reading scores in a population of lower class children, although the arithmetic scores were depressed below national norms. In interpreting this finding, the investigator suggested that reading may involve motivation arising from specific value systems and arithmetic may involve concrete acts common to society, such as marketing. In Gordon's (1965) study in Prince Edward County, Virginia, arithmetic scores were similarly found to be less depressed than reading scores in the 7- to 10-year age group. These children, having been deprived of formal education, were thought to have developed simple arithmetic skills in their naturalistic and chore experiences. However, these experiences did not provide a basis for the incidental acquisition of reading skills.

Hunt (1961) has very clearly developed the position that intelligence is not primarily a genetically determined entity but rather a function which develops in and through the process of interaction with the environment. This position is reflected in much of the work on intellectual function in disadvantaged populations. Although many studies show differential function favoring more advantage groups, much effort has been directed toward establishing evidence of social experience determinants of these differences.

Most research in this area has determined a relationship between intelligence and socioeconomic status (Clarke and Clarke, 1953; Deutsch and Brown, 1964; Dreger and Miller, 1960; Eells, 1953; Higgins and Sivers, 1958; Montague, 1964; Osborne, 1960). This relationship, however, is not seen to be permanent or irreversible (Clarke and Clarke, 1953). Deutsch (1963) noted that class differences in perceptual abilities decrease with age; Eells (1953) spoke of the cultural bias of intelligence tests and noted that children from deprived backgrounds often receive scores which are inaccurate reflections of their basic intelligence. The necessity of examining the subcultural values of the child tested was pointed out by Levinson (1961). Deutsch and Brown (1964) found that the influence of race became increasingly manifest and crucial as social level increased. Pasamanick and Knobloch (1955) noted that awareness of the examiner's skin color caused sufficient inhibition to result in decreased verbal responsiveness and thus poorer performance on language sections of IQ tests. Intelligence level was described as a function of the amount of material available for learning and the types of learning which take place (McCandless, 1952). Some investigators have characterized the lower class child as weak in conceptual ability (Siller, 1957) in such academic areas as arithmetic concepts (Montague, 1964) and in perceptual ability (Deutsch, 1963). More psychomotor and behavioral disorders and greater reading disability were found in the deprived population than in more privileged groups (Pasamanick and Knobloch, 1958). The findings by Pasamanick and Knobloch, which are based upon the study of the relationship between income level, health status, and school adjustment, suggest a continuum of reproductive errors. The incidence of reproductive error or developmental defect occurs along a continuum in which the incidence of errors is greatest in the population for which medical, nutritional, and child care are poorest and the incidence least where such care is best. This formulation, when applied to the question of possible social class or racial differences in intelligence, has led to the general feeling that racial IQ differences are a result of environmental deprivation rather than of inherent limited potential. In the definitive review of this problem, Klineberg (1963) found no scientifically acceptable evidence for the view that ethnic groups differ in innate ability.

PERCEPTUAL STYLES AND PATTERNS OF INTELLECTUAL FUNCTION

Several investigators have noted in disadvantaged children perceptual styles and habits which are inadequate or irrelevant to academic efficiency. Although high levels of perceptual sensitization and discrimination are often present, these skills tend to be developed better in physical behavior than in visual, and better in visual behavior than in aural (Riessman, 1963). Probably of greatest significance is the absence of any high degree of dependence on verbal and written language for cognitive cues. Many of the children have not adopted receptive and expressive modes traditional to and necessary for success in school.

The extent to which perceptual and expressive styles differ among children of varied backgrounds is well documented. Jensen (1963) concluded that the socially deprived child has failed to learn the verbal mediators which facilitate school learning. On measures of level of communication based on meaning, Carson and Rabin (1960) found white children to be superior to Negroes and Northern Negroes to be superior to Southern Negroes. Deutsch (1960) found lower class children to be inferior to a comparable group of middle class children on tasks of concentration and persistence, and in a subsequent study (Deutsch, 1965) he reported that lower class children are relatively poorer in auditory discrimination, in manipulation of syntactical aspects of language, and in recognition of perceptual similarities.

Leshan (1952), in a study of time concepts as employed by children in their own stories, found time orientation to vary with social class. Orientation to time was more consistent with reality in middle and upper class children. In his discussion of characteristics of disadvantaged youngsters, Riessman (1963) included slowness as a feature of their cognitive functioning. Davidson and others (1950) arrived at the same conclusion on the finding of differences in IQ estimated from timed performance tests. Deutsch (1960) reported that lower class children tended to ignore difficult problems with a "so what" attitude and that as a result learning proportionately decreased over time. Lower class children felt more inadequate in school than did other comparison groups, according to Goff

(1954). Ausubel and Ausubel (1963) found that deprived children depended more on external as opposed to internal control than did more privileged youngsters.

Ego development in disadvantaged children has been described as including low self-esteem, impaired patterns of personal-social organization, high incidence of behavioral disturbance, and distorted interpersonal relationships. Other characteristics attributed to these children are ego deflation and difficulty in accepting personal responsibility (Ausubel and Ausubel, 1963; Battle and Rotter, 1963; Goff, 1954; and Keller, 1963). Depressed self-concepts have been noted as have tendencies toward self-depreciation (Dreger and Miller, 1960; and Keller, 1963). Carroll (1945) saw the lower class ideal self as reflecting personal beauty and fame, not the moral and intellectual qualities that characterize the ideal self of the middle class child. Aggression and strong competitive feelings among children from lower class socioeconomic backgrounds were reported by McKee and Leader (1955). Deutsch (1960) found children from such backgrounds to be fearful and passive.

MOTIVATION AND ASPIRATION

The degree and direction of motivation in socially disadvantaged children are frequently inconsistent with the demands and goals of formal education, although the nature of their aspirations is usually consistent with these children's perceptions of the availability of opportunity and reward. On the other hand, symbolic rewards and postponements of gratification appear to be inoperative as positive norms in motivation. Goals for these children tend to be more self-centered, immediate, and utilitarian. There is usually no concern with aesthetics of knowledge, symbolization as an art form, introspection, and competition with self. Drive is present, but its direction and goals may not be complementary to academic achievement (Gordon, 1964). These several conclusions are drawn primarily from theoretical discussions of motivational problems in this population; the research literature is not rich on this subject.

Rosen (1956) observed high motivation to be related to high grades. He postulated that middle class children are more likely to be taught motives and values which make achievement possible than are lower class children. Edwards and Webster (1963) found that favorable self-concepts were related to higher aspiration and to greater academic achievement. They described ethnic anxiety as negatively related to self-perception and aspiration. In Gould's (1941) study only those sons who internalized parental values of aspiration were sufficiently motivated to overcome obstacles in school.

Bernstein (1960) found that achievement strivings due to parental demands for success were a more central factor in middle class motivation than in lower class motivation. Socially disadvantaged children have been reported to be less highly motivated and to have lower aspiration for academic and vocational achievement than do their middle and upper class school peers (Sewel, Haller, and Straus, 1957; Hieronymus, 1951; McCandless, 1952).

Attitudinal factors are closely related to motivational factors and are not infrequently a source of problems in educational planning for disadvantaged children. High levels of aspiration and positive attitudes toward school were more frequently encountered in middle and upper class children than in lower socioeconomic groups (Hieronymus, 1951). Consistent with this is the finding by Sewel, Haller, and Straus (1957) that educational and occupational aspirations tend to be greatly influenced by class values in favor of middle and upper classes. Wylie (1963) found that Negro and lower class children make more modest estimates of their ability to do schoolwork than do white and higher class students. Terrel, Durkin, and Wiesley (1959) determined that lower class children learn more quickly when given a material incentive than when given a nonmaterial one. The reverse is true of middle class children.

SUMMARY AND OUTLOOK

Most of the investigators and observers upon whose work our knowledge of the characteristics of socially disadvantaged children is based have developed their data against a background of experience with children from the homes of middle class white U.S. nationals. The tendency has been to describe and enumerate these characteristics in terms of their deviance from the norms of this group and to view these behaviors and conditions as deficits. Little attention has been given to a view of the behavior and conditions of socially disadvantaged children as given information which the school might use in the design of meaningful and appropriate learning experiences. By implication these studies suggest that their language, their styles, and their values are negatives to be overcome. There is no doubt that in many instances upward mobility may not otherwise be possible; however, to demean everything with which the child is identified may produce only immobility. This concern is seldom represented in these works directed at identifying and understanding the socially disadvantaged child. Even if the primary characteristics of this population were essentially negative and all of their environmental conditions were essentially unwholesome, the research effort to establish these observations would still be inadequate. In the first place, such research tends to generalize with respect to a population which is probably infinitely variable. There is probably no typical "socially disadvantaged child" but instead a wide variety of such children with widely varying characteristics. To describe them and plan for them as a group is hence in error; differential psychology is as important here as in any other area. Secondly, to establish the fact of *correlation* between certain conditions and poor school adjustment or certain characteristics and underdevelopment is not to establish the fact of *causation*. Our efforts at documenting the characteristics have not identified the cause, nor have they pointed clearly toward courses of remediation. It remains for research to determine the nature of learning facility and disability in this population; to determine those circumstances under which certain characteristics and conditions result in success and under which others result in failure; to develop more sensitive and accurate procedures for the assessment of potential for development as well as for behavioral change; and to determine those conditions necessary for appropriate development where existing pedagogical principles and technology are inappropriate to the learning experiences required for a wide variety of underdeveloped learners. Some investigations as yet unpublished and others currently in process show promise of speaking to these issues. There is as yet, however, no groundswell on the horizon.

References

Anastasi, A., and D'Angelo, R. Y. A Comparison of Negro and White Preschool Children in Language Development and Goodenough Draw-a-Man IQ. *Journal of Genetic Psychology*, 1952, *81*, 147–165.

Ausubel, D. P. How Reversible Are the Cognitive and Motivational Effects of Cultural Deprivation? Implications for Teaching the Culturally Deprived Child. *Urban Education*, 1964, *1*, 16–38.

Ausubel, D. P., and Ausubel, P. Ego Development Among Segregated Negro Children. *Education in Depressed Areas*. (Edited by A. H. Passow.) New York: Bureau of Publications, Teachers College, Columbia University, 1963. pp. 109–141.

Battle, E. S., and Rotter, J. B. Children's Feelings of Personal Control as Related to Social Class and Ethnic Group. *Journal of Personality*, 1963, *31*, 482–490.

Bean, K. L. Negro Responses to Verbal and Non-Verbal Test Materials. *Journal of Psychology*, 1942, *13*, 343–353.

Bernstein, B. Language and Social Class. *British Journal of Sociology*, 1960, *11*, 271–276.

Bronfenbrenner, U. The Changing American Child—A Speculative Analysis. *Merrill-Palmer Quarterly*, 1961, *7*, 73–84.

Carroll, R. E. Relation of School Environment to the Moral Ideology and the Personal Aspirations of Negro Boys and Girls. *School Review*, 1945, *53*, 30–38.

Carson, A. S., and Rabin, A. I. Verbal Comprehension and Communication in Negro and White Children. *Journal of Educational Psychology*, 1960, *51*, 47–51.

Clarke, A. D. B., and Clarke, A. M. How Constant Is the I.Q.? *Lancet*, 1953, *265*, 877–880.

Cloward, R. A., and Jones, J. A. Social Class: Educational Attitudes and Participation. *Education in Depressed Areas*. (Edited by A. H. Passow.) New York: Bureau of Publications, Teachers College, Columbia University, 1963. pp. 190–216.

Cohn, W. On the Language of Lower-Class Children. *School Review*, 1959, *67*, 435–440.

Dave, R. H. *The Identification and Measurement of Environment Process Variables That Are Related to Educational Achievement.* Doctor's thesis. Chicago: University of Chicago, 1963.

Davidson, K. S., et al. A Preliminary Study of Negro and White Differences on Form I of the Wechsler Bellevue Scale. *Journal of Consulting Psychology*, 1950, *14*, 489–492.

Deutsch, M. *Minority Group and Class Status as Related to Social and Personality Factors in Scholastic Achievement.* Society for Applied Anthropology, Monographs No. 2. Ithaca, N.Y.: Cornell University, 1960.

Deutsch, M. The Disadvantaged Child and the Learning Process. *Education in Depressed Areas*. (Edited by A. H. Passow.) New York: Bureau of Publications, Teachers College, Columbia University, 1963. pp. 163–179.

Deutsch, M. Early Social Environment: Its Influence on School Adaptation. *The School Dropout*. (Edited by D. Schreiber.) Washington, D.C.: National Education Association, 1964. pp. 89–100.

Deutsch, M. The Role of Social Class in Language Development and Cognition. *American Journal of Orthopsychiatry*, 1965, *35*, 78–88.

Deutsch, M., and Brown, B. Social Influences in Negro-White Intelligency Differences. *Journal of Social Issues*, 1964, *20*, 24–35.

Deutsch, M., et al. *Communication of Information in the Elementary School Classroom.* U.S. Department of Health, Education, and Welfare, Office of Education, Cooperative Research Project No. 908. Washington, D.C.: Government Printing Office, 1964.

Dreger, R. M., and Miller, K. S. Comparative Psychological Studies of Negroes and Whites in the United States. *Psychological Bulletin*, 1960, *57*, 361–402.

Durkin, Dolores. Children Who Read Before Grade One. *Reading Teacher*, 1961, *14*, 163–66.

Edwards, T. B., and Webster, S. W. Correlates and Effects of Ethnic Group Identification. *Research Relating to Children*. U.S. Department of Health, Education, and Welfare, Welfare Administration, Children's Bureau, Bulletin No. 17. Washington, D.C.: Government Printing Office, 1963.

Eells, K. Some Implications for School Practices of the Chicago Studies of Cultural Bias in Intelligence Tests. *Harvard Educational Review*, 1953, *23*, 284–297.

Gill, L. J., and Spilka, B. Some Nonintellectual Correlates of Academic Achievement Among Mexican-American Secondary School Students. *Journal of Educational Psychology*, 1962, *53*, 144–149.

Goff, R. M. Some Educational Implications of the Influence of Rejection on Aspiration Levels of Minority Group Children. *Journal of Experimental Education*, 1954, *23*, 179–183.

Gordon, E. W. Counseling Socially Disadvantaged Children. *Mental Health of the Poor.* (Edited by F. Riessman, J. Cohen, and A. Pearl.) New York: Free Press of Glencoe, 1964. pp. 275–282.

Gordon, E. W. *Educational Achievement in the Prince Edward County Free School, 1963–64.* New York: Ferkauf Graduate School of Education, Yeshiva University, 1965. (Mimeo.)

Gould, R. Some Sociological Determinants of Goal Strivings. *Journal of Social Psychology,* 1941, *13,* 461–473.

Harlem Youth Opportunities Unlimited. *Youth in the Ghetto.* New York: Harlem Youth Opportunities Unlimited (180 West 130th Street), 1964.

Hieronymus, A. N. A Study of Social Class Motivation: Relationships Between Anxiety for Education and Certain Socio-Economic and Intellectual Variables. *Journal of Educational Psychology,* 1951, *42,* 193–205.

Higgins, C., and Sivers, C. H. A Comparison of Stanford-Binet and Colored Raven Progressive Matrices IQ's for Children with Low Socioeconomic Status. *Journal of Consulting Psychology,* 1958, *22,* 465–468.

Hilliard, G. H., and Troxell, E. Informational Background as a Factor in Reading Readiness and Reading Progress. *Elementary School Journal,* 1937, *38,* 255–263.

Hofstadter, R. *Anti-Intellectualism in American Life.* New York: Alfred A. Knopf, 1963.

Hunt, J. M. *Intelligence and Experience.* New York: Ronald Press Co., 1961.

Irwin, O. C. Infant Speech: The Effect of Family Occupational Status and of Age on Use of Sound Types. *Journal of Speech and Hearing Disorders,* 1948, *13,* 224–226.

Jensen, A. R. Learning Ability in Retarded, Average, and Gifted Children. *Merrill-Palmer Quarterly,* 1963, *9,* 123–140.

John, V. P. The Intellectual Development of Slum Children: Some Preliminary Findings. *American Journal of Orthopsychiatry,* 1963, *33,* 813–22.

Klineberg, O. Negro-White Differences in Intelligence Test Performance: A New Look at an Old Problem. *American Psychologist,* 1963, *18,* 198–203.

Kohn, M. L. Social Class and the Exercise of Parental Authority. *American Sociological Review,* 1959, *24,* 352–366.

Kohn, M. L., and Carroll, E. E. Social Class and the Allocation of Parental Responsibilities. *Sociometry,* 1960, *23,* 372–392.

Leshan, L. L. Time Orientation and Social Class. *Journal of Abnormal and Social Psychology,* 1952, *47,* 589–592.

Levinson, B. M. Subcultural Values and IQ Stability. *Journal of Genetic Psychology,* 1961, *98,* 69–82.

Lewis, H. Culture, Class and the Behavior of Low-Income Families. Paper presented at the Conference on Lower Class Cultures, June 1963. Washington, D.C.: Howard University, 1963. (Mimeo.)

Maas, H. S. Some Social Class Differences in the Family Systems and Group Relations of Pre- and Early Adolescents. *Child Development,* 1951, *22,* 145–152.

McCandless, B. Environment and Intelligence. *American Journal of Mental Deficiency,* 1952, *56,* 674–691.

MacDonald, M.; McGuire, C.; and Havighurst, R. J. Leisure Activities and the

Socioeconomic Status of Children. *American Journal of Sociology,* 1949, *54,* 505–519.

McKee, J. P., and Leader, F. B. The Relationship of Socioeconomic Status and Aggression to the Competitive Behavior of Preschool Children. *Child Development,* 1955, *26,* 135–42.

Milner, E. A Study of the Relationship Between Reading Readiness in Grade One School Children and Patterns of Parent-Child Interaction. *Child Development,* 1951, *22,* 95–112.

Montague, D. O. Arithmetic Concepts of Kindergarten Children in Contrasting Socioeconomic Areas. *Elementary School Journal, 64* 393–397.

Newton, E. S. Empirical Differences Between Adequate and Retarded Readers. *Reading Teacher,* 1959, *13,* 40–44.

Olim, E. G.; Hess, R. D.; and Shipman, V. C. Relationship Between Mothers' Language Styles and Cognitive Styles of Urban Pre-School Children. Paper presented to the Society for Research in Child Development, March 25, 1965. Chicago: Urban Child Study Center, 1965. (Mimeo.)

Osborne, R. T. Racial Differences in Mental Growth and School Achievement: A Longitudinal Study. *Psychological Reports,* 1960, *7,* 233–239.

Pasamanick, B., and Knobloch, H. Early Language Behavior in Negro Children and the Testing of Intelligence. *Journal of Abnormal and Social Psychology,* 1955, *50,* 401–402.

Pasamanick, B., and Knobloch, H. The Contribution of Some Organic Factors to School Retardation in Negro Children. *Journal of Negro Education,* 1958, *27,* 4–9.

Riessman, F. The Culturally Deprived Child: A New View. *Programs for the Educationally Disadvantaged.* U.S. Department of Health, Education, and Welfare, Office of Education, Bulletin 1963, No. 17. Washington, D.C.: Government Printing Office, 1963. pp. 3–10.

Rosen, B. C. The Achievement Syndrome: A Psychocultural Dimension of Social Stratification. *American Sociological Review,* 1956, *21,* 203–211.

Sewel, W. H., Haller, A. O.; and Straus, M. A. Social Status and Educational and Occupational Aspiration. *American Sociological Review,* 1957, *22,* 67–73.

Siller, J. Socioeconomic Status and Conceptual Thinking. *Journal of Abnormal and Social Psychology,* 1957, *55,* 365–371.

Terrel, G., Jr.; Durkin, K.; and Wiesley, M. Social Class and the Nature of the Incentive in Discrimination Learning. *Journal of Abnormal and Social Psychology,* 1959, *59,* 270–272.

Wylie, R. C. Children's Estimates of Their Schoolwork Ability as a Function of Sex, Race, and Socioeconomic Level. *Journal of Personality,* 1963, *31,* 203–224.

35

Linguistic Aspects of Culturally Disadvantaged Children

Richard B. Dever

Dr. Dever is Assistant Professor in the Department of Special Education at Indiana University. With a background in Classics and Applied Linguistics, Dr. Dever approaches the field of exceptionality with a perspective quite different from most research workers. As he commented, in personal communication, "many persons in mental retardation (and exceptionalities in general) have never seen 'language' as being defined in the context of 'a language.'" His role as translator is reflected in his articles and papers on mental retardation.

This present article, supported, in part, by NICHD Grant 03352 to the University of Wisconsin Center on Mental Retardation, and written especially for this book, should open up exciting new lines of thought to the reader as well as to clarify much of the confusion that currently exists in reported research on culturally disadvantaged children. The student concerned with educational programming in the field of exceptionality should find the article invaluable.

It is strongly recommended that this article and the one that follows, A Black English Translation of John 3:1–21 with Grammatical Annotations, *be read as a unit.*

In recent years a great deal has been written and said about culturally disadvantaged children and their language. Unfortunately, not a great deal of this has been relevant to the language spoken by the children. This is partly due to the definitions of language employed in the experimental paradigms and armchair psychologizing which attempts to deal with the problem. My intent, throughout this article, is to remain as much within the conception of "language" as being "a language" as is possible. In this framework there is much to be said which is relevant to the problems of the disadvantaged, and as will be seen, certain problems can be handled only by specifying that the topic of discussion is the English or some other language.

It is very important to realize that each language is a system unto itself. That is, each language is a set of abstractions (rules, if you will) which underly the actual behavior of speaking. Further, although each language is manifested in sound, we must recognize that the sounds of a language are not the language any more than the parts of a machine are the functioning device. This analogy is an important one and can be carried further: the interrelationships between the parts of a machine are analogous to the interrelationships between the sounds and groups of sounds in language. That is, just as a machine is not the machine until the parts are functionally related, a language is not the language if the system is absent. It is very useful to realize that just as the interrelationships between the parts of a steam engine cannot be judged in terms of the interrelationships between the parts of an internal combustion engine, the systems used by the disadvantaged cannot be judged in terms of Standard English. To do so is to ask the wrong questions, and the result, of course, is the wrong answers. The relevance of this will become clear in the discussion below.

A language is a tool of a society. It is the means which humans use to carry on the affairs of their society (Francis, 1958). In the United States today, the language which is used to carry on the affairs of the large, middle-class, economically advantaged society happens to be Standard English.

If language is society's tool, it follows, then, that the degree to which a person learns the language spoken by society places the upper limits on his ability to function within that society. It will become clear in this article that culturally disadvantaged children do not learn the standard dialect of English, or Middle-Class English, as it will be called in this article. Because they do not, they cannot function in the middle-class society at the level at which they would have been capable if they had learned Middle-Class English while they were growing up. Shaw said the same thing in *Pygmalion,* i.e., that Lisa Doolittle could not leave the gutter and open up a flower shop until after she had learned the standard dialect of England at the time. The problem is probably more complex than Shaw saw it to be; i.e., there are probably many sociolinguistic forces operating which have quite adverse linguistic and perceptual effects on certain groups of children. That is, by learning a language (and by extension, a culture) which is different from that of the middle classes, a child is likely to become oriented to a different perception and organization of what is important in the world (Bernstein, 1964). In addition, it is probable that certain "in-group" pressures are operating which would mitigate the learning of Middle-Class English (Labov, 1967a), making linguistic changes difficult for the disadvantaged.

It must be noted that it is difficult to use with precision the term, "culturally disadvantaged," because it has been used in so many contexts to refer to so many different groups of children. We can, however, set forth some of the boundaries of the term as it has been used. The label "culturally disadvantaged" refers to members of certain groups which are associated with the following demographic features: the lowest incomes, the lowest rates of occupational constancy, the largest families, the most crowded homes, the poorest prenatal care, the poorest nutrition, generally lowered mean measured intelligence scores, and very often an ethnic component which carries with it the notion of social discrimination. The term has been applied to both urban and rural blacks and whites, as well as to Mexican–Americans, Puerto Rican–Americans, American Indians, and a host of other, smaller, ethnic groups such as will be found in any large city, in poor rural areas, or among other groups such as the migrant workers. Finally, in addition to the objective indices mentioned above, there is a notion buried in the use of the term which gives a feeling of hopelessness. Persons who are culturally disadvantaged are generally felt to have little control over their lives, and to be preordained to a life of poverty.

Obviously there is no one-to-one relationship between any of these groups and the fact of cultural disadvantagement. Not all children who are culturally disadvantaged fit all the above categories, nor are all the children in the above demographic categories doomed to remain in the poverty class. In spite of the fact that the term has no real precision, it will be used throughout this article because, at present, there is no better term.

The major statement to be made in this article is that culturally disadvantaged children speak a language which is different from Middle-Class English. Because of this, they experience unnecessary problems when they enter a situation in which they are forced to function in the middle-class language. The point at which most of these children make contact with Middle-Class English comes at the time they enter the school and it is here that they experience the greatest amount of difficulty. For many children these difficulties need not exist in the degree to which they are found if the proper view is taken of the problem. That is, measures could be taken which at the least could mitigate the problem before it occurs.

The present review is broken down into two main subtopics, each of which is currently an issue of debate and research. They are (1) the problem of language learning among the disadvantaged, and (2) the problem of children who speak a language different from that used for instructional purposes. These areas have received a great deal of attention in recent years, and each will be taken up in turn. It will become clear from the discussion which follows that some problems which have been thought to be important in the past probably now have to be downgraded as to their relative importance.

LANGUAGE LEARNING AMONG THE DISADVANTAGED

It now seems that this is probably a pseudo-problem in that culturally disadvantaged children do learn a language, and they learn it well. However, so much time and energy has been spent on the subject that it is necessary to examine it here.

It has been regularly reported in the literature that culturally disadvantaged children are "deficient" in language, e.g., Deutsch and Associates (1967 *passim*), Hess and Shipman (1965), Hubbard and Zarates (1966–1967), Raph (1965), and others. Statements as to the character of this "deficit" vary markedly. Some reports have stated that culturally disadvantaged children have a more "restricted" language than do middle-class children, i.e., that they have fewer modifiers, they cannot use verb forms as well, and that their vocabulary is less-well developed (Deutsch et al., 1967, *passim*); others have been more categorical in stating that the deficit is such that disadvantaged children are prevented from conceptualizing clearly and verbalizing adequately (Raph, 1965). Such statements were supported by the regular finding that culturally disadvantaged children score lower on tests of measured intelligence than do middle-class children (Kennedy, Van de Reit and White, 1963; Heber, 1969). Since intelligence test scores are widely thought of as having a verbal component (and by extension, a language component) it was logical to postulate a language deficit in these children. The next step was to decide how it got there.

Children learn language from others in their environment. Although there is yet a great deal of work to do in this area, some research has appeared to be very relevant to the question of language learning among the disadvantaged. Brown and Bellugi (1964), for example, noted that three processes normally appear to be operating in the actual learning of a language.*

The first process is one of imitation with reduction by the child of the adult utterances in the environment. The young child seems to reduce adult utterances to a form which is much like that of a telegram, i.e., it utilizes the high-content, low-function words of the adult utterance. Thus,

---

* The first of these processes is open to criticism (Olson, 1970); the reader is referred to this reference for further information.

where an adult might say something like, "I see the big chair," the child might say, "See chair." This telegraphic language, as Brown and Bellugi have called it, can communicate a situation known to the adult and the child.

The second process is quite important here and appears to be the result of a valid observation. Again it involves imitation, but it is the imitation of the child's utterance, by the adult. That is, the adult repeats the child's utterance, but expands it slightly. The resulting utterance is a perfectly formed model sentence in the adult language which apparently has, as its purpose, the effect of saying to the child, "This is a way you could have said what you just said." Thus, where a child might say something like, "There doggie," the adult might come back with, "Yes, there is a doggie." This process is so regular that the adult was compared to a computer which is programmed to teach language to a child. Brown and Bellugi state that 30 percent of the utterances of the children of the gradate students and professionals in their study were expanded on by adults.

The third process is one of induction of the latent structure. Because of space restrictions, about the only thing we can say of this here is that the language, being a system, is generated by each speaker according to rules which are not readily apparent to casual observation. The child must learn these rules in order to become a speaker of the language, and he must do it in a very short period of time. Little by little, as the interactive processes are carried on, the child induces these rules and comes more and more to approximate the adult language (McNeil, 1966). Most authorities on the subject believe that this process is largely complete by the time a child begins school. This is not to say that the child has learned all that there is to know about a language by that time. On the contrary, after he begins school he has a large amount of vocabulary yet to learn, and he must learn how to read and write. But the basic learning of the language system normally is complete by the time the child begins school.

Because of the differential in scores on tests of measured intelligence, it was natural to look for something in the disadvantaged child's environment which would mitigate his learning of a language. Results in the literature on the black inner-city child have indicated that he does not interact with adults anywhere near to the degree found by Brown and Bellugi (e.g., Hess and Shipman, 1965; Milner, 1951; and many others). It should be noted here that, to my knowledge, this lack of adult–child interaction has not been found for groups other than the black inner-city child, and my comments will have to be restricted accordingly.

This lack of interaction would make it appear that the black inner-city child ought to have a linguistic deficit, and a great deal of research time and effort has been devoted to discovering what this deficit is like. As would be expected, the deficit has been found.

John and Goldstein (1964) noticed that black inner-city children have more difficulty responding to Peabody Picture Vocabulary Test stimuli which represented action words (i.e., verbs ending in *-ing*) than they did to test stimuli representing stable objects (i.e., nouns). They reasoned that this phenomenon was due to the lack of interaction between adults and children in these environments. That is, John and Goldstein hypothesized that because *-ing*-type words represent transient actions, linguistic stabilization of these words requires interaction with mature speakers of the language. This would not be true for nouns since the objects represented by nouns are stable in themselves already, and the labels for them would be easily learned just from the child's being in an environment where they are used.

Other research has characterized the deficit as being one of poor syntactical organization, with fewer of the elaborative features found in the nondisadvantaged child's language (e.g., modifiers, qualifiers, etc.) (Deutsch et al., 1967 *passim;* Hess & Shipman, 1965).

Are inner-city children really deficient in language? At present, this is a topic of much discussion and research. Before accepting the hypothesis that they are, indeed, deficient, the possibility would be entertained that they speak what is, in fact, a different language.

Baratz and Povich (mimeo) appear to have operated within this framework in a study of the grammatical complexity of black inner-city children. They analyzed samples of black children's language and then scaled their data on Lee's Developmental Sentence Types model, which classifies deep structure rules as to their level of complexity. They then compared their results to those obtained by Menyuk (1963b) for white middle-class children. The results of this study indicated that not only was the black child not deficient in language, but also that he had a highly developed linguistic system. It was so highly developed, in fact, that the investigators were unable to find any differences in level of deep-structure complexity between their sample and the data from the white children. They did find in preparing their data, however, that the black children used a different language system from that of their middle-class counterparts. It should be noted that Lee's Developmental Sentence Types model does not allow the latter interpretation to be made simply from its use, and that Baratz and Povich do not state how they arrived at their conclusion. However, the fact that Baratz and Povich were unable to find a deficit is worthy of note, and their study should alert us to the possibility that the question has not been closed.

Garvey and McFarlane (1968) report an experiment which yields a similar interpretation. They used a test similar to Menyuk's (1963a) test, in which lower-class white and black children were asked to repeat sentences which contained critical grammatical structures in Standard English. The idea behind this test is that a child will be able to repeat only those sentences for which he has rules in his own language. If the grammatical structure differs from a functional equivalent in his own language, he will either change the sentence to conform to his own rule system, or (less frequently) will simply fail to repeat it. The results of this study indicated that, while black inner-city children were not able to repeat some of the sentences as well as were the white children, they were better able to repeat other sentences. This, too, could be interpreted as meaning that there were two different linguistic systems in use by the two groups. One of these systems, that used by the whites, was capable of processing certain structures easily, while the other system, that used by the blacks, was capable of processing other structures easily.

Other evidence that the black child may not be deficient in language at the time he starts school comes from studies of the syntagmatic–paradigmatic shift (Brown and Berko, 1960). When a young child is presented with a stimulus word and is asked to say the first word which comes to mind, he will respond syntagmatically, i.e., he will respond as if the word he says is the next word in a sentence. For example, if the very young child is presented with the stimulus *big*, he might respond *chair*. After a certain age, however (which varies with the form class of the stimulus), the child will respond with a word which is in the same form class as is that of the stimulus. That is, at a later time in life, when presented with the stimulus *big*, a child might respond *little*. This is paradigmatic response, and the age at which the shift takes place has been taken as an index of linguistic maturity. Doris Entwisle has done a great deal of work with this phenomenon over the past few years, and much of her work has relevance to the present discussion. In a summary of her work, Entwisle (mimeo) says she has found young slum children, both black and white, to be superior to young suburban white children in the number of paradigmatic responses which they give to the same stimuli. This superiority does not last very long, however, because by the third grade the suburban children catch up and surpass the slum children. Further, both groups of whites respond similarly to the stimuli, but the black children's responses are different. That is, not only are the responses of the blacks more varied than are those of the whites (this is especially true for the stimuli which are most frequently used words in the language), they are different words altogether. Entwisle interprets this as being an indication that different semantic systems are in use by white and black children. In the light of the other research cited above, this would appear to be a sound interpretation. This difference in semantic systems is greatest at the youngest ages studied, and begins to wash out as the children progress through the school years. This may be an indication that the schools may be bringing the two semantic systems closer together.

What can be said concerning the linguistic deficit found in previous research? It is quite possible that most of the research which finds deficits in "the language of disadvantaged children" has been biased. That is, the children being tested speak a language which is different (at least in part) from the language spoken by the experimenters; if the children were tested on their ability to handle the experimenter's dialect, however, a deficit had to be found. An analogy will help make this point clear. If we were to give a test to Swedish and American children on their ability to use Swedish, we would probably find the American children to be deficient in language. Our statements would, however, have to be qualified by saying that the American children are deficient in Swedish. No such qualifications have appeared in the literature dealing with disadvantaged children, and while the analogy cannot be considered to be an exact parallel, there is enough substance in it to make it an important comparison.

Another important criticism is made by the sociolinguists. The methods of data gathering may not have been appropriate in the experiments which have found linguistic deficits (Labov, 1967a). That is, many of the studies have been done in the inner city where black children live in an adult-dominated society. They quickly learn to be quiet or to talk very little in the presence of adults, and this could well be the reason for finding deficits in their language. That is, the white adult goes into the inner city, talks to a black child for a short time in an experimental situation, and then leaves. It is small wonder that the black child does not "unbend" in that little time. Labov (1967a) and other sociolinguists have found that more sophisticated techniques of data elicitation have demonstrated that the black child not only has a well-developed language, but a very rich verbal culture. To be sure, language in the ghetto is used for different purposes than it is in the middle-class white society. That is, where the middle-class white is very much interested in the transmission of information, the inner-city black is interested in the manipulation of persons (Labov, 1967a; see also Bernstein, 1964, for a similar discussion of different uses of language by middle-class and "working-class" persons in England). Each uses language to accomplish these purposes and, consequently, at least the semantic structure of each system could be expected to be different.

Perhaps the only safe generalization we can make on the basis of the research cited thus far is that if there is any deficit in the language of black culturally disadvantaged children, it is a deficiency in the use of Middle-Class English. This is quite different from saying that they are deficient in language. Note also that I am not necessarily saying that disadvantaged children do not *become* deficient in certain aspects of language after they start school, because this could, indeed, be the case. It was stated above that there is much language learning which takes place after starting school; i.e., children must learn a great deal of vocabulary, and they must learn to read and write. Much of the other learning which takes place in school is predicated on the early establishment of literacy. It is difficult to see how literacy can be established easily in a language which is both grammatically and semantically different from the one which the child speaks. If literacy does not become established early, however, the child's linguistic and conceptual growth could well be slower than normal, which would have the effect of making the child become deficient.

Before going on, a note on the term "culturally disadvantaged" is required again. Much of the research on the language of the culturally disadvantaged child has been done on inner-city black children. Although this is a perfectly legitimate area of research, the conclusions which will be drawn from such research must be limited to the groups studied. The reader should bear this in mind when reading statements on "the language of the disadvantaged," which seem to refer to all disadvantaged children. These statements appear all too often in the literature and can cause much harm. This is especially true when the statements are based on erroneous assumptions, e.g., that it is legitimate to compare black and white children's use of Middle-Class English without qualification.

THE CHILD WHO SPEAKS ANOTHER LANGUAGE

In this country today there are a large number of children who enter school speaking a language which is not the same language as that used for instructional purposes in the school. In this category are found Mexican–American, Puerto Rican–American, American Indian, and inner-city black children, as well as many other smaller groups of children from various ethnic backgrounds. In spite of the fact that few of these children receive much in the way of formal instruction in speaking English, they are usually expected to function in English from the day they begin school. That is, all instruction is carried out in English. It should be noted that a substantial minority do receive instruction in English. This is true, for example, of many American Indian children and the Puerto Rican children who live in Spanish Harlem. Even this instruction, however, is seldom relevant to the problems faced by the children. In addition, as is the case for the children who get no instruction in English, these children are usually expected to function in English while doing work in all other subjects from the first day in school. This happens in spite of the fact that it may take several years to become proficient enough in the language to profit fully from instruction in it (Committee on Labor and Public Welfare, 1967; Ohannessian, 1967).

If there is only one child who speaks a foreign language in a school, the problem is not a great one. The child will usually learn to speak English in a very short period of time because he must. For such a child, there is plenty of opportunity for linguistic interaction with the children on the playground and in the home neighborhood. When there is no other way to communicate, children tend to pick up a language very rapidly. The real problem arises when a substantial percentage of children in the school speak a foreign language. The problems generated in such a situation are well documented in various testimonies given before the U.S. Senate (Committee on Labor and Public Welfare, 1967). Some of these problems will be presented here. Children in such a situation are likely to spend their free time with their cultural and ethnic peers, not with those children who speak (what is to them) a foreign language. Many of these children are seen by the English-speaking children, and too often the staff of the school, as objects of discrimination, and the result is that there is little opportunity for language learning to take place outside the classroom. What language instruction they do receive is likely to be poorly done, with no regard to the actual needs of the situation. A negative atmosphere often prevails toward the children's native language on the part of the school personnel, and it is not unusual to see punishments meted out for speaking the native language on school property.

The combination of lack of instruction in English, lack of opportunity to learn it informally, and negative reactions of persons in power toward the native tongue has powerful effects on the children. These effects are in the areas of their self-images, their attitudes toward the learning situation, and their linguistic and conceptual development.

Children in situations such as this often grow up speaking a language which is neither English nor the native language, but a polyglot. For example, in the Southwest region of the United States, the dialect called Tex-Mex is common; it is neither English nor Spanish, but a combination used by lower-class Mexican–Americans. Again, the negative self-images of such children are well documented, and whole groups of children grow up believing that they are incompetent and worthless. And, by the time these children obtain a working knowledge of English (which, surprisingly, does occur in a fair number of children), they usually have fallen far behind their English-speaking peers in school-obtained knowledge.

The situation has lately begun to change; i.e., attempts are now being made to instruct foreign-language-speaking children in English. This instruction is taking many forms. For example, some school systems provide all instruction to all children in both English and the foreign language. In this way all the children, both English-speaking and foreign-speaking, grow up as bilinguals. This is the case in Miami, for example, where instruction of all children is being carried on in both English and Spanish in some of the schools which have large Cuban immigrant populations. In spite of attempts such as this, however, there are still too many areas in which no progress is being made.

There is a very high incidence of retardation among the groups of children who come to school speaking another language. Jensen (1961) has done some work which indicates that this retardation may, in fact, be part and parcel of the linguistic factor. Jensen presented both mildly retarded and normal English- and Spanish-speaking children with recall and serial learning tasks. In these tasks the children were required to name 12 common objects with any name they chose, and then to recall the objects after they were removed from sight. The serial task which followed was an anticipation task in which the child was required to name the same objects before they were uncovered in a row before him. Jensen found a clear-cut difference between the low-IQ and normal Anglo-American children; i.e., the low-IQ Anglos made many more errors than the high-IQ Anglos. No such difference appeared between the low-IQ and normal Mexican–American children; in fact, in the recall task, low-IQ Mexican–American children learned as fast as normal Anglo-American children, although both groups of Mexican children did less well than the normal Anglo children in the serial anticipation task. These results held up under replication.

Complementary results have been obtained by Stafford (1966) in a study involving Navaho- and English-speaking Navaho boys. Stafford presented his subjects with a concept-learning task in which they were supposed to learn which buttons in a display to press upon presentation of certain stimuli. Stafford found that the English-speaking Navaho boys were able to solve more problems of a more complex nature than were the Navaho-speaking boys. A major criticism of Stafford's design lies in the fact that teacher judgments were used to equate the two groups on intellectual ability. However, if these results could be found to withstand a more rigorous experimental paradigm, it would appear from these and other data (e.g., Jensen, 1961) that the linguistic and cultural background of children deeply affects their ability to preform certain tasks. It may well be that, as Jensen (1968) points out, low-IQ foreign-speaking children such as those mentioned above are "environmentally depressed," and that the cultural retardation so often observed in these groups would disappear under more fortuitous circumstances.*

Since I chose to place black inner-city children among the groups of children who speak another language, some justification is required. There are linguists who have stated, on the basis of their research, that the language spoken by black children is different enough from Middle-Class English to be called another language (e.g., Loflin and Sobin, 1968).

---

* In fact, Jensen's term "environmental depression," rather than "cultural deprivation" or "cultural disadvantagement," would have found use in the present article if it were not for the fact that Jensen defined it in another context.

Other linguists refuse to go this far, but all who are interested in Black English agree that there are enough differences between the two systems to cause major problems when the child begins school. Perhaps the problems of classification were solved by Stewart (1964), who said that black children speak a "quasi-foreign" language. That is, while there are many similarities between the two systems, there are also many differences, and these differences are enough to place these children in a position which is similar to children who do, in fact, speak another language.

Creole specialists, such as Stewart (1967, 1968) and Dillard (1967), have concluded that Black English is a derivation of a creolized form of the West African languages spoken by blacks when they were first brought to this country as slaves many years ago. Whether this is true, or whether it is simply a form of regionalized Southern dialects which is spoken by poor blacks and poor whites alike (Labov, 1965), is of little consequence to the present discussion. The important point is that speaking Black English creates a problem for the black child when he enters the white-oriented middle-class school.

In addition to the research presented in the previous section, it is now possible to present examples of the differences between Black and Middle-Class English which have been discovered by sociolinguists in the past few years. Many more examples can be found in the publications cited in this paper as well as in Wolfram and Fasold (mimeo) and others. It is clear that Black English is anything but deficient. In fact, in many ways it is more complex than the middle-class language. For example, in Black English there are five past-time distinctions, whereas there are only three in the middle-class dialect (Fasold, 1968). It is impossible to convey, without circumlocution, the sense of the Black English sentence "I been known that" using Middle-Class English. The speaker of Middle-Class English would have to say something like "I knew that so long ago that there is hardly any sense in talking about it." Black English has many other contrasts that are impossible in Middle-Class English. For example, there is a contrast between the two Black English sentences, "He at home," and "He be at home" (Fasold, mimeo). The first one means that he is at home now, and the second one means that he is at home, intermittently. This distinction must be made by circumlocution in Middle-Class English.

The differences between Black English and Middle-Class English are not found just in syntax, as the above examples might indicate. There are differences in the phonological systems which can cause a great deal of trouble in the school. Some phonological differences cause Black English to contain a great many homophones that Middle-Class English does not contain (Labov, 1967b). For example, *Ruth* and *roof* are homophonous; as are *poor, poke,* and *Pope;* and *Carol* and *Cal.* These phonological differences, although they might pose reading problems, are relatively minor ones. There are others which could have a greater effect in that they interact with the grammar of English. In standard English certain simplifications are possible, e.g., *can't* from *cannot*. Many more simplifications are not only possible but are mandatory in Black English, so that the following all became homophonous: *Paris, pass, passed, past;* and *miss, missed,* and *mist.* Note that in both of these examples (many others could be given) there are words which are inflected for past tense. In these words the past inflection exists for the speaker of Black English, but it is not expressed overtly (Labov, 1967b). The same phenomenon has been noted, for example, in the speaker of the Boston dialect, who "hears" the /r/ which is not overtly expressed in an utterance such as "Pahk the cah" (where a Midwesterner would say "Park the car").

In spite of the simplifications which had to be made here for space reasons, the point has been made. The black child comes to school speaking a language which is different, at least in part, from the language spoken by the white middle-class child. These differences are enough to have deep pedagogical implications. Like any child who speaks another language, the black child can be expected to misunderstand and to be misunderstood by his teachers. In learning to read, the fact that he speaks a language which is different from that used by his teachers and in his books can only be a barrier to literacy; and since literacy is a prerequisite to most of the other learning which occurs in the school, he probably will be left behind his middle-class peers in the amount of learning which he accomplishes. It is surprising that many such children learn as much as they do.

The fact that teachers are just as ignorant of the child's language as he is of theirs (Shuy, Wolfram, & Riley, 1967) does not help matters. This "reciprocal ignorance," as Labov (1967b) has called it, not only results in poor communication, but also in an inability to bridge the gap between the two systems so that effective instruction can take place. Too much of the teacher's time tends to be concentrated in attempts to eradicate socially stigmatized forms (Shuy, Wolfram, & Riley, 1967) when it could more profitably be spent in teaching the instructional language. Some attempts are now being made to teach black children the language which is used in the schools and these attempts bear close watching. Unfortunately, many of the persons involved in attempts to teach Middle-Class English to other groups of non-English speakers (such as American Indian children) do not really have a good idea either of the methods or of what must be taught and what is optional or unnecessary (Ohannessian, 1967). The same is likely to be true for persons teaching English to black children.

One reason for this is that even the interested and informed teacher needs a lot of help from linguists. There are a number of linguists today who are interested in the problems of disadvantaged children. Sometimes their interest pays off for the educator through an analysis of the contrasts between the language spoken and the target language. Such contrastive analyses can predict instructional trouble spots and suggest areas of instructional concentration before the instruction begins. Examples of contrastive analyses are to be found in most of the sociolinguistic references cited above, as well as in Saville (mimeo), Williams (1970), and others.

It should be clear, by now, that the problems are great and that easy solutions are probably not to be had. Now that the air is being cleared as to the "language deficit" of culturally disadvantaged children (and the case is being set forth in many different quarters at present), perhaps a more realistic view of the instructional task will be possible. That is, to a much lesser degree than was previously thought, disadvantaged children need developmental language instruction. What they do need, is *second* language instruction. That is, English is, to varying degrees, a second language for many disadvantaged children, and must be taught as such. This is not a new conclusion, i.e., Stewart made this statement years ago (Stewart, 1964). There are a number of programs in progress at present which are attempting to do this. Some are quite promising, such as the programs mentioned above which are attempting to make all children in the school bilingual, but these programs require completely bilingual teachers and willing communities, both of which could prove difficult to find. Other programs are trying to teach Middle-Class English to preschool disadvantaged children, e.g., the Bereiter and Engleman program (Osborn, mimeo). Preliminary results on this attempt are encouraging, and close attention is being paid to the project. Still another promising approach is one in which disadvantaged children are being taught to function in the middle-class culture from the time they are under 6 months of age (Heber, Dever, & Conry, 1968). Unfortunately, this is a very expensive approach.

In spite of the promise inherent in many of these approaches, we should recognize the possibility that it might prove very difficult to teach Middle-Class English to disadvantaged children. There are powerful forces operating in their lives which are likely to mitigate even the best-informed teaching. One of them is the fact of discrimination, which often eliminates the opportunity to interact linguistically with speakers of Middle-Class English outside the classroom; another is peer pressure against the target language (Labov, 1967a); still a third is learning which took place before the child comes to school (Ohannessian, 1967). There are many other factors, all of which stand in the way of effective teaching.

In spite of the difficulties, an attempt must be made to teach Middle-Class English to disadvantaged children. After all, it is the economically advantageous language of the country, and the children will have to know it if they should ever want to leave the ghettos and the reservations and go into the middle-class culture. We can expect to find great pressures against such teaching, both from within and without. The children cannot be expected to leave their lives, their families, and their cultures behind them. At the same time, however, the nation is under pressure to relieve the crushing burden of poverty. To say that there will be easy answers is to misunderstand the scope of the problem.

There are many unanswered questions, all of which will have to be answered. For example, one burning question concerns the testing of the use of Middle-Class English. Very little work has been done in this area, and there certainly are not enough linguists to go around for the purpose of making contrastive analyses for all disadvantaged children. Yet, unless a teacher knows what must be taught to her children and what they already know, she is likely not to be as effective as she could be. Another set of questions concerns the motivational aspects of language learning. That is, we must find out how to get disadvantaged children to want to learn the economically advantageous language. Still a third area of needed research concerns methods. Are the methods used in teaching English to speakers of other languages adequate for use with disadvantaged children, or do they need a great deal of modification? At what age should Middle-Class English be taught? What can be done in the way of materials development?

These questions are simply suggestive. There are a large number of questions yet to be answered, all of which arise from the conclusion that the language of disadvantaged children is dissimilar to the language used by the school. All of these questions boil down to the major question of how such differences interfere with the learning which is supposed to take place in school, and how the interference can be overcome by the school. With the proper view of the problem, it is unnecessary, in my view, to delay the seeking of the answers any longer.

SUMMARY

The present article dealt with the language of culturally disadvantaged children in the same context that a linguist would deal with it. That is, children learn a language while they are growing up. Reviewing the literature in this framework gives rise to the conclusion that, if there is any deficit in the language of disadvantaged children, it is a deficit in the knowledge of Middle-Class English, the language spoken in the schools and by the economically advantaged population of the United States. It follows, then, that the option of being able to become a part of the middle-class society is closed off to such children until the time when they learn to speak Middle-Class English. The pedagogical implications from this are that Middle-Class English must be taught as a second language to disadvantaged children.

References

Baratz, J., & Povich, E. Grammatical constructions in the language of the Negro preschool child. Washington, D.C.: Center for Applied Linguistics. (mimeograph)

Bernstein, B. Elaborated and restricted codes: Their social origins and some consequences. *Amer. Anthropologist,* 1964, *66* (6, part 2), 55–69.

Brown, R., & Bellugi, U. Three processes in the child's acquisition of syntax. *Harvard educ. Rev.,* 1964, *34,* 133–151.

Brown, R., & Berko, J. Word association and the acquisition of grammar. *Child Develpm.,* 1960, *31,* 1–14.

Committee on Labor and Public Welfare. *Hearings before the Special Subcommittee on Bilingual Education of the Committee on Labor and Public Welfare, United States Senate,* S.428. Washington, D.C.: U.S. Government Printing Office, 1967.

Deutsch, M., & associates. *The disadvantaged child: Selected papers of Martin Deutsch and associates.* New York: Basic Books, 1967.

Dillard, J. L. Negro children's dialect in the inner city. *Florida FL Reporter,* 1967, *5* (4).

Entwisle, D. R. Semantic systems of children. In F. Williams (Ed.), *Language and poverty: Perspectives on a theme.* Chicago: Markham (pre-publication mimeo).

Fasold, R. Isn't English the first language, too? Paper presented at the Annual Conference of the National Council of Teachers of English, Milwaukee, November 29, 1968.

Fasold, R. Tense and the form 'be' in Black English. Washington, D.C.: Center for Applied Linguistics. (mimeograph)

Francis, W. N. *The structure of American English.* New York: Ronald Press, 1958.

Garvey, C., & McFarlane, P. *A preliminary study of standard English speech patterns in the Baltimore City Public Schools.* Baltimore: The Johns Hopkins University Center for the Study of Social Organization of Schools, 1968.

Heber, R. *Epidemiology.* Madison, Wis.: Rehabilitation Research and Training Center in Mental Retardation Monograph No. 1, 1969.

Heber, R., Dever, R., & Conry, J. The influence of environmental and genetic variables on intellectual development. In H. J. Prehm, C. A. Hamerlynch, & J. E. Crosson (Eds.), *Behavioral research in mental retardation.* Eugene, Ore.: University of Oregon Press, 1968, pp. 1–23.

Hess, R. D., & Shipman, J. C. Early experience and the socialization of cognitive modes in children. *Child Develpm.,* 1965, *36,* 869–886.

Hubbard, J., & Zarates, L. An exploratory study of oral language development among culturally different children. Section IV: *Final report on Head Start evaluation and research:* 1966–67, Austin, Texas: Child Development Evaluation and Research Center, University of Texas, 1967.

Jensen, A. R. Learning abilities in Mexican-American and Anglo-American children. *Calif. J. educ. Res.,* 1961, *12,* 147–159.

Jensen, A. R. Learning ability, intelligence, and educability. In V. L. Allen (Ed.), *Psychological factors in poverty.* New York: Free Press, 1968.

John, V. P., & Goldstein, L. S. The social context of language acquisition. *Merrill-Palmer Quart.,* 1964, *4,* 265–275.

Kennedy, W., Van de Reit, V., & White, J. A normative sample of intelligence and achievement of Negro elementary school children in the Southeastern United States. *Monogr. Soc. Res. child Develpm.,* 1963, *28* (6).

Labov, W. Linguistic research on non-standard English of Negro children. In A. Dore (Ed.), *Problems and practices in the New York City Public Schools.* New York: New York Society for the Experimental Study of Education, 1965, pp. 110–117.

Labov, W. The non-standard Negro vernacular: some practical suggestions. In *Position papers from language education for the disadvantaged.* Report No. 3 of the NDEA National Institute for Advanced Study in Teaching Disadvantaged Youth, June 1967, pp. 4–7. (a)

Labov, W. Some sources of reading problems for Negro speakers of non-standard English. In A. Fraser (Ed.), *New directions in elementary English.* Champaign, Ill.: National Council of Teachers of English, 1967, pp. 140–167. (b)

Loflin, M., & Sobin, N. Transformational rules and competing generalizations. Paper presented at the Annual Conference of the National Council of Teachers of English, Milwaukee, Wis., November 29, 1968.

McNeil, D. Developmental psycholinguistics. In F. Smith & G. A. Miller (Eds.), *The genesis of language.* Cambridge: M.I.T. Press, 1966, pp. 15–84.

Menyuk, P. A preliminary evaluation of grammatical capacity in children. *J. verb. Learn. verb. Behav.,* 1963, *2,* 429–439. (a)

Menyuk, P. Syntactic structures in the language of children. *Child Develpm.,* 1963, *34,* 407–422. (b)

Milner, E. A study of the relationship between reading readiness in grade one school children and patterns of parent-child interaction. *Child Develpm.,* 1951, *22,* 95–112.

Ohannessian, S. *The study of the problems of teaching English to American Indians.* Washington, D.C.: Center for Applied Linguistics, 1967.

Olson, D. R. Language acquisition and cognitive development. In H. C. Haywood (Ed.), *Social-cultural aspects of mental retardation.* New York: Appleton-Century-Crofts, 1970.

Osborn, J. Teaching a teaching language to disadvantaged children. University of Illinois: Institute for Research on Exceptional Children. (mimeograph)

Raph, J. B. Language development in socially disadvantaged children. *Rev. educ. Res.,* 1965, *35,* 389–400.

Saville, M. Language characteristics of the disadvantaged. In T. Horn (Ed.), *Reading for the disadvantaged: Problems of linguistically different learners.* New York: Harcourt, Brace & World. (pre-publication mimeograph)

Shuy, R., Wolfram, W., & Riley, W. *Linguistic correlates of social stratification in Detroit speech.* Final Report, *CRP #6-1347,* USOE, 1967.

Stafford, K. Cognition and language: Cognition and problem-solving as affected by knowledge of English and Navaho. *Lang. & Speech,* 1966, *9,* 63–67.

Stewart, W. A. Foreign language teaching methods in quasi-foreign language situations. In W. A. Stewart (Ed.), *Non-standard speech and the teaching of*

English. Washington, D.C.: Center for Applied Linguistics, 1964, pp. 1–15.

Stewart, W. A. Sociolinguistic factors in the history of American Negro dialects. *Florida FL Reporter,* 1967, *5* (2).

Stewart, W. A. Continuity and change in American Negro dialects. *Florida FL Reporter,* 1968, *6* (1).

Williams, F. *Language and poverty: Perspectives on a theme.* Chicago: Markham, 1970.

Wolfram, W., & Fasold, R. A Black English translation of John 3:1-21; with grammatical annotations. *The Bible Translator.* (pre-publication mimeograph)

36

A Black English Translation of John 3:1-21 with Grammatical Annotations

Walter A. Wolfram and Ralph W. Fasold

Dr. Wolfram and Dr. Fasold are both Research Associates, Sociolinguistics Program Center for Applied Linguistics, in Washington, D.C.

Dr. Wolfram has authored two books, one on the Detroit Negro speech following two years of field research, and the other on field techniques in studying an urban language. In addition, he has published a number of articles dealing chiefly with Black English.

Dr. Fasold has also been actively researching and writing, having seven articles published within the past two years on Negro speech.

The reader will note that this article departs from the format set up for this book, but it is such an excellent sequel to Dr. Dever's preceding article that the editors feel its inclusion is justified. To do effective research on the culturally disadvantaged it seems imperative that the investigator can understand, accept, and work within the language system of the group being studied. Some of the problems and difficulties are highlighted in these two interesting and provocative articles.

Within the last half century the populations of many urban areas in the United States have been drastically restructured. Extensive in-migration

FROM *The Bible Translator*, April 1969. Reprinted by permission of United Bible Societies, London.

by Southern Negroes has resulted in the growth of many large isolated Negro communities. The segregated rural populations of the South have thus become the isolated Negro communities of our metropolitan areas. Although sociologists, psychologists, and anthropologists have pointed out the cultural gap that exists between the so-called ghetto culture and the culture of mainstream middle class American society, it has been only recently that the linguistic consequences of this cultural difference have been examined. Previously, the speech behavior of many lower socio-economic class Negroes was simply considered on a par with that of lower socio-economic white citizens who spoke a variety of nonstandard English. Even some dialectologists simply assumed that the speech of the uneducated Negro was no different from that of the uneducated Southern white. Recent descriptive and sociolinguistic studies of the variety of English spoken by urban ghetto dwellers (i.e., Black English [1]), however, have indicated that there are important systematic differences between Black English and Standard English.

At this point, one may ask why the speech behavior found in these isolated Negro communities should differ significantly from the nonstandard variety of English spoken by the lower socio-economic class white. In Northern urban areas, one source of difference can be found in the influence that Southern dialects have on these speech communities. But even in the rural South the Black English is characteristically different from the speech of the lower socio-economic class white, and one must ask why. For an explanation, one need only look at the distinct history of the Negro in American life, both in terms of his original immigration and his subsequent segregation. Recently, creole specialists have been particularly occupied with pointing out the historical derivation of Black English, tracing its origin to a rather widespread creole spoken in the Caribbean area. Creolist William A. Stewart notes:

> 'Of those Africans who fell victim to the Atlantic slave trade and were brought to the New World, many found it necessary to learn some kind of English. With very few exceptions, the form of English they acquired was a pidginized one, and this kind of English became so well established as the principal medium of communication between Negro slaves in the British colonies that it was passed on as a

[1] 'Black English' is appropriate as a label for the dialect of lower socio-economic class Negroes for at least three reasons. First, there is a precedent for designating dialects with color names (Black Bobo, Red Tai, White Russian). In the second place, the current use of the term 'black' in throwing off pejorative stereotypes of Negro life matches our efforts to overcome the stereotype that this dialect is simply bad English. Finally, the name 'Black English' avoids the negative connotations of terms which include words like 'dialect,' 'substandard' and even 'nonstandard.'

creole language to succeeding generations of the New World Negroes, for whom it was their native tongue.'[2]

Present day Negro dialect, according to Stewart, has resulted from a process which he labels 'de-creolization.' That is, some of the original features characterizing the creole variety of English spoken by the early Negro slaves were lost through a gradual merging of the creole with the British-derived dialects with which they came in contact. The lexical inventory of this language variety became, for all practical purposes, identical with English (a process called 'relexification' by Stewart). Due to the persistence of segregation, however, the process of de-creolization was neither instantaneous nor complete. Thus, the nonstandard speech of present day Negroes still exhibits structural traces of a creole predecessor.

Present research by linguists has focused on Black English both as a system in itself and as a variety of English which systematically differs from Standard English. Some of the differences between Standard English and Black English, though seemingly small, have important consequences for the communication of a message. Furthermore, many of the systematic differences between Standard English and Black English have been overlooked by psychologists, sociologists, and educators, who simply dismiss Black English as an inaccurate and unworthy approximation of Standard English. To illustrate this point, we may briefly cite the Black English use of the form *be* as a finite verb, in a sentence such as *He be at work*. This particular use of *be,* a well-know stereotyped characteristic of Black English, has been dismissed as simply an inaccurate attempt by the lower socio-economic class Negro to approximate the Standard English speech norm. But such is clearly not the case. A study of the grammatical and semantic function of this construction employing the descriptive technique of modern linguistic theory reveals that one function of 'finite *be*' has an 'habitual' or 'iterative' meaning for the Black English speaker. There is no equivalent category in Standard English and such a meaning can only be conveyed by a circumlocution (e.g., *He is at work all the time*). Thus, we see a clear-cut difference between the two grammatical systems. As will be seen in the annotated translation, there are a number of consequential systematic differences between Black English and Standard English.

Now let us consider the implication of the above discussion for the translation of portions of Scripture into Black English. We observe clearcut differences between the grammatical system of Black English and Standard English. The normal processes which account for dialect differences have been augmented by a creole substratum. Can one translation of the Bible using a 'simplified' or 'basic' English grammar and vocabu-

[2] William A. Stewart, 'Sociolinguistic Factors in the History of American Negro Dialects.' *The Florida FL Reporter,* Vol. 5, No. 2 (1967), p. 22.

lary be considered adequate for the uneducated Negro as well as the white? Considering the grammatical differences which exist between the two varieties of English we would have to answer in the negative. Certainly, some lower socio-economic class speakers read these translations and with some apparent understanding. We certainly would not argue that the Black English speaker is going to understand about as much of an English translation as a monolingual Hindi speaker reading an English translation. But we must raise the question, do we want a translation which will require a considerable amount of inter-dialectal 're-translation' with inevitable information loss (and some of it crucial) or do we want a translation which sounds indigenous to the people reading it? Do we want a translation which makes God sound like a white middle class American or do we want a translation which makes God's message sound appropriate for the ghetto?

Although the translation is linguistically justifiable, there remain a number of sociological factors which must be taken into account in connection with its use. The first has to do with orthography. As the reader can see, we have opted for standard orthography and conventional spelling. This is clearly preferable when the complete setting, including other printed material, official education, etc., is examined. But a linguistic question arises concerning the differences in the phonologies of Black English and Standard English. If these differences are extensive, might not the conventional spelling be so inconsistent with the phonology that a serious reading problem would result?

If the ideal alphabetic writing system is considered to be a phonemic one, and if the value of an alphabet is measured by its departure from the principle of one symbol for one phoneme, then it must be concluded that standard orthography and conventional spelling are considerably less adequate for Black English than for Standard English. For example, words which end in /θ/ in Standard English (e.g., /tuθ/ 'tooth,' /brɛθ/ 'breath') typically end in /f/ in Black English (e.g., /tuf/ 'tooth,' /brɛf/ 'breath'). Yet /f/ and /θ/ are phonemically distinct because of such minimal pairs as 'fought' /fɔt/ and 'thought' /θɔt/. As a result, while the correct spelling for 'with' in Standard English according to the phonemic principle is *with,* the correct Black English spelling by the same principle would be *wif.* Extra-linguistic factors, however, force us to go against our linguistic better judgment (if we accept the phonemic spelling principle), opt for conventional spelling, and be stuck with spelling anomalies.

But there is considerable evidence that the ideal spelling system is not one that complies with the phonemic principle. Alphabetic symbols, in an alternative view, woul nodt match phonemes, but phonological units at a more abstract level.[3] In the case of word-final /f/ in Black En-

[3] This is argued from the point of view of generative phonology in **Noam Chomsky and Morris Halle,** *The Sound Pattern of English* (New York:

glish, it can be shown that the instances of /f/ which correspond to /θ/ in Standard English are distinct from those which do not. In rapid speech, the /f/ which matches Standard /θ/ may become /t/, while the /f/ which matches Standard /f/ may not. As a result, while:

/gɛt ɔf ma bayk/ 'Get off my bike!'
/kəm bæk wɪf ma bayk/ 'Come back with my bike!'
/kəm bæk wɪf ma bayk/ 'Come back with my bike!'

are all possible in Black English,

* /gɛt ɔt ma bayk/

is not possible for 'Get off my bike!' Although /θ/ generally does not occur at the end of a word, *th* is an appropriate spelling for word-final /f/ which alternates with /t/. A number of other apparent phonemic differences between the two dialects investigated by the authors are analyzable in the same way. Conventional spelling, then, in standard orthography seems justifiable not only sociologically, but linguistically as well.

A second problem in connection with the use of the proposed translation is one of applicability. There are many young people who are poor Negro ghetto residents and potentially an audience for this translation, but have learned Standard English regardless of their background. For these people, the Black English translation would scarcely be more applicable than it would be to any other speaker of Standard English. This problem is easily overcome by sensitive rather than indiscriminate use of the translation by those involved in ghetto ministry.

A third problem is a more serious one. The degree to which the translation would be acceptable, even to *bona fide* Black English speakers is an unanswered question. Sociolinguistic research has shown that speakers who use socially stigmatized speech forms sometimes have the same low opinion of such forms as do speakers who do not use them. A possible result of this is that although the Black English translation might be clearer and more natural to some, it may not be acceptable because of the presence of these stigmatized forms.[4] This question is an empirical one and the authors plan to test acceptability in the near future. There are two factors which may tend to neutralize rejection, however. Most groups involved in ghetto evangelism seem to be largely interested in adolescents. Adolescents in general seem to reject general speech norms both consciously and unconsciously, and this tendency may lead to ac-

---

Harper & Row, 1968), pp. 49–50, and from a more structuralist point of view in Henry Lee Smith, Jr. 'The Concept of the Morphophone,' *Language* 43 (1967), pp. 318–322.

[4] This problem is not peculiar to our situation. Some missionaries to Latin American Indians report that the Indians refuse to learn to read their own language and wish only to read Spanish because of its prestige, even though their comprehension of Spanish is very low.

ceptance of the translation by this group if not the general population. The second factor is the new mood of racial pride among American Negroes. This mood, which is more pervasive in the Negro community than many whites may suspect, leads Negroes to seek those parts of their background, both in Africa and in America, which pertain distinctively to them. As a result, we see an emphasis on Negro history, 'African bush' hair styles, and neo-African clothing styles. Should the leadership of this movement ever realize that Black English, their own dialect of English, is as distinctively Afro-American as anything they are likely to find in this culture, the result will probably be dialectal pride. If this develops, the use of a Black English translation of the Bible would not only be a good idea, but a necessity.

Several comments on the actual translation and annotations used here should be explained before actually reading the passage. We have, in the first place, approached our translation task with the same rigor expected of any serious translation of the Scriptures. That is, we have attempted to be faithful to the form and content of the original manuscript. Our translation must therefore be distinguished from attempts to 'paraphrase' the Bible into contemporary cultural parallels of the original message. We have deliberately excluded contemporary or regional Black English slang. Several instances which may appear to be slang to the white middle class reader can be justified as relatively stable expressions within the ghetto which have been adopted as slang by middle class white society.

As far as the annotations are concerned, one will observe that we have mainly noted those places where clear-cut contrasts between the grammatical systems of Standard English and Black English exist. The only reference to phonological differences deals with phonology as it intersects with the grammar of Black English. Differences in the semantic content of lexical items have not generally been noted.

JOHN 3:1–21 (BLACK ENGLISH VERSION)

1. It [1] was a man named [2] Nicodemus. He was a leader of the Jews.

2. This man, he [3] come [4, 5] to Jesus in the night and say [4, 5], 'Rabbi, we know you [6] a teacher that come [5] from God, cause can't nobody [7] do the things you be [8] doing 'cept he got God [6] with him.'

3. Jesus, he [3] tell him say [5, 9], 'This ain't [10] no jive [11], if a man ain't born over again, ain't no way [12] he [6] gonna get to know God.'

4. Then Nicodemus, he [3] ask [5] him, 'How [6] a man gonna be born when he [6] already old? Can't nobody [7] go back inside his mother and get [13] born.'

5. So Jesus tell [5] him, 'This ain't [10] no jive [11], this [6] the truth. The onliest way a man [6] gonna get to know God, [6] he got to get born regular and he got to get [13] born from the Holy Spirit.

6. The body can only make a body get [13] born, but the Spirit, he [3] make [5] a man so he can know God.

7. Don't be surprised just cause I tell you that you got to get [13] born over again.

8. The wind blow [5] where it want [5] to blow and you can't hardly [10] tell where it's [14] coming from and where it's [14] going to. That's [14] how it go [5] when somebody [6] born over again by the Spirit.'

9. So Nicodemus say [4, 5], 'How [15] you know that?'

10. Jesus say [4, 5], 'You call yourself [16] a teacher that teach [5] Israel and you don't know these kind of things?

11. I'm gonna tell you, we [6] talking about something we know about cause we already seen it. We [6] telling it like it is [17] and you'all [18] think we [6] jiving.

12. If I tell you about things you can see and you'all [18] think we [6] jiving [11] and don't believe me, what's [14] gonna happen when I tell about things you can't see?

13. Ain't nobody [12] gone up to Heaven 'cept Jesus, who come [4, 5] down from Heaven.

14. Just like Moses done [19] hung up the snake in the wilderness, Jesus got to be hung up.

15. So that people that believe in him, he can give them [3] real life that ain't never [10] gonna end.

16. God really did love everybody in the world. In fact, he loved [2] the people so much that he done [19] gave up the onliest Son he had. Any man that believe [5] in him, he [6] gonna have a life that ain't never [10] gonna end. He ain't never [10] gonna die.

17. God, he [3] didn't send his Son to the world to act like a judge, but he sent to rescue the peoples [20] in the world.

18. Nobody [6] gonna judge the man that believe [5] in God [21] onliest Son; but the man that ain't believed [2], God been [22] judged [2] him cause he ain't believed [2] in God [21] onliest Son.

19. This [6] how the judging go. The light done [19] came in the world, but the peoples [20] loved [2] the dark better than the light, causse they be [8] doing wrong things.

20. Everybody that do bad, they [23] hate the light and ain't gonna come to the light cause they don't want nobody [10] to find out what they be [8] doing.

21. But the peoples [20] that act right, they [6] gonna come to the light so peoples [20] can see that God be [8] helping them with what they be [8] doing.'

Notes

1. 'It,' in Black English, can be used as an 'expletive' or 'presentative' in addition to its function as a pronoun referring to a

specific object or participant. In this usage it is equivalent to Standard English 'there.'

2. When the suffix *-ed* is realized by a stop following a base form which ends in a consonant, the stop is not pronounced (thus, the pronunciation /neym/ for Standard English /neymd/). This reflects a Black English phonological pattern in which syllable final consonant clusters in Standard English correspond to simple consonants in Black English. The pattern illustrates how phonological constraints in Black English affect the presence of certain grammatical categories.

3. A pronoun is often used following the noun subject of a sentence in Black English. 'Pronominal apposition' functions to focus on the 'topic' of the sentence and to indicate the re-entry of a participant in a discourse (see verse 4).

4. Some verbs, like 'come' and 'say' are not marked for past tense in Black English narratives, even when the context is past time.

5. Black English lacks the *-s* suffix which marks the present tense with third person singular subjects in Standard English.

6. The present tense form of the copula is not realized in a number of different syntactic environments in Black English. Generally where the contracted form of the copula may occur in Standard English the stative condition is indicated simply by word order in Black English.

7. There are two types of emphatic negative sentences in Black English involving the pre-position of a negativized auxiliary. Black English, unlike most white nonstandard dialects, permits both an indefinite subject and the main verb to carry negative markers. Thus, '. . . nobody can't do the things you be doing . . .' is a grammatical sentence in the dialect, meaning that nobody can do these things. To emphasize such a negative statement Black English speakers may prepose the negativized verbal auxiliary to the front of the sentence, much as the ordinary English yes-no question formation. Two kinds of stress pattern are associated with this structure. In verse 2, the stress pattern is 'càn't nóbody (do the things . . .),' and expresses general emphasis. In verse 4, the stress pattern is 'Cán't nobòdy (go back . . .)' which carries the overtone of disbelief.

8. The form 'be' can be used in Black English as a verb in the same constructions in which 'is, am, are, was, were' are used in Standard English, but with a different meaning. The use of 'be' as a main verb denotes iteration or habituation. In verse 2 for example, 'the things you be doing' means that Nicodemus knows that Jesus repeatedly performs miracles.

9. Quotations are sometimes introduced by the form 'say' in addition to any other quotative words such as 'tell' and 'ask.'

10. In Black English, negation is typically marked not only in the main verb phrase, but also in each indefinite determiner or

indefinite pronoun in the sentence, as well as in certain adverbs like 'hardly' and 'never.'

11. The concept 'jive' in the Negro ghetto refers to a particular form of language behavior in which the speaker assumes a guise in order to persuade someone of a particular fact. It is often used to refer to the deception of someone with flattery or false promises.
12. This construction is potentially ambiguous. It could be an example of the pre-posed negative auxiliary (see note 7). But in verse 13 for example, it could also be a stylistic variety of 'It ain't nobody who (has) gone up to Heaven' (Cf. note 1). In verses 3 and 13 the latter interpretation is indicated.
13. 'Get' (or 'got') often functions as a passive marker in Black English.
14. When a pronoun ending in /t/ like 'it' or 'that' precedes the contracted form of 'is,' the contraction /s/ is pronounced and the /t/ is not. (Cf. note 6.)
15. Sentences which would have a pre-posed verbal auxiliary in Standard English due to the formation of a content question generally have no auxiliary at all in the corresponding Black English sentence. The 'do' which would be required in Standard English in verse 9 is absent for this reason.
16. The expression 'you call yourself X' or 'you call yourself doing X' implies mild doubt that the hearer really is X or is doing X.
17. The expression 'telling it like it is' refers to making an accurate and trustworthy assessment of a situation, without any attempt to exaggerate.
18. Like Greek, but unlike most Standard English dialects, Black English distinguishes the singular and plural of the second person pronoun ('you' versus 'you'all,' pronounced /yɔl/). The 'you' in verse 12, 'the things you can see,' is really neither of these, but is the general 'you' meaning 'people' or 'one.'
19. The use of 'done' plus the past tense of a verb is a construction indicating completed action.
20. -s plural can be suffixed to forms which in Standard English form their plural in some irregular way (suppletive forms, internal change, etc.).
21. Black English lacks possessive -s so that possession is indicated only by the order of items.
22. In a construction similar to the one mentioned in note 19, 'been' can be used with the past tense of a verb. This construction indicates action in the distant past. In verse 18, the phrase is read with stress on 'been': 'God béen judged . . .' .
23. When a pronoun in apposition refers to an indefinite, the pronoun is generally plural in Black English.

Name Index

Abbott, T. B., 408
Abel, R. A., 82
Abramovitz, A., 608, 628
Achenbach, T., 133, 153–154
Agnello, J., 414
Angras, W. S., 632
Albright, M. A., 353
Allen, G., 162
Allen, K. E., 609, 610, 611, 628
Allen, P., 198, 201, 206, 210, 217, 218, 219
Allport, G. W., 35, 38, 43
Altshuler, K. Z., 364, 365, 372, 373, 392
Ames, L. B., 526
Anastasi, A., 402, 660
Anders, Q. M., 404
Andersland, P. B., 402–403
Anderson, E. G., 413
Andrews, E. G., 276
Andrews, G., 435
Anderson, V. V., 62, 65, 69, 73
Appel, J. B., 208, 214
Aristotle, 250
Aronson, A. E., 406
Aronow, M. S., 364
Arthur, B., 525
Artuso, A. A., 651
Ault, M. H., 629
Ausubel, D. P., 660, 664
Ausubel, P., 664
Avery, C. B., 372
Ayllon, T., 208
Azrin, N. H., 198, 201, 208–209, 211, 214, 216, 218

Backer, M. H., 137
Baer, D.M., 212, 606, 608, 624, 634
Bailey, P., 71
Baker, J., 611, 628, 636
Balla, D., 135, 141
Balow, B., 532

Bandura, A., 435, 604, 631, 636
Banks, M., 205, 215
Bannatyne, A., 533
Baratz, J., 676
Barbe, W. B., 529
Barker, R. G., 102, 133, 350, 358, 373, 478
Barnard, K. E., 208, 210, 212, 214, 217, 218
Baroff, G. S., 201, 203, 208, 211, 212, 216, 218, 219
Barr, M. W., 49, 50, 51, 52, 53, 64
Basilear, T., 379–380
Bateman, B., 528
Battle, E. S., 664
Baydan, N. T., 208
Bayley, N., 503
Bean, K. L., 660
Bearss, L. M., 113
Becker, W. C., 610, 633, 636
Beckey, R. E., 405
Beckham, A. S., 70
Belhomme, J. E., 52
Bellerose, B., 352–353
Bellugi, U., 674–675
Benda, C. E., 77, 79
Bender, J. F., 407, 413–414
Bender, L., 80, 526, 527, 612
Bensberg, C. J., 198
Benson, F., 85
Benson, R., 606, 620, 628
Bentler, P. M., 608, 628
Benton, J. G., 520
Berger, E. E., 382
Berger, F. M., 36, 43
Bergman, P., 588
Berko, J., 677
Berlin, C. I., 402, 408
Berlinsky, S., 350, 400, 413
Bernhardt, R. B., 412
Bernstein, B., 661, 664, 673, 678

Name Index

Bernstein, C., 63, 68
Berrera, S. E., 82, 83
Bettelheim, B., 584, 620
Betts, G. H., 322
Betts, H. B., 520
Bexton, W. H., 193
Bice, H. V., 82
Bierman, J., 502
Biggs, B. E., 459
Bigman, S. K., 369
Bijou, S. W., 82, 192, 611, 628, 629, 633, 636
Bindon, D. M., 359
Binet, A., 52, 59–61
Birch, J., 82
Birch, J. W., 358, 365, 366, 525
Birnbrauer, J. S., 198, 199, 608, 630
Bjermeland, Y. B., 403
Bjorson, J., 181, 182, 192
Blackman, L., 132
Blackwood, R. O., 201, 205, 210, 214, 219
Blake, G. D., 379
Blake, R., 285
Blakely, R., 382
Blanton, R. L., 354–355
Bloodstein, O., 439
Blumel, R. S., 439
Boatner, E. B., 379
Bobath, B., 516, 518
Bobath, K., 516, 518
Boggs, E., 88
Boland, J. R., 414
Bolles, M. M., 113
Bonaterre, 51
Bond, G. L., 531
Bonnet, J. P., 50
Bookbinder, K. F., 531
Boshes, B., 519, 524, 525
Boullin, D. J., 574
Bourne, H., 81
Bourneville, D. M., 57
Bradley, C. C., 83
Brain, R., 382
Bray, D. W., 81
Brecher, E., 77
Brecher, R., 77
Brennemann, J., 385
Brice, B. C., 407
Bridges, K. B. M., 60
Brigham, T. A., 633
Brill, R. C., 357, 358, 367
Broadbent, E., 525
Brodsky, G., 611, 628, 635, 636
Broman, S. H., 502, 509
Bronfenbrenner, U., 659
Bronner, A., 62, 71
Brown, B., 660–661, 662
Brown, D. W., 369
Brown, M. S., 323

Brown, P., 609, 624
Brown, R., 674–675, 677
Browning, R. M., 612, 636
Brueckner, L. J., 531
Bruner, J. S., 345
Brunswick, E., 39, 43
Brutten, E., 413, 414
Bryant, N. D., 531
Bryt, A., 37, 43
Buchan, L. G., 352–353
Bucher, B., 199, 202, 214, 215, 216, 218, 219, 220
Buchholz, S., 346
Bucy, P. C., 383
Budoff, M., 137
Buell, J. S., 609, 610, 634
Bugenthal, L. F. T., 415
Burchard, E. M. L., 372
Burleson, D. E., 410
Burlingham, D., 338
Burns, S. K., 195
Burr, E. T., 70
Burt, C., 283
Buscaglia, L. F., 415
Butler, F. O., 81, 85
Butler, K. G., 403
Butterfield, E. C., 137–138, 141, 152–153, 165
Buynak, E. B., 382

Cahilly, G., 181
Caldwell, B. M., 510
Calvert, J. J., 416
Cameron, A., 146–147
Campbell, M., 381, 382
Campbell, S. St. Francis, 531
Carnap, R., 38, 43
Carkhuff, R. R., 136
Carp, F. M., 412
Carroll, E. E., 659
Carroll, R. E., 664
Carrow, M. A., 401
Carson, A. S., 663
Cassel, R. H., 198
Cattell, J. M., 58
Cave, F. C., 66
Chambers, J. L., 412
Charlesworth, R., 631
Chomsky, N., 692
Chouinard, E. L., 393
Christensen, A. H., 410
Church, R. M., 211, 216
Cianci, V., 84
Clark, L. P., 81, 139
Clarke, A. D. B., 383, 662
Clarke, A. M., 383, 662
Clarke, C. A., 383
Clausen, J. A., 369

Clemens, R. L., 526
Clements, S. D., 524
Cloward, R. A., 659
Cohen, P., 382, 383, 388
Cohen, S. J., 194
Cohen, T. B., 545
Cohn, L. C., 497
Cohn, W., 661
Coleman, H. M., 533
Coleman, M., 574
Colwell, C. N., 198, 217
Condillac, E. B., 50, 51
Conry, J., 684
Cook, J., 284
Cook, R. E., 383
Cook, S. W., 370
Copernicus, 284
Cornell, W. S., 74
Corter, H. M., 136–137
Cotton, C. B., 496, 498
Cotzin, M., 87
Coulter, S. K., 630
Cox, C. M., 284
Craig, H. B., 356–357
Craig, W. N., 370, 376
Craven, D. D., 415
Crawley, S. L., 108
Creger, W. P., 383
Cromwell, O., 285
Cromwell, R. L., 162
Cronbach, L. J., 402
Croskery, J., 136
Crothers, B., 74, 75, 79
Crothers, C., 517
Cruickshank, W. M., 514
Culver, M., 245
Cutsforth, T. D., 323
Cutts, N., 82
Czermak, J., 323

Dahlstrom, W. G., 408, 414–415
Dallenbach, K., 304
D'Angelo, R. Y., 660
Daniels, G. J., 610, 629
Darley, F. L., 402, 405, 408, 410, 436
Datta, L. E., 282
Dauw, D. C., 280, 285
Dave, R. H., 659
Davies, S. P., 53, 55, 63, 65, 66, 67, 68, 69, 85
Davis, A., 146–147
Davis, D. M., 440, 455
Davis, F., 473
Davidson, G. C., 608, 616, 622, 628
Davidson, K. S., 663
Deaver, G. G., 518
de Baca, P. C., 610
de Cervantes, M., 284
De Foe, D., 285

De Graff, A. C., 383
De Hirsh, K., 384
De Jong, R. N., 531
de Labry, J., 147–148, 175
de la Fontaine, J., 284
De Martino, M. F., 87
Dembo, T., 42, 43, 102
Demings, W. E., 392
De Myer, M., 589, 603, 605, 614, 615, 616 623, 628
Denhoff, E., 510, 524
De Prospo, C. J., 84
Descoeudres, A., 74
Despert, J. L., 407
Deutsch, M., 370, 659, 660–661, 662, 663, 664, 674, 676
Dever, R., 684
Devine, J. V., 610
Diamond, M., 415
Di Carlo, L. M., 350, 365
Dickson, S., 403, 426
Dike, G. W., 401
Dillard, J. L., 682
Di Michael, S., 48, 84, 89–90
Dinsmoor, J. A., 212
Doane, B. K., 193
Dodge, P. R., 383
Doll, E. A., 60, 70, 72–73, 74, 84
Dolphin, J. E., 350
Doman, R. J., 514, 518
Doubros, S. G., 610, 628
Doughty, R., 198, 201, 206, 207, 214
Douglas, J. W. B., 385
Donvan, E., 147
Dreger, R. M., 662, 664
Drew, A. L., 531
Drillien, C. M., 502
Drummond, M., 330
Drysdale, H. H., 72
Dubnoff, B., 619–620
Duncan, M. H., 414
Dunlap, K., 438
Dunn, L. M., 165
Durkin, D., 659
Durkin, K., 147, 665
Dye, H. B., 76

Eastman, D. F., 410, 412
Eber, H. W., 479–480
Ebner, M., 644
Ecob, K., 84, 85
Edwards, A. L., 594
Edwards, M., 210, 219
Edwards, T. B., 664
Eells, K., 662
Eisenberg, L., 602
Eldred, E., 518
Ellingson, C., 524
Elliot, L. L., 354

Name Index

Elliott, J., 401
Elliott, R., 609, 624
Ellis, N. R., 162
Ellis, W. J., 87
Emerick, L. L., 412, 415
Engel, A. M., 86
Enstrom, E. A., 531
Entwisle, D. R., 677
Ericson, M., 147
Escalona, S., 588
Esquirol, E., 52
Estes, H. R., 563
Evans, J., 404

Fahel, L. S., 142
Farber, B., 226, 227, 232, 233, 235
Farrell, E., 66
Fasold, R., 682
Fay, T., 79, 515, 516, 518
Feigh, H., 34, 43
Feranchak, P. B., 404, 405
Ferguson, L. W., 407
Fernald, W. E., 53, 55, 60, 61, 65, 68, 71
Ferster, C. B., 208, 580, 603, 605, 614, 615, 616, 620, 623, 628, 634
Fiedler, M., 353, 502, 509
Finch, S. M., 588, 598
Finkelstein, P., 411
Fisch, L., 381, 382
Fishler, K., 182
Fiske, D. W., 183, 184, 193
Fitz-Herbert, 49
Fletcher, L. G., 531
Flierl, N. E., 531
Flower, R. M., 369, 382
Font, M. M., 412
Ford, F. R., 383, 384
Foshee, J. G., 136, 163
Foster, E. M., 76
Francis, W. N., 672
Freeman, G. G., 403
Freitag, G., 198, 202, 216, 589, 621, 633
French, F. E., 502
French, K. S., 503
Freud, A., 334
Freud, S., 346, 426, 562, 579
Friedman, C. J., 181, 182, 189, 192, 194–195
Friedman, E., 574
Friedman, S. B., 393
Frierson, E. C., 529, 531, 533
Frisina, D. R., 367
Frostig, M., 527, 530
Fulton, R., 284
Furth, H. G., 364, 365
Fygetakis, L., 610
Fynne, R. J., 51, 52, 53, 54

Galen, 49

Gallagher, J. J., 285
Galton, F., 322
Gans, H. J., 149, 163
Garrett, H. E., 81
Garrett, J. F., 393
Garttner, O., 323
Garvey, C., 676
Gaudia, S., 579
Gelfand, D. M., 212, 583
Gellhorn, E., 516–517
Gellman, W., 393
Gesell, A., 72, 74
Getman, G. N., 87
Getzels, J. W., 283–284
Gibson, D., 81
Gildston, P., 415
Giles, D. K., 198, 201, 206, 208, 210
Gill, L. J., 659
Ginzberg, E., 81
Girardeau, F. L., 198, 200
Gittelman, M., 610
Gjerde, C., 543
Gladwin, T., 72, 81, 124, 143, 156
Glaser, K., 526
Glasner, P. J., 413
Glueck, E., 544
Glueck, S., 544
Goddard, H. H., 58, 60, 61, 63, 64, 65, 66, 67
Godfrey, B. B., 529
Goetzinger, C., 352–353
Goff, R. M., 664
Gold, V. J., 198, 216, 621, 633
Goldberg, B. R., 181
Goldberg, I. I., 86
Goldfarb, A., 544
Goldfarb, W., 83
Goldman, R., 409
Goldsmith, O., 284
Goldstein, K., 128–132, 162, 496
Goldstein, L. S., 676
Golick, M., 533
Gonick, M. R., 350, 358, 376
Goodnow, J. J., 162–163
Goodstein, L. D., 408, 415
Gordon, E. W., 661, 662, 664
Gotkin, L. G., 275–276
Gough, H. I., 282
Gould, E., 415
Gould, R., 664
Gray, B. B., 414, 416, 610
Green, C., 142, 150–151
Greenacre, P., 342, 344–345
Greenberg, K. R., 403
Grinker, R. R., Sr., 383
Gruen, G. E., 148–149, 161–176

Hackbusch, F., 69, 70, 82
Hadley, R., 415

Name Index

Hagan, R. A., 531
Hagbath, K. E., 518
Hainsworth, P. K., 524
Halle, M., 692
Haller, A. O., 665
Halstead, W. C., 484–485
Hamilton, J., 198, 201, 206, 210, 212, 215, 217, 218, 219, 220
Hammarberg, K., 62
Haney, H. R., 412
Hanfmann, E., 113
Handford, A. H., 183, 194–195
Hannigan, H., 383
Hardy, J. B., 382, 384, 570
Haring, N., 644
Harper, P., 385
Harris, F. R., 609, 610, 611, 624, 628, 634
Harris, H. E., 439
Harris, M., 435
Hart, B., 609, 610
Harter, S., 142–143, 145
Hartmann, D. P., 212, 583
Hartup, W. W., 631
Harvey, W., 285
Havighurst, R. J., 659
Hawke, W. A., 66
Hawkins, R. P., 611, 628, 633, 636
Haydn, F. J., 285
Haylett, C. H., 563
Healy, A. B., 65, 71
Healy, W., 61, 62
Hebb, D. O., 193
Heber, R., 48, 674, 684
Hegge, T., 74, 86
Heller, T., 316
Helme, H. W., 612
Hendriksen, K., 198, 201, 206, 207, 214
Hentig, H. von, 35, 43
Hermelin, B., 132, 135, 162, 336
Heron, W., 193
Herrnstein, R. J., 208
Hess, R. D., 661, 674, 675, 676
Hewett, F. M., 585, 611, 618, 623–624, 644, 645
Hewitt, L., 552
Hieronymus, A. N., 665
Higgins, C., 662
Hill, A. S., 86
Hill, H., 440
Hill, W. F., 209
Hilleman, M. R., 382
Hilliard, G. H., 661
Hingtgen, J. N., 616, 618, 630
Hinkle, L. E., 231
Hippocrates, 49
Hirsh, E. A., 143
Hoakley, P., 69
Hofer, W., 50
Hogarth, W., 284

Hodgden, L., 139–140, 143, 150
Hofstadter, R., 658
Holden, R. H., 474, 476, 510
Hollingworth, L., 73
Holz, W. C., 198, 201, 208–209, 211, 214, 216, 218
Homburger, A., 496
Homme, L. E., 610
Honig, W. K., 212
Hood, P. H., 514
Horne, D., 530
Howe, S. G., 53
Hrdlicka, A., 62
Hsia, D. Y-Y, 194
Hubbard, J., 674
Hull, C. J., 459
Humphreys, E., 69–70
Hundziak, M., 609
Hungerford, R. H., 86
Hunt, J. M., 662
Hunt, W., 652
Hutchinson, W. L., 275
Hutt, C., 217

Ichheiser, G., 34, 43
Ingebregtsen, E., 412
Ingram, C., 74
Ingram, W., 531
Inskeep, A. D., 74
Irwin, O. C., 660
Itard, J. M. G., 51–52

Jackson, A. D. M., 381, 382
Jackson, P., 283–284
Jahoda, M., 370
Jamcs, W., 330
Jansky, J., 384
Jastak, J., 82
Jenkins, R. L., 552
Jenne, W. C., 227, 235, 285
Jenner, E., 285
Jensen, A. R., 661, 663, 681
Jervis, G., 75, 181, 182
John, V. P., 661, 674, 676
Johnson, A., 64
Johnson, A. M., 563
Johnson, D. L., 38, 43
Johnson, G. O., 87
Johnson, W., 401, 405, 406, 407, 408, 410, 436, 438, 439–440, 453
Johnston, M. K., 609
Johnstone, E. R., 64
Jones, J. A., 659
Jones, M. H., 517
Jones, R., 609, 629

Kabat, H., 516, 518
Kahn, E., 497
Kahn, H., 36, 43

Name Index

Kaliski, L., 531
Kallmann, F. J., 365, 372, 373, 392
Kanner, L., 83, 563, 588, 590, 602, 619
Kantor, J. R., 440
Kanzer, P., 147
Kaplan, A. R., 181
Kapos, E., 415
Karmen, J. L., 414, 416
Karrer, R., 181
Karsh, E. B., 214
Karsten, A., 108
Kasanin, J., 113
Kassorla, I. C., 198, 216, 621, 633
Katan, A., 341
Kaufman, M. E., 136
Keleske, L., 183, 193
Kelley, C. S., 609
Kelley, D. Mc G., 82, 83
Kelley, V. C., 383, 384, 385
Kennedy, G. M., 403
Kennedy, W., 674
Kephart, N. C., 80, 87, 527, 528, 529–530, 531
Kerlin, H. B., 56, 57, 65
Kern, W. H., 136
Khalili, A., 520
Kidder, J. D., 199
Kinder, E. F., 82
King, P. T., 415
Kinstler, D. B., 408
Kirk, S. A., 87, 372, 527, 528
Kirk, W. D., 527
Kite, E. S., 60
Kleffner, F. R., 80
Klein, E., 569
Klineberg, O., 81, 663
Klopfer, B., 82
Knight, R. P., 56
Knobloch, H., 385, 662
Knott, J. R., 459
Knott, M., 516
Knox, A. W., 61
Koch, R., 182
Kogan, N., 278–280, 283, 284
Kohl, H. R., 365
Kohn, M. L., 231, 659
Komich, M. P., 524
Kopp, H., 411
Kounin, J. S., 99–121, 123–128, 129–139, 156, 162, 163, 172
Krasner, L., 602, 627
Kreezer, G., 73
Kronenberg, H. H., 379
Krugman, M., 410
Kubzansky, P. E., 183, 184
Kuhlman, F., 60, 62, 69
Kunzelmann, H., 644
Kuypers, D. S., 610

Labov, W., 673, 678, 682, 683, 684

Lange-Eichbaum, 269
Langford, W. S., 384
Lanyon, R. I., 413
Lauer, E., 37, 43
Lawler, J. A., 198, 608
Lazarus, A. A., 607, 628, 629, 633
Leach, P. J., 132
Leader, F. B., 664
Leff, R., 212–213, 583
Lehman, E., 269–270
Lehtinen, L. E., 80, 526
Leibig, J., 285
Leiderman, P. H., 183, 184
Leitenberg, H., 209, 632
Lerea, L., 403
Le Shan, L. L., 659, 663
Levin, G. R., 612, 652
Levine, E. S., 352, 360, 364, 369, 372
Levinson, B., 662
Leviton, G. L., 42, 43
Levitt, E. E., 574
Lewin, K., 100–101, 123–128, 130, 132, 133–134, 143, 149, 155, 162, 163, 172, 478
Lewis, H., 552, 659
Lewis, M., 148, 162
Lewis, W. W., 574
Lilly, R. T., 210, 219
Lindemann, E., 193
Lindquist, E., 594
Lindsley, O., 589
Linneaus, C., 285
Locke, B. J., 205, 215
Locke, J., 50, 285
Loflin, M., 681
Lofquist, L. H., 470
Logan, W. P. D., 382
Lotze, H., 330
Lovaas, O. I., 198, 199, 202, 212, 214, 215, 216, 218, 219, 220, 582–583, 585, 589, 605, 620–621, 624, 628, 633
Lowenfeld, V., 317
Lowrey, L., 71
Luckey, R. E., 205, 216
Lunde, A. S., 369
Lunstrom, R., 381, 382
Luria, A. R., 135, 162
Luther, M., 284
Lyman, F. L., 181

Maas, H. C., 659
McAllister, M. G., 404
McBee, M., 69–70
McCandless, B., 81, 660, 662, 665
McCarthy, D., 405
McCarthy, J. J., 527, 528
McConnell, T. R., 275
McCoy, N., 175
MacDonald, M., 659
McDowell, E. D., 410
McFarland, P., 676

Name Index

McGinnis, M. A., 80
Macgregor, F. C., 37, 43
McGuire, C., 659
Mackay, R. P., 383
McKee, J. P., 664
McKee, M. M., 404
McKinney, J. D., 136–137
McNeil, D., 364, 674
McNemar, Q., 252, 283, 449
McQueen, M., 644
McWilliams, B. J., 404, 405
Maddi, S., 193
Madison, L. R., 412
Maennel, B., 66
Magaret, A., 133–134
Mahatoo, W., 193
Mahler, M. S., 568
Maier, N. R. F., 132
Malzberg, B., 76
Manson, M. M., 382
Marge, D. K., 401
Marshall, G. R., 206
Marshall, H. H., 211
Martens, E. H., 74, 76, 85
Martin, M., 611, 628, 636
Martire, J. G., 411, 415
Martyn, M., 413, 426, 429, 435
Martz, E. W., 75
Mason, B. S., 34, 43
Massa, H., 275–276
Mast, V. R., 415
Mauer, R. A., 609
Maxfield, K. E., 346
Meadow, K. P., 357–358, 370, 373
Meadow, L., 369
Meehl, P. E., 474
Mees, H. L., 579, 589, 621–622, 633
Melcher, R. T., 74
Mellone, S. H., 330
Melnick, J. L., 382
Melzack, R., 195
Melzer, H., 410
Mendelson, J. H., 183, 184, 193
Menlove, F. L., 631
Menyuk, P., 676
Metz, J. R., 589, 614–615, 623, 630, 633
Meyerson, L., 350, 358, 373
Michael, J. L., 477
Mierzejewski, V., 62
Miller, K. S., 662, 664
Miller, N. E., 453
Milner, E. A., 568, 675
Minear, W. L., 79, 517
Mitchell, D., 66, 67
Moed, G., 474
Moll, K. L., 402, 405
Möller, H., 411
Moncur, J. P., 408, 410
Money, J., 531
Monif, G. R. G., 382

Monsees, E. K., 80
Montagu, A. M. F., 382, 385
Montague, D. O., 661, 662
Montessori, M., 67
Montgomery, G. W., 375
Moore, A., 65
Moore, W. E., 406
Moores, D. F., 379
Morrison, D. C., 611, 628
Moskowitz, S., 364
Muenzinger, K. F., 218
Musick, J. K., 205, 216
Myklebust, H. R., 80, 82, 356, 372, 383, 388, 519, 524, 525
Myrianthopoulos, N. C., 503

Nadler, H. G., 194
Nakamura, C. Y., 631
Nass, M., 355
Nelson, W. E., 383, 384, 386
Nesbitt, R. E. L., 384
Newton, E. S., 661
Neyhus, A. I., 364
Nisonger, H., 88
Nolen, P., 644
Norman, R. D., 412
Nowrey, J. E., 49, 53, 55, 66
Norsworthy, N., 59
Nunnally, J. C., 354

O'Brien, R. A., 574
O'Connor, N., 132, 135, 162, 336
Odell, G. B., 383
Odom, R. G., 149–150
Ohannessian, S., 679, 683, 684
O'Leary, K. D., 610, 633, 636
O'Leary, S., 633, 636
Olim, E. G., 661
Olson, D. R., 674
Omwake, E. B., 341
Opitz, E., 183, 193
Ortiz, J. D., 352–353
Orton, S. T., 74
Osborn, J., 684
Osborne, R. T., 662
Osborne, W. J., 148
Otis, A. S., 61
Ounsted, C., 217

Pagell, W., 137
Paine, R. S., 510, 514, 517
Parloff, M. B., 282
Pasamanick, B. A., 81, 385, 662
Paterson, D. G., 61
Patterson, G. R., 608, 609, 610, 611, 628, 629, 635, 636, 644
Patterson, R. M., 74
Pauls, M. D., 384
Pavlov, I. V., 577, 602, 607
Peckarsky, A. K., 405

Name Index

Penney, R. K., 136
Péreire, J. R., 50–51
Perkins, D. W., 414
Perlstein, M. A., 79, 514
Perrin, E. H., 403
Peters, A. W., 62
Peterson, H. W., 406
Peterson, L. R., 210
Peterson, R. F., 210, 611, 628, 629, 633, 636
Peterson, W. M., 136
Phelps, W. M., 74, 75, 79, 515
Pilcher, F. H., 65
Pillsbury, W. B., 330
Piotrowski, Z. A., 72, 82
Pitner, R., 50, 59, 60, 61, 367
Pitrelli, F. R., 412
Pizzat, F. J., 415
Platner, E., 330
Plato, 49, 250
Plenderleith, M., 131, 134–135
Pocs, O., 234
Polefka, D. A., 608
Pollock, H. M., 70
Porteus, S. D., 61, 72
Post, M. A., 67
Postman, L., 35, 43
Potter, H. W., 71–72, 74
Povick, E., 676
Pressey, S. L., 253

Quarrington, B., 412
Quay, H. R., 629, 631, 644, 652
Quigley, S. P., 367

Rabin, A. L., 663
Rabinovitch, R. D., 531
Ragsdale, N., 182
Rainer, J. D., 365, 372, 373, 392
Raph, J. B., 674
Raths, J. D., 276
Raus, G. M., 514
Ray, M. H., 33, 43
Reamer, J. F., 367
Reynolds, L. G., 353–354
Richards, D. W., 83
Richardson, L. H., 412
Richmond, J. B., 510
Rickert, E. J., 610
Rider, R., 385
Rieber, R. W., 412
Riessman, F., 658, 661, 663
Riley, W., 683
Rimland, B., 574, 575, 576, 583, 598
Risley, T., 202–203, 208, 212, 214, 215, 217, 220, 579, 589, 606, 611, 621–622, 628, 633
Roach, E. G., 527
Robbins, S. D., 408, 410, 413

Robertson, J., 183
Robins, L., 548
Robinson, G. C., 383
Rockower, L., 86
Rodda, M., 353
Rogers, J. V., 214
Roney, M., 611, 628, 636
Rood, M. S., 517
Rosen, B. C., 81, 664
Rosen, J., 383, 388
Rosenbaum, B. B., 33
Rosenthal, R., 630
Rosenzweig, L. E., 86
Ross, A. O., 532
Rothstein, D. A., 392
Rotter, J. B., 664
Rousseau, J. J., 50
Roy, R. M., 382
Rubenstein, D. B., 202, 589
Rudnick, R., 581, 619
Rusk, H. A., 36, 44
Russell, G. O., 439
Russo, S., 611, 628
Rutledge, L., 355
Ruzicka, W. R., 382

Sahs, A. L., 383
St. Onge, K. R., 416
Sampen, S. E., 610, 628
Sanders, B., 152, 616
Sanders, C. C., 208
Sandler, A.-M., 336, 337
Sanford, F. H., 406
Santostefano, S., 414
Sarason, E. K., 83
Sarason, S. B., 72, 81, 83, 87, 124, 139, 143, 156
Sarbin, M. B., 365
Saskida, S., 552
Schaeffer, B., 202, 212, 589, 606, 620, 624, 628
Scheidler, E. P., 525
Scherer, M. W., 631
Sherman, J. A., 633
Schiffman, G., 532
Schild, S., 182
Schlapp, M. G., 62
Schopler, E., 598
Schroeder, P. L., 74, 497
Schrupp, M., 543
Schultz, D. A., 414
Schultz, D. P., 183
Schwarz, G., 109
Schweid, E. R., 611, 628, 633, 636
Scott, R. B., 510
Scott, T. H., 193
Seguin, E., 52–54
Selltiz, C., 370
Sergeant, R. L., 404, 406–407, 414

Name Index

Settlage, C., 183, 194–195
Sever, J. L., 382
Sewel, W. H., 665
Shallenberger, P., 144–145
Shames, G. H., 409, 413
Shank, K. H., 401
Shaw, B., 40
Shearer, W., 426
Sheehan, J. G., 413, 415, 426, 428, 429, 435, 459, 460
Sherrill, D. D., 403–404, 405
Sherrington, C. S., 516
Shipman, V. C., 661, 674, 675, 676
Shmavonian, M. B., 194
Shontz, F. C., 473, 474, 476, 479
Shotwell, A. M., 81
Schulman, E. A., 440, 444
Shuy, R., 683
Sidman, M., 212, 605
Siegal, P. S., 136, 163
Siegal, S., 189, 190, 191, 595, 596
Sigel, I. E., 364
Signurjonsson, J., 382
Siller, J., 660, 662
Silver, A. A., 532
Silverman, A. J., 194
Silverman, W. A., 382, 385
Simmons, J. J., 612, 652
Simmons, J. Q., 202, 212, 589, 606, 620, 624, 628
Simonian, K., 502
Simons, J., 634
Siqueland, M. L., 524
Sivers, C. H., 662
Skeels, H. M., 75–76, 139
Skinner, B. F., 208, 214, 578, 602
Skinner, C. W., 382
Sloane, H. N., Jr., 610, 628
Sloan, W., 82
Smith, G., 69, 74
Smith, H. L., Jr., 693
Sobin, N., 681
Solnit, A. J., 341
Solomon, A. L., 403, 404
Solomon, I. L., 412–413
Solomon, N. D., 415
Solomon, P., 183, 184, 193
Solomon, R. L., 200, 216, 220
Solomons, G., 510
Sonnega, J., 403
Spielberger, C. D., 415
Spilka, B., 659
Spitz, H., 132, 162
Spradlin, J., E., 198, 200
Sprague, R. L., 644
Spriesterbach, D. C., 436
Springer, K. J., 277
Staats, L. C., 415
Stacey, C. L., 87

Staffen, P. M., 533
Stafford, K., 681
Standahl, J., 215, 219, 220
Standlee, L. S., 415
Starkweather, E. K., 277
Stein, L., 400, 407
Steinbach, C., 66
Steinhorst, R., 610
Steisel, I. M., 181, 182, 189, 192
Stennett, R. G., 547
Stephens, L., 198, 201, 206, 210–211, 212, 217, 218, 219
Stern, W., 60
Stevens, G. D., 525
Stevenson, E. A., 366
Stevenson, G. S., 69, 92
Stevenson, H. W., 134–136, 138–139, 142, 143, 147, 148, 150, 162–166, 171, 175
Stevenson, R. L., 35
Stewart, W. A., 682, 684, 691
Stoddard, C. B., 439
Stoddard, P., 634
Stokes, J., 382
Stolurow, L. M., 275
Stone, L. J., 353
Storm, T., 146–147
Stout, G. F., 316
Stover, D. O., 612, 636
Stratton, G. M., 323
Straus, M., 665
Strauss, A. A., 79, 80, 393, 484, 497, 526
Streng, A., 372
Striefel, S., 210
Stuckless, E. R., 358, 365, 366, 379
Summer, G., 53
Suttenfield, V., 568
Swartz, M. N., 383
Sylvester, R. H., 316

Tachdjian, M. O., 517
Tarbell, G. G., 57
Tarjan, G., 85
Tate, B. G., 201, 203, 208, 211, 212, 216, 218, 219
Taylor, D., 205, 215, 218
Taylor, E. J., 36, 44
Taylor, F. D., 651
Templin, M., 401
Terdal, L. G., 136
Terman, L. M., 60, 250, 252, 284
Terrell, G., 147
Terrell, G., Jr., 665
Thomas, E., 84
Thomas, L., 415
Thompson, C., 133–134
Thompson, L. E., 632
Thorndike, E. L., 253, 577–578, 607
Titus, E. S., 367
Tizard, J. P. M., 517

Name Index

Toigo, R., 227, 235
Torrance, E. P., 274, 277–278, 280–281, 285, 287, 288
Town, C. H., 60, 71
Trapp, E. P., 404
Tregold, A. F., 62
Trost, F. C., Jr., 618
Troxell, E., 661
Trumbull, R., 183
Tuper, H. L., 412
Turnure, J. E., 151–152, 175
Twitchell, T. E., 517

Ullman, L. P., 602, 627
Unell, E., 147
Updegraff, R., 139
Usdane, W., 393

Vallet, R. S., 531
Van de Reit, V., 674
Van Riper, C., 427, 438, 439, 442, 455
Vaux, C. L., 70
Vegely, A. B., 354
Verhave, T., 209
Vernon, M., 358–359, 369, 379, 381, 383, 384, 385, 386, 388, 389, 392
Vernon, P. E., 283
Viehweg, R., 382
Vigotsky, L. S., 113
Voas, R. B., 459
Voss, D. E., 516

Wahler, R. G., 611, 628
Walker, M. S., 74
Wallace, G. L., 68
Wallach, M. A., 278–280, 283, 284
Wallen, V., 415, 416
Wallin, J. E. W., 60, 73, 82, 87
Walnut, F., 415
Walters, G. C., 214
Warner, W. L., 164
Ward, B., 403
Watson, L. S., 198, 199, 201, 205, 206, 208, 210, 213, 216, 609
Wearne, R. G., 77
Webster, S. W., 664
Weibel, R. E., 382
Weiland, I. H., 581, 619
Weiner, G., 385
Weiner, H., 201
Weir, M. W., 148, 162, 164, 171
Weisberg, P. S., 277
Weisberger, S. E., 410
Weissmann, S., 37, 43
Wellman, B. L., 139, 143
Wepman, J., 527
Werner, E., 502
Werner, H., 80, 82, 128, 131–132, 484, 497
Werry, J. S., 629, 631, 644

Westman, J. C., 525
Wetzel, R., 609, 611, 628, 636
Wexler, D., 183
Whelen, R. J., 644
Whipple, H. D., 61, 73
White, J., 674
White, J. C., 205, 215, 218
White, J. G., 610
Whitman, E. C., 413
Whitney, E. A., 51, 77, 81, 83, 84, 85
Whitney, L. R., 208, 210, 212, 214, 217, 218
Whittier, J., 609, 629
Wickman, E. K., 542
Wiesen, A. E., 201, 206
Wiesley, M., 147, 667
Wight, B. W., 474
Wilbur, H. B., 53, 55, 56
Willems, E. P., 478
Willerman, L., 502, 509
Williams, H. M., 139
Williams, J., 510
Williams, J. D., 426
Williams, M., 339
Williams, T., 198, 608
Wilmarth, A. W., 56
Wills, D. M., 336
Wilson, R. G., 410
Wingate, M. E., 413, 415, 426
Winkel, G. H., 611, 628
Winnicott, D. W., 347
Wishner, G. J., 440
Withey, L., 531
Witmer, L., 62, 66
Witt, G., 287–289
Wolf, M. M., 198, 199, 201, 206, 208, 210, 212, 579, 589, 606, 608, 609, 610, 611, 621–622, 624, 628, 633, 634
Wolff, J. L., 135–136
Wolfram, W., 683
Wolfson, I. N., 87
Wolpe, J., 607
Wood, A. C., 181, 182, 189, 192
Wood, K. S., 401–402
Wood, N., 528
Woods, F. J., 401
Woodward, M., 143
Wooley, D. W., 182
Wright, A. K., 401
Wright, B. A., 31, 32, 35, 42, 43, 44, 350, 358, 373, 469, 473, 479
Wright, H. F., 478
Wright, M. A., 609, 629
Wrightstone, J. W., 364
Wulf, F., 39, 44
Wundt, W., 317
Wyatt, G. L., 411
Wylie, A. R. T., 52, 53, 59, 63, 69
Wylie, H. L., 404, 405

Wylie, R. C., 665
Yaker, H. M., 181
Yepsen, L. N., 72
Yerkes, R. M., 60

Zarates, L., 674

Zeaman, D., 162
Zeilberger, J., 610, 628
Zelen, S. L., 415
Ziferstein, I., 627
Zigler, E., 123–156, 161–176
Zimmerman, J., 208
Zubek, J. P., 193–194

Subject Index

Achievement motivation, of stutterers, 415
American Association on Mental Deficiency, 48, 55, 56, 57, 60, 64, 87–88
Amaurotic family idiocy, 79
Aphasia, and deafness, 388, 389
Arthur Performance Scale, institutionized retardates and the, 81
Articulatory disorders, defined, 401; parental adjustment and, 401–403; personality test results and, 403–405
Aspiration level, of the deaf, 355
Aversive conditioning, and behavior change in the retarded, 197–221

Bayley Scales of Mental and Motor Development, and neurologically impaired children, 503, 505; social class differences on the, 510
Behavior modification, classroom use of, 644; defined, 602; the emotionally disturbed and, 575–583, 589, 610–626; ethics of, 625–627; parent therapists in, 610, 611, 628, 635–636; phobias treated by, 607–608; stuttering and, 459; techniques of, 603–607, 609–610 (*see also* Operant conditioning)
Bell Adjustment Inventory, and articulatory defect, 404–405; and voice disorders, 407
Bender Visual Motor Gestalt Test, and articulatory defect, 403; and the deaf, 403; as diagnostic aid in learning disabilities, 527
Bernreuter Personality Inventory and articulatory defect, 402, 404; and stuttering, 414; and voice disorders, 406
Binet-Simon Scale, 59, 60
Blacky Picture Test, and stuttering, 412–413

Blind, congenital and adventitious, compared on form perception, 313–314, 318, 332; on space orientation, 327–328, 331, 332; on space perception, 306, 320–321, 324, 332; day nursery for the, 336, 338–339; early development of the, 336; form perception in the, 306–316; number of school age, 4–5; psychotherapy and the, 336; space orientation in the, 324–331; space perception in the, 318–324; toys for the, 347
Brain-injured, characteristics of the, 496–498; sorting behavior in the, 485–487, 489–494, 495
Brain pathology, 80; in the mentally retarded, 77–78
Brandon Training School, Vt., 85
Brown Personality Inventory, and articulatory defect, 403

California Psychological Inventory, and differences in creativity, 282
California School for the Deaf, 366, 368, 386–392
California Test of Personality, and articulatory defect, 402, 404–405; and hearing loss, 354, and stuttering, 414
Cattell Infant Intelligence Scale, and neurologically impaired children, 503
Central Institute for the Deaf, 80
Cerebral palsy, 8, 77; deafness and, 386–387; estimated number of, 48; improvement in, 510; incidence in general population, 386; rehabilitation in, 513; relationship to mental retardation, 79; Rh factor and, 388; speech methods for, 74; treatment for, 515–518, 520–521; types of, 514–515
Chicago Juvenile Court, 61

Subject Index

Concept Mastery Test, 265
Creativity, defined, 273, 277; elementary school studies of, 277–281; high school studies of, 281–287; intelligence and, 275–276, 289; personality characteristics of the, 280, 282; preschool studies of, 276–277; problems in defining, 298–299; programmed instruction and, 275; teaching methods and, 275–276; tests of, 283, 285, 287
Cretinism, 50, 56; treatment of, 57
Culturally disadvantaged, characteristics of the, 673; home environment of the, 658–660, language development in the, 660–661, 674–679, 684

Deaf, adjustment of the, 350–352, 356, 372, 389–390; aspiration level of the, 355; cerebral palsy in the, 386; concepts of causality of, 355–356; the family of the, 354–355, 357–358, 365–367, 374, 376; influence of etiology on personality of the, 358–360; linguistic accomplishments of the, 364; manual vs oral methods of communication in the, 365–366, 370, 374–375; mental retardation in the, 386; multiple handicaps in the, 379–389; numbers in school, 4–5; orthopedic defects in the, 389; performance on projective techniques of the, 352–353; performance on the semantic differential of the, 354–355; personality of the, 358–360; psychosis in the, 35; visual defects in the, 389
Delayed speech, parental attitudes and, 405; personality test results with, 406
Delinquency, juvenile, and the retarded, 65–66, 71, 82
Draw-A-Person Test, 82; and creativity, 280; and deaf children, 356; and patients with facial deformities, 37

Electroencephalography, childhood schizophrenia and, 612; deafness due to Rh factors and, 389; learning disabilities and, 526; mental retardation and, 78
Elwyn State School, Pa., 53, 57
Emotionally disturbed, classroom programs for the, 644–645; family background of the, 553–557; numbers in the school, 5; symptoms of the, 553–555; symptomatic groups of the, 553–557; teachers as identifiers of the, 542–545; treated by operant conditioning, 575–576, 579–580, 581–583; operant conditioning and, 575–576, 579–580, 581–583, 589, 595–597, 610
Erythroblastosis fetalis, 358

Exceptional children, classification scale for, 8–29; survey of, 4–5

Family, the, background of the gifted, 254–255, 263; of the deaf, 354–355, 357–358, 365–367, 374, 376; effect of retarded children on, 226–245; effects on deaf children, 354–355; of emotionally disturbed children, 556–558; social class differences in, 230–231, 658–660
Faribault State School, Minn., 59
Fels Rating Scales, and delayed speech, 405
Frostig Developmental Test of Visual Perception, 527

Genetic factors, and Mental retardation, 64–65, 75, 78, 79, 180; and multiple handicaps in the deaf, 385–386
Gheel Shrine, 49
Gifted, 11, 12, 13, 16, 24; character test performance of the, 259–260; childhood interests of the, 257–259; early reading achievement of the, 257; family background of the, 254–255; female, accomplishments of the, 266; health of the, 255–256; misconceptions about the, 256; occupational achievements of the, 266–269; problems in the identification of the, 296; teacher rating of the, 260–261; underachievement in the, 297–298
Goal setting behavior, social class differences and, 664–665; in stutterers, 409
Gordon Personal Profile, and stuttering, 413
Guilford-Zimmerman Temperment Survery, and stuttering, 413

Hampstead clinic, 334, 348
Harlem Youth Opportunities Limited, 659
Hayes-Binet Intelligence Test, 306

Illinois Test of Psycholinguistic Abilities, 527
Infantile autism, differentiated from childhood schizophrenia, 83, 590; sensory sensitivity in, 588; 595–598; treated by operant conditioning, 583, 614–626; treated with punishment, 206, 216 (see also Schizophrenia, childhood)
Institutes of Justinian, 49
Intelligence, adoptive studies of, 75–76; creativity and, 275–276; cultural bias on tests of, 662; effects of social conditions on, 81–82; genetic effects on, 78–79, 180; relation to rigidity, 136–155, 163; social class differences in, 164–165, 502, 504
Iowa State Hospital for the Feebleminded, 103

Subject Index

"Kallikak, Family," the, 65
Kernicterus, 78–79, 382

Lapeer State School, Mich., 85
Law of Effect, 174
Learning disabilities, causes of, 525–526; identification of, 526; incidence of, 4–5, 524; outcome studies in, 531–532; psychological tests for diagnosing, 527; remediation of, 529
Letchworth Village, N.Y., 63

Make-A-Picture-Story, deaf and nondeaf compared on, 359
Maslow Security Index, and stuttering, 413
Meningitis, as cause of multiple handicaps in the deaf, 383–384; sequalae of, 383, 387
Mental health status, teachers as judges of, 542–545
Mental retardation, criminal behavior and, 65–66, 71, 82; custodial care for, 54–56; defined, 48; drug therapy for, 79–80; effect on the family of, 226–245; effect of institutionalization on, 141–146; etiology of, 77–82, 180; genetics of, 64–65, 75, 78–79, 180; incidence of, 4–5, 85, 386–387; and mental deficiency, distinguished, 48; normal siblings, effects on, 238–248; parent organization for, 88–89; peer acceptance of, 12; perseveration in, 136; physiologic education of, 50–54: psychotherapy for, 83, 87; relationship to marital integration, 235–237; reversal learning in, 134–135; rigidity in, 103–120, 126, 136–137, 155, 163; Rorschach used with, 72; sheltered workshops for, 86, 88; social reinforcement and, 140; sorting behavior in the, 485–487, 489–494, 495; special classes for, 66–67, 71, 73–74, 86, 89; sterilization for, 65–66; toilet training in, 609; types of, 74–77
Minimal Brain Dysfunction, 525
Minnesota Multiphasic Personality Inventory and articulatory defect, 403; and stuttering, 408, 413–414; and voice disorders, 406
Mongolism (Down's Syndrome), 56, 57, 78, 79; racial differences and, 504; sex differences and, 504; and social class, 504
Multiple handicaps, causes of, 380–386; in the deaf, 379–392; varieties of, 386–392

National Association for Retarded Children, 88–89, 122
National Intelligence Test, 251

Negro-white differences, in communication skills, 663, 675–677, 690–691; in home environment, 658
Newark State School, N.Y., 70

Operant conditioning, and the emotionally disturbed, 575–576, 579–580, 581–583, 589, 595–597, 610–626; and rehabilitation, 477–478; and the severely retarded, 199–200 (*see also* Behavior modification)
Ozeretsky Tests of Motor Proficiency, and stuttering, 411

Pacific State Hospital, Calif., 84–85
Parental Attitude Research Instrument, and delayed speech, 405
Peabody Picture Vocabulary Test, 165; and disadvantaged children, 676; and PKU children, 188–189; 190–191; relation to age of the, 192
Perkins Institution for the Blind, Mass., 53
Phenylketonuria (PKU), 79, 180–195; cause of, 181; effect of diet on, 180, 182, 574; impact of hospitalization on children with, 183–184; parental understanding of, 181; and Peabody Picture Vocabulary Test performance, 188–189, 190–191; screening for, 180; similarity to childhood schizophrenia, 182, 574
Physically handicapped, effects of summer camp experience on, 474
Prematurity, as cause of multiple handicaps in the deaf, 384–386; sequalae of, 385–386, 387, 388, 389–390; and social class factors in psychological test performance, 502
Psychotherapy, for blind children, 336; ethics of, 626–627; by parents 610, 611, 628, 635–636; for retardates, 83, 87
Punishment, childhood schizophrenia treated by, 624, 630–631; defined, 604; mental retardation, treated by; stuttering, effect on, 439; varieties of, 201
Purdue Perceptual-Motor Survey, 527

Reading difficulties, 528; remedial techniques for, 531
Rehabilitation, operant conditioning and, 477–478; psychological research and, 469–480
Rh factor, and cerebral palsy, 388; the deaf and multiple handicaps due to, 382–383; sequelae of, 382, 387, 389
Rigidity, in the deaf, 350; Lewinian concepts of, 100–102, 123–127; and mental retardation, 104–120, 124–126, 134, 136–137; relation to chronological age of,

Subject Index

Rigidity (*continued*)
104, 127, 131; satiation as a measure of, 105–106; in stutterers, 415
Rome State School, N.Y., 55, 63
Rorschach, the, and creativity, 278; and the deaf, 352–353, 359–360, 364; and the retarded, 72; and stutterers, 410–412, 414
Rosenzweig Picture Frustration Test, and articulatory defect, 403, and stuttering, 412
Rotter Incomplete Sentences Blank, and stuttering, 413
Rubella, maternal, as cause of multiple handicaps in the deaf, 380–382; sequelae of, 381–382, 387, 388, 389

Saslow Screening Test, and stuttering, 413
Satiation, as a measure of rigidity, 105–106
Schizophrenia, childhood, 83, 201, 574; and early infantile autism differentiated, 83, 590; operant conditioning as treatment for, 579–580, 581, 610–626; and PKU, 182; self-injury in, 620–621; sensory sensitivity in, 588, 595–597, 630; symptoms of, 612 (*see also* Infantile autism)
School phobia, behavior modification applied to, 608; characteristics of children with, 567–568; incidence of, 562; parents' role in, 566–567; treatment of, 563, 569–570, 608; and truancy differentiated, 563
Second-language learning, Black English and, 682–684; Cubans and, 680; Mexican-Americans and, 680–681; Navahos and, 681; problems in, 680
Self-injury, in childhood schizophrenia, 620–621; in the retarded, 199–200, 202–205, 210–211, 216, 218
Semantic Differential, for comparing deaf and normal children, 354–355
Sequential Tests of Educational Progress (STEP) and creative children, 278–279
Sheltered workshops, for the cerebral palsied, 521; for the retarded, 88
Social class, differences in response to the retarded children, 230–231, 240–241; and giftedness, 254–255; home environment and, 658–660; intelligence test score differences and, 164–165; language development and, 660–661; performance differences and, 146–148, 161–176; and reactions to neurological impairment, 502, 504–506, 510; self-concept and, 664; time orientation and, 663
Special classes, for learning disabilities, 529; for the retarded, 66–71, 73–74, 89

Speech handicapped, incidence in school age of the, 4–5; rigidity in the, 38–39; self-acceptance in the, 36 (*see also Thematic Apperception Test,* and articulatory defect; Delayed speech; Stuttering, Voice disorders)
Stanford-Binet, 61, 188, 250, 251; and neurologically impaired children, 503–505, 508; retarded and normal compared on the, 133
"Strauss Syndrome," 392, 525–526
Stuttering, conflict and, 443, 453; goal-setting behavior and, 409; parental attitudes and, 408–410; personality and, 400, 407–408; personality tests and, 408–416; recovery from, 425–426; reinforcement of, 441–456, 459–465
Syracuse State School, N.Y., 55, 62

Travistock Clinic, 400
Taylor Manifest Anxiety Scale, and stuttering, 414
Texas State School for the Blind, 306
Thematic Apperception Test, and articulatory defect, 402, 403; and retardates, 82; and stuttering, 410, 412; and voice disorders, 402, 403
Therapeutic Papyrus of Thebes, 49
Token system, classroom use of, 610, 645; in rehabilitation, 478

Usher's Syndrome, 385

Vineland Social Maturity Scale, 72–73, 82, 87, 188; deaf vs hearing compared on the, 372–373
Voice disorders, defined, 406; personality test results with 406–407

Waardenburg Syndrome, 385
Waverly State School, Mass., 53, 68, 69, 77, 85
Wayne County Training School, Mich., 74, 80, 84, 85–86
Wechsler Intelligence Scale for Children, 295; creative children studied with the, 278; deaf and hearing children compared on the, 369; and the emotionally disturbed, 645; learning disabilities diagnosed with the, 527; PKU children and the, 188–189, 190; and stutterers, 411
Wepman Auditory Discrimination Test, 527
Westinghouse Science Talent Search, 282
White House Conference, 63, 69, 89
"Wild Boy of Aveyron," 51–52
Wiley Attitude Scale, and delayed speech, 405; and stuttering, 408
Woods Schools, Pa., 87